Eu-C-II-81
Eu-C-IV

The Economic Development of Denmark and Norway since 1870

The Economic Development of Modern Europe since 1870

Series Editor: Charles Feinstein
        Chichele Professor of Economic History
        All Souls College, Oxford

1. The Economic Development of France since 1870 (Volumes I and II)
   François Crouzet

2. The Economic Development of Denmark and Norway since 1870
   Karl Gunnar Persson

Future titles will include:

The Economic Development of Italy since 1870
Giovanni Federico

The Economic Development of Austria since 1870
Herbert Matis

The Economic Development of Ireland since 1870
C. O'Grada

The Economic Development of The Netherlands since 1870
Jan Luiten van Zanden

The Economic Development of Belgium since 1870
H. Van der Wee and J. Blomme

The Economic Development of Germany since 1870
W. Fischer

The Economic Development of the United Kingdom since 1870
C. Feinstein

The Economic Development of Sweden since 1870
L. Jonung and R. Ohlsson

The Economic Development of Spain since 1870
P. Martín-Aceña

The Economic Development of the European Community
R.T. Griffiths

The Economic Development of Denmark and Norway since 1870

Edited by

Karl Gunnar Persson

Reader in Economic History
University of Copenhagen

An Elgar Reference Collection

© Karl Gunnar Persson 1993. For copyright of individual articles please refer to the Acknowledgements.

All rights reserved. No part of this publication may be reproduced, stored in a retrieval system, or transmitted in any form or by any means, electronic, mechanical, photocopying, recording, or otherwise without the prior permission of the publisher.

Published by
Edward Elgar Publishing Limited
Gower House
Croft Road
Aldershot
Hants GU11 3HR
England

Edward Elgar Publishing Company
Old Post Road
Brookfield
Vermont 05036
USA

British Library Cataloguing in Publication Data
Economic Development of Denmark and
Norway Since 1870. – (Economic
Development of Modern Europe Since 1870)
I. Persson, Karl Gunnar II. Series
330.9481

Library of Congress Cataloguing in Publication Data
The Economic development of Denmark and Norway since 1870/edited by
  Karl Gunnar Persson.
      p. cm.
  Includes bibliographical references.
  1. Denmark—Economic conditions. 2. Norway—Economic conditions.
I. Persson, Karl Gunnar, 1943– .
HC355.E27 1993
338.948—dc20   93-11089
                                                              CIP

ISBN 1 85278 683 3

Printed in Great Britain by Galliard (Printers) Ltd, Great Yarmouth

Contents

Acknowledgements ix
Introduction xi

PART I   **THE INDUSTRIAL BREAKTHROUGH**

1. Svend Aage Hansen (1970), *Early Industrialisation in Denmark*, Copenhagen: Gads Forlag, 7–28   3
2. Niels Buus Kristensen (1989), 'Industrial Growth in Denmark, 1872–1913 – in Relation to the Debate on an Industrial Breakthrough', *Scandinavian Economic History Review*, **XXXVII** (1), 3–22   25
3. Fritz Hodne (1973), 'Growth in a Dual Economy – The Norwegian Experience 1814–1914', *Economy and History*, **XVI**, 81–110   45
4. Francis Sejersted (1992), 'A Theory of Economic and Technological Development in Norway in the Nineteenth Century', *Scandinavian Economic History Review*, **XL** (1), 40–75   75
5. Jan Tore Klovland (1989), 'A Chronology of Cycles in Real Economic Activity for Norway, 1867–1914', *Scandinavian Economic History Review*, **XXXVII** (3), 18–38   111
6. Niels Kærgård (1990), 'The Industrial Development of Denmark 1840–1914', *Journal of European Economic History*, **19** (2), Fall, 271–91   132
7. Ingrid Henriksen (1992), 'The Transformation of Danish Agriculture 1870–1914', Discussion papers from the Institute of Economics, University of Copenhagen   153

PART II   **INCOME, GROWTH AND ECONOMIC POLICY IN THE 20TH CENTURY**

8. Odd Aukrust and Juul Bjerke (1959), 'Real Capital and Economic Growth in Norway 1900–56', in Raymond Goldsmith and Christopher Saunders (eds), *The Measurement of National Wealth*, London: Bowes and Bowes, 80–118   181
9. Olle Krantz and Carl-Axel Nilsson (1974), 'Relative Income Levels in the Scandinavian Countries', *Economy and History*, **XVII**, 52–69   220
10. Jan Tore Klovland (1983), 'The Demand for Money in Secular Perspective: The Case of Norway, 1867–1980', *European Economic Review*, **21**, 193–218   238

11. Rewal Schmidt Sørensen (1990), 'Changes in the Personal Income Distribution 1870–1986', translation of 'Udviklingen i den personlige indkomstfordeling 1870–1986', *Nationaløkonomisk Tidskrift*, **128**, 344–58 — 264
12. Anders Skonhoft (1990), 'Home-led or Export-led Growth? The Growth of the Norwegian Electronics Industry in the Postwar Period', *Scandinavian Economic History Review*, **XXXVIII** (1), 50–73 — 278
13. Per H. Hansen (1991), 'From Growth to Crisis: The Danish Banking System from 1850 to the Interwar Years', *Scandinavian Economic History Review*, **XXXIX** (3), 20–40 — 302
14. Niels-Henrik Topp (1988), 'Fiscal Policy in Denmark 1930–1945', *European Economic Review*, **32** (2/3), March, 512–18 — 323
15. Hans E. Zeuthen (1982), 'A Note on the Present Slump and the Depression in the 1930's', *Economic Essays in Honour of Jørgen H. Gelting*, Copenhagen: Danish Economic Association, 207–20 — 330
16. Anders Ølgaard (1979), 'Structural Problems of the Danish Economy', *The Danish Economy*, Brussels: Commission of the European Communities, 9–34 — 344
17. Ebbe Yndgaard (1982), 'Danish Industry 1964–79', *Economic Essays in Honour of Jørgen H. Gelting*, Copenhagen: Danish Economic Association, 192–206 — 370
18. Karl Ove Moene and Michael Wallerstein (1992), 'The Decline of Social Democracy', University of Oslo, March — 385

PART III INNOVATION AND TECHNOLOGICAL CHANGE

19. Ove Hornby and Carl-Axel Nilsson (1980), 'The Transition from Sail to Steam in the Danish Merchant Fleet, 1865–1910', *Scandinavian Economic History Review*, **XXVIII** (2), 109–34 — 407
20. Bjørn L. Basberg (1985), 'Technological Transformation in the Norwegian Whaling Industry in the Interwar Period', *Scandinavian Economic History Review*, **XXXIII** (2), 83–107 — 433

PART IV WAGES, UNIONS AND THE LABOUR MARKET

21. Arne Kiel and Lars Mjøset (1990), 'Wage Formation in the Norwegian Industry 1840–1985', *Scandinavian Economic History Review*, **XXXVIII** (1), 19–49 — 461
22. Christian Riis and Tore Thonstad (1989), 'A Counterfactual Study of Economic Impacts of Norwegian Emigration and Capital Imports', in Ian Gordon and A.P. Thirlwall (eds), *European Factor Mobility*, Macmillan, 116–32 — 492
23. Ulla Margrethe Larsen (1982), 'A Quantitative Study of Emigration from Denmark to the United States, 1870–1913', *Scandinavian Economic History Review*, **XXX** (2), 101–28 — 509

	24.	Peder J. Pedersen (1982), 'Union Growth in Denmark, 1911–39', *Scandinavian Journal of Economics*, **84** (4), 583–92	537
	25.	Jan Morten Dyrstad (1987), 'Resource Boom, Wages and Unemployment: Theory and Evidence from the Norwegian Petroleum Experience', *Scandinavian Journal of Economics*, **89** (2), 125–43	547

PART V   FOREIGN TRADE

	26.	Anders Ølgaard (1966), 'The Danish Terms of Trade in Foreign Trade, 1875–1963', in *Growth, Productivity and Relative Prices*, Amsterdam: North Holland, 221–43	569

PART VI   THE PUBLIC SECTOR

	27.	Fritz Hodne and Bjørn Basberg (1987), 'Public Infrastructure, Its Indispensability for Economic Growth: The Case of Norwegian Public Health Measures 1850–1940', *Scandinavian Economic History Review*, **XXXV** (2), 145–69	595
	28.	Gunnar Persson (1986), 'The Scandinavian Welfare State: Anatomy, Logic and Some Problems', *Welfare State Programme*, Suntory-Toyota International Centre for Economics and Related Disciplines/London School of Economics, Number 7, March, 1–30	620

Name Index   651

Acknowledgements

The editor and publishers wish to thank the following who have kindly given permissions for the use of copyright material.

Odd Aukrust and Juul Bjerke for excerpt: Odd Aukrust and Juul Bjerke (1959), 'Real Capital and Economic Growth in Norway 1900–56', in Raymond Goldsmith and Christopher Saunders (eds), *The Measurement of National Wealth*, London: Bowes and Bowes, 80–118.

Banco di Roma for article: Niels Kærgård (1990), 'The Industrial Development of Denmark 1840–1914', *Journal of European Economic History*, **19** (2), Fall, 271–91.

Basil Blackwell Ltd for articles: Jan Morten Dyrstad (1987), 'Resource Boom, Wages and Unemployment: Theory and Evidence from the Norwegian Petroleum Experience', *Scandinavian Journal of Economics*, **89** (2), 125–43; Peder J. Pedersen (1982), 'Union Growth in Denmark, 1911–39', *Scandinavian Journal of Economics*, **84** (4), 583–92.

Commission of the European Communities for excerpt: Anders Ølgaard (1979), 'Structural Problems of the Danish Economy', Chapter I, *The Danish Economy*, 9–34.

Elsevier Science Publishers B.V. for articles and excerpt: Jan Tore Klovland (1983), 'The Demand for Money in Secular Perspective: The Case of Norway, 1867–1980', *European Economic Review*, **21**, 193–218; Niels-Henrik Topp (1988), 'Fiscal Policy in Denmark 1930–1945', *European Economic Review*, **32** (2/3), March, 512–18; Anders Ølgaard (1966), 'The Danish Terms of Trade in Foreign Trade, 1875–1963', in *Growth, Productivity and Relative Prices*, 221–43.

Svend Aage Hansen for excerpt: Svend Aage Hansen (1970), *Early Industrialisation in Denmark*, 7–28.

Ingrid Henriksen and the University of Copenhagen for article: Ingrid Henriksen (1992), 'The Transformation of Danish Agriculture 1870–1914', Discussion Papers from the Institute of Economics, University of Copenhagen.

Macmillan Ltd and St Martin's Press, Incorporated for excerpt: Christian Riis and Tore Thonstad (1989), 'A Counterfactual Study of Economic Impacts of Norwegian Emigration and Capital Imports', in Ian Gordon and A.P. Thirlwall (eds), *European Factor Mobility: Trends and Consequences*, 116–32.

Karl Ove Moene and Michael Wallerstein for article: Karl Ove Moene and Michael Wallerstein (1992), 'The Decline of Social Democracy', University of Oslo, March.

Nationaløkonomisk Tidskrift for articles: Rewal Schmidt Sørensen (1990), 'Changes in the Personal Income Distribution 1870-1986', *Nationaløkonomisk Tidskrift*, **128**, 344-58, translated from 'Udviklingen i den personlige indkomstfordeling 1870-1986'; Hans E. Zeuthen (1982), 'A Note on the Present Slump and the Depression in the 1930's', *Economic Essays in Honour of Jørgen H. Gelting*, 207-20; Ebbe Yndgaard (1982), 'Danish Industry 1964-1979', *Economic Essays in Honour of Jørgen H. Gelting*, 192-206.

Scandinavian Economic History Review for articles: Niels Buus Kristensen (1989), 'Industrial Growth in Denmark, 1872-1913 – in Relation to the Debate on an Industrial Breakthrough', *Scandinavian Economic History Review*, **XXXVII** (1), 3-22; Fritz Hodne (1973), 'Growth in a Dual Economy – The Norwegian Experience 1814-1914', *Economy and History*, **XVI**, 81-110; Francis Sejersted (1992), 'A Theory of Economic and Technological Development in Norway in the Nineteenth Century', *Scandinavian Economic History Review*, **XL** (1), 40-75; Jan Tore Klovland (1989), 'A Chronology of Cycles in Real Economic Activity for Norway, 1867-1914', *Scandinavian Economic History Review*, **XXXVII** (3), 18-38; Olle Krantz and Carl-Axel Nilsson (1974), 'Relative Income Levels in the Scandinavian Countries', *Economy and History*, **XVII**, 52-69; Anders Skonhoft (1990), 'Home-led or Export-led Growth? The Growth of the Norwegian Electronics Industry in the Postwar Period', *Scandinavian Economic History Review*, **XXXVIII** (1), 50-73; Per H. Hansen (1991), 'From Growth to Crisis: The Danish Banking System from 1850 to the Interwar Years', *Scandinavian Economic History Review*, **XXXIX** (3), 20-40; Ove Hornby and Carl-Axel Nilsson (1980), 'The Transition from Sail to Steam in the Danish Merchant Fleet, 1865-1910', *Scandinavian Economic History Review*, **XXVIII** (2), 109-34; Bjørn L. Basberg (1985), 'Technological Transformation in the Norwegian Whaling Industry in the Interwar Period', *Scandinavian Economic History Review*, **XXXIII** (2), 83-107; Arne Kiel and Lars Mjøset (1990), 'Wage Formation in the Norwegian Industry 1840-1985', *Scandinavian Economic History Review*, **XXXVIII** (1), 19-49; Ulla Margrethe Larsen (1982), 'A Quantitative Study of Emigration from Denmark to the United States, 1870-1913', *Scandinavian Economic History Review*, **XXX** (2), 101-28; Fritz Hodne and Bjørn Basberg (1987), 'Public Infrastructure, Its Indispensability for Economic Growth: The Case of Norwegian Public Health Measures 1850-1940', *Scandinavian Economic History Review*, **XXXV** (2), 145-69.

Suntory-Toyota International Centre for Economics and Related Disciplines (STICERD), London School of Economics for article: Gunnar Persson (1986), 'The Scandinavian Welfare State: Anatomy, Logic and Some Problems', *Welfare State Programme*, Number 7, March, 1-30.

The publishers wish to thank the Library of the London School of Economics and Political Science and The Marshall Library, Cambridge University, for their assistance in obtaining these articles.

Introduction[1]

The Scandinavian Context

The Scandinavian countries, and among them Denmark and Norway, shared several important characteristics in the formative phases of their economic development. From the very start of industrialization, they were both small *and* open economies; they exploited the opportunities of increased world trade, but were also forced to adapt. Their interwar years were in some respects untypical and less sombre than in other parts of Europe. These years unleashed political forces which became important after the Second World War. The postwar welfare state expansion in Denmark and Norway had many similarities, both institutionally and quantitatively, and was a prerequisite for high growth and macroeconomic stability. If there is a lesson to be learnt from their histories it might be that trade dependence with a single economy (or a few large ones) and on raw material and agricultural exports are not necessarily obstacles to economic development and technological progress.

Growth of national income has been remarkably similar in Denmark and Norway during the last 100 years. Average yearly growth was around 2 per cent from 1860 to 1914, a half to one percentage points higher in the interwar period – but fluctuating wildly – and 4 per cent in the postwar period. Denmark was concerned (excessively, according to some observers) with its current account deficit which retarded growth in the 1950s and again in the 1970s and 1980s.[2] Both countries were the first of the Nordic nations to respond to the opportunities generated by British economic growth and import demand stimulated by the repeal of the Navigation Act and the spread of free trade from the mid-18th century onwards. That early response encouraged specialization, which explains why Denmark and probably Norway had a higher per capita income in the 19th century than Sweden, although that ranking was later reversed.[3] In particular simultaneous increases in demand for agricultural produce, fish and timber reduced seasonal unemployment in Norway, while both increased skills and a larger work effort boosted income from Danish agriculture. Early growth thus relied heavily on rich natural resources in the case of Norway and on agriculture in Denmark; dependence on the import of capital and technology was more pronounced in Norway which at that time had little innovative capacity. Timber (and later pulp and paper), fish (at first salted and dried but by the end of the 19th century fresh and preserved) and the merchant marine service together accounted for 90 per cent of Norway's export value in 1865 and 75 per cent in 1905. To this day, raw materials and semi-processed goods remain Norway's dominant export items, a pattern preserved partly because energy-intensive raw material processing has been subsidized. This is not surprising given both the abundant energy available from hydroelectricity and North Sea oil, and the strength of the 'energy lobby' in economic policy-making.

Neither the fishing industry nor the merchant marine service, which alone earned 40 per cent of Norway's export income in the entire period from 1860 to 1960, were technologically in the forefront during the early phases of industrialization. The country's decisive competitive advantage was low, but increasing, wages. Norway's long historical expertise in shipbuilding was not necessarily an advantage in the transformation from sail to steam, although it did explain early successes. Most modern shipbuilding in fact developed from mechanical engineering rather than from traditional shipbuilding based on wood. In that respect Denmark – poorly endowed with natural resources, but with a high land/labour ratio and consistent efforts to maintain and enhance soil productivity – adapted more swiftly, indicating that skills and institutional flexibility might be a substitute for varied natural endowments and cheap raw materials.

In the years preceding the First World War both Norway and Denmark were free traders, with very high foreign exposure: around 25–30 per cent of national income was exported, exerting strong pressure for internal accommodation to export sectors.[4] Industrial growth was concentrated in a few urban centres,[5] though the spread of electricity later helped industry out of its original locations. However, Danish industry was almost exclusively oriented towards the home market and remained that way until after 1945. Agriculture, with Britain as the single most important market, accounted for almost 90 per cent of export earnings by the turn of the century and remained important (with some 60 per cent around 1960), although the share of processed and semi-processed goods increased continuously. The transformation of Danish and (the similar but less known) Norwegian agriculture in the difficult last quarter of the 19th century when prices were falling is rightly contrasted with the gloomy experience in other parts of Europe, for example France, with its protectionist leanings. The transition from grain (and cattle) to dairy products and bacon in Denmark was largely a spontaneous response to changes in relative prices and export opportunities.[6]

Both Norway and Denmark developed a suitable institutional infrastructure, however, with cooperatives and local savings banks and other credit institutions. These enabled an agriculture primarily based on small and medium-sized peasant households to overcome constraints created by indivisibilities in capital equipment and imperfections in credit markets. This process was assisted by a high level of literacy. Productivity growth in Danish agriculture was impressive; despite its dominant role as an exporter, the proportion of the Danish labour force employed in agriculture, fishing and forestry before 1914 was only 35 per cent, compared to 45–50 per cent in Norway and Sweden. However, in Denmark surplus labour from rural areas was absorbed by urban employment, and emigration remained small, contrary to the experience of both Norway and Sweden.[7]

The Interwar Paradoxes

In the early 1920s Sweden had the most developed industrial base and was technologically the most self-reliant of the Scandinavian countries, with a third of its labour force in industry. This compares with a little more than 25 per cent for Norway and Denmark, even allowing a generous definition of 'industry' as regards the latter country which had a larger share employed in small-scale workshops and handicrafts. The interwar years posed similar problems for the three countries, problems generated in the 1920s by a misconceived exchange rate policy. They also enjoyed similar opportunities in the 1930s when the state was given a stronger say in economic policy and there were declining competitive pressures from Germany and the UK. The strong Anglo-Scandinavian link facilitated Norway and Denmark in following

Britain's return to the old gold parity, though with much of their motivation based on moral arguments rather than economic rationality. The expected results of an overvalued currency followed in the latter half of the 1920s: unemployment was four to five times higher in percentage terms than before 1914 when it seldom surpassed 5 per cent. After Scandinavia followed Britain off gold in September 1931, and with subsequent devaluations against the pound a few years later, growth regained its momentum but this time in an environment of elaborate foreign exchange and trade regulations. By and large Norway and Denmark had, *relatively* speaking, a reasonable economic decade in the 1930s. Unemployment remained high but industrial employment actually increased. Although Denmark experienced a moderate decline in exports, imports declined even more, thus stimulating import-substituting industrialization. Industrial labour productivity stagnated and so did real wages, but before the outbreak of the Second World War Denmark had a larger industrial labour force than at any previous date.

With its heavy dependence on agriculture and with its traditional markets becoming increasingly protectionist – Britain and Germany bought 75 per cent of Danish exports before the slump – Denmark could do little more than produce import substitutes. This was made possible by a virtual nationalization of scarce foreign exchange reserves. Consumption could be redirected towards residential building and public infrastructure, while a modestly egalitarian redistribution of income boosted demand for domestically-produced goods.[8]

Norway's (and Sweden's) export performance in the 1930s was more impressive than Denmark's due to competitive devaluation and a more diversified export sector, both geographically and in terms of products. Exports of paper, minerals and metals developed well. Norway had built up a modern industry, using foreign capital and technology and domestic electricity, in the first decades of the 20th century. Investment growth rates dropped somewhat in the 1920s and early 1930s but surpassed their prewar level in the second half of the 1930s, specifically in shipping and machinery and in residential building.[9]

Politically the importance of social democracy increased and new forms of cooperation between capital and labour evolved in the postwar period. In this respect Denmark pioneered an elaborate labour relations framework whose development had actually begun before the turn of the century. The contours of the Scandinavian model took shape, with labour-market peace traded for political reforms benefiting the working class. Agriculture was granted protection and subsidies in exchange for governmental regulation of production, although these subsidies in no way approached the levels reached in the postwar period. Although public sector spending increased and more ambitious welfare programmes were designed, the idea that Scandinavia represented an early application of Keynesian (or Stockholm school) demand management is on the whole unfounded.[10] Fritz Hodne goes so far as to argue that Norwegian fiscal policy was deflationary during the upturn in the second half of the 1930s.

Success and Failure in the Postwar Era

By almost any standard the postwar period has been a golden age for the Scandinavian countries. Growth was on or above rates for the rest of Europe, with income more equally distributed and unemployment lower. However, during most of the period Denmark's growth has been constrained by an almost permanent current account deficit caused by an undiversified export sector dominated by agriculture which did not benefit from the deregulation of trade achieved by GATT.[11] Industry began to catch up, becoming an important earner of foreign exchange in the 1950s. This mainly involved light industry, though export penetration was recorded in many markets. By the early 1960s the value of manufacturing exports surpassed that of food exports which were still concentrated on the British and German markets. In the 1960s, when many longer established industrial countries experienced a decline in their industrial labour force, this sector was still increasing in Denmark. Whether such late industrialization was far-reaching enough is debatable, given the poor prospects for agricultural sector exports and the constraint of a weak current account. Membership of the Common Market was largely dictated by the short-term needs of the agrarian sector and advocated by the powerful farm lobby; however, the Common Market agricultural policy could provide only temporary relief, having misdirected resources to less efficient uses. Other sheltered sectors, most importantly the building industry (helped by vast subsidies) and public sector employment, increased in both Norway and Denmark. Public sector employment alone accounted for between a quarter and a third of the labour force, but about half or more of the female labour force.[12] Moreover, export exposure for manufacturing has continued to increase.

While the 1960s in particular were years of great success for Denmark, with a radical change of its economic structure away from traditional products, macroeconomic stability was difficult to achieve in the 1970s with the continued strong growth of public sector employment. In the 1980s Denmark switched its economic policy regime towards that pursued in Germany (or rather it was forced to do so after having pegged the Krone to the German Mark), while Norway and Sweden continued to adhere to the Scandinavian model. The fight against unemployment remained a priority in Norway (and Sweden) well into the 1980s, while Denmark, like her fellow members of the Common Market, became more concerned with low inflation. The achievement of the Scandinavian model was to combine macroeconomic stability – low inflation and manageable current account deficits – with low unemployment, public sector *and* real income growth, as well as a respectable rate of investment. While both Norway and Sweden pursued a long period of Scandinavian modelling, the experience of Denmark was mixed. Although tax revolts started there, paradoxically it was Social Democratic Sweden which lowered marginal taxes to an extent not yet attempted in any other Scandinavian country despite being governed by Liberal and centre-right governments during part of these troubled years. The Scandinavian model required a fine balance of political favours, such as commitment to full employment and egalitarian redistribution in exchange for trade union restraint. This worked for a time, with problems appearing first in Denmark. The decline in investment, high inflation and static real take-home pay revealed the internal contradictions of this programme in the 1980s. Other factors have contributed to stagnation as well, although prevailing ideological fashions in the economics profession tend to blame only public sector crowding out. Denmark's new economic policy regime has not encouraged growth of employment, while financial deregulation has misdirected resources. Norway rushed into North Sea oil exploitation and subsequently experienced some of the familiar 'Dutch disease' symptoms, including strong wage-drift responses.[13]

The decline of the Scandinavian model is, as suggested by Moene and Wallerstein in Chapter 18, a familiar bargaining failure; interpreted in this way it was predictable that the decline should have started in Denmark where the hegemonic power of social democracy was much weaker. Does this imply the end of social democracy as a distinctive political force? That conclusion is premature. There is a certain amount of political indecision at present, but social democracy has in the past been able to seize the right moment for a political and economic revival; its coming to power in the 1930s, for instance, followed a gloomy period in the 1920s. It is equally premature to declare the end of the comprehensive welfare state in Scandinavia. Public sector growth has ended, but at a very high level of spending. It may turn out that the widespread commitment to a slightly reformed and slimmer welfare state is a forceful motive to find ways to speed up growth again after a decade of disappointing results.

Notes

1. In the editing of this book I received valuable suggestions from the members of the Copenhagen Economic History Seminar, in particular from Ole Hyldtoft, Niels Kærgård and Carl-Axel Nilsson. I have also benefited from the suggestions by Ingrid Henriksen, who has read and improved the Introduction.
2. The most comprehensive and general economic history of Norway is Fritz Hodne's *Norge's økonomiske historie 1815–1970* (Oslo, 1981) which relies on historical national accounts reconstructed by Juul Bjerke in *Langtidslinjer i norsk økonomi 1865–1960* (Oslo, 1966), as well as on contemporary economic history research by the author and associates. The Danish counterpart is Sven Aage Hansen's *Økonomisk vækst i Danmark 1720–1983* (Copenhagen, 1984). Important quantitative research on trade and historical national accounts include Ole Bus Henriksen and Anders Ølgaard, *Danmarks udenrigshandel 1874–1958* (Copenhagen, 1960) and Kjeld Bjerte and Niels Ussing, *Studier over Danmarks nationalprodukt 1870–1950* (Copenhagen, 1958).
3. See Chapter 9 by Olle Krantz and Carl-Axel Nilsson, 'Relative Income Levels in the Scandinavian Countries', in this volume.
4. The role of home market and export demand respectively has been intensively discussed, in particular in Norwegian economic historiography. Compare the contributions in this volume by F. Hodne, F. Sejerstad and A. Skonhoft (Chapters 3, 4 and 12).
5. See Ole Hyldtoft (1984), *Københavns industrialisering 1840–1914*, Herning, which is discussed at some length in Niels Kærgård's contribution to this volume (Chapter 6).
6. See Ingrid Henriksen's contribution 'The Transformation of Danish Agriculture 1870–1914' in this volume (Chapter 7).
7. See the contributions by C. Riis and T. Thonstad on Norwegian emigration, and by Ulla M. Larsen on Danish emigration in this volume (Chapters 22 and 23).
8. The alleged dominating role played by exchange controls in stimulating Danish industry is challenged by Ole Hyldtoft in 'Krise og vækst i byerhvervene' in V. Dybdahl et al., *Krise i Danmark* (Copenhagen, 1975).
9. See Odd Aukrust and Juul Bjerke, 'Real Capital and Economic Growth in Norway 1900–56' in this volume (Chapter 8).
10. See 'Fiscal Policy in Denmark 1930–1945' by Niels-Henrik Topp in this volume (Chapter 14).
11. See Anders Ølgaard's contribution to this volume (Chapter 16).
12. See my contribution on the Scandinavian welfare state in this volume (Chapter 28).
13. See Jan Morten Dyrstad's contribution (Chapter 25).

Part I
The Industrial Breakthrough

[1]

Excerpt from Svend Aage Hansen, *Early Industrialisation in Denmark*, 7–28.

Introduction

In the 1850s Denmark wass still a mainly agrarian country. Primary industries, with agriculture as the undisputed leader, accounted for about 60 % of the nation's gross product at factor cost.

Even at that time a substantial proportion of farm output — viz., about 30 %, chiefly grain — was exported [1]. Thanks to this high export ratio, the Danish nation had achieved a fairly well developed division of labour between Danish agriculture on the one hand and foreign industry on the other.

These factors explain how it was possible as early as about 1855 for commerce and other tertiary industries, whose chief function was to act as an intermediary in this division of labour, to produce about 25 % of the aggregate gross domestic product at factor cost, compared with the figure of only about 4 % which was still all that true industry accounted for. These percentages reveal certain crucial facts about the economic structure of Denmark in that age. They show that very early economic growth in the agricultural sector was accompanied by a broad commercial revolution. On the other hand Denmark had not yet enjoyed any major degree of industrial development [2]. In fact this came much later than the agricultural and commercial revolutions.

---

[1] Dansk pengehistorie 1 (1968), p. 213.

[2] The state of Danish industry prior to 1870 is treated by O. Hornby: Industrialization in Denmark and the Loss of the Duchies. *Scandinavian Economic History Review*, vol. XVII, no. 1 (1969).

1. The Debate about Danish Industrialisation.

The question when the industrial revolution actually took place has been much canvassed by Danish historians and economists. Some have favoured the 1850s and the period immediately thereafter [1]). The majority have been inclined to place the revolution in the 1870s [2]). Yet others have felt that the true revolution occurred in the nineties [3]).

If doubt has been so prevalent on this subject, the reason is to be found, firstly, in the lack of the relevant quantitative data for evaluating the development of events. Secondly, the fact that Danish industry seems on the whole to have experienced a tranquil and protracted evolution does not make it easier to pinpoint anything that can be called a revolution [4]). And in addition to this, thirdly, there is the conceptual uncertainty surrounding the use of the term »industrial revolution«.

Earlier studies of the problem have leaned rather heavily upon data about the industrial labour force. These data are culled from two sources, viz. the industrial censuses, all more or less incomplete, of 1855, 1872, 1882, 1897, 1905 and 1914 [5]), and the annual lists in the reports of the factory inspectorate for the years 1875—1914 [6]). Neither of these groups of sources on its own supplies a sufficient illustration of industrial

---

[1]) Richard Willerslev: *Studier i dansk industrihistorie 1850—1880* (1952), p. 236. Fred. Vedsø: *Danmarks industri* (1928), p. 36.

[2]) G. Nørregaard: *Arbejdsforhold inden for dansk håndværk og industri* (1942), p. 114 ff. Einar Cohn: Dansk håndværk og industri ved midten af det 19. århundrede, *Nationaløkonomisk Tidsskrift 1953*, p. 97. Povl Bagge's review of Rich. Willerslev's Studier i dansk industrihistorie in *Historisk Tidsskrift* II r. IV, p. 114 and 122. Kristof Glamann: Industrialisation as a Factor in Economic Growth in Denmark since 1700 in the *Report of the First International Conference of Economic History* (1960), p. 122.

[3]) Jens Samsøe: *Die Industrialisierung Dänemarks* (1928), p. 62. Hjalmar Gammelgaard: *Industriens muligheder og vilkår* (1926), p. 13. Vagn Dybdahl in *Danmarks Historie, Politikens Forlag*, vol. 12 (1965), p. 233. Jens Warming: *Gode og dårlige tider* (1903), p. 9.

[4]) Axel Nielsen's view, expressed in *Industriens historie i Danmark* III:1 (1944), cf. Rich. Willerslev op. cit. p. 236.

[5]) Rich. Willerslev, op. cit. p. 254—301, and publications by Danmarks Statistik and Københavns Kommunes statistiske kontor.

[6]) *Ministerialtidende B.*

trends. In the first place, the element of comparability is lacking over the long term, and secondly, the figures for the labour force itself do not offer a basis for assessing the trend of productivity, which must be presumed to have been a crucial factor in industrialisation throughout the period.

If it is desired to form a more precise picture of the industrial trend, appraisal must be based upon such macro-economic units as gross and net values of production. It goes without saying that the use of such units yields a better overall impression of the industrial trend than do single indicators such as labour force, utilization af machinery, and so on. Moreover, an exposition based upon the terminology of national accounting offers the advantage that it also permits of direct comparison being made between dimensions and growth in industry and in other economic sectors as well.

Of course, one may be predisposed to regard it as a hopeless task to procure sufficiently reliable macro-economic figures for industry bearing in mind the undoubted weaknesses of the underlying data. However, precisely because it is posssible in such calculations to combine data from a great variety of sources, all differing from one economic sector to another, it is also possible in the vast majority of cases to bridge the uncertainties and actually achieve a clearer picture of the details of industrial development.

I have undertaken calculations of this sort after a detailed scrutiny of the material available in industrial censuses, reports of the factory inspectorate, industrial reports, statistics of industrial production, information concerning state- controlled manufactures, memorial publications of industrial concerns, and so on. The results of these calculations of the gross domestic product at factor cost of industry and of other economic sectors are presented in very compressed form in table 1. More detailed information concerning individual industries is to be found in table 3 and in table I, page 71—73. It ought to be added that after 1913 the figures are culled from official statistics, and the point should further be made that the distinction between industry and handicraft is drawn in accordance with the criterion traditionally utilised in the official Danish statistics, whereby goods manufactured by firms employing six workers or more are counted as industrial products while the output of firms with five workers or fewer is regarded as handicraft.

The figures thus computed furnish a picture sufficiently detailed to shed light upon some of the issues raised to date in the debate about industrialisation. Thanks to W. W. Rostow's [1]) inspiring work on the stages of industrialisation, this debate has come to be conducted in recent years within a far more precise conceptual framework than was the case fifteen or twenty years ago, when discussion of these problems was at a peak in Denmark. A new and valuable contribution to this refining of concepts has been made recently by the studies of »the early stages of industrialisation« carried out by Rondo Cameron and his colleagues [2]). In fact the concept of »early industrialisation« as defined by Cameron is more precise, and therefore a far better tool to work with, than the term »industrial revolution«, which has been the one most commonly employed hitherto in the debate on Danish industrialisation.

Let us therefore see whether it is possible, with the aid of my figures, to place chronologically the phase of development which Cameron describes as »the early stages of industrialisation«. Conceptually he defines this phase as a transitional period in which substantial economic growth is accompanied by decisive changes in the economic structure. In regard to the latter he draws particular attention to the fact that urban production of manufactured goods, which normally forms the largest element among the secondary industries, adopts a more capital-intensive technique during this phase and grows rapidly in relation to agriculture [3]).

Of the criteria described above, the figures shed no direct light upon capital-intensity, which we shall seek to estimate

---

[1]) Especially W. W. Rostow: *The Stages of Economic Growth* (1961), translated into Danish by Gunnar Viby Mogensen under the title »*Den økonomiske udviklings faser*« (1963).

[2]) Rondo Cameron: *Banking in the Early Stages of Industrialization* (1967).

[3]) Rondo Cameron, op. cit. p. 6.

later in terms of the degree of mechanisation, cf. table 4. But the national accounting figures already available were well adapted for testing against Cameron's three other criteria of

TABLE 1.
Distribution of gross domestic product at factor cost by principal industrial categories.

	1855	1870	1890	1900	1930	1939	1956	1967
	\multicolumn{8}{c}{millions of kroner}							
Primary industries (agriculture etc.)	261	335	365	399	1202	1510	5769	7676
Manufacturing industries	18	29	63	131	663	1256	5467	15650
Handicrafts	56	79	118	132	498	772	2643	7700
Public works	0	2	4	9	107	171	553	1525
Building and construction works	19	24	30	74	310	408	2152	7825
Secondary industries, total	93	134	215	346	1578	2607	10815	32700
Tertiary industries	115	200	385	577	2925	4010	14059	41234
Gross domestic product at factor cost, total	469	669	965	1322	5705	8127	30643	81610
	\multicolumn{8}{c}{pct.}							
Primary industries	55,7	50,1	37,8	30,2	21,1	18,5	18,8	9,4
Manufacturing industries	3,8	4,3	6,5	9,9	11,6	15,5	17,8	19,2
Handicrafts	11,9	11,8	12,3	10,0	8,7	9,5	8,6	9,4
Public works	0,0	0,3	0,4	0,7	1,9	2,1	1,8	1,9
Building and construction works	4,1	3,6	3,1	5,6	5,4	5,0	7,0	9,6
Secondary industries, total	19,8	20,0	22,3	26,2	27,6	32,1	35,2	40,1
Tertiary industries	24,5	29,9	39,9	43,6	51,3	49,4	46,0	50,5
Gross domestic product at factor cost, total	100,0	100,0	100,0	100,0	100,0	100,0	100,0	100,0

Sources etc.: The data for the years 1855—1939 are based upon the results, as yet unpublished, of my own calculations. The figures for 1956—67 are the official national income data computed by the Danish Central Statistical Office *(Danmarks Statistik)*. The data are presented in terms of current prices.

»early industrialisation«, viz. 1. decisive changes in the economic structure, 2. growth of urban production of manufactured goods relative to agriculture, and 3. substantial growth of the economy as a whole.

2. The Industrial Trend.

Application of the first criterion to table 1 suggests that the periods 1890—1900, 1930—39 and 1956—67 should be singled out for the special vigour of their industrial development. The period 1890—1900 is additionally remarkable because, by virtue of a notable growth, the contribution of industry to the aggregate gross domestic product increases from 6—7 to 10 %; and this development is accompanied, moreover, by a number of other essential readjustments of the economic structure resulting, for example, in a considerable reduction (from 38 to 30 %) in the proportion of the aggregate product accounted for by primary industries. Structural readjustments of such proportions within a single decenium are exceedingly rare. In the case of Denmark, in fact, it is only the most recent times that can show anything comparable, viz. the period 1956—67, when the importance of industry and the other secondary economic sectors again increases substantially while simultaneously the contribution of the primary sectors to the overall economy is halved — from 18,8 to 9,4 %.

As well as the two periods of the 1890s and 1960s referred to above, the 1930s merit a mention on the ground of relatively vigorous industrialisation, since the contribution of industry to the aggregate gross domestic product at factor cost rises in that decade from 11,6 to 15,5 %. In other respects, however, the 1930s, when Danish industry was developing under the shelter of the quantitative import restrictions of the depression years, contrast sharply with the two other periods. This is so, for instance, in regard both to the very limited structural economic readjustments accompanying the industrialisation of the thirties, cf. table 1, and to the relatively modest total growth rate of the period, cf. table 2.

And when, as in the present context, it is upon early industry that interest is focused, it would be proper to ignore the developments of the 1960s, when industrialisation has attained a level at which it cannot justly be described as »early«.

Further, the data in table 1 show that the 1850s and 1870s can be passed over as containing any industrial revolution in the true sense. This follows from the simple fact that, throughout the period up to 1890, the industrial sector is of extremely modest significance, contributing only 4—6 % of Denmark's gross domestic product at factor cost. It is fairly clear that any industrial development occurring within such limited margins cannot have typified the development of Danish society in any way [1]. The fact that attention has been concentrated so keenly hitherto upon the industrialisation of these early periods seems attributable to two particular factors: firstly, the industrial sector's quite vigorous self-propagation, and sencondly, the intensive activity in company formation occurring during these periods.

As regards industrial growth, from the fifties to the seventies this was running at an annual average level of over 4½ %, calculated on the net value of production, cf. table 2. A rate of development of this order is to be regarded as a brisk one whether relative to the growth rates of the total economy in the same period or relative to the rate of industrialisation throughout the period from the turn of the century to the second world war. It is this high rate of growth, manifested also both in the number of new businesses and in the labour force, which explains why Richard Willerslev has regarded an industrial revolution as having taken place in the period following the middle fifties [2]. The typical boom years 1866—1876, especially, lend support to such an interpretation. In these years industrial growth, as far as can be judged from the somewhat uncertain figures of this partial period, amounted to almost 6 % *per annum*.

---

[1] Povl Bagge, *Historisk Tidsskrift* 11 r. IV, p. 121.

[2] Rich. Willerslev, op. cit. p. 207—218.

TABLE 2.
Annual growth rates per cent.

	Industry [1]	The economy as a whole [2]
1855—72	4,7	1,8
1872—82	4,4	1,7
1882—90	4,8	2,5
1890—97	7,2	2,8
1897—1905	4,4	3,1
1905—13	5,4	3,2
1920—32	1,5	3,0
1932—39	6,5	2,9
1947—56	3,5	2,6
1956—67	6,9	4,8

[1] The industrial growth rates are measured on the basis of the industry's value added at fixed prices. For the period prior to 1913 these fixed prices are arrived at by using a specially computed price index of industrial goods — cf. table II, page 74 — to reduce the current values recorded in table 3. For the period after 1913, the industrial production index in the official statistics and the fixed-price computations in the statistics of national income are used.

[2] For the period prior to 1939 the total growth rates are based on my own computations of the national income at fixed prices. After 1939 they are based on corresponding data in the official statistics.

If the 1870s are often singled out as a period of industrialisation, this is undoubtedly because, in addition to this substantial self-generated growth, the formation of joint stock companies and the trend towards concentration were very palpable features of this period of development. However, Willerslev has rightly pointed out in this regard that joint stock company formation and industrialisation cannot automatically be assumed to be coterminous. It is by no means unusual, for an incipient industrial development to be borne forward chiefly by one-man enterprises and partnerships.

Neither is the emergence of the joint stock company form in the seventies principally attributable to industry, despite the quite lively activity in promoting industrial companies up to

1875 [1]). The 30 million *kroner* of share capital invested in industrial companies at the end of the seventies still represented only 16 % of the aggregate share capital of the nation, cf. table 11. Investment in shares in that age was still directed much more towards banks and transport companies than to industry.

Somewhat similar proportions are observable in the capital financing of the C. F. Tietgen enterprises arranged through *Privatbanken*, which tend to be frequently cited because, by virtue of their grandiose size, they constitute one of the most conspicuous manifestations of the promotional operations of the seventies. As a result of these operations [2]), which in 1886 involved the placing of share capital amounting altogether to 78,5 million *kroner*, only the relatively modest sum of 18,3 million *kroner* was invested in industry, (Burmeister & Wain, the sugar refineries, the Faxe limestone quarry and the chicory factories). Most of the remainder went into transport enterprises, which thus retained their clear supremacy in the share market [3]). In view of the limited influence of the joint stock company form upon the financing of industry, too, care should naturally be taken not to overrate the extent of the competition-restraining influences already emanating from the industrial companies in the introductory phase of Danish industry [4]).

The features noted tend in themselves to support the view that Danish industrialisation took place in the form of a relatively smooth and evolutionary process of development. However, if a single era of industrialisation is to be picked out within this progression for specially vigorous growth and specially revolutionary social effects, then without question this must be the 1890s.

Prior to this period, nevertheless, there was a long introduc-

---

[1]) Rich. Willerslev, op. cit. p. 237.

[2]) See also p. 42.

[3]) Ernst Brandes: Børsen. *Tilskueren* 1886, p. 698.

[4]) Rich. Willerslev, op. cit. p. 245, cf. Kristof Glamann's review in *Svenskt Historisk Tidskrift* 1956, p. 104.

tory stage of industrialisation embracing the period from 1855 on. This period is typical in that the extent of industrialisation is so modest that fluctuations in this sector cannot have noticeably affected the economy as a whole. The crucial factors in the evolution of the economy were constituted at that time by the firmly established division of labour between Danish agriculture and foreign industry. In these circumstances the natural interest of the commercial world in keeping the exchange of goods confined to the traditional paths as long as possible most likely had a retarding effect upon the tempo of industrialisation.

At all events, the size and growth of the commercial sector justify importance being ascribed to attitudes of this sort. While the proportion of the aggregate gross domestic product at factor cost accounted for by industry rose only from 4 to 7 % between 1855 and 1890, the share of the trade-dominated tertiary sectors increased from 25 to no less than 40 % of the gross domestic product at factor cost. This is a context in which more properly to speak not of an industrial revolution but of a thirty- or forty-year commercial expansion representing the preparatory phase for the truly vigorous industrial growth of the nineties. The highly sophisticated commercial environment thus created, moreover, was to set its stamp in many ways upon the evolutionary trends and financial forms of the subsequent industrialisation.

We may attempt to form a more detailed idea of the development of industry from a sector-by-sector breakdown of the estimated figures of aggregate gross domestic product of industry at factor cost, cf. table 3.

The industrial structure that is revealed shows features particularly characteristic of a primitive industry orientated to the home market. No particular branch is dominant, and growth proceeds on a broad front determined by the common market demand factors without major differences from one sector to another.

The predominant alignment towards the home market is confirmed directly by the figures showing the trend of exports.

It is true that the value of industrial exports in absolute terms more than quadrupled during the half century from 1855 to 1905. However, even with such a growth, exports conspicuously failed to keep pace with production. The export ratio of industry measured as the proportion of gross value of production going for export therefore exhibits a steadily falling curve during the pre-industrial stage up to 1890, coming to rest at modest levels of around 10 %. The textiles sector, where competition from the great industrial countries was severe [1]), was a particular source of weakness in the export position.

The wide diffusion of Danish industry over the various sectors of a modest home market must in itself have inhibited efficiency. The same applies to the geographical dispersion prevailing during the introductory stage of industrialisation. It is interesting to find these restraints on growth and competition referred to in a survey by the economist and statistician William Scharling, one of the most experienced of contemporary observers. His reports are all the more valuable in that they date from the early nineties [2]) and therefore describe Danish industry as it was prior to its vigorous boom era [3]).

Scharling regarded the contemporary low productivity of Danish industry as a result of its being »not only small *in toto* but also remarkably diffuse in character. It is the isolated and the unique that typify our large industries, since these have disseminated themselves into every possible area and each individual enterprise again has spread itself out locally ... If we focus our attention upon true factories, ignoring those industrial establishments, such as tanneries, dyeworks, printing works, breweries etc., that are intermediate in size between factories and craft enterprises, we find almost everywhere that

---

[1]) Jens Warming: *Gode og dårlige tider* (1903), p. 27.

[2]) *Berlingske Aftenavis* 6. 8. 1892, cf. also V. Falbe Hansen og Will. Scharling: *Danmarks Statistik II* (1887), p. 495.

[3]) Scharling's view is also shared by Henry Bruun: *Den faglige arbejderbevægelse* (1938), p. 119 and 283, P. Munch i *Schultz' Danmarkshistorie* V (1942), p. 573, and Jens Warming: *Gode og dårlige tider* (1903), p. 9. Similar views are expressed by official sources in *Toldkommissions-Betænkningen af 1896.* (Section A, p. XIII).

TABLE 3.
Industrial gross domestic product at factor cost (current prices).

	1855 mill. kr.	1872 mill. kr.	1882 mill. kr.	1890 mill. kr.	1897 mill. kr.	1905 mill. kr.	1913 mill. kr.
Foodstuffs	2,0	3,9	4,6	6,7	10,6	19,8	39,7
Beverages	2,1	4,3	8,9	12,1	15,9	19,9	24,0
Tobacco	0,5	1,8	2,4	2,5	4,1	6,8	10,3
Textiles and clothing [1])	3,8	10,1	9,4	12,3	19,6	29,7	42,5
Wood and furniture	0,1	0,7	0,8	1,7	3,7	6,6	10,1
Chemical industries [2])	1,6	1,9	2,7	3,5	5,4	9,2	18,9
Stone, clay and glass	2,1	3,5	5,1	7,2	12,4	14,9	23,4
Iron and non-ferrous metals [3])	3,5	6,4	8,8	11,1	20,1	29,9	48,7
Others	0,3	0,6	0,8	1,1	1,7	2,5	4,5
Gross domestic product at factor cost, total	17,8	35,6	47,5	63,4	100,1	149,7	239,4
Gross value of industrial production	44	86	111	149	234	361	602
Industrial exports	6	12	14	16	24	27	63
Export ratio per cent	14	14	13	11	10	7	10

Sources: The figures of gross value of industrial production and gross domestic product at factor cost are based on my own computations. Industrial exports for 1852—1913 are based on Bus Henriksen and Anders Ølgaard: *Danmarks udenrigshandel 1874—1958*, Copenhagen 1960, and for 1855 and 1872 on my own adaptations of the official statistics of foreign trade. The figures prior to 1910 are more unreliable than those for subsequent years, since in those days certain industrial products were recorded in the category »other goods«. A rough correction has been made here by transferring to the industrial category half the exports of »other goods«, the same proportion as in the transitional year 1910.

[1]) Including the leather and footwear industries.

[2]) Including the rubber, mineral oil and coal industries.

[3]) Including iron- and metalworking establishments, iron foundries and engineering works, electrical industries and transport equipment industries.

they stand in isolation: nowhere in Denmark are there any agglomerations of factories of the sort found in other countries, for with us such kindred establishments are scattered over the whole country. There is scarcely a single small provincial town that does not have a factory of one kind or another; in the medium-sized ones there are four, five or six, in the large towns perhaps even as many as a dozen — but usually all different from one another. We have about the same number of engineering works as we have provincial towns — there seems to be one in every town, but only exceptionally three or four in a single town. We have a fair number of textile factories and cotton mills — but all of them are local establishments and seldom does any town have more than one or two.«

Such a situation, which is not particularly conducive to growth, is indeed typical of an introductory stage of industrialisation, certainly not of an economy made more efficient by an industrial revolution. The fact that entirely new fields of production account very largely for the subsequent growth of the economy both technically, geographically and in types of product is all of a piece with Danish industry being little developed at that time.

Examples of improved or entirely new products at the beginning of the 1890s are provided by the margarine industry, cement-making, sulphuric acid production, cable and wire manufacturing, the telephone industry and cycle-building. Something of the same sort can be noticed in fields where a new or improved technique leads to the reorganisation of production on industrial lines, as for instance in the case of bread manufacturing, soda production, and the manufacture of footwear, knitwear and ready-made clothing. A third growth area comprises that sector of industry in which large competitive new enterprises are built up from nothing, as for example the cotton-spinning mills and the woodworking industry. Finally, of course, there is substantial growth in fields where production is particularly stimulated by the pressure of demand. Examples of this are furnished by the brickworks, whose output was driven upward by the feverish pace of building construction, the shipyards, which benefited from the soaring demand for tonnage occasioned by the boom, and fertiliser and oil-cake factories, the demand for whose products was generated by the growing need of agriculture for supplies of ancillary materials [1]).

The features described explain most of the readjustments emerging from a detailed study of the industrial growth of the nineties, cf. the summaries in tables 4, 5 and 6 below. The figures contained in the latter are culled from factory inspectorate reports [2]. They ought to be reasonably comparable, since no formal changes were made in the scope of inspection during the nineties. In point of fact, however, inspection did gradually become more searching so that the figure-series probably overrate the extent of progress [3]). In relation to industry as a whole — i. e., the total number of firms with six workers or more — the inspectorate's figures towards the end of the period were quite comprehensive. Thus, the number of workers in the establishments liable to inspection adds up to 65,000 in 1897, representing 92 % of the 72,000 workers recorded at the industrial census of that year, cf. fig. 1.

The data in table 4 confirm that the nineties as a whole were characterised by considerable industrial growth but also show that in all aspects the centre of gravity fell in the latter half of the decade. This is true of the number of workers, which rose by about 25 % in 1890—95 but by no less than 50 % in the five succeeding years. Thus industry, having attracted about 36,000 new workers during the nineties, assembled a total labour force of over 78,000. The number of industrial firms shows a comparable rate of progress, rising from something over 1,900 to about 3,650 in the course of the decade. The amount of mechanical power in use is a good criterion of capital-intensity, which was increasing rapidly at the same time. In this respect too, it is the second half of the nineties that displays the fastest progress, with a doubling of power resources compared with a 33 % rise in the preceding five years. It is characteristic

---

[1]) Emil Meyer: De sidste års økonomiske udvikling, *Tilskueren 1901*, p. 60—65.

[2]) *Ministerialtidende B.*

[3]) Jens Warming: *Gode og dårlige tider* (1903), p. 22.

that in this sector a crucially important diversification occurs in the period 1895—1900 in that, from a modest beginning, the consumption of gas, petroleum and electricity expands until it accounts for more than 15 % of the aggregate power supply. This led in this same five-year period 1895—1900 to a significant shift in the ratio between manual and mechanical power employed in industry. The magnitude of the change can be expressed in terms of the average horsepower per man available in industry, which increased to 0.66 compared with 0.45—0.50 at the beginning of the period.

TABLE 4.

Establishments liable to factory inspection.

	1890	1895	1900
Number of establishments	1949	2512	3652
Number of workers	42526	52628	78206
Number of establishments using mechanical power	1702	2286	3442
Amount of mechanical power in HP	19475	25938	51591
Comprising { Steam	18805	23370	42984
Gas	670 [1])	2276	5820
Petroleum	—	245	1756
Electricity	—	47	991
Number of workers per establishment	21,8	21,0	21,4
HP per establishment using mechanical power	11,4	11,3	15,0
HP per worker	0,46	0,49	0,66

Source: Beretning fra Arbejdstilsynet, *Ministerialtidende B*.

[1]) A later source from 1901 gives this figure as 839.

The supply of labour power to the different sectors of industry supports the impression of a pattern of growth with its centre of gravity in the second half of the nineties, cf. table 5. The greatest expansion of the period took place in the timber industry, where sawmilling and other heavy woodworking processes began to reap the benefit of the expansion of forest acreages resulting from the planting of the heathlands from the

21

middle 1860s. The stone, clay and glass industries come next, the background to their dynamism being supplied by rising building construction, as already mentioned. Progress is very striking, too, in the chemicals industry, taking the form of an increasing output of fertilisers and cattle-cake. Similar handsome progress recorded by the food industries is ascribable chiefly to sugar and margarine manufacturing.

TABLE 5.

Numbers of workers employed in individual industries.

	Number of workers			Increase per cent	
	1890	1895	1900	1890—95	1895—1900
Foodstuffs	3943	5193	7776	32	50
Beverages	2180	2474	3403	13	38
Tobacco	4242	4884	5790	15	19
Textiles, clothing and leather goods	7020	8469	11856	21	40
Wood and furniture	2822	3912	7762	39	98
Paper and graphic	4032	4663	6414	16	38
Chemical, technical	3038	3973	6156	31	55
Stone, clay and glass	5347	6629	10548	24	59
Iron, non-ferrous metals and transp. equipment	9902	12431	18501	26	49
Aggregate	42526	52628	78206	24	49

Source: Beretning fra Arbejdstilsynet, *Ministerialtidende B.*

It is characteristic that the industrialisation of the nineties was rather brisker in the provinces than in Copenhagen, and that the region of most intensive growth was Jutland, cf. table 6. Reflecting this, employment in Jutland industry went up from a modest figure of just under 10,000 in 1890 to over 23,000 workers in 1900. This expansion, too, is particularly concentrated in the second half of the period, when the rate of growth of over 70 % in Jutland runs parallel with a rate of only 40—45 % in Copenhagen and the other provinces.

The low tempo of industrialisation in the capital, already noted by Willerslev, was a phenomenon as far back as the seventies, while on the other hand it was generally Copenhagen that led the way in industrialisation both in the introductory stage of industrialisation from 1855 to 1872 and in the era from the turn of century to the first world war [1]). The heavy indu-

FIG. 1.

Numbers of industrial workers.

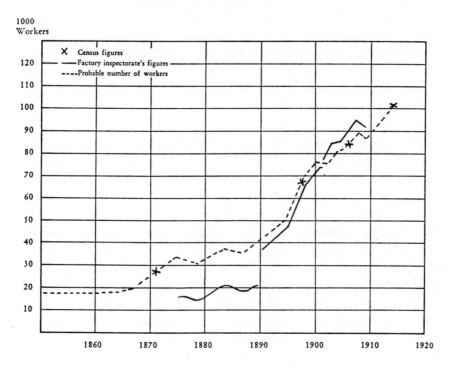

Sources: The census figures are Willerslev's extract from the official census figures published in *Nationaløkonomisk Tidsskrift* (1954). The factory inspectorate's figures for 1875—1901 are culled from the same source, while those for the subsequent years are taken from *Statistisk Årbog*. The breaks in the curve at 1890 and 1902 are due to legislative changes in the scope of inspection. The »probable number of workers« is a graphically interpolated curve which has been made continuous in an attempt to depict the fluctuations that can be deduced from the factory inspectorate's figures.

---

[1]) Rich. Willerslev: Træk af den industrielle udvikling *Nationaløkonomisk Tidsskrift* 1954, p. 249ff.

strialisation in the nineties of the provinces, especially Jutland, clearly resulted from the interaction of a variety of causes. For instance, the sharp rise in the gross turnover of farmers in the former heathlands produced a broader foundation for demand [1]. A variety of growth industries found opportunities of development in Jutland as a result, including important branches of the new timber industry, the cement industry, the margarine industry, oil mills, the knitwear industry and the cotton-spinning mills.

Certain problems touching the industrialisation of the nineties remain unresolved after studying the factory inspectorate's figures. One of these concerns the size of the industrial firm, although it is true that even here certain of the broader features of the trend can be inferred from the data. Judging from the figures, the average size of firm seems not to have changed appreciably during the otherwise far-reaching process of industrialisation, cf. table 4. Both in 1890, 1895 and 1900 the average industrial enterprise employs about 21—22 workers. Bearing in mind the large numbers of new firms established in the nineties, however, this unaltered average may well result from considerable expansion on the part of the large industrial establishments being offset by a scattering effect from the steady addition of new firms. A similar trend is observable in Swedish industry during the boom of the nineties [2].

On this question Swedish scholars have drawn attention to certain factors that undoubtedly were favourable to small businesses, factors that very likely were operative in Denmark as well. Firstly, it is easier for small firms to find a niche, either in competition with or supplementary to the bigger ones, in an era of progress and expansion than it is when economic expansion is weak. Next, the organisational problems of large-scale operation could still be intractable in an age when most workers were still recruited from the land. The shortage of technicians

---

[1] Jens Warming: *Gode og dårlige tider* (1903), p. 96.

[2] Lennart Jörberg: *Growth and fluctuations of Swedish industry 1869—1912* (1961), p. 151—52.

TABLE 6.
Distribution of industrial labour force by provinces.

	Number of workers			Increase per cent	
	1890	1895	1900	1890—95	1895—1900
Copenhagen	14555	16639	22904	14	38
Zealand (excl. Copenhagen)	11843	14088	20286	19	44
Bornholm and Lolland-Falster	2351	3034	4390	29	45
Funen	4160	5351	7541	29	41
Jutland	9586	13494	23085	41	71
Total	42526	52628	78206	24	49

Source: Beretninger fra Arbejdstilsynet, *Ministerialtidende B.*

and supervisors did nothing to ease these difficulties. At the same time the innovations in the field of powersupply positively favoured the smaller firms. As already mentioned, internal combustion engines, gas motors and electric motors were coming into use in the nineties. These machines were cheap to invest in and economical to operate even when power requirements were modest. Finally, the problem of finance was more easily surmounted when the scale on which the enterprise was to be established was not large.

It has already been stated that the founding of new enterprises must have been accompanied by major expansion among the larger industrial concerns. As well as this technical concentration Danish industry in the nineties undoubtedly also underwent a process of considerable financial concentration in the shape of merging, of individual firms. However, developments in this field cannot be followed by means of the factory inspectorate's figures, which relate only to the technical unit (the factory), not to the financial unit (the firm). Because of the absence of relevant statistics one is forced to depend almost entirely upon individual instances in order to form some impression of this important aspect of industrial development. But these are numerous enough [1]).

In the important metalworking industry during this period amalgamations between the many small iron foundries and engineering works were a frequent occurrence. A number of important concerns still in existence today — e. g., *Smith, Mygind & Hüttemeier* (1895), *Titan* (1897), *Atlas* (1897) and *Vølund* (1898) — were created in this manner. In the textile industry the tendency to concentration was much weaker, but there did nevertheless take place an amalgamation of the three largest cotton-spinning mills (1902). The paper- and woodworking industries, on the other hand, were characterised by extensive concentrations. The great majority of the paper factories merged to form *De Forenede Papirfabrikker* (United Paper Mills) in 1889, and in the woodworking industry such combines came into being as *Silvan* (1899), *De forenede Bygningssnedkerier* (United Constructional Joineries) (1897) and *Trækompagniet i København* (The Copenhagen Timber Company) (1895). The food and drink industries similarly offer a plenitude of amalgamations. Among the best known are *De Forenede Bryggerier* (United Breweries) (1890), *De Forenede Maltfabrikker* (United Malt Factories) (1895), *De danske Dampmøller* (Danish Steam Mills) (1897), *De Forenede Kaffebrænderier* (United Coffee Roasters) (1898) and *De forenede Conservesfabriker* (United Canneries) (1901). However, scarcely any other sector surpasses the concentration in the chemicals industry, where two of the biggest mergers (1897 and 1902) result in the creation of *Dansk Svovlsyre- og Superphosphat-Fabrik* (Danish Sulphur- and Phosphates Producers). Other important amalgamations led to the creation of *Sodafabrikerne* (The Soda Factories) (1896), *De Forenede Sæbefabrikker* (United Soap Factories) (1896) and *H. E. Gosch & Co. Tændstikfabriker* (H. E. Gosch Matchworks Co.) (1898

---

[1]) The account that follows is based chiefly upon *Greens danske fonds og aktier* (1902) and *Danske byerhverv* (1904—10), supplemented in places, however, by items of information from other sources.

and 1902). Finally, in the period 1898—1904 the cement industry enjoyed a vast expansion of output and sales, centring particularly upon the firm of *Aalborg Portland-Cement-Fabrik*.

The examples quoted illustrate a very comprehensive process af amalgamation which, like the other expansionary trends in industry, is particularly marked in the second half of the nineties and immediately after the turn of the century. The data support the impression that most of the amalgamations were technically motivated, since they are frequently followed by specialisation of production as between the various plants. From the economic standpoint the benefits of the amalgamations are often secured by means of cartel agreements between the great concerns thus created. The early years after the turn of the century are particularly rich in examples of this.

Altogether, the events of the nineties wrought very extensive changes upon the structure of Danish industry. Just as we have Will. Scharling's account at the beginning of the period, so also are we fortunate in having a contemporary report, by an equally experienced observer, of the industrial scene after the expansion of the nineties. This consists of a survey by professor H. I. Hannover in 1901 [1]). Hannover's assessments confirm most decisively the picture of the nineties as a period of important structural readjustments in Danish industry. After emphasising that significant industrial development began late in Denmark, Hannover goes on to state that »it was really not until the close of the present (sic!) century that, partly in consequence of the less favourable situation of agriculture and partly because cheaper transport greatly facilitated the import of iron, coal, timber etc., industrial enterprises of any significance were established in all parts of Denmark«. Regarding the trend towards concentration he continues: »Here as in other lands industry is moving in the direction of the large concern, and in more recent years particularly this has manifested itself in the conversion of many large establishments into joint stock

---

[1]) H. I. Hannover: Danske fabrikker for mekanisk industri ved begyndelsen af det 20.de århundrede, *Den tekniske Forenings Tidsskrift*, 1900—1901, p. 197—239.

companies«. Support is lent to this impression of increasing efficiency on the part of Danish industry at the turn of the century by the statistician Jens Warming's report of the considerable number of factories in foreign countries then operating in association with Danish enterprises [1]).

The features described blur somewhat the traditional view of how industrialisation occurred. The nineties seem to claim attention more than the seventies or the fifties. In the nineties the number of industrial establishments and the quantity of mechanical power grew extremely rapidly, and a marked tendency towards amalgamation opened the door to increased efficiency through large-scale operating and specialisation. At the same time the share of the national economy accounted for by industry rose from 7 to 10 %, and in this way new employment opportunities were created for 36,000 new workers, equavalent to 25 % of the decade's excess of male births and 33 % of the growth of the nation's aggregate labour force. Such a development implies that outlets were being found for considerable investment funds — which brings us to the principal theme of this paper, the problem of the financial prerequisites of industrialisation.

---

[1]) *Nationaløkonomisk Tidsskrift 1909* (p. 536).

[2]
Industrial Growth in Denmark, 1872-1913 - in Relation to the Debate on an Industrial Break-through

Niels Buus Kristensen

The industrialisation process in Denmark between the middle of the last century and the First World War can be seen as the result of a serie of fundamental structural changes in the economy and in the society in general. These changes, by establishing a certain institutional economic framework, created the conditions for an expanding capitalist economy which has been characteristic of the country's economic development since. From this perspective it is interesting to demarcate the period when the industrial break-through occured.

The present article seeks to discover, by the use of new statistics, what indications of the time-sequence of these structural changes can be obtained by a study of industrial growth between 1872 and 1913 - especially with a view to investigating whether it is possible to identify a relatively brief period in which there occured an industrial break-through.

Attention will be focused mainly upon the quantitative growth of industry, using new annual figures for industry's gross factor income between 1872 and 1913. Sv. Aa. Hansen's national income calculations, published in 1972, have remained largely unassailed and have been generally accepted as reasonable measures of industrial development.[1] The most recent research, however, suggests a need for revision of these figures as far as industry is concerned.

The core of this article comprises a presentation of new statistics for industrial value added for the period 1872-1913 - in current as well as in constant prices. The starting point consists of revisions of Sv. Aa. Hansen's figures based especially upon Ole Hyldtoft's latest findings[2] and a deflation with a new price index for industry.

Industrialisation indicating structural changes

As with many other countries, the dating of an industrial break-through has been a central concern of Danish economic history research, industrialisation often being regarded as *the* crucial economic change in the establishment of an economy with sustained growth[3].

---

[1] Hansen, Sv. Aa., *Økonomisk vækst i Danmark, I-II*, 2nd ed, Copenhagen 1977.

[2] These are to be found in Hyldtoft, O., *Københavns industrialisering 1840-1914*, Copenhagen 1984, and in new surveys (unpublished) of the numbers of workers shown by the industrial censuses of 1872, (1882) and 1897, generously made available by Hyldtoft.

[3] Cf. for example Rostow's theory of stages of economic development, or Sv. Aa. Hansen's interpretation of Cameron, in Hansen, S. Aa., *Økonomisk Vækst i Danmark, I*, pp. 290-1.

Scandinavian Economic History Review

In my judgement, industrialisation in Denmark is to be viewed as a result of a succession of fundamental changes in the economic (and political) structure. These changes can be epitomised as what may be termed the *full emergence* of a capitalist economy. What is meant with "full emergence" is that only with the establishment of a certain institutional framework does the dynamics that has characterised the capitalist economies become the driving force of economic progress.

This dynamics, which springs from the competition between individual business firms, expresses itself in three principal ways. One of the three is the constant pressures upon firms for rational production in order to meat competition. Secondly, there is what Marx called the "compulsion to accumulate", refering to the pressure to increase investment occasioned by the possibilities of the advantages of large-scale production, since the individual firm must constantly reinvest its profits in order to survive in the longer term. Last but not least, competition and the prospect of extra profits spur technological advance.

The institutional framework whose existence is the condition for the emergence of this dynamic will be described only briefly. The essential condition is the establishment of a labour market featuring *homogeneous wage-detemination* governed by certain general macro-economic variables such as productivity, unemployment, the price level and the relative strengths of labour and employers. The fulfilment of this condition is usually associated with rising agricultural productivity along with migration from country to town by a proletarianised rural labouring class.

An *institutional capital market*, featuring, for example, an extension of banking activity and joint stock company formation, is likewise a central aspect, first, in order to achieve a productive allocation of investment and, secondly, to facilitate the raising of the very large capital sums necessary for establishing a range of industries such as shipyards and railways.

At this juncture mention should be made of the *improvement of the infrastructure*, which first and foremost creates, via the improving transport network, the larger markets which are the condition of industrial mass production but which also increases the harmonisation of prices and the mobility of factors of production through which the productive apparatus can be more swiftly adapted to exogenous changes. The transport network, together with postal and telecommunication services, creates the communications system that generates an integrated social structure.

Economic factors such as the above, and the establishment of a stable *juridico-political framework*, should be seen as central prerequisities of industrialisation and and of sustained and stable growth. A satisfactory description of economic development in Denmark centring upon industrialisation must therefore focus upon these structural changes.

This having been said, however, there still remains no doubt that industrialisation can be regarded as one of the clearest indications of the full emergence of capitalism as the dominant economic structure in Denmark. It will therefore be appropriate *in the first place* to demarcate the period when the industrial break-through occured.

The Danish debate on this issue has been especially concerned with the dating of this break-through which has been the subject of some difference of opinion over the years. The following section gives a brief summary of the principal views in this discussion.

4

Industrial Growth in Denmark, 1872-1913

Main lines of the Danish industrialisation debate

Throughout this debate, which as noted above has been particularly concerned with the timing of an industrial break-through, the common understanding has been that it is very much a matter of demarcating a short period of a decade or so, in which industrial progress was specially vigorous.

To the present there have been three principal divergent opinions. From contemporary accounts of Danish industry during the period as a whole it is impossible to isolate any single period as crucial to the rise of Danish industry. However, it is a characteristic common feature throughout the period that the limited size of industry is pointed out, not only in relation to the economy as a whole but also compared with other countries. The 1850s, 1870s and 1890s are all underlined as periods of particularly vigorous advance but without any reference to an actual break-through[4].

However, once we move somewhat into the present century, when the early industrialisation process can be contemplated more retrospectively, the dominant view is that the 1870s were the years of the vigorous change. Most authors lay stress upon the underlying events as arguments for replacing of the break-through. The most important factors cited are, first, the protection against competition provided by the Tariff Act of 1863 and the loss of Schleswig-Holstein; secondly, the improved financial facilities available through the growth of the banking system, the *gründer* activity and increased joint stock company formation, and finally, the establishment of railways with consequent lower transport costs. With the exception of one author,[5] a lesser significance is assigned to quantitative yardsticks such as industrial growth, probably because of the defective character of the sources.

This view of the 1870s as the period of vigorous change was first challenged in 1952 by Richard Willerslev, who contended that as early as the 1850s industry was enjoying such profound expansion to merit that decade as worthy of the industrial break-through.[6] His view was based upon examining labour statistics taken from the industrial censuses. Willerslev's view, however, has been heavily criticised,[7] and has not gained general acceptance.

The third period to have been suggested as the period of the industrial break-through is the 1890s. With the publication of Sv. Aa. Hansen's studies in the early 1970s, this view that decisive industrialisation did not begin until the 1890s, and notably in the latter half of the decade, has won general support. This conclusion is founded chiefly upon value added calculations for both industry and the economy as a whole.

---

[4] Mainly based upon Wunder, S., *Den danske industrialiseringsdebat*, (unpublished paper) Department of Economics, University of Copenhagen, 1986.

[5] Nørregård, G., *Arbejderforhold indenfor dansk håndværk og industri 1857-1899*, Copenhagen 1943, pp. 111-15, however, estimates the quantitative development of industry on the basis of iron imports and the occupational data contained in the population censuses.

[6] Willerslev, R., *Studier i dansk industrihistorie 1850-1880*, Copenhagen 1952.

[7] Cf. Bagge, P. in *Historisk Tidskrift* 11 ser., vol. 4, pp. 105-22, and Cohn, E., "Dansk håndværk og industri ved midten af det 19. årh.", in *Nationaløkonomisk Tidskrift*, 1953.

Thus, although there have been varying opinions as to when an industrial breakthrough took place in Denmark, it has been striking that most accounts agree on a very smooth pattern of the industrialisation process.[8] So much weight has been attached to this in fact in the most recent research[9] that the term "industrial breakthrough" is either not used or directly rejected.

It is noteworthy that there has not been any notable differences in the way the concept of industry is understood. The differing views over timing are therefore to be attributed more to differing approaches and the criteria used in the appraisal of industrial development. Only in the most recent accounts are explicit links established with theoretical interpretations of the industrialisation process, and quantitative standards and statistical time series employed.

However, there is little doubt that all authors regard the growth and relative size of industry as the primary indicators of industrialisation, regardless of what yardstick and what underlying explanations may be employed. The fact that earlier accounts make only occasional use of attempts to quantify the trend over prolonged periods need therefore to be viewed in the light of the quality and extent of the available data.

Since the volume of the industrial production, measured, for instance, in terms of value added, are in theory the best measure of the quantitative development of industry, there ought to be agreement on the relevance of such returns, provided a sufficient degree of reliability can be achieved.

The only calculation of Danish industrial production which we have for the period in question are Sv. Aa. Hansen's detailed national accounts figures. Although these inevitably were based upon very simple assumptions, the reliability of the GDP figures has still not been seriously debated. However, since their appearance research has yielded new knowledge in a number of fields, making it appropriate to undertake new national accounting calculations for the period.

Such new overall calculations will involve much toil but will be particularly interesting in relation to the debate concerning industrialisation in Denmark. New figures for industrial value added are given in this article for the purpose of giving a provisional indication on the direction in which the industrialisation image shift. These new figures are based upon revisions of Sv. Aa. Hansen's calculations, taking as a starting point new data on industrial labour figures compiled by Ole Hyldtoft.

---

[8] But cf. also Nielsen, A., *Industriens Historie i Danmark*, vol. III, pp. 1-2, Copenhagen 1944, where the there is a more descriptive and detailed account.

[9] Cf. Johansen, H.C., *Den danske industris historie 1870-1970*, (manuscript) Copenhagen 1986, and Hyldtoft, O., *Københavns industrialisering 1840-1914*.

Industrial Growth in Denmark, 1872-1913

Calculation of new industrial value added figures

A proper scrutinity of the relevant factors and the mode of calculation employed in the compilation of the figures will not be undertaken here.[10] However, some account will be given to the overall method of calculation.

There are no annual figures on industrial production in Denmark until after 1916. For developments prior to that date it is necessary to base the calculations on occasional sources. The most reliable source material consists of the nationwide industrial censuses carried out in 1872, 1897, 1906 and 1914.[11] The best sources for filling in the picture in the intervening years are the annual returns of the factory inspectorate (*Arbejds- og fabrikstilsynet*) showing the numbers of workers in the inspected establishments.[12]

These are the sources, then, which constitute the principal foundation both of Sv. Aa. Hansen's work and of the calculations undertaken here. Sv. Aa. Hansen wrote with regard to his method:

> The calculations of gross domestic income are particularly detailed in the census years cited, when of course the data on industry are exceptionally copious. Furthermore, similarly detailed calculations have been made for 1890. The form of calculation best adapted to each individual industry has been selected as the most expedient, because this makes possible the best use of the very diversified source data available from one industry to another.
>
> For some industries it has been possible for calculations to be based upon almost complete production data: this applies for example to the sugar industry, to margarine manufacturing, to brewing, to distilleries and to cement works. In other sectors, production depends so heavily upon the supply of foreign raw materials that import figures have been able to serve as a good basis for production calculations. This applies, for example, to the chocolate industry, the tobacco industry, cotton spinning, the rubber industry and oil mills. The calculations for most other industries have been more difficult, because it has been necessary to combine data on the labour force culled from the industrial censuses with more diffuse production data from other statistical sources, from trade papers, from commmemorative publications dealing with individual industrial firms, and so forth. The results of these calculations detailed by industries are published in Sv. Aa. Hansen: *Early Industrialisation in Denmark*. Copenhagen 1970, pp 71-73.
>
> The gross domestic income for the intervening years is calculated more summarily...[13]

The overall procedure employed below will be similar to that adopted by Sv. Aa. Hansen. First of all new value added figures using current industrial prices are calculated for the years 1872, 1897, 1905 and 1913. After deflation, the real value added per worker is found by dividing by the respective number of workers. It is then

---

[10] For a detailed documentation of the calculations reference may be made to Kristensen, N.B., *Industriel og Økonomisk vækst i Danmark 1872-1913*, (unpublished dissertation) Department of Economics, University of Copenhagen 1987, pp. 26-70.

[11] Published for 1897, 1906 and 1914 respectively in *Statistisk Tabelværk* V.A.1, V.A.12, although it is still also the case in these years that only the labour figures can be regarded as tolerably comprehensive. For 1872 it is still necessary to link two (at least) almost concurrent censuses in order to obtain acceptable total data.

[12] Published in *Ministerialtidene* B the following year.

[13] Hansen, *Økonomisk vækst i Danmark II*, p. 336.

possible, from estimates of the trend of the increases in productivity between the four years, to work out new figures for the real industrial value added in the intervening years. With the aid of the price index used for the purpose of deflation a corresponding statistical series is obtained which measures value added in current prices.

Revision of the figures for the gross production in industry for the census years
The essential prerequisition making this compilation of new industrial growth figures possible was the work undertaken by Ole Hyldtoft in thoroughly overhauling the labour figures from the combined industrial census of 1872-73 and the 1897 census.[14] Further, new sets of industrial labour figures have been compiled for the fuller censuses of 1906 and 1914, and in terms of definition these are consistent with Hyldtoft's figures for 1872 and 1897.

As well as his calculations for these four census years, Sv. Aa. Hansen also calculated the value added for 1882 and 1890, for which there were no national censuses, which means that the source-base is inevitably rather weak. A quantitative evaluation of the consequences of applying Hyldtoft's mode of compilation to these years instead was found so unreliable that Sv. Aa. Hansen's figures for 1882 and 1890 are not included here.

The procedure employed has been to revise, industry by industry, Sv. Aa. Hansen's value added figures for the census years by multiplying the value added for each individual industry by the ratio between the new figures for the industry's workers and the number of workers which Sv. Aa. Hansen may presumably have applied to the industry in question.[15] In those industries where Sv. Aa. Hansen's basis of calculation consists of production statistics or import data, no change has been made.

Time series for number of industrial workers
The industrial value added for the intervening years is based upon an estimate of numbers of industrial workers derived from the factory inspectorate's annual reports from 1875 to 1909. However, these do have the serious weakness that the field of inspection was widened twice, 1890 and 1902 respectively, which means that figures before and after these years are not immediately comparable. Moreover, in all three periods the inspectorate's figures are far from comprehensive. The figures must therefore be transformed to a higher level in order to provide an estimate of the

---

[14] The figures have not yet been published but have been generously made available to me by Ole Hyldtoft.

[15] Sv. Aa. Hansen's procedure is described only summarily (cf. Hansen op.cit., I p. 287, II p. 335-337 and Hansen, S.Å., *Early Industrialisation in Denmark*, Copenhagen 1970, p. 23), which has hampered the calculations at a number of points.

Industrial Growth in Denmark, 1872-1913

actual trend.[16] The "fixed" points here are the four industrial census years and an estimate for 1882 based upon Hyldtoft's compilation for the latter year.[17]

Before that, however, a correction of the inspectorate's figures has been made based upon Hyldtoft's evaluation of the underestimate of the trend for the years 1872-1889, even within the inspectorate's sphere of responsability, which constitutes only a limited section of industry. Hyldtoft also contends that the trend was overestimated for 1890-1903. The estimate arrived at by Hyldtoft for 1872-1875 is likewise employed for these years, which fall prior to the inspectorate's reports.[18] Accordingly the number of industrial workers, N_t, is estimated by means (with some modifications[19]) of a linear transformation of the three *corrected* time series for the inspectorate's figure A_t:

$$N_t = N_{T1} + \frac{N_{T2} - N_{T1}}{A_{T2} - A_{T1}} * (A_t - A_{T1})$$

where "T2" and "T1" represent respectively the later and the earlier of the two "fixed" points for the inspectorate period in question, e.g. 1882 and 1872 for the first. After 1909, when the inspectorate did not publish figures, and until 1913, it is assumed that the number of workers grew at a constant rate.

The figures are illustrated graphically in figure 1, so as to afford a general view of the trend during the period. Compared with Sv. Aa. Hansen's assessment of the trend, the overall impression from the new estimated course of affairs illustrated in figure 1 is of a more stable trend, but at the same time the curve is influenced to a slightly greater degree by the movement of the trade cycle.

---

[16] Sv. Aa. Hansen has here carried out a *graphical* interpolation between Willerslev's sets of figures for 1872, 1897, 1906 and 1914, cf. Hansen, S.Å., *Early Industrialisation in Denmark*, p. 23.

[17] The source base for this year is very defective and the figures are based mainly upon the Copenhagen industrial census and Bayer's figures for the province in Bayer, J.T., *Dansk Provinsindustri*, 1885. Hyldtoft's figures are based only upon the firms actually known and are, therefore, of course certainly incomplete.

[18] Hyldtoft, op.cit., p. 56 note 31. The estimate is based upon a combination of census material and the inspectorate's pilot study.

[19] For an elaboration, see Kristensen, op.cit., p. 46-53.

Scandinavian Economic History Review

Figure 1 Numbers of industrial workers

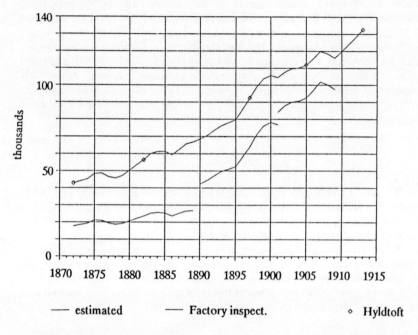

——— estimated   ——— Factory inspect.   ○ Hyldtoft

Source: Kristensen, op.cit., p. 52.

Price index for industrial production
The motive for compiling a general price index for industry is twofold. First the industrial value added in the census years has to be deflated so as that we can estimate the trend in real terms for the intervening years on the basis of time series for numbers of industrial workers. Secondly, the index is utilised to convert the annual real trend of the value added to measurements in current prices.

Sv. Aa. Hansen used for the same purpose a price index with the base year 1913, which is clearly unsatisfactory here, however, in term of reducing the index number problems.[20] This is because, in the first place, the year falls at the close of the period, and, in the second place, this is a relatively long period with vigorous industrial growth and much shifting of the relative size of individual industries. It is precisely in

---

[20] Another more serious problem is that the index from Hansen, S.Aa., *Early Industrialisation in Denmark*, which is cited as a deflator in Hansen, S.Aa., *Økonomisk vækst i Danmark*, II, p. 344, does not correspond to the deflator actually applied. If Sv. Aa. Hansen's figures for the industrial gross factor income in current and constant prices respectively are compared, the deflator used can be discovered implicitly. A graphical comparision shows at once that the two price indices are not identical despite periodically coinciding trends, cf. Kristensen, op.cit., p. 64-65.

Industrial Growth in Denmark, 1872-1913

such periods that index problems are often most severe, so that, all in all, it must be problematical to use only a single base year.

In order to reduce index number problems the price index used here has been calculated by dividing the years 1872-1913 into four subperiods with each of the census years employed as a base year. The division into periods has been effected having regard primarily to the passage in time to the census years, but also to the course of the trade cycle. Thus the price index is one with *changing* weight, where the choice of the base years can be illustrated schematically thus:

Base year	Deflation period
1872	1872-1886
1897	1886-1901
1905	1901-1909
1913	1909-1913

Finally, the indices for each period are linked together.

The price data used by Sv. Aa. Hansen were almost all extracted from J. Pedersen's and O. Strange Petersen's price history.[21] This work undoubtedly contained the most suitable aggregate price series for this purpose. The data originated in part from the weekly reports from *Mæglernes Priskurant* (Broker's Price Lists), 1855-1913, along with archive material from Den Kongelige Grønlandske Handel (the Greenland Trade Department), supplemented by six English (world market commodity) price series. In addition, Sv. Aa. Hansen extracted certain other price series from *Mæglernes Priskurant*.

If these sources alone are used, there are still important industries where price series cannot be compiled within reasonable bounds. Price series have therefore been constructed by other methods for six industries which could not very well be omitted from the index calculation.[22]

Since the movement of the price index has an influence on the growth rates calculated below, it seemed an obvious step to compare it with Sv. Aa. Hansen's index so as to estimate the extent to which the deviations from Sv. Aa. Hansen's growth pattern may be due to differences in the deflation. The general trend is in fact broadly similar, apart from 1873-76 and 1902-06. In the former period the price fall is markedly greater according to the new index, while in the second the new index exhibits a slight rise whereas Sv. Aa. Hansen's shows a clear fall.

It is difficult to determine what the causes of these differences are, since Sv. Aa. Hansen did not explain which price series he used for the individual industries.

---

[21] Pedersen, J., Strange Petersen, O., *An analysis of price behaviour*, Copenhagen 1938.

[22] The manufactures in question are: "rye bread", "margarine", "distilled spirits", "beer", "the printing industry" and "peat-making", cf. Kristensen, op.cit., p. 58-59, which also gives a detailed documentation of the price series and the basis of weighting.

Assumptions regarding productivity growth

In order to be able to compile industrial value added figures between the four census years, "all" that is lacking is an estimate of the productivity trend in the intervening years, since the average value added per worker in the census years is obtained directly as the ratio bewteen the aggregate industrial value added and the number of workers.

Sv. Aa. Hansen had chosen the simplest solution by interpolating productivity linearly between the census years. With regard to this procedure H.C. Johansen has raised the point that labour productivity is dependent upon business cycle.[23] Such a link may be due to the occurence of "labour-hoarding" during depressions. In other words, the labour force is not fully adapted to production, which brings about a degree of positive correlation between labour productivity and changes in employment.

More fundamentally, productivity may be presumed to depend upon capital per worker. Provided there are figures for the K/L ratio, the productivity performance can be estimated in countless ways using different assumptions about the production function and the relationship between technological and economic trends.[24]

The price problem, however, is the severly limited body of data. Because of these empirical problems, along with the restrictive theoretical assumptions which have to be made to calculate the productivity trend, I have preferred not to estimate the productivity trend from a calculation of the K/L ratio.

Instead, I have followed Sv. Aa. Hansen in estimating the value added per worker without empirical support for the years between the industrial censuses. However, whereas Sv. Aa. Hansen applies constant *absolute* growth, the assumption here is of constant *relative* growth per annum, so that the percentage annual rise becomes constant.

A crucial weakness of merely interpolating productivity rises is that it makes the industrial value trend too smooth, for fluctuations neither in the K/L ratio nor in technological innovations have any inffluence upon the cyclical path followed by the production trend between the census years.

Industrial growth, 1872-1913

We can now look at the figures. The time series for the value added (in current prices and deflated to 1897-level), the price index and the numbers of industrial workers are set out in appendix 1. The mode of calculation, which has been briefly described above, can be summed up in formal terms as follows:

$$GFI_t^{97} = N_t * gfi_t^{97}, \quad GFI_t = P_t^{97} * GFI_t^{97},$$

---

[23] Johansen, op. cit., p. 31.

[24] For an elaboration of this, see possibly Kærgård, N., "Produktivitetsudviklingen og de økonomisk-politiske muligheder" in *Nationaløkonomisk Tidskrift*, 1979, which also gives an estimated production function for 1904-1970.

Industrial Growth in Denmark, 1872-1913

where "t" is the year in question, "97" represents deflation to the 1897 level by reference to the compiled price index, and where "N", "P" and "gfi" are the number of workers, the price index and the value added per worker respectively, estimated by interpolation between gfi_{72}^{97}, gfi_{97}^{97}, gfi_{05}^{95} and gfi_{13}^{97}.

The exposition below will focus on value added corrected for price movements, GFI^{97}, since it is real industrial growth that is of primary interest. The trend is first examined on the basis of the census years only, these figures having the best empirical support. Next, the intervening years are brought in by reference to a graphic representation so as to produce a more detailed impression of the trend over time, which will be compared on a running basis with Sv. Aa. Hansen's figures, the latter having as mentioned formed the starting point for the new figures.

The trend shown by the industrial censuses

As may be seen from table 1, the new figures (GFI) for industrial value added lie at a higher level than Sv. Aa. Hansen's in all four of the industrial census years. There are two reasons for this. First, Hyldtoft's rearranging of the source material for 1872 and 1897 meant that a number of firms have been "discovered" which were not included in Willerslev's earlier set of figures[25] or in the industrial census of 1897. Secondly, and more importantly, there are crucial differences in demarcation as to which firms are counted as in "industry" by Hyldtoft and Sv. Aa. Hansen respectively. Hyldtoft includes all production establishments having six workers or more, except for branches comprising building activities, service trades or public works. Sv. Aa. Hansen, on the other hand, excludes "trades of the nature of handicrafts"[26] Moreover it is evident from the treatment of "dairies" and "slaughterhouses" in Hansen's national product calculations that these also are not counted as belonging to industry, either, and nor, is "peat and brown coal production", which is accounted for separately under primary occupations.

Table 1   Industrial value added according to Hansen's and to the new figures. 1872, 1897, 1905 and 1913

Value added (mill. kr)

	GFI	Hansen	% diff.
1872	43.1	35.6	21%
1897	115.4	100.1	15%
1905	169.1	149.7	13%
1913	168.0	239.4	12%

Source: Kristensen, op. cit.., 1987, p. 73.

---

[25] Willerslev, op.cit., appendix 3.
[26] Hansen, Økonomisk vækst i Danmark, I, p. 287, note to table XI.2.

Scandinavian Economic History Review

It will further be seen from the table that the relative increase produced by the revision diminishes with time. This is due mainly to the fact that the handicraft-type trades excluded by Sv. Aa. Hansen became of less importance in the later years. Ceteris paribus, this ought to be reflected in a generally lower growth rate both for the period as a whole and between the various census years, although the difference is very small from 1905 to 1913.

And of course this is the case as long as it is a matter of growth measured in current prices. It is far more interesting, however, to look at real growth; and here other things are not equal, for the new figures are deflated by the new price index. A summary of the growth according to the new (GFI97) figures and Sv. Aa. Hansen's figures respectively is presented in table 2.

It will be seen from the table that industrial growth based on the new figures is generally high - over 5% for the period as a whole and without wide fluctuations as far as can be judged from the rough breakdown into periods. It is worth noticing that growth is highest, at 5.65 %, for the very long first period, which makes it all the more interesting to study the trend within this period.[27]

Table 2 Average annual industrial real growth between the industrial census years, 1872-1913

	GFI^{97}	$Hansen^{13}$
	%	
1872-1897	5.65	5.30
1897-1905	4.10	4.43
1905-1913	4.98	5.37
Total	5.22	5.14

Note: The denominations of the columns are explained in the text.

Source: Kristensen, op.cit., p. 73.

---

[27] With regard to the interpretation of the trend shown by the figures, brief consideration should be given to what is actually being measured by the rise in GFI97 over time. On the definition of industry used here, industrial growth can be seen (analytically at least) in three ways:

a) general growth of manufacturing activity both absolutely and relatively in relation to the dominant occupation viz. agriculture, as a result of rising prosperity.

b) handicraft establishments which, in response to the general tendency towards increasing size of firms, break through the five-worker barrier and so become included in "industry".

c) finally, industry grows through the ousting of the traditional handicraft forms of production by new production methods with a greater degree of mechanisation, requiring an increased size of firm.

Industrial growth in the period thus does not represent merely an increase of production within aggregate manufacturing activity. It is also, to some extent, a result of developments in the structure of firms in the direction of larger average size.

Industrial Growth in Denmark, 1872-1913

Comparison with Sv. Aa. Hansen's figures (Hansen[13]) shows the tendency to be the same, but with a growth rate about 0.3 percentage points lower in the first period and correspondingly higher in the latter two periods. Growth over the total period is practically the same as for the new figures, despite the fact that the upward adjustment was greatest at the start of the period. The principal reason for this is to be found in the price trend at the start of the first period, when the new index shows a considerably larger fall than does Sv. Aa. Hansen's deflator. In this way the industrial level in 1872 becomes lower, and growth, both in the first period and in total, higher than if the same index had been applied.

Before we transfer our attention to developments in the years between the industrial censuses we may add a brief commentary on the productivity trend, which can be estimated by comparing table 2 with the numbers of workers. This reveals that the productivity rises in the new figures prior to 1897, at 2.45 %, are bigger than between 1897 and 1906, at 1.68 %. (A similar but less pronounced trend is found in Hansen, with 1.97 and 1.63 % respectively.) This trend harmonises badly with the prevailing view that the period from the boom of the 1890s to the First World War was characterised by increased investment and a rising K/L ratio, which would normally be expected to produce bigger productivity rises.

One of the principal interpretations propounded by Hyldtoft is in fact that the degree of mechanisation and the ratio of investment to numbers of workers increased sharply during the phase from the 1890s to 1914.[28] H.C. Johansen's calculations likewise show bigger productivity rises from 1897 to 1914 than from 1872 to 1897. Johansen uses Sv. Aa. Hansen's value added figures and labour figures at the "Hyldtoft level" for 1897, 1906 and 1914, while the labour figures for 1872 are of the same order of magnitude as Sv. Aa. Hansen's and Willerslev's, which must of course overvalue the trend at the start of the period, as Johansen himself remarks. Finally, the explosive rise of investment in urban occupations during the period 1896-1902 suggests that productivity would have risen more strongly in this period.[29]

This incongruity immediatedly suggests the possibility that the price fall at the beginning of the 1870s is overestimated. Real production in 1872 will in that case have been higher, so that the annual productivity rises during the first period will have been correspondingly smaller. To make use of Sv. Aa. Hansen's price index, however, is not sufficient to "turn the picture"; and on the other hand the fact that the tendency recurs in Sv. Aa. Hansen's figures makes it seem that the underlying GFI calculations in the census years are either too high in 1897 or too low in 1872 or 1906 *and* 1914. Both contigencies would produce a relatively increase of the productivity rises during 1897-1905. In this regard it should be remebered that the first two years are the least solid in their source-base.

---

[28] Hyldtoft, O., *Københavns Industrialisering 1840-1914*.

[29] Cf. figure XI.3 p. 282 in Hansen, *Økonomisk vækst i Danmark*, II, based upon the investment figures from Bjerke, K./Ussing, N., *Studier over Danmarks Nationalprodukt.1870-1950*, Copenhagen 1958, which however must be regarded as very unreliable. For example, investment in inventories and machinery prior to 1905 is largely based upon the imports of raw iron and ironware. Secondly, the figures for urban occupations are estimated residually from agriculture, and this gives some contrary fluctuations which do not seem realistic but more likely to be due to the rough method of estimating the total figures for inventory and machinery investment.

Scandinavian Economic History Review

The above account of developments between the census years plainly cannot describe in detail the economic climate of industry or indicate the especially successful periods with particularly vigorous industrial expansion. This is partly because the initial period of 25 years is so long that simply to label it with a single growth rate is hardly reasonable, and partly because the years singled out are arbitrarily selected from the analytical point of view.

The timing of an industrial break-through

Developments in the intervening years will now therefore be examined more closely with a view to discovering whether any particular period can be identified that is of such significance in the total growth picture as to justify its being termed as witnessing an industrial break-through. It may be observed that with regard to evaluating the trend of the figures, that as the figures are calculated, it is only the variations in the number of workers that cause the trend not to be wholly constant between the census years. As noted already, the number of workers is calculated from the factory inspectorate's annual reports, while the productivity trend is assumed to be constant.

Figure 2 Industrial value added. Deflated to 1897 level. Mill. kr.

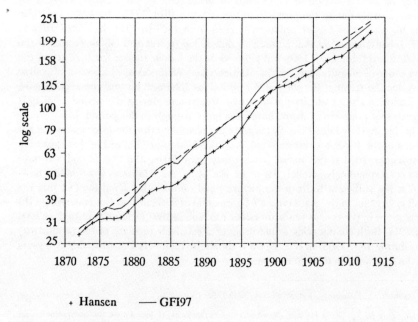

+ Hansen —— GFI97

Source: Kristensen, op.cit., p. 77.

Figure 2 illustrates the time series for industry's gross factor income measured at the 1897 price level, and compares it with Sv. Aa. Hansen's figures for the period.

Industrial Growth in Denmark, 1872-1913

The overall impression left by an inspection of the curve is of an astonishingly smooth and uniform performance throughout the entire period - an impression which is reinforced by the trend line.

Bearing in mind the uniformity of the performance, however, there are two periods which stand out from the other years. The first of these, from 1877 to 1887, is marked by the severe crisis of 1877-78 and the slump around 1886. It is interesting, however, that in both instances developments in the years immediately following not only restore the average growth level but show further increase, so that "what is lost is retrieved". Thus, the events of 1877-78 are followed by a period of high growth up to and including 1884, and the minor setback around 1886 is likewise followed by one or two good years. A similar though less characteristic tendency may be seen in 1910-13 after the bank and building construction crisis of 1908, which can be observed to some extent in industry in 1908-09.

The second period which diverges somewhat from the even pattern of growth is the second half of the 1890s, or more specifically the years 1896, 1897 and 1898, plus in some degree 1899 as well. The noteworthy feature of these years, apart from the markedly higher growth, is that the upward surge comes here after a series of relative good growth years,[30] with growth rates around an average of over 5 %.

When the figures calculated here are compared with Sv. Aa. Hansen's, also illustrated in figure 2, it can be seen that the new figures exhibit a slightly more uniform cause, though without it being possible to say that Sv. Aa. Hansen's figures show an irregular pattern. The new figures indicate greater growth than Sv. Aa. Hansen's figures up to about 1885 and rather lower growth from then until about 1897, after which the trend is generally uniform though with fractionally higher growth shown by Sv. Aa. Hansen's figures. The differences may perhaps be due not only to differences in estimating the numbers of workers from the factory inspectorate reports but also to Sv. Aa. Hansen having carried out independent calculations for 1882 and 1890.[31] Since there are no national censuses for these years (and no production statistics at all), however, the bulk of the calculations for these years are necessarily based upon estimated numbers of workers. Most of the differences for these two years, therefore, can probably be attributed to differences in estimating the total numbers of workers.

The consequences for annual growth rates of applying the different deflators are likewise negligible in relation to the annual movement as long as it is the figures for the real development that are at issue. In these, the price index is applied only with respect to the census years, so that the divergencies between the two indices become distributed over all the intervening years when one looks at the annual growth rates. The differences ascertained between the new growth rates and Sv. Aa. Hansen's agree broadly with the corrections of the inspectorate's figures affected here on the basis of Hyldtoft's estimates. There is therefore every reason to believe that the estimate of the number of workers is chiefly responsible for the differences.

---

[30] There is every reason to believe, however, that the years 1893-1894 were marked by significant unemployment, which to some extent makes the pattern similar to the period after the crisis of 1877-78.

[31] Cf. Hansen, op.cit., p. 336.

Scandinavian Economic History Review

If we now attempt to relate the results summarised above to the industrialisation debate under discussion, it is especially the interpretations of the early '70s and late '90s as break-through periods that can be evaluated.

Although the development can be observed only from 1872 onwards, it seems clear that industrial development in the 1870s was not of such a dimension as to justify the term break-through from a quantitatively point of view. Only a single year, 1875, did growth exceed the average for the period as a whole. The early 1870s therefore cannot be said to be marked by especially vigorous industrial expansion.

The last four years of the 1890s, on the other hand, with an average growth rate of 9.05 %, must well be described as even particularly expansive. Nevertheless there are two reservations which to my mind limit the extent to which one can speak of an industrial break-through during these years. The first is that a period of only four years is so short that it is difficult to reconcile it with the considerable structural changes which are generally accepted as an esssential feature of an industrial break-through. The second, as important reservation, is that this vigorous boom had no lasting effect on the overall industrial production level, for the decline that followed, from 1901 to 1905, nullified the entire increase, seen in relation to the period's average growth rate.

A long industrialisation phase

If on insists on placing a Danish industrial break-through in the period treated here, and if it is to be based upon the growth of industrial production, then in my view this break-through must be extended in time to embrace *the whole period from 1872 to 1913*, and presumably even from 1870 to 1916 if Sv. Aa. Hansen's calculations for the adjacent years are used. Such an interpretation recieves further support from the views expressed in the two most recent major studies of the Danish industrial history of the period, by O. Hyldtoft and H.C. Johansen respectively. Moreover J.P. Christensen, referring to Sv. Aa. Hansen's opinion voiced in Hansen, S.Å., *Early Industrialisation in Denmark*, (Copenhagen 1970), floated the idea as early as 1972 that Cameron's criteria for an early phase of industrialisation, to which Sv. Aa. Hansen largely adhered, ought to be combined with a considerably longer period of about 40-80 years.[32]

In order to test this thesis of a break-through lasting from about 1870 until about the beginning of the First World War, the growth of industry in this period must be seen in relation to the preceding and succeding periods. With respect to the period prior to 1872, the most reliable point for an estimate of the size of industry is 1855. Industrial growth averaged 4.7 % annually during the period 1855-72 according to Sv. Aa. Hansen's figures. This is probably overstated, since an upward adjustment of industrial value added in 1855, calculated on the same lines as has been done above for 1872, would be relatively larger for 1855.[33] Thus the annual rise in the period

---

[32] Christensen, J.P., "The Take-off in Denmark" in *Scandinavian Economic History Review XX*, 1972, p. 196.

[33] Cf. Kristensen, op.cit., p. 87.

Industrial Growth in Denmark, 1872-1913

prior to 1870 would probably be less than in 1972-1913, when average industrial growth was 5.2 %, cf. table 2.

If we look at Danish industrial development in the period subsequent to 1913 as a whole and ignoring the world wars, the industrial growth rate becomes 4.5 % for 1920-39 and 1947-75, and a mere 3.8 % for 1947-1958, i.e. immediately prior to the onset of the high boom of the 1960s. Thus this indicates that the period after 1913 also lies at a lower level of industrial growth if we view the trend over a correspondingly long period.

To sum up, the foregoing analysis of industrial growth may be said to suggest that the industrial break-through in the Danish economy ought to be placed in a relatively lenghty period from about 1870 to about 1916. It should be stressed, however, that this conclusion is only based upon a view of the industrial growth trend, and that the average growth rate does not deviate markedly from that of the period prior and subsequent to 1870-1913. An overall appraisal ought to include other indicators as well. In this connection it is but a natural step to relate industrial growth to economic development in general. This will be done by way of conclusion by looking at industry's share of the aggregate gross factor income of the period.

Relative size of industry

Industry's share of the aggregate gross factor income has beeen argued by many economists to be an essential measure of industrialisation. This measure of industrial development can be viewed in two ways. Firstly, industry's share of aggregate income affords an impression of industry's importance in the total economy. Secondly, *changes* in industry's share can be regarded as a sign of industry's independent dynamic. The greater the growth in industry's share of total gross factor income in a given period, the greater industrial growth has been relative to general growth. If industry's share are unchanged, its growth can be seen as merely a secondary effect of the nation's general development, while a rising share can be interpreted as expressing a more autonomous expansion.

Figure 3 illustrates the movement of industry's share of aggregate gross factor income in current prices. The figure shows this share calculated in accordance both with the new figures[34] for industry and with Sv. Aa. Hansen's.

---

[34] The aggregate gross factor income is here assumed to correspond to Sv. Aa. Hansen's figures, despite the increased industrial value added. This is because a roughly estimated corresponding downward adjustment of handicraft value added has been made, cf. Kristensen, op.cit., p. 88-89.

Figure 3 Industrial share of GNP at factor costs in current prices.

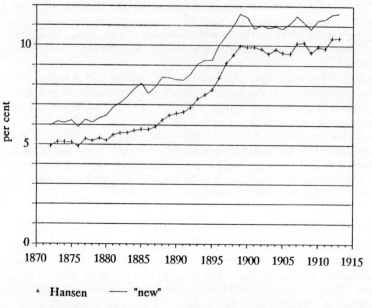

+ Hansen —— "new"

Source: Kristensen, op.cit., p. 94.

As one might already have concluded from the previous section, industry's share is generally rather higher when the new figures are used than when Sv. Aa. Hansen's are employed. Both series for the share of industry rise up to about the turn of the century, and are thereafter fairly constant. According the Sv. Aa. Hansen's figures, the share of industry generally rose at a steadily accelerating pace from year to year, reaching a peak at the end of the 1890s. From the standpoint suggested above, this can be interpreted as a constantly more dynamic trend in relation to the total economy.

The new figures offer a slightly different picture, however, inasmuch as it is possible here to distinguish two periods when the industrial share of gross factor income sharply increased while remaining broadly stable during the remaining years. In 1878 the industrial share comprised 6.1 %, but it rose to 8.1 % in the period from 1879 to 1885. Up to and including 1891 there is no tendency towards a further rise, since the share here was only 8.2 %. But between 1892 and 1899 the industrial share again rose steeply to form 11.6 % of total gross factor income, after which it does not increase any further during the period under review.

This indicator, the industrial share of total gross factor income, thus clearly indicates two periods, 1879-1884 and 1892-1899, when industrial development was markedly greater than growth in the economy as a whole.

20

Industrial Growth in Denmark, 1872-1913

Conclusion

When the two indicators treated above are viewed together, industrial development generally may be said to have been so gradual that to attach the term industrial break-through to any single subperiod is not credible.

If we want such a break-through within the overall period under discussion by reference to criteria of industrial and economic growth, then it should be placed in the whole period from 1872 to 1913, and probably from 1870 right up to and including 1916. This is supported by the fact that to all appearances industrial growth in the period both before and after this total period was at a somewhat lower level.

Such a lengthy period is naturally marked by economic fluctuations in which some years are more expansive than others. The 1890s especially may be singled out in this respect, since that decade is shown as expansive whichever indicator is employed. What is perhaps more surprising is that the period from 1879 to the middle of 1880s also seems to comprise particularly vigorous industrial expansion, while the 1870s as a whole do not differ from the average trend.

These conclusions should naturally be treated with some caution. In the first place there are several other aspects, not touched upon here, which are relevant to the discussion of an industrial break-through. And secondly, the time series compiled for industrial development are attended with a considerable element of uncertainty because of the very limited statistical material available for the period.

However, the statistics for industrial value added used here may be considereed to give a more correct picture of industrial development than do Sv. Aa. Hansen's figures, used as a starting point for the calculations. Nevertheless the new figures, like Sv. Aa. Hansen's, do have some decidedly weak points. For example the assumption of constantly rising productivity between the industrial census years could very well be refined further.

Finally, recent research suggests that there is a need for new and more thorough national accounting statistics to be produced such as has been done in the last few years, for example, for Sweden and Great Britain. For Denmark, however, such a task will be hampered by the difficulty of using the existing figures (Sv. Aa. Hansen's) as a starting point, their calculation being only sporadically documented.

Scandinavian Economic History Review

Appendix 1

Number of industrial workers and industrial value added in current prices and deflated to the 1897 level. 1872-1913.

	Value added mill.kr		Estimated number of workers
	GFI	GFI97	
1872	43.1	29.2	42877
1873	48.2	30.7	44081
1874	49.3	32.4	45340
1875	50.4	35.3	48263
1876	48.9	36.5	48690
1877	48.5	35.7	46510
1878	46.4	36.1	45836
1879	48.1	38.2	47365
1880	54.3	41.6	50346
1881	57.8	45.3	53576
1882	60.3	48.9	56441
1883	64.3	53.3	60021
1884	65.4	56.0	61495
1885	66.3	57.3	61469
1886	62.0	56.7	59369
1887	65.5	61.4	62697
1888	70.6	66.0	65837
1889	74.7	68.7	66862
1890	79.9	72.1	68467
1891	83.2	76.2	70671
1892	86.0	81.4	73684
1893	90.8	86.5	76382
1894	91.6	90.5	78000
1895	96.2	94.7	79696
1896	106.2	104.7	86039
1897	115.4	115.4	92509
1898	127.1	125.7	99142
1899	141.4	133.9	103856
1900	151.3	138.6	105762
1901	149.1	139.3	104518
1902	153.9	146.0	107769
1903	159.4	151.0	109581
1904	162.3	154.3	110112
1905	169.1	159.2	111782
1906	181.0	168.9	115415
1907	200.3	180.3	119888
1908	198.3	182.9	118334
1909	197.7	184.1	115925
1910	217.2	195.7	119868
1911	232.7	207.9	123945
1912	250.2	220.9	128160
1913	268.0	234.8	132519

Source: Kristensen, N. B., *Industriel og økonomisk vækst i Danmark 1872-1913*, (unpublished dissertation) Department of Economic History, University of Copenhagen 1987.

[3]

Growth in a Dual Economy — The Norwegian Experience 1814—1914

By FRITZ HODNE

For a majority of the advanced nations today, the key to economic growth has been the foreign sector. By entering the international trade routes and international markets, state after state has escaped the constraints of its traditional home economy. When home markets lacked infrastructure and buying power, and when the home economy was too undifferentiated to justify risk-taking in new technology, the world market, in contrast, gave each state the chance to utilize its comparative factor advantages, and specialize in areas where each had an advantage over its competitors. Moreover, with larger markets came the opportunity to realize economies of scale, since, in turn, risks became more tolerable.

The present article will discuss how far the economic growth that Norway experienced in the period 1814—1914 can be explained as a result of the country's successful integration into the world economy. It seeks to answer the following question: To what extent was the foreign sector the proximate cause of economic growth in Norway?[1]

The discussion will proceed within the framework of the dual economy model. Section I offers a brief, descriptive sketch of the model, section II considers the period 1814—1850 and the last section deals with the period 1850—1914. The first period shows the relation between stagnant foreign demand and deflation in the Norwegian economy. The last period illustrates the interrelationship between expansion in world commerce and Norway's specialization in the export field. The interaction between rising costs and technical innovation is considered, and also the performance gains realized in the transfer of labour from the agricultural into the industrial sector.

I

In the present context the dual economy model[2] consists of two sectors, the agrarian sector and the industrial sector. Agriculture has two factors,

---

[1] The article is prompted by the discussion stirred up by the appearance of two recent books on Norwegian growth.
Lennart Jörberg, *The Industrial Revolution in Scandinavia 1840—1914*, London 1970.
Sima Lieberman, *The Industrialization of Norway 1850—1920*, Oslo 1970.

[2] Arthur Lewis, Development with Unlimited Supplies of Labor, *The Manchester School*, XXII, May 1954, pp. 139—191.

labour and land; the industrial sector capital and labour. Through the industrial sector, the economy is linked to the world market. Only the open version is of interest here.

The agricultural sector is overpopulated in relation to resources and technology. The marginal product of labour, therefore, is very low, approaching zero. The wage rate, paid out in goods, is higher than the marginal product of labour. Wages may be said to be dictated more by social convention than economic maximizing behaviour. In the latter case, wages, of course, would be equal to, or higher than the marginal product of labour. This was Sir Arthur Lewis' original assumption, later elaborated in several publications by the scholars John C. H. Fei and Gustav Ranis. Dale Jorgensen, criticizing Fei and Ranis, has argued that the assumption of zero marginal product for labour is unnecessarily strict. All that is necessary, is to assume a productivity gap between the two sectors. This is the approach adopted here. For the agricultural sector the assumptions are:

1. hidden unemployment or under-employment,
2. marginal product of labour lower than the traditional or conventional wage,
3. wage-rate determined by tradition, not by the competitive market mechanism.

The industrial sector, by contrast, is urban and organized on rational economic principles. That is, productive factors, including labour, are

John C. H. Fei & Gustav Ranis, *Development of the Labor Surplus Economy: Theory and Policy*, Homewood, Ill. 1964.
— — Agrarianism, Dualism, and Economic Development in I. Adelman & E. Thorbecke, eds., *The Theory and Design of Economic Development*, Johns Hopkins Press, Baltimore & London, 1966, pp. 3—43.
H. Myint, *The Economics of the Developing Countries*, London 1964.
Dale Jorgensen, *Theories of the Development of a Dual Economy*, in Adelman & Thorbecke above, pp. 45—66.
D. M. G. Newbery, Public Policy in the Dual Economy, *The Economic Journal*, vol. 82, June 1972, pp. 567—590.
Taxation issues are dealt with in Richard Musgrave, *Fiscal Systems*, New Haven & London, Yale Univ. Press, 1969, pp. 69—167.
For the cultural aspects of dualism, rather than detailing a long list here, the reader interested in these matters, is referred to a recent scholarly summary, see
Y. Hayami & V. W. Ruttan, *Agricultural Development: An international perspective*, Baltimore, Md. 1971, especially pp. 1—66.
I have especially profited from Charles Kindleberger's books, see
Charles P. Kindleberger, *Europe's Postwar Growth. The Role of Labor Supply*, Harvard Univ. Press, Cambridge, Mass., 1967.
— *Foreign Trade and the National Economy*, New Haven, Yale Univ. Press, 1962.

paid the equivalent of their marginal product. Employment is thus determined by demand for labour, its price, both dependent on the state of technology, and the demand for industrial products. Income distribution is equally given as in the competitive model.

The term "industrial" must be taken to mean different things at different points of time. In what has been termed "the proto-industrial period" real capital per worker was low or non-existent, productivity per time unit low, but high per worker, since workers were paid their marginal product. "Industrial" then, refers to a mode of factor payment. With the advent of the factory system, machinery, and new forms of mechanical energy, productivity (in both senses mentioned above), has shown a sustained increase. "Industrial" now, thus means both a mode of factor payment and a form of production that involves large-scale capital investments in production plants and eqiupment. The assumptions for the industrial sector, in turn, are:

1. wage rate is equal to the marginal product of labour, (a subsistence wage in Ricardian sense),
2. free mobility of labour, implying an infinitely elastic supply of labour in the industrial sector,
3. "normal" price- and income elasticities,
4. for the dual economy as a whole, the rate of increase of population is a given, independent variable.

The above sketch suggests the co-existence of two economies,—hence the term "dual"—one is linked to the demand patterns of the world market, the other is largely unaffected by the forms of marginal factor payment that obtain in the market sector.

Dualism points beyond the cleavage between a market- and a non-market sector. A group of writers has stressed other dimensions.[3] Their materials are largely drawn from the tropical, under-developed states today, that have had contact with various forms of European colonialism in the past. The aim of these studies is not historical, they seek to illuminate obstacles that have to be overcome in order to set these young nations on the path of progress. However, so far from reducing the model's relevance to a country like Norway, now a mature economy, these aspects, in fact, enhances its usefulness.

The dual economy model brings out precisely those social, ethnic and cultural cleavages that characterized Norwegian society in the period

---

[3] See Hayami & Ruttan, op. cit. pp. 31—52.

under consideration, and in many ways, those cleavages still remain in force. In contrast to neighbouring Sweden and Denmark, Norway, it must be remembered, has a colonial past. It was a colony under Denmark for 400 years. From 1815 till 1905 it was allied to the Kingdom of Sweden in a personal union. Sovereignty is clearly not a significant part of the Norwegian people's heritage. Thus, as commonly observed in present-day enclave economies, foreign trade in Norway was likewise dominated by foreigners, first by the German Hansa, then (after 1560s), by Danish, Dutch, Scottish and German civil servants and entrepreneurs. These formed a political, cultural and ethnic elite, apart from the natives. Again, as in present-day developing countries, Norway never had the opportunity of setting up its own credit institutions till after 1814 —it got its first university 3 years earlier—and only after 1814 did it control its own customs tariff, its central bank, credit, and money supply.

Rural Norway was a traditional peasant culture. Urban Norway was an outward-looking commercial culture, closely in touch with European trends. This can be seen from such things as laws regarding property and inheritance, voting rights and representation in the national assembly, tax structure, poor laws and school laws. It is not usually realized, but nevertheless a pervasive fact, that economic dualism in Norway was closely matched by far-reaching legal and cultural dualism. Similarly, the main contents of Norwegian politics in the period under consideration was dominated by the urban-rural conflict, and the political mobilization of the rural periphery against the urban centre. This aspect will not be explored further here.[4]

However, parallels to dual economies today should not be carried too far. For one thing, Norway was always a free-holding peasant society. This feature reflects the combined effect of climate, geography and the extreme smallness of its population. Thus, l'ancien regime, with large-scale agrarian estates, a feudal nobility and a population of peasant serfs never took hold in Norway. Hence, the problem of economic development in Norway was largely a matter of acquiring skills, knowledge and capital, and this could only be acquired abroad.[5]

[4] Steinar Rokkan, Geography, Religion, and Social Class: Crosscutting Cleavages in Norwegian Politics, in Seymour Lipset & S. Rokkan, eds., *Party Systems and Voter Alignments: Cross-National Perspectives*, New York & London 1967, pp. 367—444.

[5] Cfr. Alan S. Milward, *The Fascist Economy in Norway*, Oxford 1972, pp. 30—31. This thoughtful, elegantly written book on Hitler's plans for integrating the Norwegian economy in a Pan German superstate, has, like Jörberg's book, the added merit of viewing Norway's

This shows that the dual economy model has explanatory value going beyond the under-developed countries of today. A recent survey of the post-war growth in Europe, for example, by Charles P. Kindleberger, employs the Lewis model with remarkable success.

We now turn to consider the interaction between the two sectors in the dual economy. Initially, a dis-equilibrium is set up in the industrial sector. This may be due, either to increased foreign demand for its products, new technology that raises efficiency, or to capital investments from outside. The increased activity results in a stepped-up demand for labour. Normally wages would rise, but with labour supply infinitely elastic, wages will remain stable while free hands move in from the agricultural sector. In this situation, unlimited supplies of labour means increased employment, stable wages, high profits and savings. With re-investment of the savings out of current production, a new round of the cycle is set up, wages going to consumption, profits to re-investments. This is, in fact, the classical Ricardian case of expansion, sustained by buoyant demand.

What happens when labour supply begins to run out? When supply turns inelastic, wages will begin to rise, and cut into profits. Wages will probably increase its share of total income, and the process of expansion will come to a halt. The capital-widening period ends, and the capital-deepening phase begins. Faced with increasing labour costs, industry will begin to cast about for new technology, which alone offers an alternative to total lay-off. New technology holds the promise to save profits in the face of increased wage-rates, even compensating for a fall in the market price of the relevant products.

Turning now to the agricultural sector, we expect the process here to match the chain of events in industry. When labour begins to move over to industry, the marginal product of labour, originally somewhat above zero, begins to rise. To the extent that total agricultural product is stable, this means that fewer hands produce more on the average than before; productivity is raised, or, in money terms, per capita income is increased.[6] As yet, labour may still be regarded as a sunken cost, with no alternative value, since its marginal product is below the institutional

---

economy as part of Europe, with the corollary of new view-points and fresh parallels, usually absent in works written by Norwegian scholars.

[6] See H. Myint, *The Economics of the Developing Countries*, London 1964, repr. 1969, pp. 86—90, who poses the pertinent question whether "zero marginal product" exists at all, hence whether "redundant" labour can be removed from the agricultural sector without a fall in production. Obviously, with unchanged techniques, those who remain behind will have to work harder. The issue is not material to the position taken here.

wage. Therefore, little or no incentive exists for substituting capital for labour. Labour emigration is as yet unable to topple the traditional agricultural system. But with continued emigration of labour out of agriculture, the productivity of those remaining behind will rise correspondingly, until the marginal product of labour matches the going wage in the market sector of the economy.

This is the crucial point, for from here on, agriculture will treat its labour as an alternative cost factor; this opens the way for the substitution of machinery for labour, a shift that is normally self-sustaining, because it is rewarded in the market. The necessity of a change in mental outlook is mentioned only in passing here. Also, when the interaction between the two sectors has gained momentum, productivity levels will be raised, of course, in both sectors. What sustains the process, therefore, is the differentials in productivity—hence factor payments—between the two sectors, that ensures the continued transfer of labour from inefficient to efficient sectors. To this extent it may be said that no advanced nation today has achieved economic growth without simultaneously improving efficiency levels in agriculture.

The Lewis model assumes growth to be achieved with unlimited labour supplies. In one sense it is a supply theory for growth. In the context of the dual economy, however, labour is seen only as a necessary condition. What triggers off the process is foreign demand, which should be regarded as the sufficient, or proximate, cause of growth. To this extent we have a demand theory.

Now, whether we call it a supply- or a demand theory, the model will assign a central role to the components of the foreign sector. Specifically, we should expect the size of the foreign sector to be at least 20 % of the GNP, preferably a good deal higher, in order to act as a pump mechanism for a massive resource transfer into the growth sector. Secondly, we should expect buoyant foreign demand for export goods and services to be related to boom conditions for the economy as a whole. Conversely, a depressed export sector would be linked with stagnation in the rest of the economy. In both cases, economic growth will be a function of foreign demand.

II

If the foreign sector acts as a trigger mechanism for the transfer of labour into the industrial sector, the size of the foreign sector as a share of GNP is of considerable interest. Norwegian national accounts series

Table 1. The Mercantile fleet, production and export of major commodities, 1791—1850.

Year	Export timber	Production iron	Production copper	Export dried & smoked fish	Export klippfish	Export salted herring & fish	Mercantile fleet
	1000 m³	tons	tons	tons	tons	tons	1000 net tons
1791	—	—	498	—	—	—	—
1792	—	5,775	—	—	—	—	—
1805	994	—	—	—	—	—	157
1817	—	3,900	—	—	—	—	138
1815—1819	597	—	—	7,784	1,463	15,521	—
1825—1829	708	—	—	15,551	5,941	33,958	113
1829	—	5,633	346	—	—	—	127
1832	671	—	—	15,748	6,093	57,584	140
1830—1835	—	6,248	—	—	—	—	143
1835	837	—	—	17,091	7,765	48,845	150
1838	894	—	—	13,467	10,264	37,706	168
1836—1840	—	5,811	673	—	—	—	175
1841—1845	—	6,337	619	12,246	8,655	58,259	220
1845	1,060	—	—	—	—	—	240
1850	1,137	—	—	15,174	11,810	56,822	284

Source: A. M. Schweigaard: *Norges Statistik*, Christiania 1840, pp. 89—91, 100—101, 114—115. M. Braun Tvethe: *Norges Statistik*, Christiania 1848, pp. 66—67, 59, 78—79, 82. *Historisk Statistikk, 1968*, Table 175.

As conversion factors are used: "1 trelast-lest"=120 cu.ft.=3.7 m³, "1 skippund"=159.4 kg. "1 fisketønne"=115.8 litres, 1 litre salted herring=0.86 kg.

go back to 1865. For estimates prior to this we are forced to rely on deductions from scattered evidence. Now, if we knew the export volume through these years, including shipping, and if we could measure the GNP percentage of exports of goods and services for one or two years in the period, we would have an estimate of the foreign sector for the entire period. This conclusion rests on the assumption that the structure of the economy remained stable. Thus formulated, the problem can be solved, at least provisionally. On the one hand, we do have fairly accurate volume figures for production and exports, on the other hand, we have "national income" estimates for two years, viz. the years 1835 and 1845.

The production figures are given in table 1.

For the moment we are interested only in the long-term trends. Consider the figures for timber exports: In 1805 they were almost as high as in 1845, 40 years later. There is thus no long term growth, but a sharp fall around 1815, a long depression, followed by a slow recovery, until the 1805-level is finally overtaken in the 1840s. The same movement is apparent in the figures for the mercantile fleet, and a similar picture of stagnation after 1815 can be seen up in the production figures for copper and iron. Only fish exports break the pattern, showing a steady rise throughout the period. We note in passing that the winter herring returned to the south-western coastal waters of Norway in 1808, after an absence of 80 years, giving the Norwegians a virtual monopoly for a cheap, nourishing mass-consumption commodity.

We now turn to professor Schweigaard and Braun Tvethe for the national income estimates in 1835 and 1845.

	1835	1845
Agricultural production	14,283	19,500
Forestry	3,000	3,750
Fisheries	3,000	4,000
Mining	611	1,000
Freight earnings in ocean transport	1,595	2,300
	22,489	
33 % addition to agricultural production to compensate for underreporting	4,285	
Total	26,774	30,550

The figures are in 1000 speciedaler, 1 spd. being equal to 4 gold kroner.

These totals do not represent the aggregate GNP for the respective years, since they do not include estimates for manufacturing, inland trade, private services and public sector services. However, assuming stability in the structure of the economy, the latter sectors may be ignored, since they can be taken to have been of the same relative size throughout the period. We know that the entire agricultural production was consumed at home. According to Schweigaard, 60 % of the forestry output was exported, and 80 % of the yields from fisheries. Braun Tvethe found that 48 % of the mining products was sold abroad in 1835, and 41 % in 1845, and he assumed the same percentages as Schweigaard for the other sectors.

The relative size of the foreign sector in the Norwegian economy in the two years may now be summarized, (table 2).

Table 2. The relative size of the Export Sector of the Norwegian Economy in 1835 and 1845.

	1835			1845		
	Total production	of which exported		Total production	of which exported	
	1000 spd.	1000 spd	%	1000 spd.	1000 spd	%
Total production	26,774	—	—	30,550	—	—
Forestry	3,000	1,800	60	3,750	2,250	60
Fisheries	3,000	2,400	80	4,000	3,200	80
Mining	611	294	48	1,000	410	41
Ocean freights	1,595	1,595	100	2,300	2,300	100
	26,774	6,089		30,550	8,160	
Foreign sector in percentage of total		22.8 %			26.7 %	

Of the estimate for total production used here, 22.8 % was exported in 1835, and 26.7 % a decade later. Compare the export figures for 1835 and 1845 with those for 1805 in table 1 above. Note further that total population was 895,000 in 1805 against 1.2 million in 1835. Further, we may assume that the labour force remained relatively stable, in keeping with the general assumption of structural stability in the economy. On this basis, it appears safe to assume that the foreign sector was larger in 1805 than in 1835, and even 1845, when the population stood at 1.3 million. It does not seem unreasonable to conclude that the foreign sector made up 30 % of the national income already by 1800. For the decade 1865—1874 the national accounts figures of Bjerke show that the export sector had increased to 28.5 % of GNP.

As a provisional conclusion we may say that the foreign sector of the Norwegian economy was of a magnitude which could act as a trigger for economic growth, in the sense that it permitted the transfer of labour from inefficient to efficient sectors. The Norwegian economy thus appears to have been very much an open economy, even in the proto-industrial period.

We now turn to some descriptive remarks, that will afford a background to the trade figures discussed so far.

The international background is well known. From 1799 to 1815 the Napoleonic wars were fought in Europe. Small neutral states were drawn into the maelstrom. Peace and economic depression followed from 1815. In the international economy, stagnation lasted well into the 1830s, broken by a few good years. Real advance was delayed until the early

1840s. In 1807 it meant disaster for Norway to be on the French side, and find itself at war with Great Britain, its biggest customer.[7] Timber exports from the towns around the Oslofjord had traditionally found their best markets in Britain. With the war this market was virtually closed, and British men-of-war blockaded the Norwegian coastal waters. From 1809 Britain, moreover, levied prohibitive import duties on the Norwegian timber, partly as a measure of retaliation against the Danish-Norwegian kingdom, partly to stimulate the export of colonial timber from Canada. British duties were ten times higher for Norwegian timber than for timber from British Canada. As late as 1846 timber shipments from Norway to England were less than half of what they had been in 1805.[8] A compensatory market was found in France from the early 1830s, but prices were low. In aggregate terms, the 1805-export level was not matched till 1842, when the old record of about 900,000 m³ was overtaken. Right up to 1830, timber merchants in traditional export towns like Christiania, Moss, and Drammen continued to export timber to clear off debts that dated back to the years before 1815. The towns simply dozed off in apathy, particularly Kristiansand and Halden. With falling prices, fixed costs and timber bought at pre-depression prices, the members of the merchant aristocracy succumbed, one by one. The place of the patricians was, with few exceptions, taken by newcomers, who were less burdened by overheads in the form of debts and social commitments.[9] An added difficulty was the heavy export duties paid to the government. Timber duties were, in fact, the largest single government revenue up to 1830.

[7] For this period, see
Jacob S. Worm-Müller, *Byen og tiden. Christiania sparebank 1822—1922*, Oslo 1922.
Nicolai Rygg, *Norges Banks historie*, I—III (Oslo 1918—1954), vol. 1 contains masses of descriptive material.
Sverre Steen, *Det frie Norge*, I—V, Oslo 1951—1962, especially vol. *Det gamle samfunn* (vol. 1) and *På fallittens rand* (vol. 2) which offers the best general survey of the post-Napoleonic depression.
Wilhelm Keilhau, *Det norske folks liv og historie*, I—XI, Oslo 1929—1938, has written vols. VIII through XI, offering in vol. VIII, a general account of this period.

[8] See in addition to titles under note 7 above:
Francis Sejersted, Aspects of the Norwegian Timber Trade in the 1840's and 1850's. *The Scandinavian Economic History Review*, vol. XVI, nr. 2, 1968.

[9] Ada Polak, *Wolffs & Dorville. Et norsk-engelsk handelshus i London under Napoleonskrigene*, Oslo 1968, the crisis in the timber trade seen from the London side.
A major source for the economic situation are the quintennial county governors' reports, beginning in 1829, issued up to 1912. The years 1830—50 are covered in *Beretning om Kongeriget Norges økonomiske Tilstand i Aarene 1830—1835*, Christiania 1837, do. for the period 1836—1840, 1841—1845, and 1846—1850, hereafter cited "Amtmennenes beretninger".

The traditional iron export also had hard times after 1815. Norway broke away from Denmark in 1814, at the same time leaving a cozy, duty-free area for its iron and glass. Denmark, in turn, imposed heavy import duties on Norwegian iron, at the same time as prices took a downward turn. This was the beginning of the end. As the English coke iron began to compete, the Norwegian charcoal-based iron-foundries, at the time the most capital-intensive ventures in the country, were forced out, one by one, though, as the caroer of Fritzøe works shows, the end was postponed into the 1860s by cost-saving innovations and product specialization. Norway, it must be remembered, had no coal deposits, and its iron deposits were small, scattered, and of low-grade quality.

A third major source of market incomes was freight earnings. (Up to this time mostly associated with the carrying trade between Norway and her foreign customers). When the bottom fell out of the timber trade in 1808, the sailing fleet was hit immediately. British seizures of Norwegian mercantile tonnage before 1814 added to the difficulties. Thus, while the sailing fleet amounted to 121,000 tons in 1800, and approached 150,000 tons in 1815, it dropped to 113,000 tons by 1825.[10] Even as late as 1835 the fleet only totalled 151,000 tons, that is, only slightly more than 40 years earlier. Jacob Aall, a central figure in the economic and political affairs of the nation at the time, looking back on this period, later declared it to have been the worst period in the entire history of Norwegian shipping. Tonnage duties to the government worsened the situation, but taxes only reduced profits, they did not determine whether or not the ships sailed or lay tied up in the buoys. This was ultimately determined by foreign demand for timber.

There is thus a direct relation of cause and effect between reduced foreign demand and depression in the industrial sector of the economy, also in the proto-industrial period.

The outstanding exception in these years was, of course, the fisheries, which provided a growing volume for export, indeed, as table 2 above shows, fish products were the biggest single earner of foreign currency right up to 1850. Again, the expansion in fishing underscores the conclusion reached above: herring and other fish were caught and marketed precisely because foreign demand remained firm throughout the stagnation years. For one thing, fish is a consumption article, not an investment input, which goes a long way to explain why demand abroad was stable.

[10] *Historisk Statistikk 1968*, Central Bureau of Statistics of Norway, Oslo 1969, table 175.

Table 3. The population of Norway 1800—1855.

Year	Total population in 1000 inh.	Total Growth %	Rural Pop. 1000	% of total	Rural Growth %	Urban Pop. 1000	% of total	Urban increase
1801	883	—	806	91.2	—	77	8.8	—
	—	+ .8	—	—	− .8	—	—	+11.5
1815	885	—	799	90.2	—	87	9.8	—
	—	+18.3	—	—	+17.3	—	—	+30.9
1825	1,051	—	937	89.1	—	114	10.9	—
	—	+13.7	—	—	+14.2	—	—	+13.0
1835	1,195	—	1,066	89.2	—	129	10.8	—
	—	+11.2	—	—	+ 9.5	—	—	+25.5
1845	1,328	—	1,167	87.8	—	162	12.2	—
	—	+12.2	—	—	+10.8	—	—	+22.2
1855	1,490	—	1,292	86.7	—	198	13.3	—

Source: *Historisk Statistikk 1968*, table 13.

Moreover, the population increase in Europe accelerated after 1815, with the advent of peace and the return of the soldiers. A growing population needed more food, and fish is a cheap type of nourishment for the poor, which is why demand for fish was inelastic. Finally, new markets for klippfish, that is, dried and salted cod fish, were found in Spain and Portugal during these years. Since the Newfoundland codfisheries were disrupted during the war years, the Norwegians were quick to step in to fill the vacuum.

Admittedly, the post-war depression hit all the countries in the Atlantic economy, but no nation at the time, or since, for that matter, seems to have had such a large foreign sector as Norway. The presumption is, therefore, that the stagnation in the foreign sector had adverse linkage effects that were relatively stronger in Norway than elsewhere.

What happened to the other sectors of the economy after 1815?

Only a few of these linkage effects can be dealt with here. As the model anticipates, stagnation in the market sector of the economy meant that the population increase would have to be absorbed largely in the non-market sector. The exception again would be the towns and areas associated with the fisheries. These expectations are largely confirmed by the actual population figures for the period. Consider first the aggregate population figures in table 3.

From 1801 to 1815 the urban population, reflecting the boom conditions in the market sector up to 1808, grew by 11.5 %, while rural population actually dropped by .8 %. After 1815, the urban population continued to grow, but now more in step with the increase in the rural districts. More detailed evidence would show that the urban growth was now largely confined to the towns serving the fisheries. Relative urban stagnation was especially marked in the decade 1825—35, when the rural districts showed a growth higher than that of the towns, 14.2 % versus 13 %. Note that there are no statistical pitfalls here, such as, changes in existing town boundaries or the creation of new towns. These trends were to be dramatically reversed in the latter half of the century.

The aggregate population grew markedly after 1815. This was due to the elimination of periodic famines, the introduction of vaccination and better nourishment, following the systematic cultivation of the potato. Total population increase 1815—1845 amounted to 443,000 inhabitants, of this the rural districts absorbed 368,000 or 75 %, the remaining 75,000 fell on the towns.

Parallel to the shift away from the market sector—fisheries excepted — cultivation of new land took a sharp upward turn. With less money for grain imports, people were forced to cover a higher percentage of their food requirements from their own soil. Similarly, the rural labour force expanded more quickly than the non-agricultural labour force, that is to say, stagnation in the foreign sector forced second-best resource allocation upon the country. The potato became a strategic element of the diet in these years. Between 1820 and 1865 total farm acreage just about doubled, that of the potato quadrupled. No general statement can be made on productivity developments in agriculture, but, in the best areas around the Oslofjord, the counties of Akershus, Vestfold and Hedmark, evidence suggests that crops improved considerably. No such evidence exists regarding agriculture in the west and north.[11]

With more people on the land, the "husmenn", a rural class that emerged in the 16th century, as the rural proletariat, now swelled to uncomfortable proportions. The husmenn were farm-workers, or tenant small-holders, with a family and a plot of land, rented on good, and sometimes on bad terms, in return for labour services to the farmer. With more applicants for vacant husmanns-plots, rent conditions were tightened. Their number increased from 48,000 in 1825, to 67,000 in 1855. With an average family of 6, the husmenn-class thus made up

---

[11] Stein Tveite, *Jord og Gjerning*, Kristiansand 1959, passim.
Fartein Valen-Sendstad, *Norske Landbruksredskaper 1800—1850-årene*, Lillehammer 1964, English summary pp. 303—316.

more than a quarter of the total population. Still, they were not the bottom stratum. Below the husmenn were the growing number of really landless rural workers, mostly without a family, the so-called "drenger" and "innerster", whose prospects were truly Ricardian in the 1840s. We touch here on the social problem of pauperism, the dominant social issue of the day. Compare the fact that the Storting passed draconic poor-law bills twice in less than twenty years, in 1845 and 1863. In 1825 the number of paupers on the public dole, which was organized in rural areas by passing the old and decrepit dependents from farm to farm, stood at 21,000. By 1845 the figure had doubled to 39,000. The corresponding figures for the towns were 3,500 and 7,000 persons. The provisions in the poor-laws against vagrancy and begging were understandably harsh.[12]

As mentioned above, the fisheries represented the exception in this period. Like the American prairies later, the coastal waters of the Lofoten islands were now drawn more closely into the Atlantic market economy. The frontier of the Atlantic economy was pushed, not only westwards along the great American plains, but also northwards along the semi-arctic fjord territories of Norway. The Lofoten fisheries were remarkably stable; the products found an inelastic, but stable demand and a steadily growing market in the Latin parts of Europe, and from the 1850s, also in Brazil. The herring fisheries, by contrast, were more unstable, but catches were truly enormous and markets were readily found in the Baltic and in the inland districts of Scandinavia. Something akin to the Klondyke atmosphere hung over the coastal towns and townlets engaged in the fisheries during these years, Stavanger, Haugesund, Ålesund, Kristiansund and Molde. Especially the three northernmost counties, Nordland, Troms, and Finnmark, received an astonishing stream of settlers from outside. These outlying districts, now largely regarded as declining, population-losing areas, had a population growth up to 1900 that surpassed in relative terms, all the other rural counties.[13] An exception, of course, was the county of Akershus, that surrounded the capital Oslo. Thus, while most of the 18 rural counties of the kingdom doubled their population during the century, the three northernmost counties tripled theirs, and Finnmark alone quadrupled its population. Towns like Tromsø, and Bodø, shot up from next to nothing to substantial

[12] Helge Seip, *Kommunenes økonomi*, Oslo 1949, pp. 28, 40.
M. Braun-Tvethe, *Norges Statistik*, Christiania 1848, p. 375.
[13] *Historisk Statistikk 1968*, table 5.

towns by the standards of the time.¹⁴ The interplay between international demand and expansion of market sector-activities is clear and direct.

Added light on the character of the interaction is shed by a consideration of the balance of payments-situation after 1815.¹⁵ With peace and depression, export incomes dwindled. In the long run imports would be adjusted accordingly, but meanwhile the country faced a balance of payments-deficit. The dis-equilibrium in the foreign sector resulted in a series of devaluations over the years 1813—1822. Import bans, government borrowing abroad, or export of precious metal offered no satisfactory solution to the problems in those days, any more than they do today. In consequence the nation's money had to be devalued, though several political figures expressed apprehensions on behalf of the national honour. With independence in home affairs in 1814, the country was in a position to create its own national bank and its own separate national currency. The lengthy debates within the government and in the Storting demonstrate that those who had to make the decisions interpreted the situation in the terms sketched here, that is to say, they understood that the nation faced a trade deficit, adverse terms of trade, hence, that it was impossible to introduce convertibility for the new money at once. In 1818 convertibility was, therefore, postponed indefinitely. This decision was, in effect, a ban on metal export. Instead the groundwork was laid for a policy of long-term deflation,—along the familiar pattern: the devaluations would raise the price of foreign goods at home, while Norwegian exports became less expensive abroad. In the long run, the detorioration of the exchange-rate was bound to improve the country's terms of trade, and ultimately lift the exchange-rate for the Norwegian speciedaler towards par. This occurred finally in 1842, when par exchange was introduced by law.¹⁶

---

¹⁴ *Tabeller over Folkemengdens Bevegelser i Aarene 1856—1865*, NOS Christania 1868, pp. 191—192.
 Tabeller over Folkemengdens Bevegelser i Aarene 1886—1900, NOS Christania 1906, appendix nr. 4, pp. 79—81.
¹⁵ For the difficult monetary questions, see
N. Rygg, op. cit., vol. 1, passim.
W. Keilhau, *Den norske pengehistorie*, Oslo 1952, pp. 48—97.
S. Steen, *Det frie Norge*, vol. II, pp. 126—206, vol. III, pp. 24—70, 271—288.
Gunnar Jahn et. al., *Norges Bank gjennom 150 år*, Oslo 1966, pp. 1—58.
F. Sejersted, Review of Jahn op. cit., in *Historisk Tidsskrift*, 1968, pp. 149—172.
¹⁶ Partial convertibility had been in effect from January 1st 1823, but at a very heavy discount. In modern terms, the country's Central Bank authorities were allowed to "float" the Speciedaler within a specified band, beginning with the band of 190—175, the actual

The currency story 1815—1842 shows to what extent international demand and tariff policies influenced an open economy like Norway's. Clearly, the currency decisions reflected concern for the external, rather than the internal value of the speciedaler. Internally, the money, far from depreciating in value, underwent a revaluation, which accounted for the deflationary pressure right up to 1842. This was possible in part because the home producers, again except the fishermen, worked without imported materials. (Salt, of course, had to be imported.) To the extent that best technology at all existed abroad, the prospects for profits for Norwegian entrepreneurs were less sanguine than they otherwise would have been.

It does not follow that the authorities, with a different set of currency and credit policies could have removed the more deep-seated causes of the depression. These must be sought fundamentally in the failure of foreign demand after 1815, that hit the major export goods of the country directly, and indirectly hit the carrying trade of the sailing fleet.

On the whole, the survey above does reveal the sensitivity of the Norwegian economy to the international business cycle, and how far exports determined the allocation of labour. A measure of the influence exerted by the foreign sector is its size. As shown, already by 1805 export of goods and services probably accounted for a third of the Norwegian total income. By 1825 it had dropped below 20 %; it hovered around 20 % in the 1830s, and around 25 % a decade later. Labour was pushed out of the marker sector. The post-Napoleonic depression, in short, meant a reallocation of inputs away from the export sector over to agriculture. The one bright spot was represented by the fisheries, but apart from that, unfavourable trading conditions forced the adoption of various second-best allocations of resources, with a consequent loss of potential income.

III

Turning to the period 1850—1914, our concern will be to show the interaction,—beginning in the 1850s,—between world demand and the expansion of market activities in the dual economy. The discussion will be limited mainly to the development of Norwegian shipping,

---

exchange rate of the paper money to be adjusted passively to the rate recorded on the stock exchange. This was in effect a de facto devaluation, the fourth in 9 years. What happened up to 1842, was that the external balance, through deflationary measures, was regained, step by step. Pari passu the exchange rate improved till it was pegged at par level in 1842.

which affords the classical example. Since, as will be shown, the foreign sector in this period came to represent about a third of total GNP, and since shipping made up 39 to 45 % of the foreign sector, it appears warranted to consider shipping as an indicator of the shifting forms of the interaction. Shipping, in fact, will directly comprise 13 to 15 % of the total Norwegian economy.

The international setting was favourable in the 1850s. By virtue of its industrial lead in coal, iron, textiles, chemicals and machinery, Britain by 1850 had become the hub of the world economy. Its pound acted as reserve currency for international settlements; the discount rate of the Bank of England was a standard followed by the other national banks. In 1846 and 1849 Britain opted for a future as an industrial nation by repealing old restrictions on trade (the Corn Laws), and sea-borne transport (the Navigation Acts). Free trade became the declared policy of Britain. The program was taken up by other European states in the years 1850—1870. By 1862 the great powers of Europe had turned the Continent into a single low-tariff area.

Population growth, international migration, gold discoveries, railways and the telegraph, extensive foreign lending and borrowing at low rates of interest, gave a massive boost to international trade in the 1850s. In per capita terms, world trade grew at a decennial rate of 33 % between 1800 and 1913, in the period 1840—1870 it reached a peak rate of growth of 53 % per decade.[17]

An important factor facilitating the international expansion was improved technology in the construction of ships and shipping machinery, in the use of fuels and in navigation. In consequence, freights dropped steadily, especially in two periods, viz. the years 1815—1851 and 1875—1909. In the first period the freight declines took place on outward voyages in the Baltic, Mediterranean routes and on the North-Atlantic run. In the latter period the drop in freights occurred in the long hauls, helped, of course, by the opening of the Suez Canal in 1869 and the Panama Canal in 1901. Reflected in the freight declines were a range of improvements, including the sailing-ship designs, more intensive use of the ship per year, resulting from improvements in cargo handling

---

[17] For a modern text, see
A. G. Kenwood & A. L. Loughead, *The Growth of the International Economy 1820—1960*, London, 1971.
Simon Kuznets, Quantitative Aspects of the Economic Growth of Nations: x-Levels and Structure of Foreign Trade: Long-term Trends, in *Economic Development and Cultural Change*, Part II. January 1967.
C. P. Kindleberger, *Foreign Trade and the National Economy*, New Haven, 1962.

and dock facilities. Advance also stemmed from the use of the double and triple compound expansion engine, which cut coal consumption from 10 lbs per hp per hour, to nearly 1 lb after 1900, while the power of the marine engine increased about forty times. The introduction of iron, and later steel, in ship-building made possible a steady increase in carrying capacity and continuous opportunities for cost-cutting.[18]

Reduced freights had far-reaching significance for world trade. For one thing, bulky goods whose value is low in relation to volume, could now enter world trade. Goods that only in exceptional times had been traded internationally, now came to dominate the carrying trade, viz. coal, grain, timber, iron ores—and emigrants.[19]

The point to note here is that free trade and expansion in world commerce cleared the way for national specialization and international division of labour and resource use. In turn, the small peripheral states were given an opportunity for growth they otherwise would not have had. Poor internal factor endowments could now be overcome through international exchange of a few goods for a wide variety of inputs and consumer goods. These observations seem especially pertinent to a country like Norway.[20]

It possessed a very small range of resources, hence economic growth was, in the logic of things, destined to take place through specialization in the international economy. Therefore, it was, perhaps, only natural that the shift to economic liberalism met with very little opposition. Matching trends abroad, the home authorities removed most of the obstacles, legal and otherwise, to the free movement of labour and capital in the period 1839—1872. Thus, in 1839 the guilds were abolished, internal commerce was thrown open by a series of laws beginning in 1842, saw-mill privileges were likewise repealed by law in 1860, and the customs tariff was given a free-trade profile over the years 1842—1872. However, rural land, the largest single capital asset of the country, remained an exception to the free resource use, as the institution of the "odel"-right was retained, due to the unanimous insistence on the part of the country's farm population. "The odel" functioned, in effect, as the legal equivalent to entail in Britain and the fideicommiss in contem-

---

[18] H. J. Dyos & D. H. Aldcroft, *British Transport. An Economic Survey from the Seventeenth Century to the Twentieth*, Leicester University Press 1969, pp. 231—299.

[19] Douglass C. North, Ocean Freight Rates and Economic Development 1750—1913, *Journal of Economic History* vol. XVIII, no. 4, 1958, pp. 537—555.

[20] Douglass C. North, *The Economic Growth of the United States 1790—1860*, Englewood Cliffs, N. J.: Prentice Hall, 1961, a perceptive study of the US in the period, using postulates and materials similar to those used here for Norway.

porary Prussia; both represented the determination on the part of the old society to incapsulate itself from the hardships implicit in the unhampered market economy.

As in England, government revenue became, restricted to a few import duties on the consumption of sugar, coffee, tobacco and alcohol, that is to say, government revenue was autonomously determined by the income elasticities for these goods. When a third of GNP depended on the proceeds from the export sector, it followed that government revenue was in fact, directly determined by the international business cycle.

Norway, as said, found its field of specialization in the international carrying trade. Consider the key figures. In the years 1850—1880 the country sailed up from 8th place to becoming the third largest shipping nation of the world—after Britain and Germany. Its sailing fleet jumped from 288,000 net tons to 1,500,000 tons by 1880, the number of sailors swelled from just under 19,000 to 62,000 by 1878.[21]

These figures point to the fact that the fleet during the period outgrew its old function of carrying goods to and from Norwegian harbours. Already by 1872 80 % of the freight earnings stemmed from international carrying trade. While the fleet that served the carrying demands of the Norwegian economy doubled during the years 1860—1880, the part that sailed exclusively in international trade quadrupled. This shift meant that henceforth the fortunes of Norwegian shipping were almost exclusively determined by the international business cycle.[22]

In consequence, the Norwegian economy became more open, for with the expansion in foreign demand for shipping services, the relative size of the foreign sector climbed upwards. This was a repetition of a pattern observed for the last boom period in the years 1800—1808. Table 4 summarizes the development up to 1914.

The table shows that the decade averages, both on the export and the import side, represented close to a third of the entire GNP during most of the period after 1865. By 1905 the export sector had passed beyond even this level. There was a slowing-down or a halt in the decades 1875—1884 and 1885—1894, which points to the general stagnation in the international economy, and again in the decade 1895—1905.

---

[21] Historisk Statistikk 1968, table 175.
[22] The standard work on the history of Norwegian shipping is Jacob S. Worm-Müller, et. al., *Den norske sjøfarts historie I—III*, in 6 separate parts, (Oslo 1923—51). Of relevance for this present period, vol. II, part 1 and 2.

Table 4. Exports and imports of goods and services at current prices. Moving decade averages. 1865—1914.[23]

Decade	Absolute figures. Mill. kroner			Percentage shares of gross domestic product at current prices		
	Exports	Imports	Export surplus	Exports	Imports	Export surplus
1865—1874	166	157	+ 9	28.5	27.0	+1.5
1870—1879	202	200	+ 2	28.8	28.6	+0.2
1875—1884	214	214	—	28.8	28.8	—
1880—1889	217	209	+ 8	30.3	29.1	+1.2
1885—1894	226	236	−10	30.1	31.5	−1.4
1890—1899	258	297	−39	29.7	34.1	−4.4
1895—1904	297	346	−49	29.3	34.0	−4.7
1900—1909	354	396	−42	30.5	34.0	−3.6
1905—1914	490	520	−30	33.6	35.6	−2.0

Table 5. Composition of exports at current prices. Percentage figures, total export of goods and services=100. Selected years 1865—1915.[24]

	1865	1875	1885	1895	1905	1915
Fish, whale-oil and other products from hunting	21.8	20.1	16.4	17.4	15.6	14.6
Timber, wood, pulp, paper and paper products	23.6	19.0	19.7	20.4	21.9	14.0
Products from mining; metals and chemical products	2.9	3.3	3.2	2.4	3.4	11.7
Other industrial products	5.3	6.7	9.2	11.0	9.7	13.7
Gross freight earnings by ocean shipping	41.4	45.2	43.3	38.9	32.5	39.9
Other exports	5.0	5.7	8.2	9.9	16.9	6.1
Total exports of goods and services	100.0	100.0	100.0	100.0	100.0	100.0

We turn to the composition of exports, to appraise the relative importance of shipping in the national economy (table 5).

The table brings out the dominant position of shipping and shipping services in the country's export sector. Above 45 % of total exports originated in the ocean-borne carrying-trade around the peak year of 1875. It thereafter decreased till 1900 when it again picked up momentum and by 1915 freight earnings had reached about 40 % of total export incomes.

[23] Juul-Bjerke, *Langtidslinjer i norsk økonomi 1865—1960*, Statistisk Sentralbyrå, Oslo 1966, table 27.
[24] Ibid., table 30.

If we view the development in terms of the anticipations generated by the dual economy model, we note that the initial stimulus came from abroad. During the capital-widening phase 1850—1880, growth of the fleet depended on high international demand for freight services, and at home, on cheap, elastic supply of labour, moving in from the rural sector. The situation permitted high profits, savings and reinvestments of current profits in conventional technology, i.e. sailing vessels. Gross freight earnings increased from 53.2 million kroner in 1865 to 71.1 million kroner in 1870. Six years later they had soared to 103.3 million kroner. Fairly reliable evidence indicates that net returns on capital averaged 16 % over the years 1866—1870.[25] As noted above, the labour force in shipping trebled while total tonnage quintupled. Ton/man ratio improved somewhat, up from 15 tons per man in 1850 to 23 in 1876, still, the figure underscores the capital-widening rather than the capital-deepening character. Compare the fact that of the total tonnage in 1876 only three per cent represented steamships, while the rest was sail tonnage. Business management was altogether the captain's domain. He negotiated contracts, independent of home base, picking up cargoes wherever they could be found. That is to say, incomes represented voyage freights rather than time freights. The company form was loose, with a partnership company being set up separately for each ship contracted, which underscores the haphazard, amateurish operation methods of newcomers.

It was a matter of course—and concern—that the Norwegian assets were the low wages for crew and officers, the poor fare for both, and the second-best technology that the Norwegian sailing ships represented. English and American ships could not compete on the routes that the Norwegians entered, and gradually left the field, first the long-haul routes, involving bulky and durable goods, then the short-haul routes involving non-durables, such as fruit from the West-Indies to the U.S.

World price trends slumped after 1873.[26] It was marked in consumption goods and industrial products, and was severely felt in shipping freights. Industrial wages on the other hand, having risen especially in

---

[25] A. N. Kiær, *Den norske Skibsfarts Økonomi*, Christiania 1871, Scattered figures also found in Worm-Müller, op. cit. and the Reports of the County Governors.

[26] Douglass North, *Ocean Freight Rates*, above.
Dyos & Aldcroft, op. cit. 265—269.
E. A. V. Angier, *Fifty Years of Freight 1869—1919*, London 1920, provides a precise record and commentary on the developments in the freight markets.
J. Worm-Müller, op. cit. II, 2. passim.

Table 6. Average tonnage increase or decrease for selected countries 1860—1886.

	Great Britain	USA	Germany	Norway	France
Steam					
1860—1870	8.2	8.4	10.7	9.7	8.2
1870—1880	10.2	−2.0	9.7	16.5	4.2
1880—1886	8.0	−4.5	13.5	13.0	11.5
Sail					
1860—1870	1.3	−4.7	1.7	5.7	−0.33
1870—1880	−1.6	0.7	0.6	4.4	−2.8
1880—1886	−2.8	−0.4	−2.1	0.0	−4.9

Source: *Tabeller vedk. Handelsflaaderne 1850—1886*, NOS, Christiania 1887, p. 68.

1871—1875, failed to adjust downwards to the same degree. The resulting profit squeeze in shipping posed the typical challenge: How to compensate for permanently higher variable costs in the face of continually falling freight rates. We will limit ourselves to some analytical remarks. The British, with easier access to capital, predictably switched to steam. At the same time they concentrated on liner company routes, which were subsidized by the British Government in return for mail carrying. The Americans, who in the fifties had been unrivalled on the clipper runs, now packed up and left the field altogether, leaving the US coastal trade, and even the Great Lakes traffic, almost exclusively to foreigners. Comparative costs made shipping no longer a profitable venture for American capital. The Germans, like the British, sought refuge in liner companies, and the French and Italian governments began subsidizing their ship-yards. In short, the capital-deepening phase had begun in international shipping.

The Norwegians, on the other hand, continued to make money undisturbed for while, since they operated with lower variable costs than their competitors. This is indicated in table 6.

The table shows that while the foreigners were selling off their sailing tonnage, the Norwegians continued to make money on this type of tonnage well into the eighties, although they also bought steam-ships.

In the stagnant eighties, freights kept sinking under the impact of the growing use of steamships. These boasted larger carrying capacity per gross ton than the sailing vessels, a greater independence of winds, and hence a better utilization of the capital. They also represented greater speed and reliability, which can easily be seen from contemporary

Table 7. The Norwegian mercantile fleet 1850—1910. Selected years, in 1,000 net tons, and Gross freight earnings in ocean transport.

Year	Sail 1000 t	Steam 1000 t	Total 1000 t	in percent		Gross freights 1000 kroner
				Steam	Sail	
1850	284	—	284	100	0	—
1855	405	—	405	100	0	—
1860	532	—	532	100	0	—
1865	706	—	706	100	0	53,200
1870	961	13	974	99	1	71,135
1875	1,310	42	1,352	97	3	90,538
1880	1,461	58	1,519	96	4	97,800
1885	1,449	114	1,563	93	7	82,779
1890	1,503	203	1,706	88	12	112,800
1895	1,284	321	1,605	80	20	93,021
1900	1,003	505	1,508	67	33	143,911
1905	814	664	1,478	55	45	115,523
1910	63	893	1,526	41	59	139,941

Source: *Historisk Statistikk 1968*, table 175, 195.

insurance rates and ship-wreck statistics. Finally, they offered economies of scale, above all, because of lower manpower requirements.

One or two examples will suffice to show the downward freight trend. Ships sailing with ballast up to Archangel to load board and props for England in 1862 received 77 sh per standard, in 1900 50 sh. For coal to Rio de Janeiro in 1860, the rate was 30 to 40 sh. per ton, by 1900 it had slumped to 15/20 sh. Coffee in bags on the run from Rio to Europe in 1861 paid from 50 to 75 sh. per ton, against 25 sh. in 1875 and 15 to 20 sh. by 1900. On the cost side, wages decreased somewhat in nominal terms, but so did food prices, hence, real wages for the sailors held up fairly well.

Experience in the eighties convinced the most obdurate that the profit squeeze was of a permanent nature. Competition from steamships simply intensified, while the easier travel opportunities to the US set a floor to wages on Norwegian ships. The contours of the gradual conversion to steam is seen in table 7, which gives the overall figures.

One interesting feature in the table is that only around 1890 did the sailing fleet reach its peak level of 1,503,000 tons net, and not till 1907 did steam tonnage outstrip sail, (viz. 814,000 against 751,000 tons). Nor was the transition to steam a direct exchange—ton equivalent by ton equivalent—of one type of tonnage for another, for as the table suggests, the fleet in fact diminished somewhat during these years, 1890 —1910, down from about 1.7 million tons to 1.5 million tons. Allowance must, of course, be made for the higher cargo capacity of steamships, but, even so, it is clear that the rate of growth approached zero level after 1885. All in all, the transition from the second best to the best technology was an uncertain and slow process.

This is a general observation; a more detailed review of the matter will show a marked contrast between developments in Bergen and Oslo on the one hand, and Sørlandet on the other, the three shipping regions of Norway. Oslo, for example, offered more credit facilities, entrepreneurship, and the whole economy was more diversified there. Outward-looking Bergen had sufficient amounts of capital, entrepreneurship and forged ahead as pace-setter in steam shipping; also because Bergen in contrast to Oslo, apparently lacked alternative outlets for its pool of risk capital. Sørlandet, in comparison, lacked the necessary entrepreneurship, and its risk capital was scattered. Sørlandet, in short, seems to have lacked the resources for the new and risky venture, both in terms of organization, capital and technology. We cannot go into a detailed discussion here about the causes for success or failure. The fact remains that the economy of Sørlandet went into a decline during the period 1890—1910, following a series of bank failures in the preceeding decade. In terms of the dual economy model, our concern here is what happened to the stream of labour that, up to now, had been flowing from the rural into the market sector.

With the gradual introduction of steam, the mercantile fleet was no longer able to absorb rural labour at the same rate as before 1876. Compare for example, the decennial growth rates of the labour force on board. For four straight decades the labour force showed a growth above thirty per cent per decade, from 11,279 men in 1835 to 60,281 men in 1875. In the following three decades the growth stopped and turned negative, down .1 % 1875—1884, and in the following two decades, down 6 % and 8.9 % respectively. In 1904 the number of men on board had dropped to about 50,000 sailors.

In other words, labour now being barred from expanding employment in the home industrial sector, was forced into seasonal unemployment, underemployment, or simply pushed back into the agrarian sector. But in contrast to the years after 1815, when a similar process occurred, there was another alternative in the 1880s: America. As the home industrial sector failed to expand in step with the growth in the work force, Norwegians emigrated to the USA in waves of growing proportions, in the 1860s, above all in the 1880s, and again in the decade after 1900.[27] The causal relationship between stagnation in shipping and emigration in the eighties is revealed by the fact that in the nineties, the counties of Rogaland, Vest Agder and Øst Agder delivered the greatest flow of rural emigrants. In order to evaluate this result, it should be emphasized that the economy of Sørlandet offered no job alternatives in manufacturing, and even the herring fisheries failed during this period. Since the Oslo region and Bergen converted to steam, the labour surplus of these areas could be absorbed, partly in shipping as before, partly in industrial employment, whereas the population of the Sørlandet had no alternatives to shipping when sailing ships were laid up for good. It is against this background that the record-high emigration rate from Sørlandet should be viewed. (It was double the national average in the decade 1895—1904).

In retrospect, the rise of Norwegian shipping would seem to confirm the anticipations inherent in the dual economy model. Surplus labour may sustain a high level of demand once the growth process has got under way, it cannot initiate a growth process. Labour is a permissive rather than an initiating factor. The determining factor is foreign demand. As long as cheap labour gave Norway a comparative advantage, growth was buoyant. When freight-rates dropped below the critical point at which the sailing fleet, even with subsistence wages, could no longer be profitably used, stagnation set in, first in shipping, and from there the ripples spread to the entire economy. This goes to show that growth in the Norwegian economy, as illustrated by Norwegian shipping, was a function of foreign demand. This is a bald statement that needs qualifications. We shall consider two.

First, look at the national income figures. According to Bjerke GNP per capita tailed off from 763 kroner to 743 kroner, that is .3 % annually, during the decade 1877—1887.[28] A similar set-back occurred in the years 1899—1905, when per capita GNP eased downwards from 933 to 916 kroner, or .2 % annually. In comparison, gross freight earnings in 1896 stood at the same level as they had done 20 years before, around 103 million kroner.[29] In view of the dominant position of the

---

[27] For Norwegian emigration, see the standard work:
Ingrid Semmingsen, *Veien mot vest*, 2 vols. Oslo 1941—50, cfr. a recent demographic study.
T. Moe, *Demographic Developments and Economic Growth in Norway, 1740—1940*, Ann Arbor, Mich., USA, 1970, (mimeograph).

[28] Juul Bjerke, op. cit., p. 39.

[29] *Historisk Statistikk*, table 195.

Table 8. Total labour force and its distribution by industry, 1865—1910. Absolute figures and per cent.

Sector	1865	1875	1890	1900	1910
Agricultural					
Agriculture, forestry, fishing and whaling	59.8 %	51.8 %	49.2 %	40.7 %	39.0 %
Non-agricultural					
a) manufacturing	13.6 %	18.1 %	21.9 %	26.3 %	25.0 %
b) services	20.5 %	27.5 %	27.5 %	30.3 %	32.3 %
Total labour force, thousands	654	731	781	883	920

Source: *Bjerke*, op cit., table 21. Note that the figures do not add up to 100 % because of a fraction whose occupation is unknown.

Table 9. Gross domestic product at current prices by industry. Absolute figures and percentage distribution for selected years 1865—1910. (Figures before 1910 calculated on the assumption of constant ratios between final output and gross product in each industry).

Sector	1865	1875	1890	1900	1910
Agriculture, forestry, fishing and whaling	33.8 %	32.7 %	27.2 %	22.4 %	23.7 %
Manufacturing	21.0 %	21.2 %	22.5 %	24.4 %	26.2 %
Services	45.2 %	46.1 %	50.3 %	53.2 %	50.1 %
Total GNP in millions kroner	480	771	780	1,115	1,435

Source: *Bjerke*, op. cit., table 24.

carrying trade in the Norwegian economy at the time, there can be no doubt that there is a direct causal link between stagnation in gross freight earnings and the parallel levelling-off in national income.

Since shipping's labour absorbing power up to 1880 mostly reflected foreign demand, and since economic growth can be achieved simply by moving labour from low- to high-productivity sectors, it is of considerable interest to appraise how much of the advance in the Norwegian economy can be explained as a result of sectoral re-allocations within the labour force, for example moving Sørlandets labour force from agriculture into shipping. We need to know total labour force, total GNP, percentage figures for the labour force employed in each sector, and the percentages of overall GNP stemming from each sector. To begin with compare table 8, which gives the figures for the labour force. Bjerke has computed the contribution to total GNP by the various

Table 10.[31] GNP per worker, by industrial sectors. Current prices in kroner.

Sector	1865	1875	1890	1900	1910
Agriculture, forestry, fishing and whaling	415	666	552	695	948
Manufacturing	1,133	1,235	1,026	1,172	1,635
Services	1,618	1,914	1,827	2,217	2,419
Average GNP per worker	734	1,055	999	1,263	1,560

sectors for the same period. The computation is based on the kind of figures that was used for the years 1835 and 1845 in table 2 above, that is, they represent gross value of final deliveries from each sector. Major structural shifts in the composition of the labour force are discernible in tables 8 and 9. One inference is that the average gross productivity—as measured in money units—was four times higher in the service sector than in agriculture in 1865.[30] The recorded shift towards employment in the market sector, in itself implies a shift towards higher productivity levels, since labour, in the competitive market setting, is paid the value of its marginal product. Part of the economic advance undoubtedly reflects better technology, skills, and organization. But how much of the increase in GNP per worker mirrors changes in the sectoral composition of the labour force? Table 10 thus gives the total productivity growth as 321 kroner in the decade 1865—1875. We now ask, what were the gains due simply to re-allocation of labour?

Now, multiplying the sectoral estimates of GNP per worker in 1865 by the sectoral labour force for 1875, we obtain a measure (partly hypothetical) of the GNP per worker that would have been achieved in each sector in 1875, if labour in each sector had been as productive at that date as it was in 1865. Next, the sectoral figures may be added up to yield the average GNP per worker for the whole economy, and the resulting difference between the GNP averages for the two years will indicate the gain achieved through the sectoral shifts alone. An illustration of this method of computation is offered in table 11.[32]

[30] Juul Bjerke, op. cit., p. 57.
[31] Table 10 is easily seen as based on table 8 and 9, that is overall GNP divided by the work force (by sectors).
[32] The method has been used on Swedish data, see
Y. Åberg, *Produktion och produktivitet i Sverige 1861—1965*, Uppsala 1969.
Cfr. P. Munthe, *Den økonomiske sirkulasjon*, 3. ed., Oslo 1971, pp. 160—164, for transfer gains in the Norwegian economy in the twentieth century. The present author is indebted to Munthe for this section.

Table 11. Transfer gains achieved through re-allocation of labour 1865—1875. (Current kroner).

(Hypothetical) GNP per worker in 1875:	
Agriculture	415 × .518 = 215
Manufacturing	1,133 × .181 = 205
Services	1,618 × .275 = 445
Average GNP per worker 1875	865

Since the average gross productivity level of 1865 was 734 kroner, we may now isolate the gain due to intersectoral labour re-allocation:

	in kroner	
Transfer gain:	(865—734) = 131	(40.8 %)
Productivity advance	(1,055—865) = 190	(59.2 %)
Total GNP growth per worker, 1865—1875	321	(100 %)

Considering the importance of shipping for the whole economy at the time, it is interesting to note that in the decade when shipping showed its record high absorption of labour, a hefty 40.8 % of the performance gains in the Norwegian economy were due to re-allocation of labour into more productive types of employment. Similarly, when in the following decade, the rate of increase in shipping employment plunged to zero, and even turned negative, the transfer gains shrunk to very modest proportions, as can be seen from the figures in table 12. Of course, we cannot tell for sure how much of the gain prior to

Table 12. Performance gains achieved through shifts in the composition of the labour force, 1865—1910, in current kroner.

Decade	1865—1875	1875—1890	1890—1900	1900—1910
Transfer gain	131	70	52	17
Productivity gain	190	—126	212	280
Total GNP growth per worker	321	— 56	264	297

1875, reflects the influence of shipping, but, in view of the importance of freight earnings on the export side, and the labour intensive character of operations, we may conclude, with a good deal of confidence, that almost half of the transfer gains up to 1875 mirrored the fortunes of shipping. They reflect, in other words, the influence of international demand patterns.

After 1875, labour absorption into shipping levelled off, and, at the same time, re-allocation gains dropped steadily. That is, when shipping ceased being a source of transfer gains in the economy, the overall economic growth as measured in terms of GNP per worker, turned negative, down 56 kroner in the years 1875—1890. Although not quantifiable, there is a strong presumption that this kind of correlation expressed a causal link. This is another way of saying that Norwegian shipping ceased to be labour-intensive, and swung over to a more capital-intensive period.

Table 12 indicates that after 1890, economic growth in Norway came to depend on the productivity gains, achieved either through more advanced skills and technology, or better organization. Parallel to this, production gradually became more capital-intensive. This is demonstrated by the conversion to steam in shipping, it is also seen in the new hydro-electric industries established in the decades 1895—1914, which were characterized by massive inputs of capital and relatively little labour. As seen above, gains from labour re-allocations were correspondingly low.

In this connection it must be emphasized that all the investment capital for the electro-chemical industry and the mining industries came from abroad, as did the demand for their products. Excess labour from the rural sector continued to emigrate as before—800,000 in fact, left the country in the period 1840—1920—and here the importance of the free labour market in the US for Europeans right up to 1924 cannot be overestimated. The emigration rate from Norway, it should be added, was surpassed only by that of Ireland.

From the point of view of Norway's economic growth, the role of the external world may now be indicated. The outside world

— absorbed the country's excess labour,
— supplied the largest share of the necessary investment capital, both for the private sector and for government infrastructure, as well as for modernization of the farms,

— provided the markets for the country's very limited range of marketable goods, and
— supplied the major share of the country's food requirements.

These generalizations from shipping to conclusions about the overall economy, should of necessity be regarded as exploratory, i.e. as suggested lines for further inquiries.

We would like to see, for example, how the dual model fits the developments in the other major exports businesses, e.g. the fisheries and the timber and pulp industry.

Was there a similar relationship between home costs and changing foreign demand after 1875, and was there a parallel swing to capital-deepening product functions? The implications are that, at least for the pulp & paper industry, such an interplay between fixed wage rates and cost-reducing technology can easily be established.[33] To that extent the dual economy model would prove a fruitful framework both for explanation and prediction.

[33] Cfr. F. Sejersted, *Historisk introduksjon til økonomien*, Cappelen A/S, Oslo, 1972, stensil, pp. 11—13.

Norway's School of Business administration, Bergen

[4]

A Theory of Economic and Technological Development in Norway in the Nineteenth Century

Francis Sejersted

Introduction

In the course of the nineteenth century, an industrial revolution took place in Norway, and the nation became integrated into the developed part of the world economy. What had been a pre-industrial society, with primary industries and a predominant self-sufficiency, became a developed country, acquiring the political and social structures and the self-sustaining economic-growth mechanisms typical of developed countries. Economic growth was especially pronounced in the years from 1835 to 1875, at least quantitatively. The factors underlying that development have been the subject of considerable research by economic historians in recent decades.

Fritz Hodne has vigorously propounded the applicability of the theory of export-led growth.[1] Economic development in Norway was determined by an external factor, demand from export markets. The opening up of foreign markets from the 1840s was of strategic importance. Hodne supports his argument by pointing to the unassailable fact that all Norway's traditional outward-looking industries, fish and timber exports, and shipping, benefited from exceptionally favourable conditions in the period between the post-Napoleonic War crisis and the Great Depression at the end of the 1870s, that is the most important period of development from the point of view of economic growth. It may be noted that the theory of export-led growth not only dominates Hodne's view of the mid-nineteenth century, but also his approach to industrialised Norway's development to the present.

In the exposition of his theory, Hodne emphasises that its underlying assumption is that such factors as foreign trade, technology or institutions are not decisive in themselves, but rather the individual entrepreneur.[2] This does not prevent him, however, from basing his argument firmly on the theory of export-led growth, because he clearly if tacitly presupposes a constant tendency to exploit economic opportunity. Such a premise is more characteristic of economic than of historical science (being inherent in the so-called maximisation assumptions). Given certain institutional and technological conditions - such as a provision under the rule of law for the free exchange of goods, a system of transport which makes it possible to exploit markets,

---

[1] Hodne, F., *Norges økonomiske historie 1815-1970*, Oslo, 1985, Ch. I.

[2] *Ibid.*, p. 25.

A Theory of Economic and Technological Development in Norway

and the like - new market opportunities may in themselves appear to trigger developments.

The account given by Ivan T. Berend and Gyørgy Ranki of the industrialisation of the European periphery rests on similar arguments.[3] They attach decisive importance to structural and institutional conditions, and then bring in market opportunities as the triggering factor. As with Hodne, growth is demand-led almost by definition. If certain countries in the European periphery (such as the Balkan countries) failed to respond to market impulses, this was because of the absence of the institutional prerequisites. It is as if external markets are simply the last in a series of necessary conditions; once it too is fulfilled, growth follows so to speak "of its own accord".

Kristine Bruland has criticised Berend and Ranki among other historians because, in their description of Europe's industrialisation, they "concentrate - in what might be called a 'Gerschenkronian' fashion - more on the prerequisites of industrialization and technological change than on the process by which it actually occurred".[4] One needs to deal more specifically with how opportunities were utilised, and not least by whom. Attention is shifted - also when the triggering factor is being sought - to the supply side. Bruland's main concern is the emergence of the modern Norwegian textile industry. She emphasises that the initiative for this early industrialisation came from England. From the 1840s on, England exported not only finished goods but whole factory systems. The English sought active partners in countries where the conditions were right, and exported whole factory packages, including engineers and sometimes even workers.

It is important to call attention, as Bruland does, to this kind of industrialising initiative from outside, because such mechanisms are rarely emphasised in studies of the industrialisation of the European periphery. Later in the century a parallel process can be seen emanating from Norway: when the modern sawmills found their scope restricted by shrinking supplies of raw materials, Norwegian entrepreneurs moved their businesses, sometimes with Norwegian machines and manpower, to Sweden and Finland, and ultimately Russia.[5] Or, to take another example, when the time was ripe for harnessing water-power to produce electricity, Norway experienced another wave of industrialisation, again in large part on initiatives from outside.

Bergh, Hanisch, Lange and Pharo are explicit in their criticism of the export-led growth theory as they wish to shift attention from the demand to the supply side. Having established how heavily the Norwegian economy depended on exports, they continue: "In quite a number of cases that dependence has been so heavily emphasised that domestic developments in this country appear to be little more than a reflex to developments on the world market....We wish instead to underline the need

---

[3] Berend, I.T./Ranki, G., *The European Periphery & Industrialization 1790-1914*, Cambridge, 1982.

[4] Bruland, K., *British Technology and European Industrialization: the Norwegian Textile Industry in the Mid-nineteenth Century*, Cambridge 1989, p. 13.

[5] Sejersted, F., Veien mot øst, in Langholm, S./Sejersted, F., (eds.), *Vandringer: Festskrift til Ingrid Semmingsen*, Oslo, 1980, pp. 163-201.

to view much of the rhythm in the Norwegian economy in the light of domestic rather than foreign factors."[6] Unlike Hodne but like Bruland, they see much of the dynamic being generated on the supply side: unlike Bruland, on the other hand, and her example from the textile industry, they maintain that circumstances at home rather than abroad determined the rhythm of economic development.

Development theorists have recently taken more interest in the development of the European periphery. Attention normally focuses on how the various countries responded to the challenge of the industrial revolution in Britain and later in Central Europe, and on what we have referred to as the "supply side". To some extent, deliberate policies can be discerned, aimed at removing institutional or other barriers to economic development. The classical study in this tradition is Alexander Gerschenkron's.[7] Interestingly enough, his analysis so to speak turns the normal analysis, as represented for instance by Hodne, on its head. Instead of regarding institutions as necessary preconditions, and the emergence of markets as a triggering factor for economic development, Gerschenkron does the opposite: the market potential is, as it were, given, and the creation of institutions is seen as the triggering factor.

A recent study has been carried out by Dieter Senghaas.[8] In his view, the normal process for peripheral countries was to be "peripheralised", that is to become suppliers of raw materials without developing themselves. The problem then is to explain how some countries managed to avoid this "normal" process and develop. He distinguishes between six responses to this challenge. The six strategies were, more or less, successful in terms of economic development. Among the sources of support for his analysis are Friedrich List's theories of protective tariffs. Senghaas finds that Norway adopted strategy no. III, alternating successfully between free trade and protective tariffs. Development began with an upturn in the export of raw materials; this is followed by some protection, aimed at promoting import substitution, first of consumer goods and then of capital goods. The last phase (after World War II) saw the return of free trade. Compared to Gerschenkron, Senghaas attaches more importance to economic or market incentives, in that he sees the alternation between protection and free trade as a continuous attempt to lay down institutional constraints aimed at creating "correct" market incentives.

Taking as our point of departure the discussions and theories mentioned, we shall seek to present an analysis of the historical process by which Norway became a "developed" country. We may note in this connection that, as the problem has been defined, a shift is in some way assumed in the causes underlying economic development. The question is, how did Norway make the transition from a preindustrial to a

---

[6] Bergh, T./Hanisch, T.J./Lange, E./Pharo, H., *Norge fra U-land til I-land: Vekst og utviklingslinjer 1830-1980*, Oslo, 1983, p. 229.

[7] Gerschenkron, A., *Economic Backwardness in Historical Perspective*, New York, 1962. Bruland's critique of Gerschenkron (see above) for only being concerned with conditions is not quite accurate. He would hardly claim that development is automatic once the conditions exist. His main point is precisely that certain countries can be seen to have adopted deliberate political strategies to develop their institutions so as to exploit the opportunities demonstrated by developments in Britain.

[8] Senghaas, D., *The European Experience: A Historical Critique of Development Theory*, Leamington Spa, 1985.

A Theory of Economic and Technological Development in Norway

developed society with its own built-in growth mechanisms? The mechanisms explain the growth of later phases, but, of course, not how they themselves came about. It is thus assumed that different mechanisms drive development at different times.[9] The main purpose of this study is to show how Norway became a capitalist country as the dynamics of development shifted from the demand side to the supply side, or from market pressure to supply-side pressure.

Pressure from the market

Some preconditions

In the 1840s we see the first contours of a qualitatively new society. We shall analyse the development process from about 1840. The preceding development had, however, created some preconditions of fundamental importance.

First, something like an agricultural revolution had taken place. The most conspicuous change was the breakthrough of potato farming during the Napoleonic Wars. It has been calculated that in normal years before 1809, the potato crop yielded about 1/10 of the calorific value of the grain harvest. By 1835, it had increased tenfold, reaching the same level in terms of calorie value as the old grain harvest. In the meantime, the latter had increased by about 50 per cent, and livestock production by about 75 per cent. In terms of calorific value, the total increase was thus about 65 per cent, with potatoes accounting for about half. After 1835, too, relatively rapid growth was maintained, mainly in the production of grain.[10]

Secondly, there had been a population explosion arising from a dramatic fall in the mortality rate following the Napoleonic Wars. From 1815 to 1865 the population grew from about 900,000 to about 1,700.000 - almost double.[11] The remarkable fact is, however, that although the population increased sharply, food production grew even more. It seems evident that, on the average, people ate better as the nineteenth century wore on.

Thirdly, as an outcome of the Napoleonic Wars the old union of Denmark and Norway was dissolved. This cleared the ground in such a way that a new constitutional, semi-democratic state could be built almost from scratch. A paramount consideration for the new regime was to limit political power and to establish a firm framework of conditions for economic activity - equality of treatment, the protection of property, and a stable currency system. There was a reaction against the mixture of political and economic activity which the former system of privilege had led to. A clear distinction was to be made between the private and the public sector.

The mercantilistic system had been well suited to a consolidated *grande bourgeoisie*, but the crisis of this system during and after the Napoleonic Wars undermined it. The new political system paved the way for a broader bourgeoisie. It held out a

---

[9] Cf. the chapter Dynamikken i utviklingen in Sejersted, F., *Historisk introduksjon til økonomien*, Oslo, 1985. See especially the section on the difference between revolutionary changes which destroy their own cause and cumulative changes which reproduce their own cause.

[10] Sejersted, F., *Den vanskelige frihet* (vol. 10 of Cappelen's *Norges Historie*), Oslo, 1978, p. 95-125.

[11] Drake, M., *Population and Society in Norway 1735- 1965*, London, 1969.

promise to anyone with initiative: it was a much more open system. At the same time, the fall of the old bourgeoisie had cleared the stage. An outstanding feature of the first half of the nineteenth century is the tremendous force with which a new small industrial and trading bourgeoisie emerged.

The revolutionary growth of middle-class society in this period can best be illustrated by comments made around 1840 by two "survivors" from the old *grande bourgeoisie*, looking back on earlier developments.[12] The elder, Haagen Mathiesen, declared that "the middle class no longer exists", whereas his somewhat younger contemporary, Jacob Aall, noted that "everything in our country is middle class, somehow". This is not quite the contradiction it appears to be: our observers simply lacked an adequate terminology for a new state of affairs. Mathiesen registered the absence of the old *grande bourgeoisie*, whereas Aall observed the broad new petty bourgeoisie.

It is useful to note that the new political system did more than promote ownership by protecting property. It also laid important new foundations for local cooperation, chiefly through the new system of local government brought about in 1837.[13]

Expansion in the export industries

The export of fish recovered quickly from the Napoleonic Wars, not least because of the plentiful occurrence of cod and herring in the fishing seasons. While exceptionally rich catches were maintained well into the century, prices on the European market tended at the same time to rise - a chance coincidence of favourable circumstances.[14]

Timber exports had been hit hard by the postwar crisis, but began to experience distinct growth from the 1830s. Because of the British duty on timber, much of these exports went to other markets than Britain, principally France. The gradual reduction of the British import duty from 1842 to 1851 proved to be a powerful stimulus to exports.[15] Thus developed a favourable pattern of events: first, the old industry was forced by the British protection of Canadian timber to look for new markets; strengthened by this, it then found new export opportunities as the British duty was removed.

In the twenty-five years from 1841 to 1866, exports of fish and timber taken together doubled. By the end of the period, they accounted for about 12 per cent of gross national product. Shipping alone accounted for a similar percentage. This meant that of the industries engaged in foreign trade, growth was especially rapid in shipping; as early as the 1830s, Norway had begun systematically building up a position as a carrier for other countries.

---

[12] Sejersted, 1978, *op.cit.*, p. 284.

[13] Steen, S., *Lokalt selvstyre i Norges bygder*, Oslo, 1968.

[14] Solhaug, T., *De norske fiskeriers historie 1815-1880*, I-II, Oslo, 1976. - A standard work on the fisheries.

[15] Sejersted, F., *Fra Lindenud til Eidsvold Værk*, Vols. II-2 & III, Oslo, 1972 & 1978. The two volumes give an analysis of the Norwegian timber trade in the nineteenth century.

A Theory of Economic and Technological Development in Norway

Figure 1 Number of vessels 1800-1900

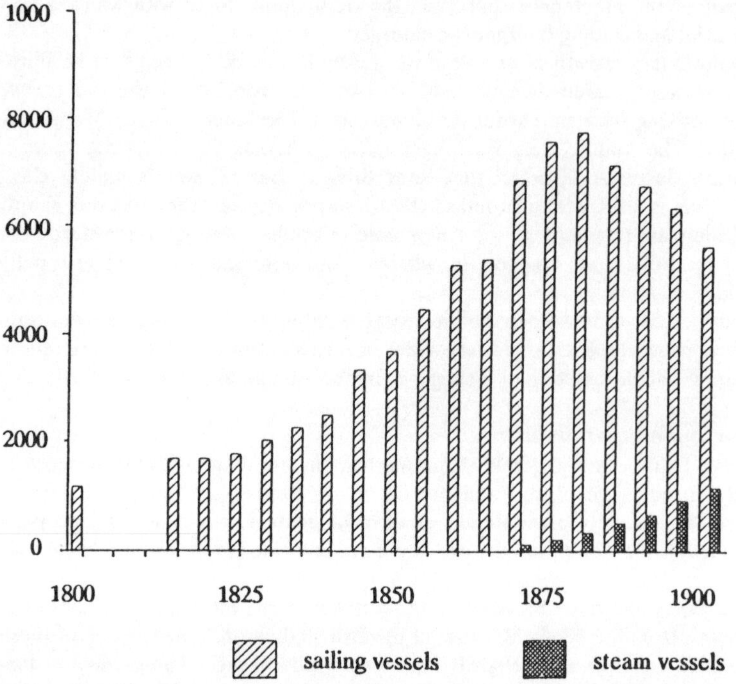

[Bar chart showing number of vessels from 1800 to 1900, with sailing vessels (hatched) and steam vessels (dotted). Y-axis: 0 to 10000 (labels shown: 1000, 8000, 6000, 4000, 2000, 0). Sailing vessels grow from about 1000 in 1800 to a peak of nearly 8000 around 1875-1880, then decline to about 5500 by 1900. Steam vessels appear near 1875 and grow to about 1000 by 1900.]

△△ sailing vessels   ▪▪ steam vessels

Sources: All diagrams are based on figures published by the Central Bureau of Statistics.

A decisive boost came with the rapid expansion of the timber trade from the Swedish Baltic ports, to Britain and elsewhere. The British Navigation Acts were no obstacle, as Britain regarded Sweden and Norway as one nation. Norway was accordingly well placed when Britain repealed the Navigation Acts in 1849, and, further, when shipping boomed during the Crimean War which began in 1851. In the twenty-five years from 1841 to 1866, the Norwegian merchant fleet grew by some 250 per cent.

In his account of development in Scandinavia, Senghaas emphasised the significance of this first phase of large exports of raw materials. As such, this was not peculiar to Scandinavia apart from the fact that its exceptional volume was enough in itself to have spin-off effects in the economy as a whole and thus counteracted the tendency to form enclaves. The development was also "exogenously determined and dependent".[16] The growth of shipping, however, is a case apart and more difficult to account for. There was no comparative advantage to speak of, beyond a certain sea-

---

[16] Senghaas, *op.cit.*, pp. 87 and 89.

faring tradition, which Norway was not alone in having. Competition was apparently on equal terms. But in view of the circumstances surrounding the Navigation Acts and the union with Sweden, however, the build-up of Norwegian shipping independently of Norwegian trade can be said to have benefited from a sort of protective mechanism in what was strategically a very important phase.

Norway's national product appears to have grown considerably from the early 1830s to the crisis years at the end of the 1870s, and the growth also appears to have been relatively steady. Despite the uncertainty of all our estimates, it seems clear that the growth rate was comparable to those of later developing economies.[17] To this growth the traditional export industries made a substantial contribution. On this basis, Hodne concludes that Norway's economic growth was "driven by 'market suction' in export markets" (see above). This needs some qualification since, as noted above, there was also considerable expansion in the country's principal industry, agriculture.

The question also arises as to whether growth in the Norwegian exporting industries was due to a passive response to new opportunities abroad, or to an active adaptation on the supply side to exploit opportunities which may have existed before. "Market suction" presupposes the first answer. Although signs can be seen of domestic initiatives, for instance when timber exports gained access to French markets in the 1830s, one has to agree with much of what Hodne says. The export industries developed as a reaction to developments in European markets, a reaction which was to have a considerable impact on the nation's economic development in general.

One reason for the general significance of growth in the export industries was that they themselves did not develop merely as enclaves: further, it was not merely by virtue of their volume that they had notable spin-off effects.[18] To a very large extent, the production on which they depended was based on seasonal work by farmers, who caught fish or felled timber in the off season. The same applies to sawmills, whereas shipbuilding and shipping were closely integrated in local coastal communities, whose young men went to sea for a time before establishing themselves as dual farmers and fishermen. For a long time there was no fundamental change in this traditional organisation of the export industries. A very large proportion of the population was directly engaged in activities connected with the exceptional growth of these industries, the spin-off from which thus had an immediate impact on the community.

Technological conservatism in the export industries

The growth of the export industries was extensive in nature, that is it largely remained within established patterns and relied on traditional technology. Not only was the shipping expansion predominantly based on the traditional jointly-owned

---

[17] Cf. Bergh et al. *op.cit.*, and Hodne, *op.cit.*, p. 43 ff.

[18] This is Senghaas's argument (*op.cit.*, p. 89), based where Norway is concerned among other things on Hodne, F., Growth in a Dual Economy: The Norwegian Experience 1814-1914, *Economy and History* 16, 1973, pp. 81-110. Hodne's model assumes that the export industries to some extent were enclaves, a view to which, as will be evident, we do not subscribe.

A Theory of Economic and Technological Development in Norway

shipping firm, with each ship a commercial unit owned by many members of the local community; the ships themselves were traditional sailing vessels, built according to age-old handicraft traditions by numerous small builders along the coast. Technologically, Norway was behind the other large shipping nations.

The expansion in fish exports was essentially due to a natural increase in the fish stocks reaching the coast to spawn in late winter. In this case there was, as indicated above, a fortunate coincidence of increased stocks and a growing demand in export markets. There was no technological revolution underlying this expansion. The fishing methods used remained traditional, in coastal waters from open boats. Not until late in the century did deep-sea fishing from more advanced vessels occur on any scale.

Methods of felling, sawing and transporting timber also remained traditional. The old waterwheel-driven sawmills, for instance, were the only ones seen up to the 1860s, thanks to the old mercantilistic sawmill privileges which in effect blocked the adoption of new steam technologies. Not until these privileges were withdrawn in 1860 could the new technology take over in the industry. When it did, it brought with it relocation, restructuring, and all-year-round operations.

A striking general feature of these developments, then, was the organizational and technological conservatism of the major export industries. Technological renewal came relatively late, not until after the rapid expansion. Indeed it seems as if agriculture, which produced for domestic markets where it had a market orientation, was more inclined towards qualitative technological innovation, as indicated earlier. The lack of technological innovation on the supply side confirms Hodne's theory that the actual impulses promoting growth were generated in overseas markets.

Nonetheless, such growth as may have been due to qualitative supply-side improvements cannot be entirely attributed to foreign demand, or at least not without clarifying certain premises. It is important to bear in mind that it is precisely this qualitative change that we are attempting to explain. In a broader perspective, growth was necessarily linked to the transformation of Norwegian society into a modern industrial society based on modern technology and possessing built-in, self-sustaining growth mechanisms. But our observations on growth in the export industries has revealed that it was precisely where "market suction" was strongest that the impulses towards technological renewal were weakest. This usefully reminds us that growth is one thing, but that qualitative change as a basis for further growth is quite another. Further analysis needs to take this as its point of departure.

What the argument had so far established, however, is that the contours of a qualitatively new society which began to appear in Norway in the 1840s appeared during a period of rapid growth of the traditional industries, and that this growth had begun before significant signs of qualitative change. It seems likely that this growth was at least one of the basic prerequisites for their appearance.

Institutional change, with special reference to the peculiar dynamics of the monetary and credit system of the 1840s
There was to be a remarkable concentration on qualitatively new initiatives in the 1840s. This decade saw the appearance of the first modern textile factories, the first modern mechanical engineering workshops, the first private commercial bank, and

preparatory steps for the building of the first railway. The first "modern" labour movement, the Thrane movement, also emerged in this decade. In short, it is precisely in the 1840s that one begins to see the outlines of a new economic society in Norway.

Let us return to institutional conditions, as embodied in the political system. We have mentioned that, together with the collapse of the old bourgeoisie during the crisis, the new liberal constitution of 1814 prepared the ground for the emergence of a new wider middle class, and in effect also for the new large group of freeholding farmers. But even with the ground prepared, it took time for these new groups to establish themselves and consolidate their positions. They needed time to grow up. There can be little doubt that the expansion of the export industries from the 1830s onwards was an important factor in the growth and consolidation of the new bourgeoisie. New institutional conditions also came into being in due course. One very important step in this connection was the establishment of a new monetary system following the wartime hyperinflation. Consideration of the monetary system leads us on to discussion of the development of the credit system.

For the new political regime, a stable monetary system was a basic cornerstone, but to clear up the currency chaos after the Napoleonic Wars was to take time. Norway did not establish a system with the value of money fixed on a silver standard until 1842. There had been deflation by fits and starts since the early 1820s. Legislation in 1816 established a central bank, *Norges Bank*, and gave it a monopoly to issue bank notes. Such a monopoly was unusual in the Europe of the day. The intent of the monopoly was to help guarantee the value of the bank notes. A par value was also fixed at the same time. However, the Bank was forced by the pressure of circumstances to postpone the exchange of notes for silver so as to permit inflation to continue: it only became possible to halt inflation in the 1820s, as the balance of trade improved. To move the exchange rate up to par, a system was devised whereby notes were initially exchanged for silver at market rates (which were well below par at that time). Given a cyclical upturn, the market value of the notes would also tend to rise, and the exchange rate would be allowed to follow it up. The exchange rate was never lowered, however, showing that it was used to prevent the market rate from falling. The system achieved periods of improvement in the exchange rate until par was finally reached in 1842. A side-effect of this policy was that it tended to quell any sign of an upturn until par was reached. The positive effect of the final exchange at par was considerably enhanced by a large increase in the funds available for lending by the central bank.

An ordered monetary system, the abandonment of the par policy, and an increase in the volume of credit, were certainly very significant preconditions for the blossoming of economic initiatives in the 1840s. Essentially, it suddenly became possible to borrow. The strict par policy had been a reaction to the excesses of bank-note mercantilism during the Napoleonic Wars, but its rigid implementation was also due to the fact that policy was very much conducted by civil servants. In addition to representing strict orthodoxy, they also improved their incomes. On the other hand, the par policy harmed business and industry and during the long period of its adherence, there was also a mercantile opposition, inspired by mercantilist monetary principles. There was tension between what can be described as the "educated bourgeoi-

A Theory of Economic and Technological Development in Norway

sie" and "the money bourgeoisie". In retrospect, it would also be fair to argue that the bank notes ought to have been devalued much earlier, for instance early in the 1830s. That would have eased the economic situation without any risk of an inflationary relapse.

In the 1840s there appears to have been an exceptional increase in credit volumes, and it is pertinent to point to the stabilisation of money as an important contributory factor. The 1840s saw the first capitalist boom in Norway, in the sense that it appears to have been founded on increasing borrowing. In the previous economic system with its lack of exits, favourable cycles had often been exploited to consolidate operations and pay back debts. The desire on the part of the new bourgeoisie to exploit a boom by borrowing was something new. It can be seen as evidence of new opportunities and of an increasing business optimism. In its own day it was regarded with amazement. The Governor of Christiania, for instance, wrote that "Many rise to prosperity although it is well known that they owe the means with which to begin and maintain their businesses more to their credit than to their wealth". [19] The transition, the release of being rid of the par policy, may in itself have been a stimulus.

The expansionary upturn of the 1840s was to come to a dramatic end with a characteristic monetary crisis towards the end of the decade. The general view at the time was that the main task of the central bank was to maintain the value of money. During the crisis, with the need for short-term loans at its most urgent, it accordingly had to call in funds in order to maintain the statutory relation between banknotes and silver: a mechanism through which the sources of credit run dry as the thirst for credit grows. The expansion of credit during the preceding boom, of course, had made the need for credit even more acute than it would otherwise have been. This sudden crying need for credit in an expansive economy gave rise to two initiatives, both originating in the merchant opposition. One was the establishment, by Fritz H. Frølich, a restless spirit and leading entrepreneur of the period, of Norway's first commercial bank. The second, urged by Adolf B. Stabell, the merchant opposition's leading spokesman in the Storting, was that the state rised loans, the funds to be mediated to the industrial sector by means of government discounting commissions.

It is important to note that although the better ordered monetary system of the 1840s laid the foundations for rapid credit expansion, and despite the presence of a generally active middle class, it was not until the monetary crisis of the end of the decade that an essentially new initiative was taken with the establishment of the first private commercial bank. The move was not due to the growth in credit, but to the shortage of credit that followed. A second point is how willing the government, led by the civil servants or "educated bourgeoisie" was to intervene on behalf of the money bourgeoisie to tide it over the crisis.

For such measures there were earlier precedents. Private banking was less well developed in Norway than in comparable countries. This is frequently attributed to the monopoly granted to the new central bank, *Norges Bank*, established in 1816, to issue bank notes. Since the issuing of bank notes was a normal way of funding pri-

---

[19] Sejersted, F., *Norges Bank og høykonjunkturen i 1840-årene*, Oslo, 1968, p. 20.

vate banks, this practically amounted to a banking monopoly for the semi-official note-issuing bank. To make up for the lack of a private banking system, the administration set up the so-called "discounting commissions", which were really state-owned commercial banks.[20]

On the other hand local autonomy brought with it the establishment of numerous local savings banks, a development which was especially pronounced in Norway. They were semi-official in nature, since their Boards were often identical with the Municipal Boards. They became important instruments of industrial development, on a small scale and at the local level. Later they were to be obstacles to the efforts of the big commercial banks to become nationwide.[21] Taking them into account with the semi-public note-issuing bank - easily the country's largest banking institution - and the public discounting commissions, it is clear that mid-century banking in Norway was predominantly public in nature.

In other words, Norway does not fit into the Gerschenkron schema according to which one would expect a combination of a passive state and an active private banking system. As private banking developed in the second half of the nineteenth century, however, public banking withdrew from the direct market. Nevertheless Norway never developed a really strong commercial banking system.[22]

The special demographic situation of the 1840s

Returning to population growth, we find that it, too, contributed to the creation of a unique situation in the 1840s. Let us quote that keen-eyed observer of the contemporary scene, Eilert Sundt:

> After 1841 there emerged a numerous, a suddenly and extraordinarily multiplied, generation of young people aged between 20 and 30. The many extra willing hands considerably expanded industry, as can be seen from the fact that much greater numbers than before were able to earn their livelihoods and found themselves in positions to marry and raise families. The many extra hands also created a surplus, whereby many were disappointed in their expectations, as could be seen from the fact that many, although old enough, were obliged to refrain from matrimony (marriages thus being many in absolute but few in relative terms), and that more severe and numerous moral and civil problems arose than there had been before.[23]

---

[20] Egge, Å., *Statens diskonteringskommisjoner. Finansdepartementet som statsbank i det 19. århundre* (Ph.d. dissertation, Oslo, 1988).

[21] Strømme Svendsen, A. et al., (eds.), *Studier i sparing og sparebankvesen i Norge 1922-1927*, Oslo, 1972.

[22] Sejersted, F., Bank og samfunn. Forretningsbankenes forhold til næringslivet, TMV, Memorandum series 3, 1989.

[23] Sundt, E., *Om Giftermaal i Norge*, Oslo, 1967 (1st edition 1866), p. 152.

A Theory of Economic and Technological Development in Norway

Figure 2 Births and deaths 1800-1900

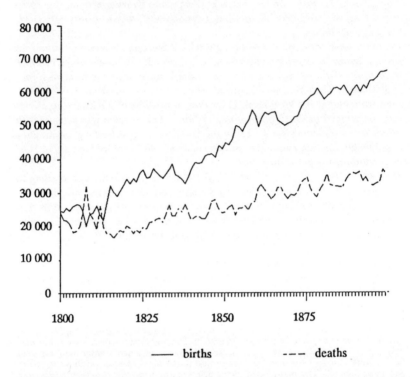

——— births   - - - deaths

There were, then, unusual numbers of young working-age people. On the one hand, they could not all find work. One sees signs of a proletariat forming at the bottom of society. In economic terms, there was a surplus of cheap labour. On the other hand, as we have seen, times were good or even very good, as witness Eilert Sundt's comment on the rapid expansion of industry. It was a period of increasing wealth. The Governor's report on the first half of the 1840s thus regrets "the increasing luxury and lavish lifestyle even among farmers and plain artisans .... manifested especially in a greater consumption of imported foods and use of costly foreign textiles".[24] Rapidly rising demand was in other words coinciding with a plentiful supply of cheap labour, economically a very favourable combination. We note in particular a rapidly rising demand for textiles, which meant - not least - cotton. A new market was formed, as yet for foreign goods, though of course the possibility of import substitution, to which we shall be returning, did exist.

Proletarisation, the "moral and civil problems", were a consequence of the population explosion, and meant not only cheap labour but also a threat. The enormous

---

[24] *Beretninger om kongeriget Norges økonomiske tilstand i aarene 1840-1845*, p. XXXI.

51

population pressures could all too easily have stifled the favourable economic trends. Of course the new economic society helped to solve the population problem in the long run by creating more opportunities, but the first real solution only presented itself in the form of emigration to America. Only Ireland experienced larger relative emigration than Norway. In the nineteenth century, it was Norwegian society's safety valve, and enabled the population explosion to be turned to economic advantage.

Modernisation as an ideology
That the mercantile classes won the support of the Storting and the administration when they requested government help, for instance in raising loans abroad, was no coincidence. The new liberal regime was founded on the idea of economic expansion. The rule of law, the protection of property, a stable monetary system, freedom of contract: every arrangement found its principal motivation in the idea of "the wealth of nations", in Adam Smith's words, or "the increase of national wealth", as the leading political figure, professor Anton Martin Schweigaard, was to put it. The contemporary economic scene as a whole shows distinct features of a large-scale political plan aimed at the economic development of the nation, with a relatively extensive use of public measures. The driving force, the ongoing initiatives, belonged to the private realm; but the point is the extent to which they formed part of an overall plan. The instrumental view of the market was that it was a useful mechanism. But it was that very instrumental and relativistic view which made it easy to disconnect it if it failed to function as intended. As has been maintained, "capitalism was staged by the state".

We should therefore not be deceived by seeing so many initiatives left to the private sector. Politically, the paramount consideration was modernisation, a strategic perspective which one can see revealed, not only in the more or less constant framework conditions, but also in the conspicuous elements of pragmatic policy directed at economic development. The state's interpretation of its mandate to provide favourable conditions was a wide one. Its attitude is well illustrated by the efforts to establish a system for supplying credit when the market proved inadequate. The numerous semi-public savings bank are another example, at the local level, of the extent of the mixed economy. The purchase of the country's first steamship was a state initiative. The state established a mortgage bank for landowners, and a scholarship fund to enable young technicians to go abroad to learn about the latest technologies. The government took a hand in railway construction and in developing a telegraph network. The Storting even went so far as to grant loans to private individuals if it felt that the measure in question would contribute to social modernisation. A number of the government measures were launched in the "spring thaw" of the 1840s. In 1845 a new Ministry of "home affairs" was established under the dynamic Frederik Stang. It could equally well have been called a "ministry for modernisation".

In the nineteenth century, in other words, Norway had a political regime with a long-term strategy to modernise the country. In retrospect we can also see what a surprisingly good grasp they had of the necessary instruments of policy. The continuous weighing of public against private instruments proved very effective, with competition balancing cooperation at both the local and the national level. That is precisely the balance assumed in Senghaas's theory of economic development.

A Theory of Economic and Technological Development in Norway

The normal view taken of nineteenth-century Scandinavian economic development has been to regard it as largely autonomous, with a minimum of government initiative or overall planning. Institutional conditions favoured economic development, for instance in the scarcity of feudal "remains", while at the same time the administration provided the necessary infrastructure. Although recent literature has tended to see a more prominent state role, a general view has persisted that developments in Scandinavia were relatively autonomous and were based on a fortunate conjunction of conditions, with the state relatively passive. This is the account given, for instance, by Berend & Ranki, Hodne, and Jörberg.[25] They point not only to passivity or limited activity on the part of the state, but equally to the distinct demarcation between the administrative and industrial sectors, the "small degree of connection between state and industry" which Rolf Torstendahl emphasises as typical of classic industrial capitalism in general.[26]

As will have been seen, we would place greater emphasis than these authors do on the role of the state, and not least its constant interaction with industry, as it appears, in the governmental willingness to compensate for market inadequacies. We see this most clearly in the part played by the administration in building up a system of credit facilities. At the local level, the impression of cooperation between the public and private sectors is considerably strengthened by the extensive "grey" mixed economy zone seen there. On the other hand, Berend and Ranki are certainly right to emphasise, in comparing the Balkans and Scandinavia, that state intervention alone is not enough to bring about economic development in a backward country. There must be driving forces in the private sphere with which the public sphere can collaborate.

The cooperative harmony between public and private institutions in Norway was based on the predominant ideology of modernisation, which found its clearest expression in the policies and the generation of senior civil servants - the educated bourgeoisie - which dominated the political agencies and the administration from the 1840s onwards.

In 1854 an industrial fair was held in Christiania, inspired, of course, by the great world exhibition in London in 1851. That sharp observer Eilert Sundt commented on what he saw as "a turn for the better in attitudes and ideas. The "educated world" is taking a growing interest in the distinctive callings and skills of the working world".[27]

One can also see the modernisation ideology in the new "broad money" bourgeoisie, which was enabled by its very breadth to generate so many initiatives. The period gave birth to countless entrepreneurs. We have already mentioned Frølich and Stabell. Frølich, in particular, was a source of many new initiatives, establishing

---

[25] Berend/Ranki, *op.cit.*, Hodne, *op.cit.*, Jörberg, L., The Nordic Countries 1850-1914, in Cipolla, C.M., (ed.), *The Fontana Economic History of Europe, The Emergence of Industrial Societies*, Vol. 4, Part 2, London, 1973.

[26] Torstendahl, R., Teknologi och samhällsutveckling 1850-1980. Fyra faser i Västeuropeisk industrikapitalism, in Nybom, T./Torstendahl, R., (eds.), *Byråkatisering och maktfördelning*, Lund, 1989, p. 87.

[27] Quoted from Frølich, T.H., *F.H. Frølich og hans samtid*, I-V, Oslo, 1912-38, Vol. II, p. 139.

Norway's first match factory, a kerosine factory (for lamp oil), the first factory for the manufacture of steel pen nibs, and much else besides, all around 1850. However, he was only one of many.

What existed in Norway, then, looks very much like an ideology of industrialisation, as described by Gerschenkron:

> To break through the barriers of stagnation in a backward country, to ignite the imaginations of men, and to place their energies in the service of economic development, a stronger medicine is needed than the promise of better allocation of resources or even the lower price of bread. Under such conditions even the businessman, even the classical daring and innovating entrepreneur, needs a more powerful stimulus than the prospect of high profits. What is needed to remove the mountains of routine and prejudice is faith - faith, in the words of Saint-Simon, that the golden age lies not behind but ahead of mankind.[28]

This industrialisation ideology was just as strong in government agencies as it was in the private sphere. Nor was it simply directed at industrialisation in a narrow sense, but at something broader or perhaps vaguer, which the term "modernisation" captures. Such an ideology was naturally greatly influenced by developments in Europe, and not least in Britain, with which Norway had had such close contacts. Such an ideology at the least provides us with a pointer in our search for something more than preconditions, namely a "driving force".

A striking aspect of the ethos of the rapidly expanding petty bourgeoisie was the low-church movement started by Hans Nilsen Hauge. This movement flourished in the years after 1814. Beginning as a rural movement, it appears to have contributed a good deal to a new spirit of independence amongst farmers and thus to the agrarian breakthrough in political life. It would seem to have been a factor behind the dynamic development of local autonomy. In accord with the Protestant ethic, thrifty financial management was one of its leading characteristics, and this acquired added importance as the movement spread to the towns. Efforts were made within the movement to help upwardly mobile farmers' sons to establish themselves as town merchants and industrialists. Hauge himself had explicitly formulated the programme of helping these "God's children" to take over "trade, factories and other large enterprises" from "the worldly wise, the false and the evil". In a number of towns, Hauge's followers were to constitute a highly successful part of the bourgeoisie, most notably in Stavanger and Bergen, but also in such towns as Drammen, Kristiansand and Trondhjem.[29]

The movement's importance lies, in the first place, in the moral legitimacy it gave the profit-seeking businessman at a critical moment in the development of the modern industrial society of Norway. There was a clear tendency at this time to regard the entrepreneur and the businessman as "the moral man". This had hardly happened before and should not happed again.

---

[28] Gerschenkron, *op.cit.*, pp. 128-129.

[29] Sejersted, F., *Om det gode samfunnsavhengighet av moralsk tvilsomme handlinger*, TMV Working paper, Oslo 1919; Strandbakken, P., *Protestantisme, kapitalisme og sosial endring* (Mag. thesis, sociology), Oslo, 1987.

A Theory of Economic and Technological Development in Norway

This religious movement may also help to explain some of the strength, spiritual independence and democratic attitudes of the petty bourgeoisie. Taking a broader social perspective, we may also see similar characteristics in the Norwegian working class as it was to emerge.

About the mid-nineteenth century, then, we can see a modernisation ideology combining with a general feeling of optimism and with many new initiatives. We can also see new features emerging in the social structure and new forms of social organization which seem to point forward to a modern society. However, this was but a beginning, and there was little to be seen of the qualitatively new technological development which was to be so important in the time ahead. Where the roots of technological transformation are to be found remains a problem.

The roots of the modern textile industry

The year 1842 stands out in Norwegian economic history principally because Norway acquired a currency linked to the silver standard, but also for other reasons. A new Trade Act adopted the same year removed many old privileges. A new scale of customs duties proved to be a big step in the direction of free trade, though some protection was retained, for instance, for finished goods. There were important events outside Norway, too. Britain began scaling down its timber duties, which had an immediate impact on Norwegian timber exports; even more important was the withdrawal of the British ban on machinery exports. That was what made Britain "the workshop of the world" in earnest: in addition to exporting the products of the system, Britain began systematically exporting the system itself, initially modern cotton spinning and weaving mills.[30]

Neither the opportunity to import British machinery, nor such protective tariff barriers as remained, led to an immediate blossoming of industry. What did happen in the boom was a very marked increase in imports of cotton textiles, which grew by 300 per cent from 1840 to 1846, mostly consisting of finished cotton garments. We may recall the Governor's contemporary lament at the widespread "luxury", with ordinary people buying foreign clothes. A market for this modern product thus formed very rapidly. Around 1846, developments took an interesting turn: imports of finished garments and cotton yarn fell dramatically, and imports of raw cotton rose correspondingly, in a clear, almost dramatic case of import substitution.[31] By then, Adam Hiorth and Knud Graah had started their modern spinning mills in Christiania, and Peder Jebsen had set up a modern weaving mill in Bergen.

---

[30] Earlier attempts had been made to establish "Manchester mills" in Norway: in Fredrikshald in 1813 and at Solbergfoss in 1820. Cf. Parmer, T., How Industrial Technology first came to Norway in Bruland, K., *Technology Transfer and Scandinavian Industrialisation*, New York, Oxford, 1991.

[31] Import figures are available in *Norges Offisielle Statistikk*. Cf. also Grieg, S., *Norsk Tekstil*, I-II, Oslo, 1948.

Figure 3 Imports of textiles 1828-1865

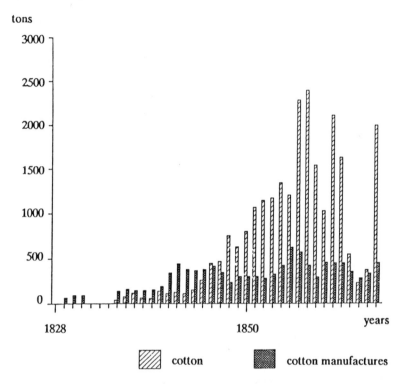

A couple of years later, Jebsen built a spinning mill near Bergen, and Halvor Schou built a weaving mill in Christiania. A modest but up-to-date industry was thus being established in Norway. We may note the clear signs of demand-led development: a market was formed first, and then an industry. In a sense it was consumers rather than manufacturers who took the initiative.

We have seen, however, that demand by itself was not enough to generate qualitatively-new initiatives in production. It takes more to break through what Gerschenkron has called "routine and prejudice". We have indicated the general feeling of optimism and the contemporary modernisation ideology which no doubt played a part, but there were other factors too. Kristine Bruland has shown that the new initiatives came at least as much from the British as from the Norwegian side. Britain was in fact exporting complete "factory packages", comprising technical operatives as well as machinery: "Norwegian textile industrialization was not so much an imitation as an *extension* of British developments following the development of a differentiated capital goods industry in the U.K.".[32] Of course a series of favourable conditions also

---

[32] Bruland, 1989, *op.cit.*, p. 6.

A Theory of Economic and Technological Development in Norway

had to exist, and we have accounted for most of them. The last was the almost explosive market formation of the 1840s. But conditions are, as Bruland emphasises, not enough. One cannot simply assume that demand more or less automatically generates output, and especially not in the case of something qualitatively new. Such beginnings have to be explained in terms of a positive initiative, and in this case it largely came from abroad. One can still regard Hiorth, Graah, Jebsen and Schou as entrepreneurs and trail-blazers, but with a little more reservation than has been customary. To some extent at least they should be seen as agents of the British.

Two further points should be noted at this juncture. The first is that the idealistic, Gerschenkronian explanation based on an ideology of industrialisation is not sufficient to account for new initiatives. The second is that increasing demand could, of course, have been satisfied by means of imports. That import substitution did take place, establishing a modern industry in Norway, can not be attributed, generally speaking, to favourable conditions, but more particularly to the existence of moderate tariff barriers protecting finished goods. It is often claimed that development in Scandinavia, and especially in Norway, can be accounted for by protective tariffs, because tariff policy generally was so favourable to free trade.[33] As already indicated, we are more inclined to Senghaas's view, and would argue that the moderate use of protective barriers within a system dominated by a free trade ideology was very helpful. A little went a long way. Whatever one's reservations with regard to simplistic conclusions from demand to output, a third point to note is that demand, or to be more precise market formation, played a decisive part in the establishment of Norway's first modern industry.

The mechanical engineering workshops and the "vacuum"

The second major modern industry to be introduced in the 1840s was mechanical engineering. The emergence of modern workshops coincided with the closing down of the old iron works, and the two events were connected. Iron consumption began to increase rapidly from 1835, and trebled in the next ten years. To begin with, the old ironworks in southeastern Norway tried to meet the demand, but declined from 1840 on and were supplanted by cheap imported iron. Some of them, nevertheless, sought to survive by adapting their production. Some continued to manufacture hardware from imported iron, and some ventured into mechanical engineering. By 1836, both Næs and Bærums Verk had acquired large lathes. Bærums Verk supplied the mills along the Akerselv river, where the first textile mills were also to be situated. The old iron works were not ideally located, however, because their original locations had been determined by charcoal supplies, whereas for the new workshops closeness to ports and their customers was much more important. The factories along the river found it inconvenient to use Bærums Verk, and it was their need that stimulated the establishment of Norway's first modern mechanical engineering workshop, Akers mek. verksted. This firm was founded in 1841 by a young naval lieutenant, P.S. Steenstrup. He had been captain of Norway's first steamship, "Constitutionen", bought by the state, and had been to England where he had

---

[33] Cf. Berend/Ranki, *op.cit.*, p. 64.

studied its engineering industry. In 1840 he had been assigned to design the Navy's main shipyard in Horten, but two years later *Morgenbladet* reported that the steamship Christiania had to be sent to Sweden for repairs, because the naval yard lacked the necessary tools.[34] So the need existed, and expansion appears to have been a response to it. Clearly this was a public sector initiative, intended to meet military needs. Note, incidentally, that in his study of Akers mek., Dag Solstad describes it as the workshop of the official classes right up to World War I.[35] It reflects the commitment to modernisation of the governing group, the educated bourgeoisie; or their recently awakened interest in "the distinctive callings of the working world".

Trondheim got its first mechanical engineering workshop in 1832 and Christiania its second, Myrens mek. verksted, in 1848. But demand outpaced supply. Writing of Oluf Onsum's establishment of Kværner Brug in 1853, Kristian Anker Olsen writes: "Studying the surviving contemporary sources, newspapers and periodicals and letters, one finds frequent laments at the "vacuum" which had not been filled".[36] The "vacuum" thus appears to have been a decisive incentive.

We should bear in mind that the "vacuum" was the need of other industries for workshops capable of repairing their new mechanical acquisitions. It was not so much a question of import substitution, but rather of an infrastructural prerequisite for importing and using steamships and new machines. The subsequent move from repairs to manufacture and import substitution was a second phase. The fact that the mechanical engineering industry was essentially established in two stages goes far in explaining the breaking down of the traditional barriers to the qualitatively new in the case of this major industry.

How was capital raised for these new enterprises? It is true that studies of early modern industry usually exaggerate the problem of capital accumulation. Very small amounts of start-up capital were needed. Steenstrup's needs, for instance, amounted to a modest 8,400 specie dollars. The problem lay rather in the absence of any system for raising "venture capital". There was little flexibility in the supply of capital, because it was not customary to invest outside one's own business. Steenstrup raised his initial capital by forming a partnership with two wealthy men, in addition to being granted a loan by the Storting. The legislative assembly, in other words, was free in special cases to commit "venture capital". Hiorth also brought in some wealthy men when he started his textile mill. Graah was supported by a rich brother-in-law, whereas Schou had money of his own.

As it happened, the good times had produced something approaching pressure for capital: timber exports were providing high yields at the time, but there was, as we saw, limited scope for ploughing capital back into the industry. There was an incen-

---

[34] Lødrup, H.P., *Akers mek. Verksted*, Oslo, 1951, pp. 22-23

[35] Solstad, D., *Medaljens forside*, Oslo, 1990.

[36] Anker Olsen, K., *Kværner Bruk*, Oslo, 1953, p. 40.

A Theory of Economic and Technological Development in Norway

tive to look beyond one's own enterprise for investment opportunities. In the generally optimistic atmosphere of the time, some of the old timber merchants thus felt able to invest small amounts elsewhere, and so providing a certain amount of "venture capital".

The first railway

In one sector, however, large sums were necessary. In Norway, as in other countries, the railway required new forms of capital accumulation. The railway was a truly revolutionary innovation, and one would expect to find strong driving forces behind the building of the first one, which was opened in 1854 and ran from Christiania to Eidsvold. There was along this stretch of country, especially from Christiania to the north end of lake Øyeren, heavy demands for timber transport from the Glomma watercourse. This need had previously given rise to plans for a canal, which had come to nothing. The question of an "iron road" was raised in 1824. The ever-active Frølich took up the idea around 1840, but it was not until the favourable business cycle had become very evident that plans began to take definite shape. Transport had then once again become the bottle-neck which made it almost impossible for the Christiania timber trade to respond to market signals.[37] And so it was typically enough one of the big Christiania timber merchants, Westye Egeberg, who also owned sawmills in the Romerike district, who took the initiative. He had a route surveyed and the costs calculated for a railway from Christiania trough Romerike to Eidsvold. It was also indicative of the harmony prevailing between the administration and the commercial sector that the project obtained official support in the form of a public railway commission which reported that the old transportation system was inadequate.

The crisis of the late 1840s temporarily halted the plan, but it was soon revived. Englishmen built the railway, half the capital being English, and the other half equally divided between the Norwegian state and private investors. Easily the largest private shareholders were the four largest sawmill owners in Romerike, and the railway proved enormously useful to them. Transport costs fell; timber utilisation improved greatly because they were enabled to market cheaper grades; and the value of property rose. It was also very significant that the timber reached its destination more quickly: Tostrup and Mathiesen were able to release as much as 20,000 specie dollars which had been bound up in stores, twice as much as they had paid for their shares in the railway. Yet the share purchase had been regarded as an amazingly large investment outside one's own enterprise. It is unnecessary to add that the railway made a profit from the start. So, the railway proved the solution to what had for so long been a bottle-neck in the Christiania timber trade, an efficient answer to an urgent need.

More clearly than anything else, it also demonstrated to the man in the street the great potential of the new technology. It pointed the way ahead to a new and better form of society. It may have contributed more than anything else to the feeling of being at the threshold of a new era. Some, however, also registered the socially re-

---

[37] Cf. Sejersted, F., *Den gamle bedrift og den nye tid*, Vol. III of *Fra Linderud til Eidsvold Værk*, Oslo, 1979.

volutionary nature of the new technology, and were alarmed at the violent pace of development and wanted to put the brakes on. The public sawmill commission of 1854, for instance, warned against turning the steam engine loose in the sawmills, invoking the "fear" which had arisen "at the exceptionally rapid development recently in the use of steam, also in our country".[38] What they chiefly had in mind was no doubt the 45 miles of track up to Eidsvold. On the whole, however, it seems people were quite clearly looking forward to the new society.

As had so often been the case elsewhere, Norway's railway also called for new forms of organization and association to raise the necessary capital. Limited-liability joint-stock companies were not unknown,[39] but they were rare. Capital accumulation was usually in the form of personal wealth. From the point of view of economics, the difficulty was not principally that this kept capital accumulation too limited: it was only with the railway that became a problem. The main problem was that the capital was split up with each succeeding generation. One sees a curious manifestation of this in the treatment given in the 1840s to the new legislation relating to inheritance. The main argument against equal rights for women to inherit was that they would "increase the splitting up of estates". It was essential, so it was held, that "large fortunes, once they have been accumulated, be maintained within the families".[40] The line of thought reveals a problem which was felt to be urgent in the country's current phase of rapid economic development. The solution was eventually to be found elsewhere than in limiting the right of women to inherit. In the longer term, the joint-stock company was the most important solution, pioneered in Norway, as mentioned, in connection with the railway. In Norway, however, development was slow, both in corporate formation and in commercial banking. Limited companies were not adequately regulated by law until 1910. Forms of financial organization remained traditional for a long time in Norway, and the railways became a state responsibility.[41]

Conclusion

A number of factors coincided to make conditions in the 1840s exceptionally favourable for Norwegian economic development. But the qualitative changes of a technological nature, what we have called the outline of a new society, find no immediate or direct explanation in economic conditions alone. Besides, it is striking that qualitatively new methods of production or organizational structures gained little ground in the really expansive sectors of the economy, that is the three principal export in

---

[38] The commissions's recommendation in *Stortingsforhandlinger 1854*. d. 4, O. no. 39.

[39] Cf. Olsen, E., *Danmarks økonomiske historie siden 1750*, Copenhagen, 1967, pp. 125-128. The law relating to shares was apparently quite advanced in Denmark-Norway as early as in the 1700s.

[40] *Stortingsforhandlinger* 1851, D. 5, U, p. 37.

[41] Alfred D. Chandler jr. argues in *Scale and Scope. The Dynamics of Industrial Capitalism*, Cambridge, Mass., 1990, p. 415, that whereas the railway in the U.S.A. paved the way for new forms of organization in the private sector, the administration of the German railways must be regarded as an extension of public bureaucracy.

A Theory of Economic and Technological Development in Norway

dustries, timber, fish, and shipping. The good times enjoyed by those industries were the principal source of the big demand boom. And we have noted repeatedly how behind even qualitatively new ventures there lay clearly articulated demand. The textile mills were an immediate response to the explosive increase in demand for cotton goods. The mechanical engineering workshops came in answer to the countless complaints about a "vacuum" which nobody would fill. The first private commercial bank was a result of an acute credit squeeze after a very expansionary period. The railway overcame a particular bottle-neck in the transportation system which had been recognised as a serious problem for over fifty years. And so on. These are all cases of clearly demonstrated and defined concrete needs for precisely what the new technology was capable of delivering. One gets the impression of production to order. And in fact the new instruments began showing profits the moment they were set in motion.

In view of the clearly defined demand, the widespread modernisation ideology, and the general optimism, new ventures were strikingly hesitant. Considerable force was evidently needed to break down traditional barriers, and some of the more important initiatives had to come from above and from outside, from the state administration and from Britain. The government bought the first steamship. The initiative behind the textile mills was largely British. The mechanical engineering workshops developed slowly, partly continuing a tradition from the old iron works, and partly as repair workshops. The state played a part, for instance in meeting military needs. Like the textile mills, the railway also arrived, broadly speaking, as a package from Britain, and here, too, the state was heavily committed. When the market proved unable to generate a satisfactory credit system on its own, the state provided a supplement in the form of a government commercial banking system.

There is, then, much to be said for Fritz Hodne's argument that Norwegian economic development in the mid-nineteenth century was led by demand in export markets. It was the main factor behind the good times which among other things created a domestic market for the new products and services. But demand is not the only answer: new developments only came grudgingly, and not in automatic response to demand. Other factors have to be taken into account to explain qualitatively new ventures. We see then how elements of the new economic and technological system find hesitant footholds. The next question is what happens once they gain that foothold. The establishment of Den norske Creditbank will give some indication.

Supply-side pressure

An utopian dream
Mention has already been made of the establishment in 1848 of the first Norwegian private commercial bank, Christiania Bank og Kreditkasse, when we saw how that establishment, like most other significant new developments in the financial life of the time, was prompted by a specific need, or rather by the imbalance between the need and the means of satisfying it. That also appears at first glance to have been the

case when the considerably larger Den norske Creditbank was established in 1857. Writing about its origins, Ebbe Hertzberg states that it was created "by the unaided force of circumstance".[42] On the same subject, Jens Arup Seip goes a step further, arguing that underlying the bank's establishment there was an utopian kind of dream.[43] The actual initiators were two members of the "educated bourgeoisie", Ole Jacob Broch and Torkel H. Aschehoug. They were neither wealthy, nor greedy for capital, but keenly interested in the new society that was taking shape, and motivated by faith in "the golden age". They took the idea for the Creditbank from the Crédit Mobilier, the Saint-Simonists' bank.

The governing idea was to bring together and allocate all the country's available capital, in order to devote it to systematic modernisation. That goes a great deal further than anything that could have been brought about by the "unaided force" of Norwegian "circumstance", and its realisation was also far from utopian. On the other hand, it could more than meet any needs as yet articulated - or any "unaided force of circumstance". It became a very large bank, with two million specie dollars of original capital, and promptly had difficulty in finding suitable investments. It engaged in speculation in the Oppland region which led to the so-called "Oppland crisis" in 1866, which proved a serious blow. Subsequently it did not operate as the investment bank it had been intended to be.

Den Norske Creditbank appears to be the first example on a large scale of initiative and leadership which took developments beyond the "unaided force of circumstance". As we have seen, the modernisation ideology can be traced further back in time; but we also saw that where truly qualitatively new ventures were concerned, nothing happened until there was a clearly defined need. In the case of the establishment of Den norske Creditbank, however, it is no longer the clearly defined need, the market, which is the driving force, but rather a dream of the market of the future. Developments were in other words in the process of freeing enterprising spirits from specifically articulated needs. To put it differently, these were the first indications that developments in production were going their own way, parting company with market developments, a process which can be seen particularly clearly in the area of infrastructure in general.

---

[42] Hertzberg, E./Rygg, N., *Den norske Creditbank 1857-1907*, Christiania, 1907. p. 7.

[43] Arup Seip, J., Assosiasjon og konkurranse: en bankhistorie, in *Tanke og handling i norsk historie*, Oslo, 1968.

A Theory of Economic and Technological Development in Norway

Figure 4 Numbers of industrial workers

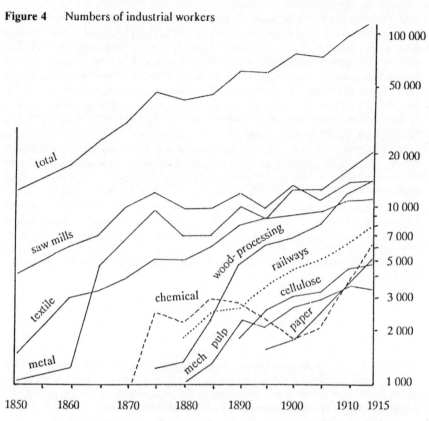

Note: The curves are based on printed statistics: *Beretningen om Kongeriket Norges Økonomiske Tilstand* (up to and including 1865), *Statistikkene over Fabrikanlæg* (to 1895), and *Industristatistikken* (from 1895). The principal source for the railways is *Statistiske oversikter* 1948, 10. rekke, no. 178. The bases for the statistics have undergone certain changes which make more detailed comparisons over longer periods more difficult, especially the extension of the basis when *Industristatistikken* began in 1895. However, the change do not significantly affect the overall picture. It is more important to note the inaccuracy which arises because the curves show numbers of workers rather than of man/years. The statistics only give man/years for the latest years, where an arbitrary adjustment has had to be made for the sake of comparison.

Infrastructure, mechanical engineering and railways

A characteristic feature of developed, capitalist, industrialised economies is the strong position of their capital goods industries. In addition to offering technical solutions to the problems that arise elsewhere in the manufacturing industries, a developed mechanical engineering industry is in itself a dynamic force, which contributes to technological innovation and new investment. That was precisely how the British industry functioned in relation to the establishment of Norway's first modern textile industry in the 1840s. The quantum leap in Norwegian mechanical engineering occurred in the 1860s. A foothold had been secured by means of a system of

63

public scholarships and through repair workshops, which had also built up their competence by mediating imports of British machinery. The 1860s were not characterised by the quantum leap alone, but also by the fact that they coincided with a decline in machinery imports.[44] This indicated that Norwegian workshops had become independent and competitive manufacturers of capital goods, making import substitution possible in that sector, too. And that came about without the help of even a moderate protective tariff. Machinery could be freely imported. In other words, one of the foundations for dynamic industrial development had been laid on Norwegian soil.

The engineering industry developed partly in concert with the extension of the railways. We have seen how the first railway was initiated in response to a specific transport need. It was also sufficiently employed to be profitable right from the start. This demonstration by the railway had an enormous impact as an example. It opened up new opportunities and aroused the popular imagination. Norwegians are familiar with the enthusiasm felt by the author Aasmund Olavsson Vinje after he had begun the journey described in *Ferdaminni* by taking the train to Eidsvold: "It is human thought which here, Creator-like, breathed life in through the nose of the lump of earth, and made coal and water and fire and ore its servant". In many ways the railway became the symbol of the new society, and it is perhaps not surprising that it provides many clear examples of a development based on what we have called supply-side pressure, that is a development based more on a vision of the future than on articulated demand. The railway was an important part of the infrastructure, and the "gospel of communication" was an article of contemporary faith.

The Randsfjord line, from Drammen via Hønefoss and opened in 1869, illustrates the construction of a railway as infrastructure. There were too few goods to carry to begin with, and the railway had financial difficulties for many years. As Andreas Ropeid wrote, "It was not really clear to everyone what goods the railway was to carry"; it had been "built for the future".[45] The future was wood-pulp mills. Together with the lines to Krødern and Kongsberg opened in 1871 and 1872, the Randsfjord line was one of the reasons why that region became the centre of the pulp industry in the 1870s and 1880s (see below). The Meraker line from Trondhjem and across to Sweden is another example. It was opened in 1882. There had been no clearly articulated need for transport, and for the first few years the results were poor. Gradually more and more use was made of it, and it became a precondition for economic activity. Timber and pulp from Sweden could be shipped from Trondheim, and in the other direction the railway opened up opportunities for substantial herring exports to Sweden.

Where the railways are concerned, then, we see a development of a first venture in response to clearly articulated needs, to later expansion in response to the clearly demonstrated effects of the first venture, and with the intent rather of laying the foundation for future progress than of serving existing customers.

---

[44] Bruland, K., Norsk mekanisk verstedsindustri og teknologioverføringen 1840-1900, in Lange, E., (ed.), *Teknologi i virksomhet. Verstedindustri i Norge etter 1840*, Ad Notam, 1989, p. 41.

[45] Ropeid, A., *Hønefossboka*, Vol. 2, 1965, p. 235.

A Theory of Economic and Technological Development in Norway

Figure 5   Railways. Length of line 1855-1900

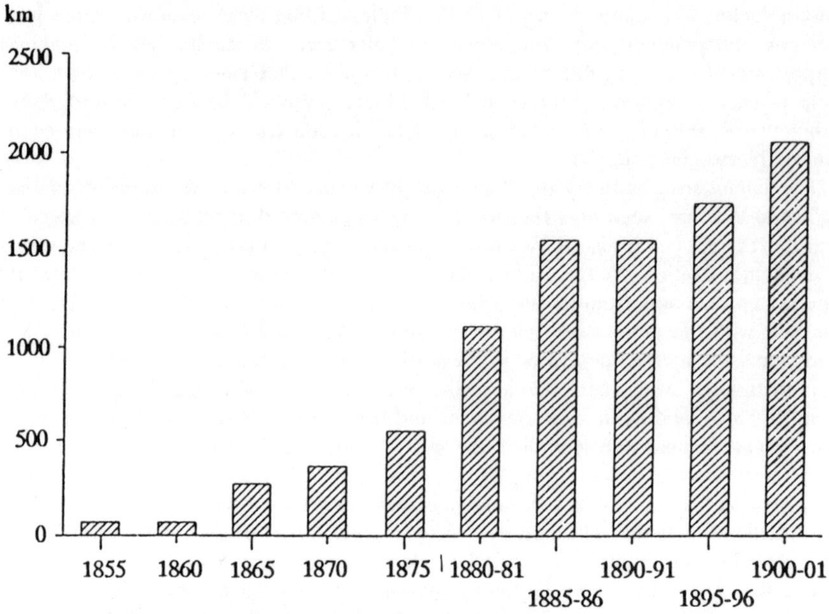

km

[Bar chart showing railway line length in km from 1855 to 1900-01. Values approximately: 1855: ~0, 1860: ~0, 1865: ~250, 1870: ~350, 1875: ~550, 1880-81: ~1100, 1885-86: ~1550, 1890-91: ~1550, 1895-96: ~1750, 1900-01: ~2050]

The timber industry turns dynamic
One reason for the development of the engineering industry was the marked increase in demand due to railway construction as well as developments in other sectors. An especially significant change was the very rapid technological modernisation of one of the big export industries, timber. Its technological conservatism had been closely related to the old system of privilege, which had in effect prevented a modern industry based on steam-driven sawmills from developing. It underwent rapid modernisation when the privileges were withdrawn from 1860.[46] Another reason for the changes was the shortage of raw materials, especially along the Skien and Drammen rivers; along the Glomma, raw materials were still relatively plentiful. The more intensive exploitation along the Skien and Drammen rivers had been due to greater accessibility to the forest and the waterfalls which determined the location of the old water-driven sawmills. When steam-driven sawmills became viable, this changed, leading to a radical relocation and an incredibly rapid development of a new steam sawmill industry in Fredrikstad, at the mouth of the Glomma. Several of the entrepreneurs came from the old industry in Drammen.

---

[46] Sejersted, F., En gammel produksjonsmåte mobiliserer til selvforsvar, in Sejersted, F., (ed.), *Vekst gjennom krise. Studier i norsk teknologihistorie*, Oslo, 1982.

65

There was more to this development than the creation of a market for machinery. It seems likely that it could not have taken place, at least not at the same rate, without the active involvement of Myrens mechanical engineering workshop. Myrens was run by Jens Jensen, one of the state scholars who had been sent to England to study the latest technology. In addition to supplying the new industry with most of its machinery, he also took a hand in the technological planning. It is worth noting that the modernisation went beyond the actual sawing process, to include the development of a greater degree of processing than had been customary. Fredrikstad made a speciality of planed timber, and Myrens made the planes. The special blend of competition and cooperation which arose, with a number of competing timber companies cooperating closely with the same supplier of machinery, was an important reason why the industry became so dynamic.

That it was dynamic could be seen, not only in the creation of Fredrikstad as a modern industrial centre, but also in the setting up of establishments abroad.[47] Concurrently with the Fredrikstad developments, extensive Norwegian establishments took place in Sweden, where, to quote Ernst Söderlund, "the expanding timber handling industry in Norrland offered these outstanding experts from one of the world's technologically most advanced timber industries higher incomes and greater opportunities for profit than the declining or stagnating production in their own country".[48] Carsten Jacobsen and Hans Rasmus Astrup were among the best-known figures, but there were many others. Many of the establishments used Norwegian machinery supplied by Myrens.

In Finland a modern sawmill industry was established in the early 1870s, and here too Norwegians played a leading part, with Hans Gutzeit especially prominent. He arrived from Fredrikstad in 1872, bringing capital, machinery from Myrens, and sawmill hands, and established what quickly grew into the notable Gutzeit concern.

A final wave of enterprise creation, from the 1890s on, took place in Russia. It peaked during World War I, and was brought to a sudden stop by the Revolution. Such enterprise had been quite substantial: in 1917, the newspaper *Archangelsk* claimed that the Norwegians were trying to take over the whole of the forest industry of North Russia. An exaggeration no doubt, but nevertheless suggesting the scale of the activity.[49]

The strikingly dynamic character of the Norwegian sawmill and timber-exporting industries in these years is a clear demonstration that Norway was fast becoming a modern industrial nation. Its origins lay in the modernisation of an old industry but, as we have seen, the process was by no means "automatic". The timber industry remained technologically conservative for a long time. A dynamic modern timber industry grew up only when the traditional activities experienced difficulties owing to dwindling supplies of raw materials, at a time when the foundations had been laid for a modern capital goods industry. Entrepreneurs were doing what the British had

---

[47] Dealt with in Sejersted, F., Veien mot øst, in Langholm, S./Sejersted, F., (eds.), *Vandringer. Festskrift til Ingrid Semmingsen*, Oslo, 1980.

[48] Söderlund, E., et al., *Svensk trävaruexport under hundra år*, Stockholm, 1951, pp. 117-118.

[49] Sejersted, Veien mot øst, *op.cit.*, p. 188.

A Theory of Economic and Technological Development in Norway

done earlier: that is, expanding beyond national boundaries to exploit international opportunities in the form of access to raw materials and of markets for finished goods. This Norwegian "road to the east", as it has been called, was part of a general economic imperialism. Geographical expansion is a characteristic of the dynamic European capitalism of the time. Norway took part, if only economically, in that imperialism.

Wood pulp - a new technological concept

The dynamic nature of the timber industry was closely linked to technological innovation, and this applies to an even greater extent to the wood-processing industry. Following modest beginnings in the 1860s, it made a breakthrough of sorts in the boom of the 1870s and went on growing rapidly during the subsequent major crises of the 1870s and 1880s.[50] The wood-processing industry was based on a completely new technological concept, the use of wood pulp to produce paper.

The demand for paper had grown rapidly during the nineteenth century, and the search for an alternative raw material to textile fibres began early. Wood fibre was to be the solution, and the first production of mechanical pulp took place in Germany in the 1840s. Paper, and products based on wood fibre generally, would gradually find other applications, too: the technological base had been laid for a new growth industry.

A remarkable feature of the development of the Norwegian wood-pulp mills is that the bulk of the expansion took place along the Drammen and Skien rivers, that is in the very areas where the traditional sawmills had run into difficulties because of the dwindling supplies of raw materials. As much of the large-dimension timber was cut, the centre of gravity of the sawmill industry began to move eastwards, to Fredrikstad, Sweden, Finland and Russia. The pulp industry, however, could manage with smaller-dimension timber and moved into the vacated areas. Besides, whereas sawmills were switching from water wheels to steam engines, pulp grinding used turbines and was able to harness the waterfalls which the sawmills were moving away from. These factors help to account for the rapid expansion of the wood-pulp industry. There were input factors ready and waiting for the opportunities opened up by the new concept - pulp.

---

[50] The breakthrough by the Norwegian wood pulp industry has been the subject of some discussion. Cf. Mikkelsen, P.R., *Tremasseindustri 1863-1895. En studie i industrielt gjennombrudd*, Master's thesis, Oslo, 1975; Sejersted, F., *Den gamle bedrift og den nye tid*, Vol. III of *Fra Linderud til Eidsvold Værk*, Oslo, 1979, pp. 270 ff., and Teknisk utvikling i sagbruks- og treforedlingsindustrien under krisen i 1880-årene in Sejersted, F., (ed.), *Vekst gjennom krise*, Universitetsforlaget, 1982; Lange, E., Norsk tremasse på det britiske marked, *Historisk Tidskrift*, 2, 1988; Halvorsen, O., Tremasseeksporten 1870-95, *Historisk Tidsskrift*, 1, 1990.

Figure 6 Export of mechanical and chemical wood-pulp. Annual average 1866-1900

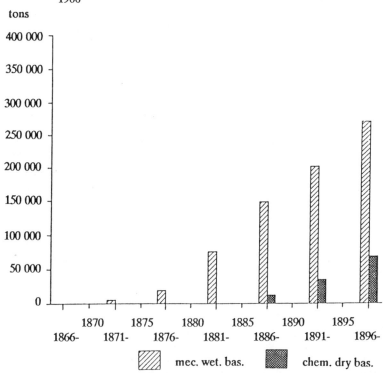

While the new product of wood pulp aroused great expectations, with visions of rapidly expanding markets, there had not been any distinct "market suction". This development was thus not demand- led. Of course people expected to be able to sell the product. But the inspiration lay in a vision of the future market, a vision in the minds of supply-side entrepreneurs. In 1905 G. Thilesen, one of the industry's leading men, put the situation in a nutshell: the wood pulp mills had largely been "in the hands of owners with little or no knowledge of the consumers and indeed little idea of export trade" - quite a comment on our first modern export industry. Unfamiliarity with markets may indeed have been a condition for the emergence of the new industry. The dynamics of its development came from the supply side, and seems to some extent to have been "technology-led". This was not peculiar to the Norwegian industry. The trend in Europe at this time was for the technically rather than the commercially competent to become the leaders of industry.[51]

---

[51] Torstendahl, R., *Bureaucratisation in Northwestern Europe, 1880-1985. Domination and Governance*, Routledge, 1991, pp. 16-17.

A Theory of Economic and Technological Development in Norway

Nevertheless, the availability of raw materials and a vision of a future market were not enough to account for the supply-side dynamics in the emergence of the wood-processing industry. They may serve to explain why things happened where they did, and may also in a way have triggered events; but nothing would have happened unless certain other material conditions had also been present, conditions characteristic of modern industrial societies.

A significant factor underlying the rapid and relatively early expansion of the wood pulp industry was technical competence, developed in the capital goods industry which had been established in the 1860s. Like the sawmills, the pulp industry developed in close cooperation with the mechanical engineering industry, and especially with Kværner Brug. The fundamental technological breakthrough had occurred outside Norway, but Norwegian industry had been sufficiently developed to make use of it and to make its own independent contribution to further development. It was also significant that the expansion of the pulp industry was so rapid that in a relatively short space of time it gathered around itself engineers who could be regarded as wood pulp specialists.

The new technology, and the existence of specialist engineers to handle it, had other origins also. It appears that Norwegian mechanical engineering workshops were well advanced for instance in turbine design, which found their first use on any scale in the milling industry, the technology of which closely resembles that of woodpulp mills. In fact some engineers moved from milling to become pulp industry entrepreneurs, for example, Hansen of Kittilsen and Hansen, and Heyerdahl of Union, both in Skien. Such cases of "technological convergence" demonstrate well how much of the dynamic can be attributed to technological development.

Much of the wood pulp industry's development took place in the 1870s. The technology appears to have "matured" by the end of the decade. In other words, the concept had been relatively clearly defined, the technology had become easier to transfer, and the path of further development had become quite clear.

Supply-side dynamics in a capitalist economy also include the entrepreneurial factor, part of which consists of the supply of venture capital. The good profits made by the old timber industry in the first half of the 1870s, and the limited opportunities for expansion at home, have already been noted. Such a situation inspired ventures abroad, but also led some imaginative spirits who had caught the modernisation germ to explore new paths at home. One prominent entrepreneur was Christian Anker, of the old factory-owning family in Fredrikshald. In 1869 he established the Skaaningsfos wood pulp mill, and in 1873, with his cousin H.C. Mathiesen of the large timber company Tostrup and Mathiesen, he founded the large Hønefos mill. H.C. Mathiesen invested considerable sums in ventures of this kind, and thus figured prominently in the building up of Union in Skien. It was thanks to his substantial fortune that these relatively large businesses survived the difficult 1880s.[52] These are just a few examples of what might be referred to as a wood-pulp entrepreneur cul-

---

[52] Cf. Sejersted, 1979, *op.cit.*

ture, corresponding to that of the engineering environment. These two fields can be seen to have joined forces in quite a number of cases.

In the 1880s, the general crisis, which was far-reaching in Norway, caught up with the wood pulp industry, too, but the situation served to enhance its great potential. There was a marked drop in prices, but an even sharper increase in exports, so that in sum the industry's contribution to Norwegian economic development was positive. One reason, for this was a substantial improvement in productivity. This was principally founded on economies of scale (increasingly large plants) and organizational innovations. Some interplay between falling prices and improving efficiency seems likely. Falling prices impelled rationalisation and the better utilisation of technology, while increasingly efficient production made it possible to lower prices and thus win new markets. There was great elasticity of demand for the product - on paper. It was at about this time that daily newspapers began to reach a wider general public, in Norway too. The wood pulp industry thus provides a good example of how a modern industry possessing the potential for technological development can overcome a crisis brought about by economic depression.

Agriculture and local cooperatives
In the second half of the nineteenth century, Norwegian agriculture underwent dramatic change. We have already seen how, during the crisis years of the Napoleonic Wars, agriculture developed new features that made it more dynamic in the period that followed. As communications steadily improved, domestic farming was marked by an increasing market orientation. From the mid-century new factors came into the picture, principally renewed competition from imported grain, Black Sea rye in the 1850s, but especially wheat from the American prairies in the 1880s. New industries sprang up on the basis of the imported grain: breweries and big flour mills which supplied the growing urban markets.

Norwegian agriculture met this foreign competition by making a large-scale switch from crops to livestock, especially in the last two decades of the century. Until about 1865, the farming population had been increasing. From then and concurrently with the major change to livestock, the farming population began to fall, whilst its productivity steadily increased. Agriculture can be said to have been impressively innovative while at the same time transferring workers to the new industries.

At least to some extent, Norwegian agriculture's ability to meet the new competition must be traced to a capacity to adapt to changing circumstances, which had been developed earlier in the century. That flexibility had been related to the development of individually-owned freehold farms. But the switch to animal husbandry required more than adaptability: it required capital investment and a credit system, and it called for the efficient processing of farm products, in other words for dairies. One extension of local autonomy had been the development of savings banks all over the country. Together with the mortgage bank initiated by the central administration in 1851, the savings banks provided the credit facilities which made it possible for individual farmers to achieve transition.

A Theory of Economic and Technological Development in Norway

The savings banks were a new type of local cooperation in the "grey zone" between the public and private sectors. The development of a local dairy industry, which was very rapid from the 1880s on, was the next substantial example of a similar type of local cooperative. Local small industries were developing on the basis of modernised agriculture, with the same savings banks providing the credit. Lars Thue has emphasised how prominently this type of local cooperative figures in Norway's modernisation. The same structures provided the foundations on which the telephone network and the electricity supply system were to develop, both early and rapidly.[53] Local cooperatives were thus instrumental in spreading new technologies, and contributed significantly to the new supply-side dynamism.

The great crisis and the new outward-looking industries

The "great depression" of the 1870s and '80s has been the subject of much international discussion by economic historians. Its principal feature was falling prices, and to some extent declining production. These years were also the point of departure for the rapid development of strong new industrial countries, Germany and the U.S.A. In some respects it was chiefly a crisis for Britain. It has also been considered as related to a change of technological paradigms. Followers of Joseph Schumpeter often speak of the "second industrial revolution". The potential for growth using the old iron and steam-based technology was nearing exhaustion. The solution to this lay in the innovation and development of new technologies based on steel, chemicals and electricity. At the organizational level, it would call for integration into larger units. The crisis itself was thus structural, a painful process of adjustment to a new technological paradigm.[54]

In many ways, Norwegian economic development provides a good illustration of this structural crisis, with its distinct combination of declining traditional industries and expanding new ones. The depression made itself strongly felt in Norway, where it hit the old export industries, which had accounted for so much of the growth since the 1830s, especially hard. The timber industry suffered a decline from which it never fully recovered: from 1874 to 1887 the exports of timber by value almost halved. Over the same period, freight revenues in overseas trade fell from about NOK 103 million to about 76 million. The fisheries, too, had hard times as herring catches proved less dependable than earlier in the century. The crisis hit the Stavanger district especially hard. As Juul Bjerke has emphasised, the reason why this profound crisis in the old export industries had such serious consequences was that new export industries did not develop up until the 1880s.[55]

---

[53] Thue, L., Hvorfor Norge ble et rikt land? Lokale kooperasjoner og økonomisk vekst, unpublished Ms., 1991.

[54] Cf. for instance Freeman, C./Perez, C., Structural crises of adjustment, business cycles and investment behaviour in Giovanni, D./Freeman, C./Nelson, R./Silverberg, G./Soete, L., (eds.), *Technical Change and Economic Theory*, London, 1988.

[55] Bjerke, J., *Langtidslinjer i norsk økonomi 1865-1960*, Samfunnsøkonomiske studier, 16, Statistisk Sentralbyrå, Oslo, 1966.

Figure 7 Exports by the principal new export industries, in current prices (NOK millions)

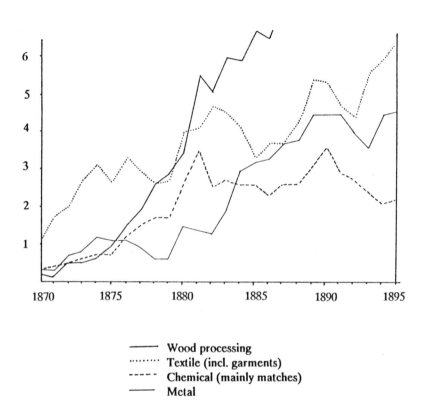

— Wood processing
······ Textile (incl. garments)
---- Chemical (mainly matches)
— Metal

We noted earlier how the technologically-advanced the sawmill industry expanded by establishing itself outside Norway. More important still, we noted the establishment of a pulp industry which, although not large in itself, had begun to adapt to export markets before the crisis, and thus had secured a base from which to expand rapidly during the crisis: it was in the course of the crisis that Norway became the leading exporter of mechanical pulp. We also noted the development earlier, alongside the technologically conservative export industries, of some modern import-substituting industries, notably textiles and metal in addition to match manufacturing, which grew rapidly in the 1870s. Falling demand during the crisis hit those industries, but they showed their potential in those same 1880s by developing as export industries.

It is important to be aware of the degree of technological innovation underlying the new orientation towards exports. In the metal industry, there was some decline in shipbuilding and machinery, whereas such items as horse-shoe nails, fish hooks and nails expanded and were sold abroad. Much of the increase in textile exports in

A Theory of Economic and Technological Development in Norway

the 1880s was achieved by the garment industry. Developments in shipping paralleled those in the metal industry. Whereas total tonnage declined from 1878 onwards, a special sector, steamship tonnage, grew relatively quickly in the first half of the 1880s. Some other products which won markets in the 1880s represent a qualitatively new direction, for instance condensed milk, brisling sardines from the Stavanger Preserving Co., oxalic acid from the Gresvik chemicals plant, and Peter Møller's steamed cod-liver oil. Like wood pulp, these were based on domestic raw materials and new technologies derived at least in part from the new technological paradigm. Among the new industries which were not particularly geared to exports but were based on the new paradigm, mention can be made of nitroglycerine, margarine, and cement. This was also the time when electrotechnology, a field in which Norway made an early start, was introduced. The first telephone arrived in 1880; the manufacture of dynamos began in 1883; and the first power station to sell electricity started in 1885.

None of this output counted for much quantitatively, but it did point the way ahead out of the crisis, and it revealed the existence in Norway of what one might call self-reinforcing capitalistic mechanisms. It is noteworthy that some of this qualitatively new orientation as to both markets and technologies took place at a time of rapidly falling prices, so there was no market suction or demand pressure - on the contrary. It is precisely during the crisis that it becomes clearest that the dynamic factors are to be found on the supply side. In some degree it would also make sense to see the crisis contributing to the transformation. Falling profitability in traditional manufacturing made it tempting to innovate where technological opportunities for a brighter future could at least be glimpsed. During the crisis one can also see signs of what Schumpeter called "creative destruction". It was not until old industries got into difficulties that input factors became available, and the space too in which entrepreneurs could try out what the new technological paradigm had to offer. The crisis thus also brought with it a painful process of restructuring.[56]

The crisis of the 1880s was also political. It ended with the fall of the senior civil servants' regime and the introduction of parliamentarism. An important aspect of this crisis was that its roots can be seen in an economic and social crisis. What was in dispute was not only who was to rule, but also how. Political reforms paved the way for a central government which could be given new responsibilities, especially in social policy.[57] The most important change in the function of the state was the prominence now given to redistribution. Central government took upon itself, as it were, the task of alleviating the most harmful effects of industrial development. One reason why the new state did not from the beginning assume new responsibilities in production was precisely that institutions and mechanisms had now been developed which gave economic development a self-reinforcing dynamic. It was in accord with this that central government withdrew from its direct commitment to supply credit.

---

[56] On the Schumpeter tradition and the "function" of crisis in a process of economic development, see Sejersted, F., *Rutine og Valg*, TMV Working Paper No. 5, Oslo, 1990.

[57] Sejersted, F., *Demokrati og rettsstat*, Oslo, 1984. Cf. the same author's *Den norske "Sonderweg"*, TMV Working Paper Series, No. 35, Oslo, 1991.

73

The discounting commissions were abolished, and *Norges Bank* discontinued its operations in the market, leaving private credit institutions to take over.[58]

Epilogue

The turn of the century was a period of rapid industrialisation in Norway. Mechanical engineering was to be one area of rapid development, and especially shipbuilding. The process seen earlier in timber and wood processing came to be repeated in the modernisation of Norway's merchant fleet. This industry remained faithful to the old technologies for a long time, but once modernisation began it was based on and carried out in close liaison with Norway's capital goods industries.[59]

The 1890s also saw a developing production of chemical pulp, or cellulose, a product typifying the new technological paradigm of the period. A number of factories, such as Borregaard's, were built in Norway. But Norway was never to acquire such a leading position as it had done in the field of mechanical pulp. The 1890s saw also the beginnings of the big wave of industrialisation based on hydropower. An interesting point in this connection, however, is the trend which emerged towards marginalisation. Norwegians were not prepared themselves to organize the exploitation of hydropower. The initiative was taken by foreigners, and the result was that not only the loan capital but also the equity capital was largely in foreign hands. Was the capitalist system, then still not fully developed?

We have seen how, over time and through a long process, Norway developed features which we definitely recognise as belonging to a modern industrial society. The necessary structural conditions existed from the start, but that was not enough to account for development. A growing demand in Europe for traditional Norwegian goods and services explains a good deal, but was not the whole answer. The difficulty lies in explaining why Norway was not marginalised, that is simply turned into a supplier of raw materials to more highly developed countries. In this respect the role of central government stands out. The modernisation of the nation was a deliberate strategy, and it was carried out on the basis of a clearly articulated ideology of modernisation. The willingness of the central authorities to take action in many areas departs to some extent from the picture we are usually shown. Nevertheless, we have seen how strong the forces, and not least the market forces, had to be to enable new industries to secure a foothold. This they did, to some extent, outside the traditional Norwegian industrial sector. But once they had secured their footholds, particularly in mechanical engineering, that established the premises on which in the next instance the large traditional industries were modernised and made dynamic. The characteristic feature, and the clearest sign that Norway was on the road to modern industrial capitalism, was that development had become self-reinforcing, or that the driving force, to a large extent, shifted to the supply side. This emerges most clearly from the developments during crisis of the 1880s.

---

[58] Sejersted, F., Review of Jahn, G. et al., Norges Bank gjennom 150 år, in *Historisk Tidsskrift*, Vol. 47, 1968. See also Egge, Å., *Statens diskonteringskommisjoner, op.cit.*

[59] With Andersen, H., Norsk skipsbyggingsindustri gjennom 100 år, in Lange, E., (ed.), *Teknologi i virksomhet. Verkstedindustri i Norge etter 1940*, Oslo, 1989.

A Theory of Economic and Technological Development in Norway

The economic structure which developed in Norway over the course of the nineteenth century proved very well suited to the type of production found in the first phase of industrialisation. The general technological environment and the mechanical engineering industry which emerged proved well able to modernise the sawmills, service the wood-pulp mills, and convert the merchant fleet to steam. Norway was less favourably placed, however, to exploit the modern, more scientifically-based technology of the new technological paradigm at the end of the century. The capital accumulation and credit supply systems which had emerged, like the infrastructure generally, had lent themselves very well to smaller business units and local cooperatives, but proved inadequate for large units. Norway had developed a strong petty bourgeoisie, with an industrial structure in which small and medium-sized enterprises predominated. No *grande bourgeoisie* grew up to correspond to those in the countries which became the leading nations in the next stage of development, with the "second industrial revolution" at the end of the century, Germany, the USA and, to some extent, Sweden.[60] There is reason to believe that the capitalist structure and dynamic which was built by development in the nineteenth century have remained, for better or worse, a leading characteristic of Norway as an industrial nation to this day.

---

[60] These matters are discussed in more detail in Sejersted, Den norske "Sonderweg", *op.cit.*

[5]

A Chronology of Cycles in Real Economic Activity for Norway, 1867-1914

Jan Tore Klovland

Introduction

Business cycles, defined as "recurrent sequences of persistent and pervasive expansions and contractions in economic activities"[1], have been a distinctive feature of the experience of capitalist countries as far back as our historical records on aggregate economic activity go. Indeed, Schumpeter maintained that "[a]nalyzing business cycles means neither more nor less than analyzing the economic process of the capitalist era ... Cycles are not, like tonsils, separable things that might be treated by themselves, but are, like the beat of the heart, of the essence of the organism that displays them".[2]

In the United States empirical research on business cycles has a long and broad tradition, especially within the National Bureau of Economic Research (NBER).[3] In Scandinavia, and more particularly, in Norway, the empirically oriented and largely descriptive business cycle analysis, concerned with identifying cycles and dating turning points, never gained such widespread attention as in the United States.[4] There is little doubt that these differences in method and scope to some extent must be attributed to the authority of the macroeconomic tradition associated with Ragnar Frisch. In the interwar years Frisch worked on several theoretical and empirical aspects of business cycle analysis.[5] Subsequently, however, his econometric research program became more oriented towards applied work on areas like national income accounting, economic planning models and input-output analysis.

---

[1] Moore, G.H./Zarnowitz, V., The development and role of the National Bureau of Economic Research's business cycle chronologies, in *The American business cycle*, edited by Gordon, R.J., University of Chicago Press, Chicago 1986, p.520.

[2] Schumpeter, J.A., *Business cycles*, McGraw-Hill, New York 1939, p.V.

[3] The classic contributions in this tradition include Mitchell, W. C., *Business cycles: The problem and its setting*, National Bureau of Economic Research, New York 1927 and Burns, A.F./Mitchell, W.C., *Measuring business cycles*, National Bureau of Economic Research, New York 1946. For a more recent survey of the NBER methods of busines cycle analysis see Moore/Zarnowitz, *op.cit.*

[4] The study by Jörberg, L., *Growth and fluctuations of Swedish industry 1869-1912*, Almqvist & Wiksell, Stockholm 1961, on the cyclical fluctuations of Swedish industry between 1869 and 1912 seems to be rather exceptional in the Scandinavian literature.

[5] Frisch, R., Propagation problems and impulse problems in dynamic economics, in *Economic essays in honour of Gustav Cassel*, George Allen & Unwin, London 1933, remains one of the classics in business cycle theory. Cf. also Andvig, J.C., Ragnar Frisch and business cycle research during the interwar years, *History of Political Economy*, vol. 13.

A Chronology of Cycles in Real Economic Activity

As was more or less the case in the rest of Europe, there was little evident interest in classical business cycle analysis. This approach, being associated with the pejorative measurement-without-theory label launched by Koopmans[6], seemed to be outdated in light of the recent advances in macroeconomic theory and the sustained growth of European economies in the early postwar years.

Consequently, the painstaking gathering, sifting and scrutinizing of a wide range of individual time series were superseded by large-scale econometric model building. Despite the undisputed subsequent achievements of the econometric approach, some would nevertheless argue that important empirical aspects of macroeconomics were crowded out in this process. Serendipity had to give way to system stringency, and degrees of freedom literally had to be sacrificed as the models were to fit into the straitjacket of the annual national accounting framework. It must be acknowledged, however, that the computer-intensive exercises in national accounting akin to the early generations of econometric models served quite well for purposes with which economic planning authorities were concerned.

As the belief in the perpetual bonanza of the postwar economy gradually weakened, particularly in the more turbulent 1970s, there seemed to be a revival of interest in business cycle analysis. The analysis of cycles in the postwar Norwegian economy by Wettergren is evidence of this.[7] In recent years systematic monitoring of business cycles has gained more attention by economic analysts in Norway as well.[8]

Previous studies on business cycles in Norway

Although business cycle analysis never came to the forefront of macroeconomic research in Norway, it is important to recognize that there do exist several valuable contributions by individual economists and historians. J. Einarsen[9], who was inspired by Frisch, made an important theoretical and empirical contribution in his study of investment cycles in the Norwegian shipping industry. Gjermoe made an elaborate study of the cycles in the interwar period and analyzed several time series for earlier periods as well.[10] His contributions are firmly in the tradition of empirical business cycle analysis, thus being outside the mainstream macroeconomic tradition in Norway at the time.

---

[6] Koopmans, T.C., Measurement without theory, *Review of Economics and Statistics*, vol 29, 1947.

[7] Wettergren, K., *Konjunkturbølger fra utlandet i norsk økonomi* (SØS no. 36), Central Bureau of Statistics, Oslo 1978. Aukrust, O., *Norges økonomi etter krigen* (SØS no. 12), Central Bureau of Statistics, Oslo, 1965, also contains much interesting material for the early postwar years.

[8] See for example Solheim, J.A., Konjunkturovervåkningsarbeidet i Norges Bank, *Penger og Kreditt*, vol. 12, 1984, for a survey of the work on business cycle analysis at Norges Bank.

[9] Einarsen, J., *Reinvestment cycles and their manifestation in the Norwegian shipping industry*, University Institute of Economics, Oslo, 1938.

[10] Gjermoe, E., *Konjunkturene i mellomkrigstiden i Norge og utlandet*, Central Bureau of Statistics, Oslo, 1951, Konkursene fra 1895 til nu, *Statistiske Meddelelser*, vol. 40, 1922, Seddelomløpet 1851-1922, *Statistiske Meddelelser*, vol 41, 1923 and Seddelomløpet i Norge, Sverige og Danmark, *Statistiske Meddelelser*, vol. 42, 1924.

19

Scandinavian Economic History Review

For the half-century before the First World War, which is the period we will be focusing on here, extensive work on business fluctuations are to be found in some recent historical studies of individual industries. Solhaug[11] contains a detailed study of fluctuations in prices and export volumes of the Norwegian fisheries up to 1880. The other major export industry, the wood and timber trade, is less systematically covered, although Sejersted presents much useful information on price fluctuations in the early years.[12]

Contributions by economists include Aschehoug, E. Einarsen and Rygg.[13] E. Einarsen provides an extensive compilation of time series data from the foreign trade statistics and excerpts from annual trade reviews. Aschehoug suggested using the currency circulation as an indicator of business fluctuations. However, none of these authors presented any index or time series which measures fluctuations in aggregate economic activity in Norway on a monthly or quarterly basis. This paper is intended as a first step towards constructing such data for the period 1867 to 1914 by estimating a monthly indicator of real economic activity.

The construction of the GDP indicator

Basically, our approach is to employ monthly data on such indicators as the volume of foreign trade, shipping activity, and railway freight receipts to form a monthly index of aggregate real economic activity. Some comments on the measurement, reliability and relevance of these series as short-term indicators of gross domestic product (GDP) are necessary in order to evaluate the results of this paper.[14]

The data

Quantities of Merchandise Exports and Imports: Beginning 1867 monthly data on the quantities imported and exported of the principal commodities were published by the Central Bureau of Statistics. In the early years the number of commodities included in the monthly returns was small, but they nevertheless represented 40-50 per cent of the total value of imports and more than 80 per cent of the value of merchandise exports. The number of commodities increased over the years, but on the other hand foreign trade became more diversified. Accordingly, in terms of value

---

[11] Solhaug, T., *De norske fiskeriers historie 1815-1880*, Universitetsforlaget, Bergen 1976.

[12] Sejersted, F., *Fra Linderud til Eidsvold Værk (III): Den gamle bedrift og den nye tid*, Dreyer, Oslo, 1979. For a general survey of the development of the Norwegian economy, see Hodne, F., *Norges økonomiske historie 1815-1970*, J.W. Cappelen, Oslo 1981.

[13] Aschehoug, T.H., Den cirkulerende seddelmængde som økonomisk barometer, *Statsøkonomisk Tidsskrift*, vol. 7, 1893 and De økonomiske kriser og depressioner i det 19de aarhundrede, *Statsøkonomisk Tidsskrift*, vol. 12, 1898. Einarsen, E., *Gode og daarlige tider*, Gyldendal, Copenhagen and Kristiania, 1904. Rygg, N. *Norges Banks historie*, part 2, Oslo 1955.

[14] A listing of the data and a more detailed description of the data and their sources can be found in Klovland, J.T., A chronology of cycles in real economic activity for Norway, 1867-1914, *Discussion Paper no. 02/87, Norwegian School of Economics and Business Administration*, 1987. The main sources of data were *Statistiske Meddelelser* issued by Central Bureau of Statistics of Norway, supplemented by the newspapers *Morgenbladet* and *Den Norske Rigstidende*, *The Economist*, NOS *De Offentlige Jernbaner* and *Konsulatberetninger* (published by the Norwegian Foreign Office).

A Chronology of Cycles in Real Economic Activity

shares, the coverage declined slightly towards the end of the century and somewhat more distinctly thereafter. Still, the monthly data are presumably a good indicator of foreign trade activity throughout the period.

The monthly trade data were adjusted in several ways by using the annual trade statistics to obtain consistency over time. For a number of import articles adjustments were also made for changes in the quantities remaining in the bonded warehouses at the end of the year, so that the series reflect the quantities consumed rather than imported. Each item was seasonally adjusted and then aggregated to three sub-indices of exports (fish, wood and other products) and of imports (cereals, foodstuffs and other products). The weights used in deriving these indices were average value shares of each article in two years, one at the beginning and one at the end of each of four sub-periods of 10-15 years for which indices were constructed.

Tonnage of Norwegian vessels engaged in foreign trade: Gross freight earnings from ocean shipping accounted for 43.8 per cent of the total value of exports of goods and services in 1870-1874. Although this percentage fell to 30.5 in 1909-1913, it is evident that it would be of great importance to have an indicator of the short-run fluctuations in the volume of shipping. It seems impossible to get a wholly satisfactory measure of this. However, the monthly British Board of Trade returns on the tonnage of Norwegian vessels entered inwards and cleared outwards with cargoes at UK ports presumably contain some information on the fluctuations in Norwegian shipping activity. The percentage of freight earnings originating from voyages to and from UK ports was considerable (27.9 per cent in 1872, 26.5 per cent in 1892 and 21.0 per cent in 1910).[15] In the period 1868 to 1896 the correlation coefficient between a measure of aggregate deflated earnings from ocean shipping and the tonnage of Norwegian vessels engaged in trading between UK and foreign ports is 0.95; eliminating the common trend by taking first differences of the logarithm of the series gives a correlation coefficient between annual growth rates of 0.64. The degree of correlation is lower in the years 1899-1913, being 0.83 in level form and 0.25 between growth rates. This reflects the diminished relative importance of the UK trade.[16]

Railway freight receipts: Data on railway freight traffic have been widely used as an indicator of economic activity, especially in earlier periods for which no production

---

[15] Calculated from *NOS Norges Skibsfart.*

[16] To compute the contribution of ocean shipping to real GDP the Central Bureau of Statistics used *The Economist's* index of shipping freights as a deflator (*NOS National Accounts 1900-1929*, Oslo, 1953, p.41). This index is not available prior to 1898 and no information is given as to which procedure was followed in earlier years. Here, use was made of the Norwegian freight rate index presented in Fischer, L.R./Nordvik, H.W., Maritime transport and the integration of the North Atlantic economy, 1850-1914, in *The emergence of a world economy 1500-1914. Papers of the IX. international congress of economic history*, edited by Fischer, W./McInnis, R.M./Schneider, J., Franz Steiner, Wiesbaden, 1986.

indices exist.[17] Such a series can be constructed on a monthly basis back to 1867 for Norway as well.

Two objections as to the usefulness of railway freight receipts as an indicator of real economic activity immediately come to mind. Since it is not a physical volume series, such as freight ton-miles, changes in freight rates may distort the picture. Secondly, train mileage increased dramatically over this period, from a mere 270 kilometres in 1868 to 3085 in 1913. Concerning the first issue, it turns out that railway freight rates were changed rather infrequently in the latter half of the period, being kept virtually constant between 1892 and the First World War. Moreover, in earlier years it is possible to adjust the series by deflating it by annual data on freight receipts per ton-mile. The increase in the length of lines needs only to concern us if it proceeded at an uneven pace, since we will only be using data in the form of deviations from a linear time trend. Various attempts were made to adjust the data for short-run changes in line length, but there did not seem to be any strong effects on freight receipts from variations in line length once the secular trend was taken into account.

Railway investment expenditure: The 1870s were characterized by a high rate of public investment in railway construction. It is possible to construct a series which reflects quite well short-run fluctuations in nominal investment expenditure from the early 1870s and into the first half of the 1880s. Then the publication of such data was discontinued, presumably because the level of activity was greatly reduced. To convert this series into real terms it was deflated by a series of wages paid to public road and railway workers.[18]

The rate of unemployment among union members: This series is an obvious candidate in this context, but the problem is that it is only available from July 1903. In addition, union membership was relatively low and the statistics do not cover all unions.

The GDP indicator

Together with the other seasonally adjusted monthly series the six indices of merchandise trade formed the input to the simple regression method which was used to produce monthly estimates of the main components of GDP. From the expenditure side gross domestic product is defined in terms of private consumption (C), private investment (I), government expenditure (G), exports (X) and imports (M): GDP = C+I+G+X-M. For each sub-period and for each component regressions were run on annual data to establish a relationship between GDP (in constant prices) and selected cyclical series. The explanatory variables included in a

---

[17] See Hultgren, T., *Railway freight traffic in prosperity and depression* (Occasional Paper No. 5), National Bureau of Economic Research, 1942 and Burns, A.F./Mitchell, W.C., *op. cit.*, for evidence from the United States and Goodhart, C.A.E., *The business of banking, 1891-1914*, Weidenfeld and Nicholson, London 1972 for the UK.

[18] The average of piece wages and daily wages paid to railway construction workers were computed as from December 1874 from *Stortingsproposisjon no. 1*, 1882. This series was extended backwards by using similar data relating to public road workers (raised by 8 per cent) which are available from the Wedervang Archive at the Norwegian School of Economics and Business Administration.

A Chronology of Cycles in Real Economic Activity

particular equation had to meet a criterion of a priori plausibility; for example, imports of cereals and foodstuffs were considered as candidates in the equation for consumption but not in the investment equation. A further criterion was that the variable helped track the annual movements of the dependent variable in the posited direction. A linear time trend and a constant were always included as explanatory variables as well. Assuming the same relationship to hold on a monthly basis, it is then possible to construct monthly estimates of the GDP components by using the coefficient estimates from the annual regression.[19] By construction, this version of the interpolation procedure ensures that the monthly series exhibits the same long-run trend as the annual series, but it does not make the sum of monthly data equal to the annual (national accounts) data in each year.

In the annual regression equations it turned out, quite plausibly, that private consumption was most firmly related to imports of cereals and foodstuffs, while other imports (which includes articles such as machinery, coal, cotton, hemp, petroleum and woollen goods) played the most important role in the investment equations. Railway freight traffic was of significance in almost every equation. Presumably, it is so important because it picks up fluctuations in the home trades and construction activity not reflected in the import variables.

We end this section by some reflections on the reliability of the data series presented here, notably the monthly indicator of real gross domestic product. There is little doubt that the individual time series that were used as inputs to this analysis - the various sub-indices of the volume of foreign trade, shipping activity, railway freight receipts and, in the last decade, unempolyment figures - seem rather fragile when considered individually. It is an unfortunate fact that we lack indicators of production or retail sales, which play a major role in contemporary business cycle analysis. The regression procedure used to construct the monthly indicators of the GDP components essentially allows data correlation (on an annual basis) to determine the weights of each of the candidate series, so that if a cyclical indicator does not contribute to explaining the annual movements in, say, investment expenditure, its effective weight in the monthly indicator series will be zero. Together with priori reasoning about the relevance of the cyclical variables in each case this procedure may help to weed out the less useful input series.

It stands to reason that such an indicator has an inherent bias towards the market-related sector of the economy. Short-run fluctuations in the consumption of locally produced goods, for example due to crop failures, are scarcely reflected in the data. This makes the indicator less accurate as an estimate of GDP, but the problem is not acute in business cycle studies since such short-run supply disturbances are often neglected anyway.

When compared with the official annual estimates of real GDP in the national accounts (Y) it seems to be the case that the indicator has a somewhat wider cyclical

---

[19] This method is due to Chow, G.C./Lin, A., Best linear unbiased interpolation, distribution, and extrapolation of time series by related series, *Review of Economics and Statistics*, vol. 53, 1971 and is widely used. See, for example, the quaterly data base for the US economy 1875-1983 constructed by Gordon, R.J./Veitch, J.M., Fixed investment in the American business cycle, 1919-83, in *The American business cycle*, edited by Gordon, R.J., University of Chicago Press, Chicago, 1986 and Balke, N.S./Gordon, R.J., Historical data, in *ibid*.

amplitude. At the cyclical trough years it is on the average 0.8 per cent below Y; at peak years it is 0.9 per cent higher than the national accounts figures. The standard deviation of annual changes is about 20 per cent higher than that of Y. The official GDP estimates may be unduly smoothed because some items have been interpolated between benchmark years, but it nevertheless seems to be the case that our indicator exaggerates the cyclical movements. It is also evident that the monthly estimates of GDP are rather choppy, basically due to the fact that the foreign trade figures are rather erratic. Some form of smoothing, for example the 13-month centred moving average employed here, presumably gives a better estimate of the underlying state of economic activity.

Dating turning points in the Norwegian economy, 1867 to 1914

In this section the estimated values of the monthly GDP indicator are presented with a view to dating cyclical turning points. By focusing on a single variable in the identification of turning points of economic activity we depart from the traditional business cycle analysis which focuses on a variety of time series, both real and nominal, representing diverse economic activities. The explicit or implicit weighting system used in the latter approach is inevitably somewhat arbitrary. Gross domestic product seems to represent a more well-defined and widely accepted concept of aggregate economic activity.[20]

It is important to note that the GDP indicator is derived from primary data on physical quantities. The business fluctuations studied in this paper are therefore fluctuations in the volume of aggregate economic activity; no systematic information is provided on prices and profitability. While the latter subjects have traditionally occupied an important role in business cycle analysis, cycles based on data in physical units (often referred to as "deflated" cycles)[21] do have a more clear-cut interpretation during periods of secular changes in the general price level.[22] Nevertheless, compilation and analysis of monthly price series, particularly shipping freight rates, is certainly of vital importance to a further progress in business cycle research in Norway, but is beyond the scope of this paper.

Figures 1, 3 and 5 show the seasonally adjusted real GDP indicator smoothed by a centred 13-month moving average.[23] In order to highlight the cyclical movements of the variable Figures 2, 4 and 6 present 13-month moving averages of GDP after

---

[20] See Cloos, G.W., How good are the National Bureau's reference dates?, *Journal of Business*, vol. 36, 1963 and Zarnowitz, V., On the dating of business cycles, *Journal of Business*, vol. 36, 1963 for further debate on this issue.

[21] See Mintz, I., Dating United States growth cycles, *Explorations in Economic Research*, vol. 1, 1974.

[22] As is well known (see e.g. Schwartz, A.J., Secular price change in historical perspective, *Journal of Money, Credit and Banking*, vol. 5, 1973), the period from the early 1870s to about 1896 was characterized by declining prices in gold standard countries, while the trend moved in the opposite direction from 1896 until the First World War had ended. The consumer price index for Norway compiled by Ramstad, see Minde, K.B./Ramstad, J., The development of real wages in Norway about 1730-1910, *Scandinavian Economic History Review*, vol 34, 1986.

[23] Note that since a logarithmic scale is being used a variable with a constant growth rate will be represented by a straight line.

A Chronology of Cycles in Real Economic Activity

Figure 1 The GDP indicator (in logs)
(13-month moving average 1867-882)

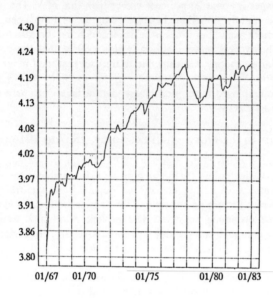

Figure 2 Growth cycles. GDP indicator 1867-1882

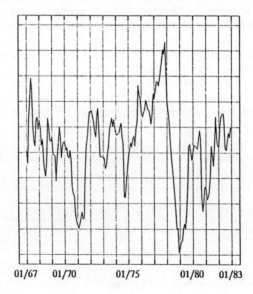

purging it of its underlying trend value. Several alternative methods exist for estimating the trend value of the series[24], and it should be recognized that the estimates of the cyclical component may be somewhat sensitive to the actual choice made. Here, a 75-month moving average was used, which allows for a slowly changing trend growth over time.[25]

The dating of the turning points is done by visual inspection of the smoothed values of the cyclical GDP series. The cycles we try to identify thus correspond to the concept of *growth cycles* (deviations from growth trends) rather than *classical cycles*, which refer to absolute declines in aggregate economic activity.

The cycles which we are primarily interested in here are cycles of relatively short duration. In the traditional business cycle literature these are referred to as either Kitchin cycles (about three years from peak to peak) or Juglar cycles (nine years).[26] We will not try to impose a rigid pattern of Kitchins and Juglars on our time series, but we nevertheless face the problem of defining criteria for identifying cycles. Particularly in view of the less than perfect coverage and quality of our data it is clear that one cannot attach a cyclical downturn to every dip in the series. Technical rules, like those applied by Mintz[27], are of some help; for example, it will be required that the minimum duration of a cycle phase is five months, that like turning points cannot be less than twelve months apart and that there can be no peak or trough when there are like turns without an intervening turn in the opposite direction. Such rules are, however, still rather arbitrary and the identification of turning points must in the end be a matter of judgement.

As noted above, the method of trend estimation and degree of smoothing of the data may also affect the apparent cyclical movements. Hence, it stands to reason that the chronology of growth cycles presented here must be regarded as tentative only. For convenience we locate cyclical turning points at a specific month, in line with the NBER tradition, but there is no presumption that the cycle phases can be determined unambiguously with such precision.

---

[24] Crafts, N.F.R./Leybourne, S.J./Mills, T.C., The climacteric in late Victorian Britain and France: A reappraisal of the evidence, *Journal of Applied Econometrics*, vol 4, 1989, give a discussion of some of the relevant technical aspects of trend estimation and provide an application to a long-standing issue in British economic history.

[25] In Klovland, *op. cit.* two other methods were used, a deterministic linear time trend fitted to four sub-periods and a stochastic trend method due to Beveridge, S./Nelson, C.R., A new approach to decomposition of economic time series into permanent and transitory components with particular attention to measurement of the "business cycle", *Journal of Monetary Economics*, vol 7, 1981. In most cycles these turning points were within 4 months of those found here.

[26] The longer cycles are identified with the names of Kuznets (20 years) and Kondratieff (50 years), although recent empirical research tends to view the latter as more or less a statistical artifact (Solomou, S., *Phases of economic growth, 1850-1973. Kondratieff waves and Kuznets swings*, Cambridge University Press, Cambridge 1987). In Schumpeter, *op.cit.* and Lewis, W.A., *Growth and fluctuations 1870-1913*, George Allen and Unwin, London 1978, the historical origins of the different cycle concepts are traced and related to fluctuations in international economic activity over the period considered here.

[27] Mintz, I., *op. cit.*

A Chronology of Cycles in Real Economic Activity

The late 1860s and the 1870s
There is some evidence that cyclical fluctuations in *industrial* activity were rather mild in North Europe in the latter half of the 1860s. Spree argues that this was the case in Germany.[28] Jörberg notes that changes in industrial production in Sweden were small in the late 1860s, with a possible trough in 1869.[29] The agricultural sector was still by far the most important one and crop failures played a dominant role in creating fluctuations in real income.

These findings also seem to be consistent with the data for Norway. This is, however, not readily apparent from the curves of the GDP indicator in Figures 1 och 2, which are somewhat affected by problems of seasonal adjustment in 1868 and 1869 (due to changes in the coverage of the monthly trade statistics) and some uncertainty as to estimating the trend growth in the early part of the sample. Disregarding spurious seasonal movements it seems to be the case that there were rather small deviations from trend growth between 1867 and 1870. Although E. Einarsen[30] was able to identify 1869 as a "minimum year", this conclusion cannot be verified on the basis of our data. Some slackening of the pace of business activity may have occurred in 1868 or 1869, but any recession is likely to have been mild.

The first clearly visible turning point in our data is a trough in February 1871. The recession in Norway centred around the winter months of 1871 is evident from data on merchandise exports and imports as well as railway freight traffic. The volume of wood and timber exports declined moderately as from August 1870, but rebounded sharply in March 1871 when the unusually severe winter weather lost its grip (the mean temperature of the three-month period from December 1870 to February 1871 seems to have been one of the lowest ever recorded).[31] The fall in the quantity of exports of fish products (both codfish and herring) was more spectacular, being affected by loss of markets as well as by bad catches.[32]

The clearly manifested recession in 1871 is at first rather puzzling. It is scarcely noted in the annual reviews in the domestic newspapers reproduced in Einarsen or by later contributors to business cycle history in Norway.[33] The fact that domestic supply disturbances seem to have been an important factor in this recession may go some way towards explaining this neglect. However, a closer look at contemporary international sources on business matters makes it likely that a slump in demand from abroad may have played an important role too. *The Economist's Commercial History and Review* of 1871 referred to "the contraction of business, caused by the

---

[28] Spree, R., *Die Wachstumszyklen der deutschen Wirtschaft von 1840 bis 1880*, Duncker & Humblot, Berlin 1977.

[29] Jörberg, L., *op.cit.*

[30] Einarsen, E., *Gode og daarlige tider*, Gyldendal, Copenhagen and Kristiania, 1904, p.51.

[31] *Statistiske Oversikter*, Central Bureau of Statistics, 1948, Tables 1, 2 and 3.

[32] Solhaug, T., *op. cit.*, p.637 and p.648.

[33] Einarsen, E., *op. cit.*

war in the final half of 1870".[34] Accoring to Kindleberger[35] and Schumpeter[36] both France and Germany experienced a setback due to the Franco-German War. Furthermore, according to the NBER chronology the United States experienced a cyclical trough in December 1870.[37]

After this brief recessionary interlude the economy entered into an unusually prolonged period of sustained growth. According to Figure 2 the expansion lasted until November 1877. There were a few short periods of more sluggish growth, notably at the end of 1872 and during 1874, but these episodes do not qualify as independent cycles in overall economic activity.

It is evident that the great international boom of 1871-1873 gave a strong impetus to increased economic activity in Norway. The tonnage of Norwegian ships cleared and entered with cargoes at UK ports showed a spectacular increase already in the spring of 1870, remaining at a very high level until the summer of 1874. The volume of merchandise exports grew strongly from the spring of 1871. The first phase of the boom period is thus clearly dominated by external demand forces. Later on the indicators of domestic demand responded as well. The growth of the volume of merchandise imports and railway freight traffic gained steadily in momentum; indeed, showing little weakness until the second half of 1877.

Accordingly, we find little evidence of any recession in 1874/75, which seems to run counter to the established view.[38] There are at least two main factors which may account for this. First, previous authors on this subject have mainly been occupied with export activity, whereas our focus is on a broader range of sectors. There is indeed a short period (about 9 months) of significantly weaker merchandise exports and shipping activity beginning in the summer of 1874. These contractionary forces are counterbalanced by the sustained buoyancy of domestic demand, however. Secondly, it is important to bear in mind that we are concerned with cycles in *real* economic activity rather than nominal fluctuations. If we had set the turning points with reference to nominal indicators, it is highly likely that a cyclical trough would have emerged in 1874 or 1875.

There are several reasons why real economic activity was so resilient after this episode. Merchandise exports recovered after a cyclical low in January 1875. Export activity held up well until early in 1878, partly due to building booms in Britain and

---

[34] Supplement to *The Economist*, March 16, 1872, p.68. It also turns out that a general indicator of nominal business transactions such as the amount of daily clearing (excluding stock exchange settling days) at the Bankers' Clearing House in London showed a marked deceleration in the second half of 1870 (see *ibid* p.68 and the *Review* of 1870, p.53).

[35] Kindleberger, C.P., *Economic growth in France and Britain 1851-1950*, Harvard University Press, Cambridge (Mass.), 1964, p.12.

[36] Schumpeter, J.A., *op. cit.*, p.362.

[37] See Moore, G.H./Zarnowitz, V., *op.cit.* for a convenient summary of the NBER turning points for USA, UK, France and Britain.

[38] See Einarsen, E., *op.cit.*, pp.88-95 and Rygg, N., *op. cit.*, pp.143-145. Aschehoug, T.H., *op. cit.*, p.46, maintained that there was no real "crisis" in Norway, although he conceded that by 1875 the expansion was over.

A Chronology of Cycles in Real Economic Activity

Germany.[39] The volume of exports also benefited from excellent catches of codfish and herring along with an expansion of markets for Norwegian salted and dried cod.[40] The volume of ocean shipping and freight earnings reached a new high in 1876, which also gave an impetus to domestic shipbuilding.[41]

Another important factor was the strong expansion in railway investment beginning in the autumn of 1873. The level of this activity peaked in October 1877, almost coincidentally with real GDP. Its repercussions on domestic expenditure on other investment goods and on consumption were important factors in promoting an expansionary climate in this period. The railway investment programme was largely financed by foreign government loans and consequently stimulated absorption (domestic expenditure on consumption and investment) even more than production. Given the background of weakening international economic activity in the second half of the 1870s the public railroad construction programme, inadvertently it must be presumed, came to serve as a forceful example of countercyclical economic policy.[42]

The Norwegian economy went down resoundingly in 1878, along with the major industrial countries.[43] In our data the trough of the growth cycle is in December 1878, but on an annual basis 1879, rather than 1878, is the trough year.[44] This downturn was severe. From the peak in November 1877 our indicator of GDP (using 13-month averages as in Figure 1) fell 7.4 per cent in twelve months and there was hardly any growth until the summer of 1879. The episode of mild recovery and renewed deceleration that followed in 1880 is too short to qualify as a separate cycle.[45] 1881 must be characterized as a year of continued depression, although there was some improvement towards the end of the year.

The 1880s

It is well known that the cyclical pattern of the 1880s was quite different from the extravagances of the 1870s; export growth was sluggish, domestic railway investment

---

[39] Lewis, W.A., *op. cit.*, p.37. Einarsen, E., *op.cit.*, p.111, also pointed to the fact that several European economies seemed to have experienced a partial rebound of economic activity in 1876 and 1877. The peak year for Swedish manufacturing industry was 1876, cf. Jörberg, L., *op.cit.*, pp.222-248.

[40] Solhaug, T., *op.cit.*, pp.594-615 *et passim*.

[41] See Gjølberg, O., *Økonomi, teknologi og historie. Analyser av skipsfart og økonomi 1866-1913*. Unpublished PhD thesis, Norwegian School of Economics and Business Administration, 1979. Fischer, L.R./Nordvik, H.W., *op.cit.*, have recently argued that a commonly used freight rate index like the one compiled by Isserlis, L., Tramp shipping cargoes and freights, *Journal of the Royal Statistical Society*, vol 101, pp.53-134, 1938, overstates the fall in freight earnings in the mid 1870s.

[42] This episode has an interesting parallel in the deliberate countercyclical policy that was pursued almost exactly 100 years later, cf. Skånland, H., Når den brede vei blir smalere. Aktuelle problemstillinger i norsk økonomi, *Statsøkonomisk Tidsskrift*, vol 92, 1978, pp.1-15.

[43] Lewis, W.A., *op.cit.*, pp.34-38.

[44] The NBER turning points for Germany, USA, UK and France are all in 1879. In Sweden 1879 was also a very marked trough year, cf. Jörberg, L., *op.cit.*, p.241.

[45] It has a parallel in Britain, where the short-lived surge in economic activity in the first half of 1880 was attributed to increased demand from America. *The Economist*, July 3, 1880, p.765.

Figure 3 The GDP indicator (in logs)
 (13-month moving average 1881-1896)

Figure 4 Growth cycles. GDP indicator 1881-1896

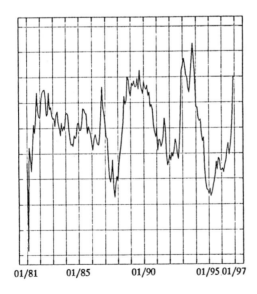

A Chronology of Cycles in Real Economic Activity

activity tapered off and the profitability of many industries was low due to the severe international price decline. Owing to the generally subdued state of trade it is difficult to trace any spectacular boom periods. At the first peak in the GDP growth cycle, occurring in May 1882, real gross domestic product had hardly regained the level of the previous peak in June 1877. This is somewhat surprising in view of the highly synchronized Juglar peak among the major countries of the world in 1882-1883.[46]

The economy decelerated slowly towards the deepest trough in October 1887, interrupted by three minor cycles, which are difficult to fit into our chronology because they are so short and the amplitudes are rather weak. The peak in 1882 and the trough in 1887 also coincide with the established view in Aschehoug[47], Einarsen[48] and Rygg[49]. After the trough in October 1887 growth picked up rapidly and remained above the average of the period (about 1.7 per cent per year) well into 1890. The peak of this growth cycle is rather uncertain. It is located at September 1889, but as Figure 3 in particular shows, economic activity was high in 1890 as well.

The export cycles present a rather different picture. The volume of fish exports moved countercyclically as from 1883, increasing strongly throughout the depression period. Prices, however, responded to the state of demand, and as pointed out by Einarsen[50], export *values* conform much better to the cyclical pattern than volume figures do in this period. Export volumes of wood, timber and wood pulp staged only a partial recovery from the depressed level in the late 1870s - the building boom to be expected in Britain in the 1880s never materialized.[51] The short flurries of increased shipping activity only managed to create one short period of prosperity, the one in 1889.

The 1890s

As we approach the 1890s the ubiquitous gloom recedes, and, although still subdued, the economy enters on a path of slightly higher growth. After a shallow recession in November 1891, growth picked up again, particularly during the autumn of 1892 and throughout 1893. The peak in October 1893 is too evident to ignore, but the expansion of economic activity does not seem to have been broadly based. It is most visible in some export industries, primarily several fish products as well as pulp and paper; the expansion of the latter industries reflecting heavy prior investment. The subdued activity in home industries is evident from the indicator of railway freight traffic. These factors may go some way towards explaining why 1892-1893 has not been

---

[46] Lewis, W.A., *op.cit.* p.41.

[47] Aschehoug, T.H., *op. cit.*

[48] Einarsen, E., *op.cit.*

[49] Rygg, N., *op. cit.*

[50] Einarsen, E., *op. cit.*

[51] See Lewis, W.A., *op.cit.*, p.53 and Thomas, B., *Migration and economic growth*, Cambridge University Press, London 1973.

Figure 5 The GDP indicator (in logs)
(13 month moving average 1895-1914)

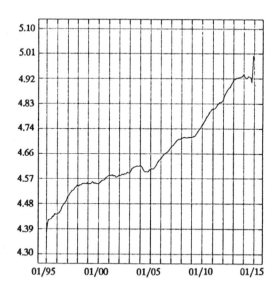

Figure 6 Growth cycles. GDP indicator 1895-1914

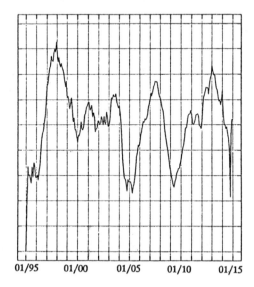

A Chronology of Cycles in Real Economic Activity

generally considered as an expansionary period.[52] Except in the United States these years are not particularly buoyant; indeed Sweden experienced a trough in 1893 according to Jörberg[53], although there is a short export cycle similar to the one in Norway in this year.

After a fragile export boom had ended in 1893 real economic activity fell throughout 1894, both relative to trend and in absolute terms. The trough was in March 1895, being well synchronized with the European Juglar depression in the winter months of 1895. From then on a long period of expansion set in, creating a spirit of enterprise not experienced since the 1870s.

Few other episodes of business cycle history in Norway have been more thoroughly dealt with than the spectacular building boom, particularly in Kristiania, in the second half of the 1890s. Its fascinating details cannot detain us here;[54] we only note from Figures 5 and 6 that it occurred during a period of unusually strong growth in real economic activity. During the next three years following the trough in March 1895 real GDP grew at a rate of 4.6 per cent per year. The growth cycle peak can be dated to December 1897, when the most spectacular growth ended. Then the economy held steady for a period of two years, rather than actually falling. The collapse of the financial boom, which is identified with the failure of a large merchant house in June 1899[55], might have contributed to the slowdown of real economic activity. But the crisis was mainly of a local character and on the international scene there was little indication of any significant slackening of the speed of the engine of growth until well into 1900.[56]

There was in fact a short period of renewed expansion in 1900, undoubtedly connected with the temporary surge in foreign trade. Merchandise exports (excluding fish products) showed considerable strength between the summer of 1899 and early 1901. So does our indicator of shipping activity, which had remained high ever since 1897. However, this wave is probably too weak to be classified as a separate cycle in total economic activity.

1900 to the First World War

The trough of the downswing that started at the beginning of 1898 is difficult to pin down exactly. January 1900 is the most likely candidate, but as Figure 5 shows, it is more correct to speak of a pause in growth than a full-scale depression. The ensuing expansion consisted of two minor waves; the first one is the Boer war cycle discussed above, the second peaking in August 1903 in line with the trading partners. This episode was at most a Kitchin flurry, but we recognize it as a cycle since it is well

---

[52] Cf. Rygg, N., *op. cit.*, although he notes, p.227, the favourable export performance in 1893.

[53] Jörberg, L., *op. cit.*

[54] Se Rygg, N., *op. cit.*, and some of the numerous bank anniversary volumes, in particular Keilhau, W., *Kristiania Hypothek- og Realkreditbank 1866-1936*. Oslo 1936. A detailed blow-by-blow account of the financial aspect of the boom and its aftermath can be found in the financial weekly *Farmand*.

[55] The total number of failures also increased significantly in the second half of 1899, see Gjermoe, E., *op. cit.*

[56] Schumpeter, J.A., *op.cit.*, p.426 and p.447.

manifested in the data and corresponds very well to the experience of the major European countries.[57]

After the turn of the century it was obvious that exports had become less heavily dependent on the old staples of timber and fish.[58] These natural resources now increasingly formed the basis of manufactured products like pulp and paper and tinned food. In addition the exploitation of waterfalls promoted a rapid expansion of the chemical industry. The broadening of the industrial base in Norway is likely to have made her even more exposed to fluctuations in aggregate economic activity abroad.

The last ten years before the First World War was a period of relatively strong growth in real gross domestic product (3.2 per cent per year). Episodes of absolute decline in GDP (classical cycles) were few and mild, but the growth cycles stand out clearly in Figure 6. We date the troughs at April 1905, May 1909 and October 1914; peaks are clearly visible in July 1907 and January 1913. The temporary setback in 1911 is obviously related to labour disputes and is disregarded in this connection. This chronology is consistent with the detailed industry-by-industry account given in Rygg.[59] The timing of the cycles is also what one would expect from the highly synchronized pattern among the leading European powers.[60] The latter conclusion is not entirely dependent on our reliance on foreign trade figures - the same pattern emerges from the course of the "domestic" indicators such as railway freight traffic and the unemployment rate.

When the war came in 1914 the downswing was already well established, having started in January 1913. The onset of the war naturally implied severe distortions to international trade, which is clearly reflected in the figures. It also appears that economic activity recovered quickly afterwards. Whether this cyclical pattern would have been the same, though more subdued, without the war is, of course, a hypothetical issue. From the experience of previous cycles it does not seem to be wholly unlikely.

Some properties of the suggested chronology of growth cycles

The results of the preceding analysis are summarized in Table 1, which contains the turning dates, duration and growth rates of the cycle phases. Four of the low-rate phases identified here are characterized by a retardation of growth rather than by an absolute decline in real economic activity. Yet there is little doubt that these periods must be classified as years of economic stagnation in relation to the underlying growth potential of the economy. The long period of low-phase growth in the mid-

---

[57] According to the NBER chronology France (May), Great Britain (June) and Germany (August) all peaked in 1903 after a brief upswing.

[58] In the first Juglar expansion, 1871-1877, the proportion of fish (including cod-liver oil and roe) and timber and wood in total merchandise exports was 81.9 per cent. In the last expansion period from 1909 to 1913 it averaged 32.1 per cent, sharply falling throughout the cycle.

[59] Rygg, N., op, cit., p.285-352.

[60] Moore, G.H./Zarnowitz, V., op. cit. See also Table 2.

A Chronology of Cycles in Real Economic Activity

eighties, stretching over more than five years, stands out in particular. The average duration of the eight cycle phases identified here is 65 months, with 26 months allocated to the low-rate phases and 39 months to the high-rate phases.[61]

Table 1   A chronology of growth cycles in real gross domestic product for Norway, 1867-1914

	Dates of peaks and troughs		Duration in months		Average annual rate of growth	
Cycle no.	Trough (T)	Peak (P)	Low-rate phase (P to T)	High-rate phase (T to P)	Low-rate phase (P to T)	High-rate phase (T to P)
1	1871 Feb	1877 Nov	-	81	--	3.3
2	1878 Dec	1882 May	13	41	-7.8	2.4
3	1887 Oct	1889 Sep	65	23	0.5	5.4
4	1891 Nov	1893 Oct	26	23	0.1	4.9
5	1895 Mar	1897 Dec	17	33	-3.0	7.9
6	1900 Jan	1903 Aug	25	43	0.2	2.4
7	1905 Apr	1907 Jul	20	27	-0.5	4.5
8	1909 May	1913 Jan	22	44	1.0	5.4
9	1914 Oct		21	-	-0.5	-

Notes: The growth rates are continuously compounded annual rates of growth in the real GDP indicator, being calculated from 13-month averages of real GDP centred at the turning points.

Table 2 presents a comparison of turning points of growth cycles in Norway with the NBER business cycle chronologies for Britain, Germany and France. When reviewing these figures it should be recalled that the NBER chronology relates to classical cycles rather than growth cycles, and that turning points are set on the basis of a variety of real and nominal time series, including financial market variables.

With a few important exceptions, to be discussed below, the timing of turning points between Norway and her trading partners is quite close. Using the average figures for the three foreign countries, the difference in timing is less than 6 months in 9 out of the 13 cases. Considering the differences in cycle concepts, data quality as well as the leeway introduced by our eyeball dating procedure, we conclude that the majority of cycles in real economic activity in Norway was well synchronized with the pattern of business cycles in the major European countries.

From these data two time-periods stand out as being characterized by differences in turning points. These are the two turning points in the late eighties and the cycle around the turn of the century. Both episodes seem to be connected with well-known

---

[61] Mintz, I., *op. cit.*, found that for the post-WWII US economy up to 1969 the average growth cycle lasted 36 months. The duration of the high-rate phases was about 1.5 times that of the low-rate phases, which is quite similar to our results.

special factors in Norway. The difference between classical cycles and growth cycles is also of importance here.

Table 2 Lead (+) or lag (-) in monthly turning points in Norway against Britain, Germany and France

Cycle no.	Trough in: Norway	UK	Germany	France	Average
2	1878 Dec	+6	+2	+9	+5.7
3	1887 Oct	-16	-14	-2	-10.7
5	1895 Mar	-1	-1	-2	-1.3
6	1900 Jan	+20	+26	+32	+26.0
7	1905 Apr	-5	-2	-6	-4.3
8	1909 May	-6	-5	-3	-4.7
9	1914 Oct	-1	-2	-2	-1.7
Average		-0.4	+0.6	+3.7	+1.3

Cycle no.	Peak in: Norway	UK	Germany	France	Average
2	1882 May	+7	-4	-5	-0.7
3	1889 Sep	+12	+4	+16	+10.7
5	1897 Dec	+30	+27	+27	+28.0
6	1903 Aug	-2	0	-3	-1.7
7	1907 Jul	-1	0	0	-0.3
8	1913 Jan	-1	+3	+5	+2.1
Average		+7.5	+5.0	+6.7	+6.4

Notes: The turning points for Britain, Germany and France correspond to the NBER chronology of classical cycles reproduced in Moore/Zarnowitz, *op. cit.* There are no cycles recorded for these countries corresponding to cycle no. 1 and cycle no. 4 in Norway in Table 1.

The protracted low-growth period that ended in October 1887, more than one year later than in Britain and Germany, is not associated with any obvious external causal factor.[62] The severity of this depression emanated from its duration and the protracted decline in prices rather than from any period of abrupt fall in economic activity. In 1886 both commercial and savings banks recorded heavy losses; net

---

[62] In Sweden, too, 1887 seems to represent a cyclical low, but Jörberg, L., *op. cit.*, notes that "the trough of 1887 was very slight in comparison with that of the previous cycle".

A Chronology of Cycles in Real Economic Activity

aggregate profits of commercial banks were even negative.[63] The failure of Arendals Privatbank in September 1886 triggered off a wave of failures among banks on the southern coast of Norway.[64] Our tentative hypothesis is that the domestic financial difficulties and the ensuing drawn-out liquidation processes added to the depressed state of trade. A more definitive treatment of this episode, however, is not possible without access to price data.

The upper turning point for Norway in 1889 precedes the NBER dates, albeit only by 4 months in the case of Germany. Because of the strong underlying trend of growth in this period the peak of the growth cycle is well ahead of the classical cycle, which in this case certainly would have taken place in 1890, cf. Figure 3.

According to Keilhau[65] the downswing in the late 1890s was felt earlier in Kristiania than at any other place in the world. Keilhau attributed this to the collapse of speculative activity in 1899.[66] Although the crisis was primarily of a local character, its repercussions were felt throughout the country by a tightening of credit markets. Finally, nominal business cycle indicators may have behaved quite differently from data on real economic activity in this case, since the last Juglar boom of the century engendered a significant price increase.[67]

Finally, we note from Figure 6 that there is a second trough in September 1901 in the rather irregular cycle between 1897 and 1903. If we had chosen this date for Norway it would have coincided exactly with the cyclical low in Britain.

Some concluding remarks

The main purpose of this paper has been to present a chronology of cycles in real economic activity in Norway. The cyclical pattern identified for the Norwegian economy in this time period turned out to be quite similar to the experience of the major European countries. A few cycles seem to fit less well into the European chronolgy, but the available historical narratives of these episodes give some plausibility to the hypothesis that these cases were indeed associated with particular circumstances in Norway.

If supported by more rigorous testing than has been carried out here, would the hypothesis of a domestic economy being highly synchronized with cyclical movements in the large European countries conform to the existing theoretical and empirical knowledge? Most macroeconomic models would be consistent with the

---

[63] The issue is well treated in Hoffstad, E., *Det norske privatbankvæsens historie*, Forretningsliv, Oslo 1928.

[64] Between 1885 and 1889 two commercial banks and five savings banks suspended payments.

[65] Keilhau, W., *op. cit.*, pp.48-49.

[66] As noted above, growth in economic activity remained high until the middle of 1899. The peak of a corresponding classical cycle would in this case presumably be fixed at a later date than the growth cycle turning-point in December 1897.

[67] In Britain the price level continued to rise until July 1900, according to the Sauerbeck wholesale price index (*Journal of the Royal Statistical Society*, 1938, p. 380). In the year to March 1900 the annual rate of inflation was running as high as 14.3 per cent.

existence of strong links between countries operating under fixed exchange rates and few impediments to trade and capital flows. The channels of transmission would include the foreign demand for domestic goods as well as price and interest rate links. Such mechanisms would provide a positive correlation between income movements in different countries as long as the disturbances originated from the demand side of the economy. On the other hand, to the extent that income fluctuations were caused by supply schocks (e.g. productivity changes) the correlation would tend to be negative.[68]

The available empirical evidence shows that there were fairly tight interest rate and price level links between Norway and her trading partners during the gold standard period.[69] However, Easton[70] found little contemporaneous correlation between real output (annual national account figures adjusted for trend) in Scandinavian countries on the one hand and several major countries on the other after 1879. This is possibly a reflection of the theoretical ambiguity concerning the net effect of demand and supply factors noted above. On the other hand, the evidence from his causality tests does give some support to the hypothesis that the United Kingdom, and to a lesser extent Germany, was the hub around which the Scandinavian countries revolved. The evidence from Table 2 is not wholly inconsistent with this view, particularly with respect to the timing of the troughs.

No single index of economic activity can ever reflect all the different shades of prosperity and depression characterizing the individual trades and activities of an economy at a particular point in time; quantification does not obviate the need for detailed historical narratives. In the light of the preceding discussion we nevertheless conclude that the monthly GDP indicator, in spite of the underlying severe data limitations, represents a useful summary measure of fluctuations in real economic activity in Norway in this period.

---

[68] See Wood, G.E., Comment, in *A retrospective on the classical gold standard, 1821-1931*, edited by Bordo, M.D./Schwartz, A.J., Chicago University Press, Chicago 1986, pp. 538-544.

[69] See Bloomfield, A., *Monetary policy under the international gold standard: 1880-1914*, Federal Reserve Bank of New York, New York, 1959 on the correlation of discount rate changes among European countries. Edison, H.J./Klovland, J.T., A quantitative reassessment of the purchasing power parity hypothesis: Evidence from Norway and the United Kingdom, *Journal of Applied Econometrics*, vol. 2, 1987, pp.309-333, found that there were significant price level links between Norway and the United Kingdom in the long run.

[70] Easton, S.T., Real output and the gold standard years, 1830-1913, in Bordo, M./Schwartz, A.J., *op.cit.*

[6]
The Industrial development of Denmark 1840-1914

Niels Kærgård
University of Copenhagen

1. Introduction

The date when the industrial breakthrough in Denmark took place has been discussed for a long time. The most specific theories from recent decades are those of Richard Willerslev (1954 and 1952), Svend Aage Hansen (1970) and Ole Hyldtoft (1984). Willerslev argues for an early revolution starting in the 1850s, while Hansen lays stress on the rapid growth in the 1890s. Hyldtoft tries to combine these two different views in a theory of long cycles. Hyldtoft does not see the cycles as substantial change in the aggregate growth rate, but mainly as a change in the composition of the factors of production. He divides the development into phases of capital deepening and of capital widening. In the periods 1840-1965 and 1896-1914 both the growth in the stock of capital and the rate of technological progress are very substantial, while the period 1865-1896 is characterized by a consolidation of already introduced techniques.

Some of the differences in attitude between the authors could be explained by the fact that Willerslev and Hyldtoft are historians, while Hansen is an economist. Hansen bases his theory mainly on figures for the aggregate national product, while Willerslev and Hyldtoft prefer more disaggregated series. They are especially interested in employment and in the amount of mechanical power in the manufacturing industries in Copenhagen (Hyldtoft's book deals with industrial growth in Copenhagen 1840-1914).

Niels Kærgård

In this paper the industrial growth in Denmark is analyzed by means of methods utilised in mathematical statistics — methods which have not been used at all in the debate.

Two sections concentrate on the development in mechanical power. Section 2 tests whether changes in the characteristics really took place between the chosen periods and tries to estimate an optimal division in periods. Section 3 tries to explain the development in mechanical power by a logistic curve modelling the introduction of steam engines. In section 4 a number of other indicators are introduced, and a common trend is estimated by use of the methods of principal components. The paper ends with a short conclusion.

2. The different phases in the development

There are several different series for the development of mechanical power, but none of them is complete for the total period 1840-1914. In fig. 1 the data are summarized. It is clear that a change in the growth rate in 1865 is not a very distinct event and that a similar change in 1896 is indistinct because of lacking data.

A more evident separation into three periods is seen in fig. 2 where mechanical power per employee is shown. The only extant data, however, are based on industrial censuses for eight different years for the period 1831-1914, and two of these (1831 and 1839) are previous to the period discussed in this paper.

A combination of the different series from fig. 1 could be used in connection with the broad definition of Copenhagen and the unbroken series from 1840-1875 and 1902-1909, supplemented by the industrial census data from 1897 and 1914 and adjusted down to the level of the other series by means of data from the years with both kinds of observations.[1]

---

[1] The relation between the two types of data is estimated for the years where both observations are available (ie. 1847, 1855, 1873, 1906). The industrial census data is

The industrial development in Denmark 1840-1914

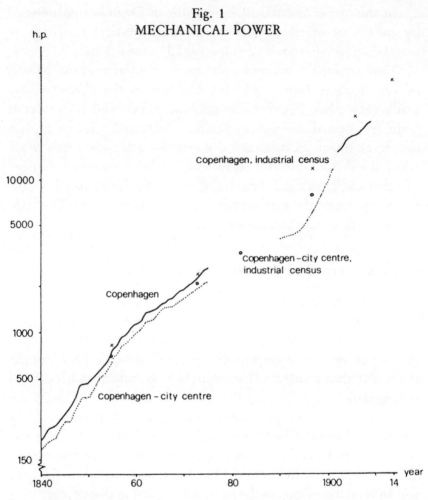

Fig. 1
MECHANICAL POWER

Source: Hyldtoft (1984) p. 54.

A log-linear trend is estimated for these data as shown in fig. 3.A. The estimated relation is:

$$\log HP_i = -117.2 + 0.067\,i$$
$$\quad\quad\quad (1.6)\quad\ (0.001) \tag{1}$$
$$\quad R^2 = 0.99 \quad D.W. = 0.11 \quad N = 45$$

estimated to be 33% higher than the other data. The Industrial census data from 1897 and 1914 is then reduced by 33% and used together with the other data.

Niels Kærgård

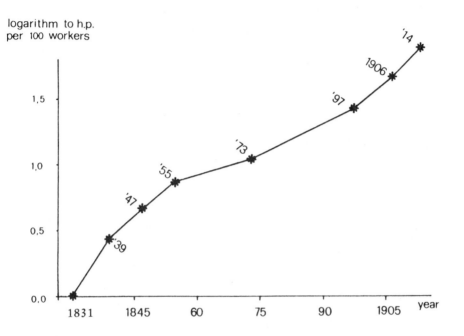

Fig. 2
THE DEVELOPMENT OF MECHANICAL
POWER FOR WORKERS 1830-1914

Source: Hyldtoft (1984) p. 52.

where log HP_i is the mechanical power extant in year i. The figures in brackets are the deviation of the coefficients, R^2 the degrees of explanation, D.W. is Durbin-Watson's test for autocorrelation and N is the number of observations.

It is seen that the log-linear trend is a rather exact description of the series — the degree of determination is about 99%, but D.W. indicates that there is a systematic deviation from the trend.

The problem is whether this systematic pattern of the deviation could be explained in the different phases for the three periods (1840-1865, 1865-1896, 1896-1914), as assumed by Ole

Hyldtoft. In fig. 3.B log-linear trends are estimated for the three periods separately. They are composed by a Chow-test for *switch in the relation*.[2] The test compares the sum of the squared residuals for the three trends, SSR_u, with the same sum when the three trends are restricted to be equal, SSR_R; it is the sum of squared residuals in fig. 3.B and fig. 3.A. The test-quantity is F-distributed. The actual test is:

$$\frac{(SSR_u - SSR_R)/(f-k)}{SSR_R/f} = \frac{(0.606 - 0.080)/4}{0.080/39} = 64.1 \quad (2)$$

where f is the number of degrees of freedom in the restricted estimation and k is the number of restrictions. It is seen that the test is extremely significant, and it could be concluded that Hyldtoft is right in assuming that there are different phases.

The next question is then whether 1865 and 1896 are the right demarcation points between the phases. Data for the years close to 1896 are so scarce that tests are impossible, and only the switch in 1865 should be tested. The unbroken series 1840-1875 are used as data and the model by R.E. Quandt for relations with shifting regimes is the statistical framework.

In this model (see Quandt, 1958 and Goldfeld & Quandt, 1976. An elementary introduction to the topic is found for instance in Johnston, 1984 chap. 10.2 and 10.4) the development is described with two different trends as in fig. 3.B. The model is:

$$\begin{aligned} y_i &= \alpha_o + \alpha_1 i + u_{i1} \quad \text{for } i \leq t \\ y_i &= \beta_o + \beta_1 i + u_{i2} \quad \text{for } i > t \end{aligned} \quad (3)$$

where y_i is the mechanical power in year i, t the year for the switch, α and β are parameters measuring the two different trends and u_{i1} and u_{i2} are normal, independent distributed re-

---

[2] The Chow-test and other similar test are discussed in Brown, Durbin & Evans (1975), Farley, Hinick & McGuire (1975). An introduction to the test is in Johnston (1984 pp. 207-225) and an application for instance in Rasmussen & Kærgård (1980).

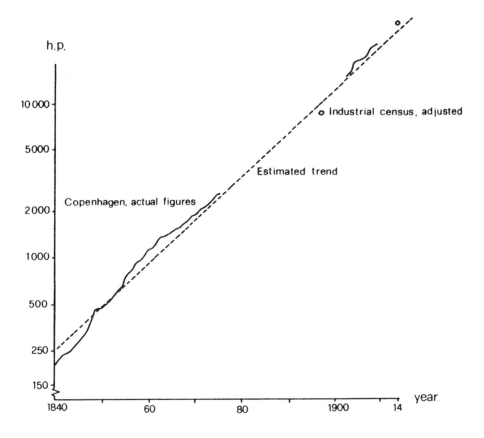

Fig. 3A
MECHANICAL POWER IN THE
INDUSTRY OF COPENHAGEN

siduals with mean O and deviation σ_1, σ_2. There are then 7 parameters to estimate (α_0, α_1, β_0, β_1, σ_1, σ_2 and t).

The method developed by Quandt is a maximum-likelihood-method. The maximum-likelihood function is:

$$\ln L = -\frac{n}{2} \ln 2\pi - \frac{n}{2} - \frac{t}{2} \ln s_1^2 - \frac{n-t}{2} \ln s_2^2 \quad (4)$$

The industrial development in Denmark 1840-1914

Fig. 3B

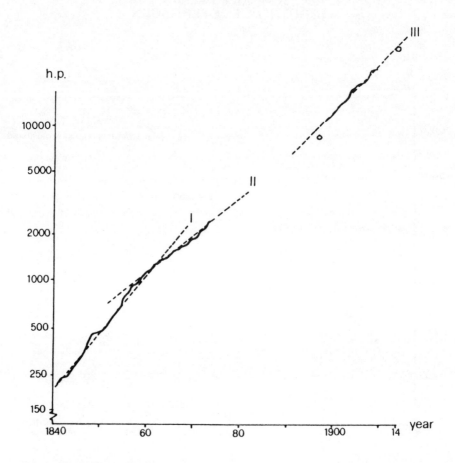

Source: See fig. 1.

where n is the total number of observation and s_1 and s_2 are maximum-likelihood-estimates of σ_1 and σ_2. If t is fixed, then ln L could be calculated (s_1 and s_2 could be found by OLS for the two subsamples and (4) then calculated). The value of ln L is then calculated for different values of t, and ln L as a function of t is shown in fig. 4.

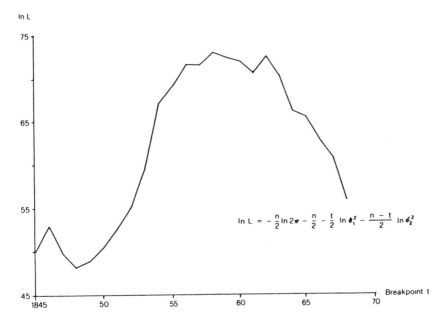

Fig. 4
THE LOG-LIKELIHOOD FUNCTION
FOR DIFFERENT BREAKPOINTS

$$\ln L = -\frac{n}{2}\ln 2\pi - \frac{n}{2} - \frac{t}{2}\ln \hat{\sigma}_1^2 - \frac{n-t}{2}\ln \hat{\sigma}_2^2$$

It is seen that 1858 is the optimal estimate of t, but that the likelihood-function is rather flat from 1856 to 1862. The statistically optimal breakpoint is consequently about 7 years earlier than proposed by Ole Hyldtoft on the basis of more diffuse criteria, and the statistical analysis is strongly against an assumption placing the phase change after 1863.[3]

3. A theory of the development

In the last section it is concluded that the development of mechanical power in manufacturing industry in Copenhagen

---

[3] A more profound discussion of the statistical estimation of the model is found in Kærgård (1988) where different statistical assumptions are tested, but the main conclusion is the one given here.

could be divided into different phases. Hyldtoft's hypothesis, as mentioned in the introduction to this paper, is that there are long-run fluctuations in the economy, the Kondratieff-waves. In this section a theory of diffusion of steam engines and electric and kerosene engines will be in focus. The theory will be the topic of statistical testing and its relation to the Kondratieff-waves will be discussed.

In the theory of diffusion it is normally assumed that the development is described by a s-shaped curve: At first the development is accelerating, but later it is characterized by a slower approximation to a saturation point. This picture is consistent with what is known from Hyldtoft and others, namely that the high growth rate in the first phase (1840-65) is caused by the production of steam engines, and the high growth rate in the third phase (1896-1914) is derived from electric and kerosene engines. Is so the development should be similar to the picture in fig. 5.

Fig. 5

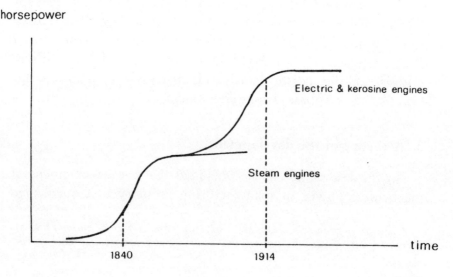

Niels Kærgård

As seen in the earlier section of this paper there are very few data from the latter part of the period, and statistical analysis should consequently be concentrated on the period 1840-75, as in section 2.

For the sake of simplicity a logistic diffusion function is chosen. The function:

$$HP_i = \frac{K}{1 + be^{-aKi}} \qquad (5)$$

where HP_i is mechanical power in year i, K the saturation level, and a and b are parameters, is rather inflexible (it is symmetric around the point where $HP_i = K/2$), but it is simple to work with, because it could be linearized (and then visually tested) as:

$$\Delta HP_i/HP_i = [aK] - a\,HP_i \qquad (6)$$

The growth rate ($\Delta HP_i/HP_i$) is a linear function of the stock HP_i. For the whole period 1840-1875 the function does not look attractive. Until 1855 there are unsystematic fluctuations, and after 1868 the growth rates are too high, perhaps as a consequence of the introduction of the new type of engine. A logistic function of the form (6) is hence estimated for the shorter period 1855-1868. The result is:

$$\Delta HP_i/HP_i = 0.177 - 0.000088 HP_i$$
$$(0.042)\ (0.000033) \qquad (7)$$

$$R^2 = 0.37 \qquad D.W. = 2.81 \qquad N = 14$$

The relationships and the observations are shown in fig. 6.

It is seen that the degree of explanation is rather low (0.37), but this is to some extent a consequence of a negative autocorrelation as indicated by the Durbin Watson test, and this is a simple consequence of the use of a variable like ΔHP_i. If big investments in engineering are made in a certain year, common sense will tell us that most of the needs for engine power in the firms are fulfilled, so that the investment in the next period will

The industrial development in Denmark 1840-1914

Fig. 6
THE DEVELOPMENT IN MECHANICAL
POWER 1855-1868

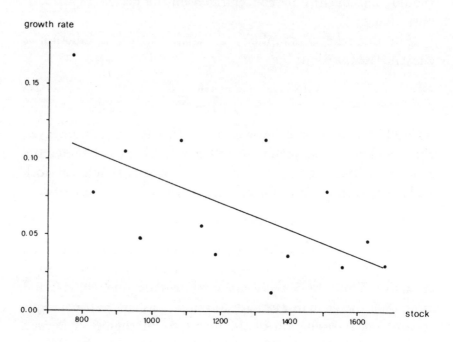

be small. These are arguments in favour of some sort of smoothing. If one uses the average of a period's growth rate and the next period's growth rate as dependent variables, R^2 will change to 0.66 and if one uses period i and i−1 instead of i+1, then R^2 will be 0.73.

If one tests the residuals for indications of mis-specifications, none of these are found. Mean and variance in the first half of the sample period are not significantly different from those in the latter half. Nor is there any difference between mean and variance of the residuals in the middle part of the sample compared with residuals from the first and the last years.[4] It seems

---

[4] The t-values for testing a difference between the means in two samples is never bigger than 0.7, and the F-value for testing a difference in variance is never bigger than 1.75. There is absolutely no indication of significant differences.

as if the estimated model is valid, but is characterized by a lot of unsystematic noise.

To sum up, one could say that the development straddling the characteristic breakpoint around 1860 may be explained by a theory of a logistic diffusion process, and that it is possible to estimate such a process, but that the estimation results are dimmed by a lot of unsystematic noise. A diffusion process for steam engines seems to be the most convincing theory in order to explain the development in mechanical power for the period 1840-75. Compared to a model founded on Kondratieff's and Schumpeter's theories (as advocated by Hyldtoft, 1984) the difference is perhaps minor, but it is not yet documented that the development in mechanical power has parallels in the general process of development or at least in the development in the stock of capital. In the next section this is investigated by means of some other indicators.

4. Alternative development indicators

In this section several potential indicators of the development in the Danish capital stock for the period 1840-1914 are taken into consideration. As no obvious possibilities are available a broader set of possibilities is considered, and the attempt is made to let the statistical analysis itself to determine the most suitable.

The possible indicators are the ones for mechanical power (see fig. 1) MHP, two series for the amount of fire insurance (the difference between them is due to the included area, see Cohn, 1958, and Falbe-Hansen & Scharling, 1885) FIRE 1 and FIRE 2, and a series for the real value of loans from the private banks in Copenhagen (see Danmarks Statistik, 1969) LOAN.

Some series of national accounts data for Denmark are also used. These are gross national product GNP and value added in manufacturing industries GNPI, both in real terms and both taken from Hansen, 1974. A series for the capital stock is calculated from Hansen's investment series, KT.

The quality of the Danish national accounts for this period is debatable, and some data which are more well-defined (but perhaps less relevant for our purpose, too) are taken into consideration. These are the population in the productive age groups (the 15-65 year olds taken from Hansen, 1974), NP, the real value of the note circulation, NOTE, and the real Danish money stock, M/P (both taken from Hansen 1968).

All the series are shown in fig. 7. The idea in the following is to use the factor analysis and the theory of principal components to find some common movements in the series. The method is explained in, for instance, Theil, 1971, and Koutsoyiannis, 1977. The main principle is to construct an index which includes a maximal part of the variation in all the series. This index is found as an eigenvector corresponding to the biggest eigenvalue in the (X'X)-matrix, where X is the data matrix. The second principal component is then an index which takes the maximal part of the remaining variation, and is uncorrelated with the first component. This is the eigenvector corresponding to the second biggest eigenvalue. One can continue until there are as many principal components as series in X and then all the variation in X is determined by the principal components. But normally only a few principal components are necessary for determining the main part of the variation in x. In Theil's analysis of 17 series for the American economy for the period 1922-38 (see Theil, 1971, pp. 50-55) he found that only 3 components are necessary for a proper explanation of the series. Furthermore each of his three components has a straight — forward interpretation — one is an expression for the general income level, one for the growth in income, and the last is a linear trend.

This technique needs a complete X-matrix, and as it is seen in fig. 7 this is not possible for the whole period and with all the series included. It is chosen to use a selection of series around the interesting breakpoint about 1860, and an X-matrix consist-

Fig. 7
INDICATORS FOR THE DEVELOPMENT

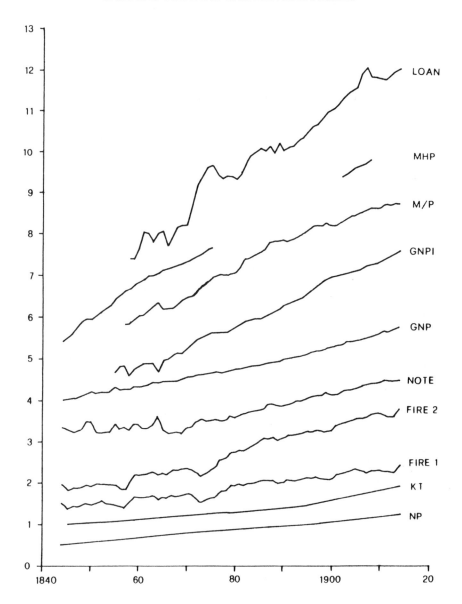

Source: All variables are logarithmic transformed. A scale correction is added to the series which means that it is impossible to read the level from the figur. The notation is explained in the text.

ing of the series KT, MHP, FIRE1, FIRE2, GNP, NOTE and NP for the period 1846-1875. The principal components are calculated and the correlation between them and the series in X is shown in table 1. It is seen that all the series — except the note circulation, NOTE — are strongly correlated with the first component. The second component is correlated with the note circulation, but with no other variables. There is no remaining variation for the last 5 components.

The same conclusion could be found in table 2 where eigenvalues corresponding to the components are shown. These measures show how much each component explains; the eigenvalue is the sum of correlation coefficients for each component in table 1 squared. The part of the variation in X which is explained by the first n components is shown, too. It is often mentioned as a rule-of-thumb that the eigenvalue should exceed one for the necessary components.[5] Table 2 confirms that only 2 components are necessary for a satisfactory explanation.

Only the first component is then possible as an estimate of a general development index. This component is shown in fig. 8 (the variable is normalized to mean zero and deviation one). The index is rather trended but with a few years of extreme growth just before 1860. There is a break in the trend, but in contrast to fig. 1 there is no change in the growth rate in the first part of the curve, compared to the latter part. There is a change in the level in 1858/1859, and the development is explained by a dummy for such a change, and by a trend:

$$PC1_i = -157.0 + 0.084\ i + 0.56\ d \qquad (8)$$
$$(9.4) \quad (0.005) \quad (0.09)$$
$$R^2 = 0.99 \qquad i = 1846\text{-}75 \qquad D.W. = 1.51$$

where $PC1_i$ is the development index from fig. 8 for the year i and d is a dummy variable which is 0 for 1846-58 and 1 for

---

[5] See Koutsoyiannis, 1977 pp. 433-434 for a discussion of the possibility for testing.

Niels Kærgård

Table 1
CORRELATION BETWEEN THE PRINCIPAL COMPONENTS
AND THE VARIABLES
(Factor Loadings)

Variable, logarithmic transformed	Principal component no. 1	2	3	4	5	6	7
Capital stock, KT	0,98	0,05	0,18	0,01	0,02	0,03	0,02
Mechanical power, MHP	0,98	0,06	0,15	−0,08	0,06	−0,04	0,00
Fire insurance amount, Copenhagen center, FIRE1	0,82	−0,43	−0,36	−0,08	−0,05	0,01	0,00
Fire insurance amount, Copenhagen FIRE2	0,93	−0,22	−0,26	0,10	−0,06	−0,01	−0,00
Gross National Product, GNP	0,97	0,14	0,14	0,05	−0,11	−0,02	0,00
Real note circulation, NOTE	0,33	0,90	−0,28	−0,01	0,00	0,00	−0,00
Population 15-65 year, NP	0,98	0,03	0,17	−0,01	0,01	0,03	−0,02

Table 2
EIGENVALUE AND EXPLAINED
PART OF THE VARIATION

Principal component no. J	Related eigenvalue	Part of variation explained by the first j principal components
1	5,498	0,785
2	1,069	0,938
3	0,382	0,993
4	0,025	0,996
5	0,021	0,999
6	0,004	1,000
7	0,001	1,000

The industrial development in Denmark 1840-1914

Fig. 8
DEVELOPMENT INDEX

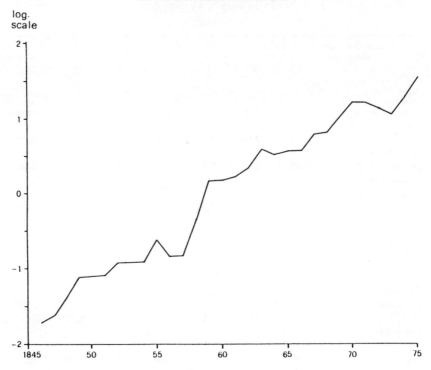

Source: The index is the first principal component of the series on fig. 7.

1859-75. This relation is better than all possible combinations of separate trends of the type in fig. 3, as evaluated with a F-test statistics.

All the series in X are rather trended and a differentiation of the series could then be a natural procedure. If the analysis from table 1 and table 2 is repeated for the matrix ΔX the results will be as shown in table 3 and table 4. These results are quite different from the former. The first 4 components have eigenvalues bigger than one, and all 7 components should be used before the explained part of the variation exceeds 0.99: compared to the case in table 2 where this was reached with only 3 components.

287

Table 3
CORRELATION BETWEEN THE PRINCIPAL COMPONENTS
AND THE VARIABLES
(Factor Loadings)

Variable, (growth rate = dif. ln X)	Principal component no. 1	2	3	4	5	6	7
Capital stock, KT	0,37	0,40	0,03	0,73	0,38	0,14	0,02
Mechanical power, MHP	−0,10	−0,08	−0,83	0,40	−0,37	0,04	−0,02
Fire insurance amount, Copenhagen center, FIRE1	−0,90	0,34	−0,10	−0,02	0,08	0,03	0,23
Fire insurance amount, Copenhagen, FIRE2	−0,91	0,27	0,02	−0,02	0,11	0,19	−0,21
Gross National Product, GNP	−0,45	−0,70	−0,08	0,28	0,29	−0,07	−0,03
Real note circulation, NOTE	−0,02	−0,90	−0,04	−0,05	0,12	0,41	0,05
Population 15-65 year, NP	0,30	0,20	−0,68	−0,48	0,42	−0,02	−0,02

Table 4
EIGENVALUE AND EXPLAINED
PART OF THE VARIATION

Principal component no. J	Related eigenvalue	Part of variation explained by the first j principal components
1	2,090	0,299
2	1,693	0,540
3	1,171	0,708
4	1,008	0,852
5	0,572	0,933
6	0,363	0,985
7	0,104	1,000

This is an indication of the fact shown in table 5 that the correlation matrix for the ΔX-matrix generally consists of very low figures.

Table 5
CORRELATION MATRIX FOR THE VARIABLES

	Capital	Power	Fire insu., Center	Fire insu., Cph.	GNP	Notes	Population
KT	1.00	0.6	−.18	−.18	−.19	−.30	−.03
MHP		1.00	.11	.02	.16	.05	.17
FIRE1			1.00	.88	.17	−.25	−.09
FIRE2				1.00	.18	−.14	−.18
GNP					1.00	.51	−.23
NOTE						1.00	−.09
NP							1.00

The conclusion must be that with a broader set of development indicators, an index could be constructed for a common fluctuation (except for the note circulation), but this index has other characteristics than the series for mechanical power. The common trend is, however, only a very rough picture of the development, and if one is using growth rates instead of levels the common fluctuation disappears.

5. Conclusion

The paper discusses the economic growth in Denmark for the period 1840-1914, with special reference to the Copenhagen area. It is shown that if mechanical power is used as a growth indicator the development could be divided into different phases, as three different growth functions (for the three periods 1840-1865, 1865-1896 and 1896-1914) describe the development significantly better than one common growth function. The statistically optimal choice of demarcation point between the two first periods is found to be 1858, which is remarkably earlier than the 1865 used by historians.

The change from high to low growth rate is explained by a logistic diffusion function for steam engines, estimated for the period 1855-1868.

But this is based only on data for mechanical power, and if other indicators such as Danish national income figures, the amount of fire insurance and note circulation are taken into consideration the conclusion changes dramatically. If the series are combined by the methods of principal components no indication of a change in growth rate is found. There are indications of a rather complex picture with different movements in the growth rates for the different series. It seems as if one should be very careful with conclusions based on only a few indicators (for instance mechanical power). The long waves in the mechanical power data seem to be a special event and not a sufficient indication for a general Kondratieff-cycle in the Danish economy.

The industrial development in Denmark 1840-1914

REFERENCES

Brown R.L., J. Durbin and J.M. Evans (1975). 'Techniques for Testing the Constancy of Regression Relationships over Time', *Journal of the Royal Statistical Society*, series B, pp. 149-192.
Cohn E. (1958). *Privatbanken i KjØbenhavn gennem Hundrede Aar 1857-1957*, II. Half volume, Copenhagen.
Danmarks Statistik (1969). Kreditmarkedsstatistik, *Statistiske undersØgelser nr. 24*.
Falbe-Hansen V. and W. Scharling (1885). *Danmarks Statistik I*, Copenhagen.
Farley J.V., M. Hinich and T.W. McGuire (1975). 'Some Comparisons of Tests for a Shift in the Slopes of a Multivariate Linear Time Series Model', *Journal of Econometrics*, pp. 297-318.
Goldfeld S.M. and R.E. Quandt (1976). 'Techniques for Estimating Switching Regression', in Goldfeld and Quandt (ed.): *Studies in Nonlinear Estimation*, Cambridge, Massachusetts.
Hansen S.Aa. (1968). Perioden 1818-1914, in K.E. Svendsen, S.Aa. Hansen, E. Olsen and E. Hoffmeyer, *Dansk Pengehistorie*, The Bank of Denmark, Copenhagen.
Hansen S.Aa. (1970). *Early Industrialization in Denmark*, Copenhagen.
Hansen S.Aa. (1972-74). *Økonomisk vækst i Danmark I-II*, Copenhagen.
Hyldtoft Ole (1984). *KØbenhavns Industrialisering 1840-1914*, (with English summary), Herning.
Johnston J. (1984). *Econometric Methods* (3. edition), New York.
Koutsoyiannis A. (1977). *Theory of Econometrics* (2. edition), London.
Kærgård N. & T.V. Rasmussen (1981). 'A growth model of the Danish Economy', in: Janssen, Pau and Straszak (ed.), *Dynamics Modelling and Control of National Economics*, Oxford.
Kærgård N. (1988). Kinked Exponential Model with Unknown Breakpoints, (unpublished), Copenhagen.
Quandt R.E. (1960). 'Test of the Hypothesis that a linear regression system obeys two separate regimes', *Journal of The American Statistical Association*, pp. 324-330.
Theil H. (1971). *Principles of Econometrics*, Amsterdam.
Willerslev Rich (1952). *Studier i dansk industrihistorie 1850-1880*, (with English summary), Copenhagen.
Willerslev Rich (1954). 'Træk af den industrielle udvikling 1850-1914', *NationalØkonomisk Tidsskrift*, p. 242-262.

[7]
The Transformation of Danish Agriculture 1870–1914

Ingrid Henriksen

Introduction

Few other subjects within modern economic history have had such unanimous praise lavished upon them as the performance of Danish agriculture during the period from about 1870 to the First World War. This historiographic tradition spans from Lord Ernle (1912) to Charles Kindleberger (1951), just to mention two prominent non-Danish scholars. This paper starts by re-examining the presumed success story. The analysis is based mainly on official statistics and on the results of recent Danish historical research within the field.[1]

(Two comprehensive English language versions of Danish agricultural history exist: Einar Jensen's (1937), and Jens Christensen's shorter version from 1983. Both, but especially Jensen's book, offer a great body of statistical information.)

Parts of the 'accepted wisdom' will be contested, although the present stage of research does not allow for a more fundamental reevaluation. Rather my purpose is to open up a few perspectives for further investigation.

1. Agriculture in the Danish Economy

A good starting point for evaluating the performance of agriculture at the macro-level is to compare the Danish structural changes with those of other European countries which passed through the same stages of development, as suggested by Crafts (1985, ch. 3). According to the data on value added and labour force a rather peculiar feature of Denmark around 1870 is the observed lack of an industrial–agricultural productivity gap. Crafts (p. 56) explains this as a result of Danish agriculture's high productivity.

Inspired by Crafts (and by the work of Chenery-Syrquin) Wunder (1987) has calculated the Danish development path with rising per capita incomes from 1870 to 1910. The assumption behind Wunder's analysis is, that GNP per capita is a central variable in describing the stage of development of a particular economy.

The figures are presented in Table 1.1. The European norm is recalculated from Crafts, whereas the national data are somewhat different (due mostly to different delimitations of sectors) from those used by Crafts. On the whole, the same picture is revealed: in 1870 (here at a per capita income of 563 1970 US dollars) Danish agriculture comes close to

Table 1.1 Denmark's development transition

Year	1840	1870	1890	1900	1910
Per capita income level (1970 $US)	402	563	708	900	1050[1]
Crude birth rate	30	30	31	30	28
European norm	36.5	34.0	32.0		28.8
Crude death rate	21	19	19	17	13
European norm	26.4	23.7	21.6		18.2
Percentage of labour force in primary sector	49.3	46.8	43.3	40.0[2]	36.4
European norm	64.3	54.6	47.4		35.2
Percentage of male labour force in industry[4]	19.5	20.9	24.7	27.5	27.3[3]
European norm	17.0	24.6	30.4		40.1
Percentage of income in primary sector	53.0	50.1	37.8	30.2	30.3
European norm	46.5	38.0	31.6		20.9
Percentage of income in secondary sector[5]	16.9	16.4	19.2	20.6	19.8
European norm	21.3	24.6	27.5		31.9

Notes:
[1] The European norm for $1.050 is calculated by means of linear interpolation between $900 and $1.130. The bias, however, will be minimal, since the distance to $1.050 is small and development in most variables, is monotonous.
[2] 1901
[3] 1911
[4] Male *and* female labour in crafts and industry.
[5] GDP in industry, crafts and public utilities.

Sources: Crafts (1985), pp. 54, 55 and 62. Johansen (1985), pp. 111–18, 260–62, 389–92, 399–401. Hansen (1974 II), pp. 245–6, 20, 170 and I, p. 16. Wunder (1987), p. 56.

maintaining a fraction of national income equal to the proportion of agricultural labour in the total labour force. In 1910 the gap reappears, due to faster productivity growth in the urban sectors. On the other hand, the tendency for the *relative* labour productivity of European agriculture to lose momentum (except in Britain and France), is less strong in Denmark. In other words, the productivity gap remains smaller than the European norm throughout the period. Considering the dominant position of agriculture in the economy (see below on foreign trade) it may seem surprising that its relative share in the total labour force in 1870 is less than the European norm. Since industry also takes up a smaller place, the tertiary sector must account for the difference. An obvious suggestion is that the relatively high productivity of agriculture is associated with a highly commercialized economy. On the eve of the First World War, the pattern is reversed such that agriculture's share of the labour force in Denmark exceeds the European norm. This can best be explained by looking at the modest export penetration by Danish industry combined with the export oriented nature of Danish agriculture.

One must expect the small productivity difference between the two sectors to be mirrored in equally small real wage differences between rural and industrial labour. For various reasons (see below on labour) our knowledge of the wages of agricultural workers before 1921 is far from satisfactory. An early study by Pedersen (1930, p. 119) based on evidence from five estates, suggests that there was hardly any difference between the real income of a day labourer in agriculture and an industrial worker in a provincial town. Ølgaard (1976) has used Pedersen's figures and the information gathered through the official Statistical Bureau for 1897, 1905 and 1910 to construct a time series index of wages in agriculture and urban trades 1875/76 to 1912/13. A comparison of the two equivalent groups of urban workers and agricultural day labourers exhibits an almost parallel increase in yearly nominal wage. Agricultural servants experience a larger increase than the two other groups. A more precise comparison between wage developments of servants in agriculture and industrial workers ought to consider the shortening of working hours in urban trades, something which did not occur in agriculture during the period. It may prove an impossible task to come up with a fully satisfactory analysis of the real wage span for this period.

Table 1.2 Agricultural export values, 1875–1915

	Total export value thousand kroner	Per cent Total animal export value	Per cent Total vegetable export value	Export quota
1875	137,000	58	42	38
1880	136,000	51	49	40
1885	118,000	68	32	37
1890	162,000	81	19	43
1895	190,300	87	13	48
1900	250,600	88	12	53
1905	346,000	86	14	58
1910	444,600	91	9	61
1915	790,000	97	3	64

Source: Statistisk Tabelværk: *Kongerigets Vare-Indførsel og Udførsel*, from 1897 *Danmarks Vare-indførsel og udførsel*, Calculations by Christensen 1983, p. 87.

The somewhat atypical pattern of development of a nineteenth-century industrializing country is best explained by the division of labour between British industry and Danish agriculture, which was manifest as early as 1870, based on comparative advantages. As indicated in Table 1.2, the export quota of Danish agriculture is 38 per cent in 1875 and rises to 64 per cent in 1915. The importance of the British market is illustrated by the fact that it represented 49 per cent of Denmark's total agricultural export value in 1875–79 and 73 per cent in 1905–09 (Nüchel Thomsen 1966, p. 176). For specific products such as butter and pork the proportion bought by British customers exceeded 90 per cent around 1900[2]. Viewed from Britain, the Danish producers supplied 15.1 per cent of all imported butter in 1877–81 rising to 43.3 per cent in 1909–13, while during the same period bacon imported from Denmark rose from a minuscule 0.7 per cent to 48.2 per cent, and eggs from 3.6 to 23.9 per cent (Nüchel Thomsen 1966, p. 150). The growing market shares are at the same time a demonstration of the competitiveness of Danish farm products.

A basic element of the Danish success story is that it began in the nineteenth-century free trade era when the vital British market was kept open for most products. As pointed out by Boserup (1992, p. 57), this placed Denmark in a fundamentally different and much more favourable position than today's raw material producers, who are discouraged by the agricultural subsidies and dumping policies of the EEC and the USA. Most barriers encountered by exporters were on the important German market. Bismarck's 1879 tariff act and the increase in duties following in 1885 and 1887–90 sharply reduced the export of live cattle. An outbreak of swine disease in 1887 momentarily halted export of live pigs to Germany and dramatically affected the conditions of Danish producers. This incident led to the establishing of co-operative bacon factories in order to expand sales on the British market. In 1895 Germany put a definitive ban on the import of live pigs. A Swedish tariff act in 1888 stopped the Danish export of flour. Finally, in 1892, both Britain and Germany prohibited the import of live cattle, and later that year, sheep.

Denmark, for good reason, upheld her own free trade position during the crises of falling farm produce prices in the 1880s and early 1890s. Proposals to impose tariffs on grain, cattle and butter were turned down by farmers on several occasions, most importantly in a committee set up by the Danish Royal Agricultural Society in 1887 and again in 1892 at a meeting of Farmers Association representatives. Clearly, the majority of farmers realized the advantages accruing from free imports of cheap animal feed during the ongoing process of transition from vegetable to animal production (cf. below). Even in the late 1880s when prices of animal products also started to fall, it was generally understood that from the viewpoint of a net exporter protection was self-defeating. Instead, the Danish agrarian movement directed its energy towards removing the relatively modest foreign industrial tariffs which, it was claimed, were harmful to agriculture's sectoral terms of trade. By maintaining free trade, the Danes adhered to a national tradition of liberalism, a reflection of a small economy without any domestic mineral resources. The reaction of the Netherlands during the same period is probably the closest parallel.

2. The Growth of Output and Productivity

So far, no clear indication has been given as to the absolute productivity of agriculture. A comparison has been made with other sectors, and it has been suggested that the export success of agriculture was based solely on comparative, if not (from the outset) on absolute, advantages in farm products over Denmark's trading partners.

Table 2.1 Growth of GDP in 1929 prices by sector, 1869–1914 (per cent p.a.)

	Total growth rates		Growth per head of labour force	
	Agriculture[1]	*Urban trades*	*Agriculture*	*Urban trades*
1868–76	0.8	3.5	0.2	2.4
1876–94	0.7(1.1)[2]	3.0	0.7(1.1)[2]	1.7
1894–1914	3.0	3.6	2.7	1.9

Notes: [1] Including fishing, gardening and forestry.
[2] The production result was abnormally low in 1894. When calculation is based on 1875/79–1890/94 the growth rates obtained are 1.1 per cent.

Source: Hansen (1972), p.239.

Table 2.1, constructed by Hansen, presents the best data available on growth of value added and labour productivity (Hansen 1972, p. 239). The material used has been criticized by Christensen (1985, p. 73) because of the shaky estimate of domestic consumption on which the final production value is partly based. The account of the exact value of raw materials and other intermediate inputs seems open to doubt. Nevertheless, when the three sub-periods 1868–76, 1875/79–1890/94 and 1894–1914 are considered, the figures leave an unmistakable impression of accelerating growth. The achievements of Danish agriculture, as of other countries, can best be illuminated in an international perspective. It is both a difficult and, sometimes, an unrewarding task to try to make international comparisons of productivity at the aggregate level. There is lack of agreement on which methods to employ. A recent interesting attempt, which includes the Danish case, has been made by van Zanden (1991). His approach is a direct comparison, in which all agricultural outputs are converted into wheat units as the 'constant' numerator to obtain gross output figures for 15 European countries during 1870 to 1910. The results for Danish agriculture compare very favourably with those of other modern economies, when examining growth of production per head, production per hectare and total productivity.

Some caveats must apply, however.

1. The Danish (and perhaps the Dutch) data are particularly biased in their use of gross production figures instead of value added. That is, they are probably less suitable as

indicators of true performance than figures of any other country during this period. Van Zanden chooses to ignore the size of intermediate inputs but suggests that the biases are in roughly the same proportion among the richest West European countries. Danish import statistics for the same period, however, tell a story of extraordinarily large inputs especially in the form of fodder (cf. below).
2. If the index number problem is *not* circumvented by van Zanden's method, though he claims that it is, another serious bias arises from the fact that productivity growth was particularly evident in the originally high-priced processed foods (butter and bacon).
3. Data on labour input is lacking (and for this van Zanden is not to blame). It may very well be that the growing number of smallholders, who were also day labourers on farms and estates, increased their hours of work compared to farm servants (cf. section 3 below).

Even allowing for the possible biases mentioned above, there is hardly any doubt that Danish farmers ranked among the highest producers in Europe.

When measured in terms of value, the growth of productivity cannot be separated from the development in output composition. In this case, attention focuses on the transition from vegetable to animal products. The key figures at the aggregate level are shown in Table 2.2. On the one hand, the share of animal products in the total agricultural production exhibits its steepest increase from the early 1880s. This is also true for the relative share of animal products in agriculture's export value. Thus, one traditional interpretation of the

Table 2.2 *Agricultural production value, 1850–1915*

	Total production value (in thousand kroner)	Percentage distribution	
		Value of total vegetable production	Value of total animal production
1850	128,200	43	57
1860	198,400	39	61
1870	304,000	35	65
1875	356,000	26	74
1880	337,400	26	74
1885	320,300	17	83
1890	376,200	15	85
1895	394,000	8	92
1900	472,400	9	91
1905	600,000	5	95
1910	731,200	9	91
1915	1,236,600	6	94

Source: Christensen (1983), pp. 58 and 86.

change to animal husbandry carries some weight. It tends to stress the importance of innovations in technology and organization during the 1880s.

On the other hand, both the share of animal products in total agricultural production and in export value begin to increase as early as the 1860s – nearly 20 years before the agricultural crisis, co-operatives and cream separators. One explanation of the seemingly premature change, often cited in the Danish literature, is that it reflects peasants' response to impoverishment of the soil by grain crops. It is argued that by selling off their grain instead of feeding it to their animals, during the period of rising grain exports from the 1830s, the farmers took away the 'original power' from their land without replenishing it by manuring. This interpretation has been challenged by the agricultural economist S.P. Jensen. Good statistical records of the acreage of crops going back to 1861 show that even in the regions best suited for the purpose, no more than 50 per cent of the arable area was ever sown with grain crops, and it is doubtful whether the pervasive breeds of grain could have absorbed more nutrients, especially nitrogen, than they already received.[3] Furthermore, the decline in yield sometimes observed following repetition of the same crop can most often be explained by plant diseases, which thrived under such conditions.

The main explanation for when and why product mix changed is more likely to be found in the alteration of price relations *already* underway prior to the grain crisis of the seventies. From 1848–57 to 1867–77 wheat prices went up 100.9 per cent and barley 120 per cent, while beef prices rose by 137.2 per cent and butter by 127.6 per cent (Nüchel Thomsen 1966, p. 124). The change in relative prices reflects the larger income elasticity of animal products and the long-term trend of rising incomes in Denmark and abroad. This view is supported by the works of the Grand Old Man of Danish agrarian history, Fridlev Skrubbeltrang (1934–45, pp. 291–2) and the two economists Henriksen and Ølgaard's work with export statistics (1960, pp. 10–11).

One implication of the early reorganization of production is that the time- and capital-consuming process of building up herds of milk cows was well underway before the introduction of modern dairy technology impelled animal husbandry towards further productivity gains. It may have provided Danish farmers with an advantage over their competitors in Britain and The Netherlands, where the number of livestock per person (of the agricultural population) was lower in 1870 (cf. van Zanden 1988, p. 38).

A strong concurrent motive for the transition to animal farming was, of course, the possibility of acquiring relatively cheaper fodder. The figures showing imports of these goods in Table 2.3 illustrate the point. In spite of being well endowed with land for fodder growing, Denmark fully exploited the advantages of cheaper inputs like oilseed cakes and maize. A calculation by Ølgaard (1966, p. 234) based on foreign trade data indicates an improvement from 1875/76 to 1912/13 in the overall terms of trade, mainly due to the relative price increases for processed foods exceeding those of various raw materials and industrial products. Still, the price of one decisive input wages, did *not* favour animal husbandry. Money wages per person employed in agriculture more than doubled between 1875 and 1913.

A somewhat simpler approach to productivity comparisons with a more limited field of application is to measure physical units. Grain yields in Danish agriculture lagged behind those of The Netherlands, Belgium and Britain for most of the nineteenth century, only to catch up around 1900. It seems that the northwest European countries by then converged

Table 2.3   Agricultural imports, 1875–1915 (in thousand tons)

Year	Grain	Fertilizer	Fodder
1875	71	0.1	15
1880	134	0.1	17
1885	183	0.3	31
1890	260	0.5	70
1900	606	6.0	210
1905	710	13.0	359
1910	657	102.0	481
1915	702	228.0	517

Source: Christensen (1983), p. 90.

toward an intermediate plateau of kilos per hectare reflecting the state of technology at the time. Growth was resumed in the next century as the result of more systematic breeding (to obtain grains with higher yield and more stiff-strawed so as to be able to absorb more fertilizer) combined with new nitrate fertilizer.

When all vegetable products are converted into a common denominator (as done by Jensen 1988, p. 256) the increase in the productivity of land is *sustained* in Denmark. This is due to the still existent growth potential of grasses and root crops.

With respect to milk production, Danish farmers overtook their European competitors in 1900. Probably more crucial than litres of milk per cow were the enormous advances in dairy processing, i.e. kilos of butter per 100 kilos of milk (cf. section 5 below) .

3.   Factor Endowments

3.1   Agricultural Land

The high land/man ratio undoubtedly contributed to the high labour productivity of Danish agriculture. Total area, including meadows and grassland, increased by about 11 per cent from 1871 to 1911, almost completely offsetting the slight rise in agricultural population. The increase, seen in Table 3.1, is found in the years up to 1888. (The boost in land reclamation in these years followed upon Denmark's loss of Schleswig-Holstein to Germany in 1864.) Thereafter the total agricultural area stagnated at a level of about 75 per cent of the total area.

The relatively advantageous position of the Danish rural population in a European context is highlighted in the above mentioned study by van Zanden. From 1870 Denmark held the leading position with 2.9 hectares of cultivated land per head of agricultural population, falling to 2.6 in 1910, surpassed only by Ireland. The equivalent figures for Holland are 1.4 hectares in 1870 and 1.2 in 1910, and for all 15 countries in van Zanden's study they are 2 and 1.7 hectares respectively.[4]

3.2 Capital Investment in Agriculture

According to Hansen (1972, p. 281 ff), the main period of transition to animal husbandry in the 1880s and 1890s is distinguished by a major expansion in purchased raw materials such as oilseed cakes, etc., while fixed investments remained at a comparatively low level. Although he has strong reservations about the estimated investment figures, Hansen nevertheless presents an assessment of agricultural net investments as a percentage of total agricultural income, showing first an increase in the mid-1890s from a level of about 4–5 per cent to about 7–10 per cent and then a boom from 1903 to 1907, where investments are believed to have reached 14–15 percent, thereafter falling to 9–10 per cent. Investment estimates are based partly on the valuation of agricultural machinery 1875–1913 made for one of the big credit associations. In addition to the apparent surge in acquisitions of machinery between 1905 and 1909, there exists evidence of a major increase in the building of farm houses during the same period in order to accommodate the growing stock of animals.

Breaking down investments, the long-term gradual increase in the number of milk cows has already been mentioned. This development accelerates slightly from the 1880s. The major contribution to the increase in livestock investments, however, springs from a five fold increase in the number of pigs from 1881 to 1914 and from a doubling in the number of calves, heifers and bulls, due to the rising turnover of milk cows, as production intensified (Jensen 1988, pp. 260–61). Increasing use of machines and the greater need for transport are reflected in the steadily growing number of horses after 1881.

An inventory of the various kinds of machinery on farms of different size was not made until 1907. Two points are worth mentioning. First, labour-saving machinery was almost entirely confined to vegetable production in the narrow sense (indirectly serving animal production of course). A labour-saving device such as the milking machine, first introduced into many British stables during the First World War (Taylor 1976, p. 595), did not really gain momentum in Denmark until the 1930s. Innovations during the first decade of this century included threshers (to an increasing degree driven by steam instead of horse-drawn), reapers, mowers (sometimes utilized as reapers), reaper-binders and sowing machines.

Publicized testing of the costly equipment (state sponsored after 1892) guided hesitant investors. According to Jensen (1988, p. 275), bad reviews had the beneficial effects of either causing the product to be improved or to disappear from the market.

When comparing the use of threshers (24.5 per cent of the holdings), reapers (10.3 per cent) and sowing machines (12.2 per cent) in 1907 with that of some other European countries in the study by van Zanden, Danish farmers look well-supplied, although relatively more Swiss farmers used a reaper and more German farmers a thresher.

The second noteworthy point is the extent to which machines were shared (20–30 per cent of the sowing machines and reapers), hired or lent as an alternative to ownership. Although the expected 'threshold acreage', below which no farmer would buy a machine, is established in the material, it appears that small size did not altogether preclude the use of machinery.

Soil improvement in the form of drainage culminated somewhat earlier than other investments – 1.6 per cent of the arable land having been drained in 1861, 21 per cent in 1881 and 26 per cent in 1907. The same goes for marlin and chalking, which dropped in the

1870s except for newly reclaimed land, only to reappear after 1910 as agricultural science was able to extract new benefits from it.

3.2.1 Financing agricultural investments

The growing demand for funding concomitant with rising investments was still chiefly met by self-financing. According to a rough estimate made by Hansen (1972, p. 283), based on the growth of indebtedness between 1900 and 1914, about 70 per cent of total investments during this very active period must have been financed out of retained profits.

This is not to say, however, that financial institutions were not of growing importance. During the 1880s, credit associations overtook savings banks in advancing mortgage loans to agriculture. Other sources of capital, such as loans offered by entailed estates and by the Public Trustee's Office, continued to be significant. In 1901 the latter made up 36 per cent of total mortgage loans, against 46 per cent by credit associations and 18 per cent by savings banks.

In addition to this, agriculture despite the liberalist spirit pervading the period, was financially favoured by the state in more than one way. Grants, including loans to smallholders, are dealt with in Section 3.3 below. In addition a general state loan fund was established in 1904, of which agriculture was able to secure the bulk of the funds.

Even though demand for agricultural capital rose substantially throughout the period 1870–1914, due to the ever-growing commercialization of the sector, higher rates of investment and the increasing problem of buying out the shares of other heirs to a farm (cf. section 4 below), the necessary funds were nevertheless available. Self-financing still played a major part. Moreover, it is stated by contemporaries, that agriculture, particularly after 1900, had no difficulty in attracting loans. If correct, this statement accords well with available information on the relatively small productivity gap between agriculture and industry, (cf. Section 1). Of course the earlier decades of falling product prices and falling prices of property had caused indebtedness (debt as a percentage of property value) to rise temporarily. Consequently, in the bleakest years of 1885–89, 10 per cent of all sales were foreclosures. On the whole, however, accumulated savings even in those days were enough to meet the demand from gradually raising livestock.

3.2.2 Human capital

The literacy of the Danish rural population during the last quarter of the nineteenth century ranked generally high, together with that of the populations of Norway, Sweden, Scotland, Switzerland and the Protestant parts of Germany. The school law of 1814 made instruction (though not school attendance) mainly in reading, writing and religion, mandatory for children under the age of 14. It is generally believed that the legislation was operative around 1830 at the latest (Bjørn 1988, p. 107). The constitution of 1849 stated that instruction in primary schools was free of charge to all parents of limited means. The earliest reliable account of the consequences assesses the learning of Danish recruits in 1881. It is established that 22 per cent had severe problems in reading and 43 per cent in writing. This result may be positively biased, as the recruits were young and could remember their recent schooling, and as they were physically fit (to be soldiers), the handicapped young men having been excluded (Dybdahl 1982, pp. 107–9).

The first primary schools probably had to put up with poorly-educated teachers and lack of materials. Furthermore, the law and amendments up to about 1890 were dominated by the concern that children were part of the work force, in deference to the peasants' own wishes. Only gradually was education viewed as an asset to rural society, ahead of other considerations. Village children attended school only three days a week, and a number of school holidays were conveniently placed around sowing, harvest, and ploughing time (Christensen 1988, p. 393). All this having been said, the majority of Danish villagers in 1870 were in fact able to read, and thereby also to share in the new ideas propagated through newspapers and in popular agricultural journals.

The 'folk high schools', residential colleges set up for rural youth from the mid 1840s and most vigorously from the late 1860s, are often mentioned in international literature as essential in relation to the professional training of the Danish peasant class. Their emphasis, however, was on the national heritage, i.e. subjects like national literature, history and Christianity, and on improving and broadening basic knowledge in reading, writing and arithmetic. Only some of the colleges taught agricultural subjects. Accordingly, their indisputable influence on economic development was mainly indirect: bolstering the vital peasant culture and consequently paving the way for co-operatives, etc. (cf. Section 5 below).

Genuine agricultural schools were set up somewhat later, along the same lines as these adult schools. The young male students typically followed a five-month winter course – the season during which their work was needed less. Around 1900, a total of 700 students a year followed a course at an agricultural school, rising to 1300 in 1914. This is roughly about 5 per cent of the 20-year-olds in agriculture during that year (Christensen 1988, p. 400). Two schools, from 1879 and 1889, specialized in the theoretical training of dairymen.

Scientific education and research in agriculture was launched in Denmark with the establishment of The Royal Veterinary and Agricultural University in 1858. The University's graduates were to become advisers to peasants' and smallholders' associations (cf. Section 5 below).

3.3 Labour on the Land

According to the censuses the total population in agriculture varied little in absolute numbers, from 788,735 in 1870 to 1,003,716 in 1911. An estimate of the size of the agricultural work force, shown in Table 3.1, reveals the same impression of a modest increase interrupted by a minor decline in the late 1880s and early 1890s. As expected, the agrarian share of the total work force declined significantly – from 52 in 1870 to about 39 per cent in 1914[5] (Hansen 1974, pp. 230–31). As already stated in Section 1, however, this still left Denmark with a relatively larger agrarian workforce than the European average in 1914. Relative productivity in agriculture and industry, as depicted in Section 1, reflected this development at the macro-level. It appears as if agricultural labourers had little to gain by way of higher wages from switching to urban employment. Still, we lack a more thorough explanation for the high retention of labour on the land.

The key to understanding the perseverance of rural labour in Denmark during the late nineteenth century most probably lies in the prevailing opportunities to acquire a house of one's own, or more specifically, a house with a small plot of land. During the century that followed the great land reforms of the 1780s, the class of cottagers and smallholders

Table 3.1 The agricultural population, 1870–1911

Year	Number of persons dependent on agriculture[1]	Work force[3] estimated by Hansen (1974)
1870	788,735	486,000
1880	888,931	510,000
1890	882,336[4]	503,000
1901	980,605[5]	511,000
1911	1,003,716[5]	529,000

Notes:
[1] These figures are employed by Wunder (1987) and reproduced in Table 1.1
[2] Including assistant wives of farmers and an estimate of the number of married women working for others plus children over the age of 15, reduced by an estimate of children in the educational system. Agriculture in this column includes fishing, gardening and forestry.
[3] According to *Statistisk Tabelværk* V litra A no. 5, p. 162 the decline from 1880 to 1890 may be due merely to a change in the work on the collected material.
[4] From 1901 onwards an attempt is made to distinguish between servants doing agricultural work and domestic servants (not included).

Sources: *Statistisk Tabelværk* V litra A, no.5. *Statistisk Tabelværk* V litra, no.10. Hansen (1974), pp. 230–31.

trebled, and in 1880 they comprised about 65 per cent of the total rural population (Christiansen 1975, p. 8).

The importance of parcelling out is corroborated by the data on overseas emigration from rural districts. Hvidt, in his study of Danish emigration (1868–1914), found that 62 per cent of the rural emigrants were farm servants, i.e. people without a house of their own (Hvidt 1971, pp. 215, 245, 250). Further evidence is provided by local emigration studies. The Lolland–Falster region, for example, experienced a rather large outflow of rural labour. These islands maintained feudal relations for a longer period than most other areas of Denmark. Large estates predominated and the number of smallholdings was limited. In western Jutland, where land was readily available and relatively cheap, emigration was correspondingly lower.

Further confirmation of the relation between landless labourers and emigration is obtained from the fact that the composition of the agricultural labour force was beginning to change during 1870 to 1914. The absolute number of farm servants living with their employers declined after 1870, and most rapidly after 1890. The higher wage gains of this group (cf. Section 1) indicate that these, mostly young people, were harder to retain. Their work was taken over by the ever-increasing number of smallholders, who depended on wage labour for maintaining their families.

From the point of view of agricultural employers, the altered workforce also reflected a change in the demand for labour. The need for female servants to perform a number of tasks declined as dairies, bakers and brewers became specialized urban occupations[6]. Estates and large farms employed more or less permanent male day labourers during the year, whereas middle-sized farms preferred to supplement the work of their live-in servants with that of casual day labourers during peak seasons. The employers of permanent day labourers relied on the cottagers' wives to perform the ever more important daily milking work.

A day labourer at that time can best be defined as a wage earner with a household of his own. There remain problems in further delimiting the group, although a rough estimate of its size was given above. The term 'day labourer' is often used synonymously with the terms 'cottager' or 'smallholder'. However, not all smallholders were dependent on wage work and not all day labourers had a house (rented, held as a tenant or owned). Some rented part of a house from their employer. If we confine ourselves to the cottager/smallholder definition, the number of cottages increased by 29 per cent during 1873–1905, whereas the arable land belonging to them increased by only 10 per cent. (After 1905 comparison is made difficult by a change in the measurement of land from quality to mere area.) It appears that the group seems to have been generally impoverished, although the number of completely landless cottages started to decline slightly after 1885.

3.3.1 The workers' standard of living

Coinciding with the rise of an urban labour movement in Denmark, public interest in the living conditions of agricultural workers resulted in special inquiries on the subject from the 1870s onwards. Unfortunately, the results do not lend themselves to a more precise comparison over time. Smallholders on average spent half their time working for others. As stated in Section 1, the development of day labourers' wages seems to have followed that of urban workers. To the extent that it was sought and necessary, employment was still far from secure, especially for casual day labourers (Witte 1977, pp. 120–21).

Payment in kind, though declining in importance, was far from being totally abolished. A particularly intriguing feature was the tilling of the smallholders' plots using the employers' horses and plough. For quite a number of cottagers, this made up a large part of the payment for their work, and as it was most often performed during evenings and Sundays, tilling their own plots added to already long working days.

Children of cottagers, from the age of about 9 or 10 years old, are likely to have worked extensively during the summer season, although the exact figures are not known. Two of the myths of Danish history are that this did not basically interfere with their schooling, which was secured for all children according to the 1814 law, and that farmers' and cottagers' children shared similar conditions in the village schools. Nissen's (1973) study on school absenteeism of different social classes in a rural district reveals that farmers' children in 1880–85 were absent without due cause from 6 per cent of the lectures, cottagers' children from more than 16 per cent. The small fines for illegal absence were paid for by the employers of the children.

Any estimation of total yearly working hours per person for the cottagers is subject to numerous difficulties. It would be of great interest for any assessment of living conditions, and would also help toward an accurate calculation of labour productivity. Maybe the smallholders with a small plot were, in the terms of the Russian economist Chayanov, a 'self-exploiting' group in their role as part-time farmers. Data on farm prices per hectare in the years immediately following the First World War indicate that the smallholder generally envisaged a lower rate of return on his capital outlay and thereby expected to work harder than did the owner of a medium-sized farm (Bjerke 1950, p. 62).

A study of household budgets of rural labourers between 1872 and 1890 points to an improvement in the standard of living: food expenses dropped from 80 to 70 per cent, approaching 60 per cent in 1907 (which must still be considered extremely high) (Hansen 1972, p. 260).

Finally, in evaluating the living conditions of Danish agricultural workers it must not be overlooked that emigration from rural areas in neighbouring Norway and Sweden far exceeded the Danish rate, and that rural emigration from Sweden to Denmark was considerable, probably an indication of Denmark's relatively higher standard of living.

3.3.2 The state and rural labour

Until the 1870s, the cottager was destined for the role of assistant to larger farms and estates. The above-mentioned expansion in the number of smallholdings corresponds toward the end of the nineteenth century with the Danish demographic transition period, which halved mortality and initially left fertility unchanged. As will be shown in Section 4, the medium-sized farms remained mostly intact (largely undivided through inheritance), giving up only fringes for cottages. Thus, the excess rural population had the option of either migrating or trying to make a living under these conditions. Consequently, around the 1870s the public was concerned about rural over-population and the reported poverty among the landless or near-landless classes. Twenty-five years later, the picture was almost reversed: urban and overseas migration caused the rural population to stagnate or even decline slightly while at the same time the transition to animal husbandry increased the labour requirements of agricultural production.

Legislation concerning smallholdings mirrors the shift. The 1880 law on Subsidized Credit Associations for Smallholders aimed at giving loans on a scale too small for the established credit associations. The state guaranteed a minimum interest on the bonds issued. The two associations established according to the law acted as a support for the more well-to-do smallholders, especially after the decline in land prices in the 1880s.

Some 20 years later, the shortage of labour, which had been observed on estates and bigger farms from about 1890, generated the 1899 Law on Procurement of Plots of Land for Farm Workers. The state was to assist landless labourers to acquire these plots by granting them state loans of up to nine-tenths the mortgage value of the property. Repayment by the holder did not have to start until five years later and was on very favourable terms. The irony of this law, however, was that by limiting the amount of land acquired to a maximum of about 4–5 hectares, a ready supply of available agricultural workers could be ensured! As it turned out, during the first five years after the law's enactment, almost 90 per cent of the buyers of state grant plots were day labourers (Witte 1977, p. 128). This was quite in accord with the intention of the law. According to a survey from 1907, a smallholder with a state grant plot was still dependent on working for others for an average of 155 days a year.

The years around the turn of the century brought about a change in more than one way, even to this under-privileged group. First of all, the viability of small plots now hinged on new opportunities to market a larger part of their product for a better price. This opportunity had arisen due to the co-operative producers' associations. Once established on the initiative of farmers, the dairies and slaughterhouses could make the best possible use of even small deliveries of milk and pigs, thus enabling smallholders to maintain a family on considerably less land than by grain-growing alone. Secondly, the year 1901 brought about the victory of parliamentary democracy in Denmark, in the sense that the majority party in the *Folketing*, The Liberal Farmers' Party (*Venstre*) came into office. The Liberals replaced a Conservative government whose agrarian policy had been much influenced by estate owners. Supported by the Smallholders' Associations and by a new political party, the Radical Liberals, the cottagers and smallholders now enacted a number of laws furthering their wish to replace their old status as labourers with a small plot with a new one as small producers. The 1906 Law on Societies for the Parcelling Out of Land made it possible to obtain public loans for the purchase and parcelling out of estates and larger farms. A 1909 prolongation of the 1899 Law on State Grants raised the limit of the loans and enabled smallholders to enlarge their holdings beyond the original maximum size. Preliminary considerations on expropriations of estate land to be parcelled out were interrupted by the First World War.

To sum up, the sparse amount of wage data points to an initially narrow span between agriculture and industry. Presumably just as important for retaining rural labour were the prospects for young people without property to establish households of their own. This was made possible through the willingness of estates and large farms to sell or rent small plots of their land in exchange for labour; thus, they retained a stable work force of day labourers and their families. The state, representing the interests of agricultural employers until the turn of the century, actively promoted the tendency by making cheap loans available.

4. Land Tenure

Danish system of land ownership has often been cited by development economists to illustrate the point that equity and efficiency are not mutually exclusive (cf. for example Warriner 1969, p. 392 ff. and Senghaas 1985, p. 90). The questions to be raised are therefore, 'How equal was the land distribution?' and 'How efficient was the medium-sized farm, normally regarded as the vanguard of late nineteenth, early twentieth century development?'

Table 4.1 provides an indication of the number and size (measured in quality terms) of Danish estates, farms, and smallholdings between 1860 and 1905 (after the latter year the measure of size changes to area proper, which makes a direct comparison less relevant). The data indicate that the middle-sized farm with from 1 to 8 'tønder hartkorn' (roughly 10 to 60 hectares for the country on average) retained its share of total land, while there was a definite restructuring within the middle-sized group in favour of the smaller farms. The large farms (8–12 'tønder hartkorn') shrank both in number and in their share of arable land. Estates of more than 12 'tønder hartkorn' expanded in both number and size through 1905; thereafter their numbers declined. This is despite the fact that the period is normally seen as the heyday of the medium-sized farm. At the same time the number of smallholdings with little land increased until 1905, cf. Section 3.3 above on rural labour.

Some brief remarks on the origin of the 1870 structure may be useful. It is rooted in the fact that peasant land was the main taxable object from the time of the early absolute monarchy in the late seventeenth century. Consequently, estate owners were prevented from adding the land of their tenants to the demesne (which they might have wanted to do

Table 4.1 Farms by size according to hartkorn (Danish unit of land valuation based on estimated productivity)

With a *hartkorn* of:	1860		1885		1905	
	Number	Total Hartkorn	Number	Total Hartkorn	Number	Total Hartkorn
Less than 1	139,286	[1]	188,526		212,520	43,128
1–2	17,600	25,557	20,979	30,150	23,060	33,123
2–4	20,793	61,274	23,397	67,876	24,365	70,457
4–8	27,474	157,498	24,636	139,887	23,327	132,005
8–12	4,284	39,988	3,953	37,152	3,765	35,525
12–20	1,054	15,592	1,145	17,092	1,174	17,635
20–	824	36,471	896	39,517	919	40,547

Notes: [1] For 1873 the number of small holdings of a *hartkorn* less than 1 is 165,264 and their total *hartkorn* is 39,331.

Source: Rasmussen (1988), pp. 223 and 225.

for various reasons) (cf. Smout 1987). This left the farm structure intact and the major part of the land – probably close to 90 per cent – to be worked by peasants. The late eighteenth century land reforms had a generally emancipatory effect. Abundant labour had made tying of labour to the land dispensable. More crucially the reforms paved the way for two developments: a successful and comparatively rapid enclosure of commons and consolidating of farms was undertaken, often in unison with the peasants. (The losers, in this country as everywhere else, were the landless poor, to the extent that they were excluded from grazing rights of the commons. The landless were left even more dependent on paid work for peasants and owners than before.)

Soaring grain prices from the late 1790s facilitated the freehold purchases by more than half the peasants, leaving most of the remainder to effect it during the economic regeneration of the 1840s and 1850s. It may still be a bit of a puzzle to Danish historians, as to why the estate owners so willingly let go large parts of their land. (Owners of entailed estates, of course, were prevented from doing so.) Perhaps the capitalized value of interests and instalments were correctly weighted against future land rents, or perhaps some owners (land speculators in particular) were in urgent need of an injection of capital. Official policy, especially after the constitution of 1849, sympathized with this development. In 1885 only eight per cent of the farmers' land was still held by tenants.

One aspect of the structural development from 1870 to 1914 depicted above is the growing burden of generational change upon agriculture. More children surviving to adulthood meant more heirs, since all siblings had the right to inherit. More heirs leaving the countryside meant more buying out of their shares. Finally the longer life of parents meant that more adult children sought to establish families of their own, before they could inherit. Given all these factors, one might have expected an outcome with even more fragmentation than that which actually took place. Contemporaries praise the well-functioning credit system of savings banks and credit associations for the smooth running of the process. In addition, there was presumably a general tendency to maintain the farm in a relatively undivided state, leaving some younger sons as lower status smallholders[7].

Deliberate parcelling out of plots in order to retain labour – and sometimes also to liquidate part of one's capital – was nonetheless the most influential force behind the observed fragmentation, cf. Section 3.3 above.

The expansion of estate farming until 1905 can be ascribed to various factors: the elite of the Danish estates throughout the first three-quarters of the nineteenth century were the bearers of technological and commercial renewal. The co-operative producers and export associations of the latter part of the century built comfortably upon this foundation. Secondly, some estates (though far from all) were better equipped to adjust to the fall in grain prices in the 1870s. According to Christensen (1985, pp. 94–5) their production already had a more adequate balance between vegetable and animal production than did the farms. Consequently, when relative prices changed they were able to shift quite quickly to animal production. The estates possessed the necessary capital for an expansion into livestock and for investments in animal feed. Only from the early 1890s were they squeezed between falling prices of animal products and rising wages. Unlike the farms, the estates could not resort to the low wage and control costs of family labour. Thirdly, most Danish estates, like those of other north-west European countries, successfully substituted labour for capital to the extent this was at all possible at the time. The growing number of harvest and sowing machines has already been mentioned.

Various accounts of the use of capital by middle-sized farms speaks in their favour. Evidently, producers' co-operatives were a means of exploiting the benefits of large-scale processing. The sharing and hiring arrangements of steam-threshers and other such machines can be seen as the response to economies of scale in primary production. By analogy, the advisory services of farmers' unions is a means of overcoming the indivisibility of expert information. This type of evidence is borne out by different kinds of local studies elucidating how farmers reacted to price developments by changing their investments. A few peasant diaries handed down tell us of local pioneers in production (Bjørn 1982, pp. 22–3, Jensen 1985)

By 1870 the Danish farm structure, whether beneficial or not, was probably due as Smout suggests, to 'a stroke of luck'. It was the outcome of political, demographic and technological forces of the preceding two centuries. A conclusion regarding its merits will in part depend on the level of analysis. From a narrow sectoral point of view, the question is whether an alternative structural arrangement would have led to higher efficiency (keeping in mind that macro-evidence does not suggest a more efficient use of resources outside agriculture, at least not until the last part of the period). Danish researchers are not in complete agreement on this point. Most tend to find the structure favourable on the whole, applying some of the arguments mentioned above. From a broader social point of view, Senghaas (1985) points out the beneficial effects to development of an appropriate distribution of resources. The distribution of land was equal enough to allow for a rise in productivity and income and, thus, a demand, for domestic manufactured goods. However it was not so equal (i.e. fragmented) that it prevented the generation of necessary savings.

5. The Institutional Setting

When interpreting the economic development of Danish agriculture between 1870 and 1914, the institutional background plays a major role. The self-organization of peasants through co-operatives (from the 1880s) is often cited. The co-operatives enabled the medium and even small-sized farms to utilize the advantages of large-scale farming by establishing a superstructure which could provide the benefits of large-scale technology in processing and marketing farm products as well as the supply of important raw materials. (The principal participants in co-operative dairies held farms of 0.5–40 hectares of land, and herds of 1–15 milk cows.) However, the foundation of co-operatives and other vital institutions of economic significance was laid in the self-organization of the middle peasant class back in the 1840s. Co-operative organizations can thus be seen as the principal instrument in the continuing struggle for political, economic, and social emancipation of the peasants. According to the most authoritative Danish historian in this field, Bjørn (1988, p. 368) many characteristic features of co-operative organization could be seen in the various forms of associations formed by peasants earlier on.

Most important among the socio-economic organizations were the farmers' associations, which were massively joined by peasants from the 1860s. In 1896, membership came close to 70 per cent of the potential membership. Besides articulating the peasants' general interests, as time went by the unions effectively came to take charge of much of the work of informing peasants about new technology in the transition to intensive animal husbandry. Thus, the unions initiated research activities, lectures, discussions, cattle shows, etc.

One of the most important features of the unions' activities in Denmark was the organization of advisory services to peasants on a semi-public basis. State-supported encouragement of new products and methods, either directly or via organizations like The Royal Agricultural Society, already existed in Denmark as well as in other north-west European countries. From 1890 to 1910, however, a new form emerged, in which the local or regional peasants' (and later on also smallholders') unions hired and instructed consultants in cultivation or cattle breeding, while the state covered half of the expenses. This way of organizing advisory services enabled the peasants to extract the kind of advice suitable to their particular local conditions and type of holding in a much better fashion than some form of 'lecturing from above', and thus helped to bridge the gap between agricultural science and its users.

Much the same can be said of the consultants hired by the smallholders' associations after their start in 1900 (Christiansen 1975, p. 5). The later formation of the smallholders' unions reflects the low status of their members. This is equally mirrored in the much broader goal of these unions. The majority of the peasants' unions' activities were confined to technical and economic questions, while the smallholders' unions also sought a general emancipation of the class they represented. Their proposals for new legislation often had a social and political aspect.

The establishment of new local savings banks from the 1850s is another important example of collaboration within the economic area. They originated in real or imagined difficulties in obtaining loans from urban savings banks. By starting their own financial institutions, the peasants were able to pursue their economic and political aims. Small local savings banks were the major source of credit in financing the first co-operative dairies of the 1880s. It could be added that the peasants gained an ever increasing influence over the credit associations (first established in 1850), through their representatives in the councils and through their role on the local level as property assessors. In the 1880s credit associations overtook savings banks as the main providers of outside capital to agriculture.

This brief survey of some institutions should nevertheless have made clear the early emergence of a *collective peasant consciousness* based on persistent and determined self-organization. Some writers even go so far as to refer to the solidarity of the open fields (prior to the enclosures of the late eighteenth century). This is not entirely accurate when we examine the start of co-operative dairies. These originated in western Jutland, where open fields even in the eighteenth century had little significance. Besides there exist fairly accurate records of the first establishments, from where their inspiration came, which group took the initiative, and what motivated them.

The evidence points to individual economic gain as the all-pervading motive in an environment characterized by high social cohesion. The latter is accounted for by most authors by the *homogeneity* of the middle peasant group with respect to property size and line of production.

Some commentators, e.g. Kindleberger and Clapham, refer to *owner occupancy* in explaining why the co-operative movement caught on in some places more than others. Co-operative accounts being open to inspection, tenant farmers feared their landlords might raise the rents if the landlord found the peasants too prosperous (Kindleberger 1951, p. 45). Clapham (1968, p. 112) when addressing the question of the virtual absence of co-operatives in Britain attributed this to social ambitions on the part of the individual tenant, who may have had his eyes fixed on a 'station well above him'.

Kindleberger and others also stress the importance of *education*, which in Denmark helped increase the quantity and quality of necessary communication.

Finally, the importance of the out-group to the cohesion and efficiency of the group in question is touched upon by Kindleberger. In this case, however, it may not be so much the Danish antagonism towards Germany (after the military defeat in 1864) as the continuous opposition to landed aristocracy (who, though small in number, maintained a strong political position after the constitutional reform of 1866) and to townspeople, who were said to exploit peasants.

The above examination of general co-operative ventures indicates that Danish peasants in the latter part of the nineteenth century were socially-conscious, well-educated, determined in pursuing their goals and suspicious of outsiders. Still, this may not satisfactorily explain the almost exclusive choice of co-operation in dealing with economies of scale in dairying. The following is an attempt to clarify this development in the light of modern institutional theory.

5.1 Dairies in the Late Nineteenth Century as a Case of Vertical Integration

It will be argued that producers' co-operatives were the most efficient response to the technology and property distribution that characterized dairy production at this specific time and place.

The point of departure is the following. Some important inventions during the 1870s in cold-storage (originating in the USA) and in centrifugal cream separators (from Germany[8]) quickly reached Denmark and were further developed here. These discoveries paved the way for a substantial productivity gain in butter production. Economies of scale using this technology required milk from at least 300 cows a day, while a middle-sized farm at the beginning of the 1880s possessed an average of only 10. From the outset, and still in the early 1890s, butter from Danish estates, because of its superior quality was quoted at a price about 30 per cent higher than peasant butter in the English market. (Prior to the introduction of cold storage it was necessary to be able to churn large quantities of milk frequently.)

Now the obvious response to new opportunities would be for enterprising capitalists to start dairies based on purchased milk from the surrounding farms. In fact, Wade (1981 p. 54) in his study of institutional determinants of technical change in three European countries, maintains, that 'The (Danish) creamery need not have been co-operative in institutional form. Processing capacity could have been achieved with individual or corporate-owned creameries.'

However, dairies established as private undertakings *did* in fact exist in Denmark prior to and parallel to the establishment of the first co-operatives. Why, then, were they unsuccessful and why were they ousted by the co-operatives from an early date?

Table 5.1 indicates the establishment of private and co-operative dairies. The first co-operative dairy was established in 1882 but new starts accelerated after 1885. It will be seen that while private dairies preceded co-operatives, they were outnumbered by co-operatives by around 1890. In his thorough study of private enterprise dairies (often somewhat confusingly denoted as 'joint'; dairies) Bjørn (1977, p. 77) points out that these were met with criticism even *before* the alternative organizational solution of co-operatives was reached. The majority of private enterprises were initiated in two ways: either by the owner of a large farm investing in modern equipment and needing to buy even more milk in order to utilize the advantage of scale, or by a skilled dairyman. From the early 1880s the

Table 5.1   Dairies by ownership

Year	Number of Co-operatives	Number of Private enterprises[1]
1888	388	468[2]
1894	907	215
1898	1013	260
1901	1067	209
1905	1087	207
1909	1163	255

Notes: [1] Exclusive of estate dairies and some small farm dairies that added the milk of a couple of neighbouring farms to their own.
[2] According to Bjørn (1977, p. 72) the number of private dairies in the mid-1880s was at least 500. At that time the number of co-operative dairies did not yet exceed 50.

Sources: Bjørn (1977), p. 71 for 1888 and
Bjørn (1982), p. 121 for the following years.

technology applied was basically the same in these enterprises as in the co-operatives a bit later on.

The criticism of private enterprises related to three points. First, the quality of the product suffered, because the owners of the dairy were unable to control how the cows were fed and the way in which the milk was treated by the suppliers. (This may still be a problem in a co-operative venture.) While the quality therefore surpassed that of ordinary peasant butter from individual farms it did not quite reach that of estate butter. Another cause for concern was that milk deliveries were too small, and the farms delivering it were spread over a large area, which made the costs of transportation high. A third problem was that private undertakings were generally too modest in equipment and scale from the beginning, and that funds for expansion were harder to obtain for the individual owner. In contrast, members of the co-operative were jointly responsible for loans from savings banks. (This problem certainly could have been overcome by corporate organization, which was also attempted in some places, though to no avail.)

Producers' co-operatives in food processing, as with dairies, may from the point of view of institutional theory be regarded as a form of *vertical integration*: primary producers took control over the higher step in the production process by collectively owning the plant. Within the same framework, private enterprise dairies can be regarded as adapting themselves to market forces when purchasing milk from individual farmers, who would of course try to obtain the highest price possible for their product, but who take no responsibility for the outcome after delivery.

Internal organization (in the form of vertical integration) of the transfer of a good or service across a technologically separable interface is preferred to market procurement where asset specificity is great (Williamson 1989, p. 151). By asset specificity Williamson refers to the degree to which an asset can be redeployed to alternative uses and by alternative users without sacrifice of productive value (p. 142). On the one hand, markets promote high-powered incentives. On the other, they impede the ease of adaption as the bilateral dependency of the relation between two parties builds up.

To put it simply, if an input can be utilized alternatively by another producer, at another time or place, market procurement is always favoured. If this is not so – if the asset is specific to a few uses – the two parties involved increasingly come to depend on each other. Beyond a certain degree of asset specificity, vertical integration is the most efficient institutional solution to the problem of minimizing transaction costs (the costs of transferring a good or service across a technologically separable interface). This simplified version of the theory leaves out important assumptions, but it should suffice to illustrate the main point.

Now what is the relevance of all this to milk producing farmers and butter producing dairies in late nineteenth-century Denmark? Special circumstances made fresh liquid milk, with a high content of butterfat, a very specific asset to dairying. Vertical integration, i.e. integrated control over all steps in the process, therefore became a solution preferable to separate ownership (private farms and private enterprise dairies) and use of market transformation. Milk was a highly perishable product, which at that time had to be transported on gravel roads by slow wagons. Most of the milk could only be used for butter production within reachable distance. Seen from the processing angle, smooth production was dependent upon deliveries of sufficiently large quantities of high quality milk. The capital investments involved on both sides were substantial. (Asset specificity obviously has a relation to the notion of sunk cost.) Once a herd of milking cows was established or once a creamery had been built, the parties depended on each other for sales and deliveries. Mutually damaging hold-up situations could be ended by co-operatives.

The point concerning vertical integration can be further underlined by the fact that the concomitant organizational development in pig breeding and bacon factories deviated somewhat from that of milk and butter production. In contrast to a gallon of milk, the site specificity of a live pig is smaller and so is the physical specificity. It can be kept for longer and consequently travel longer and be sold to more customers. This may provide part of the explanation for why private undertakings were at least much more competitive in this field of production.

5.2 The Gains from Modernization

The activities of co-operative dairies and bacon factories, and from the 1890s of export associations, succeeded in raising the price of peasant products to the level formerly reserved for 'estate' products. Even if much is ascribed to co-operation, it alone did not bring results. 'It was the instrument through which science and technical knowledge were brought to bear upon the problems' (Jensen 1937, p. 329). The fact that with the use of a cream separator the amount of butter extracted from the milk went up by 25–30 per cent is illustrative. It could be added equally correctly that specialization helped to achieve high quality products. Following the difficulties encountered by Denmark's exports of live cattle and pigs to her traditional markets, these were replaced by two products, bacon and butter.

The institutional developments in food processing, etc. in these years meant a challenge to estate production. The larger farms and estates, having larger herds of milk cows, were better able to employ a cream separator. Consequently, they joined the cooperative dairies very late or not at all. They were confronted however, with problems in the primary step of production, which did not hit the peasant farms to the same degree. First, the growing scarcity (and rising wage) of labour (cf. Section 3 above) made itself felt more strongly where family labour could not be drawn upon. Secondly, working with animals and the different activities related to them seems to present a case of decreasing returns to management. As Pollak (1985, p. 591) states in his account of the family farm from an institutionalist's point of view, 'The family farm can be regarded as an organizational solution to the difficulty of monitoring and supervising workers who, for technological reasons cannot be gathered together in a single location'. Recurrent complaints about the quality of milking workers were heard from large dairy estates in these years.

Simplifying somewhat, it can be stated that medium-sized farms with the given technology had the best of both worlds: they reaped control advantages in the sphere of primary production, and economies of scale in processing and marketing.

Summary and Conclusions

A few years after the Second World War, the United Nations Food and Agriculture Organization (FAO) published a study on the evolutionary changes of Danish agriculture during the previous 200 years. The implication was that the Danish experience held a lesson for developing nations. The foreword refers to the general interest in and possible application of the Danish agricultural model (Skrubbeltrang 1953, p. iii). Is such an interest still justified in the case of developing countries or the countries in Eastern Europe facing an immediate restructuring of their land tenure and allocative system?

The early Danish 'Green Revolution' that boosted output per worker took place in the fundamentally different and much more favourable environment of an open and growing market for processed foods, quite different from that facing new entrants on the market today.

Any ambition to quantify the development of labour productivity in more precise terms is frustrated by the deficient data on the actual labour input of the large and expanding group of smallholders. They probably worked for less than the market wage acting according to their main goal of establishing a household and owning even a small plot of land. On the other hand, available evidence on the performance of Danish agriculture at the macro level contradicts any notion of gross inefficiency caused by underemployed labour.

The FAO study paid much attention to land tenure problems, emphasizing the importance of the Danish medium-sized, owner-operated farms. Our overview of Danish research tends to substantiate that this form of tenure, at the state of technology dominant around 1900, had definite advantages. The farm type at that time apparently adapted well to new patterns of production, and the farmers in many cases knew how to compensate for small scale by pooling their efforts. Combined with the co-operatives, the farms seem to have reaped the control advantages belonging to modest scale in primary production and the economy of scale belonging to modern processing of foods. Do these advantages hold true universally? According to one school of thought the institutional framework is determined by the technological level. Modern technology therefore makes owner-occupancy and moderate farm size anachronistic. Nonetheless, the parcelling out of land in Denmark went even further in the twentieth century, having been influenced by rather strong agriculturalists' organizations. The process was not reversed until the late 1950s. For the past 30 years, Danish agriculture has been radically restructured towards larger units, so that in 1987 the average farm size of 32.5 hectares still exceeded that of all other EEC countries except Britain. This increase in farm size was of course sustained by a marked growth in urban employment possibilities. Owner-occupancy came under pressure from the late 1970s, when many young farmers in particular found themselves almost desperately in debt to credit associations and banks. The high cost of establishing a modern, highly mechanized farm business, the high interest rates and anticipated gains from entrance into the EEC that pushed up property prices (up to membership in 1973) all brought about this critical situation. Owner-occupancy, however, is not being seriously contested – neither by farmers or by politicians.[9]

Co-operative ventures in processing and marketing of farm products were by no means confined to Danish agriculture although they are often mentioned as a uniquely Danish accomplishment contributing to high growth in an international context. This article has tried to provide an additional argument for this form of organization, particularly in the case of co-operative dairies, by emphasizing vertical integration. Vertical integration of primary production and processing was the solution adopted to minimize transaction costs with the given state of technology and distribution of property. Consequently, although the substance of co-operatives has changed somewhat in today's industrial countries[10] the organizational concept may still be applicable under other circumstances.

Notes

1. I am indebted to Dr. S.P. Jensen and Dr. Gunnar Persson for valuable comments. I am solely responsible for any remaining errors.
2. When the c.i.f. value of exports is applied as in this case, the export is generally overestimated compared to a valuation 'ex farmer' and more so as time goes by, since processing of agricultural goods increases.
3. More nitrogen would mean softer straw which caused the grain stalks to wilt.
4. There is no general agreement on the concept of agricultural land best suited for international historical comparisons. The definition chosen has obvious implications for the interpretation of the results. Van Zanden's use of cultivated land places Danish agriculture in a favourable position, whereas a wider concept which includes permanent pastures and meadows as well as rough and mountain grazing, chosen by O'Brien and Prados del la Escosura (1992, p. 517) places the United Kingdom far ahead of every other European country with respect to land/man ratio, and Denmark on a level with Germany and France.
5. It must be noted that the agrarian share of total population used by Wunder in Table 1.1 is not directly comparable with Hansen's share of the total labour force in Table 3.1.
6. It may also be worth noting that dairying in Denmark, as elsewhere in western Europe, was traditionally a women's occupation. Co-operative dairies, however, changed the prospects of women fundamentally during the 1880s and 1890s. Under various pretexts they were ousted by men, first as leaders and then gradually altogether (Christensen 1988, pp. 389-90).
7. The right of inheritance was equal as mentioned already. Nevertheless, the testator according to a law of 1769 amended in 1837, could favour one of his heirs by charging a particularly low price for the farm when selling it to this heir in his own lifetime.
8. The principle of centrifugal power to separate the cream from the milk is reported to have been applied in Germany in the 1860s. The Swede Laval and the Dane Nielsen are mentioned as simultaneous inventors of the continuous cream separator.
9. The acquiring of a smallholding as a sort of state tenant was made possible in 1919 – much inspired by the ideas of Henry George. The law was moderately successful, but still twice as many prospective holders preferred the old system of state grant loans to actually buying their land.
10. In Denmark at least, there has occurred a heavy consolidation of co-operative ventures since the 1960s and the original participation by members has been reduced.

Bibliography

Bjerke, Kjeld (1950), *Omsætningen og salgsprisen for landejendomme 1902-1942*, København.
Bjørn, Claus (1977), 'Fællesmejerierne – En fase i Dansk Mejeribrugs Udvikling 1860-1890' *Bol og By. Landbohistorisk Tidsskrift*, 2, række I.
Bjørn, Claus (1982), 'Dansk mejeribrug 1882-1914', in Claus Bjørn (ed.), *Dansk mejeribrug 1882-2000*, København.
Bjørn, Claus (1988), in Claus Bjørn et al. (eds), *Det danske landbrugs historie III. 1810-1914*, Odense.
Boserup, Ester (1992) 'En kommentar til Thorkild Kjærgaards disputats om Danmarks grønne revolution', *Fortid og Nutid*, hæfte 1.
Christensen, Jens (1983), *Rural Denmark 1750-1980*, Copenhagen.
Christensen, Jens (1985), *Landbostatistik. Håndbog i dansk landbohistorisk statistik 1830-1900*, København.

Christensen, Jens (1988), in Claus Bjørn et al. (eds), *Det danske landbrugs historie III. 1810–1914*, Odense.
Chistiansen, Palle Ove (1975), *Husmandsbevaegelse og jordreform i Danmark*, København.
Clapham, J.H. (1968), 'Machines and National Rivalries (1887–1914)', with an Epilogue (1914–1929), *An Economic History of Modern Britain*, Cambridge.
Crafts, N.F.R. (1985), *British Economic Growth During the Industrial Revolution*, Oxford.
Dybdahl, Vagn (1982), 'Det ny samfund på vej 1871–1913', *Dansk social historie, bind 5*, København.
Ernle, Lord (Rowland E. Prothero) (1912), *English Farming Past and Present*, London.
Hansen, K. (ed.) (1934–45), *Det danske landbrugs historie. Femte bind*, København.
Hansen, Svend Aage (1972), *Økonomisk vækst i Danmark, bd. I: 1720–1914*, København.
Hansen, Svend Aage (1974), *Økonomisk vækst i Danmark, bd. II: 1914–1975*, København.
Henriksen, Ole Bus og Anders Ølgaard (1960), 'Danmarks Udenrigshandel 1874–1958', (with an English introduction), *Studier fra Københavns Universitets Økonomiske Institut*.
Hvidt, Kristian (1971), *Flugten til Amerika. Drivkræfter i masseudvandringen fra Danmark 1868–1914*, København.
Jensen, Einar (1937), *Danish Agriculture. Its Economic Development. A Description and Economic Analysis Centering on the Free Trade Epoch 1870–1930*, Copenhagen.
Jensen, S.P. (1985), 'Landbrugets systemskifte 1870–1914 belyst gennem dagbøgerne og regnskaber fra en enkelt gård', *Bol og By. Landbohistorisk tidsskrift*, nr. 2, pp. 56–101.
Jensen, S.P. (1988), in Claus Bjørn et al. (eds), *Det danske landbrugs historie III. 1810–1914*, Odense.
Kindleberger, Charles (1951), 'Group Behavior and International Trade', *Journal of Political Economy*, 59 (1).
Nissen, Gunhild (1973), *Bønder, skole og demokrati*.
Nüchel Thomsen, Birgit og Brinley Thomas (1966), *Dansk-engelsk samhandel 1661–1963*, Århus.
O'Brien, Patrick K. and Leandro Prados de la Escosura (1992), 'Agricultural Productivity and European Industrialization, 1890–1980', *Economic History Review*, XLV (3), pp. 514–36.
Pedersen, Jørgen (1930), *Arbejdslønnen i Danmark. Under skiftende konjunkturer i perioden ca. 1850–1913*, København.
Pollak, Robert A. (1985), 'A Transaction Cost Approach to Families and Households', *Journal of Economic Literature*, XXIII, pp. 581–608.
Rasmussen, Jørgen Dickmann (1988), in Claus Bjørn et al. (eds), *Det danske landbrugs historie III. 1810–1914*, Odense.
Senghaas, Dieter (1985), *The European Experience. A Historical Critique of Development Theory*, New Hampshire.
Skrubbeltrang, Fridlev (1934–45), in K. Hansen (ed.), *Det Danske Landbrugs Historie*, Femte bind, København.
Skrubbeltrang, Fridlev (1953), 'Agricultural Development and Rural Reform in Denmark', *FAO Agricultural Studies nr. 22*, Rome.
Smout, T.C. (1987), 'Landowners in Scotland, Ireland and Denmark in the Age of Improvement', *The Scandinavian Journal of History*, 12, pp. 79–97.
Taylor, David (1976), 'The English Dairy Industry, 1860–1930', *Economic History Review*, XXIX (4), pp. 585–601.
Wade, William Windsor (1981), *Institutional Determinants of Technical Change and Agricultural Productivity Growth. Denmark, France, and Great Britain, 1870–1965*, New York.
Warriner, Doreen (1969), *Land Reform in Principle and Practice*, Oxford.
Williamson, Oliver E. (1989), 'Transaction Cost Economics', in R. Schmalensee and R.D. Willig (ed.), *Handbook of Industrial Organization*, I.
Witte, Jørgen (1977), 'Landarbejdernes kår 1850–90, *Bol og By. Landbohistorisk Tidsskrift*, 2, række I.
Wunder, Sven (1987), 'Aspekter af dansk industrialisering – en teoretisk-kvantitativ indfaldsvinkel i N. Buus Kristensen og S. Wunder, To analyser af dansk industrialisering før 1914', *Blåt memo nr. 161 fra Københavns Universitets Økonomiske Institut*.
Zanden, J.L. van (1988), 'The First Green Revolution. The Growth of Production and Productivity

in European Agriculture, 870-1914', *Research memorandum 42. Vrije Universiteit. Faculteit der Economische Wetenschappen en Econometrie,* Amsterdam.

Zanden, J.L. van (1991), 'The First Green Revolution: The Growth of Production and Productivity in European Agriculture, 1870-1914', *Economic History Review,* **XLIV** (2), pp. 215-39.

Ølgaard, Anders (1966), *Growth Productivity and Relative Prices,* København.

Ølgaard, Anders (1976), 'Arbejdslønnen i byerne og landbruget i Danmark 1875-1955, *Memo nr. 49 fra Københavns Universitets Økonomiske Institut.*

Part II
Income, Growth and Economic Policy in the 20th Century

Excerpt from *The Measurement of National Wealth*, 80–118.

4

REAL CAPITAL AND ECONOMIC GROWTH IN NORWAY 1900-56

By Odd Aukrust and Juul Bjerke
The Central Bureau of Statistics of Norway

INTRODUCTION

THE main purpose of this article is to present a review of the growth of real capital in Norway since the turn of the century. Attention has also been devoted to the relationship between the growth of real capital, employment, and net national product, however.[1]

In Section I some of the fundamental problems involved in computations of the value of the real capital are discussed. Attention is drawn to some of the defects and limitations which often are attached to estimates of the real capital stocks. Section II gives a description of the main features of the methods which have been applied for the Norwegian computations. Section III contains a summary of the principal results of the real capital computations. A more detailed statement of results is given in the Appendix. The last two sections comprise a closer analysis of the figures derived. Section IV is devoted to an analysis of the variations in the marginal capital–output ratio since 1900, with special emphasis on the remarkable postwar trend. Since 1948 the marginal capital–output ratio has been of the order of magnitude 5:1 as against 3:1 in earlier periods. In Section V it is pointed out that this may be explained by a production function of the Cobb–Douglas type with a trend component.

I. DEFINITION AND VALUATION PROBLEMS

In computations of the value of the stocks of real capital there are two vital questions which must be decided. The first is the question of defining the real objects one wants to include in the term real capital. The second, and far more difficult, problem consists in selecting a system of weights ('prices') which can be used in the aggregation of highly divergent real objects on the basis of a common unit of measurement.

---

[1] The work on this study has been carried out with the financial assistance of the Social Science Research Council.

The capital concept

In this study the concept of real capital is given a somewhat narrow scope. It embraces *all man-made durable real objects in private and public enterprises, including dwellings, and buildings and constructions of general government with the exception of military installations*. Durables are all real objects with a life expectancy of one year or more. Inventories, livestock, land, standing forests, and real objects in the hands of consumers have been excluded from the real capital concept, mainly because statistical sources do not permit annual estimates of these items to be made with any accuracy. The reader should bear this in mind when reading the analytical sections of the paper.

In order to permit some comparisons of the Norwegian figures with figures of other countries, rough estimates of the omitted items have been attempted for one single year, viz. for the end of 1953. These estimates, which are in current prices only, are included in Appendix, Table V. Apart from cars, the figures given do not include estimates of the value of durables in the hands of households, however.

The aggregation problem

To arrive at a convenient system of weights ('prices') for use in the aggregation of real objects of highly different nature it is necessary to operate on the basis of properties which the real objects have in common and which can be measured. Moreover, it is essential that the weight system be based on properties which are relevant from an economic-analytical point of view. However, we are immediately faced with the problem that there are almost no two real objects which are entirely identical in a technical sense. Even highly standardized categories of capital, such as automobiles, etc., will often have different technical qualities. In addition to these purely technical diversities, differences as regards total life and remaining life will make a comparison of various categories of real objects difficult. For these reasons one can hardly hope to arrive at a weight system on the direct basis of the technical properties of real objects.

There seems, however, to be two characteristics of capital objects as defined above which might serve as a basis for an economic measurement of the real capital. The first is that the production of capital objects entails a certain absorption of real resources (production costs). The second characteristic is that a certain production or earning capacity [1] is connected with the capital objects. These qualities seem to permit two different solutions to the aggregation problems. One method, which may be termed the *retrospective method*, implies looking back and using the costs of production as basis for the weight system. The second method, *the prospective method*, implies looking ahead and attempting to determine the weight system on the basis of the future earning capacity of the various real objects. Market prices, or substitutes for these in the absence of market prices, may be taken as an approximation to the latter weight system.

It is the first aggregation method, the retrospective, which has been applied in the Norwegian capital computations, and in the following section some features of this method will be analysed. The second method will also be discussed, however, as a comparison of the results derived from the two different methods is of interest.

The retrospective method

As has already been mentioned, this method implies that the costs of production for the various capital objects are taken as a starting-point. We are then faced with the choice between use of historical costs of capital and replacement costs in the valuation. For well-known reasons replacement costs are preferable. By the use of replacement costs a set of figures is derived for real capital in current value.

These figures will reflect the volume of real productive resources incorporated in the capital equipment as well as the current prices of these resources. To arrive at a volume concept for real capital (meaning by this the volume of accumulated productive resources absorbed) the current-value figures must be deflated with an appropriate cost index, that is an index reflecting the price trend for productive resources. To provide reliable expressions for such indices is not easy, but in principle it presents similar problems to those involved in other forms of price or cost indices.

Special problems arise in the estimation (in current value) of objects which are partly obsolete. To estimate all real objects,

---

[1] See Raymond W. Goldsmith, 'The Growth of Reproducible Wealth of the United States of America from 1805 to 1950', *Income and Wealth, Series II*, p. 249.

old as well as new, at full replacement cost would be tantamount to giving partly obsolete objects the same weight as completely new objects of the same category. The only way to avoid this is to base the valuation of partly obsolete objects on depreciated replacement costs. There is the difficulty, however, that several depreciation methods are possible (linear, progressive, and degressive). The choice between these will affect the computation result and lead to capital concepts of somewhat different content. Within the retrospective method, therefore, a number of variants are possible, depending on the depreciation system used. The choice among these variants can be made on a conventional basis only.[1] In the Norwegian computations constant depreciation allowances have in principle been used, i.e. equally large depreciation allowances each year through the life of the capital objects (the 'straight-line method').[2]

At a given time there will always be some real objects in use which have been rendered obsolete by technological and economic development, so that there can be no question of replacing them with identical units. For such objects it seems reasonable to base the estimates on the replacement costs of real objects by which the obsolete objects may be replaced, with proper adjustments for differences in the potential earning capacity of the two types of capital objects.

The prospective method

Under *the prospective method* the value of the capital items should reflect their future earning capacity. This must be determined on the basis of the future input and output flows which are associated with the different items. If we regard the prices of the various input and output categories and the discounting factors as given quantities at all times, and the future

---

[1] From the point of view of the individual company it may seem reasonable to provide for depreciation so that the value of the capital objects decreases in step with their remaining earning capacity. If this principle is to be strictly applied, it would be necessary to know the development over time of the output and input factors connected with the various capital objects. In practice, one will have to be content with more or less satisfactory approximations. *Stuvel* has pointed to linearly decreasing depreciation as a possible method. See G. Stuvel, 'The Estimation of Capital Consumption in National Accounting', *Review of Economic Studies*, 1955–56, Vol. XXIII (3), No. 62, pp. 183–185. Provided that the time function for the earning capacity of the capital objects decreases parabolically over the period, this method will be in agreement with the principle mentioned above. If, on the other hand, the earning capacity decreases linearly over the life period, the straight-line procedure will produce the desired result.

[2] Actually this principle may not always be fulfilled, cf. p. 90.

INCOME AND WEALTH

input and output flows are known, the earning capacity of the different capital items may in principle be estimated.

When the prospective method is used, one would in practice base the valuation on the market prices of the capital items, since as these can be taken as approximate expression of their earning capacity. Problems arise for the (quite numerous) categories of capital objects which are not usually sold in the market. In such cases one will have to guess what the market prices would have been if a market had existed. Another point in the prospective method is that no fundamental problems arise in the valuation of partly outworn capital objects, or objects which have been rendered obsolete by the technological and economic developments. The earning capacity or market prices give us the solution directly in both cases.

To arrive at figures for the value of the real capital measured in fixed prices under the prospective method one should in principle take the starting-point in a set of given (fixed) prices on all input and output factors and a set of discounting factors. In practice, the usual procedure is to deflate the figures in current prices by price indices designed to reflect the price trend for capital objects with a given potential earning capacity.

Comparison of the two methods

There is reason to believe that the results obtained under the two methods, in so far as the value of capital in terms of current prices is concerned, will not show very large deviations. The reason is that in most cases the market prices of capital goods are not likely to deviate much from their (depreciated) replacement costs as calculated by any standard method of depreciation under the retrospective method. It is obvious, for example, that the market price of new capital equipment cannot be far from its costs of production. But for partly obsolete objects, market prices may also be assumed to be fairly close, on an average, to depreciated replacement costs. This will be the case if and when the depreciation method actually used approximates, on an average, to the falling earning capacity of capital goods with increasing age.[1] With most of the standard depreciations methods discussed above this may not be too far from the truth.

For the value of capital in terms of *fixed* prices, on the other hand, the two methods will usually produce different results.

---

[1] See Raymond W. Goldsmith, *loc. cit.*, p. 251.

This is a consequence of the different meaning of the price-change concept in the two valuation methods. Under the *retrospective method* a series of figures for the value of the real capital in terms of fixed prices will reflect the quantity of productive resources which are incorporated in the capital equipment at various times. But the figures are not supposed to be influenced by the fact that as a result of increased technological knowledge it has gradually become possible to combine these productive resources in a more effective technique. Under the *prospective method*, on the other hand, one tries to compute figures in fixed prices which take into account both the increase in the volume of incorporated productive resources and improvements in technique. For here one uses price indices for capital objects which as far as possible are equal from a technological efficiency viewpoint. It is reasonable to assume that gradually increasing technological knowledge will make it possible to produce more effective capital objects with given investment of productive resources. It is to be expected, therefore, that the real capital volume will show a sharper increase over a period if the computations are performed under the *prospective valuation method* than if they are based on the *retrospective method*.

The choice between the two evaluation methods also depends on the objective of the computations. If the purpose is to study the role of capital as a factor of production, the *prospective method* may seem preferable. Volume figures for the capital computed on the basis of this method will, as pointed out above, also reflect improvements in the productive capacity of the capital as a result of more effective technique. That will not be the case to the same extent with volume figures computed under the *retrospective method*. This point is of significance if we want to use figures for the real capital in a production function to 'explain' the production trend over a lengthy period. If in this case we use capital data computed under the *retrospective method* we must include in the production function a special variable in order to allow for the effects of the gradual change in the technological level.[1]

[1] When real capital is to be used as explanatory variable in a production function there may be reason to question both of the valuation methods mentioned here. Under both methods partly obsolete capital objects will be given a substantially lower value than corresponding new objects, on the assumption that they have a lower *remaining* production capacity. But this probably does not give

INCOME AND WEALTH

If the primary purpose of the capital computations is regarded as part of the work on what Ingvar Ohlsson [1] terms 'statement of results' the *retrospective method* seems to be the most satisfactory. Two arguments may, as far as we can see, be raised in support of this:

(i) It is natural to require of our capital data that they (in terms of fixed prices) be consistent with the national account figures (also expressed in fixed prices), i.e. that the capital growth over a period according to the capital estimates shall equal the accumulated net investments over that period according to the national accounts. But in a national accounting system, prepared for the purpose of measuring 'economic results', net investments have to be estimated so as to give a measure of the volume of the productive resources which have been used to increase the capital of the society. It follows that in the capital computations also we must regard the capital as 'accumulated productive resources', which means that the *retrospective method* must be applied. Provided that the same principles are applied in the estimation of the depreciation in both cases, this will result in capital stock figures at constant prices which are consistent with the current national accounting figures at constant prices.

(ii) In analysing economic results it is often necessary to use stock data and current data together, for example, in analyses where the capital is regarded as the accumulated result of the production of earlier periods. It is therefore desirable that the two sets of data be based on identical valuation principles, i.e. that the capital data, like the current data, are computed on the basis of the production costs of the commodities.

In both cases a deeper reason for the choice of valuation principle lies in the fact that the production costs express a fundamental transformation relationship between the objects, as they

---

a satisfactory expression of the relation between the *current* production capacity of old and new equipment, for example, a ten-year-old railroad car in the short run may be of as good service as a completely new one. It is presumed that this factor may be disturbing for short-term analyses, where the age structure of the capital may vary appreciably, and where changes in the value of the capital therefore will not always provide a good measure for the changes in its production capacity.

[1] Ingvar Ohlsson, *On National Accounting*, Stockholm, 1953.

approximately measure the quantities of productive resources which are incorporated in them.

II. COMPUTATION METHODS

In this section a brief outline will be given of the computation methods of the Norwegian capital estimates. The employment data which are used in sections III–V will also be described in some detail.

Capital computations

Figures for the real capital volume have been computed on an annual basis for the period 1900–55 with the exception of the war years 1940–45. For all years the real capital has been classified into the following four groups: buildings and constructions in private and public enterprises; buildings and constructions of general government; ships and boats; machinery, tools, and transportation equipment excluding ships. More detailed data by industry as well as by type are available for three years, viz. the years 1900, 1939, and 1953. All results are expressed in 1938 prices.

The computations have been performed in three steps, or by three different types of computations. Step (1) was to determine figures for gross investment, measured in 1938 prices, for each year in the period under review and for each capital group. Step (2) consisted in direct and detailed computations of the value of the real capital stocks (in 1938 prices) at a few benchmark points, namely at the end of the years 1899, 1920, 1939, and 1953. Steps (1) and (2) together gave the data required to compute (separately for each capital group) the total net investments and the total capital consumption within each of the periods 1900–20, 1921–39. In step (3) these preliminary results were used to compute annual figures for the capital consumption in each capital group, also in terms of 1938 prices. Together with the annual gross investment figures (step (1)) and directly computed capital data for bench-mark years (step (2)), this permitted a simple determination of the annual stock data. The computations at the various steps have been described in further detail in the following.

It is characteristic of the computation method applied that it is based on computations of gross investments for all years and independently derived estimates of capital stocks for bench-mark

88 INCOME AND WEALTH

years, and that the results of these computations are controlled against each other by studying the implications they entail for the development of capital consumption. The capital-consumption data are useful *per se*, and will be used in the Norwegian national accounts.[1]

Step (1): Computation of annual gross investment figures

The gross investment data used in this study have been taken from earlier published national accounting data and are mainly estimated by the commodity-flow approach, i.e. on the basis of import statistics and Norwegian production of capital goods. Further details on the computations in fixed and current prices may be obtained from official publications.[2] The lack of gross investment data for the years 1940–45 is the main reason why this article contains no capital-stock figures for these years.

Step (2): Capital computations for bench-mark years

For no year are census results available which permit a computation of capital stocks based on complete and homogeneous material. The computations for bench-mark years made for this study are therefore based on data collected from highly variable sources, often supplemented with approximate corrections and estimates. As a general rule, total figures must be presumed subject to smaller relative margins of error than the more detailed specifications presented.

For the years 1899, 1939, and 1953 the capital-stock figures are based on detailed computations for each single group of capital objects, made separately for each individual industry. The computations for 1920 are more summary, and their main purpose has been to provide some basis for judging whether capital consumption over the fifty-year period have developed proportionally with the capital volume (see p. 90 below). The

---

[1] In our opinion it would be difficult to find a better method for computation of the level of capital consumption, as it guarantees that the national accounting data on capital consumption will be consistent with the gross investment data and with the best estimates that can be made of the size of the capital stocks at different points of time. The need for capital consumption data for the national account was, as a matter of fact, one of the main reasons for undertaking this study.

[2] Organization of European Economic Co-operation, *National Accounts Studies – Norway*, Paris, 1953, pp. 100–101. Central Bureau of Statistics of Norway, *National Accounts 1900–1929* (NOS. XI. 143), pp. 10–13, *National Accounts 1930–1939 and 1946–1951* (NOS. XI. 109), pp. 50–51, and *National Accounts 1938 and 1948–1953* (NOS. XI. 185), pp. 37–38.

nature of the statistical sources used in the direct capital computations vary from industry to industry and from capital object to capital object.

For some categories of capital it has been possible to base the computations on direct volume data and production costs data, sometimes supplemented by data on the age structure of capital. Dwellings, ships and boats, automobiles, roads and railroads are examples of groups of capital objects for which we have been able to make direct use of volume and cost data.

For other categories of capital objects the computations are based on value data, generally measured in current prices. These data are sometimes fire-insurance values, in other cases book values. The book values represent in some cases depreciated capital values, in others cumulated historical costs before depreciation. Manufacturing and mining are examples of industries where data on fire-insurance values have been available. For post, telegraph and telephone, and for railway and tramway rolling stock the computations are based on book values.

For the components of the capital equipment where computations are based on value data in current prices one of the difficult problems has been the conversion from current prices into 1938 prices. The price indices used for these computations have in most cases been those used for the fixed-price estimates for gross investment in the national accounts for the period 1900–55.

Step (3): Computation of annual capital consumption data

With the aid of data from step (1) and step (2) the sum total of the capital consumption over a period of years can be determined.[1] In our case the computations provide figures for the total capital consumption for the period 1900–39 and for the two sub-periods 1900–20 and 1921–39, separately for each of the four object groups of real capital discussed in paragraph 20. (A computation of capital consumption by industry is not possible, however, as gross investment data by industry are not available for the whole period 1900–39.)

[1] We have $D_{t/t+\theta} = J_{t/t+\theta} - (C_{t+\theta} - C_t)$, where $D_{t/t+\theta}$ and $J_{t/t+\theta}$ denote capital consumption and gross investment respectively in the period from t to $t + \theta$ and $C_{t+\theta}$ and C_t the size of the real capital at the end of the period and at the beginning of the period. $D_{t/t+\theta}$ can be set as balance when the right hand elements are known.

INCOME AND WEALTH

The next problem is to distribute the total of capital consumption thus estimated over the different years in the period. This can be done by assuming that each year's capital consumption varies in a given way with the depreciated value of the real capital at the beginning of the year (both expressed in 1938 prices).[1] The simplest assumption would be to assume that capital consumption throughout the period has been proportional to the capital value. However, the computations for the two sub-periods 1900–20 and 1921–39 indicate that the capital-consumption ratios (capital consumption in 1938 prices as a percentage of the real capital measured in 1938 prices) must have been higher after 1920 than before 1920 for all categories of capital objects. It seems natural to deduce from this that in the course of the period 1900–39 a gradual shortening of the 'normal' life of capital has taken place. We have therefore based our computations on the assumption that capital consumption as a percentage of the capital value has shown a linear rise over this period. In other words, we have assumed, for each kind of capital, that the capital consumption ratio p_t can be written

$$p_t = a + bt$$

where a and b are positive constants, and where t denotes the time. The magnitude t may assume values from 0 (in 1900) to 39 (in 1939).

We now have sufficient data to be able to determine the absolute magnitude of the capital consumption in each year and the capital at the beginning of each year. The procedure is as follows: It is possible to determine the constants a and b for each group of capital through the figures derived for the value of the real capital at the end of 1899, 1920, and 1939 and the capital consumption figures for the sub-periods 1900–20 and 1921–39. The capital-consumption ratios for each year then follow automatically from the above formula. But when the capital-consumption ratios are known and data are available for gross in-

---

[1] The straight-line method which was chosen for the present study requires the value of capital as new to be used as a basis for this distribution. Unfortunately, this could not be done for lack of data, and the method actually used must be viewed as an approximation to the former. It is justified in that the two methods will give identical results when applied to a stock of capital goods with a given age distribution. However, since the distribution by age of the various categories of capital cannot be expected to have remained constant over the period in question, the results obtained must be assumed to deviate somewhat from the values one should have got, had the straight-line method been strictly applicable.

vestments in each year it is a simple matter to compute annual capital-stock figures and annual capital-consumption data, starting from a direct estimate of the capital stock of one year, say the end of 1899.[1]

The computations for the post-war period are based on a form of extrapolation of bench-mark data for 1953. It is assumed that the capital-consumption percentages for the years 1946–56 can be determined through the same formula (with the same constants) as for 1900–39. Annual capital-consumption figures and stock figures for the real capital have then been computed as before, on the basis of these depreciation ratios, the already available annual investment figures, and the direct estimate of the capital stock in 1953.

Computation of employment data

For the period 1930–56, with the exception of the war years, annual employment figures in terms of man-years have been published in the official national accounts.[2] These figures are based on detailed computations for individual industries.

The employment data used in this article for the years prior to 1930 have a far weaker statistical foundation. They are not based on detailed computations for each individual industry. The data have been derived largely by backward extrapolation of the national accounting total for man-years in 1930. In the extrapolation the size of the working population, estimated on the basis of population censuses for 1900, 1910, 1920, and 1930, has been used as an indicator. A correction has been attempted for variations in unemployment, however. These corrections are based on data on unemployment among trade-union members.[3]

III. MAIN FINDINGS

The real capital data derived from the computations are presented in detail in the Appendix and in excerpts in Tables I–III below. Some comments on the figures are given in the following paragraphs.

---

[1] Capital consumption in 1900 is derived by applying the capital-consumption ratio for 1900 to the estimate of the real capital at the end of 1899. When gross investments for 1900 are known the size of the capital at the end of 1900 follows from this. With this as basis, the capital consumption for 1901 and the capital at the end of 1901 can be determined, and so on.
[2] See *National Accounts 1930–1939 and 1946–1951* (NOS. XI. 109) and *National Accounts 1938 and 1948–1953* (NOS. XI. 185), table 39.
[3] See *Statistiske oversikter 1948* (NOS. X. 178).

INCOME AND WEALTH

The growth of the total volume of real capital

The volume of capital has grown continuously since 1900, apart from the war period 1940–45. On the basis 1900 = 100, the volume of capital at the end of 1955 was 390 (Table I). This implies an average rate of growth of 2·4 per cent per annum.

TABLE I

Real Capital [1] by Type at the End of Selected Years

Year	Value of Fixed Real Capital Million krona in 1938 prices	As Percentage Value Fixed Real Capital at 1938 Prices				Index of Total Fixed Real Capital 1900 = 100
		Buildings and Constructions of General Government	Buildings and Constructions of Enterprises	Machinery and Transportation Equipment Excl. Ships and Boats	Ships and Boats	
1899	7,250	14·5	73·5	6·8	5·2	100
1905	8,075	14·3	72·3	7·7	5·7	111
1910	8,961	13·4	71·5	9·1	6·0	124
1915	10,550	12·7	70·7	10·2	6·4	146
1920	12,203	11·9	72·0	10·5	5·6	168
1925	13,351	13·2	70·9	10·1	5·8	184
1930	14,990	13·2	68·2	10·5	8·1	207
1935	16,319	13·6	68·4	10·9	7·1	225
1939	18,874	13·2	66·4	12·5	7·9	260
1945	16,461	15·5	69·4	10·1	5·0	227
1950	21,578	14·1	64·9	12·7	8·3	298
1955	28,284	13·0	62·3	16·7	8·0	390

The rate of growth of capital shows large variations as between quinquennia (Table II). The most rapid growth in real capital before the last world war occurred between 1910 and 1920 and in the years 1935–39. In both these periods the rate of growth was well over 3 per cent per annum. The growth was notably slow in the five-year periods 1900–5 (1·7 per cent per annum), 1920–25 (1·8 per cent), and 1930–35 (1·7 per cent).

Between 1939 and 1945 there was a decline in total real capital of some 13 per cent.[2] The decline was due not so much to the

[1] Structures and equipment only.
[2] This is a somewhat lower figure than that computed by the Central Bureau of Statistics in 1946. The Bureau at that time arrived at an estimated capital reduction of 18·5 per cent, but this estimate included inventories, personal furniture, and movables, where the capital reduction was particularly large (Statistisk Sentralbyrå, *Nasjonalinntekten i Norge 1935–1943* (NOS. X. 102), p. 159).

decrease in the number of capital objects as to the fact that the average remaining life of capital dropped sharply. This fact must be borne in mind in considering changes in the real capital volume in relation to the net national product (the capital–output ratio) from 1939 up to the first post-war years.[1]

TABLE II

Growth of Real Capital [2] by Groups. Average Rates of Growth for Five-year Periods

Period	Increase in Real Capital, Absolute Figure Million krona in 1938 prices	As Percentages of Increase in Real Capital			Average Rate of Growth, All Groups Per cent per annum
		Buildings and Constructions	Machinery and Transportation Equipment, Excl. Ships	Ships and Boats	
1900–05	658	71·0	17·8	11·2	1·7
1905–10	886	70·0	21·6	8·4	2·1
1910–15	1,589	74·5	16·6	8·9	3·3
1915–20	1,653	87·1	12·7	0·2	2·9
1920–25	1,148	87·5	4·7	7·9	1·8
1925–30	1,639	59·1	13·9	26·9	2·3
1930–35	1,329	88·0	15·3	−3·3	1·7
1935–39	2,555	64·2	23·0	12·8	3·7
1939–45	−2,413	43·6	28·5	27·9	−2·3
1945–50	5,117	60·0	20·9	19·1	5·6
1950–55	6,706	64·0	29·3	6·7	5·6

After the last world war the growth of real capital has been considerably stronger than for any other period in this century, viz. 5·6 per cent per annum on the average for the period 1945–55. It is remarkable that in spite of the capital reduction during the War we find the same rate of growth for the period 1939–55 as a whole as for the period 1900–39. The growth of capital in the years 1946–55 has, in other words, been sufficiently rapid to offset entirely the setback due to World War II.

Capital structure by type

The growth has not been equally strong for all groups of real capital. Estimated for the period 1900–55 as a whole, we find average rates of growth of 4·2 per cent per annum for machinery

[1] See p. 102.
[2] Structures and equipment only.

and transportation equipment (ships excluded), 3·3 per cent per annum for ships and boats, and 2·2 per cent per annum for buildings and constructions. To some extent the figures reflect the extensive mechanization which has taken place over the period in question

As a result of this there has been a marked change in the composition of capital. Buildings and constructions still represent the largest group, but have dropped from 88·0 per cent of total real capital (measured in 1938 prices) in 1900 to 75·3 per cent in 1955. In the same period the ratio for machines and transportation equipment (ships excluded) increased from 6·8 to 16·7 per cent and for ships and boats from 5·2 to 8·0 per cent.

The relative decline in the building and construction capital has been a stable feature in the development through the whole century. Only during the two world wars has there been a temporary increase in the relative importance of this capital group, and exclusively because the merchant fleet was substantially reduced through war losses.

The growing relative importance of machinery and transportation equipment (ships excluded) has also been a comparatively stable feature of the picture. Apart from a time of relative stagnation at the beginning of the twenties, it is only for the war years 1939–45 that the ratio for machinery and transportation equipment shows decline.

For ships and boats the trend has been more irregular. In this group we find periods of progress as well as periods of decline. The progress was most pronounced in the periods 1900–16, 1924–31, and 1945–55. There was an absolute decline towards the end of, and immediately after, World War I and in the period 1931–34.

Government building and construction measured as a proportion of total real capital has shown a slight downward trend through the period. The growth of real capital in this group has nevertheless been somewhat more rapid than for building and construction as a whole.

Real capital by industries

As pointed out earlier, it has not been possible to compute annual figures for real capital by industries, as pre-1930 gross investment data by industry are not available. Directly computed capital figures for the years 1900, 1939, and 1953, however, show the main lines of the development.

There has been increase in real capital within all industries, but the growth has been somewhat varied. The growth has been relatively weak within agriculture and forestry and housing, and particularly strong for mining, manufacturing, electricity development, and shipping.

TABLE III
Real Capital [1] by Main Industry Groups in 1900, 1939, and 1953

Industry Group	Absolute Figures Million kroner in 1938 prices			Percentage Distribution		
	1900	1939	1953	1900	1939	1953
Agriculture and forestry	1,112	2,090	2,382	15·3	11·1	9·4
Fishing and whaling	113	352	385	1·6	1·9	1·5
Mining and manufacturing	555	2,552	4,067	7·6	13·5	16·0
Electricity and gas	30	1,100	2,083	0·4	5·8	8·2
Dwellings	3,062	6,200	7,289	42·3	32·8	28·7
Sea transport	340	1,389	1,932	4·7	7·4	7·6
Other transport	446	1,418	2,038	6·1	7·5	8·0
Merchandise trade and services	540	1,281	1,815	7·5	6·7	7·1
General government	1,052	2,492	3,444	14·5	13·3	13·5
Of which: Highways and bridges	540	1,320	1,726	7·4	7·0	6·8
Total	7,250	18,874	25,435	100·0	100·0	100·0

The trend is reflected in the individual industries' ratio of the total real capital. For agriculture and forestry this ratio dropped from 15·3 per cent in 1900 to 9·4 per cent in 1953. (It should be observed that the figures do not include land and ground, livestock and standing forests. The relative decline would probably have been even bigger if these items had been included.) For housing there is a decrease from 42·3 per cent in 1900 to 28·7 per cent in 1953, or relatively a slightly weaker decrease than for agriculture and forestry. For all other sectors the ratio shows a rise or standstill.

The increase is particularly marked for electricity, mining, and manufacturing. For these sectors as a whole the ratio has trebled between 1900 and 1953, namely from 8 to 24 per cent. These

[1] Structures and equipment only.

industries accounted for almost one-third of the total net investment in the period. The growth has been most rapid in electricity, where the ratio advanced from 0·4 per cent in 1900 to 5·8 per cent in 1939 and to 8·2 per cent at the end of 1953.

Sea transport has also increased its ratio of the total real capital quite appreciably. The ratio rose from not quite 5 per cent in 1900 to about 7·5 per cent in 1939, a level reached again in 1953, when the effects of the tonnage loss during the War had been overcome.

The ratio has increased for other transport as well, viz. from 6·1 to 8·0 per cent. The rise is small, however (from 13·5 to 14·8 per cent), if capital of general government in highways and highway bridges is included in this group. The entire growth relates to highway and air transport, and post, telephone, and telegraph. The railroad ratio of the total real capital has remained unchanged.

For service trades other than transport the ratio has dropped. For machinery and transport, however, there is also a strong relative rise.

The data presented above on the composition of the real capital by industry and object do not alter the picture suggested by other evidence on economic developments in this century. It confirms the view that the most marked feature of the picture is the relative decline of agriculture, the rapid relative growth of manufacturing, and the exploitation of water-power as a source of energy. The relative expansion in sea transport and the increasing role of machinery and transport equipment compared with building capital are also points worth noting.

Relation between real capital, employment, and production

In the course of the fifty-six years under review the real capital in Norway has almost quadrupled. The average rate of growth has been 2·4 per cent per annum. In *per capita* terms the corresponding rate of growth has been about 1·6 per cent per annum. The tables give a strong impression of the extent to which the wealth of a modern society is a result of the efforts of the latest generation. About three-quarters of the real capital in existence in Norway today has been created since the turn of the century, only one-quarter is a heritage from earlier times.

The growth in employment has been considerably slower. The number of man-years in 1956 was only about 60 per cent higher than in 1900, corresponding to an average annual rate of growth of some 0·8 per cent. This, of course, means that production has become more 'capital-intensive'. In 1956 there was over 2·5 times as much capital behind each worker as at the turn of the century. The growth of real capital per man-year has been a relatively stable feature since 1900. It is only during the last world war and exceptionally in the 1920s that employment has risen more rapidly than the capital, so that the capital–labour ratio has dropped.

Production has risen more rapidly than both capital and employment. With 1900 = 100 the net national product in 1955 was 457. This corresponds to an average rate of growth of 2·8 per cent per annum, or 2·0 per cent if the growth is calculated per man-year and 2·0 per cent if estimated *per capita*. Thus, while production has undoubtedly become more 'capital-intensive' in the sense that the capital–labour ratio has risen, it has not also become more 'round-about', if by that we mean that the real capital represents more years of 'accumulated production' now than half a century ago. On the contrary, while the real capital expressed in fixed prices in 1900 represented about four years' national product, the average capital–output ratio in 1956 had dropped to approx. 3·3.

TABLE IV

Average Rates of Growth for Net National Product, Real Capital,[1] and Employment in Selected Periods

Period	Average Percentage Growth per Annum in Real Capital Volume	Average Percentage Growth Per Annum in Number of Man-years	Average Rates of Growth for Real Capital Volume per Man-year	Average Rates of Growth for Net National Product
1900–05	1·7	0·4	1·3	0·4
1905–10	2·1	0·8	1·3	3·5
1910–15	3·3	1·3	2·0	4·3
1915–20	2·9	1·6	1·3	3·1
1920–25	1·8	−0·6	2·5	0·4
1925–30	2·3	0·4	2·0	5·3
1930–35	1·7	0·9	0·8	1·3
1935–39	3·7	2·3	1·3	4·6
1930–46	−1·4	0·4	−2·0	0·5
1946–48	6·0	2·7	3·3	8·7
1948–51	5·5	0·9	4·7	3·7
1951–55	5·6	0·4	5·1	3·3

[1] Structures and equipment only.

98 INCOME AND WEALTH

The growth in the period 1900–56 has by no means been steady. Table IV indicates that there have been sharp fluctuations in the rates of growth of both real capital, employment, and national product. The table further shows that there is a comparatively high degree of co-variation between the three series. On the whole, we find that periods of rapid capital increase have also been periods of rapid growth in employment, and these are naturally also the periods when the rise in production has been greatest. Particularly striking is the co-variation between the rate of growth of real capital and the rate of growth of national product. It is worth noting, however, that the period following the last war is different both in this and other respects. One point often made is, for example, that the growth in the national product after 1948 does not seem to be in any reasonable proportion to the exceptionally rapid growth in the real capital in these years. In the remainder of this paper the co-variation between capital, employment, and production will be subjected to closer analysis.

IV. THE CAPITAL–OUTPUT RATIO

The idea of a constant marginal capital–output ratio

Studies from several countries, particularly the United States and Great Britain, have shown that a remarkable stability can be found in historical data in the relationship between the volume of capital and the volume of national product, totally or marginally. Sometimes this stability is interpreted as an economic law, from which the impression is gained that the size of production is determined by the volume of capital alone. Economic growth models of the Domar–Harrod type are examples of models which characteristically assume a constant marginal capital–output ratio.

It should be stressed, however, that *a priori* we have no reason to expect such a simple connection between increments in real capital and national product. On the contrary, production theory suggests that the marginal productivity of capital is not likely to be a constant, but a quantity which will vary with the size of the capital itself, as well as with employment and the technological level. Consequently, we cannot expect that a given increase of real capital will always lead to a proportionate increase of the national product, irrespective of what is happening to employment and to technology. Yet another argument may be added. Various kinds of capital will as a rule have different marginal productivity from a social point of view. The effects on the national product of a particular capital increase is therefore not independent of the 'mix' in which the capital increase takes place. 100 million kroner more invested in highways, for example, might lead to a different increase in the national product than the same amount invested in new housing.[1]

Against this background we shall in the following pages consider the actual trends in real capital and national product in Norway for the period after 1900. The main features are

TABLE V

Increments in Real Capital [2] and Net National Product for Bench-Mark Periods

(Figures in 1938 prices)

Period	Real Capital Increment	Net National Product Increment	Marginal Capital–Output Ratio
	Million kroner	Million kroner	$1 \div 2 = 3$
	1	2	3
1900–16	3,300	1,049	3·15
1916–30	3,950	1,326	2·99
1930–37	2,351	816	2·88
1939–56	10,136	3,199	3·17
1900–56	21,078	6,731	3·13
1946–51	5,126	1,767	2·90
1947–51	4,430	1,011	4·38
1951–56	6,741	1,230	5·48

illustrated in Graph 1 below, where correlated values of national product and real capital have been drawn for each year except the war years 1940–45 (the fine line). The graph should be studied together with Table V, where the increment in real capital and national product is shown for bench-mark periods.

The period 1900–39

For the period before the last world war real capital and national product have risen largely in step. This is particularly clear if we focus our attention on boom years in the period

[1] For an elaboration of this reasoning see Odd Aukrust, 'Effect of Investments on National Product', *Statsøkon. Tidsskrift*, 1957, No. 2.
[2] Structures and equipment only.

100   INCOME AND WEALTH

Growth of real capital and net national product 1900-39 and 1946-56

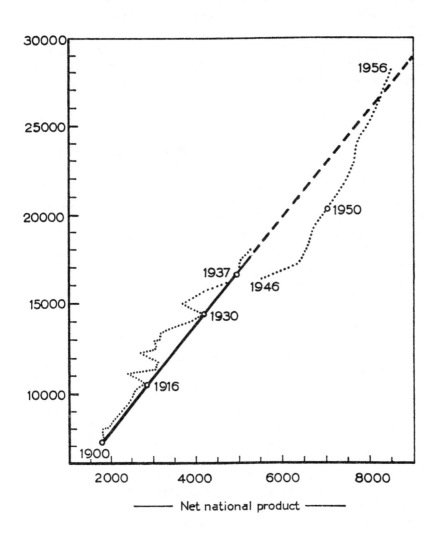

(which in Norway were 1900, 1916, 1930, and 1937) and disregard intermediate years when production capacity was not fully utilized. By and large, an increase in real capital of 300 million kroner (in fixed prices) has resulted in a rise in the annual national product of 100 million kroner, i.e. the marginal capital coefficient has been 3·0 for the period as a whole. This is shown by the fitted, fully drawn-in straight line in the graph.[1]

The graph further indicates that this ratio has kept remarkably constant in the different cyclical periods, measured from peak to peak. Table V shows that the marginal capital coefficient for the period 1900–16, was 3·15, for the period 1916–30, 2·99, and for 1930–37, 2·88. For the period 1930–39 it was 3·19.

But the graph also indicates that there are substantial year-to-year deviations from the straight line. It is justified to conclude from it that the physical production potentials were not fully utilized in inter-peak periods. The area above the fitted line thus roughly measures the 'loss in production' resulting from insufficient aggregate demand in the inter-war period. It is necessary to add, however, that not even in 1930 and 1937 was actual production capacity fully utilized, as there was extensive unemployment in both these years.

The period 1946–56

For the period following World War II the historical line has a course which on several points deviates radically from the trend before 1939. True, the marginal capital–output ratio for the whole period 1939–56 (3·17) does not differ much from the ratio derived for the pre-war period. But within this period the ratios shows substantial variations. Altogether, there are several features of the trend which seem peculiar: (i) There is a notable shift in the historical line between 1939 and 1945. Already in 1946 production was well above the pre-war level, despite the fact that real capital was considerably lower than in 1939. (ii) At the same time the national product showed a very rapid growth in the first two post-war years. For these years we find considerably lower values both for the average and the

[1] The line is a regression line for real capital (C_+) with respect to national product (Y_+), estimated on the basis of observations for 1900, 1916, 1929, and 1937. The formula of the line is $C_t = 3·00\ Y_t + 1,840$.

marginal capital–output ratio than those we know from the pre-war years. (iii) A change occurs in 1948. From then on the marginal capital–output ratio has been decidedly higher than in the inter-war period and at the same time increasing. It was 4·38 for the years 1947–51 and 5·48 for the years 1951–56, or 4·99 for the whole period 1947–56.

How are these facts to be explained? The most simple explanation is perhaps to regard the course of the historical line in the early post-war years as an 'accidental and transitory' deviation to the right from the underlying long-run trend, followed by a normalization, e.g. as a consequence of variations in total demand. This is tantamount to acceptance of the hypothesis that the long-run marginal capital–output ratio is a constant and suggests that for coming years we must again expect to find the value of the marginal capital–output ratio at around 3·0.

As we have pointed out on p. 98, however, there is no reason to expect the marginal capital–output ratio to remain stable over time, rather the contrary. In particular, we have to assume that this ratio will itself be a function of employment, volume of capital, and production technique. A more subtle explanation for the post-war trend than that suggested in the previous paragraph is therefore required.

The following factors provide an explanation for the shift in the historical line from 1939 to 1946: (i) Employment was somewhat higher in 1946 than in 1939. (ii) Parallel with the rise in employment there was an extensive shift of labour from sectors with low net product per man-year to sectors with high net product. (ii) It is probable that our capital figures, as computed, exaggerate the decrease during the War in the current production capacity of the capital.[1]

The low marginal capital–output ratio in the early post-war years can be plausibly explained as follows: (i) The capital increase in those years was accompanied by a very sharp rise in employment. (ii) The marginal productivity of capital was high, because the real capital volume per employed was lower than before the War. (iii) Simultaneously with the capital increase there was a rapid technological change. In 1946 the results of six to seven years of rapid development abroad were suddenly at our disposal.

It is more difficult to explain the high and rising capital–output

[1] Cf. p. 92.

ratio from 1948 onwards. It has been suggested that the investment structure may have had some effect, and that may be true. But the main factors appear to be the following: (i) The rate of increase in employment has been somewhat slower in 1948 than earlier in the century, and substantially slower than in the first two post-war years. (ii) Because of the high investment level in post-war years, real capital per employed has risen rapidly (from 12,000 1938 kroner in 1946 to 18,000 kroner in 1956). The marginal productivity of capital has therefore dropped. (iii) The decreasing demand pressure since 1950 has probably curbed the production increase. (This is the factor that was originally suggested above as the *only* explanation, but which we rejected as such.) (iv) Because the average age of the capital has been declining, its productivity has risen less than the capital volume, as measured in this study.

The explanation of the post-war development given in the preceding paragraphs contains quite different implications for the future than the simple explanation originally advanced. If we admit that the volume of production does not only depend on the volume of capital, but assume more complicated production functions, it cannot be taken for granted that the marginal capital–output ratio will drop again to its former level of about 3·0. On the contrary, it is quite possible that in the future we must again reckon with a ratio of the present order of 5·0 or higher. Whether the one or the other will be the case is a question of great importance for the future prospects of our economy. With our present net investment rate (15–18 per cent per annum) a marginal capital–output ratio of 5·0–6·0 corresponds to a rate of growth for the national product of 2·5–3·6 per cent per annum. A marginal capital–output ratio of 3·0 will with the same investments give a rate of growth of 5·0–6·0 per cent per annum. The difference is so great that further attempts to investigate the shape of the aggregate production function are well justified.

V. SOME EXPERIMENTS IN FITTING A PRODUCTION FUNCTION TO DATA

(a) *Selecting the form of the function*

Attempts to estimate relatively strongly aggregated production functions have frequently been made. The earliest and the majority of these experiments have concerned individual manufacturing groups or manufacturing in general,[1] but some have also been applied to agriculture.[2] A few studies have adopted production functions for the whole national economy.[3]

Most of these studies have used functions of the Cobb–Douglas type or variations of this. In its original form this was written as an exponential function of the type.

$$Y = AC^\alpha L^\beta \qquad . \qquad . \qquad . \qquad (1)$$

where the magnitudes A, α, and β are constants, and where Y, C, and L denote the production volume, input of capital, and labour respectively. In the early studies by Cobb and Douglas it was assumed that the sum total of the exponents α and β equalled 1 (which is tantamount to assuming that the production law has *pari-passu* character). The function above can then be written somewhat more simply, namely as

$$Y = AC^\alpha L^{1-\alpha} \qquad . \qquad . \qquad . \qquad (2)$$

where there are only two constants α and A. In later works efforts have also been made to estimate the constants α and β freely, i.e. assuming that the sum total does not necessarily equal 1.

The Cobb–Douglas function in its original form does not take into consideration changing techniques. This has been done in some later studies, where attempts have been made to allow for the effect of technological improvements by introducing a trend factor, while maintaining the general form of the Cobb–Douglas function. In his attempt to estimate a production function for the overall U.S. economy in the period 1921–41, Tint-

---

[1] The most well-known research works are perhaps those done by C. W. Cobb, P. H. Douglas, and a number of his collaborators. Cf. for instance C. W. Cobb and P. H. Douglas, 'A Theory of Production', *American Economic Review*, Vol. 18. Supplement 1928. P. H. Douglas, *The theory of Wages*, New York, 1934. M. L. Handsaker and P. H. Douglas, 'The Theory of Marginal Productivity Tested by Data for Manufacturing in Victoria', *The Quarterly Journal of Economics*, Vol. 52 (1937/38). G. T. Gunn and P. H. Douglas, 'Further Measurement of Marginal Productivity', *The Quarterly Journal of Economics*, Vol. 54 (1939/40). M. Bronfenbremer and P. H. Douglas, 'Cross-section Studies in the Cobb–Douglas Function', *The Journal of Political Economy*, Vol. 47 (1939). G. T. Gunn and P. H. Douglas, 'The Production Function for American Manufacturing in 1919', *The American Economic Review*, Vol. 31 (1941).

[2] G. Tinter, 'A Note on the Derivation of Production Functions from Farm Records', *Econometrica*, Vol. 12 (1944).

[3] G. Tintner, 'Some Applications of Multivariate Analysis to Economic Data', *Journal of the American Statistical Association*, Vol. 41 (1946), pp. 496–500. J. Tinbergen, 'Zur Theorie der langfristigen Wirtschaftsentwicklung', *Weltwirtschaftliches Archiv*, 1942, p. 509.

ner¹ used a relation which is linear in the logarithms to Y, C, L and in the variable time. Tinbergen's earlier work involved a production function of the type

$$Y = \epsilon^t C^\alpha L^{1-\alpha} \qquad . \qquad . \qquad . \qquad (3)$$

V. E. Smith [2] has tried to estimate the constants in a production function for the Canadian automobile industry in the period 1918–30 by the formula

$$Y = AC^\alpha L^\beta (10^{ht+gt^2}) \qquad . \qquad . \qquad (4)$$

For our purpose it is natural to regard the net national product as a function of the production factors real capital, labour, and 'technique'. We shall assume that the shape of the functional relationship is such that the three factors of production enter into it symmetrically in the same manner as in production functions of the Cobb–Douglas type. The factor 'technique' is defined broadly so as to include the general level of technical knowledge, the efficiency of management and workers, the industrial structure, etc. So defined, the 'volume of technique' cannot be measured, however, and for our purpose we shall simply assume that it can be represented by an exponential function e^{ht}, where t denotes time and h the rate of growth of the 'volume of technique'. The plausibility of this assumption is, of course, debatable. It leads to the following formula for the production function of the overall economy

$$Y_t = AC^\alpha_t L^\beta_t e^{t\gamma} \ [3] \qquad . \qquad . \qquad . \qquad (5)$$

which written in logarithmic form becomes

$$\log Y_t = \log A + \alpha \log C_t + \beta \log L_t + \gamma \log e \cdot t \qquad (6)$$

Here Y_t is the net national product in year t measured in 1938 kroner, C_t the real capital volume at the end of year t also measured in 1938 kroner, L_t employment in year t measured by number of man-years, and t the time measured with 1925 as

---

[1] G. Tinter, loc. cit.

[2] V. E. Smith, 'Nonlinearity in the Relation between Input and Output: The Canadian Automobile Industry 1918–1930', *Econometrica*, Vol. 13, 1945.

[3] We have $Y_t = AC^\alpha_t L^\beta_t (e^{ht})^\lambda$, where λ denotes the elasticity of net product with respect to the 'volume of technique'. Inserting the letter γ for $h \cdot \lambda$ we get the expression in formula (5) above. The elasticity λ cannot be estimated separately, since we have no direct estimates of the 'volume of technique' or its rate of growth h. The rate of growth in production resulting from improvements in 'technique', in which we are primarily interested, can, however, be ascertained by the estimate of γ which measures the combined effect of both h and λ.

base year. A, α, β, and γ are constants, the numerical value of which can be estimated on the basis of the available data.

A structural relationship of this type cannot be expected to hold exactly. We therefore choose to give it a stochastic formulation:

$$\log Y_t = \log A + \alpha \log C_t + \beta \log L_t + \gamma \log e \cdot t + u_t \quad (7)$$

where u_t is a stochastic residual with expectation zero and variance γ_u^2. If we assume that the variables are observed without measurement errors and that C_t and L_t are non-stochastic variables, the parameters A, α, β, and γ can be estimated by minimizing the sum of the square deviations on log Y_t in (7).

(b) *Computation results*

Estimates computed on the basis of observations for the periods 1900–39 and 1946–55 give the following numerical values for the constants in the production function:

est $A = \hat{A} = 2 \cdot 262$; est $\alpha = \hat{\alpha} = 0 \cdot 203$; est $\beta = \hat{\beta} = 0 \cdot 763$; est $\gamma = \hat{\gamma} = 0 \cdot 0181$

with dispersions for α, β, and γ of respectively

$$\hat{\delta}_\alpha = 0 \cdot 101 : \hat{\delta}_\beta = 0 \cdot 191 : \hat{\delta}_\gamma = 0 \cdot 0029.$$

If these estimates are used and the stochastic residual is disregarded the production function becomes

$$Y_t = 2 \cdot 262 \cdot C_t^{0 \cdot 203} \cdot L_t^{0 \cdot 763} \cdot e^{0 \cdot 0181 \cdot t} \quad (8)$$

Formula (8) says: (i) A partial increase of the volume of real capital by 1 per cent will, *ceteris paribus*, raise the national product by 0·2 per cent. (ii) A partial increase of labour by 1 per cent will, *ceteris paribus*, raise the national product by 0·76 per cent. (iii) With constant capital volume and constant employment the national product will, as a result of gradually improving 'techniques', increase at the rate of approximately 1·8 per cent per annum.

The values for net national product for the years 1900–55 which can be derived from formula (8) and the available data on C and L on the whole fit in well with the actual observations. Table VI illustrates this, showing the magnitude of the percentage deviations (without regard to signs) between computed and actual values of the national product in the years under review.

As will be seen, the fit is particularly good for the post-war period, when the deviations apart from 1946 in no year exceed 2 per cent. For the inter-war period, when the production showed sharp short-run fluctuations, the deviations are notably larger.

TABLE VI

Comparison between Computed and Actual Figures for National Product

Numbers of observations (years) grouped according to the size of the percentage deviations between computed and estimated figures.

Period	Number of years in the period	Of which with percentage deviations				
		Less than 1%	1·0–2·9%	3·0–4·9%	5·0–6·9%	7% and more
1900–16	17	5	5	4	3	0
1916–39	23	5	8	3	2	5
1946–55	10	5	4	0	1	0
1900–55	50	15	17	7	6	5

As we already have seen, the estimates for the dispersion of the parameters in the production function are in some cases considerable. In particular, the dispersion is relatively large for the elasticity with respect to capital. If a rejection region of 0·05 is chosen we cannot reject the hypothesis $\alpha = 0$. The other parameters are, on the other hand, with this critical region significantly different from 0.

An impression of the reliability of the estimates may also be gained by studying their sensitivity to the choice of period. In the table below the results for the whole period 1900–55 are compared with estimates computed on the basis of data for some part-periods. (The figures in brackets give the estimated dispersions for some of the structural coefficients.)

Period	$\hat{A}$	$\hat{\alpha}$ ($\hat{\delta}_\alpha$)	$\hat{\beta}$ ($\hat{\delta}_\beta$)	$\hat{\gamma}$ ($\hat{\delta}_\gamma$)
1900–55	2·262	0·203 (0·101)	0·763 (0·191)	0·0181 (0·0029)
1917–55	6·085	0·282 (0·105)	0·513 (0·193)	0·0198 (0·0028)
1917–39	0·045	0·719 (0·795)	0·619 (0·288)	0·0118 (0·0169)
1922–39	0·057	0·622 (0·645)	0·390 (0·263)	0·0160 (0·0130)

108   INCOME AND WEALTH

Some of the parameters are found to depend strongly on which period the computations were made for. Another general feature is that the estimated dispersions are much bigger when the observations, for the post-war period are not included in the estimates.

We may add that insertion in (7) of the estimates for the periods 1917–39 and 1922–39 gives a very poor fit for the post-war years. The computed values for the net national product which these estimates give are far above the actual (largely because of the high values for $\hat{\alpha}$). On the other hand, the fit is affected only slightly if the estimates for 1900–55 are replaced with the estimates for the period 1917–55.

(c) *Conclusions*

The computations discussed in the foregoing can be judged from two rather different viewpoints. First, they may be regarded as experiments in macro-economic curve fitting. Second, the computations may be viewed as an attempt to determine the constants in a macro-economic structural relation.

From the first point of view the computations are an example of how it is possible to arrive at a comparatively simple macro-relation which gives a good fit for a relatively long period for an economy like the Norwegian. The actual development of three macro-economic variables (net national product, real capital volume, and employment volume) and time has been found to be such that a Cobb–Douglas function with a trend component gives a very good description of the actual course of events in the period 1900–55.

If the computations are interpreted as an attempt to determine the parameters in a production function, the results assume an entirely different meaning. For in that case the computation results are supposed to *explain* the growth of net national product in terms of capital input, labour input, and technique, considered as independent variables.

A necessary condition for this interpretation is that the shape we have chosen for the production function can be given an economic justification. In micro-analysis we are probably justified in regarding production functions of the Cobb–Douglas type as fairly well-founded hypotheses on the production laws. Whether one can expect to find stable production functions of equally simple shape in macro-analysis is an entirely different matter. Even more fundamentally, this is a question which concerns not only the shape of the function. It also raises the problem as to whether it is at all possible to explain production trends in macro-analysis merely by studying changes in macro-variables, without specifying, say, in which industries such changes occur. The basis for much of the macro-economic analysis, however, is presumably that it is possible to disregard such changes between factors in micro-analysis. On this basis it does not seem entirely unrealistic to reckon with a production function in macro-analysis of the type we have chosen.

There is little in our computation results to indicate that such a macro-type production function cannot be a useful hypothesis, rather the contrary. It is particularly interesting in this context that the production trend in the post-war period, which so obviously contradicts the idea of a constant marginal capital–output ratio, seems to have quite a natural explanation in the light of the production function estimated from the observations through the whole period 1900–55. Nevertheless, we would warn against placing too much confidence in the value of the parameters estimated, for several reasons. (i) Our choice of function shape is rather arbitrary. In this study the main reason for this choice is that a function shape of this type has to a great extent common usage in economic analyses. (ii) Particularly dubious is the assumption that technique, considered as a factor of production, can be represented by a trend component of such a simple time shape as the one we have used. (iii) The estimates on the value of the parameters are based on the assumption that the volume of employment and real capital can be regarded as two non-stochastic variables, and this is probably unrealistic. (iv) Substantial margins of error must be allowed for the observed variables, especially the employment data before 1930. Moreover, our capital data apply to capital in existence, while in the product function real capital in actual use is probably the relevant variable. (v) Finally, we may add to this list that the estimated dispersions for the constants are relatively large. This also applies to the estimates which were computed on the basis of the observations for the whole period 1900–55. However, having stated these qualifications, we shall in conclusion venture to discuss some implications which seem to follow from our estimates.

(d) *An economic interpretation of the computation results and their implications*

The most striking conclusion that can be drawn from our computation results is that the role of capital as a production-increasing factor appears to be considerably smaller than generally assumed. On the basis of (8) we can derive the following general formula for the relationship between the relative increase in national product, employment, capital, and technique (time):

$$\frac{dY_t}{Y_t} = \frac{0.76}{(0.191)} \frac{dL_t}{L_t} + \frac{0.20}{(0.101)} \frac{dC_t}{C_t} + \frac{0.0181}{(0.0029)} dt \quad (9)$$

(Figures in brackets indicate estimated dispersions.) This means that: (i) An increase in labour by 1 per cent, with constant capital and with given technique, will raise the national product by 0·76 per cent. (ii) An increase in the capital by 1 per cent will, with constant labour and given technique, increase the national product by 0·20 per cent. (iii) The national product will have a tendency to grow at a rate of 1·81 per cent per annum even with unchanged labour and capital, simply as a result of gradual technical improvements.

If the formula holds, it permits us – for any period – to say something about the 'causes' of the percentage rise in the national product which has been achieved. For the period after 1948 employment has increased by an average of 0·6 per cent per annum and the real capital volume by 5·6 per cent per annum. According to the estimated production function, this warrants an annual rate of growth for the national product which may be computed thus:

Growth as a result of:
1. Rise in employment: 0·76 . 0·6 = 0·46 per cent per annum
2. Rise in capital: 0·20 . 5·6   = 1·12 ,, ,, ,, ,,
3. Improved technique etc.:   1·81 ,, ,, ,, ,,

Aggregate rate of growth   3·39 per cent per annum

The actual rate of growth in the period was virtually the same as indicated by the formula, viz. approx. 3·4 per cent per annum on average. Of this growth, only about one-third should therefore be attributable to the growth of capital.

This result should probably not be taken too literally, however. Even apart from the uncertainty connected with the constants in the product function (cf. the dispersion estimates), the interpretation of the trend component presents difficulties. In the foregoing we have assumed the trend component to represent 'technique' (in the widest sense) as special factor of production on line with labour and capital. It is certainly unrealistic, however, to assume that the rate of the technological progress is completely independent of the rate of increase in the capital volume. To put it differently, it is almost certain that the increase in the national product of 1·81 per cent per annum which has been ascribed to technique in the foregoing, would *not* have occurred without a simultaneous increase of the capital.

Even allowing for considerable margins of uncertainty for the parameters derived, they give a convincing explanation of the high and rising values which we found in Section IV for the marginal capital–output ratio for the years around 1948. If we transform the expression of the relative increments in formula (9), we get the following expression of the marginal capital–output ratio

$$\frac{dC_t}{dY_t} = \frac{1}{\frac{Y_t}{dC_t}\left(0 \cdot 76 \frac{dL_t}{Lt} + 0 \cdot 0181 \, dt\right) + 0 \cdot 20 \frac{Y_t}{C_t}} \quad (10)$$

The formula states that the marginal capital–output ratio varies inversely with the rate of growth in labour (dL_t/L_t), and rises with the fraction of national product devoted to investment, e.g. the net investment ratio (dC_t/Y_t) and the size of the average capital–output ratio (C_t/Y_t). For the years after 1948 the net investment ratio has averaged approximately 17 per cent, the increase in labour approximately 0·6 per cent per annum, and the average capital–output ratio approximately 3·2. This should, according to (10) give a marginal capital–output ratio of 5·12. The actual figure was, as previously mentioned, 5·13. (The close agreement between the computed and the actual figure is, of course, only a reflection of the fact that our production function fits so well with the data for the period in question.) With a net investment ratio of the order of magnitude we had in the interwar period, about 10 per cent, and equal conditions otherwise, the value of the marginal capital–output ratio would have been approximately 3·45 according to the formula. This puts an entirely new light on the trend in recent years. The high marginal capital–output ratio after 1948 is in no way 'contradictory to the experience of earlier times', on the contrary, it seems to have a natural explanation in our high investment level.

If the effects of a capital increase on the national product are as slight as our estimates suggest, it means that the chances of speeding up the growth in the national product by expanding the scope of investments are smaller than hitherto assumed. A transformation of the formula above gives us the following expression of the net investment ratio (dC_t/Y_t) which is required to achieve a given rate of growth for the national product (dY_t/Y_t) when the increase in labour (dL_t/L_t) is given and when the average capital–output ratio (C_t/Y_t) is also given.

$$\frac{dC_t}{Y_t} = \frac{1}{0\cdot20} \cdot \frac{C_t}{Y_t} \left(\frac{dY_t}{Y_t} - 0\cdot76 \frac{dL_t}{L_t} - 0\cdot0181 dt \right) \quad (11)$$

In the following table we have compiled rounded rates of growth for the national product derived from alternative assumptions for the net investment ratio and changes in employment. The table is based on an average capital–output ratio corresponding to the ratio in Norwegian economy today, namely approximately 3·40.

Net Investment Ratio (dC_t/Y_t)	Employment Increase Per cent per annum (dL_t/L_t)			
	0	0·5	1·0	1·5
	Rates of Growth for National Product Per cent per annum			
0	1·8	2·2	2·6	3·0
10	2·4	2·8	3·2	3·5
15	2·7	3·1	3·5	3·8
20	3·0	3·4	3·7	4·1
30	3·6	4·0	4·3	4·7

It is clear that the rate of growth of the national product is affected comparatively little by the level of investment. Without any increase in employment it is necessary to have as high investment ratio as 20 per cent in the next years to accomplish a 3 per cent growth per annum in the national product. If we reckon with an employment increase of, for example, 0·5 per cent per annum, a net investment ratio of 15 per cent (somewhat lower than the average in Norway in the last years) will give a growth in the national product of approximately 3·1 per cent per annum. To raise the rate of growth to 4 per cent would – if our computations are realistic – require a net investment ratio of no less than 30 per cent.

In light of the above, it appears that the rate of growth which can be attained in a society like the Norwegian depends to a much smaller extent than was hitherto believed on the investment policy followed. Whether the rate of investment within reasonable limits is high or low, the national product with constant employment will rise by 2–3 per cent per annum, largely because the technical factor alone automatically warrants a growth which here has been estimated at roughly 1·8 per cent per annum. The pace can be increased somewhat beyond this by maintaining a high investment level, but not very much.

If this is correct, it has obvious economic-policy implications. A stringent economic policy designed to maintain a high investment level becomes much harder to justify. One question which naturally arises in this connection is whether the trend factor here termed 'technique' in itself is an invariable or whether it can be influenced, for example by placing more emphasis on the education of efficient management, technicians, and workers. This is an interesting and important question. If the answer is positive, the low effect of investment suggested above gives a hint that a higher rate of growth could possibly be obtained, by releasing resources now devoted to investment for a greater effort in education and research, for example. However, to this the present study can provide no answer.

APPENDIX OF TABLES

TABLE I

Fixed Real Capital[1] by Type at the End of the Years 1899–1939 and 1945–1955

At constant (1938) prices. Millions of kroner

End of Year	Total Fixed Real Capital	Of which			
		Government Building and Construction	Building and Construction of Enterprises	Machinery, Tools, and Transport Equipment Excl. Ships	Ships and Boats
1899	7,250	1,052	5,351	472	375
1900	7,417	1,073	5,451	505	388
1901	7,583	1,093	5,551	532	407
1902	7,724	1,114	5,631	557	422
1903	7,840	1,131	5,695	578	436
1904	7,970	1,145	5,770	600	455
1905	8,075	1,156	5,835	622	462
1906	8,212	1,165	5,913	649	485
1907	8,395	1,174	6,024	689	508
1908	8,581	1,183	6,147	731	520
1909	8,746	1,195	6,260	770	521
1910	8,961	1,207	6,405	813	536
1911	9,239	1,224	6,580	860	575
1912	9,567	1,248	6,782	924	613
1913	9,905	1,278	6,994	991	642
1914	10,224	1,311	7,217	1,044	652
1915	10,550	1,336	7,460	1,077	677
1916	10,904	1,354	7,756	1,116	678
1917	11,098	1,370	8,026	1,145	557
1918	11,340	1,393	8,253	1,164	530
1919	11,745	1,424	8,507	1,228	586
1920	12,203	1,454	8,782	1,287	680
1921	12,403	1,506	8,909	1,278	710
1922	12,573	1,590	9,002	1,280	701
1923	12,804	1,671	9,136	1,300	697
1924	13,070	1,727	9,315	1,320	708
1925	13,351	1,769	9,470	1,341	771
1926	13,536	1,813	9,560	1,339	824
1927	13,736	1,856	9,674	1,354	852
1928	14,082	1,896	9,852	1,412	922
1929	14,500	1,939	10,037	1,500	1,024
1930	14,990	1,982	10,227	1,569	1,212
1931	15,317	2,030	10,368	1,599	1,320
1932	15,482	2,076	10,536	1,628	1,242
1933	15,662	2,116	10,702	1,651	1,193
1934	15,926	2,160	10,911	1,694	1,161
1935	16,319	2,214	11,165	1,773	1,167
1936	16,851	2,280	11,481	1,899	1,191
1937	17,564	2,365	11,814	2,058	1,327
1938	18,192	2,422	12,141	2,204	1,425
1939	18,874	2,492	12,528	2,360	1,494
1945	16,461	2,545	11,423	1,673	820
1946	17,157	2,614	11,781	1,788	974
1947	18,256	2,698	12,289	2,004	1,265
1948	19,311	2,796	12,802	2,240	1,473
1949	20,413	2,913	13,374	2,465	1,661
1950	21,587	3,040	14,006	2,744	1,797
1951	22,760	3,159	14,631	3,070	1,900
1952	24,051	3,287	15,327	3,483	1,954
1953	25,435	3,444	16,055	3,879	2,057
1954	26,868	3,636	16,776	4,337	2,119
1955	28,284	3,839	17,477	4,719	2,249

[1] Structures and equipment only.

TABLE II
Fixed Real Capital[1] by Industry and by Types of Assets at the End of the Years 1899, 1939, and 1953

At constant (1938) prices. Millions of kroner

Industry, Type of Asset	1899	1939	1953
Agriculture and forestry	1,112	2,090	2,382
Building and construction	1,014	1,880	2,043
Machinery	92	188	301
Transport equipment	6	22	38
Fishing	108	282	280
Fishermen's sheds, piers, etc.	23	49	42
Boats	60	185	185
Equipment	25	48	53
Whaling (boats)	5	70	105
Mining and manufacturing	555	2,552	4,067
Building and construction	332	1,277	1,902
Machinery, etc.	215	1,236	2,100
Transport equipment	8	39	65
Electricity and gas	30	1,100	2,083
Building and construction	21	900	1,718
Machinery, etc.	9	200	365
Business buildings (buildings)	454	930	1,250
Dwellings (buildings)	3,062	6,200	7,289
Shipping (ships)	310	1,239	1,767
Railway transport	378	964	1,343
Railroad construction	355	843	1,223
Rolling stock	23	121	120
Tramways, etc.	17	98	95
Tramway, etc., construction	14	79	75
Rolling stock	3	19	20
Road transport (transport equipment)	5	133	232
Air transport (aircraft)	—	3	20
Communication (building and communication installations)	46	220	348
Wholesale and retail trade	50	198	336
Transport equipment	8	50	86
Other equipment	42	148	250
Harbour construction	30	150	165
General government building and construction	1,052	2,492	3,444
Highways and bridges	540	1,320	1,771
Other building and construction	512	1,172	1,673
Other industries	36	153	229
Transport equipment	—	3	9
Other equipment	36	150	220
Total fixed real capital	7,250	18,874	25,435
Of which:			
Building and construction of enterprises	5,351	12,528	16,055
Government building and construction	1,052	2,492	3,444
Ships and boats	375	1,494	2,057
Transport equipment excl. ships	53	390	590
Machinery and other equipment	419	1,970	3,289

[1] Structures and equipment only.

TABLE III
Total Fixed Real Capital [1] and Net Domestic Product at Constant (1938) Prices, and Total Employment in Thousands of Man-years 1900–39 and 1946–55

Year	Total Fixed Real Capital Millions of kroner 1	Net Domestic Product Millions of kroner 2	Total Employment Thousands of Man-years 3	Average Capital-Output Ratio $4 = 1 \div 2$	Real Capital per Man-year Kroner $5 = 1 \div 3$
1900	7,417	1,821	977	4·07	7,592
1901	7,583	1,860	987	4·08	7,683
1902	7,724	1,882	993	4·10	7,778
1903	7,840	1,858	996	4·22	7,871
1904	7,970	1,850	999	4·31	7,978
1905	8,075	1,860	1,002	4·34	8,059
1906	8,212	1,931	1,005	4·25	8,171
1907	8,395	2,019	1,008	4·16	8,328
1908	8,581	2,085	1,013	4·12	8,471
1909	8,746	2,119	1,023	4·13	8,549
1910	8,961	2,213	1,027	4·05	8,725
1911	9,239	2,302	1,041	4·01	8,875
1912	9,567	2,406	1,055	3·98	9,068
1913	9,905	2,528	1,071	3·92	9,248
1914	10,224	2,589	1,090	3·95	9,380
1915	10,550	2,726	1,107	3·87	9,530
1916	10,904	2,870	1,124	3·80	9,701
1917	11,098	2,605	1,142	4·26	9,718
1918	11,340	2,455	1,161	4·62	9,767
1919	11,745	3,084	1,178	3·81	9,970
1920	12,203	3,171	1,202	3·85	10,152
1921	12,403	2,734	1,107	4·54	11,054
1922	12,573	3,037	1,122	4·14	11,206
1923	12,804	3,127	1,179	4·10	10,860
1924	13,070	3,099	1,201	4·22	10,883
1925	13,351	3,245	1,173	4·11	11,382
1926	13,536	3,241	1,097	4·18	12,339
1927	13,736	3,380	1,096	4·06	12,533
1928	14,082	3,573	1,151	3·94	12,235
1929	14,500	3,888	1,188	3·73	12,205
1930	14,990	4,196	1,187	3·57	12,628
1931	15,317	3,791	1,153	4·04	13,284
1932	15,482	3,999	1,178	3·87	13,143
1933	15,662	4,093	1,192	3·83	13,139
1934	15,926	4,253	1,213	3·74	13,129
1935	16,319	4,480	1,240	3·64	13,160
1936	16,851	4,808	1,276	3·51	13,206
1937	17,564	5,012	1,309	3·50	13,418
1938	18,192	5,102	1,330	3·57	13,678
1939	18,874	5,353	1,358	3·53	13,898
1946	17,157	5,555	1,394	3·09	12,308
1947	18,256	6,311	1,441	2·89	12,669
1948	19,311	6,567	1,467	2·94	13,164
1949	20,413	6,772	1,489	3·01	13,709
1950	21,587	7,073	1,499	3·05	14,401
1951	22,760	7,322	1,509	3·11	15,083
1952	24,051	7,629	1,522	3·15	15,802
1953	25,435	7,812	1,522	3·26	16,712
1954	26,868	7,915	1,537	3·39	17,481
1955	28,284	8,323	1,534	3·40	18,438

[1] Structures and equipment only.

TABLE IV

Fixed Real Capital[1] by Type for Selected Years

Current prices. Millions of kroner

End of Year	Total Fixed Real Capital	Of which			
		Government Building and Construction	Building and Construction of Enterprises	Machinery, Tools, and Transport Equipment Excl. Ships and Boats	Ships and Boats
1900	3,456	456	2,382	332	286
1905	3,559	484	2,398	352	325
1910	4,291	552	2,914	463	362
1915	6,855	770	4,566	778	741
1920	25,629	2,771	17,248	3,051	2,559
1925	17,108	2,142	11,932	1,962	1,072
1930	12,209	1,548	8,243	1,337	1,081
1935	12,800	1,656	8,675	1,509	960
1939	19,588	2,656	12,804	2,464	1,664
1946	32,802	5,113	21,830	3,506	2,353
1950	51,154	7,053	30,939	6,495	6,667
1955	90,763	12,753	52,169	13,874	11,967

[1] Structures and equipment only.

TABLE V
National Wealth of Norway at the End of the Year 1953
Millions of kroner at current prices

		Total [1]	Of which [1] Public [7]
A. *Enterprises*	total	89,700	9,767
I. Reproducible assets	total	86,655	9,767
1. Structures	total	45,977	8,203
(a) Dwellings [2]		22,013	..
(b) Agricultural		5,413	
(c) Other		18,551	8,203
2. Equipment	total	21,078	1,564
(a) Agricultural		831	..
(b) Other		20,247	1,564
3. Inventories [3]	total	19,600	..
(a) Livestock		1,300	..
(b) Other agricultural		800	..
(c) Other		7,500	..
(d) Standing timber		10,000	..
II. Non-reproducible assets, land	total	3,045	..
(a) Agricultural		3,045	..
(b) Forest		..	..
(c) Other		..	..
B. *Government* [4]	total	10,642	
I. Reproducible assets	total	10,642	
1. Structures [5]		10,642	
2. Equipment		..	
3. Inventories		..	
II. Non-reproducible assets, land	total	..	
C. *Consumer durables*	total	550	
1. Passenger cars and other vehicles [6]		550	
2. Other		..	
D. *Foreign assets*	total	−1,370	
1. Monetary metals		185	
2. Other net foreign assets		−1,555	
Total		**99,522**	

[1] .. Not available; not included in totals.
[2] All dwellings.
[3] Livestock and standing timber included.
[4] Only general government (military assets not included). For the distinction between general government and government enterprises and public corporations (which are entered under A. Enterprises, column public) see – *A System of National Accounts and Supporting Tables*, United Nations, pp. 11, 12.
[5] Roads, bridges, and public schools included.
[6] Only privately owned cars, wholly or partly in use for private consumption.
[7] Only government enterprises and public corporations, for a further explanation see [4].

[9]

Relative Income Levels in the Scandinavian Countries

By OLLE KRANTZ and CARL-AXEL NILSSON

I

Denmark, Norway, and Sweden all have national accounts that cover more than a century and that are, at least in principle, similarly constructed. The Danish series start already at the beginning of the 19th century, while the Norwegian and Swedish ones start around 1860. From the point of view of quality, the Swedish series seem to be considerably more uneven than the Danish and Norwegian ones.[1]

In at least two studies dealing with the economic history of the Scandinavian countries these income data have been used to compare the income levels in the countries studied. Both works form part of general surveys of Europe during the 19th century.[2]

Jörberg states that, by the middle of the 19th century, Denmark and Norway had an income level per capita that was about one third higher than that of Sweden. Around 1910, incomes in Sweden had apparently increased roughly to the Danish and Norwegian level (p. 376 ff, 387). From the growth series published by Jörberg it appears, however, that in his actual discussion he somewhat exaggerates the relative development of Swedish income, particularly in comparison to that of Denmark.

Milward and Saul have chosen the years 1911—15 as their starting point (p. 531 ff). In this period, they claim, the Danish income level was about 10 % higher than the Swedish one which in its turn, was about as high as that of Norway. The differences that can be observed in the rates of growth indicate that incomes had been higher in Denmark than in Sweden around 1870 and that Norway topped both Sweden and Denmark at that time. Milward and Saul emphasize the intricacy of income levels comparisons—the distribution of incomes and

---

[1] For our comparison of incomes, we use data about the GDP per capita. The terms 'income' and 'GDP per capita' are used synonymously and with no particular specification. The comparisons had been more meaningful if data about income per occupied person had been used. However, lack of sufficiently reliable occupation data prevented this.

[2] Jörberg, L., The Nordic Countries 1850—1914 (1970) in Cipolla (ed) The Fontana Economic History of Europe (1973), and Milward/Saul, The Economic Development of Continental Europe 1780—1870 (1973), cha. 8, The Economic Development of Scandinavia, in which the period up to 1914 is treated.

the development of prices may have been different in the countries compared.

In this study, we intend to clarify the problems involved in this kind of comparisons and to carry out an investigation resulting in—though approximate—better supported assumptions about relative income levels than is the case in the investigations referred to. We have also considered it convenient to see the patterns of change in a longer time perspective. The comparison has thus been extended to include the 20th century as well.[3]

When comparing the situation around 1870 with that of 1910, Jörberg appears to found his arguments on current price data. Milward and Saul draw on current prices to discuss the period 1911—15, but base their conclusion about the situation around 1870 on series showing the real rates of growth. Both Jörberg and Milward/Saul seem to suppose that the rates of exchange—1:1:1 during most of the period discussed—also reflect the rates of internal purchasing power.[4]

However, it is not possible, without qualification, to base comparisons on series in current prices. The relation between the countries, shown by these series, changes and is influenced by differences in the development of prices as well as by the fact that the patterns of consumption do not remain the same at different levels of income. It is, of course, only differences in real development that should be allowed to determine the changes of the relative level of income that are calculated.

Using series in fixed prices when describing the relative situation between one year and a reference period, for example 1911—15, the results will not necessarily be more reliable. The choice of a reference period determines the outcome and, consequently, has to be specifically ex-

---

[3] Problems arising in comparisons of incomes are discussed, for instance, by Gilbert, M., and associates, Comparative National Products and Price Levels, (1958).

[4] It should be pointed out that in writing this article we have had recourse to later and probably better national accounts series for Denmark (S. A. Hansen, stencil 1973) than Jörberg and Milward/Saul have had. The latter have used Bjerke, The National Product of Denmark 1870—1952, Income and Wealth, vol. V (1955), while Jörberg used Bjerke/Ussing, Studier over Danmarks nationalprodukt 1870—1950 (1958), (Studies of the Danish National Product . . .). As far as the rates of growth are concerned, these works do not differ very much. The levels, however, are different. For instance, the difference around 1910 at current prices between Sweden and Denmark is about 10 % according to Bjerke, 15 % according to Bjerke/Ussing and 20 % according to Hansen. As appears from what follows, these differences are only of marginal importance to the results that have been obtained in the present study.

It should also be pointed out that in this study we have made certain revisions of the Swedish national accounts series.

Cf. appendix.

plained. And, as we have already mentioned, rates of exchange are not necessarily relevant in comparing incomes.

The ideal solution would be to base an examination of the differences in income levels on purchasing power equivalents of each country and year. These equivalents ought to be taken from identical, actual budgets for each year and each country. In this way, these equivalents could be related directly to each year's income values at current prices.

If such a method is adopted, "the only" remaining problem is to select a country whose product mix could serve as a point of reference. That problem can be solved—as e.g. Kuznets has suggested—by consistently choosing the product mix of the country with the highest income level. The differences between the countries will thus be less compared to the opposite procedure.

II

In its main outlines, the pattern of change shown by ranking Denmark, Norway, and Sweden according to the size of per capita income during the period 1860—1970, is well established. At the beginning of the period, the income levels of Denmark, and Norway, with slight differences between them, are higher than those of Sweden. Denmark's superiority is based, primarily, on more efficient farming, Norway's on a larger and more effective shipping sector.

Primarily, the rapid growth of British industrialization during the first part of the 19th century affected the economies of Denmark and Norway earlier than that of Sweden.

During the later part of the period, at any rate during the 1950s, Sweden had the highest income level, while differences between those of Denmark and Norway remain very small. Sweden's superiority can be explained, above all, by the fact that Sweden's industry is larger and more efficient than that of the other two countries.

Swedish industry received considerable stimulus from the rapid industrialization of the Continent, by means of export of raw materials and semi-manufactured goods for further industrial use, as well as export of finished investment goods.

The pattern of change Sweden vis-à-vis Denmark is particularly clear. Before the first world war workers went from Sweden to Denmark where the real wage level was higher. It can also be shown that Danish capital and know-how were superior to Sweden's in many areas. One example of this is the fact that Danish merchants were responsible, to a certain extent, for the export from the south of Sweden during the 1860s and 1870s.[5] Another example is that still towards the end of the 19th century a certain amount of goods was imported to the south of Sweden via Danish trading companies.[6]

After the second world war workers moved in the opposite direction because real wages were higher in Sweden. Swedish capital and knowhow began to penetrate the Danish economy, particularly in the production of capital consumption goods and in the distribution of goods.

At the same rate that the Swedish economy developed faster than the Danish, the Danish crown fell in value in relation to the Swedish one. The rate of exchange was around 1870 1:1, in the 1950s it was 1:0.75 (Sweden=1). This is in agreement with the differences in price structure as a result of differences in the composition of export goods.

III

Continuous budget data about Scandinavian countries that would make it possible to draw up yearly purchasing power equivalents are scarcely available. A lot of research, in any case, would have to be done and still the results would probably be only rough approximations for long periods. In these circumstances, we shall have to resort to some sort of simplified procedure. And simplification must mean that we select one or several years as years of reference, and estimate purchasing power equivalents for these years. In doing so, as has been pointed out earlier, we must be aware that the choice of years will have great influence on the results. And the results can be very differing.

The procedure to be followed when one year or several years are selected as years of reference, is for the purchasing power equivalents of these years to be applied to the per capita product of the same years at current prices. We then obtain a ratio which indicates the real relation between the per capita products of the countries. This ratio is multiplied by an index of the per capita product at fixed prices during the remaining years of the period. The resulting figures will express the ratio of the per capita products of the countries during the other years,

---

[5] Nielsen, A., Den Skandinaviske Myntunion, 1917, (The Scandinavian Monetary Union), page 2 f. A certain part of Swedish exports from the Western side of the country was also organized by Norwegian merchants.

[6] Nilsson, C.-A., Järn och stål i svensk ekonomi 1885—1912, 1972, (Iron and Steel in the Swedish Economy . . .), page 102.

and the changes in the ratios will depend on the different growth rates of the countries.

This procedure also implies that the ratio of any year (the comparison year during the period) is determined by the purchasing power equivalents of the year of reference, by changes in the countries' relative price structures between the year of reference and the year of comparison and, finally, by the per capita income ratio at current prices during the year of comparison. The process, thus, consists in converting the purchasing power equivalents for the year of reference into purchasing power equivalents for the year of comparison, with the help of price changes.

Formularized, the procedure can be described in the following way where, for the sake of simplicity, only one sector is supposed to exist. P represents production per capita, E purchasing power equivalents, a and b two countries, f fixed prices, c current prices, r year of reference, and y year of comparison. The GDP ratio in index form during the year of comparison will be as follows, the year of reference being the base year:

$$\frac{\frac{P^a_{yf}}{P^a_{rf}}}{\frac{P^b_{yf}}{P^b_{rf}}} = \frac{P^a_{yf}}{P^b_{yf}} \cdot \frac{P^b_{rf}}{P^a_{rf}} \qquad (1)$$

The GDP ratio for the year of reference is

$$\frac{P^a_{rc}}{P^b_{rc}} \qquad (2)$$

The ratio of the purchasing power equivalents becomes

$$\frac{E^a}{E^b} \qquad (3)$$

(2) multiplied by (3) expresses the real ratio between the countries during the year of reference and this real ratio is multiplied by (1) to get the ratio between the countries during the year of comparison:

$$\frac{P^a_{yf}}{P^b_{yf}} \cdot \frac{P^b_{rf}}{P^a_{rf}} \cdot \frac{P^a_{rc}}{P^b_{rc}} \cdot \frac{E^a}{E^b}$$

Reformulating the expression we get the following result:

$$\underbrace{\frac{\frac{P^a_{rc}}{P^a_{rf}}}{\frac{P^b_{rc}}{P^b_{rf}}}}_{(g)} \cdot \underbrace{\frac{P^a_{yf}}{P^b_{yf}}}_{(h)} \cdot \underbrace{\frac{E^a}{E^b}}_{(k)}$$

The term (g) refers to the changes in the price relations of the countries between the year of comparison and year of reference, (h) refers to the ratio between the per capita incomes of the countries during the year of comparison at current as well as at fixed prices, and (k) to the ratio of the purchasing power equivalents during the year of reference.

IV

The method of simplification used in this study has been to estimate the purchasing power equivalents for the years 1873 and 1952. Starting from these years, we have then calculated separate equivalents for 1898 and 1927 as well. These four years thus constitute our years of reference.

1952

There is already an investigation of cost of living in the Scandinavian capitals for this year.[7] It is based on calculations of how much the quantity of goods represented by all the countries' budgets would cost in the different capitals. These sums of money can be used when calculating purchasing power equivalents, which, however, must be looked on as approximations and which are very likely to differ in some way from the "true" equivalents. The reasons for this are, first of all, that the investigation covers the capitals only, and so cannot be considered completely representative of the countries; and besides, it is likely that the extent of deviation from the results of a study based on each country as a whole is different for each country.

It is for instance, possible that the economic structure of Copenhagen differs more from the rest of Denmark than that of Stockholm does from the rest of Sweden. In the absence of a more detailed investigation, it is difficult to determine, with any degree of certainty, how this affects the purchasing power equivalents. What small corrections have been made below are based on assumptions and not on an actual investigation.

A second limitation of the possibilities of determining correct purchasing power equivalents is that the cost-of-living investigation only deals with personal consumption. In calculations of the kind outlined above, we ought to include purchasing power equivalents for at least the most important items of the GDP, i.e. public and private consump-

---

[7] Levnadskostnader och reallöner i de nordiska huvudstäderna, Nordisk statistisk skriftserie 1, 1954, (Nordic statistical review, Cost of living and real wages in the Nordic capitals).

tion as well as investments. For this reason we have had to resort to further approximations.

Certain items have been selected from the 1952 cost-of-living study which have been considered to correspond to public consumption and investments. Finally, the whole budget has been taken to correspond to private consumption. The purchasing power equivalents have then been calculated for the three GDP sectors with the help of the budgets of the three countries involved.

It seemed convenient to use a combination of purchasing power equivalents from the different countries. It appeared that in each country's budget there was some sector-equivalent which was quite absurd when compared to the corresponding equivalent in the budgets of the other two countries. Otherwise the differences between the countries were small within each sector, and one sector-equivalent could be chosen from each country.

The result of these calculations and adjustments was as follows:

Country	Private consumption per capita		Public consumption per capita	
	Purchasing power equivalents	In (a) Swedish (b) Norwegian currency crowns	Purchasing power equivalents	In (a) Swedish (b) Norwegian currency crowns
a) Sweden	100.0	3865	100.0	861
Denmark	99.0	3939	75.4	513
b) Norway	100.0	3710	100.0	677
Denmark	109.3	4350	87.3	594
	Investments per capita			
a) Sweden	100.0	1238		
Denmark	77.9	1110		
b) Norway	100.0	2341		
Denmark	118.1	1683		

	Sums per capita			
	In (a) Swedish (b) Norwegian currency crowns	In domestic currency crowns	Purchasing power equivalents	GPD ratio
a) Sweden	5964	5964	100.0	107.2
Denmark	5562	6085	91.4	100.0
b) Norway	6728	6728	100.0	101.5
Denmark	6627	6085	108.9	100.0

The ratio between for instance, Sweden and Denmark would thus be 107.2:100 and to obtain the ratios during the other years we should have to multiply the real per capita income index of these years (where 1952=100) by the figures just mentioned. However, the deviation of the economic structure of the capitals from that of the rest of the country can affect the result. We have assumed that the Danish capital has a higher concentration of industry than the Swedish capital. Therefore, the purchasing power equivalent has been decreased by 2.5 % in relation to that of Sweden. Denmark's purchasing power equivalent is thus 89.2, and the GDP ratio between Sweden and Denmark is 110:100. This is the ratio that has actually been used in the following calculation.

1873

During this year, all three countries changed over to the gold standard with 1:1:1 as the rate of exchange. Denmark and Norway introduced the crown as their monetary unit according to a relation between the earlier units and the Swedish crown which was roughly—but not exactly—the same as the rate of exchange prevailing up to 1873. At the same time, the gold standard was introduced with somewhat different relations between gold and silver in the three countries. The resulting exchange rates, thus, remained roughly the same as earlier.[8]

During the same year, the Scandinavian Monetary Union was founded, at first with only Sweden and Denmark as members; Norway joined the other two in 1876. The fact that Norway joined the Union somewhat later had no effect on the monetary system of 1873.

The official reports made when the Monetary Union came into being do not seem to contain any information that makes it possible to work out purchasing power equivalents. For this reason, we have assumed that the agio between the purchasing power equivalents and the exchange rates in 1873 were the same as in the early 1950s. Thus, for instance, the internal purchasing power of the Danish crown is assumed to be higher than that of the Swedish in 1873. This assumption is supported by the difference that can be observed in the relative price development between the countries as calculated with implicit GDP prices. The correspondence between the changes in the exchange rates and the changes in the ratio of prices is almost total.

---

[8] Nielsen, A., op. cit. page 18.

The result is the following:[9]

Country	GDP per capita		GDP ratio
	Purchasing power equivalents	In a) Swedish b) Norwegian currency crowns	
a) Sweden	100	302	57.6
Denmark	120	524	100.0
b) Norway	100	413	90.0
Denmark	105	459	100.0

1898 and 1927

It is, of course, not satisfactory to have only two years of reference at such a distance from each other as 1873 and 1952. For this reason, we have tried to work out purchasing power equivalents for two more years. Schematically, 1898 and 1927 have been selected, 25 years after 1873 and 25 years before 1952. The choice of the new years of reference can be defended from a factual point of view, too. The relative price development between the countries is such that all four years of reference have been taken from periods with relative price structures that are different.

The new equivalents have been derived from those of 1952 and 1873 with the help of the GDP deflators of the countries involved. This means that the new equivalents only approximate to the actual ones since the original budgets still form the basis of the constructions.

The new equivalents of 1927 produce income ratios between Sweden and Denmark on the one hand, and between Norway and Denmark on

[9] A simple comparison of prices has been made for the period 1871—75 and has shown differences in the price structure between Sweden and Denmark that support the conditions of purchasing power observed here. Two groups of goods were compared. The one contained grain, potatoes, peas, butter and pork. The other one comprised flour, pearled grain, sugar, coffee, and paraffin-oil, i.e. goods with a higher degree of refining. By measuring to a certain extent weighted averages of the prices of each group, the price structure of the countries was compared. It turned out that the price level of group two, as compared to group one, was about 25 % lower in Denmark than in Sweden. This result is consistent with the assumption that the Danish crown has a purchasing power that is about 20 % higher than the Swedish one. (Sources: Myrdal, G., Cost of Living in Sweden 1830—1930, London 1933. Pedersen, J., Petersen, O. Strange, An Analysis of Price Behaviour 1855—1913, Copenhagen & London 1938.)

the other, which in 1927 are somewhat smaller than if the original equivalents of 1952 had been used.[10] On the other hand, the new equivalents for 1898 do not result in any difference, compared with the results obtained with 1873 as the year of reference.[11] The results are summarized in the following tables:

Country	Private consumption per capita		Public consumption per capita	
	Purchasing power equivalents	In a) Swedish b) Norwegian currency crowns	Purchasing power equivalents	In a) Swedish b) Norwegian currency crowns
1927				
a) Sweden	100.0	1168	100.0	115
Denmark	119.8	1410	68.0	103
b) Norway	100.0	1139	100.0	134
Denmark	124.1	1460	102.9	156
	Investments per capita			
a) Sweden	100.0	192		
Denmark	117.0	299		
b) Norway	100.0	247		
Denmark	124.0	317		

	Sums per capita			
	In a) Swedish b) Norwegian currency crowns	In domestic currency crowns	Purchasing power equivalents	GDP ratio
a) Sweden	1475	1475	100.0	81.4
Denmark	1812	1584	114.4	100.0
b) Norway	1520	1520	100.0	78.6
Denmark	1933	1584	122.0	100.0

[10] It would have been possible to calculate certain purchasing power equivalents for a number of years in the inter-war period with the help of the purchasing power surveys carried out by the International Labour Office. These surveys are based on a common budget for a number of countries. (Data from these surveys are published i.a. in Sociala Meddelanden.) They refer, however, to a limited basket of goods—mainly food—and thus do not cover the same field as the 1952 survey. This is the reason why they have not been used instead of the 1952 figures. However, it can be noted that the surveys mentioned point into the same direction as the data used here.

[11] A price study, similar to that described in note 9, was made for the period 1896—1900. The

Country	GDP per capita		GDP ratio
	Purchasing power equivalents	In a) Swedish b) Norwegian currency crowns	
1898			
a) Sweden	100	399	59.2
Denmark	133	674	100.0
b) Norway	100	459	80.1
Denmark	113	573	100.0

V

The results of the calculations based on the purchasing power equivalents and the income ratios presented in the preceding section are shown in diagram 1. The Norwegian and Swedish income levels have been related to the Danish one since the Danish level is higher during the greater part of the period. The diagram contains four curves for Norway and Sweden. The years of reference have been used to represent the following periods of comparison:

1873:	1861 (1865)—1888
1898:	1884 —1912 [12]
1927:	1908 —1939
1952:	1935 —1970

During the 1860s and 70s the Norwegian income level was approximately 10 % lower than the Danish one and further decreased towards the end of the 19th century to a new and considerably lower level. From the first decade of the 20th century onwards, this trend changed and in the 1950s the Norwegian incomes are about the same as the Danish ones.

relative difference of prices between the countries had increased so that the relative price in Denmark for group two was about 40 % lower than in Sweden. This result is consistent with the supposed changes in the purchasing power condition between 1873 and 1898. Another comparison of prices for the years 1908—12 shows a return to the differences in relative price structure that was established for 1871—75. This is, in its turn, consistent with the supposed changes of the purchasing power relations between 1898 and 1927. This type of price analysis is less suited for the 1920s. The deflation following upon the war inflation had different paces in the two countries and the return to the gold standard came at different times.

[12] The curve with 1898 as base year corresponds to the preceding. Cf. p. 61.

Relative Income Levels in the Scandinavian Countries

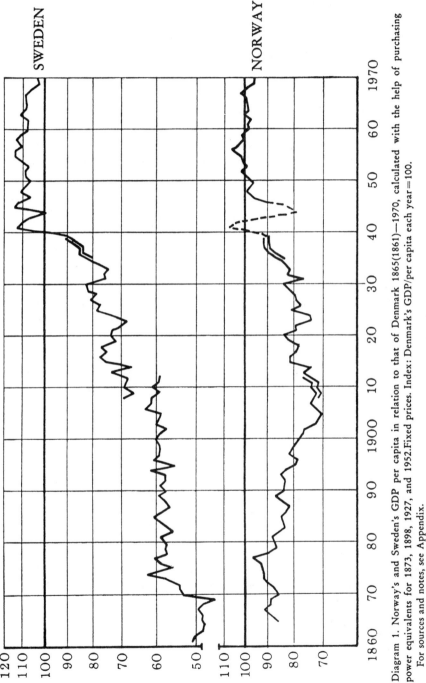

Diagram 1. Norway's and Sweden's GDP per capita in relation to that of Denmark 1865(1861)—1970, calculated with the help of purchasing power equivalents for 1873, 1898, 1927, and 1952. Fixed prices. Index: Denmark's GDP/per capita each year=100. For sources and notes, see Appendix.

The Norwegian income ratio shows a tendency to change by rather distinct stages. The decrease during the 19th century is concentrated to a few years around 1880 and a ten-year-period around 1900. The increase during the 20th century is irregular, but it is obvious that the Norwegian level increases particularly sharply during two short periods: the early 1910s and the late 1930s.

The Swedish income level in the 1860s was about half as high as that of Denmark. Then it increased compared to the Danish one and the Danish income level is definitively overtaken during the 1940s. It is possible that this trend ended towards the end of the 1950s when a period of very high growth rate started in Denmark.

It has been pointed out earlier (p. 53) that the choice of years of reference has a great influence on the results obtained. The comparison between Sweden and Denmark offers ample proof of this statement. If a year around 1910 had been chosen as the year of reference for a period covering 1895—1925, the curve would have shown that the distance from Denmark was considerably smaller around 1910 than what the curve for the period 1884—1912 actually shows. It is thus probable that the curves showing the relation between Sweden and Denmark during the 19th century underestimate the degree at which the Swedish income level has approached the Danish one.[13]

As was the case with Norway—though even more marked—we find a tendency of the changes of the Swedish income ratio to be concentrated to short periods. There is a sharp increase in the early 1870s,[14] and another one during the 1930s.

It may now be suitable to go back to the statements about income levels in Scandinavia cited introductorily. Our investigation shows a considerably greater difference of incomes between Sweden and Denmark around 1910 than Jörberg, and Milward & Saul estimated. This is the result, regardless of the years of reference chosen as our starting point.

It appears indirectly from the diagram that the Swedish income level does not attain the Norwegian one until the inter-war period. Around 1940, the Swedish incomes then definitively reach a higher level than those of both Norway and Denmark.

---

[13] Cf. also note 11.
[14] It is uncertain, nevertheless, whether the change 1870—74 really was quite so abrupt. The Swedish national product series for the 1860s is notoriously bad.

VI

We have considered it reasonable to add to the comparison of total incomes a comparison concerning total consumption only. Such a comparison provides us, of course, with better material for describing differences in standards of living. It also makes it possible to distinguish relative patterns of change in the relation between consumption, on the one hand, and investments/export surplus, on the other. The years of reference are, as before, 1873, 1898, 1927, and 1952. In the case of 1952 and 1927 we have used the equivalents shown on pages 58 and 61.[15]

The consumption equivalents for 1873 have been determined by considering their relation to the overall equivalents. The relative price development between consumption and the total GDP has determined whether the relation of the consumption equivalents to the overall equivalents is different in 1873 and 1952.

Compared to e.g. Sweden, prices in Denmark rose less, as far as consumption was concerned, between 1873 and the early 1950s, than they did in total. As a result, the purchasing power of the Danish crown in consumption increased, compared to the total purchasing power. Thus, the difference between the consumption equivalents and the total equivalent is less in 1873 than in 1952. Nevertheless, the price development was not such as to make the consumption equivalent in 1873 less than the overall equivalent.

The consumption equivalents for 1898 have been determined according to the same principles as were used in the case of the overall equivalents.[16]

---

[15] We have not considered it necessary to adjust the figures for the small bias caused by the fact that they relate to the capitals only.

[16] The following equivalents have been determined for Sweden—Denmark:

	Sweden	Denmark
1952	100	95.5
1927	100	114
1898	100	132
1873	100	125

The following equivalents have been determined for Norway—Denmark:

	Norway	Denmark
1952	100	105
1927	100	110
1898	100	113
1873	100	115

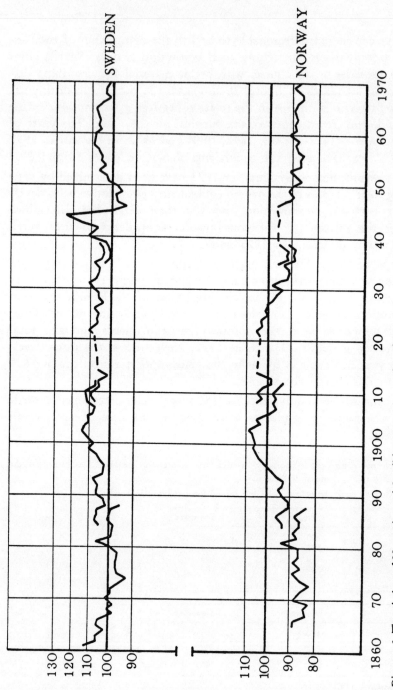

Diagram 2. The relations of Norwegian and Swedish consumption to that of Denmark related to the corresponding total income ratios 1865(1861)—1970.
For sources and notes, see Appendix.

In the case of Sweden's relation to Denmark, there is a marked tendency (see diagram 2) towards a more favourable comparison in consumption than in the total GDP. This is shown by the fact that the levels in the diagram surpass 100. The changes in the curve show the changes of the Swedish consumption ratio as compared to the Danish one. During an early period, up to the end of the 1870s, investments increase more in Sweden than in Denmark, as the downward curve of the diagram shows. The opposite is true of the years around the turn of the century. The great Swedish export surplus during the first world war takes the curve down to a lower level again. It is natural that the curve should fluctuate heavily during the 1940s. The war created an enormous Danish export surplus and was followed, first, by an increase of consumption in Denmark, then, during the 1950s, by an increase of investments.

In the case of Norway, the diagram shows a tendency contrary to that of Sweden. During long periods, the relation to Denmark shows a less favourable comparison in consumption than in the total GDP. This has to do with the well-known fact that the investment ratio in the Norwegian economy is very high.

Towards the end of the 19th century the Norwegian consumption ratio increased in relation to the Danish one. This was a period when investment activities were high in the Danish economy, and when the Norwegian economy, generally, showed a very slow rate of growth. When heavy investments increase in Norway after the turn of the century, the consumption ratio shows a pronounced decrease in comparison with the Danish one. This is a tendency that continues to the end of the 1930s, possibly with a break during the 1910s.

VII

Even though this investigation may not have established the exact income relations between the Scandinavian countries, it seems probable, however, that the relations that have been estimated between them here, are fairly reliable and likely. A more careful budget analysis for 1952 than the one used here cannot result in very different estimates of purchasing power equivalents. Furthermore, it is very likely that an investigation of the 1873 budget would result in equivalents and differences of income between the countries that do not differ very much from the ones given here. Finally, budget analyses for the intervening years would have to show drastic shifts in relative consumption patterns, if the results were to reveal relations of any considerable difference from those shown by this study.

Appendix

Sources

All of the series for *Denmark* are taken from Hansen, S. A., *Økonomisk vækst i Danmark 1720—1970*, (Economic Growth in Denmark 1720—1970), Bilagetabeller (stencil, 1973). In this work, however, the GDP at market prices is not included as it is in the Swedish and Norwegian series. Instead, we have the GDP at factor costs and "rådighetsbeløb", which is worked out by adding the import surplus to the GDP—or subtracting the export surplus—and by adding indirect taxes and subtracting subsidies. Thus, the "rådighetsbeløb" is the sum of consumption and investments. To obtain the GDP at market prices, indirect taxes minus subsidies have been added to the GDP at factor costs. The same result is, of course, obtained if the import surplus is subtracted from, or the export surplus added to the "rådighetsbeløb".

As to *Norway*, data for the GDP at market prices have been taken directly from the *Nasjonalregnskab 1865—1960*, (National accounts 1865—1960), (NOS XII 163), for the periods 1865—1939 and 1946—1960. For the period 1940—45 data have been estimated with the help of *Norges økonomi etter krigen*, (Norway's economy since the war), p. 57 (Samfunnsøkonomiske studier 12, Oslo 1965). Finally, *Historisk statistikk 1968*, and *Statistisk årsbok för Norge*, (Norway's statistical yearbook), have been used for the period 1961—1970. From these publications, population data have also been taken.

The *Swedish* series for the GDP at market prices have been taken from Johansson, Ö., *The Gross Domestic Product of Sweden and its Composition 1861—1965*, (Uppsala, 1967) for the period 1861—1950 and from *Statistiska Meddelanden N* (Statistical Review), 1972: 93, for the period 1951—1970. Population data have been taken from *Historisk Statistik 1* and from *Statistisk årsbok för Sverige* (Sweden's Statistical Yearbook).

Östen Johansson's national products computation series display certain obvious weaknesses.

The GDP calculations are only brought up to the total items consumption and investments at fixed prices by deflating with the price indices which are implicit in the calculations of production accounts. But the last step towards a total GDP series is not taken. Instead, this is obtained by a deflating procedure which is completely independent of the earlier calculations; to do this, the cost-of-living index is used. The GDP calculations at current prices are summed up by Ö. Johansson in two total series, one by sector of origin and the other by type of expenditure, i.e. consumption, investments, etc. However, it is only the first of these two series that is published at fixed prices, and both the total sum and the sector sums are deflated with the same cost-of-living index.

This does not seem to have been observed by scholars who have used Johansson's data to make special studies. For instance, one might ask how gross investment ratios may be calculated in a relevant way.[17]

---

[17] Compare for instance, Lundberg, Kapitalbildningen i Sverige 1861—65 (1969), in which such ratios are given.

It turned out—when we calculated the income relations between Sweden and Denmark—that when Ö. Johansson's series deflated with the cost-of-living index were used, the results for the 1910s and 1920s did not seem plausible. For this reason, the subseries by type of expenditure at fixed prices given by Ö. Johansson were summed up for the period 1908—1950. These series have been used in the present investigation, with a few adjustments of obviously wrong figures.

A corresponding summing-up for the later part of the 19th century turned out to be to a certain extent, less suitable, among other things, because the implicit consumption index deviated markedly from the cost-of-living index. However, from 1880 onwards, we were able to use the series at fixed prices given by Ö. Johansson. For the period before 1880 other deflators have been used.

The foreign trades series at fixed prices published by Ö. Johansson show such weaknesses for the period up to 1908—12, that they have been replaced by data from Fridlizius, G., Sweden's Exports (*Economy and History,* Vol. VI).

The revisions made of the Swedish GDP figures have only been discussed in brief outline here. We shall give a more detailed presentation of them in a forthcoming paper which will contain a number of other revisions as well.[18]

---

[18] In the present volume of Economy and History there are a couple of articles which criticize the present national product data. See Bengtsson and Johansson, and Holgersson.

THE DEMAND FOR MONEY IN SECULAR PERSPECTIVE

The Case of Norway, 1867–1980

Jan Tore KLOVLAND*

Norwegian School of Economics and Business Administration, 5000 Bergen, Norway

Received June 1982, final version received October 1982

This paper presents some evidence from Norwegian data on some of the long-standing empirical issues of money demand. The choice of a scale variable and the issue of simultaneous equations bias is subjected to some recently developed statistical tests. The outcome favours a permanent income model of money demand. No significant simultaneity bias was detected. Various specifications of explanatory variables, like the own yield on money, interest rates and price expectations as well as the issues of price level homogeneity and stability between subperiods are also considered in the paper.

1. Introduction

Ever since the appearance of the pioneering empirical work on the demand for money in the United States by Friedman (1959), Meltzer (1963), Chow (1966) and Laidler (1966), the determinants of the demand for money have been subjected to extensive empirical investigation in many countries. The sustained preoccupation with the properties of the demand-for-money function arises naturally from the strategic role that this relation plays in virtually all models of price and income determination. In addition, the demand for money is the key relation in the models within the tradition of the monetary approach to the balance of payments and exchange rates.

Laidler (1980, p. 221) has recently summed up the empirical evidence on the demand for money thus: 'As far as empirical work is concerned, perhaps the most striking development in the last decade has been the extensive analysis of data on economies other than the United States and the capacity of the basic hypotheses about the nature of the demand-for-money function, originally established utilizing U.S. data, to survive such extensive testing. The frequency with which a positive real income (or wealth) elasticity of demand for money, a negative opportunity cost elasticity, and a unit price level elasticity of demand for money have been found to be well-determined

---

*I am indebted to Stanley Fischer and an anonymous referee for helpful comments on an earlier version of this paper.

is quite remarakable'. But still, there are a number of unsettled issues, such as the choice of the appropriate scale variable, the role of the own rate of return on money and of price expectations as well as the stability over time of the demand-for-money equation.

The purpose of this paper is to present some evidence from Norwegian data, covering the period of 114 years between 1867 and 1980, on some of these long-standing issues of money demand. By using data that are constructed in a fairly consistent way over such a long period this provides a valuable test ground for an empirical analysis of the nature of the long-run demand for money in a small, open economy.

This paper is organized as follows. The specification of the basic model is presented in section 2. Section 3 contains a discussion of the choice of estimation method. Several alternative empirical specifications of scale, rate-of-return and price variables are considered in section 4. A rigorous test for simultaneity bias is carried out in section 5. Then the issue of the stability between subperiods is briefly considered. A concluding section contrasts the findings of this study with the evidence on the long-run demand for money from other countries.

2. The basic model

By now it seems to be almost universal agreement that the set of explanatory variables in a long-run demand-for-money function should include a scale variable, a set of opportunity cost variables, and possibly also a variable capturing the secular swings in velocity caused by the process of monetization and changes in financial structure. We now give a brief description of the variables contained in our basic model, leaving a more detailed specification analysis to section 4.

Permanent income is used as the scale variable in the basic model. Real per capita permanent income, y_t^P, is computed as a geometrically distributed lag on real per capita gross domestic product, y_t, with account taken of the trend rate of income growth, g_t.[1] Thus,

$$y_t^P = (1-\lambda)y_t + \lambda(1+g_t)y_{t-1}^P, \qquad 0 \leq \lambda < 1. \tag{1}$$

A grid search over the possible values of λ showed that a λ value of 0.97 gave the lowest standard error of the equation, but neither coefficient estimates, their t-ratios nor residual variance were particularly sensitive to alternative values of λ greater than 0.5 (see footnote 9 below). As discussed in

---

[1]The value of g_t was obtained by regressing the logarithm of measured income on time trends, i.e., $\ln y_t = \gamma_0 + \gamma_1 t + \gamma_2 t^2$. Then g_t was set equal to the estimated value of $d \ln y_t/dt = \hat{\gamma}_1 + 2\hat{\gamma}_2 t$, and the initial value of permanent income was computed as $\exp(\hat{\gamma}_0)$, where $\hat{\gamma}_0$, $\hat{\gamma}_1$ and $\hat{\gamma}_2$ denote the estimated values.

more detail below, the monetization process and other structural factors that impinge on the long-run demand for money are likely to be strongly correlated with the trend rate of income growth. Any failure to capture all such effects, even by introducing a separate explanatory variable as we in fact do here, may bias the estimate of λ upwards, so that y^P is getting close to a pure time trend. This particular problem, together with the general problem of autocorrelated residuals, is the reason why we would not expect the grid search method, or some more direct method of estimating λ by making use of the Koyck transformation, to lead to any reliable estimate of λ in this case. Therefore, in the regressions reported here, λ was set equal to 0.67, which is the estimate obtained by Friedman (1957) and later used in a number of demand-for-money studies.

The yield on long-term government and state bank bonds, RL, is considered to be the chief variable representing the yield on alternative financial assets. A variable measuring price level expectations, π^A, was also included as an opportunity cost variable. These were modelled according to the adaptive expectations formula

$$\pi_t^A = (1-\mu)\pi_t + \mu\pi_{t-1}^A, \qquad 0 \leq \mu < 1, \tag{2}$$

where $\pi_t = \ln(P_t/P_{t-1})$. P is the implicit deflator for gross domestic product. On the basis of a grid search in some preliminary regressions μ was fixed to 0.3 in the subsequent empirical analysis.

Over the past century the long-run course of the income velocity of money in Norway displays a U-shaped pattern, which is remarkably similar to the ones observed in many other countries.[2] Jonung (1978) provides an explanation of this empirical observation along Wicksellian lines, arguing that the downward trend in velocity in the first part of the period was essentially due to the monetization process, i.e., the spread of the banking system and the growing use of money for transactions purposes. On the other hand, the turn and subsequent rise in velocity in the interwar years must be ascribed to the increased financial sophistication as well as the higher security and stability provided by the modern welfare state.

Since such structural factors to some extent may be correlated with the trend rate of income growth, it is important to account for the separate effect of these factors in the demand-for-money function to avoid a serious bias in the estimate of the income elasticity. Following the suggestion by Tobin (1965), previous work on the long-run demand for money in Norway by Klovland (1978), and in Norway and some other countries as well by Bordo and Jonung (1981), has found that the currency–money ratio may be the best, although still far from perfect, empirical proxy for the secular changes in financial structure.

[2] Some evidence on this is presented in Bordo and Jonung (1981).

A three year moving average of the current and two past values of the deposit–currency ratio, DCR, was used to capture such effects. The results from the study of the short-run demand for money in the period 1925 to 1939 in Klovland (1982) indicate that this variable may also pick up the effect on the demand for money of the increased riskiness of bank deposits in the interwar period, which was due to the widespread bank failures at that time.

This leads to an estimating equation of the form

$$\ln(M/P)_t = \beta_0 + \beta_1 \ln y_t^P + \beta_2 \ln RL_t + \beta_3 \pi_t^A + \beta_4 DCR_t + u_t, \quad (3)$$

where M/P is real per capita money balances and u is the disturbance term. The data on the money stock and the long-term rate of interest are computed as annual averages of quarterly and half-yearly observations, respectively, throughout 1918; thereafter these are averages of monthly figures. The money stock is broadly defined, including currency and all unrestricted deposits with commercial banks, savings banks, and postal depositary institutions. The choice of a broad version of the money stock, which includes demand deposits as well as time and savings deposits, is motivated on two grounds. First, savings deposits have always constituted the bulk of bank deposits held by the household sector. Such deposits have essentially been withdrawable on demand during most of the period.[3] Second, as argued by Laidler (1980) in general terms, and indeed being confirmed by the historical evidence from Norway, the demand function for a narrow money stock is more affected by financial innovations and structural changes in the banking system.

3. The choice of estimation method

As is well known, the presence of serially correlated error terms is likely to inflict a serious downward bias to the ordinary least squares estimates of the standard errors. Moreover, although the OLS coefficient estimates are unbiased, their sampling variances may be high compared to those obtainable from more efficient estimation methods. Thus, the inferences drawn about the true relationship between money demand and its determinants may be significantly different when the equation is estimated by more efficient methods.

It may be argued that long-run demand-for-money equations are very likely to be plagued by autocorrelated residuals, because of the inherent difficulties in modelling the changes in payment patterns and financial

---

[3]In more recent years savings deposits accounts may be used for transactions purposes by means of the bankgiro system as well.

structure over time. This suspicion is indeed confirmed by an inspection of some of the early well-known long-run studies of the demand for money, which in general also failed to adjust their regression equations for serial correlation.[4] As witnessed by the recent reestimation by Lieberman (1980) of the influential study by Chow (1966) this failure may have biased the conclusions that were drawn from this important work.

However, some doubts can be raised as to whether the conventional method of correcting for serial correlation is legitimate in the case of the estimation of the long-run demand for money.[5] Most often, it is assumed that the disturbance terms u_t follow a first-order autoregressive process

$$u_t = \rho u_{t-1} + \varepsilon_t, \qquad 0 \leq \rho < 1, \tag{4}$$

where ε_t has the white noise properties.

Eq. (4) can alternatively be written as

$$u_t = \sum_{i=0}^{\infty} \rho^i \varepsilon_{t-i},$$

which makes it clear that the effects of omitted factors of the economic model, operating through the disturbance terms, are all supposed to decay exponentially with time and at the same rate.[6] This implicit assumption does not seem to be particularly suitable to such omitted factors as those pertaining to institutional features of financial markets and the secular spread of the money economy, which are obvious candidates in a long-run money-demand equation. On the contrary, it makes more sense to hypothesize that the possible effects of such factors will persist into the future without decay, causing permanent shifts in the intercept of the equation over time.

A procedure more suitable to the estimation of economic models subject to structural changes over time is the adaptive regression model developed by Cooley and Prescott (1973). The structure of the model is assumed to be

$$y_t = \alpha_t + \beta_1 X_{1t} + \cdots + \beta_\kappa X_{\kappa t} + u_t.$$

The special feature of this model is that the intercept, α_t, is subject to random sequential changes over time,

$$\alpha_{t+1} = \alpha_t + v_t.$$

---

[4] A tabular survey of the main results from some of these studies is presented in section 7.
[5] The following discussion draws on Cooley and Prescott (1973).
[6] Although the decay process may be more complex the same principle would apply to a second-order autoregressive process under the usual assumptions about the ρ's.

The stochastic processes, u_t and v_t, are assumed to be independently and normally distributed, both with zero means and variances given by

$$\text{var}(u_t) = (1-\gamma)\sigma^2, \quad \text{var}(v_t) = \gamma\sigma^2, \quad 0 \leq \gamma \leq 1. \tag{5}$$

The crucial parameter in this model is γ, which can be interpreted as measuring the importance of permanent relative to transitory changes in the intercept term.[7]

The results from applying the various estimation methods to our basic model on annual data from 1867 to 1980 (excluding the years 1940–1951) are given in table 1.[8] As was expected, the residuals from OLS estimation of the equation are strongly positively autocorrelated. The coefficient estimates, and, of course, even more so the standard errors, are somewhat changed when maximum likelihood estimation of the first-order autoregressive model (AR1) is performed. Since the Durbin–Watson statistic still indicates the presence of autocorrelation in the residuals, a second-order autoregressive model (AR2) is then applied. This method appears to remove the remaining serial correlation, while coefficient estimates and standard errors are not much different. Finally, in spite of the differences in the assumed error structure, the estimation results obtained with the adaptive regression model (ADR) are quite similar to those obtained with the conventional autoregressive models.

Accordingly, the basic results from estimating the money-demand function over this long time span stand up quite firmly against alternative assumptions about the error terms. In short, the main results are a permanent income elasticity of about 1.2, an interest rate elasticity of -0.3, and a semi-elasticity with respect to the expected rate of inflation of -0.7. In addition, the variable measuring the impact of monetization and financial sophistication, DCR, exerts a significantly positive influence, as expected. All coefficient estimates are quite precisely determined to judge from the high t-ratios.[9]

---

[7]Note that if γ is zero, all disturbances are transitory, and the model is identical to the standard linear regression model.

[8]The data from the war years and the first postwar years are excluded because of the rather abnormal economic conditions prevailing then, like the widespread rationing of goods, price controls and the freeze of deposits. However, the qualitative findings of this study are not substantially affected when data from these years are included, although individual coefficient estimates are somewhat different. The equation estimated by the adaptive regression technique over the full sample period 1867 to 1980 is (t-ratios in parentheses)

$$\ln(M/P)_t = \text{const.} + 0.396 \ln y_t^P - 0.159 \ln RL_t - 0.853\,\pi_t^A + 0.024\,DCR_t, \quad \gamma = 0.98,$$
$$\qquad\qquad\qquad (2.89) \qquad (3.19) \qquad (9.48) \qquad (2.16)$$
$$SEE = 0.0414.$$

[9]When $\lambda = 0.97$ is substituted for $\lambda = 0.67$ in the permanent income formula (1) the resulting coefficient estimates are: $\ln y = 1.205$, $\ln RL = -0.263$, $\pi^A = -0.634$, $DCR = 0.062$, with $\gamma = 0.98$ and $SEE = 0.0270$, when estimated by ADR. As can be seen from table 1, these estimates are close to those reported in regression 1.4.

Table 1

Demand-for-money functions 1867–1980 (excluding 1940–1951); various estimation techniques.[a]

Eq. no.	Estimation method	$\ln y^P$	$\ln RL$	π^A	DCR	SEE	DW	ρ_1	ρ_2	γ
1.1	OLS	1.243 (108.4)	−0.520 (13.46)	−0.184 (1.71)	0.121 (45.80)	0.0695	0.311			
1.2	AR1	1.219 (17.22)	−0.313 (8.06)	−0.658 (9.85)	0.064 (7.66)	0.0284	1.285	0.986 (58.78)		
1.3	AR2	1.220 (13.02)	−0.288 (8.13)	−0.720 (11.82)	0.051 (5.30)	0.0262	2.011	1.39 (15.32)	−0.40 (4.41)	
1.4	ADR	1.207 (12.97)	−0.309 (7.72)	−0.663 (9.70)	0.062 (6.92)	0.0289				0.98 (9.51)

[a] SEE is the standard error of estimate, DW is Durbin–Watson's d-statistic, ρ_1 and ρ_2 are the parameters of the autocorrelation process, and γ is defined in eq. (5) of the text. All equations include an intercept. Estimation of the AR1 model is done with the modified Cochrane–Orcutt procedure developed in Beach and MacKinnon (1978). The method used for the AR2 model is the grid search method described in Savin (1978). The estimates of ρ_1 and ρ_2 are constrained to lie within the stability triangle defined by $\rho_1 + \rho_2 < 1$, $\rho_2 - \rho_1 < 1$, $|\rho_2| < 1$. The method of estimation of the ADR model is described in Cooley and Prescott (1973). For all methods, except OLS, the t-ratios are computed as the ratio of coefficient estimates to *asymptotic* standard errors.

4. Alternative empirical specifications

4.1. The scale variable

Models of the demand for money in which money is held for transaction purposes imply that some measure of current income or bank debits is the proper scale variable in an empirical demand-for-money function. On the other hand, in models where the asset motive serves as the basic rationale for holding money, the empirical specification calls for a wealth or permanent income variable. Numerous empirical studies have attempted to discriminate between the transactions and asset demand approach by means of goodness-of-fit criteria from regressions with alternative scale variables but the issue does not yet seem to have been settled in this way.[10]

Table 2

Demand-for-money functions 1867–1980 (excluding 1940–1951); adaptive regression estimates with alternative scale variables.[a]

Eq. no.	Coefficient estimates with absolute values of asymptotic t-ratios in parentheses						
	$\ln y^p$	$\ln y$	$\ln w$	$\ln RL$	π^A	DCR	SEE
2.1	1.207 (12.97)			−0.309 (7.72)	−0.663 (9.70)	0.062 (6.92)	0.0289
2.2		0.652 (7.17)		−0.330 (6.17)	−0.694 (7.57)	0.040 (3.46)	0.0387
2.3			1.294 (8.97)	−0.328 (7.65)	−0.648 (8.87)	0.061 (6.29)	0.0309
2.4		0.220 (2.47)	1.089 (7.96)	−0.326 (7.81)	−0.666 (9.30)	0.062 (6.64)	0.0302

[a] All equations include an intercept. The adaptive regression parameter γ was estimated to 0.98 in all equations.

Table 2 sets out the results from estimation of the demand for money with permanent income y^p, current income y, and non-human wealth w, respectively, as scale variables. All variables are deflated by population and the implicit price deflator for gross domestic product. There are in fact no satisfactory data on wealth available, but a crude measure of total non-human wealth was obtained in the tradition of Stone (1964) by using benchmark estimates of fixed real capital and accumulation of private and public saving.

[10] Laidler (1977) gives a review of much of the relevant evidence. Lieberman (1979, 1980) has recently claimed that transactions variables, i.e., bank debits and current income, are superior to wealth and permanent income in explaining the demand for money in the United States.

We first consider the relative performance of the three scale variables over the full estimation period as reported in eqs. 1 to 3 of table 2. The choice of scale variable has little effect on the coefficient estimates of other explanatory variables, but the elasticity with respect to the scale variable varies considerably. On the basis of the standard error of the equations permanent income would have been preferred, followed by wealth, and then current income.

However, one may question whether such relatively small differences in residual standard errors provide any firm basis for concluding that any one of these specifications performs significantly better than the others. To obtain more reliable information on this issue, we suggest the application of two recently developed, and somewhat related, statistical tests for model specification. These are the J-test described in Davidson and MacKinnon (1981) and the N-test developed by Cox, Pesaran and Deaton. Here we give a brief outline of the steps involved in performing the J-test; for a description of the N-test see, e.g., Pesaran and Deaton (1978).

By computing these statistics one can test the validity of a regression model against the evidence provided by a non-nested alternative hypothesis. This use of the tests has to be distinguished from the procedure followed in pure model selection. In the latter case we are merely seeking to infer which of the two models is the better one. While the test statistics can also be used for model discrimination our use of the tests will be directed towards significance testing of the alternative hypotheses.[11]

Consider the two non-nested hypotheses

$$H_1: m = X_1\beta_1 + u_1 \quad \text{versus} \quad H_2: m = X_2\beta_2 + u_2,$$

where m is the vector of observations on the dependent variable, X_1 and X_2 are the matrices of explanatory variables in the two models, β_1 and β_2 the corresponding vectors of coefficients, and u_1 and u_2 the disturbance vectors. When H_1 is the maintained hypothesis, step 1 consists of estimating model 2 to obtain the predicted values $X_2\hat{\beta}_2$. Then the value of the J-statistic is obtained as the asymptotic t-ratio of the estimate of α from the regression

$$m = (1-\alpha)X_1 b_1 + \alpha X_2 \hat{\beta}_2 + u'_1.$$

The J-statistic can be shown to be asymptotically normally distributed with zero mean and unit variance when H_1 is true. The maintained hypothesis is then rejected if the value of the test statistic exceeds the critical value.

---

[11]For a further discussion of the difference between discrimination and significance testing see Fisher and McAleer (1979).

It is important to note in this connection that in testing non-nested hypotheses the acceptance or rejection of a specific hypothesis has no implication for the alternative hypothesis; the question we ask in these pairwise tests is whether the performance of the alternative model against the data is consistent with the truth of the maintained hypothesis. Therefore, we must subsequently reverse the role of the two hypotheses and repeat the test procedure. This can lead to either one, both or none of the models being rejected.

To avoid the problem that different values of autocorrelation coefficients or differences in intercept shifts do not make the models strictly comparable, OLS estimation was used, with the filter $(1-0.75L)^2$, where $LX_t = X_{t-1}$, applied to all data.[12] The calculated values of the test statistics are given in table 3. Hypotheses H_1, H_2 and H_3 correspond to permanent income, current income and wealth as scale variables, respectively.

Table 3
Calculated values of test statistics for the J-test and the N-test.[a]

Maintained hypothesis		Alternative hypothesis		
		H_1	H_2	H_3
H_1 (permanent income)	J	0.0258	−1.260	1.470
	N		1.270	−1.745
H_2 (current income)	J	10.733	0.0393	5.811
	N	−15.010		−9.094
H_3 (wealth)	J	11.480	6.539	0.0407
	N	−18.367	−10.645	

[a]The italic figures are the standard errors of the equation. The critical value is 1.645 with a two-tailed test at the 5 per cent significance level.

When H_1 is the maintained hypothesis, it is not rejected according to the J-test, neither when H_2 nor when H_3 is the alternative hypothesis. With the N-test the conclusion is the same with respect to H_2, but when H_3 is the alternative hypothesis the absolute value of the calculated N-statistic is slightly higher than the critical value from a two-tailed test.[13] On the other hand, both H_2 and H_3 are rejected against H_1 and also when they are tested against each other. Accordingly, there is fairly strong evidence against the models with current income and wealth as scale variables, while permanent income performs much better.

[12]This is the filter advocated by Sims (1972) in order to ensure that the residuals are approximately white noise.
[13]However, if the purpose were explicitly one of discrimination between the two hypotheses we would use a one-sided test. The critical value is then 1.96, implying no rejection of H_1 in the latter case either.

However, some empirical models of money demand use both current income and wealth as scale variables. The justification for entering wealth into an equation with income as scale variable might be to capture the demand for money arising from financial transactions. Alternatively it may simply be a recognition of the fact that money is demanded both for transactions as well as store-of-value purposes, and that the two variables are not equally efficient in accounting for both purposes.

Eq. 4 of table 2 gives the estimates of such a model including both current income and wealth as scale variables. The income elasticity is estimated to 0.22, whereas the elasticity of the demand for money with respect to wealth is 1.09. The coefficient estimates of both variables are significantly different from zero. The standard error of the equation is still slightly higher than that of our basic equation with permanent income as a scale variable. Once again, we suggest that a comparison between the two non-nested hypotheses H_1 (permanent income) and H_4 (current income and wealth) be made on the basis of the rigorous specification tests. When H_1 is the maintained hypothesis, the value of the J-statistic is 0.315. When H_4 is the maintained hypothesis, the computed value is 7.685. Thus, there is decisive evidence that we must reject H_4 in favour of H_1.

The outcome of these tests shows clearly that current income and wealth, neither alone nor combined, provide an adequate specification of the scale variable in our demand-for-money functions. On the other hand, the permanent income model stands out quite well in the light of the sample evidence and the alternative hypotheses tested here. We finally note that the specification tests provide quite unambiguous evidence on the relative performance of the various models considered here, even though the differences in the residual standard errors of the estimated equations appear to be relatively small.[14]

4.2. The own yield on money

Although a significant portion of broad monetary aggregates usually consists of interest-bearing bank depositis, few empirical studies have taken explicit account of the own yield on money. There are two main approaches to measuring the rate of return on money. The first one utilizes some weighted average of the actual rate of interest paid on the various bank deposit categories contained in the money stock.[15] Of course, in theory it is

---

[14]However, differences in the standard error of estimate are somewhat larger with the OLS-estimation on the prefiltered data, as can be seen from a comparison of the results in tables 2 and 3. The residual standard error of model 4 with prefiltered data is 0.0334.

[15]Artis and Lewis (1976) and Smith (1978) use the difference between the interest rate on alternative financial assets and an average interest rate paid on money in demand-for-money functions fitted to data from the United Kingdom.

the marginal rather than the average rate that should be used, but such data are usually hard to obtain.

The second approach is associated with the concept of the marginal return on money in a competitive banking system, as developed by Klein (1974). The major advantage of this measure is that it in principle includes the effect of explicit interest payments as well as the implicit yield on bank deposits due to reduced loan rates and service charges to depositors. However, the assumption of a perfectly competitive banking industry may be rather restrictive. Furthermore, as pointed out by Carlson and Frew (1980) this rate of return variable may perform seemingly well in empirical demand-for-money functions due to the fact that it is correlated both with the return on alternative assets as well as with the dependent variable itself.

Table 4 shows the results from entering both of these alternative measures of the rate of return on money into our basic equation. RMA is constructed as a weighted average of the rate of return on currency (zero), demand deposits and time deposits, with weights equal to each component's share of the money stock. From this gross rate of return is deducted an expected loss rate on bank deposits, estimated as a geometrically distributed lag on actual

Table 4

Adaptive regression estimates of the demand for money 1867–1980 (excluding 1940–1951); alternative specifications of rate-of-return variables.[a]

Eq. no.	Coefficient estimates with absolute values of asymptotic t-ratios in parentheses					
	$\ln y^P$	$\ln RL$	π^A	DCR	Other variables	SEE
4.1	1.207 (12.97)	−0.309 (7.72)	−0.663 (9.70)	0.062 (6.92)		0.0289
4.2	1.162 (12.21)	−0.233 (4.05)	−0.699 (9.93)	0.064 (7.17)	−0.058 ln RMA (1.83)	0.0286
4.3	1.186 (12.50)	−0.260 (4.34)	−0.686 (9.61)	0.062 (6.91)	−0.032 ln RMB (1.11)	0.0289
4.4	1.190 (12.69)	−0.276 (5.68)	−0.674 (9.80)	0.062 (6.94)	−0.024 ln RS (1.22)	0.0289
4.5	1.190 (12.63)	−0.273 (5.54)	−0.673 (9.73)	0.062 (6.81)	−0.031 ln RS + 0.010 ln RS^E_{t+1} (1.15) (0.37)	0.0290
4.6	1.218 (10.05)	−0.403 (8.05)		0.091 (8.32)	−0.293 π^E_{t+1} (4.03)	0.0376
4.7	1.161 (9.34)	−0.444 (8.94)		0.081 (6.87)	−0.237 π^E_t (3.21)	0.0386
4.8	1.244 (12.22)	−0.336 (7.74)		0.067 (6.93)	−0.567 v^A_t (7.88)	0.0317

[a] All equations include an intercept. The adaptive regression parameter γ was estimated to 0.98 in all equations.

loss rates. RMB is computed as a variant of the formula derived by Klein (1974), i.e.,

$$RMB = RI \cdot (1 - H/M) + RB_1 \cdot (B_1/M) - RDL \cdot (D/M), \qquad (6)$$

where H is the stock of high-powered money, RI is the yield on investment made by banks (proxied by short-term market interest rates), B_1 is those bank reserves which yield a positive rate of return equal to RB_1 (treasury bills which are eligible in meeting primary reserve requirements), RDL is the expected loss rate on bank deposits and D is total bank deposits.[16]

As can be seen from eqs. 2 and 3 of table 4 neither of these measures of the return on money met with any success in the estimation of the demand for money. Both variables take on a negative coefficient, contrary to a priori expectations. With a two-tailed t-test neither of them is significantly different from zero, however. It is likely that the positive correlation between the own rate variables and the bond yield accounts for the slightly reduced absolute value of the coefficient of RL and the small negative coefficients of RMA and RMB. However, attempts at alleviating the problem of collinearity by entering the yield differential instead of two separate rate-of-return variables resulted merely in a wrongly signed coefficient and reduced explanatory power of the equation. Similarly unsuccessful were several other regressions with alternative own rate measures such as the unweighted highest obtainable yield on time deposits and alternative estimates of RMB based on other measures of RI.

The complete failure of all of the own rate variables in the empirical analysis of the demand for broad money may seem somewhat surprising in view of the fact that explicit interest has always been paid on time deposits, and, during most of the period, even on demand deposits.[17] The results may suggest that these empirical counterparts of the true rate of return on money balances, as perceived by money holders, are rather poor. It seems reasonable to conclude that other factors than explicit interest payments may exert a major influence on the own yield on money. The modelling of such factors,

---

[16]The formula is derived by first defining $RMB = RD \cdot (D/M)$, where RD is the marginal rate of return on deposits paid by a competitive banking system. The major marginal costs associated with offering deposits are the interest foregone on the additional non-interest-bearing bank reserves B_0 and the interest-bearing reserves B_1, since the yield on the latter is lower than market rates RI. Thus marginal costs are $MC = RI \cdot (B_0/D) + (RI - RB_1) \cdot B_1/D$. By assumption, $RD = RI - MC$. By using the definitions of the money stock, $M = C + D$, where C is currency held by the public, and of high-powered money, $H = C + B_0 + B_1$, one obtains eq. (6) of the text by finally adding the term measuring expected losses on bank deposits.

[17]These findings are also in marked contrast with the results reported in Klovland (1982) which showed a strong positive influence of the RMB variable on the quarterly demand for money in Norway, 1925–1939. It appears that this period was rather outstanding as to the wide fluctuations in the effective rate of return to depositors because of heavy losses on bank deposits and the strong downward trend in the earnings of an impaired banking system.

like variations in the range of services offered to depositors and compensating balances requirements under a system of credit rationing, may be of importance if progress towards a correct measure of the yield on money is to be made.

4.3. The yield on alternative financial assets

During most of the period considered here long-term government and state bank bonds have been a relevant substitute for money holdings. The bond market activity was particularly significant during the interwar years, but ever since 1852 there was a market for state bank bonds. However, since the early 1960s the non-bank private sector's purchases of bonds have been small due to the interest-pegging policy of the monetary authorities.

On the other hand, there has never been any regular market for short-term financial assets like treasury bills etc. In the nineteenth century private bills drawn on Hamburg and London circulated among businessmen and were even used as a general means of payment to some extent; in more recent years private lending through non-bank intermediaries has grown in importance since bank credit has been rationed. Thus, although bonds were clearly the most important financial assets throughout most of the period, we cannot exclude that variations in short-term market rates may have affected the demand for money as well in some periods.

Recent theoretical work by Friedman (1977) and Fisher (1978) as well as empirical work by Heller and Khan (1979) indicates that the demand for money is affected by the whole term structure of interest rates rather than by one or two single rates. Accordingly, the classical issue in the money-demand literature of finding *the* correct long or short rate now seems to be less relevant. In principle, the demand-for-money function should include some parameters that sufficiently describe the yield curve as explanatory variables, but such data are only available for part of the period considered here. Instead we add a short-term market interest rate RS into the equation to summarize information on the short end of the yield curve.[18] As can be seen from regression 4.4, the short-term interest rate bears a small, negative coefficient, but the t-ratio is only 1.22. The coefficient of the long-term interest rate is slightly reduced in absolute value; otherwise the equation is little affected. This lack of significance of the short rate may be attributed to the institutional characteristics of the Norwegian financial system noted above, but it may also reflect the ambiguity of the direction of the influence

---

[18]The data on RS had to be constructed by splicing series of the most relevant short-run market rates that were available within each time period. These are 1867–1920, the discount rate on bills quoted by Bank of Norway; 1921–1959, the yield to maturity of one-year state bank and government bonds; 1960–1980, the implicit 3-month yield on Norwegian kroner calculated from the interest parity formula.

of short-term rates on the demand for money that appears in the models developed by Friedman (1977) and Fisher (1978).

In the model considered by Fisher (1978) an *expected* rate of interest exerts a *positive* influence on the demand for money. To investigate the empirical evidence on this specification, a time series of expected short-term interest rates in the next period, RS^E_{t+1}, was constructed by running least-squares regressions of the actual rate, RS_t, on five lagged values in several subperiods,

$$RS_t = \theta_0 + \sum_{i=1}^{5} \theta_i RS_{t-i},$$

and using the estimated parameters to compute $RS^E_{t+1} = \widehat{RS}_{t+1}$. It appears from eq. 4.5 that the coefficient of $\ln RS^E_{t+1}$ is positive, but of a very small magnitude, and very far from being significantly different from zero.[19] Thus, neither the short-run interest rate nor its expected value in the next period performs particularly well in the long-run demand-for-money equation considered here.

4.4. Inflation expectations

Our basic equation, reprinted for convenience in the first line of table 4, makes use of the conventional adaptive expectations formula, which can be derived from a distributed lag scheme with geometrically declining weights, i.e.,

$$\pi_t^A = (1-\mu) \sum_{i=0}^{\infty} \mu^i \pi_{t-i}, \qquad (7)$$

where π_t is the actual inflation rate in period t and where μ was set equal to 0.3 in the empirical application.

We now briefly consider two variants of an alternative to (7). Instead of restricting the lag weights a priori these were obtained by regressing the actual inflation rate on five lagged values, to obtain the predicted rate of inflation,[20]

$$\pi_t = \mu_0 + \sum_{i=1}^{5} \mu_i \pi_{t-i}. \qquad (8)$$

---

[19]The same qualitative results were obtained in regressions that also included the alternative own rate variables.

[20]Separate regressions were run for the periods 1867–1914, 1915–1939 and 1952–1980, since they differ with respect to exchange rate regimes.

In the last subperiod the rate of change in the implicit price deflator for the United States' GNP was substituted for the corresponding domestic variables as explanatory variables.

An estimate of next period's inflation rate is then computed as $\pi^E_{t+1} = \hat{\pi}_{t+1}$. Alternatively, we use the expectations formula for this period's inflation rate, $\pi^E_t = \hat{\pi}_t$. The latter measure may perhaps be rationalized on the grounds that there is an information lag on actual price changes to the public, so that it is only past values of inflation that are of relevance to this period's desired real money balances. Finally, we follow Friedman and Schwartz[21] in using the expected rate of change of nominal income, v^A_t, as a measure of the expected yield on physical assets. This variable was constructed in an analogous way to (7), with $\mu = 0.4$.

It appears from the results reported in eqs. 4.6 to 4.8 that all these measures exert a significantly negative influence on the demand for money. But all are inferior to the adaptive expectations measure π^A_t in terms of residual variance of the equation.

In sum, these results based on alternative expectations mechanisms corroborate our findings that inflation expectations exert a significantly negative influence on the demand for money. While the menu of expectations formulae presented here is rather small, it should be noted that it includes both the conventional adaptive expectations mechanism and a variant of Sargent's (1973) 'partly rational' expectations, which utilizes information on the past history of price level changes only.

4.5. Homogeneity with respect to the price level

The logarithm of the price level was added as an explanatory variable to our basic equation to test whether the real per capita demand for money is homogeneous of degree zero in the price level. For the whole sample period the estimated coefficient of $\ln P$ was 0.149, with a 95 per cent confidence interval ranging from 0.079 to 0.219. Similar point estimates were obtained for several subperiods. Thus, somewhat surprisingly the hypothesis of a unitary elasticity of nominal money demand with respect to prices seems to be rejected.

This result might, however, also be due to statistical problems. One such problem is the collinearity between money balances, the price level and real income, which all exhibit a strong positive time trend. Another problem may be connected with the short-run dynamics of the adjustment of real money balances to a changing price level. A regression model that may go some way in alleviating these problems is the error correction mechanism advocated by

---

Regressions on the domestic values resulted in a $F_{5,24}$-value of only 1.09, which is not significantly different from zero at the 5% level. One reason for the superior performance of the US inflation rate, intended as a proxy for the world inflation rate, may be the extensive use of price controls in Norway, which may have severely distorted the extraction of information on the underlying inflation rate contained in the past values of domestic inflation rates.

[21] See Schwartz (1975).

Hendry (1979). When estimated by ordinary least squares over the whole sample period, excluding 1940–1951, the resulting estimates were (where $\Delta x_t = x_t - x_{t-1}$)

$$\Delta \ln\left(\frac{M}{P}\right)_t = -0.961 + 0.232\,\Delta \ln y_t - 0.241\,\Delta \ln r_t - 0.443\,\Delta \ln P_t$$
$$\quad\quad (3.78)\quad (2.70)\quad\quad\quad (5.36)\quad\quad\quad\quad (8.67)$$

$$+0.419\,\Delta \ln P_{t-1} + 0.087\,\Delta DCR_t - 0.149\,\ln\left(\frac{M}{P}\right)_{t-1}$$
$$\quad (8.57)\quad\quad\quad\quad (8.24)\quad\quad\quad (3.51)$$

$$+0.180 \ln y_{t-1} - 0.084 \ln r_{t-1} + 0.019\,DCR_{t-1} + 0.009 \ln P_{t-1},$$
$$\quad (3.84)\quad\quad\quad (2.47)\quad\quad\quad (3.54)\quad\quad\quad (0.58)$$
$$\tag{9}$$

where $R^2 = 0.799$, $SEE = 0.0256$ and $DW = 1.626$.

In (9) the coefficient estimate of $\ln P_{t-1}$ takes on a small positive value, but it is no longer significantly different from zero. Accordingly, our previous conclusion that the zero homogeneity of the demand for real balances with respect to the price level should be rejected is no longer supported by the data.

The steady-state solution to (9), assuming that $\Delta \ln y = \Delta \ln r = \Delta DCR = 0$, and that $\Delta \ln P = \pi$, is[22]

$$\ln(M/P) = \text{const.} + 1.208 \ln y - 0.566 \ln r - 0.570\pi + 0.127 DCR$$
$$+ 0.061 \ln P. \tag{10}$$

These estimates are fairly close to the direct estimates of the equilibrium equation reported above in regression 4.1, providing additional support for our conclusion that the estimated long-run coefficients are quite robust to alternative methods of estimation.

5. Testing for simultaneity bias

If the rate of interest or other explanatory variables in the demand-for-money function are correlated with the error term of the estimating equation, the OLS estimates of the coefficients will be biased. In estimating the demand for money with single-equation techniques one should of course investigate whether this potential simultaneity bias is significant. This consideration is,

---

[22] The method of solution is explained in Currie (1981).

however, often neglected in empirical work; at best, some informal comparisons between ordinary least squares (OLS) and instrumental variable (IV) estimates of the coefficients are made.

In this paper the issue of simultaneity bias will be rigorously tested by means of a test statistic for specification errors recently developed by Hausman (1978). Denoting the OLS and IV estimates of the coefficient vector by $\hat{\beta}_0$ and $\hat{\beta}_1$, and their variance–covariance matrices by $V(\hat{\beta}_0)$ and $V(\hat{\beta}_1)$, respectively, it can be shown that the test statistic m, defined by

$$m = (\hat{\beta}_1 - \hat{\beta}_0)'[V(\hat{\beta}_1) - V(\hat{\beta}_0)]^{-1}(\hat{\beta}_1 - \hat{\beta}_0), \tag{11}$$

is asymptotically distributed as χ^2 with degrees of freedom equal to the number of variables in the estimating equation. If $(\hat{\beta}_1 - \hat{\beta}_0)$ is large relative to its variance, the null hypothesis of no specification error will be rejected.

In order to make the OLS and IV estimates of the same equation strictly comparable, and also to cope with the problem of autocorrelated residuals, the data were prewhitened with the same filter as before, $(1 - 0.75L)^2$. As can be seen from the Durbin–Watson statistics reported in table 5, this filter removes most, if not all, autocorrelation in the residuals.[23]

In the instrumental variable estimation all explanatory variables were treated as endogenous. As instruments were used the current and lagged values of a series of foreign bond yields, lagged values of the central bank discount rate for bills, population and all explanatory variables lagged once.

The results are set out in table 5. Inspection of the coefficient estimates reveals that there is in most cases little difference between the outcome of the two estimation methods. One exception is the permanent income elasticity in the subperiods 1867–1913 and 1914–1939. Also the OLS and IV coefficient estimates of DCR in the first subperiod differ quite much. Once again these results are a reminder of the difficulty of pinning down the true income elasticity of the demand for money in a time period of great changes in the financial system.

However, in none of the five time periods is the value of the m-statistic greater than its critical value, which is 9.49 at a 5 per cent significance level. Consequently, the hypothesis of specification error due to simultaneity problems can be rejected. This conclusion is in line with the evidence from informal comparisons of OLS and IV estimates of the demand for money made by Goldfeld (1973) and numerous other researchers.[24]

---

[23]The Durbin–Watson d-statistic is in the indeterminate range for all OLS subperiod regressions. An exact test would reject the hypothesis of no serial correlation at the lowest significance level, 3.6 per cent, in the case of the 1914–1939 period.

[24]The formal analysis of the extent of simultaneity bias in the Canadian short-run demand for money by Gregory and McAleer (1981) also concluded that the simultaneity bias was statistically insignificant.

Table 5

Demand-for-money functions, various periods; ordinary least squares and instrumental variable estimates with prefiltered data.[a]

Time period	Estimation method	Coefficient estimates with absolute values of t-ratios in parentheses							
		$\ln y^P$	$\ln RL$	π^A	DCR	SEE	F	DW	m
1867–1980 (excluding 1940–1951)	OLS	1.111 (20.68)	−0.209 (5.21)	−0.780 (13.18)	0.082 (7.76)	0.0258	187.60	2.217 [n.a.]	
	IV	1.124 (18.43)	−0.164 (2.33)	−0.934 (4.63)	0.089 (4.28)	0.0269		2.242	1.490
1867–1913	OLS	1.829 (6.86)	−0.369 (3.75)	−0.678 (7.15)	0.048 (2.89)	0.0194	39.08	2.309 [0.8123]	
	IV	1.299 (2.94)	−0.332 (1.94)	−0.967 (3.94)	0.092 (3.09)	0.0236		2.191	4.672
1914–1939	OLS	0.488 (1.26)	−0.197 (2.28)	−0.779 (6.47)	0.069 (2.87)	0.0382	34.73	2.719 [0.9640]	
	IV	0.783 (1.29)	−0.196 (1.53)	−0.760 (2.46)	0.065 (1.93)	0.0392		2.621	0.462
1867–1939	OLS	1.215 (8.98)	−0.228 (4.11)	−0.760 (10.53)	0.084 (6.57)	0.0289	95.76	2.403 [0.9460]	
	IV	1.348 (7.33)	−0.206 (2.59)	−0.762 (3.75)	0.069 (2.99)	0.0295		2.312	1.504
1952–1980	OLS	1.218 (5.93)	−0.144 (3.61)	−0.877 (8.98)	−0.016 (0.38)	0.0145	41.06	1.641 [0.1060]	
	IV	1.211 (4.11)	−0.121 (2.30)	−0.757 (4.04)	−0.044 (0.72)	0.0154		1.498	1.269

[a] The data were prefiltered with $(1-0.75L)^2$, were $Lx_t = x_{t-1}$. All estimated equations include an intercept. The figures in brackets below the values of the Durbin–Watson d-statistic are the values of the cumulative distribution function of d evaluated by the Pan Jie-Jan method. The m-statistic is defined in (11) of the text.

In spite of the *theoretical* importance of the problem of simultaneity bias in the estimation of the demand for money, which has been widely acknowledged ever since Teigen's (1964) pioneering work in this field, there is by now much evidence which indicates that the problem is not of particular *empirical* importance. A priori the seriousness of the problem would seem to depend on both the exchange rate system as well as the openness and size of the country.[25] In a small, open economy operating under fixed exchange rates international arbitrage in securities markets tends to reduce the degree of endogeneity of interest rates considerably. In absence of political risk free capital mobility will limit the range of variation in domestic interest rates to the narrow band around the interest parity value determined by transactions costs. In the gold standard period, 1880–1913, this is what seems to be a fair description of the market for bonds which is of relevance here. The simple correlation with a comparable foreign interest rate, a series of long-term Danish bond yields, is 0.90. The largest yield differential between annual averages of the two rates was 31 basis points, which is well below the rough estimate of transactions costs in covered interest arbitrage of one half per cent made by Keynes (1923).

Furthermore, in the postwar period the level of interest rates in Norway has largely been administered by the monetary authorities. Thus, the only period in which the problem of simultaneity bias with respect to the interest elasticity of money demand seems to be of potential importance is the 1914–1939 period, where exchange rates were flexible during many years. However, as can be seen from table 5, in this period the computed value of the m-statistic is particularly low, implying that the hypothesis of biased OLS estimates is very far from being rejected.

6. The stability between subperiods

On the basis of the OLS-estimates given in table 5 we may compute the relevant F-statistics to test for stability between subperiods. First, testing for stability between the periods 1867–1939 and 1952–1980, we get an F-value of 0.79, well below the critical value of 2.33 at a 5 per cent significance level. Likewise, breaking the pre-World War II period into the two subperiods 1867–1913 and 1914–1939 gives an F-value of 2.12, which is also below the critical value, 2.37. Consequently, the conventional F-test does not indicate any instability between the subperiods considered here.

Nevertheless, it is clear from the adaptive regression estimates of the demand for money presented in table 6 that the point estimates of several coefficients differ substantially between the various subperiods. This concerns in particular the estimated permanent income elasticity, which is as high as

[25]These issues have recently been discussed by Poloz (1980) and Gregory and McAleer (1981).

Table 6

Adaptive regression estimates of the demand for money; various subperiods.[a]

Time period	ln y^P	ln RL	π^A	DCR	SEE
1867–1980 (excluding 1940–1951)	1.207 (12.97) [1.025, 1.389]	−0.309 (7.72) [−0.231, −0.388]	−0.663 (9.70) [0.529, −0.796]	0.061 (6.92) [0.044, 0.080]	0.0289
1867–1913	1.522 (7.23) [1.109, 1.935]	−0.417 (4.56) [−0.238, −0.596]	−0.611 (5.24) [−0.382, −0.839]	0.056 (4.51) [0.032, 0.081]	0.0205
1914–1939	0.742 (2.34) [0.121, 1.362]	−0.230 (2.43) [−0.045, −0.415]	−0.685 (5.48) [−0.440, −0.930]	0.076 (3.69) [0.036, 0.117]	0.0404
1867–1939	0.991 (5.76) [0.654, 1.330]	−0.264 (4.62) [−0.152, −0.376]	−0.657 (8.83) [−0.511, −0.803]	0.077 (7.17) [0.056, 0.098]	0.0298
1952–1980	0.854 (5.36) [0.542, 1.166]	−0.165 (2.65) [−0.043, −0.288]	−0.746 (4.04) [−0.385, −1.108]	0.058 (1.60) [−0.013, 0.130]	0.0207

[a] All equations include an intercept. The adaptive regression parameter γ was estimated to 0.98 in all equations.

1.522 in the pre-World War I period, while being below unity in the two more recent subperiods. Again, one may suspect that this divergence at least in part reflects the secular influence of the institutional factors discussed above. Also, there seems to be a drift towards somewhat lower absolute values of the interest elasticity of the demand for money in recent years. In view of the particular institutional features of the bond markets in the more recent decades this is what might be expected.

But on the whole, the estimates for the various subperiods and the results of the F-tests show that the estimated model of the demand for money is quite robust to the choice of time period. In spite of the fundamental changes on both the real and financial side of the economy the long-run demand for money in the postwar period has been affected by the same variables and in roughly the same proportions as in the three quarters of a century preceding World War II.

7. A brief summary of the evidence on the long-run demand for money

In this final section we contrast the evidence on the long-run demand for money emanating from this study with some main results obtained from other countries. Table 7 gives a selective survey of coefficient estimates of the

Table 7

A tabular survey of the evidence on the long-run demand for broad money in various countries.

Country	Reference	Time-period	Scale variable[b]		RL[c]	RS[d]	Other variables included[f]
USA	Friedman (1959)	1870–1954	y^P	1.81			$\bar{P}$
	Meltzer (1963)	1900–1929	w	1.41	−0.42		
		1900–1958	w	1.32	−0.50		
	Courchene and	1902–1929	w	1.28	−0.20		
	Shapiro (1964)	1902–1958	w	1.27	−0.53		
	Laidler (1966)	1892–1916	y^P	1.75	−0.30		
			y^P	1.64		−0.12	
		1919–1940	y^P	0.79	−0.55		
			y^P	1.25		−0.14	
	Klein (1974)	1880–1918	y^P	1.83	(−0.13)	(−0.11)	RM
		1880–1970	y^P	1.37	(−0.06)	(−0.29)	RM
	Aghevli (1975)	1879–1914	y	0.94	−0.83		S
	Meyer and	1897–1960	y^E	1.07	−0.27		
	Neri (1975)		y^E	1.13		−0.09	
	Gandolfi and	1900–1929	y^P	1.42		(−0.11)	$y^T, \bar{P}$
	Lothian (1977)						
	Klein (1977)	1879–1972	y^P	0.95	(−0.05)	(−0.06)	RM, PU
	Stauffer (1978)	1900–1920	y	0.95			S
	Bordo and	1880–1972	y^P	0.88		(−0.02)	y^T, S
	Jonung (1981)						
UK	Kavanagh and	1880–1961	y	1.27	−0.46		
	Walters (1966)						
	Laidler (1971)	1900–1913	y^P	1.24	−0.27		
		1920–1938	y^P	0.79	−0.45		
			y^P	0.93		−0.08	
	Mills and	1923–1974	y	1.10	−0.62		
	Wood (1977)						
	Graves (1980)	1911–1966	y	0.27		(−0.10)	
	Bordo and	1876–1974	y^P	0.82		(−0.03)	y^T, S
	Jonung (1981)						
Canada	Bordo and	1900–1975	y^P	0.46		(−0.03)	y^T, S
	Jonung (1981)						
Italy	Spinelli (1980)	1867–1913	y^P	1.77		−0.05	
		1914–1936	y^P	1.47		−0.15	

long-run demand for money from several countries. Since the evidence from postwar data are extensively surveyed elsewhere[26] we focus on equations estimated on data prior to World War II. The selection of the results from one particular among the many estimated equations usually reported in each study must necessarily involve some arbitrariness, but the tabulated results

[26]See, e.g., the tabular survey of results from European countries by Fase and Kunć (1975) as well as surveys by Boorman (1980), Laidler (1977) and Feige and Pearce (1977).

Table 7 (continued)

			Estimated elasticities[a]			
Country	Reference	Time period	Scale variable[b]	Rl^c	π^{ee}	Other variables included[f]
Sweden	Lybeck (1975)	1890–1913	y^L 0.97		−0.62	
		1925–1938	y^L 1.07	−0.63	−7.49	
		1890–1968	y^L 0.98	−0.12	−1.02	
	Bordo and Jonung (1981)	1880–1974	y^P 0.37	(−0.03)	(−0.34)	y^T, S
Finland	Suvanto (1976)	1920–1939	y^P 1.60		−5.10	
Norway	Bordo and Jonung (1981)	1880–1974	y^P 0.88	(−0.04)		y^T, S
	This study	1867–1913	y^P 1.52	−0.31	−0.61	S
		1914–1939	y^P 0.74	−0.42	−0.69	S
		1867–1939	y^P 0.99	−0.23	−0.66	S
		1867–1980	y^P 1.21	−0.31	−0.66	S
			w 1.29	−0.33	−0.65	S

[a] Semi-elasticities are reported in parentheses.
[b] y is current income, y^P is permanent income, y^E is expected income, $y^L = y + y_{-1}$, w is non-human wealth.
[c] Long-term rate of interest.
[d] Short-term rate of interest.
[e] Price level expectations; coefficients refer to $d\ln(M/P)/d\pi^e$, where π^e is some function of $\ln(P_t/P_{t-1})$.
[f] RM = marginal return on money, $\bar{P}$ = permanent prices, PU = price level uncertainty, S = variables intended to measure secular changes in the financial system of various kinds, y^T = transitory income.

should nevertheless give the flavour of the main results. We have tried to make the results as comparable as possible by including only estimates made with a broad version of the money stock.

On the whole our results for Norway seem to be quite consistent with the body of the evidence from other countries. The most salient features to be noted from table 7 include a relatively high scale variable elasticity (1.2–1.8) estimated from data up to World War I and somewhat lower values (0.7–1.2) for the interwar period (except Sweden); an elasticity with respect to long-term interest rates[27] in the range of −0.2 – −0.6, and a notable absence of price expectation variables for all but Nordic countries. It is also evident that studies that take account of the influence of institutional factors of some kind, like Aghevli (1974), Klein (1977), Stauffer (1978), Graves (1980), and Bordo and Jonung (1981), report much lower scale variable elasticities than other authors who do not take account of such factors, like, e.g., Friedman

[27] Note also that the elasticity of the demand for money with respect to long-term rates is usually higher in absolute value than the ones estimated with respect to short-term rates.

(1959) and Klein (1974). On the other hand, the inclusion of a number of variables in the demand-for-money function in order to capture the effects of changing institutional and structural factors may introduce additional statistical problems, like multicollinearity between these proxy variables and the scale variable.[28]

In sum, this study has shown that the demand for money in Norway over the past century can be well explained by the set of factors suggested by theory and evidence from other countries. In view of the very long estimation period employed here it is of some interest to note that the demand for money seems to respond to the same set of explanatory variables qualitatively in the same way at the end of the period as it did at the beginning a hundred years ago.

In contrast to most previous empirical work in this field, this paper has made the long-standing issues of the choice of a scale variable and the severity of simultaneous equations bias subject to rigorous statistical tests. The outcomes of these tests are in favour of a permanent income model of money demand, with the yields of substitute financial and real assets as additional explanatory variables. Our results also corroborate the considerable amount of informal evidence that the extent of simultaneity bias in demand-for-money equations is only of modest importance as a practical matter. On the other hand, the results presented here also indicate that there still are a number of unresolved issues in the estimation of the long-run demand for money, of which two of the most important ones seem to be the measurement of the own rate of return on money and the modelling of how the process of monetization and financial sophistication affects the secular fall and rise of the income velocity of money.

[28]Graves (1980), e.g., introduces such a trend-like variable as the per cent of population living in urban areas into the conventional demand-for-money equation, which may in part explain his unusually low income elasticities.

References

Aghevli, Bijan B., 1975, The balance of payments and money supply under the gold standard regime: U.S. 1879–1914, American Economic Review 65, 40–58.
Artis, M.J. and M.K. Lewis, 1976, The demand for money in the United Kingdom: 1963–1973, Manchester School 44, 147–181.
Beach, Charles M. and James G. MacKinnon, 1978, A maximum likelihood procedure for regression with autocorrelated errors, Econometrica 46, 51–58.
Boorman, John T., 1980, The evidence on the demand for money: Theoretical formulations and empirical results, in: John T. Boorman and Thomas M. Havrilesky, eds., Current issues in monetary theory and policy (AHM Publ. Corp., Arlington Heights) 315–360.
Bordo, Michael D. and Lars Jonung, 1981, The long-run behavior of the income velocity of money in five advanced countries, 1870–1975: An institutional approach, Economic Inquiry 19, 96–116.
Carlson, John A. and James R. Frew, 1980, Money demand responsiveness to the rate of return on money: A methodological critique, Journal of Political Economy 88, 598–607.

Chow, Gregory C., 1966, On the long-run and short-run demand for money, Journal of Political Economy 74, 111–131.
Cooley, Thomas F. and Edward C. Prescott, 1973, Tests of an adaptive regression model, Review of Economics and Statistics 55, 248–256.
Courchene, Thomas J. and Harold T. Shapiro, 1964, The demand for money: A note from the time series, Journal of Political Economy 72, 498–503.
Currie, David, 1981, Some long run features of dynamic time series models, Economic Journal 91, 704–715.
Davidson, Russell and James G. MacKinnon, 1981, Several tests for model specification in the presence of alternative hypotheses, Econometrica 49, 781–793.
Fase, M.M.G. and J.B. Kuné, 1975, The demand for money in thirteen European and non-European countries: A tabular survey, Kredit und Kapital 8, 410–419.
Feige, Edgar L. and Douglas K. Pearce, 1977, The substitutability of money and near-monies: A survey of the time-series evidence, Journal of Economic Literature 15, 439–469.
Fisher, Douglas, 1978, Monetary theory and the demand for money (Martin Robertson, Oxford).
Fisher, Gordon and Michael McAleer, 1979, On the interpretation of the Cox test in econometrics, Economics Letters 4, 145–150.
Friedman, Milton, 1957, A theory of the consumption function (Princeton University Press, Princeton, NJ).
Friedman, Milton, 1959, The demand for money: Some theoretical and empirical results, Journal of Political Economy 67, 327–351.
Friedman, Milton, 1977, Time perspective in demand for money, Scandinavian Journal of Economics 79, 397–416.
Gandolfi, Arthur E. and James R. Lothian, 1977, Did monetary forces cause the Great Depression?, Journal of Money, Credit, and Banking 9, 679–691.
Goldfeld, Stephen M., 1973, The demand for money revisited, Brookings Papers on Economic Activity, 577–638.
Graves, Philip E., 1980, The velocity of money: Evidence for the U.K. 1911–1966, Economic Inquiry 18, 631–639.
Gregory, Allan W. and Michael McAleer, 1981, Simultaneity and the demand for money in Canada: Comments and extensions, Canadian Journal of Economics 14, 488–496.
Hausman, J.A., 1978, Specification tests in econometrics, Econometrica 46, 1251–1271.
Heller, H. Robert and Mohsin S. Khan, 1979, The demand for money and the term structure of interest rates, Journal of Political Economy 87, 109–129.
Hendry, David F., 1979, Predictive failure and econometric modelling in macroeconomics: The transactions demand for money, in: Paul Ormerod, ed., Economic modelling: Current issues and problems in macroeconomic modelling in the UK and the US (Heinemann, London) 217–242.
Jonung, Lars, 1978, The long-run demand for money — A Wicksellian approach, Scandinavian Journal of Economics 80, 216–230.
Kavanagh, N.J. and A.A. Walters, 1966, The demand for money in the U.K., 1877–1961: Some preliminary findings, Oxford Bulletin of Economics and Statistics 28, 93–116.
Keynes, John M., 1923, A tract on monetary reform (Macmillan, London).
Klein, Benjamin, 1974, Competitive interest payments on bank deposits and the long-run demand for money, American Economic Review 64, 931–949.
Klein, Benjamin, 1977, The demand for quality-adjusted cash balances: Price uncertainty in the U.S. demand for money function, Journal of Political Economy 85, 691–715.
Klovland, Jan T., 1978, The demand for money in Norway, 1866–1939, Mimeo. (Norwegian School of Economics and Business Administration, Bergen).
Klovland, Jan T., 1982, The stability of the demand for money in the interwar years: The case of Norway, 1925–1939, Journal of Money, Credit, and Banking 14, 252–264.
Laidler, David, 1966, The rate of interest and the demand for money: Some empirical evidence, Journal of Political Economy 74, 55–68.
Laidler, David, 1971, The influence of money on economic activity: A survey of some current problems, in: G. Clayton et al., eds., Monetary theory and monetary policy in the 1970s (Oxford University Press, London) 75–135.

Laidler, David, 1977, The demand for money: Theories and evidence (Dun–Donnelley, New York).
Laidler, David, 1980, The demand for money in the United States — yet again, Carnegie-Rochester Conference Series on Public Policy 12, 219–271.
Lieberman, Charles, 1979, A transactions vs. asset demand approach to the empirical definition of money, Economic Inquiry 17, 237–253.
Lieberman, Charles, 1980, The long-run and short-run demand for money, revisited, Journal of Money, Credit, and Banking 12, 43–57.
Lybeck, Johan A., 1975, Issues in the theory of the long-run demand for money, Swedish Journal of Economics 77, 193–206.
Meltzer, Allan H., 1963, The demand for money: The evidence from the time series, Journal of Political Economy 61, 219–246.
Meyer, Paul A. and John A. Neri, 1975, A Keynes–Friedman money demand function, American Economic Review 65, 610–623.
Mills, T.C. and G.E. Wood, 1977, Money substitutes and monetary policy in the U.K., 1922–1974, European Economic Review 10, 19–36.
Pesaran, M.H. and A.S. Deaton, 1978, Testing non-nested nonlinear regression models, Econometrica 46, 677–694.
Poloz, Stephen S., 1980, Simultaneity and the demand for money in Canada, Canadian Journal of Economics 13, 407–420.
Sargent, Thomas J., 1973, Rational expectations, the real rate of interest, and the natural rate of unemployment, Brookings Papers on Economic Activity, 429–472.
Savin, N.E., 1978, Friedman–Meiselman revisited: A study in autocorrelation, Economic Inquiry 16, 37–52.
Schwartz, Anna J., 1975, Monetary trends in the United States and the United Kingdom, 1878–1970: Selected findings, Journal of Economic History 29, 138–159.
Sims, Christopher A., 1972, Money, income, and causality, American Economic Review 62, 540–552.
Smith, David, 1978, The demand for alternative monies in the U.K.: 1924–77, National Westminster Bank Quarterly Review, Nov., 35–49.
Spinelli, Franco, 1980, The demand for money in the Italian economy: 1867–1965, Journal of Monetary Economics 6, 83–104.
Stauffer, Robert F., 1978, A reinterpretation of velocity trends in the United States, 1900–1920, Journal of Money, Credit, and Banking 10, 105–111.
Stone, Richard, 1964, Private saving in Britain: Past, present and future, Manchester School 32, 79–112.
Suvanto, Antti, 1976, Permanent income, inflation expectations and the long-run demand for money in Finland, Scandinavian Journal of Economics 78, 457–469.
Teigen, Ronald L., 1964, Demand and supply functions for money in the United States: Some structural estimates, Econometrica 32, 476–509.
Tobin, James, 1965, The monetary interpretation of history, American Economic Review 55, 464–485.

[11]
Changes in the Personal Income Distribution 1870–1986

Rewal Schmidt Sørensen

Summary

The reduction in the inequality of the income distribution of households in Denmark is primarily concentrated in two periods: the 'take-off' phase (1870–1900) and the Second World War and nearby years (1938–48). Changes in the age structure of the population have been instrumental in equalizing the income distribution prior to the Second World War, while the opposite is true after the war. Social policy has dominated the redistributive efforts of Government, although not as much as previously believed. Changes in the industrial structure counteracted a more equal distribution in the period 1939–61. Two new inequality measures are suggested.

The personal monetary income in a period is presumably the most significant determinant of economic welfare of the individual person in a market economy, as income determines the potential monetary consumption of an individual per period – without changing the wealth of the individual person. For that reason alone, distribution of personal incomes is of interest as seen from a socio-scientific point of view. However, there have been very few Danish research efforts in this area (cf. e.g. Viby Mogensen, 1987), and it is very difficult to catch sight of a cohesive survey of the period 1870–1986, for which statistics are available. The available surveys (e.g. Bjerke, 1957; Caspersen, 1961; Egmose, 1985; and DØR, 1967) typically cover only a relatively short period of time and/or contain calculations of distribution for a few selected years.

This article[1] summarizes the results of a new analysis of changes in the personal income distribution, where, by and large, all available tax-related statistics were included. The main emphasis is on the period from the beginning of the 1900s, and up to the end of the 1960s, as it seems that this period is weakly illustrated in earlier surveys.

First, a range of important problems involved in the measurement of income distribution are discussed.

The Annual Income Method Versus Life Income Calculations

If analyses of distribution are based on annual data, the so-called annual income method, attention must unconditionally be focused on the changes, as the inequality level, viewed separately, cannot provide a meaningful interpretation. However, the annual income method gives rise to a number of problems, as the estimated measurements of distribution depend on, e.g., differences in economic activities and the age structure of the population during each year. It has been proposed to replace the annual income method with life income calculations (see, e.g. Dich, 1973). In practice, these must be effected on the basis of cross-sectional data. Consequently, calculation of life income measurements of distributions for selected years based on life income calculations will be pure abstractions.

Conversely, measurements of distribution estimated via the annual income method will describe the actual observed distribution of income, which is clearly preferable.

However, a fruitful utilization of the annual income method presupposes that income distribution of the total population (the total distribution) is, as far as possible, split up, with a view to determining the factors which have caused the observed changes in the income distribution.

In practice, it is, of course, the primary statistical data that determine the possibilities of splitting up the total distribution. The results presented in the empirical survey are based on calculations where it has been endeavoured to use the data material in an optimum way.

Selection of Measurements of Distribution

Data on income arranged according to increasing size clearly call for making attempts at 'fitting' data with a theoretical distribution function, and, thereafter, using the estimated parameters of the function as measurements of distribution. The best known attempts within this tradition are use of the logarithmic normal distribution and the Pareto distribution. Generally speaking, it must be ascertained that the construction of such 'closed' measurements of distribution rarely succeeds, as the theoretical distribution function hardly ever 'fits' the data in a satisfactory way – typically, there are problems involved in a simultaneous adaptation 'at both ends'. The method is best used for distribution of wages and salaries, where the population is relatively homogeneous.

In practice, 'free' measurements of income distribution are therefore used, where it is endeavoured to aggregate the characteristic features of the distribution into one figure. Generally, these measurements are an expression of the inequality of the distribution based on some definite preconditions of which weights must be attached to the redistributions of income at different income levels. Typically, these 'preconditions of weights' are an integral part of the measurements of distribution, but during recent years measurements have also been constructed, where the 'preconditions of weights' can be specified via a parameter.

In Denmark it is traditional to use the maximum equalization coefficient, MEC, in the analyses of distribution, which in my view is a very good choice: the MEC is superior to all other measurements of distribution as regards interpretation. The MEC indicates the shares of the total incomes, which have to be transferred from the population with single incomes above the mean value (average income), of the total distribution, to the others, in order to achieve an equal distribution, *viz.*:

(1) $\text{MEC} = F(\mu) - \Phi(\mu)$; where :

$F(\mu)$ = share of the population with single incomes, which are smaller or equal to μ
$\Phi(\mu)$ = this population's share of the total income

The most significant drawback of the MEC is that it is not affected by redistributions on the same side of the mean value. Traditionally, this has been offset by means of the so-called decile calculations, where the population is divided into ten equal shares, which are compared to the pertinent income shares. Together with the MEC, this results in no less than 11 figures, whose changes have to be studied during the period of analysis. It is obvious that this is not a very neat way of solving the problem, as 'the secret' of measurements of distribution is to provide a reasonably adequate description of the distribution by means of the fewest possible figures.

Consequently, calculation of the two following supplementary MECs is suggested:

(2) $\text{MECP} = \dfrac{F(p)}{F(\mu)} - \dfrac{\Phi(p)}{\Phi(\mu)}; \quad \text{MECR} = \dfrac{1-\Phi(r)}{1-\Phi(\mu)} - \dfrac{1-F(r)}{1-F(\mu)};$ where :

p = average income of the population with single incomes less than or equal to μ, i.e. the average income of 'the poor'
r = average incomes of the others, i.e. 'the rich'

The MECP thus indicates the shares of the income of 'the poor', which have to be transferred from those with single incomes in the income interval [p;μ] to those in the interval [0;p], provided that all 'the poor' are to have the same income, p. The MECR is defined in the same way, and indicates the shares of the income of 'the rich', which have to be redistributed so that all 'the rich' have the income, r. The terms 'poor' and 'rich' are only used for the sake of convenience.

It goes without saying that the MECP and MECR are subject to the same type of criticism as the MEC, as, e.g., redistributions of single incomes below p do not affect the MECP. But, in practice, the MECP and MECR combined with the MEC seem to provide a rather complete description of changes in the income distribution – much better than the decile calculations.

If changes in the income distribution are analysed by estimating only the MEC, MECP and MECR for the total distribution, a uniform picture of the underlying reasons for the changes is obtained. Therefore, a decomposition of the total distribution is necessary. If the following symbols are introduced:

N = number of persons (or rather, units of taxation) in the total distribution
n_k = number of persons in the sub-population k
a_k = share of persons in group k, whose incomes are smaller or equal to the mean value of the total distribution, μ

p_k = average income for a_k i.e. 'the poor' of group k – where 'the poor' is defined in relation to the mean value of the total distribution

group k's contribution to the MEC of the total distribution will accordingly be as follows:

$$MEC_k = \frac{n_k a_k}{N} - \frac{n_k a_k p_k}{N\mu}$$

and hereafter we arrive at the following discrete version of the MEC:

(1a) $\quad MEC = \sum_{\forall z} \frac{n_z}{N} a_z - \sum_{\forall z} \frac{n_z}{N} \frac{a_z p_z}{\mu}; \quad z = 1,\ldots,k,\ldots$

This formulation can, for example, be used as basis for quantifying the impact on the income distribution caused by changes in the age structure. If the standardized maximum equalization coefficient is defined for period 1:

(3) $\quad SMEC_1 = \sum_{\forall z}\left(\frac{n_z}{N}\right)_1 (a_z)_0 - \sum_{\forall z}\left(\frac{n_z}{N}\right)_1 \left(\frac{a_z p_z}{\mu}\right)_0; \quad z = 1,\ldots,k,\ldots$

where $(n_k/N)_1$ indicates the k'th age interval's share of the total population in period 1 – then the $SMEC_1$ can be interpreted as the MEC, which would have been measured in period 1, if only the age distribution had changed from period 0 to 1.

It is obvious that calculations based on direct standardizations are built on a partial consideration, and as a consequence of this, the SMEC-calculations alone must be seen as an illustrative quantification of the importance of changes in the age structure for the income distribution. The decomposition of the MEC of the total distribution can be further refined, as the MEC can be split up into the maximum equalization, which can be achieved by redistribution within and between the groups, respectively (internal and external equalization). Moreover, elasticities can be estimated, which show the sensitivity of the MEC versus changes in the size of the groups, average income, etc. It falls outside the scope of this article to discuss these relatively complicated deductions, but for more information cf. Sørensen, 1989. The analysis of the interaction between changes in the structure of the business sector and the income distribution in paragraph 4 is primarily based on such calculations.

Empirical Problems of Measurement

There are only minor technical problems involved in selecting 'the correct' measurements of distribution, cf. above, when compared to the empirical problems of measurement, which the use of the Danish tax-related statistics give rise to. The most important problems are dealt with below, but, owing to considerations of space, only a rough summary is given.

When comparing calculations of distribution for several periods of time, it would be perfect, if the income concept and the population are similar throughout the whole period.

It is obvious that the population as regards contents will always vary over time, as demographic changes affect the composition of the population. However, at least one requirement must be met: the population must as regards the concept, i.e. the unit of taxation, be the same throughout the whole period of analysis. It goes without saying that comparisons of measurements of distribution estimated on the basis of data concerning income for the taxation unit 'the household' and 'all persons liable to pay tax' are meaningless – as regards comparisons of both the level and the changes of the measurements of distribution.

In the period 1870–1968, the unit of taxation in the tax-related statistics covers all persons except married women (married women's income is included in the husband's income), and children under the age of 18 years who have no income.

As cohabitation in this period is generally identical with marriage, the unit of taxation in the tax-related statistics must be considered a rather good proxy for 'the household' – and thus for the consumption unit.

From 1976 and onwards information about income of 'single persons and married couples' is available, which, with two (significant!) exceptions corresponds to the previous unit of taxation. First, there has been a marked change in the way people live their lives together, which implies that the categorization of marital status is less suitable as proxy for the 'household'. Second, income of all persons above the age of 15 years (exact age) is assessed; as a consequence of this many persons who have a zero-income are included.

Either circumstance indicates that the statistically measurable inequality level is increased from 1976 – and therefore the level cannot be compared with earlier figures. Owing to the fact that the stock of married couples is still relatively large, it must, however, be assumed that a certain degree of comparability in respect of the changes is reasonable.

With the introduction of taxation at the source (Pay-As-You-Earn system) in 1970 'all persons liable to taxation' is the most commonly used unit of taxation. As 'all persons liable to taxation' also cover a large number of married women whose income is zero, the calculations of distribution based on this unit of taxation are not comparable at all with figures before 1970 – neither in respect of level or changes. Moreover, the use of 'all persons liable to taxation' as the unit of taxation implies that the correspondence between the unit of taxation and the consumption unit is lost completely, which must be regarded as unfortunate.

As with the unit of taxation, it is a condition that the income concept is similar in the periods that are compared. However, the determination of the concrete contents of the income concept used in the tax-related statistics is rather problematic, as it is affected by changes in tax legislation, which are not determined at all, out of consideration for the data being used in the analyses of distribution. Moreover, a change in the understatement will affect the measurements of distribution. There are no direct possibilities of rectifying these drawbacks, which imply that the results must be interpreted with some caution.

Differences in the three formal income concepts, which are used in the period 1870–1986, must be taken into account in the analyses of distribution.

Up to and including 1966 the concept 'assessed income', which can be defined as the taxable income with deduction of last year's assessed tax (the so-called tax allowance), is used. The assessed income is therefore an approximative expression of the disposable income, which indicates the taxation unit's possibilities of private consumption.

In the period 1967–68 the distribution of taxable income of 'the households' is known, but these data cannot be used for comparison with figures before or after due to changes in the income concept and unit of taxation, respectively, cf. above.

From 1970 the statistics generally cover information on the distribution of gross income as well as taxable income. However, a number of changes in the definition of gross income in the period 1970–76 imply that the taxable income alone is suitable for illustrating changes in the distribution in the whole period 1970–86.

The use of the taxable income in the analysis implies that the distribution of the taxation unit's possibilities of monetary consumption, private as well as public consumption, must be examined.

As taxable and assessed income will generally be highly correlated, changes in the distribution of the two income concepts can presumably be compared (assuming that the unit of taxation is the same!) – whereas the levels will differ on account of the progression in central government tax.

The practical circumstances mentioned above further substantiate the need for focusing attention on *changes* in the personal income distribution in the empirical survey.

The Empirical Survey

Discussion of the empirical survey is divided into to two sections. First, the results are analysed in close connection with the main features in the economic-political changes during the period, and thereafter the consequences of a range of structural changes for the personal income distribution are quantified.

Changes in the Personal Income Distribution 1870–1986

The 'take-off' phase in the Danish economy, 1870–1900, is followed by a heavy fall in the level of the economic inequality, cf. Figure 1.

A significant reason for the sharp income equalization in the rural districts is the exodus of farm workers from the rural districts to the urban areas, which implies that persons with low incomes leave the rural districts. The exodus from farming, combined with the structural alteration in agriculture to labour-intensive livestock production means that the demand for farm workers is increased and this affects the wages and salaries favourably. The equalization in the rural districts is further supported by the advance of the co-operative movement, which generally leads to more homogeneously finished products and more uniform prices – independent of the size of the farms.

The equalization in the urban areas must be attributed to the low concentration of enterprises, and the advance of the labour movement – particularly by the end of the 1800s.

The period from the turn of the century until the First World War was influenced by heavy economic growth, partly stimulated by the strong international demand, which followed in the wake of the many military operations and brisk investment activities in China, Japan and Russia.

On the labour market this resulted in a low rate of unemployment and steady incomes for the employees. Coupled with the labour movement's mounting influence and minor social

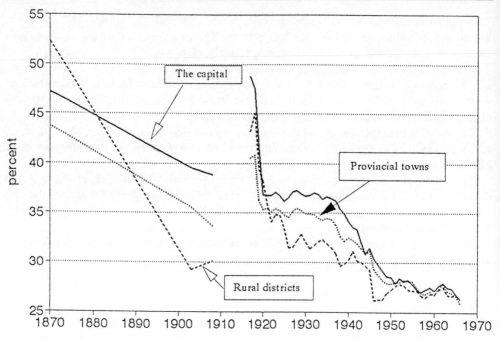

Note: In the period 1870–1937, the total assessed incomes below DKK 800 are based on estimates.
Source: Sørensen 1989, Annex 3, page 6.

Figure 1: The MEC in 'rural/urban' areas 1870–1966

initiatives, this implied that the equalization in the urban areas continued. In the rural districts the international boom seemed to favour the self-employed farmers and, therefore, this resulted in a minor increase in the skewness of the income distribution.

The outbreak of war was followed by heavy price increases, which, to a great extent, favoured the self-employed in the form of increased profits – trade particularly experienced a 'boom in earnings' during the war. The wages and salaries of the employees could not keep up with inflation, as a result of, for example, the collective wage agreements of 1911, where the nominal trend of wages and salaries was fixed for a five-year period. Public employees particularly experienced a sharp fall in real earnings. The consequence of this was an almost explosive skewness in the income distribution.

The fall in real wages and salaries during the war, and inspired by the Russian Revolution, there was a steep increase in the number of members of the syndicalistic labour movement, which greatly influenced the collective wage agreements during the first post war years. As a consequence, the skewness in the income distribution in the urban areas nearly returned to the same as before the war – this was also accounted for by improved employment possibilities. The end of the war saw a heavy fall in prices for agricultural products, which resulted in a reduction in the earnings of the self-employed farmers – and the inequality level was also normalized in the rural districts.

The remaining years of the interwar period were characterized by a relatively stable inequality level for Denmark as a whole – despite major changes in economic activities during this period. However, in the rural districts there were considerable year-on-year variations, which were attributable to a combination of the labour-intensive production form in agriculture, and the hired workers, to an increasing degree, had to be considered as fixed overheads in the short run. In the short run, farmers could not compensate for falling prices by dismissals of hired workers, as the livestock had to be looked after, irrespective of price trends. The non-agricultural industries were in a more favourable position in this respect; thus the self-employed persons were able to maintain their relative income position in times of economic recession. Moreover, the stability of the income distribution in urban areas was also favoured by the gradual extension of social legislation, including unemployment benefit, which peaked temporarily in Steincke's social reforms of 1933.

The earnings situation of agriculture throughout the 1930s was changed radically with the German occupation of Denmark, which heralded a veritable golden age for agriculture. As agriculture during the German occupation had to base the livestock production on self-sufficiency in feed grain, the large- and medium-sized farms benefited from the generous prices paid by the Germans, as these were primarily engaged in grain production – the inequality was markedly increased in the rural districts and 'peaked' in 1941. Generally speaking, the German occupation acted as an incentive to the rate of employment, partly due to the good export potentials to Germany, and partly due to a transition to replacement production with a lower degree of productivity. Moreover, the building of fortifications for the Germans implied that alternative employment possibilities were offered to workers from the rural districts.

The boom during the Second World War and the first postwar years resulted in the greatest equalization of the income distribution of the century, if adjustment of the level immediately after the First World War is not taken into account. The transition to peacetime economy in 1945 influenced, in particular, agriculture, which had to accept a considerable decrease in earnings, which was beneficial to the income equalization in the first postwar years.

There was only a minor income equalization in the period from the end of the 1940s to 1966, however the fluctuations in connection with this trend were smaller year by year. Figure 1 also shows that the rural districts are no longer 'playing solo', but, generally, follow trends in the urban areas. The reason why is the decreasing emphasis on the income distribution of agriculture in the rural districts, which is 'filled up with' persons moving to the suburbs – i.e. taxation units with an urban characteristic as regards income. Moreover, a range of agricultural support systems from the end of the 1950s and onwards are carried out, and the remaining farms are compensated for the steadily aggressive deterioration in terms of trade versus the non-agricultural industries. The reason why the income distribution was stabilized at the end of the 1940s must primarily be viewed against the background of the growing regulation of the population's income. These regulations were carried out by means of a steadily increasing extension of social legislation, where the criteria of receiving social benefits were largely a result of the cessation of income. On the labour market, the efforts of the trade union movement must be stressed, as this, in an efficient way, formulated demands for higher wages and salaries as a result of increasing profits in trade and industry. The time when the self-employed could benefit unilaterally from changes in economic activities is past history now. Moreover, the stability in the income distribution is supported by the favourable employment situation – particularly from the end of the 1950s.

Changes in the period 1870–1966 are summed up in Figure 2.

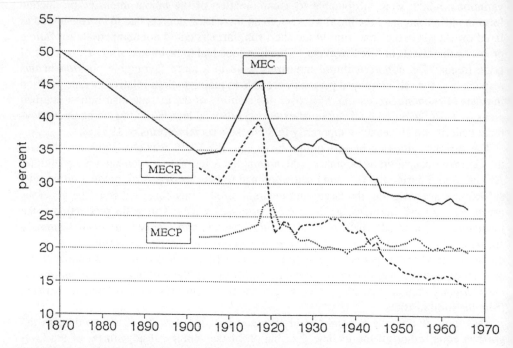

Note: The income concept is the assessed income.
Source: Sørensen 1989, annex 3, page 18.

Figure 2: *The MEC, MECP and MECR for all Denmark 1870–1966*

When considering the MECP and MECR an impression of changes 'at both ends' of the distribution is also achieved. If the extreme fluctuations during the period around the First World War are left out, the long-term trend is clear. Income distribution among the households whose income was above average has been markedly equalized, which is presumably attributable to the increased activity rates of women, whereas the distribution among 'the poor' has been more or less stable. The smaller increase in the level in the MECP during the German occupation is attributable to a sharpening of the social legislation in this period.

There is a general misunderstanding that the personal income distribution, compared with earlier periods has been markedly equalized after the introduction of taxation at source (Pay-As-You-Earn system) in 1970 (see, e.g., Egmose, 1985). The misunderstanding is due to, cf. above, the meaningless comparison of measurements of distribution estimated on the basis of various units of taxation; this clearly appears from Figure 3.

The calculations of distribution based on the unit of taxation 'all persons liable to taxation' stresses the impression of a sharp equalization in relation to earlier periods.

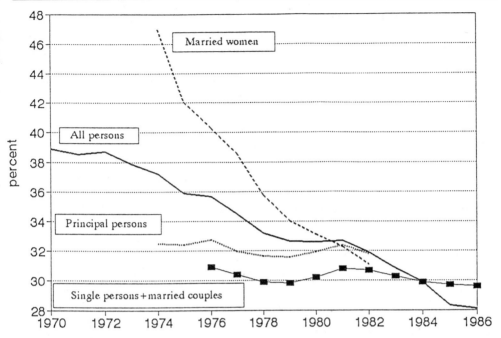

Note: It is not possible to construct time series for the whole period 1970–86 for all four units of taxation. The income concept is taxable income.
Source: Sørensen 1989, annex 3, pages 47 and 53.

Figure 3: The MEC for selected units of taxation 1970–86

However, the only more or less relevant comparison is measurements of distribution based on the taxation unit 'single persons & married couples', which only shows a weak tendency towards an equalization during the period 1976–86.

The reason for this sharp equalization in connection with the unit of taxation 'all persons liable to taxation' is further illustrated by means of the Figure. It is the equalization of married women's income distribution that mainly accounts for this – a consequence of the heavily increased activity rates of women, which decrease the number of zero-income assessments. The reason why this does not appear from the income distribution of 'households' indicates that the increased activity rates of women are mainly attributable to the emancipation of women, which has influenced all social classes – independent of the husband's level of income.

Income Distribution and Structural Changes

The age structure of the population was changed radically in the 1900s, primarily as a result of the falling fertility rates. The impact on the income distribution appears from the SMEC-calculations in Table 1.

Table 1: Income distribution and age structure 1915–66

Index 1939=100	1915	Average 1921–23	1939	1945	1955	1966
MEC	131	110	100	91	92	77
SMEC	105		100	101	105	106

Source: Sørensen 1989, annex 3, pages 68–70.

It is only possible to make calculations for the years 1915, 1939, 1945, 1955 and 1966 owing to insufficient data. For 1915 the population and income data are very inadequate (the population census 1 February 1916), as a consequence of this the SMEC has been calculated 'backwards' (i.e. the SMEC for 1915 = the MEC for 1915; assuming that incomes were similar to those in 1939 and the age structure similar to that in 1915).

The figures show that changes in the age structure from 1915 to 1939 have favoured the equalization. It goes without saying that a comparison of the SMEC and the MEC for 1915 is not very interesting on account of the extreme conditions during the war, consequently, the more 'normal' level for the MEC is represented by the average of the 1921–23 figures. Generally speaking, it can be ascertained that changes in the age structure during the interwar period account for about 50 per cent of the equalization.

The elderly people's share of the adult population was increased after the Second World War. This helps to explain changes in the other SMECs; provided that only the age structure was changed in the period 1939–66 the inequality level would have been about six per cent higher in 1966 than in 1939. The fact that the inequality was heavily reduced, the more remarkable this is.

When changes in the industrial structure's significance for the income distribution are to be quantified directly in relation to the MEC, rather complicated elasticity calculations are necessary, which the available data material only allows for the period 1936–61.

In Table 2 the MEC's elasticity as regards the size of each industrial group $E(MEC, n_k)$ (i.e. percentage changes in the MEC, when the size of an industrial group is increased by one per cent) is estimated for 1939, and hereafter a standard calculation is effected.

It is obvious that the significant changes in the industrial structure during the period (column B) have counteracted the income equalization, as the MEC would have been about five per cent higher, if only the size of the industrial groups had been changed in the period 1939–61. Only the fall and increase, respectively, in the number of housemaids, and workers within the building trade and industry have favoured the equalization.

As the income distribution has, in actual fact, been equalized during the period, the next question is whether the equalization is attributable to redistributions within or between the groups. Here calculations indicate that the equalization primarily can be attributed to redistribution within industrial groups. Popularly, it can be said that the income solidarity during the period is only extended to one's own industrial group – and does not cut across the demarcation lines.

Finally, the income equalization in respect of public finance is to be analysed. The analysis is based on surveys of the years 1937, 1949, 1955 and 1963, which it is possible to

Table 2: Industrial structure and income distribution 1939–61

k		(A) E(MEC, n_k) in 1939 (per mille)	(B) Change in number of assesments 1939–61 (per cent)	(A)*(B) (per mille)
1.	Self-employed in agriculture	–0.3	–11.3	3.4
2.	Hired workers in agriculture	–0.1	–14.2	1.4
3.	Workers, building trades and industry	–0.7	23.1	–16.2
4.	Others in agriculture	about 0	–16.1	0
5.	Masters in building trades	about 0	–20.9	0
6.	Other self-employed	about 0	7.4	0
7.	Salaried employees	about 0	38.3	0
8.	Public service and clerical workers	about 0	57.0	0
9.	Managers and factory owners	0.2	91.7	18.3
10.	Shop owners	0.2	1.4	0.3
11.	The professions	0.2	65.3	13.1
12.	Housemaids	0.2	–45.2	–9.0
13.	Apprentices and pupils	0.1	151.9	15.2
14.	Others	0.3	78.8	23.6
Total		0.0	22.7	50.1

Source: Sørensen 1989, page 107.

make reasonably comparable – although earlier summaries have not paid attention to the problems involved.

Traditionally, the equalization in respect of public finance has been quantified by comparing the taxes and duties paid and social security benefits received by a group with a certain income. The distribution of taxes and duties and social security benefits is based on rough estimates. Furthermore, the total equalization is split up into fiscal equalization (= taxes and duties distributed proportionately with the income with deduction of paid taxes and duties) and socio-political equalization (= total equalization with deduction of fiscal equalization), respectively.

Any meaningful comparison of the results estimated in this way presupposes that the population, which is analysed every year, is similar as regards concepts, and that the same income concept is used with the proportionate distribution.

The fact that the above-mentioned circumstance was not taken into account has led to the erroneous conclusion that the fiscal element in the equalization in respect of public finance was completely insignificant in 1937 (the population analysed in Olsen and Kampmann, 1948 covers only employees with income above the tax limit). In the 1963 survey (DØR, 1967), it was ascertained that the difference between the fiscal and socio-political element is eliminated in 1963 – however, it is a result which is only attributable to the fact that the 1955 figures estimated on the basis of total income are compared with the 1963 figures based on assessed income. If these circumstances are rectified we arrive at the results in Table 3.

Table 3: Equalization in respect of public finance 1937–63

	1937	1949	1955	1963
1. Percentage of total income	6.2	4.8	6.1	8.9
fiscal share	17.9	32.4	42.7	31.1
socio-political share	82.1	67.6	57.3	68.9
2. Percentage of assessed income	7.5	6.5	8.5	10.8
fiscal share	25.0	44.8	52.9	48.6
socio-political share	75.0	55.2	47.1	51.4

Source: Sørensen 1989, page 114.

In the period 1937–63 there is a clear tendency towards an increased equalization in respect of public finance – however, this increase was interrupted by a minor fall in 1949. When the distribution of fiscal and socio-political equalization is analysed, it is important to use total income (i.e. gross income), as this is the foundation of evaluating the progressiveness of taxation, although the actual rules governing taxation are based on assessed income.

It appears from the figures that the socio-political equalization is predominant throughout the whole period, but that the fiscal policy almost 'catches up with' this equalization in the middle of the 1950s, and thereafter ground is lost in respect of the socio-political element.

There are no surveys of changes after 1963 which can be compared with the period 1937–63. However, a survey of conditions in 1976 and 1981 (Hansen, 1985) indicates that the total equalization in respect of public finance is reduced from 1976 to 1981, and that the fiscal element is still declining. The latter factor is a continuation of the tendency from 1955 to 1963 – and is primarily attributable to the circumstance that the share of VAT of public receipts is increased.

Conclusion

It has been suggested 'to throw a veil of oblivion over' analyses of distribution based on the annual income method (cf. Dich, 1973, p. 205). The results presented here should have made it probable that it is actually possible to 'wring out' interesting information from annual income data.

The fact that the Danish tax-related statistics are not suitable for describing changes in the personal income distribution is not surprising: the statistics only describe the population's ability to pay taxes (at best), as defined in the tax legislation.

However, there is nothing wrong with the annual income method as far as methodology is concerned. Provided that the concept of economic inequality could be objectively and precisely defined as regards which weights should be given to requirements, age, efforts, etc. in relation to the income – and data collected with a view to analysing this – the annual income method would be perfect for analyses of distribution.

Life income calculations only systematically seek to make adjustments for the age variations of the incomes, which constitute rather an inadequate 'solution'. Before a generally acceptable definition of the economic inequality concept has been laid down, the annual income method is still the best basis of analyses of distribution.

This article focused on the reasons for changes in the personal income distribution, which it was possible to quantify on the basis of data. The survey seems to have resulted in a more varied picture of Danish changes in the distribution than earlier surveys.

Note

1. The article is based on my thesis (M.A. economics), Sørensen 1989. I am grateful for the assistance I have received from Gunnar Viby Mogensen, M.A. economics. Any errors, omissions, etc. are, of course, entirely my responsibility.

References

Bjerke, Kjeld (1957), *Changes in Danish Income Distribution 1939–52. Income & Wealth Series*, VI, pp. 98–154.
Caspersen, Sven (1961), *Den personlige indkomstfordeling i Danmark 1908–56*. Thesis.
Dich, Jørgensen, S. (1973), *Den herskende klasse*, København.
Egmose, Sven m.fl. (1985), *Uligheden, politikerne og befolkningen*, København.
Hansen, Finn Kenneth (1985), *Fordelingspolitikken og den virkninger*, København.
Olsen, Poul Bjørn og Kampmann, Viggo (1948), 'Indkomstudjævningen i Danmark', *Socialt Tidsskrift*, 24 pp. 49–66.
Sørensen, Rewal Schmidt (1989), *Udviklingen i den danske personlige indkomstfordeling i 1900-tallet*. Thesis. København.
Viby Mogensen, Gunnar (1987), *Historie og Økonomi*, København.
Det Økonomiske Råd, DØR (1967), *Den personlige indkomstfordeling og indkomstudjævningen over de offentlige finanser*, København.

[12]

Home-led or Export-led Growth?
The Growth of the Norwegian Electronics Industry in the Postwar Period

Anders Skonhoft

Introduction

During the postwar period the electronics industry has advanced to become a key industry, if not the key industry, behind technological transformation, structural changes and economic growth in the western industrial countries. Since the publication in 1982 of the book "Unemployment and Technical Innovation", by Christopher Freeman and others,[1] it has gradually become not uncommon to regard the electronics industry as the *modus operandi* of a new technological system which has emerged during the past 20-30 years.

The imputing of such importance to the electronics sector as the leading sector of a new technological system implies, firstly, that innovations and technological changes in the electronics industry have had and are having, directly and indirectly, far-reaching effects on macroeconomic growth and productivity. Secondly, that these innovations have applied and are applying fixed trajectories to a very great deal of the other innovative activity and technological renewal which is going on in these developed industrial countries.

Prior to the Second World War the electronics industry was first and foremost a consumer goods industry: the sector's main products were supplied for private consumption and consisted primarily of radio sets. However, the war laid the foundations of a dramatic switch of production- and market-orientation in the direction of technical electronics. The series of technological revolutions which took place during the course of the 1950s, 1960s and 1970s have therefore manifested themselves in most dramatic fashion as product innovations in the investment goods industry. The result has been a more effective utilisation of resources in a large number of production processes.

During the early postwar years, Norwegian electronics firms scarcely represented any sort of economic sector or branch. A few firms manufactured electronic products, often having other items, such as electro-mechanical equipment and apparatus, as their main products. The best-remembered feature of the electronics industry as a functional economic activity immediately after the war is the relatively large number of small radio factories which existed.

Thanks are due to Jan Fagerberg for constructive comments.

[1] Freeman, C. et al., *Unemployment and Technical Innovation*, Frances Pinter, London, 1982.

Home-led or Export-led Growth?

The situation was much the same all through the 1950s. However, a fairly significant production of telecommunications products evolved during the 1960s, and this was the most important product group by volume around the middle of that decade. The production of electronic consumer goods became less important, and by the end of the 1970s it had dwindled to an almost negligible activity. Norwegian computer production was established during the second half of the 1970s, while production of electronic instruments and apparatus accelerated notably in the early 1970s. In many ways, therefore, the development of the Norwegian electronics industry ran fairly parallel to that found in many other developed industrial countries.[2]

The period from the beginning of the 1950s to the 1970s, when technical electronics production was growing and the manufacture of electronic consumer goods virtually disappeared, will be characterised below as the *establishment phase* of the Norwegian electronics industry. The new electronics industry became established, while the older segment, the producers of radios and TV sets, vanished from the scene. What we shall analyse in this article is a number of aspects of the growth of this new electronics industry.[3]

We shall begin by giving a macro-level description of the growth and demand trends. We shall then analyse the pattern of growth from a Keynesian *demand perspective*. The question which we shall ask ourselves more specifically is this: were the strongest demand impulses received by the Norwegian electronics industry in the 1950s, 1960s and 1970s from export markets, or was the home market of greater importance? In other words, was the growth of this branch mainly home-led or export-led? Implicit in this analytical perspective is an assumption that the supply side, represented by physical production capacity and profitability, was not an effective constraint to the development of production in this period.[4]

There are a number of studies which analyse macroeconomic growth processes in such a perspective, and Choi[5] provides a comprehensive discussion recapitulating the export-led growth theory. On the other hand there are relatively few analyses of in-

---

[2] For a brief account of the most important features of structural and technological change in the electronics industry, see Tilton, J.E., *International Diffusion of Technology, the Case of Semiconductors*, The Brookings Institution, Washington, 1971.

[3] The sector classification in the NOS industrial statistics (NOS Industristatistikk) does not give a clear-cut definition of the electronics industry. Our definition of electronics production and electronic products is therefore based on the list of goods in the Brussels nomenclature (BTN). The electronics industry is demarcated in this article in such a way as to embrace originally 11 product groups (electronic consumer goods not included). These groups are merged in the analysis. A detailed description of the data is given in the Statistical Appendix.

[4] We employ the concepts "home-led growth" and "the strongest growth impulses from the domestic market" more or less synonymously. This is a somewhat imprecise use of concepts. If factors on the supply side did form an effective limitation on the quantity produced, terms such as "export-led growth" or "home-led growth" are rather misleading. With limitations of this type it would be proper in a Keynesian demand perspective to give a milder interpretation of the concepts. Thus, for example, it would be more correct to speak of "stronger growth impulses from the home market than from the export market" or "stronger growth impulses from the export market than from the home market".

[5] Choi, K., *Theories of Comparative Economic Growth*, The Iowa State University Press, Ames, 1983.

dustrial growth at the sector and *branch* level from this starting point. Linder[6] is an important exception, but he offers only a qualitative discussion of possible cause-effect mechanisms underlying the growth of new industrial activity starting from growth impulses via the home market. A discussion of important aspects of Norwegian industrial development starting from growth impulses via the export market is to be found in Hodne,[7] for example. The theoretical framework of this work, however, is far less ambitious than that of Linder. As far as is known there are no studies which attempt to test in an analytical way whether growth impulses from the home market have been stronger than growth impulses from the export markets for particular activities in industry. An important aspect of the present work is that we shall carry out just such tests.

The article is organized as follows. The first section gives a description of certain principal features of the development of the Norwegian electronics industry. The growth pattern and the development of demand are discussed, and the most important features of structural change are highlighted. The data presented in this section form the starting point for the subsequent analysis. Thereafter, various theories and mechanisms of home-led and export-led growth are discussed. The next section follows up with the statistical analysis, in which the theories of home-led and export-led growth respectively are examined in greater detail. The article concludes with a number of synoptic observations in the last section.

Growth, transformation and demand development

The electronics industry[8] has been the most vigorously-growing branch of Norwegian industry during the postwar period.[9] Whereas the volume produced by Norwegian industry in the aggregate trebled during the thirty-year period 1950-1979, the result shown by our calculations is that the quantity produced by the electronics industry increased by a factor of over 50 in the same period. While electronics production constituted an extremely modest 0.3% of total industrial production in 1950, the proportion had risen to 3.5% by the end of the 1970s.[10] In spite of the much more vigorous growth of the electronics industry compared with industry as a whole,

---

[6] Linder, S.B., *An Essay on Trade and Transformation*, Almquist and Wicksell, Uppsala, 1961.

[7] Hodne, F., *Norges økonomiske historie 1815-1970* (The economic history of Norway, 1815-1970), Cappelens forlag, Oslo, 1981.

[8] See the Statistical Appendix for a more detailed description of definitions and principles of calculation (cf. note 3).

[9] Generally speaking such a statement would depend on which classification of branches was selected. The electronics industry as defined here corresponds approximately to a branch classification at the three-digit ISIC level. There is little likelihood that any other branch in Norway, even at the five-digit ISIC level, grew faster than the electronics industry in this period.

[10] The value added at current prices in the electronics industry is calculated at 10.3 million *kroner* for 1950 and 1,294.0 million *kroner* for 1979 (see the Statistical Appendix). In 1950 the value added of Norwegian industry overall was 3,624 million *kroner* (NOS *Nasjonalregnskap* 1949-62); the corresponding figure for 1979 at current prices was 36,594 million *kroner* (NOS *Nasjonalregnskap* 1962-78).

Home-led or Export-led Growth?

Figure 1 Employment (graph a) and value added (graph b). Millions of *kroner*, 1970 prices. Whole electronics industry.

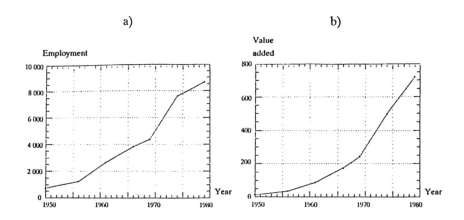

Source: Own material.

therefore, the electronics industry represented a fairly modest activity in terms of direct production and employment even at the end of the 1970s.

Figure 1 shows the trend of numbers employed and value added at fixed prices (1970 = 100) over the period 1950-79. The figures are calculated for the years 1950, 1956, 1961, 1966, 1969, 1974 and 1979, and are intended to represent the peaks of successive business cycles. The trend is linearised between the individual years.

As the figure shows, it is difficult to discern any long-term wave motion in the growth pattern. Production grows steadily in volume by over 15% annually until the middle of the 1960s. The rate of growth declines somewhat in the latter half of the 1960s, rising again in the first half of the 1970s. In the latter half of the 1970s the rate of growth falls off once more. The general tendencies towards stagnation which set in during the second half of the 1970s in Norwegian industry (and industry in all OECD countries) thus did hit the electronics industry, but not with the same intensity and scope.

Far-reaching structural changes are concealed behind the aggregated growth pattern shown by figure 1. This is apparent from table 1, which shows the distribution of total gross output value between four main groups of products: 1) Computers and office machinery, 2) Components, 3) Telecommunications material, and 4) Instrument production. The output value for the whole sector totalled at current prices is given at the bottom of the table.

Scandinavian Economic History Review

Table 1 Proportion of gross output, main groups of products. Gross output value, whole branch, totalled in millions of *kroner* at current prices.

	1950	1956	1961	1966	1969	1974	1979
Computers and office material	0.0	0.0	13.2	10.5	6.4	9.1	19.7
Component production	0.0	0.0	0.4	0.4	0.5	0.6	1.5
Telecommun. material	100.0	85.7	77.4	68.6	75.5	65.7	59.3
Instrument production	0.0	14.3	8.9	20.4	17.6	24.5	19.6
Total production	22.6 (100)	61.5 (100)	151.1 (100)	329.4 (100)	418.6 (100)	1278.2 (100)	2371.3 (100)

Source: Own material.

The manufacture of telecommunications material has always been the dominant product group in Norwegian electronics production. The production of instruments started in the middle 1950s but was not specially significant in terms of volume until the first half of the 1970s. Around the middle 1960s a few firms began producing computers and office materials on a modest scale. After the middle of the 1970s this production became fairly extensive and represented possibly the most dynamic segment of the Norwegian electronics industry in the 1970s. One important characteristic of Norwegian electronics production, finally, is the fact that the component-producing part of the industry, viz. the manufacture of radio valves, transistors and - later on - integrated circuits, was almost entirely absent during the whole of this period.

Home-led or Export-led Growth?

Figure 2 Gross output value, imports and exports in millions of kroner at current prices. Whole electronics industry.

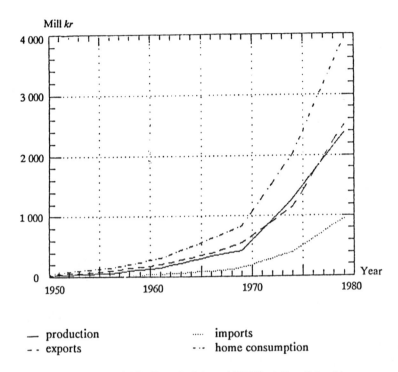

— production ..... imports
- - exports --- home consumption

Sources: Own material, OECD Trade Statistics and NOS Norsk Utenrikshandel.

Figure 2 shows production (gross output), imports, exports and home consumption for the whole branch at current prices for the same period as before. Home consumption, or domestic demand, is calculated on the basis of the data given for production, exports and imports. By definition, home consumption corresponds to production plus imports minus exports when changes in stocks are disregarded.

The figure shows that electronics imports constituted a significant proportion of internal market demand over the whole period. The significant share of the Norwegian electronics market taken by foreign producers emerges more directly from table 2, which shows the import ratio for the whole sector and the same four main groups of products as before. The import ratio, defined as imports as a percentage of home consumption, is fairly stable, hovering around 55-65%. A fairly stable import ratio at the same time signifies, of course, that the share of the entire Norwegian electronics market enjoyed by Norwegian producers was likewise stable during this period.

Table 2 Import ratio in %. [(imports/domestic demand)100].

	1950	1956	1961	1966	1969	1974	1979
Computers and office material	n.a.	n.a.	93.5	96.0	104.5	87.2	86.3
Component production	n.a	n.a	99.6	98.9	98.7	95.9	85.8
Telecommun. material	n.a.	n.a.	45.1	44.7	42.9	40.5	47.1
Instrument production	n.a.	n.a.	88.5	62.2	73.6	48.2	62.6
Total production	62.0	67.8	66.9	62.0	66.6	56.6	63.8

Source: As figure 2.

In all categories of goods except instrument production we find the same degree of stability over time in the market shares accounted for by foreign and home producers respectively. The import ratio is particularly high for components and computers and office machinery products. The high import ratio for components is self-explanatory. As already shown, Norwegian electronics firms have generally not been producers of components. At the same time the demand for this type of product has been relatively substantial because components are the basic input factor for the segment of the electronics industry carrying out assembly production. The import ratio in the computers and office machinery group was over 100% in 1969. This must be interpreted as re-exports of imported products if possible changes in stocks are disregarded.

The export ratio, defined as the proportion of production that was exported, is shown in a similar manner in table 3. There is a fairly clear tendency for the export ratio to increase in the 1950s and again in the latter half of the 1970s. For the individual product groups the export ratio fluctuates fairly widely from year to year. The export ratio for the computers and office materials group is over 100% in 1969. This too must be interpreted as due to the existence of re-exports.

Home-led or Export-led Growth?

Table 3 Export ratio in % [(Exports/production) 100].

	1950	1956	1961	1966	1969	1974	1979
Computers and office material	n.a.	n.a.	77.5	86.7	130.9	51.1	65.3
Components production	n.a.	n.a.	83.3	57.1	52.6	20.0	20.0
Telecommun. material	n.a.	n.a.	21.5	17.2	21.9	29.1	31.9
Instrument production	n.a.	n.a.	63.7	35.2	47.8	29.9	40.4
Total production	13.3	24.4	33.0	28.3	33.6	31.3	40.0

Source: As figure 2.

In the light of what we have seen we can now sum up the following two main features of the development of the Norwegian electronics market and Norwegian electronics production during this period. Firstly, internal market demand in the 1950s, as later, was met to a significant degree by imports. The import ratio was somewhat in excess of 60% throughout, and was remarkably stable. The great importance of the market share held by foreign producers on the Norwegian electronics market may be seen also from the fact that throughout the period, with the exception of certain years in the early and middle 1970s, the quantity of imports exceeded the volume of home production (figure 2).

Secondly, the growth in the quantity produced which was going on throughout the 1950s and 1960s to a large extent represented deliveries to the domestic market, large in percentage terms but modest in volume. Exports gradually assumed greater significance and at the end of the period the export ratio approached 40%.

In the analysis that follows we shall be attempting to look somewhat more concretely at the importance of the home market as against the export market for the growth of the Norwegian electronics industry. As has been noted, the Keynesian analytical perspective we adopt implies that the growth of production is assumed to have been demand-constrained throughout the period of analysis. Production capacity is built up over time and this production capacity is presumed to have been large enough to cover demand all the time; if producers had wanted to produce more, profit considerations would have caused them to do so had they found the markets.

This supposition probably comes fairly close to reality. Given this perspective we reduce the theoretical growth analysis to a determination of whether it was growth impulses via the home market or the export market that were strongest in the establishment phase of the Norwegian electronics industry. Before starting the analysis, however, we must present the most important theoretical viewpoints with regard to export-led and home-led growth processes. This leads on to the empirical interpretation we give of an export-led and a home-led industrial growth process respectively.

Export-led versus home-led growth

To what extent growth processes can be said to be export-led has been the subject of a long and wide-ranging debate in the literature. Many have stressed the great importance of export-led growth. Thus Beckerman,[11] Kaldor,[12] Lamfalussy[13] and Thirlwall,[14] for example, have argued that differences of competititiveness and export activity are the central factors in understanding why the growth rates differed in the well-developed industrial countries during the period immediately after the Second World War. For a brief résumé, see Choi.[15]

The adherents of the theory of export-led growth have propounded several cause-effect mechanisms to buttress the theory. One principal mechanism is that growth of exports will stimulate the sectors which can exploit the advantages of scale. This will apply primarily to the industrial sectors. A shift of the balance of economic activity in favour of bigger production units and larger-scale production will furnish the basis for increased productivity and reduced unit costs. Competitiveness improves, exports rise and production rises. This is a chain of reasoning which we find in Kaldor, for example.

Another principal mechanism associated with the theory of export-led growth is that growth of exports protects the trade balance and makes possible a growth of investment activity. The nation's productive capacity increases, and effective domestic demand is stimulated by the multiplier effects. This is the cause-effect chain for which, for example, Beckerman argues. An extremely simple variant of this model is given by Thirlwall,[16] who shows under easily-grasped conditions that a growth pattern which precisely ensures a balance in the foreign trade produces a proportional relationship between the export growth rate and the growth rate of the national product.

The export-led growth theory is basically a macroeconomic growth theory, not a theory of industrial development. However, parts of the theory can also be assigned the status of a theory of industrial development, as is done by Cornwall.[17] The growth of a new branch or sector of industry in a country can be interpreted as ex-

---

[11] Beckerman, W., Projecting Europe's Growth, *The Economic Journal* 72, 1962, pp. 912-925.

[12] Kaldor, N., *Causes of the Slow Rate of Growth of the United Kingdom*, Cambridge 1966; Kaldor, N., Conflicts in National Economic Objectives, *The Economic Journal* 81, 1971, pp. 1-16.

[13] Lamfalussy, A., *The United Kingdom and the Six; an Essay on Economic Growth in Western Europe*, Richard Irwin, Homewood, Ill., 1963.

[14] Thirlwall, A.P., *Balance of Payment Theory and the UK Experience*, (3 ed.), Macmillan, London, 1986.

[15] Choi, *op.cit.*.

[16] Thirlwall, *op.cit.*, chapter 10.

[17] Cornwall, J., *Modern Capitalism. Its Growth and Transformation*, Martin Robertson, London, 1977.

Home-led or Export-led Growth?

port-led if entrepreneurs and individual firms first attempt to establish market shares and sales abroad, (perhaps) exploiting the local national market afterwards.

Cornwall, on the other hand, designates a growth pattern as home-led ("homespun growth") if firms and entrepreneurs in a new branch of industry first seek to penetrate the home market and then as a second stage endeavour to establish market shares at international level. The mechanisms underlying such a development may be linked to certain factors on the supply side. For example it is argued that firms may be able to establish advantages of scale by developing the domestic market, which in turn may furnish the basis for cost advantages *vis-à-vis* competitors abroad. Sales and production at home exert an irrigating influence on export markets over time.

A more specific and somewhat different theory of home-led industrial development is adduced by Linder.[18] Linder contends that growth of new industrial activities in a country *always* (or nearly always) takes place within the domestic market. Only when the possibilities there are exhausted and some form of market saturation sets in do producers attempt to move towards production for export. As a general rule, therefore, exports of industrial products and foreign trade are - in Linder's view - merely an extension of the trade that goes on inside a country's boundaries.

In the actual description of the gradual market reorientation away from the domestic market to the export markets, Linder and Cornwall are largely in agreement (though more as a potential trend of development in Cornwall). The mechanisms underlying a pattern of home-led industrial growth, however, are different in Linder inasmuch as he believes that it is the *qualitative* structure of home market demand that determines the type of products which domestic industrial manufacturers will produce and which - later on - they can export.

The emphasis laid on the qualitative structure of the home market implies that in a country which (for one reason or another) has, for example, a substantial involvement in shipping, there is a considerable possibility that industrial activity will be established with a special orientation from the outset towards parts of this market. Manufacturers of new products will in the initial stages align themselves towards market segments of this type rather than towards possible export markets because on the home market they have better information and can establish simpler search mechanisms than they can abroad. Various forms of producer-user links are often held to play an important role in this respect.[19] In such a step-by-step market dynamic from home market to export market, prices and costs are presumed to play a secondary role. Conclusions as to which factors are decisive in establishing the structure of a country's economy can therefore be very different from predictions based on the theory of comparative advantage.

---

[18] Linder, op.cit.. Andersen, E. et.al., *The Importance of the Home Market for the Technological Development and the Export Specialization of Manufacturing Industry, Duplicated*, Aalborg University, Aalborg, 1981, give a fairly comprehensive discussion of this theory. This work also suggests links with the product-cycle theory (see below).

[19] This perspective is developed especially by Lundvall, B.Å., *Product Innovation and User-producer Interaction, Duplicated*, Aalborg University, 1985.

The so-called product-cycle theory can be interpreted as an extension of Linder's theory of home-led growth (Hirsch,[20] Vernon,[21] van Duijn and others,[22] see also Posner.[23] The product-cycle theory supplements Linder's theory at an important point in that it introduces dynamic developmental relationships for industrial growth *between different countries* which are at different stages of development. In contrast to Linder (and Cornwall), this theory gives a fairly good explanation, for example, of why a home-led growth process becomes exhausted and stops.

Criticisms can be levelled at Linder's home-led growth and industrial development theory on several planes. In the first place it may be objected that the theory can appear somewhat mechanistic and unhistorical in that it asserts that (almost) all new industrial activity in a country will evolve in response to growth impulses from the internal market. As a basic position there is reason to believe, for example, that Linder's theory fits in better with the growth of various types of product-assembly industries in developed industrial countries than with the establishment of processing industries in less industrialised countries. Secondly, there is the objection that the theory is so open and general that the empirical implications seem unclear. How, for example, is it possible to give a precisely-detailed account of what the qualitative structure of home market demand consists of? And thirdly, the theory must be regarded as stylised in the sense that it is difficult to believe that only growth impulses from the home market have significance for industrial growth - even in an extremely early phase of growth - in small open economies.

Analysis

The empirical model

As has been pointed out by Lubitz[24] and others, the empirical implications of the macroeconomic theory of export-led growth are not clear and unproblematical. One of Lubitz' main points is that a high positive correlation between the growth rates of national product and export volume respectively does not necessarily lend support to the theory. This is the most usual way of testing the theory, but Lubitz contends that such a correlation cannot be accepted without further ado as substantiating the mechanisms underlying the theory.[25] There is also a certain amount of controversy as to how the individual variables are to be represented. For example, should export activity be expressed as a growth rate, as an export ratio (exports as a proportion of

---

[20] Hirsch, S., *Location of Industry and International Competitiveness*, Clarendon Press, Oxford, 1967.

[21] Vernon, R., International Investment and International Trade in the Product Cycle, *Quarterly Journal of Economics*, 1966, pp. 191-207.

[22] van Duijn, J. et al., *The Long Wave in Economic Life*, Allen and Unwin, London, 1983.

[23] Posner, M.V., International Trade and Technical Change, *Oxford Economic Papers*, 13, 1961, pp. 323-341.

[24] Lubitz, R., Export-led Growth in Industrial Economies, *Kyklos*, 27, 1973, pp. 307-321.

[25] In Lubitz' empirical model, *op.cit.*, the extent of investment activity is also one of the factors brought in as a variable of explanation.

Home-led or Export-led Growth?

GNP), or as an absolute change? The different modes of representation frequently reflect differing views as to how the mechanisms underlying an export-led growth process operate. This debate seems not to have resulted in any final clarification.[26]

The empirical implications of an export-led and a home-led industrial growth process respectively may seem to be somewhat simpler than for the export-led macro-theory. One of the main reasons for this is that it is meaningless to link trade balance barriers with the development of particular economic activities. An obvious empirical interpretation of a home-led pattern of growth à la Cornwall is that export ratios will be small yet rising steadily as a result of a gradual orientation towards markets as the new activity burgeons. The same interpretation can also be given by Linder's theory, but here the domestic "quality" of the demand for the sector's products comes in as an additional factor. An empirical interpretation on the lines of Cornwall, an export-led pattern of industrial growth could be that export ratios will be high while at the same time there will possibly be a tendency for these to be reduced as time goes on because of a gradual orientation towards the home market as production becomes better established.

As remarked in the previous section, it may seem difficult to give a more detailed descriptions of what goes on within the home market's qualitative structure. Nor do we have any data that might be able to say anything particularly precise about this because our data are limited to include production and trade flows for some selected year. We therefore have no opportunity to study the core of Linder's industrial growth theory statistically, but we shall offer a few tentative comments at the end of the article. However, the other aspect of the theory of a home-led pattern of growth - that the export ratios will be low but growing - can easily be studied in greater detail. As we have already seen in section 2, the growth tendencies of export ratios can be regarded in this respect as supporting this theory. We shall also look at this in more detail at the end.

In the calculations which follow we shall lay more emphasis than do Cornwall and Linder on a somewhat different interpretation of the links between growth and the trend of market shares, in that we shall enquire instead whether the strongest impulses behind the growth of the Norwegian electronics industry have come from the home market or from export markets. The empirical problem will then be to study the connections between development of production and development of the different components of demand. This analytical approach is founded on an *a priori* assumption that both the home market and the export market can have been important to the growth of the new industry - even in the very earliest years.

From such a basic position it will be natural to formulate an empirical model featuring a simultaneous relationship between production development, export demand and growth of home demand. When applying our hypothesis that the growth of the Norwegian electronics industry was demand constrained throughout the establishment phase, such an approach may be further justified, for example, by taking as a starting point a reduced form of a model containing only two equations - one of them (actually an identity) expressing the relationship between supply and use of

---

[26] See the concluding discussion in chapter 5 of Choi, *op.cit.*.

electronics products, and the other saying that the import ratio (i.e. imports as a proportion of home consumption) is fixed.[27] The use of such a simultaneous model makes it possible to investigate in greater detail which of the two demand components contributed most to the growth of production.

The next question, then, is how this relationship is to be represented. In a first formulation we shall express the various magnitudes as annual average growth rates. As has been said, this is the representation most commonly found when the macroeconomic export-led growth theory is being tested. However, because the starting level for many of the goods and production flows in the Norwegian electronics industry is very low and the calculated growth rates are therefore extremely sensitive *vis-à-vis* the starting level, we shall also represent the relationships as absolute changes.

As far as we can see there is nothing in the theories saying that a representation in the form of growth rate is necessarily better than a formulation in terms of absolute change. We can obviously get into a situation where the different representations can give different conclusions, but this is a quite ordinary problem of specification.

(1) gives the model when the specification is at growth rate form. g is the average annual growth rate of production, d is the growth rate of domestic demand over the same period, and e is the growth rate of exports, also reckoned over the same period as production.[28]

(1) $g = \alpha_0 + \alpha_1 d + \alpha_2 e$

A priori we expect both α_1 and α_2 to be positive. If both coefficients are positive and significantly different from zero, both demand components explain the variation in production growth. In such a situation the question of which of the two demand components has contributed most to explain growth is usually resolved by taking an average. The domestic market's contribution is then the mean value of the growth rate of domestic demand multiplied by the appropriate regression coefficient, while the contribution of foreign markets is the mean value of the export growth rate multiplied by the regression coefficient.

(2) shows the corresponding model when the specification of the model is given in terms of absolute changes. ΔX is production changed from one moment in time to another, ΔD is domestic demand changed in the same period, and ΔE is changed exports. The interpretation of this model formulation is as above.

---

[27] The relationship between supply and use of electronics products is given by the identity (disregarding changes in stocks) $B + X = D + E$, where B = imports, X = production, D = home consumption and E = exports. A fixed import ratio gives the import function $B = b D$. Substituted into the balancing equation this gives $X = (1 - b)D + E$. Differentiating gives $dX = (1 - b)dD + dE$. In growth rate form we get $dX/X = [(1 - b)D/X]dD/D + (E/X)dE/E$.

[28] For obvious reasons the introduction of time-lags in the variables of explanation can have something to be said for it. However, the observations we have are rather scanty and will become even fewer if the variables of explanation are given with time-delays.

Home-led or Export-led Growth?

(2) $\Delta X = \beta_0 + \beta_1 \Delta D + \beta_2 \cdot \Delta E$

It is worth noticing that the interpretation we give of the type of growth pattern in these models does not imply anything about the size of the export ratios or their trend over time. On the other hand (2) can - as indicated above - be directly interpreted as though this model reflected fixed import ratios (see note 27).

The models are estimated in two data series. First we look at the sector as a whole, then we use the data material for the individual commodity groups along with the whole sector. For the whole sector we have altogether seven points for measuring production, exports and domestic demand (cf. e.g. table 2). Between these seven measuring points, which are intended to represent the peaks of successive business cycles, we have six observed growth rates and absolute changes. When the models are estimated for the whole sector and we have a pure time-series regression, therefore, we have only six observations. All growth rates and absolute changes are given in current prices and the growth rates are calculated as average annual geometrical growth rates.

For the individual commodity groups we have five observations for the trade flows (cf. tables 3 and 4). By using this disaggregated material we consequently get four observed growth rates and absolute changes for exports and domestic demand. Since we have four commmodity groups this gives sixteen observations in all. Along with the six observations for the sector as a whole, these combined cross-sectional and time-series data give 22 observations altogether.

Calculations

Table 4 shows the results from the time-series regression for the whole sector when the models are specified in growth rate form, model (1). The complete regression is shown at the bottom of the table as (c), while the individual regressions are shown at the top of the table as (a) and (b). When both market components are included simultaneously, the sign of the regression coefficient for growth on the domestic market will, as expected, be positive, while the sign of the regression coefficient for growth in the export market comes out as negative. Compared with (a) and (b) there are clear indications of multicollinearity, and the regression where only the domestic demand component is included fits best to the growth model. The regression coefficient for growth on the domestic market becomes positive in (a) and is significantly different from zero at the 1% level.

The interpretation of this regression coefficient is that a 1% increase in the demand growth rate (in nominal terms) gives an increase of 1.55 percentage points in the growth rate of production. This is equivalent to saying that an increase of 1% in domestic demand gives an increase of 1.55% in production, which means that the impact of domestic demand on growth declines in relative terms when the volume of demand becomes larger. Inasmuch as demand increases over time, this means at the same time that the calculation is telling us that the relative importance of the domestic market has decreased over time. This conforms to actual developments.[29]

---

[29] The individual regression between production growth and growth of domestic demand in growth rate form, $g = \alpha_0 + \alpha_1 d$, gives by integration the formula $X = Ae^{\alpha_0 t} D^{\alpha_1}$. t is the time and e is

Table 4 Regression calculation equation (1), growth rates, Whole sector, time series 1950-79 (N=6)

(a) g =   −7.02   + 1.55 d $R^2 = 0.86$
          (−1.53)   (4.99)
                       *

(b) g =   6.06   + 0.49 e $R^2 = 0.32$
          (0.86)   (1.39)

(c) g =   −7.14   + 1.77 d   − 0.16 e $R^2\text{adj.} = 0.80$
          (−1.43)   (3.69)   (−0.64)
                      **

Estimating method: Ordinary least squares method.
* significant at 1% level
** significant at 5% level (t-value in parentheses)

Table 5 gives the results of the corresponding calculations when the variables are specified in terms of absolute changes, model 2. The complete model (c) fits very well with the data, and both the regression coefficients are significant at least at the 5% level. However, the coefficient for export growth now also has the wrong sign. Comparison of (c) with (a) and (b) shows that there are quite clear indications of multicollinearity with this specification of the model as well. Since (a) fits the data rather better than does (b), the conclusion is that the growth in the domestic market alone best explains the growth of production even with this sample and with this specification of the model.

---

the base figure in the natural logarithmic system. $\alpha 1$ can therefore be interpreted as an elasticity between production and domestic demand. If $\alpha 1 > 1$ the ratio between D and X will decrease when D exceeds a certain level, i.e. the relative importance of the domestic market diminishes. The ratio between domestic demand and production was on average somewhat below 2.0 for the period as a whole. This ratio is indicated by figure 2, but can be read more clearly from table A1 in the Statistical Appendix. It can also be seen from this table that the ratio declines over time.

Home-led or Export-led Growth?

Table 5 Regression calculation equation (2), absolute changes. Whole sector, time series. 1950-79 (N=6)

(a) $\Delta X = \quad -7.84 \quad + \quad 0.62\, \Delta D \qquad\qquad R^2 = 0.98$
$ (-0.17) \qquad\;\; (13.14)$
$ *$

(b) $\Delta X = \quad 63.39 \quad + \quad 2.08\, \Delta E \qquad\qquad R^2 = 0.92$
$ (0.81) \qquad\;\;\; (6.61)$
$ *$

(c) $\Delta X = \quad -60.17 \quad + \quad 1.19\, \Delta D \quad - \quad 2.01\, \Delta E \quad R^2_{adj} = 0.99$
$ (2.46) \qquad\;\; (8.05) \qquad\;\; (-3.91)$
$ *** \qquad\qquad * \qquad\qquad\; **$

Estimating method: Ordinary least squares method.
* significant at 1% level
** significant at 5% level
*** significant at 10% level (t-value in parentheses).

The above calculations are based on only six observations. As has been noted, we can enlarge the basis of observation if we look at the trend of all four main groups of products and the whole sector combined. We then have 22 observations. The results derived from these combined cross-sectional and time-series calculations are shown in the growth rate specification, model (1), in table 6. We shall come back to the conditions underlying the relation (a*).

This estimate gives results differing somewhat from those yielded by the corresponding model specification above (table 4). Both the regression coefficients in the complete model (c) have the signs expected and are significant at the 5% level. The explanatory power of the model is, however, rather weak. Multicollinearity is now no problem and the complete model can be regarded as the best adaptation of the data. The mean value of the export growth rate is 16.6% per year, while the mean value of the growth rate on the domestic market is 13.9% per year. On average, therefore, exports contribute to a production growth rate amounting to 9.8% per year (0.59 x 16.6). The domestic market, on the other hand, contributes on average to a growth rate of 11.9% (0.85 x 13.9) per year, i.e. somewhat more.

Table 6 Regression calculation equation (1), growth rates. Four commodity groups and whole sector (combined time series and cross-section) 1950-1979.

N = 22
(a) g =   2.10   +   1.04 d $R^2 = 0.21$
         (0.32)   (2.28)
                        **

N = 22
(b) g =   5.10   +   0.69 e $R^2 = 0.26$
         (1.09)   (2.67)
                        **

N = 22
(c) g = -5.06   +   0.85 d   +   0.59 e $R^2_{adj} = 0.33$
        (-0.76)   (2.03)   (2.43)
                        **   **

N = 20
(a*) g = -9.39   +   1.87 d $R^2 = 0.81$
        (-2.98)   (8.78)
          *   *

Estimating method: Ordinary least squares method.
* significant at 1% level
** significant at 5% level (t-value in parentheses).

Detailed study of the data shows that there are two extreme observations which cause the correlation between production growth and growth on the domestic market to be so low in this calculation. This may be seen in figure 3a, which shows observations and estimated regression line for equation (a) from table 6. For the sake of comparison the corresponding relation for model (b) from table 6 is given in figure 3b. As can be seen, the observations are spread more evenly around the regression line here.

The observation at the bottom of figure 3a is for commodity group 1, Computers and office machinery 1966-69, while the observation at top left is for commodity group 2, Components 1974-79. If we exclude these two observations and calculate the regression between the production growth rate and the growth rate of domestic demand, the results will be as shown in (a*) of table 6. The growth of the domestic market alone now explains a significant proportion of the growth of production. It can be seen that when the two observations are excluded this simple model is better adapted to the data than does the complete model (c).

Home-led or Export-led Growth?

Figure 3 Graph a; observations and estimated regression line home-led growth, model (a) table 6. Graph b; observations and estimated regression line export-led growth, model (b) table 6

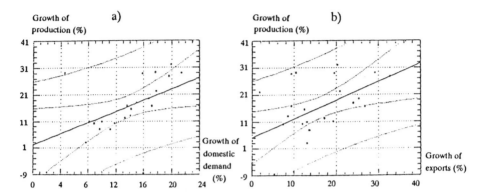

We have no *a priori* grounds for believing that any other characteristics should be linked to the two above-mentioned observations compared to the other observations. To exclude them and make an estimate from the remaining part of the sample is therefore an *ad hoc* manoeuvre in the highest degree. Nevertheless it is on this more *ad hoc* basis that we prefer to interpret the results of the calculations in table 6 as supporting the theory that the strongest growth impulses came from the home market and that the growth was primarily home-led.

Table 7 shows the results when growth expressed as absolute changes is estimated from the combined cross-sectional and time-series data, equation (2). The results run fairly parallel with the earlier calculation of equation 2 from table 5. The primary effect of these calculations is likewise to lend support to the theory that the strongest growth impulses came via the home market and that growth was mainly home-led.

The conclusions which we can draw from the calculations we have carried out are not entirely clear and unambiguous. In three instances the figures lend support to the theory that the strongest demand impulses came via the home market. In the fourth calculation the impression is more mixed. If we eliminate two extreme observations from the material in this calculation, however, the conclusion changes somewhat. The exclusion of these two observations from the calculation produces the result that growth on the home market alone explains over 80% of the growth in all

Table 7 Regression calculation equation (2), absolute changes. Four commodity groups and whole sector (combined time series and cross-section) 1950-79, N = 22

(a) $\Delta X =$ -6.44   +   0.63 ΔD $R^2 = 0.95$
             (-0.36)   (20.15)*

(b) $\Delta X =$ 28.34   +   2.14 ΔE $R^2 = 0.90$
             (1.15)   (13.45)*

(c) $\Delta X =$ -14.63   +   0.82 ΔD -   0.70 ΔE $R^2_{adj} = 0.95$
             (-0.77)   (4.93)*   (-1.19)

Estimating method: Ordinary least squares method.
* significant at 1% level, (t-value in parentheses).

four calculations. All in all, therefore, we interpret the calculations as supporting the theory that the electronics industry in Norway has grown primarily as result of demand impulses from the domestic market. A less precise interpretation is that the growth stimuli received from domestic demand seem to have had more impact on growth than have demand impulses from abroad.

Concluding remarks

The idea of its being possible for a new industrial activity in a small open economy to spring forth chiefly as the result of demand impulses from the domestic market is an interesting conclusion. It is also far from being a self-evident result. For in the fairly recent industrial history of Norway there is probably a whole series of important examples where growth and development patterns have been of a contrary character - viz. export-led. The establishment and expansion of power-hungry industry over the past 40-50 years is probably the supreme example of such a process.

The impression formed as a result of the above calculations, of a primarily home-led growth of the Norwegian electronics industry, is strengthened further when we look at the trend of exports and export ratios. As shown in table 3, there is a clear tendency for the export ratio for the sector as a whole to increase over time. In 1950 the export ratio was 13.3%, whereas in 1979 it was 40%.[30] As has already been remarked, such a market development is what we should expect with a home-led

---

[30] If we fit a linear time trend to the movement of the export ratio, a, so that t=0= 1950 (the first observation year), this gives the regression equation (t-values in parentheses):

a = 18.09 + 0.74 t   N=7, $R^2 = 0.77$
    (5.73)   (4.13)

The increase of the export ratio therefore awards fairly well to a time trend.

Home-led or Export-led Growth?

growth process on Linder-Cornwall lines. Home market demand is the initiating growth factor behind industrial growth, but little by little as the new activity becomes more "mature", markets elsewhere assume ever-increasing significance and the export ratios increases.

We can also detect faint echoes of the stress laid by Linder on the qualitative importance of the domestic market for the growth of a new industrial activity in its very earliest stage. For example, production of navigation and other maritime electronic equipment was certainly of significance in the 1950s and 1960s. These products were supplied to the fishing and merchant fleets, which were important sectors of the Norwegian production system during this period - sectors which, in Linder's view, can manifestly be said to represent a special "quality" of home market demand.[31]

The main weight of domestic demand in this early part of the establishment phase, however, came from the public sector, i.e. primarily telecommunications and defence.[32] This type of demand had a much greater effect in the 1950s and 1960s than in the 1970s. In the 1950s and 1960s telecommunications material formed the dominant product group in the Norwegian electronics industry (see table 1) and it was Televerket (the Telecommunications Authority) which was the most important customer for these products. The first phase of the Norwegian electronics industry's growth, therefore, partook to some extent of the character of a publicly-administered growth process.

Finally, it is a natural step to enquire what effect protection of the domestic market in the form of customs and quota restrictions may have had on the home-led growth process. In an article on Norwegian industry in the 1950s and 1960s, Balassa[33] contended that Norwegian import protection in the form of duties on industrial products was lower than that imposed by Norway's most important trading partners during this period. Moreover, most of the quota restrictions on imports of industrial products were abolished in Norway around 1960.[34] There are also clear signs suggesting that the trade barriers against imports of electronics products into Norway were more modest than the trade barriers encountered by Norwegian products abroad during this period.

Using a survey of customs tariffs as a starting point, we have calculated the average (unweighted) percentage duty on imports of electronic products into Norway to have been around 10% at the end of the 1950s. The corresponding average rate has been reckoned at about 20% for Great Britain and 15% for the EEC countries as a

---

[31] See Skonhoft, A., Framveksten av ny industriell aktivitet i en liten åpen økonomi (The growth of new industrial activity in a small open economy), *Arbeidsnotat*, Trondheim, 1986.

[32] Ibid.

[33] Balassa, B., Industrial Development in an Open Economy, the Case of Norway, in *Artikkel* nr. 30, Statistisk Sentralbyrå, Oslo 1969.

[34] Balassa has calculated the average customs tariff on industrial products in Norway at 11.7% in 1958. The corresponding customs tariff for EEC countries was 14.5%. See Balassa, *op.cit.*, p. 10. See Aukrust, O. et al., *Norges økonomi efter krigen* (Norway's economy after the war), Samfunnsøkonomiske studier nr. 12, Statistisk Sentralbyrå, Oslo, 1965. In chap. VI there is a broader discussion of Norwegian commercial policy during the early postwar period.

whole.[35] Since quota restrictions on imports of industrial products were virtually abolished in Norway at the start of the 1960s, there were probably rather fewer obstacles to imports of electronic products into Norway than there were to Norway's exports of electronic products to its most important trading partners at the end of the 1950s. However, this asymmetry probably became less marked during the 1960s because of the establishment of EFTA in 1959.

This suggests that what we have interpreted as a home-led growth process did not take place under cover of a specially protected domestic market. If the customs duties of Norway's most important trading partners had been more in line with the Norwegian tariff, the export ratio of Norwegian producers would probably have been rather higher in the 1950s and 1960s. The market share of foreign producers on the Norwegian electronics market, on the other hand, would have been little affected if these producing countries had reduced their customs tariffs to the Norwegian level. A lower level of customs duties and an absence of quota restrictions both in Norway and among Norway's trading partners, on the other hand, would probably have entailed the possibility both that the Norwegian producers' export ratio might have been higher and that their share of the Norwegian market might have been lower.[36]

---

[35] The table below shows the customs tariffs in % 1958 applied to 14 electronic products by Norway, Great Britain and the EEC countries. The number in the first column refers to the product number in the Brussels nomenclature (the BTN system). See the Statistical Appendix.

	Norway	Great Britain	EEC		Norway	Great Britain	EEC
84.51	10	15	15	85.16	10	20	15
84.52	10	16	12	85.17	10	20	15
84.53	10	17.5	11	85.21	5	25	18
84.54	10	16	15	90.17	10	20	16
85.13		20	15	90.20	5	33.5	11
85.14	5	20	17	90.26	18	20	15
85.15	10	20	17	90.28	15	25	16
				Unweighted average	7.8	20.6	14.9

Sources: Pep, *Atlantic Tariffs and Trade*, Allen and Unwin, London, 1962.

[36] On the assumption more symmetrical customs tariffs, i.e. if the tariffs of Norway's trading partners were in line with Norway's, it is reasonable to suppose that imports, B, would have been unchanged while exports, E, would have been higher - i.e., $dB = 0$ and $dE > 0$. If we assume that domestic demand, D, is not affected, then we also have $dD = 0$. From the balancing equation $B + X = D + E$, therefore, we find that $dX = dE > 0$ (we assume that there are no barriers on the supply side). The import ratio, $b = B/D$, remains unchanged under the given conditions. The export ratio is defined as $a = E/X$. By differentiation we easily find that $da > 0$. In the absence of customs duties, both exports and imports would probably have been higher. It is simple to demonstrate that under otherwise similar conditions as above, this would lead to a higher export ratio and a higher import ratio.

Home-led or Export-led Growth?

Statistical Appendix

Sources and definitions
The data base is made up partly of data for individual firms which, when totted up for all firms, give figures for the whole sector, and partly of aggregated sector and commodity data. Export and import data are obtained in aggregated form, while base material for production figures etc is obtained at company level. The reason for our having taken the microdata road is connected with the fact that the branch classification which we find in the public statistics (published in NOS Industristatistikk) does not define the electronics industry effectively when we are using fairly long time series.

The company data file gives production figures (defined as gross output value) for 14 groups of electronic products along with principal economic figures such as value added, numbers employed and so on for all Norwegian electronics firms for selected years. The measurement points are 1950, 1956, 1961, 1966, 1969, 1974 and 1979.

The data base is derived from the *Statistisk Sentralbyrås* (SSB) *Industristatistikk* (the Industrial Statistics of the Central Bureau of Statistics, SSB), and the concept of what constitutes a firm follows the SSB definition. In other words, whatever is defined as a firm or company in our company data file is also defined as a firm or company in the NOS industrial statistics.

The method employed in order to identify from SSB's registers what we define as electronics firms is as follows. As a first step all firms in occupational group 3712 (cable and wire factories), 3719 (production of other distribution material) and 3720 (signals, radio and telecommunications material) according to the old ISIC code, and occupational group 3825 (production of office machinery), 3832 (production of signals, radio and telecommunications material) and 3851 (production of technical and scientific instruments) according to the new ISIC code, were picked out. The new ISIC code applies to all years from 1966 onwards, while the old ISIC code applies to earlier years. In all about 325 firms were singled out in this way. In other words, altogether about 325 firms with production in the above-cited occupational groups during one or more of the years specified were recorded.

As a second step the original statistical schedules which the firms submit to SSB (this is the basic material for the NOS Industrial Statistics) were examined so as to ascertain what sort of products the firms produced during the particular years. If in at least one of the years the firm produced what we have defined below as electronic products, the firm has been included in our company data file and in this respect defined as an electronics firm. Altogether there were 148 such firms.

The definition of electronics production is based upon the lists of goods in the Brussels nomenclature (BTN). The products are categorised in the following 14 main groups:

1) 84.51 Typewriters
2) 84.52 Calculating machines
3) 84.53 Punch-card machines and computers
4) 84.54, 84.55 Other office machines
5) 85.13, 85.14 Telecommunications equipment
6) 85.15100-85.15459 Radio apparatus
7) 85.15500.1815559 TV apparatus
8) 85.15901-8515909 Parts under 85.15
9) 85.15 ex. groups 6), 7) and 8), Radar and navigational apparatus
10) 85.21 Radio valves, semiconductors
11) 90.17 Electro-medical instruments
12) 90.20 X-ray apparatus
13) 90.26, 90.28, 90.29, 85.16, 85.17 Measuring equipment
14) 92.11, 92.13 Gramophones etc.

71

In conformity with the above, an electronics firm in our data files is a firm which, in one or more of the years 1950, 1956 ... 1974 and 1979, was recorded in one of the above-mentioned ISIC occupational groups and at the same time produced articles figuring in one or more of the BTN commodity groups specified.

This definition implies that firms which are recorded in ISIC occupational groups other than those specified above, and which at the same time produced electronic products falling within the above-specified commodity-grouping, are not included in our data files. There will be some such firms, but their numbers are probably extremely modest in practice.

Total production in the individual commodity groups, total production of electronic products, value added and numbers employed in the whole branch are thus arrived at by totting up the figures for all firms. In this article we are concerned only with production of technical electronics, electronics production for consumer use therefore being excluded. Consumer electronics are defined as commodity group 6), commodity group 7) and commodity group 14). Total electronics production (gross output value) for the individual years therefore corresponds to the sum of the production of the individual firms over commodity groups 1) to 14) excluding the three commodity groups with consumer electronics, i.e. 11 commodity groups in all.

These 11 commodity groups are merged to form 4 main commodity groups (cf. e.g. table 1). Groups 1) to 4) are merged to form main group 1) Computers and office machinery; group 10) corresponds to main group 2) Component production; groups 5), 8) and 9) correspond to main group 3) Telecommunications material; and groups 11), 12) and 13) correspond to main group 4) Instrument production.

Trade data for the years from 1961 onwards inclusive are based upon OECD Trade Statistics. Data for the same 14 product groups as above have generously been made available by the Department of Production, University of Ålborg. The figures are given here in US $ which are converted to NOK by using the average annual exchange rate. The exchange rate is found for example in the UN International Trade Statistics 1983. For the years 1950 and 1956 we have ourselves extracted the data from NOS Utenrikshandel.

Calculations

Value added at fixed prices (figure 1): Manufactured value at current prices is derived from the company data file described above. Price index calculation based on the ISIC-group production of electrical apparatus and material. Source: *NOS Nasjonalregnskap* 1949-62 and *NOS Nasjonalregnskap* 1962-78. Numbers employed (figure 1) aggregation as above.

Tables A1-A5 show gross output value, imports and exports in current prices (mill. kr.) for the four main commodity groups and the whole sector. These tables form the basis of compilation of all tables and figures (except figure 1) in section 2. The tables also form the starting point for the analysis in section 4.

Home-led or Export-led Growth?

Table A1 Whole sector

	1950	1956	1961	1966	1969	1974	1979
Production	22.6	61.5	151.1	329.4	418.6	1278.2	2371.3
Imports	32.0	98.0	204.6	385.3	553.8	1146.0	2506.7
Exports	3.0	15.0	49.8	93.3	140.6	399.5	948.2
Home consumption	51.6	144.5	305.9	621.4	831.8	2024.7	3929.8

Table A2 Commodity group 1: Computers and office machinery

	1950	1956	1961	1966	1969	1974	1979
Production	0	0	20.0	34.6	26.9	116.7	467.5
Imports	n.a.	n.a.	64.6	109.2	192.2	388.3	1023.2
Exports	n.a.	n.a.	15.5	30.0	35.2	59.6	305.5
Home consumption	n.a.	n.a.	69.1	113.8	183.9	445.4	1185.2

Table A3 Commodity group 2: Component production

	1950	1956	1961	1966	1969	1974	1979
Production	0	0	0.6	1.4	1.9	8.0	34.5
Imports	n.a.	n.a.	27.0	53.0	69.0	148.1	166.9
Exports	n.a.	n.a.	0.5	0.8	1.0	1.6	6.9
Home consumption	n.a.	n.a.	27.1	53.6	69.9	154.5	194.5

Table A4 Commodity group 3: Telecommunications material

	1950	1956	1961	1966	1969	1974	1979
Production	22.6	52.7	117.0	226.1	316.2	840.0	1405.1
Imports	n.a.	n.a.	75.3	151.3	185.6	405.4	852.7
Exports	n.a.	n.a.	25.2	38.8	69.2	244.6	448.2
Home consumption	n.a.	n.a.	167.1	338.6	432.6	1000.8	1809.6

Table A5 Commodity group 4: Instrument production

	1950	1956	1961	1966	1969	1974	1979
Production	0	8.8	13.5	67.3	73.6	313.5	464.2
Imports	n.a.	n.a.	37.7	718	107.0	204.2	463.9
Exports	n.a.	n.a.	8.6	23.7	35.2	93.7	187.6
Home consumption	n.a.	n.a.	42.6	115.4	145.4	424.0	740.5

[13]

From Growth to Crisis
The Danish Banking System from 1850 to the Interwar Years

Per H. Hansen

Introduction

Banking history has had little attention in Denmark if compared to many other countries. The purpose of this article is to present some current topics of interest in Danish banking history from about 1850 to the interwar years. Special emphasis will be laid upon the relations between banks and industry as well as the boom and bust phases of the banking system during the period.

Section two of this article deals with the legal setting in which the banks operated and section three outlines the structure of the banking system and its relative importance to the economy in general. Section four presents the rather incomplete knowledge about the banks' relations to industry and finally, in section five, attention will be paid to the banking crises of the period with special regards to the 1920s and to the role of the Nationalbanken, the Danish central bank, as a lender of last resort. Section six will summarize the article with some concluding remarks and suggestions for further research.

The legal setting

Even though Danish banking was never a free banking regime it developed in a very favourable climate providing liberal conditions for the operations of banks. Entry into banking and the development of banking services remained free until 1919, when the first commercial bank act was passed through parliament. These liberal conditions left space for innovations in financial services, like the cheque, cash credits, branch banking, investment banking and was in general favourable to the development of banking in Denmark. On the other hand it cannot be denied, that some of the worst calamities in the banking crises of 1877-78, 1907-08 and the 1920s might have been avoided if bank regulations had been enacted earlier.

In *Banking and Economic Development* Rondo Cameron claims that "where banking was left most free to develop in response to the demand for its services, it produced the best results."[1] A Danish study inspired by the approach of Cameron contends that absence of regulation was advantageous to the growth of industrial manufacturing in Denmark.[2]

---

[1] Cameron, R., *Banking and Economic Development. Some Lessons of History*, New York, 1972, p. 25.

[2] Hansen, S.Aa., *Early Industrialization in Denmark*, Copenhagen, 1970, p. 64.

From Growth to Crisis

The main reason for the absence of prudential regulation was the very liberal economic climate that dominated the Danish economy until the First World War.[3] In 1880 the savings banks had been regulated by law because of the crisis of 1877-78. But in fact this crisis hit the commercial banks harder, and the committee preparing the savings banks bill explicitly commented that there was no need to regulate commercial banks, since their customers were business men able to judge the solidity of the individual banks. The savings banks' customers, on the other hand, were unable to do this. In modern economic theory this would be labelled the information problem. According to the committee asymmetric information was a problem in respect to savings banks but not to commercial banks.

This attitude was to change in the aftermath of the banking crisis of 1907-08, when the state, the Nationalbanken and the main banks provided assistance to troubled banks which later had to be liquidated. As was the case thirty years earlier it was a banking crisis that initiated legislation. Now it was realized that bank customers did not possess full information, and a board was appointed to prepare a bill on commercial banks. When a commercial bank act finally passed through parliament in 1919 it provided for some differentiation between savings banks and commercial banks, better presentation of accounts, auditing, rules concerning solvency, solidity and liquidity and restrictions on the right to own and lombard own shares etc. The bank act also established, as a separate public body, the office of the bank inspector who was authorized to investigate the banks' adherence to the law. A proposal on interest rate ceilings, meant to reduce competition between banks and savings banks, had been part of the original bill in 1913 but was rejected by the House of Lords committee on the grounds that "money is an international good, the price of which is determined by the laws of supply and demand."[4] Another interesting point is that, when the committee reported in 1913, it had drawn up a section which listed the lines of business that the banks should be allowed to do. In this list investment banking activities were absent. When the House of Lords committee reported on the bill in 1913, they inserted "the preparation and founding of companies" into the bill on the grounds that legislation was not intended to limit the existing lines of business, and the committee found it a necessary part of bank operations in a small country like Denmark.[5] Promotion and founding of companies did get a place in the bank act, but with another, and more conditioned text. According to this the bank could "participate in the founding of companies, according to the circumstances".

In general it may be said, that the bank act of 1919 instituted the principles of information and control in order to secure the payments system and the deposits of

---

[3] Thomsen, N., *Industri, stat og samfund 1870-1939*, Odense, 1991, p. 199.

[4] Betænkning over forslag til lov om bankselskaber. Afgivet af Landstingets udvalg den 7. marts 1913, *Rigsdagstidende 1912-13*, col. 1159-72, col. 1160-61.

[5] Hansen, P.H., Bank Regulation in Denmark up to 1930, Paper presented to the First European Analytical Economic History/Historical Economics Conference, Copenhagen, 19-21 July 1991, p. 16.

the public.[6] Unfortunately, the negotiations for the bank act were procrastinated for so long that the chance to prevent the banking crises of the 1920s was lost. It was generally agreed that it was an adequate and good law, but the excesses of the First World War had influenced on the banks' balance sheets. As a reaction against the severe banking troubles through the decade of the 1920s many demands for a revision of the bank act were heard. Again, it took about 8 years from the process started until a new law was passed through parliament in 1930.

The commercial bank act of 1930 set out to utilize the experience of the 1920's banking troubles in order to avoid a return of the calamity. Thus, it was little surprise, that it ended up more severe than the former one. During the preparation, much more severe proposals had been submitted, among others limitations on entry. According to this, entry should be subject to approval on the conditions that it was supposed to be advantageous to the society in general. It is some paradox, that the committee appointed to prepare a revised bank act, proposed to introduce a new kind of market deficiency, monopoly, while trying to reduce the effects of another, information deficiencies. The proposal was defeated, and the final law, passed on April 15 1930.

Contrary to the law of 1919, this one had been drafted by a committee consisting of the various interest groups, for instance bankers organizations, unions etc. Thus, a considerable measure of corporatism had been introduced into the bank legislative process. This was not the case in the legislative process in 1910 to 1919, when politicians were the main participants. The most significant addition to the bank act was that lending to a single borrower was restricted to a maximum of 35 per cent of the bank's equity, or 50 per cent if the board and directors gave their unanimous approval. Exactly this sort of lending had been one of the main causes of the bank failures in the 1920s. Furthermore, liquidity and solvency regulations were made more rigorous, and the banks' right to own shares and real estate was restricted.

It is too early to pass judgement on prudential regulation of banking in Denmark until 1930. As in other countries, there is a close correlation between banking crises and legislation. Parliamentary negotiations constantly emphasized the need to protect the payment system and the economy in general and there was some sentiment for a protection of the depositors interests.[7] This fact emphasizes the importance of analysing the legislative process in the light of theories of regulation, because the statements concerning bank regulation by public authorities and experts tend to stress the need for protection of the public interest. While this motive is relevant of course, the regulatory process should be analysed also from the point of view of other interest groups involved, first of all the banks. Did the banks profit from the legislation or did the costs exceed possible benefits? The approach of the economic theory of regulation may be fruitful in order to analyse this problem.[8]

---

[6] Olsen, E./Hoffmeier, E., *Dansk Pengehistorie 1914-1960*, Copenhagen, 1968, pp. 134-146, and Hansen, *Bank Regulation* ...

[7] Hansen, *Bank Regulation* ...

[8] About the economic theory of regulation, see Stigler, G.J., The Theory of Economic Regulation, *The Bell Journal of Economics and Management Science*, vol. 2, spring, 1971, pp. 3-21, and Pos-

From Growth to Crisis

The banking system

By every measure, around the middle of the 19th century, Denmarks economy was dominated by agriculture which was specializing in grain production. In the following years a still larger part of this production was exported to England, and the agricultural production was to a high degree export orientated, which it continued to be, also after the transition to animal production which took place from about 1870.

Industrial development, on the other hand, was still in its infancy and manufacturing thus dominated by handicraft production. In general manufacturing was producing for the home market, and joint stock industrial companies were few.

The distribution of GDP at factor prices within certain sectors between 1850 and 1930 is shown in table 1.

Table 1 Distribution of GDP at factor prices. 1929 prices

Year	Agriculture	Industry	Commerce etc.	Construction	Transport
1850	403	84	57	35	11
1860	433	126	75	49	17
1870	519	170	121	55	30
1880	532	226	196	61	51
1890	596	325	297	71	81
1900	657	462	474	158	150
1910	861	657	721	166	246
1920	755	831	1081	110	311
1930	1430	1324	1431	310	546

Source: Johansen, H.Chr., *Dansk økonomisk statistik*, Copenhagen, 1985, pp. 395-397.

In 1850, the credit market too was insignificant. The only major credit institution was the Nationalbanken, established in 1818, and besides that 35 savings banks and one commercial bank existed. The year after, in 1851, a credit association (building society) bill was enacted, and in the following years some credit associations were set up.

Until 1845, the Nationalbanken lent money on a certain scale, but the primary objective of this bank was to stabilize the monetary system, which had been destroyed during the Napoleonic wars, due to hyperinflation. The Nationalbanken was given monopoly of note issue and the task of bringing back the Danish Rix dollar to parity. This goal was achieved in 1838, and in 1845 the bank declared its notes convertible into silver. At the same time, inflexible reserve requirements for the bank's

---

ner, R.A., Theories of Economic Regulation, *The Bell Journal of Economics and Management Science*, vol. 5, autumn, 1974, pp. 335-358.

note issue were introduced, and this meant that the bank's potential for lending was severely restricted.[9]

The lending of the Nationalbanken, especially lombarding securities and discounting of bills of exchange, could not fulfil the needs of the business community. The activities of many Danish commercial firms were financed by Hamburg merchant houses, but still there was a credit vacuum around the middle of the century. This vacuum was filled out by a wave of commercial joint stock bank foundings in the provinces. Until 1857, 13 provincial banks were established, and all with the explicitly stated objective of promoting "commerce, industry and agriculture". In Copenhagen two banks were founded, the most important being the Privatbanken (the Private Bank) in 1857 under the leadership of C. F. Tietgen. The founding of a commercial banking system took off in this period, because Denmark experienced a boom in the economy, concentrated around the exports of the agricultural sector.

At this time, self-financing and private sources of credit were predominant in relation to financing of industrial and commercial activities. Agriculture on the other hand probably borrowed some funds from the savings banks whose lending was directed primarily towards that sector.

In 1857, the crisis put an abrupt end to the establishment of new banks, but in the first half of the 1870s, a new boom in bank foundings took place. Table 2 illustrates the later development in the banking and savings banks system:

Table 2   Deposits of commercial and savings banks (mill. kr.)

Year	Commercial Banks Deposits	Commercial Banks Equity	Commercial Banks Number	Savings Banks Deposits	Savings Banks Number
1870	27	17	18	118	168
1880	78	54	41	254	443
1890	176	71	46	454	516
1900	310	101	86	582	512
1910	701	235	135	811	521
1920	4,037	587	208	1,459	505
1930	2,344	445	180	2,097	532

Source: Johansen, *Dansk økonomisk statistik*, pp. 263-270 and *Banktilsynet 1920-1945*, Copenhagen, 1945.

Already from the beginning of the 1870s, the banking system had taken on the structural characteristics, that were to dominate for almost 100 years. Thus, from the beginning of the 1860s, the Nationalbanken had taken on the macro- as well as the micro functions of a central bank, that is managing the monetary system on the one

---

[9] In 1875, Denmark converted to a gold standard, and in 1908 the charter of 1818 was renewed, the most important change being the adoption of more flexible reserve requirements based on a percentual coverage.

From Growth to Crisis

hand and acting as a bankers bank on the other.[10] This was the result of a combination of the Bank's inability to handle the crisis of 1857 in an adequate way and the appointment of a new manager Moritz Levy. In the commercial banking world, the three big Copenhagen main banks, Privatbanken, Landmandsbanken (the Agricultural Bank) (1871) and Handelsbanken (the Commercial Bank) (1873), dominated the banking system and acted as a sort of money center banks, since the provincial banks used them as correspondents and carried out transactions in foreign exchange mainly through them. In 1880, the three main banks held 72.1% of all banks' balances, in 1890 62.3%, 1900 62.9%, 1910 59.5%, 1920 56.5 and in 1930 52.1%.[11] These data seems to show that the relative importance of the main banks was decreasing, but actually these banks took on an increasing importance in the credit market due to, among other things, their operations on foreign markets and their role as correspondents to provincial and medium sized Copenhagen banks. This meant that the ability of the Nationalbanken to manage the liquidity as well as the banking system was impaired.[12]

Also, Landmandsbanken and Handelsbanken started up with a strategy of establishing branches in the provinces, collecting savings there and, to some degree, canalizing them to the capital.

The relative size of the banking system may be expressed in relation to the GNP. In 1870 the total assets of the banks were 7% of GNP, in 1880 17%, 1890 27%, 1900 34%, 1910 54%, 1920 67%, 1930 53% and in 1940 43%. The figures emphasizes the increasing importance of the banking system right up to 1920 when the banking crisis of the 1920s led to a decline during the decades of the 1920s and 1930s.

In relation to the operations it carried out, the Danish banking system was a universal banking system. The banks not only advanced working credits to industrial and other firms, but also engaged in investment banking activities through the issuing of shares and debentures in connection with creation of new as well as expansion of existing firms. Also, bankers were represented in many of the boards of industrial and commercial companies; not only the larger companies situated in the capital, but also smaller provincial companies. This mixed banking tradition was established during the period from 1865 to 1875 through the activities of C. F. Tietgen and the Privatbanken, and carried on by the main banks and some provincial banks in the 1880s and 1890s. Section four goes into more detail on this subject.

While the amalgamation movement in European banking was leading to a concentration of banking, the Danish banking system continued to be relatively decentralized in the period under treatment. That is not to say, that no mergers or acquisitions of smaller banks took place, but as is evident from table 2 the structure of the banking system with a lot of independent banks continued to exist. However, two banks, the Landmandsbanken and Andelsbanken did engage in acquisitions. The Landmandsbanken, especially in the years 1912 to 1921, when it took over 16 provin-

---

[10] On this subject, see Goodhart, C., *The Evolution of Central Banks*, Cambridge, Mass., 1988.

[11] Statistiske Undersøgelser, nr. 24: Kreditmarkedsstatistik, Copenhagen, 1969, and De Danske Banker. Indberetning til Handelsministeriet om de danske bankers virksomhed, 1930 and 1931.

[12] Hansen, Sv.Aa./Svendsen, K.E., *Dansk Pengehistorie 1700-1914*, Copenhagen, 1968, pp. 354-363.

cial banks and savings banks with total assets of 150 mill. kroner. In 1922, just before it crashed, it took over a troubled medium sized Copenhagen bank with assets of more than 100 mill. kroner.[13] The acquisitions met with a lot of opposition. Axel Nielsen, a professor of economics at the University of Copenhagen, warned against the concentration of the banking system and the power of the big banks related to it. Also, the local communities where banks were taken over or attempted to be taken over protested, and quite often a new local, independent bank was founded when the old one was taken over.[14] The Andelsbanken (the Cooperative Bank) was primarily establishing new branches and offices, and at an astonishing speed. The Andelsbanken was founded in 1914, with strong relations to the cooperative movement. In 1915 it opened 6 branches, in 1916 10, in 1917 30, in 1918 32 and in 1919 23 branches. 35 of these branches were acquired through take overs of 11 local banks and savings banks and their offices.[15]

Table 3   Number of Copenhagen banks' provincial branches

Bank	1900	1905	1910	1915	1920	1925	1930
Landmandsbanken	8	8	8	11	21	47	47
Handelsbanken	7	7	7	7	7	30	40
Andelsbanken[a)]	-	-	-	6	112	104	-
Dansk Andels- og Folkebank	-	-	-	-	-	5	23

Source: *Statistisk Årbog* 1900, 1905, 1910, 1915, 1920; *De Danske Banker. Indberetning til Handelsministeriet om de danske bankers virksomhed 1926 and 1930. Beretning til Rigsdagen fra det i henhold til lov af 8. august 1925 nedsatte rigsdagsudvalg angående Andelsbanken*, Copenhagen, 1926, p. 12.

[a)] The figures for 1920 and 1925 are from 1921 and 1924 respectively. The bank failed in 1924. Instead, the cooperative movement founded the Dansk Andels- and Folkebank.

In 1921, the provincial branches of the Copenhagen banks had public liabilities of 565 mill. kroner or 34% of the three banks total public liabilities. The corresponding figures for 1925 and 1930 are 269 and 32% and 301 and 33%.[16] A large part of the deposits of the branches was time deposits.[17] The main banks, with the exception of Privatbanken, that had no branches at all, funded a third of their assets from their

---

[13] Beretning om forholdene i Den Danske Landmandsbank. Hypothek- og Vekselbank m.m. Afgivet af den ved Kgl. ordre af 21. september 1922 nedsatte kommission, Copenhagen, 1924, pp. 22-39.

[14] Nielsen, A., *Bankpolitik, Første del: Beskrivelsen*, Copenhagen, 1923, p. 363; Beretning om forholdene ..., pp. 20-39, *Finanstidende*, 31 July, 21 August and 11 September, 1918.

[15] Beretning til Rigsdagen fra det i henhold til lov af 8. august 1925 nedsatte rigsdagsudvalg angaaende Andelsbanken, Copenhagen, 1926, pp. 11-14.

[16] Figures for the period before 1921 are not available.

[17] De Danske Banker ..., 1921, 1925 and 1930.

From Growth to Crisis

provincial branches. From time to time the provinces claimed that the main banks channelled these funds away from the local area, to the advantage of the business life of the capital.

The only bank merger of any importance was in 1919, when two medium sized banks, the Københavns Laane & Diskontobank (the Copenhagen Loan- and Discount Bank) and the Revisionsbanken i København (The Auditing Bank in Copenhagen) merged into Københavns Diskonto and Revisionsbank (The Copenhagen Discount and Auditing Bank) with total assets of 440 mill. kroner.[18]

The composition of assets and liabilities of the banks changed, of course, during the many years under investigation. In tables 4 and 5, the assets and liabilities of the banking system are split up into different groups.

Table 4   Assets of Danish banks 1870-1939. Per cent

Year	Bills	Lending	Foreign assets	Securities	Other assets	Cash	Total
1870-79	33.03	33.98	6.99	12.85	9.00	4.16	100
1880-89	26.18	31.18	8.49	15.59	13.35	5.22	100
1890-99	21.53	35.24	7.35	17.51	14.45	3.92	100
1900-09	19.82	44.12	5.01	14.99	13.32	2.74	100
1910-19	15.03	45.83	4.95	16.54	14.72	2.93	100
1920-29	13.94	54.29	3.12	12.58	13.02	3.06	100
1930-39	12.78	52.17	2.71	14.31	12.24	5.78	100

Source: Johansen, *Dansk økonomisk statistik* ..., pp. 263-265.

Discounting bills of exchange formed a strongly decreasing part of total assets during the period, while other forms of lending, especially cash credits and lending against securities gained considerably in importance. This is in accordance with the general view, that industrial financing by banks became more common in the run of the 70 years.

Noticeably, the share of securities in the assets portfolio did not vary significantly, but more detailed study into this area is necessary. For instance, the composition of the securities portfolio itself before 1921 is not known i.e. how large a part of the portfolio was made up of shares? Furthermore, the values are, of course, in current prices, saying nothing about the nominal values or the price when acquired by the bank.

---

[18] Statistiske Undersøgelser ..., pp. 58 and 114, *Finanstidende*, No. 11, 1919.

Table 5 Liabilities of Danish banks 1870-1939. Per cent

Year	Equity	Deposits	Foreign liabilities	Other liabilities	Total
1870-79	38.04	50.27	.00	11.68	100.00
1880-89	30.26	63.00	.00	6.74	100.00
1890-99	25.44	68.05	.00	6.51	100.00
1900-09	21.96	70.02	.00	8.01	100.00
1910-19	17.30	75.44	.00	7.26	100.00
1920-29	12.77	76.64	3.00	7.60	100.00
1930-39	14.91	76.26	1.78	7.05	100.00

Source: Johansen, *Dansk økonomisk statistik* ..., pp. 267-269.

When it comes to the composition of liabilities, the most distinct characteristic is the very dominant position taken by equity in the years prior to 1900. There is no doubt, that some relationship exists between this high ratio of capital to total liabilities and the development of mixed banking in Denmark.[19] However, another reason for the high capital ratio must be emphasized too. In the initial stages of commercial banking the banks seem to have been, to some degree, unaware of the potential role of deposits from the public and since note issue was a monopoly of the Nationalbanken the banks started out with high capital ratios. Deposits with the banks increased quite fast, however, and the banks began to rely increasingly on deposits for their funding. This meant of course that maturity transformation became a more important part of the banking business, even though a large part of the deposits could undoubtedly be characterized as savings banks deposits.

During the First World War, the banks were saturated with deposits. This was due to a heavy increase in the general liquidity caused primarily by a very favourable balance of payments during the war. As a consequence, for the first time since about 1890, Denmark became a creditor nation.[20] The Nationalbanken did nothing to restrain this increase in liquidity and the money that flowed into the banks had to be placed somewhere. During the first half of the war the banks increased their lending on cash credits very strongly, but in the last year and a half it became harder to lend

---

[19] Tilly, R., Banking Institutions in Historical and Comparative Perspective: Germany, Great Britain and United States in the Nineteenth and Early Twentieth Century, in *Journal of Institutional and Theoretical Economics*, Vol. 145 No. 1, March 1989, pp. 189-209. Tilly finds positive correlation between the willingness of the bank of issue to rediscount banks' bills and the banks' engagement in investment banking. His study incorporates banking in Germany, Great Britain and USA. It is not obvious, that such a correlation exists in the Danish case since the practice of investment banking was developed before the rediscounting practices were firmly cemented. However, more research into this question is necessary, since the early relations between banks and the Nationalbanken are not quite clear.

[20] Cohn, E., *Danske Pengeforhold 1914-1936*, Copenhagen, 1961, p. 33; Hansen, *Dansk Pengehistorie* ..., pp. 347-353; Johansen, H.Chr., De private banker under den første verdenskrig, *Om Danmarks historie 1900-1920. Festskrift til Tage Kaarsted*, Odense, 1988, pp. 165-168.

From Growth to Crisis

out all the money deposited with the banks. For the provincial banks this dilemma seems to have been solved by placing big deposits with the correspondent main banks in Copenhagen which on their part invested the funds in foreign assets.[21]

In the autumn of 1920 a period of severe contraction in the business of banking began. The international decline in the price level and the corresponding troubles of companies spilled into the asset portfolios of the banks. That, however, is the subject of section five.

Banks and industrial finance

Ownership and investment in industry was mainly Danish, since only very little direct foreign investment took place. To the degree that domestic savings were insufficient capital import was undertaken through the sale of securities, especially bonds. This capital import was carried out by banks, credit associations and from 1906 through a public institution, Kongeriget Danmarks Hypothekbank (the Royal Danish Mortgage Bank).[22]

Knowledge about industrial finance in Denmark may be described as impressionistic. Very few studies into the subject have been undertaken and consequently we know too little. However, we do know that self-financing was far the biggest source of funds for industry in the period under consideration, but also that institutional capital played an increasingly important role. Especially up to 1914 and perhaps even longer industrial firms relied heavily on ploughing back profits for financing.[23]

Basically, there are at least two ways in which to look at the role of banks in industrial finance, from the point of view of the bank and the company respectively. Also of interest is the question about how different branches within the industrial sector were financed. This section will present some, rather inconclusive, evidence on these aspects.

As mentioned above, the Danish banking system was a universal banking system. The operations of mixed banks can be structured into 5 functions: 1) the founding function, related to the creation of companies or mergers between existing ones. 2) The issuing function, associated with the banks' provision of equity or debenture capital through underwriting activity. 3) The working credit function. 4) The managerial function, exercised through the appointment of company board members by the bank and 5) the concentration function, i.e. the attempts to restrict competition through horizontal mergers in the branches of industry in which the bank had interests. These functions apply especially to the German banking system, which has come to stand as a model for mixed banking.[24]

---

[21] Johansen, *De private banker ...*

[22] Johansen, H.Chr., Banking and Finance in the Danish Economy, 1870-1914, in Cameron, R. (ed.), *International Banking*, Oxford University Press. (Forthcoming).

[23] Nielsen, P.B., Industriens investeringsmønstre og finansielle struktur 1840 til 1914, unpublished Ph.D. dissertation, University of Copenhagen, 1988, p. 197.

[24] Hansen, *Early ...*, p. 42, and Tilly, R., Germany. 1815-1870, in Cameron, R. (ed.), *Banking in the Early Stages of Industrialization*, Oxford, 1967, pp. 151-182.

In Denmark the Privatbanken was actively engaged in promoting companies in the field of communication such as Det forenede Dampskibs-Selskab (the United Steamship Company) (1866), Det Store Nordiske Telegraf-selskab (The Great Northern Telegraph Company) (1869) and Kjøbenhavns Telefon A/S (the Copenhagen Telephone Company) (1881). Furthermore, the Privatbanken also founded some large industrial firms like De Danske Sukkerfabrikker (The Danish Sugar Factories) (1872), Burmeister & Wain (1872), Tuborgs Fabrikker (Tuborg Breweries) (1873) and De danske Spritfabrikker (The Danish Distilleries).[25] Quite early the Privatbanken acquired a considerable placing power in relation to its investment banking activities. This placing power was related to the bank's intimate relations with companies and several provincial banks. Among the provincial banks using the Privatbanken as correspondent, was the Fyens Disconto Kasse (the Discount Bank of Funen), which frequently took over shares of the issues underwritten by the Privatbanken.[26] The importance of placing power is illustrated in the monograph on Citibank:

> ... investment banking depended on more than the ability to originate an issue. Of almost equal importance were placing power (relationships with prospective institutional and individual investors) and banking power (the resources to provide short-term credit to syndicate members and brokers to enable them to finance their positions in an issue while it was being sold to the ultimate investors).[27]

Being a correspondent bank to the provincial banks, the Privatbanken also had the banking power to support these with loans in connection with the placing of issues. It should be mentioned that even though the Privatbanken was acting as underwriter of company equity and debt, its main investment banking activity was in the area of arranging public loans for governments and local authorities.[28]

Some provincial banks engaged in investment banking activities too, although on a smaller scale. As a case study, Fyens Disconto Kasse, can be mentioned. Fyens Disconto Kasse was the largest provincial bank, located in Odense which was the second largest town in Denmark, and with industrial activity higher than average. Through guaranteed issues of debentures and shares the Disconto Kasse participated in the founding of transport and communication companies like railroads, telegraph and shipping companies and industrial firms in among others paper-, textile- and sugar-production. Through its portfolio of securities, the bank financed the capital basis of several companies and in the years between 1870 to 1878 the bank held an increasing portfolio, a very large part of which was shares and debentures. In 1870 the portfolio was 9% of total assets and 38.5% of that was in shares and debentures, the other part in royal bonds and credit association bonds. In 1871 the figures were 7.3 and 55%, in 1872 10.1 and 64.3%, in 1873 14.7 and 68.7, in 1874 14.6 and 85.4, in 1875

---

[25] Hansen, *Early* ..., pp. 42-43.

[26] Hansen, P.H., Fyens Disconto Kasse. En undersøgelse af bankens kreditformidling, med særligt henblik på industriens finansiering, unpublished masters thesis, Odense, 1989 pp. 69-71.

[27] Cleveland, H. van B./Huertas, T.F., *Citibank 1812-1970*, Cambridge, Mass., 1985, pp. 33-34.

[28] Nielsen, *Industriens* ..., p. 194.

From Growth to Crisis

16.4 and 87.7, in 1876 16.9 and 100, in 1877 15.6 and 98.4, in 1878 16.6 and 96.7 per cent.[29] These figures demonstrate that the portfolio policy of the bank was directed towards high yield securities with corresponding risk exposure,[30] but that was not the only reason why the bank engaged in investment banking. A genuine wish, by the entrepreneurial minded manager of the bank, to promote industrial development should also be stressed. In 1874 this resulted in an addition to the articles of association which read:

> Against commission, the bank performs lending and share issuing for local authorities, railroads and other companies. The terms of these activities are subject to negotiations.[31]

Also, a new issue of shares which increased the capital by 100% from two to four million kroner was carried out. This was done for the explicit reason that the banks capital base should be strengthened in order to enable the bank to carry on its issuing function.[32] This investment banking policy of the bank was to bring heavy losses in the second half of the 1870s, when the price of shares and debentures in the portfolio declined strongly and the newly founded companies had problems with their earnings.

Besides its investment banking activities, the bank also engaged in other sorts of industrial financing through lending on securities, discounting bills of exchange and, most important, through cash credits. Working credits were also supplied to the companies founded with assistance from the bank. In the years 1847, 1867, 1875 and 1885 the total lending to industry,[33] including shares and debentures, was 7.3, 8.4, 16.5 and 22.36 per cent respectively of total lending in these years. If the figures for shares and debentures are deducted for 1885, the figure will be 19%, which equals the amount lent to industry by Danish banks in 1969.[34]

In the 1890s the Landmandsbanken, at that time by far the largest bank in Denmark, also engaged in investment banking by founding some of Denmark's largest industrial companies.[35]

In several instances the managers of the banks were seated on the boards of the companies they financed, and they also interfered with the business. Thus, when Dalum Papirfabrik (The Paper Factory of Dalum) founded in 1872 with the help

---

[29] Hansen, *Fyens* ..., pp. 59-86.

[30] Similar results have been found by Tilly, R., German Banking 1850-1914: Development Assistance for the Strong, *Journal of European Economic History*, Vol. 15, No. 1, Spring 1986, pp. 113-152.

[31] Hansen, *Fyens* ..., pp. 57 and 62.

[32] Ibid.

[33] In this case, the term industry refers to industrial firms as well as handicraft.

[34] Hansen, *Fyens* ..., p. 123, and Hansen, P H., Fyens Disconto Kasse 1846-86. Indlån og udlån, *Erhvervshistorisk Årbog* 1989, Århus, 1990, pp. 98-137.

[35] Schovelin, J., *Den Danske Landmandsbank. Hypothek- og Vekselbank. Aktieselskab. 1871-1921*, Copenhagen, 1921, pp. 379-380.

from Fyens Disconto Kasse got in trouble later in the 1870s the bank granted new loans on the explicit conditions that the bank was given direct influence upon the management of the factory. This was accepted and on a later general assembly of the company the chairman emphasized that the company had only survived because of the financial support of the Fyens Disconto Kasse.[36]

According to a recent study investment banking lost importance in banking operations in the years prior to 1914, when the banks concentrated on the provision of working credits and the companies' long term debt was financed through the anonymous market and abroad.[37] It is true that the decline in the capital ratio of the banks points in this direction, but no studies have been carried out on this subject. Indeed, the debentures and shares issued in the hectic years following the outbreak of World War One were floated through the banks but whether they acted merely as distributors without any guarantee or underwriting risks has not yet been investigated.

A clue can be given, however, by going through prospectuses published by companies in connection with issue of shares and debts. This has been done for the period June 1916 to January 1930 and the result is seen in table 6.[38]

This information seems to support the view that the banks not only floated the issues but acted as investment banks taking over or guaranteeing the issue of shares and debentures. That the banks were eager to carry out this line of business can be seen from the case of the Syndicate of Danish Banks. The syndicate was founded in 1917 by about 25 provincial banks with the purpose of "taking over such bank operations that single members of the syndicate would not be able to handle." It seems likely that the primary purpose of the syndicate was to participate in investment banking activities.[39]

A look at the securities portfolio of the banks (table 7) confirms, that banks were engaged in trading with shares and debentures, even though the risk exposure was far from that in the Fyens Disconto Kasse in the 1870s.

---

[36] Hansen, Fyens Disconto Kasse 1846-1886. En Undersøgelse ..., p. 73.

[37] Johansen, Banking and Finance ..., p. 23.

[38] Of the 85 issues, 72 were issued from 1916 to 1919. The method used to produce table 6 is, that all issues have been registered according to the bank handling the issue, the amount, and whether the issue was just floated, guaranteed or taken over. In many instances, the text read, that the issue was taken over by a syndicate, or just that the shares not taken by the public would be taken over. I have interpreted statements like these as evidence, that the issue was guaranteed and that the bank was involved in this. Finally it is important to notice, that not all issues were advertised in Finanstidende. For instance, in 1818, 35 prospectuses for industrial issues were published, but 90 issues were actually performed in that year. (Statistisk Årbog 1919, p. 112) In spite of these limitations the figures of table 6 must be taken to express the fact, that banks did act as investment banks.

[39] *Finanstidende* no. 31, 2 May 1917, p. 637.

From Growth to Crisis

Table 6 Share issues, industrial companies 1916-30. 1000 kr.

Bank	Number	Amount Shares	Amount Debentures	Guaranteed Number	Guaranteed Amount
Main Banks	38	67,500	16,500	29	66,400
Other Copenhagen banks	23	23,750	4,000	17	21,250
Banks and stockbrokers	4	9,070	---	2	6,000
Provincial banks	4	1,200	400	3	900
Provincial and Copenhagen banks	6	25,500	---	6	a)25,500
Syndicate of Danish banks	3	1,000	1,950	3	2,950
Stockbrokers	6	4,550	---	3	3,000
Companies	1	600	---	-	---
Total	85	133,170	22,850	63	126,000

Source: *Finanstidende* 1916-1930.

a) The big amount are due to two issues by The Privatbanken and the Århus Privatbank for to a total of 23.000 kr.

Table 7 Banks securities portfolio 1921-30. % and mill. kr.

Year	Bonds %	Debentures %	Quoted shares %	Unquoted shares %	Total %	Total amount mill. kr.
1921	70	10	8	12	100	592
1922	64	11	9	16	100	586
1923	53	12	10	25	100	603
1924	52	12	7	29	100	511
1925	55	14	7	24	100	415
1926	55	16	6	23	100	365
1927	55	15	6	24	100	357
1928	68	12	8	12	100	410
1929	71	9	8	13	101	425
1930	76	7	7	10	100	490

Source: *De Danske Banker*, 1921, 1922, 1926, 1931.

When it comes to the working credit function of the banks little is known too but it is possible to give a few hints. In the period from 1908 to 1914 for instance we know that 48% of the lending discussed in the management meetings of the Privatbanken went to industry, 18% to the commercial sector and 23% to the transport and communications sector.[40] 48% to industry seems to be a large proportion, but part of the explanation may be that the Privatbanken had intimate links with some of the biggest industrial companies in Denmark. For that reason the Privatbanken's lending may be skewed towards industry. To balance this, data for another main bank are presented for 1932, when the Handelsbanken reported its lending to the Nationalbanken. The Handelsbanken, which was known not to have as intimate relations with industry as the two other main banks, had lent a total of 334.5 mill. kr. in almost 16,000 loans. Of these 24% went to industry in 844 loans, while the commercial sector received 33% in 2,600 loans, the transport sector 7% in 142 loans and agriculture 10% in 4,899 loans.[41]

This is fragmentary evidence and hard to compare, since the data for the Privatbanken represent the total turnover in loans for a longer period, while the data on the Handelsbanken are a cross sectional view in 1932. In spite of this it should be concluded that the banks placed a considerable proportion of their funds in industry through commercial as well as investment banking activities.

Even though the Danish banking system had distinct characteristics of a mixed banking system it should also be stressed that the connections between banks and industry were only seldom as intimate as in the German case. However, in the terms of Rondo Cameron,[42] it can be said that the Danish banking system was not only permissive, accommodating all credit worthy borrowers, but actively promoting new investment opportunities.

Now, when we turn to the banks' role in industrial financing seen from the industrial companies, it should be said that the picture is a little more varied.

The banks' provision of mortgage loans to the tobacco and the iron industry respectively have been investigated for the period 1840 to 1914 and it was concluded that the banks played a minor if increasing role in this sort of lending. Banks supplied 9.4 and 14.2% of the total mortgage loans to the tobacco and the iron industry respectively during the whole period, but from 1895 to 1914 the figures were 14.6 and 17.9 per cent. In general, institutional credit took over the role as the most important source of funds from private credit in this period, and in the last part, i.e. from 1895 to 1914, the banks were more important than credit associations and savings banks. An important, if not surprising, observation in the study is that there were differences in the credit needs of the two branches because the iron industry was more capital intensive than the tobacco industry. Also the kind of funds needed were different since the tobacco sector relied heavily on working credits like supp-

---

[40] Nielsen, Industriens ..., p. 191.

[41] Minutes of the directors of the Nationalbanken, vol. 4, with supplements. Supplement 2691.

[42] Cameron, R., *Banking in the Early Stages of Industrialization*, Oxford, 1967, p. 2.

From Growth to Crisis

liers credits, while the iron industry was increasingly dependent on long term funds for capital investment.[43]

The industrial companies' funding was, as mentioned before, to a high degree supplied by ploughing back profits. However, external funds were needed to. The published accounts of most industrial companies for the period until 1930 tells us very little about the composition of liabilities and no systematic research has been done to overcome this lacuna. Again, however, some information can be found.

As an example the medium sized textile factory, Mogensen and Dessau, can be used. Established in 1902 as a joint stock company, the share capital was one million kr. half of which was taken over before going public. At the same time a debenture loan of 600,000 kr. was issued. Both issues were floated by the Privatbanken and the Fyens Disconto Kasse, and it would probably be a good guess that the banks took over a part of the shares as well as the debenture loan. The manager of the Fyens Disconto Kasse had a seat on the board of the company, and so had the manager of the biggest savings bank in Odense. Table 8 shows the liabilities of the company for selected years.

Table 8   Mogensen & Dessau, liabilities. 1000 kr.

Year	Equity	Debenture loan	Creditors	Acceptances	Bankcredit	Other
1908	1312	550	184	198	282	69
1910	1450	500	165	197	372	131
1917	2035	325	251	222	97	597
1919	2180	275	955	310	628	400
1923	1700	175	901	1195	2240	42
1926	1900	100	1221	311	2081	-
1929	1716	---	962	305	1849	1
1935	1120	---	833	214	2458	192

Sources: *Greens Danske fonds og aktier*, vol. 2, 1908, 1910, 1917, 1919, 1923, 1926, 1929, and 1935.

In per cent the bank credit, being mainly cash credit, was in 1908 11%, 1919 13%, 1917 3%, 1919 13%, 1923 36%, 1926 37%, 1929 38% and in 1935 49%. Thus, bankcredit takes on a strongly increasing role from the beginning of the twenties. If one takes a look at the profits this is hardly surprising since the company made large profits during World War One and its aftermath. In 1922 the game was over and the loss was 920,000 kr. Then followed two years with small net earnings but from 1925 to 1929 the bottom line went into red again. In other words, the company became more dependent on bank-credit during the twenties and thirties. In fact this was the

---

[43] Nielsen, Industriens ..., pp. 134-180.

case for many industrial companies in the interwar years, and quite a few reconstructions took place with assistance from the banks.[44]

In 1928, a committee was appointed with the task of preparing a revised bill on commercial banking. During its work the committee wanted information about the banks' financing of joint stock companies and an investigation was carried out as a cross sectional study for the year 1925. The study comprises 195 companies, each with a share capital of more than 1 mill. kr., 119 companies were industrial, 50 were commercial and 26 were in shipping. Table 9 displays the most important results.

Table 9   Bank financing of 195 joint stock companies 1925

Sector	Companies' assets	Companies' equity		Bank-credit		Shares/debentures in bank portfolios	
	mill.	mill.	%	mill.	%	mill.	%
Industry	1134	408	36	233	21	76	7
Trade	693	319	46	73	11	25	4
Shipping	295	140	47	20	7	37	13

Source: Forslag til lov om banker. Fremsat i Folketinget den 15. januar 1930 af Minister for Handel og Industri Hauge. In *Rigsdagstidende* 1929/30, Tillæg A, col. 4497-4656, col. 4587-4594.

Table 9 confirms the general impression that industrial companies were dependent on bank credit in the 1920s. If bank credit is related to equity instead of total assets, this is emphasized even more. Bank credit was 57% of equity for industrial companies whereas the same figures were 23% and 14% for trade and shipping respectively.

The investigation continues with a study into the distribution of bank credit to companies split up into size-, age- and profit groups. Finally the investigation divides the companies into those independent of and those dependent on the bank. Unfortunately this is done on an aggregate level without distinguishing between industry, trade and shipping. The study concludes that one third of the companies were totally dependent on the banks.

The circumstantial evidence presented here allows the conclusion that the banks funded an increasing part of the liabilities of industrial companies and that they used an equally increasing share of their funds to finance industry. Cash credits gained considerable importance during the period under investigation whereas investment banking activities, while still of importance, declined in comparison with the hectic 1870s and 1890s. During the international crisis of the 1920s many industrial companies got into trouble and had to be supported by the banks. Obviously, there were

---

[44] Johansen, H.Chr., *Industriens vækst og vilkår 1870- 1973*, Odense, 1988, pp. 133-194.

From Growth to Crisis

differences between various branches of industry but this subject, as so many others, remains to be studied.

In times of crisis

At the same time as industrial companies were most dependent on banks the banking-system itself was hit by a severe crisis. During the period 1920 to 1932, 35 Danish banks were liquidated, 19 were forced to merge with other banks and 17 were reconstructed with help from the state, the Nationalbanken and the main banks. In total 57 banks made losses for their shareholders.[45]

Table 10 Writing offs in Danish banks 1921-1932. (Mill. kr.)

Year	Total Assets	Losses on loans	Losses on securities	Total Losses	In % of assets
1921	4,921	64.2	3.9	69.6	1.41
1922	4,423	240.1	24.2	265.3	6.00
1923	4,213	62.6	5.5	68.7	1.63
1924	3,859	19.0	29.3	49.0	1.27
1925	3,398	141.8	55.5	202.9	5.97
1926	3,085	14.5	5.7	21.1	0.68
1927	2,956	29.3	0.4	31.5	1.07
1928	2,887	75.1	1.3	77.5	2.68
1929	2,969	12.4	0.2	13.5	0.45
1930	3,059	16.2	0.2	17.4	0.57
1931	2,874	11.2	40.7	52.7	1.83
1932	2,777	15.5	1.5	18.7	0.67

Source: *Banktilsynet* 1920-1945.

Bad loans, of course, were the reason for the banks' troubles, but below it all was the deflation of the 1920s that led to insolvency. First the decline in the general price level that reached Denmark in the autumn of 1920 and later the deflationary monetary policy with the aim of reestablishing the gold standard which had been suspended since the early days of the war.

The most spectacular bank failure was that of the Landmandsbanken in 1922. After numerous rumours about the bank the bank inspector initiated an investigation in which he concluded that the bank had lost 70% of its equity. The Landmandsbanken was the largest bank in Scandinavia with total assets of 1.4 billion kr. and equity of 160 mill. kr. There was general agreement between the government,

---

[45] Hansen, P.H., Banking Crises and Bank Regulation: Denmark in the Interwar Period, *Papers in Business History. Report from the BHU International Conference 1991*, Vol. 8, London School of Economics and Political Science, pp. 1-20, pp. 7-8.

the Nationalbanken and the bank inspector, that the bank was too big to fail. In spite of the fact, that the bank had lost so much equity that according to section 16 in the bank act it had to call a general assembly in order to restore its capital, the truth about the losses was kept a secret and the Nationalbanken put up 30 mill. kr. in reserves in the bank. Already in September the bank had to be reconstructed, and this time the the equity was written down to 10 mill. kr. and 100 mill. kr. in preferred share capital and reserves were put up by the state, the Nationalbanken and some large joint stock companies.[46] The troubles of the Landmandsbanken only stopped when the state in 1923 guaranteed all claims against the bank. The bank's situation was finally taken care of in 1928, when the bad assets were isolated in a special liquidation entity while new share capital was paid up by the state alone.

The Landmandsbanken was not the first bank to get into trouble, however. Already in 1921 the Nationalbanken had had to act as lender of last resort providing assistance to troubled banks.[47] Until 1924 the Nationalbanken readily rendered this assistance to most troubled banks. In case of large banks, these were assisted even when they were not only illiquid but also insolvent. In fact, the Bank went even further and helped put up share capital in new banks founded in areas where a local bank had failed. Another sort of assistance provided by the Nationalbanken was attempts at supporting the share prices of troubled banks by buying shares in the market. The latter sort of operations were done when managers of large banks met in the Nationalbanken and expressed their fear that declining share prices would initiate a run on their banks.[48]

In most cases the Nationalbanken tried to involve the main banks in the lender of last resort action, and in case of a large bank failure it was also attempted to involve the state. Likewise it often discussed the cases with the bank inspector even though he was employed by the state and the Nationalbanken was a private joint stock company.

During the period 1920 to 1932 40 banks applied for assistance from the Nationalbanken, while 30 other banks were reconstructed or liquidated without applying for help.

After 1924 it seems that the Nationalbanken changed its policy concerning lender of last resort operations. In 1924 and 1925 it allowed two large Copenhagen banks

---

[46] Andersen, P.N., Laanerenten, Copenhagen, 1947, pp. 189-190; Mordhorst, K., *Dansk Pengehistorie*, Vol. 3, Copenhagen, 1968, pp. 128-134.

[47] On the concept of lender of last resort see for instance Kindleberger, C.P., *Manias, Panics and Crashes. A History of Financial Crises*, 2nd ed., London, 1989, pp. 172-200; Guttentag, J./Herring, R., Emergency Liquidity Assistance for International Banks. in Portes, R./Swoboda, A. (eds.), *Threats to International Financial Stability*, Cambridge, 1987, pp. 150-186; Solow, R.M., On the Lender of Last Resort, in Kindleberger, C.P./Laffargue, J.P. (eds.), *Financial Crises: Theory, History and Policy*, Cambridge, 1982, pp. 237-248; Rockoff, H., Walter Bagehot and the Theory of Central Banking, in Capie, F./Wood, G.E. (eds.), *Financial Crises and the World Banking System*, London, 1986, pp. 160-180; Baltensperger, E./Dermine, J., The Role of Public Policy in Ensuring Financial Stability: A Cross Country Comparative Perspective, in Portes, R./Swoboda, A. (eds.), *Threats ...*, pp. 67-90, and the classic: Bagehot, W., *Lombard Street. A Description of the Money Market*, London, 1873.

[48] Hansen, Banking Crisis ..., p. 10.

with assets of 418 and 171 mill. kr. to fail. The same banks had been supported earlier in the 1920s by the Nationalbanken and a shift in policy seems to be the explanation. In 1924 the Nationalbanken had embarked on a policy of deflation in cooperation with the Government. This was expressed by a manager of the Bank, when he said that in the period prior to 1924 the protection of production was more important than protection of the money, while about 1924 protection of the money was given foremost priority. In reality the manager expressed a Keynesian view of economic policy before this had come into prominence. Thus a shift in monetary targets must be taken into consideration when trying to explain the lender of last resort operations of the bank in the 1920s.[49] Among other conditions affecting the Nationalbanken's policy towards troubled banks are the huge outlays in connection with the failure of the Landmandsbanken that may have frightened the Bank and also led to a certain return of inflation and a deteriorating exchange rate in the years 1922 and 1923. Also personal and political aspects i.e. the interests of the different interest groups involved should be taken into consideration.

Summary

The commercial banking system in Denmark was founded in the period from 1850 to 1875 with the explicit purpose of promoting trade, industry and agriculture. Danish banking developed a practice of mixed banking and thus was a universal banking system although not with quite the same intimate relations between banks and industry as in Germany. Investment banking activities were facilitated because of the high capital ratios of the banks. Financial innovations like cash credit and branch banking was introduced early in Danish banking and enabled the banks in combination with the issuing function, to service industry. Favourable to these developments was the very liberal climate with absence of bank legislation right up to 1919.

Industrial financing by banks has been studied too little on the basis of primary source material. However, in this article some evidence has been presented to show that banks were engaged in financing industry's working credit as well as long term investment needs. Most industrial companies, however, were financed primarily by ploughing back profits, and the proportion of bank credit on the balance sheets of industrial companies seems to have grown considerably only from around 1920. Even though the capital ratios of banks constantly declined since the 1870s the banks continued to act as investment banks for industrial as well as other companies. Evidence presented in this article seems to indicate that this line of banks' business did not cease to exist in the period treated.

During the booms of 1870-75, 1901-06 and World War One, the banks built up portfolios that had to come down again. Thus the banking system was hit by crises in 1877/78, 1907/08 and in the 1920s, the latter being the most severe. This points to a clear correlation between booms and busts of the banking business. A close correlation also exists between crises and prudential regulation in the financial sector. One of the primary aims of regulation was to limit information deficiencies, while attempts at limiting competition were defeated during the legislative process.

---

[49] Ibid., pp. 16-18.

Protective regulation,[50] like lender of last resort activities, was employed in all three crises by the Nationalbanken. The crisis in the 1920s, which is the only one treated above, demonstrates that lender of last resort operations cannot be carried out regardless of the general economic and monetary situation, which also influences the monetary targets of the policy of the Nationalbanken.

The research agenda in Danish banking history is filled up with important subjects of investigation. In this article only some of the areas have been presented. These may be especially relevant since they are connected to recent research in banking history in other countries.

The role of banks in industrial financing should be analysed on the basis of a comprehensive examination of sources like bank and company records. Even though there are big gaps in this material and access in some cases may be hard to obtain, there are possibilities of fruitful research. An approach setting out to work on the basis of the concepts of institutionalism is still needed in Denmark in regard to banks.

The regulation of banking and the lender of last resort operations of the Nationalbanken in the period from 1870 to 1930 have not been subjected to systematic research. Analysis of the regulatory process and the Nationalbanken's role in emergency rescue operations should be performed on the basis of the relevant theories of regulation and central banking.

Finally studies into the consolidation process of banks in the aftermath of crises ought to be carried out in order to discover the reaction of a bank organization to crisis and the possible consequences to the credit needs of business.

---

[50] On this concept se Baltensperger, E./Dermine, J., The Role of Public Policy in Ensuring Financial Stability: A Cross Country Comparative Perspective, in Portes, R./Swoboda, A., *Threats to International Financial Stability*, Cambridge, 1987, pp. 67-90, 72-73.

FISCAL POLICY IN DENMARK 1930–1945

Niels-Henrik TOPP

University of Copenhagen, DK-1130 Copenhagen K, Denmark

1. Introduction

The subject of this article is the debate in Denmark in the period from 1930 to 1945 on the use of the budget as a means of affecting economic activity. The aim is to examine the introduction of the new views on fiscal policy and to explain their fate among Danish economists and politicians.

2. Neoclassical fiscal policy

A description of neoclassical economic theory may serve as a starting point for an analysis of the change in attitude to fiscal policy which took place in the period 1930–1945. Until the end of the 1920s the principle of a self-regulating economy found overall support. Through continuous adjustments in prices and wages the competitive forces of the market economy would ensure an economy forever moving towards a state of equilibrium in which optimal use was made of the resources of society. Economic policy should first of all ensure the optimal functioning of the markets, and monetary policy should be directed towards supporting economic development. The main objection to an expansionary fiscal policy was exactly that it would disturb the free formation of prices, and that it led to a crowding-out of private demand. A set of standard rules had to be observed if the government was to carry out 'a sound fiscal policy'. Since each generation ought to pay for the public expenditures from which it would benefit, it was considered of the greatest importance to keep a balance of annual budgets and a low level of public debt.

3. The new views on fiscal policy

Deflation and the rapid rise of unemployment in the beginning of the 1930s clearly showed that the workings of the free markets – at least in the short run – did not lead to the desired equilibrium. This development changed the views on fiscal policy. Though in principle in favour of a balanced budget policy many Danish economists like F. Zeuthen (1935) believed that the economic conditions called for an expansionary fiscal policy and argued that crowding out would be negligible due to the severe unemployment. It did not constitute a lasting solution to the problems but might be defended on humanitarian grounds.

In the same period the need for a systematic use of a countercyclical fiscal policy was pointed out in the current debate among economists. This view was closely attached to the theoretical work of Gunnar Myrdal (1934) and was based on a concept of balancing the budget over a period of some years. In this respect it can be seen as a further elaboration on the neoclassical ideas. On the other hand, Myrdal's countercyclical budget policy does anticipate a new attitude to fiscal policy. It emphasized that fiscal policy was an integral part of a stabilization policy and that what was important in the short run were the effects on the economy rather than a balanced budget.[1]

Since high unemployment seemed to persist, even the assumption that the economies were self-regulating in the long run was called in question and finally abandoned. This dramatically changed economic policy, as it became clear that the government could no longer rely on some independent forces of the economy to bring about an adequate level of activity, but would itself have to take the responsibility for achieving this aim. The *General Theory* from 1936 is traditionally thought of as laying the foundations for the new philosophy of fiscal policy. Keynes, however, was not alone in questioning the ability of the free market to stabilize the economy at a level of full employment. The *Stockholm School* also contributed to the development of the theoretical foundation for an expansionary fiscal policy, and the Swedish economists had a great influence on their colleagues in Denmark; see Topp (1987).

4. Jens Warming and Jørgen Pedersen

The theory of the multiplier has a very long tradition in Denmark; see Topp (1981). In Julius Wulff (1896) the now well-known multiplier formula was established, and Wulff was the first to make a generalization by means of algebraic symbols. The multiplier was, however, based on an import leakage, whereas savings were not considered. In the late 1920s F. Johannsen and Jens Warming took an interest in the multiplier theory. Warming made two interesting contributions to the theory.[2] Warming (1928) pointed out

---

[1] In Sweden and Norway this new line of thought came to dominate both the theoretical and political debate and, together with the influence of J.M. Keynes, became a major source of inspiration for Danish economists in the 1930s; see Topp (1987, chs. 6 and 11).

[2] Jens Warming is best known in Denmark for a number of handbooks on descriptive economics but has made a number of remarkable theoretical contributions. Warming was the first to draw attention to the identification problem and his article on fisheries economics has been translated into English; see Kærgård (1984) and Andersen (1983).

that the effects of savings on derived demand had to be taken into consideration and that a calculation of the multiplier in a small open economy like Denmark therefore had to be based on a combined savings and import leakage. Warming can be said to anticipate the Keynesian theory of effective demand. His articles and books from the period 1928–1933 on macroeconomic topics offered a comprehensive discussion of the now familiar interaction between investment, income and savings, where savings were automatically adjusted to fluctuating investment by means of changes in income, the essential equilibrating variable. Furthermore, he presented a multiplier based on a marginal propensity to spend less than 1.[3]

Warming's second contribution was his calculation of the effects of fiscal policy. Around 1931 it is possible to find a number of economists in Denmark and abroad advocating that an expansionary fiscal policy be carried out until full employment was obtained. At the same time one may find economists calculating the secondary employment effects of public outlays. Warming (1931), however, was the first to take the full consequences and combine the two aspects. He not only argued that it was the duty of the government to run a deficit in its budgets for as long as unemployment persisted, he also calculated the magnitude of the budget deficit required. This deficit, he said, had to be maintained for some years, until the increase in demand for consumption goods had stimulated private investments sufficiently. This was indeed an extraordinary achievement and points directly to the use of empirical macroeconomic models during and after the Second World War.

Jørgen Pedersen was the second Danish pioneer of fiscal theory in the 1930s. Early in the 1930s he developed views on economic theory and policy rather similar to those of Keynes. Through numerous articles in journals and newspapers Pedersen kept on attacking the politicians for sticking to a 'sound' policy of budget balance instead of using the budget as a means of combating unemployment. At the beginning of the decade just like other economists Pedersen had argued that the budget should go on balancing over the trade cycle. In about 1933, however, he began to question whether it was reasonable to assign any specific importance to the actual size of the public debt. By 1935 Pedersen had come to the conclusion that the interest in the development of the debt was merely a reminiscence of the experience

---

[3]The basic ideas were fully developed prior to the publication of R.F. Kahn's (1931) now famous article on the multiplier. In fact, Kahn's article prompted Warming (1932) to write an article for the *Economic Journal*, in which he presented his own ideas and argued that just like Wulff and F. Johannsen, Kahn had ignored the savings leakage when calculating the multiplier. In short, according to Warming Kahn wasn't a Keynesian. Neither was Keynes himself for that matter in 1932, and as pointed out by Neville Cain (1979) Warming's 1932 article may be regarded as one of the many sources which inspired Keynes to the important development of his ideas on economic theory in the period 1932–1934.

of private business. Pedersen (1935) believed in what A.P. Lerner (1943) later labelled *functional finance*; to him all that mattered were the effects of fiscal policy on economic activity. This approach was fully developed in Pedersen (1937).[4] Alvin H. Hansen (1941, pp. 140–144) made extensive use of J. Pedersen's 1937 article. In Denmark his ideas were taken up by the new generation of economists, who were influenced by Keynes and the *Stockholm School*.

5. Fiscal policy in Denmark 1930–1940

Although the works of Jens Warming and Jørgen Pedersen had created the necessary foundation for an expansionary fiscal policy, such a policy was not implemented in Denmark. This was mainly due to the fact that the overall economic conditions did not invite such a policy. During the 1930s Denmark was having an almost permanent deficit on the balance of payments, and from 1933 to 1937 the foreign exchange reserves were negative. Moreover, the limited room for manoeuvre was preempted to carry out an expansionary monetary policy in order to ease the debt problem in the agricultural sector. A further important reason for the lack of success of the new ideas on fiscal policy was the economic philosophy of the major political parties. Although Socialdemokratiet (the Labour Party) and Venstre (the Liberals) were political opponents favouring, respectively, a socialist planned economy and the classical adjustment policy, both were in fact advocating a balanced budget, the latter out of belief in classical economic theory, the former out of a reluctance to pay interests on a public debt to the capitalists. The Labour Party did favour expanding public expenditures, but on a tax-financed basis, since tax payments were primarily levied on the higher incomes. The Danish economic policy was deliberately out of line with the policy pursued by the Labour governments in other Scandinavian countries. The Danish Labour government pursued a traditional Labour policy which involved some element of planned economy. The Norwegian and Swedish Labour Parties were never allowed to go that far, but introduced expansionary fiscal policy as the second best solution.

6. The Keynesian revolution in Denmark

The appearance of the *General Theory* in Denmark did not give rise to

---

[4]'In my opinion public finance logically belongs in the same category as all other activities of the government. In practice, any government activity should be judged in terms of its contributions to a political end. We may therefore conclude that the fiscal transactions of the government, ... are not economic activities which may be measured in terms of the balance-sheet of the public sector. This balance-sheet tells nothing about the soundness of given measures. The appropriateness of such measures appears only in their impact on individual citizens, the welfare of whom is the political goal.' Pedersen (1937 (1975, p. 27)).

any major theoretical debate such as can be found in other countries. Their acquaintance with the thoughts of the *Stockholm School* left many Danish – as well as Swedish – economists with the feeling that the *General Theory* offered little that was new: many of its ideas had already been included in the Scandinavian debate. On the other hand it is clear from the substantial number of references to the *General Theory* in Danish books and articles that the book had a great impact on especially young economists in the late 1930s.[5]

The theoretical development of fiscal policy and economic stabilization taking place in Denmark during the Second World War was, however, not solely based on the Keynesian model. Especially in the works of Kjeld Philip the influence of the *Stockholm School* was clear. The point of departure of his thesis from 1942 was the observation that fiscal policy measures primarily influence the reaction of private agents through alterations in their stocks of liquid resources. One of his main conclusions was that the effectiveness of fine-tuning economic activity would be diminishing because the public would gradually anticipate the fiscal policy measures; Philip (1942).

The introduction of the Keynesian model into the analysis of fiscal policy was made by Jørgen Gelting, who was the first to present the balanced budget multiplier; Gelting (1941). During the War Gelting was involved in the government planning of the Danish post-war economic policy. In the government abstract of the 1944 Beveridge Report on Full Employment the first Danish empirical model was published: *Meddelelser* (1945). The model was set up by Gelting, was partly inspired by Kaldor's model in Beveridge's book, and tried to estimate the extent to which various fiscal instruments needed to be changed in order to achieve full employment. Gelting's model was more than a mere translation of the Beveridge–Kaldor construction. It had its own special features and some of them – like the consumption function – were developed prior to the publication of Beveridge's book; see Andersen and Topp (1982). Gelting included the 1945 model in his thesis; Gelting (1948). The thesis was the first Danish work on the theory of public finance based directly on the Keynesian model.[6]

7. Fiscal policy during the Second World War

Despite the growing acceptance of Keynesian policy among professional economists and the radical changes in the economic policy demanded by the circumstances, the attitude of politicians towards fiscal policy did not change

---

[5]The list includes P. Nyboe Andersen, Hans Brems, Jørgen Gelting, Isi Grünbaum, Bent Hansen and Kjeld Philip.

[6]'Today Gelting's book has nothing new to tell us; all of it is intermediate textbook stuff now, but had the book been published in English in 1946, it would have been a leading – perhaps even the leading – work for its time on Keynesian fiscal theory.' Hansen (1975, p. 33).

much during the German occupation. In the period 1940-1945 the Danish economy was particularly influenced, on the one hand by a drastic curtailment of imported raw materials and, on the other hand an aggregate demand stimulated by considerable German purchases during the whole period.

During the first years of the occupation the demand was further increased by a fiscal deficit. In reality, therefore, the breakthrough of a new fiscal policy was signaled in 1940 when an employment plan was carried out in order to reduce unemployment. For the first time an extensive debt financing of public outlays was implemented. In the summers of 1941 and 1942 a shortage of labour became apparent. On the advice of the so-called Professorial Committee a deflationary economic policy was carried out from 1943 to counter an inflationary pressure.

The Professorial Committee argued that the economy was characterized by excess demand; Betænkning (1943). The German purchases and the Danish employment policy had resulted in a rise in income and employment, but because of the shortage of raw materials supply could not meet demand. The result was that the population saved up more idle balances than was desirable. The Committee therefore recommended that the tight price and wage control be supplemented by a contractive fiscal and monetary policy in order to reduce the excess demand.

The report was sharply criticized by Jørgen Pedersen, which resulted in an extensive debate between him and H. Winding Pedersen from the Committee. In Jørgen Pedersen's opinion the economy showed no sign of excess demand. Although the unemployment figures had dropped somewhat a degree of unemployment still existed, which to him was a clear sign that the supply was not limited but did in fact meet the demand. A deflationary policy would only create greater unemployment, while its stabilizing impact on prices would be small.[7]

Even though Parliament had accepted an expansionary policy in 1940 and the reverse type of policy in 1943, with a few exceptions the political debate showed no understanding of macroeconomic effects. In political circles the doctrine of balanced budgets still met with wide approval, and it was widely held that only a sound fiscal policy would permit a stable economic development. In fact, prestige of the Committee and the Central Bank rather than arguments put forward made politicians accept a delfationary policy in 1943.

---

[7]The differences of opinion about the effects of the economic policy may be illustrated within the framework of a simple fixed-price model. It is obvious that Jørgen Pedersen described the Danish economy as a Keynesian unemployment regime. The Committee and H. Winding Pedersen, on the other hand, argued that the households were constrained on the supply side. Furthermore, they maintained, unemployment had been eliminated during the years 1940-1942, which meant that the state of the economy must have changed from a classical unemployment regime to a regime of suppressed inflation, Topp (1987, chs. 14-15).

Only in the post-war programmes of the political parties can new views on fiscal policy be seen. It was now taken for granted that a full employment policy could be pursued successfully, and fiscal policy had become accepted as a means of regulating economic activity. This change was partly a result of the foreign debate on economic policy, partly a result of the increasing political influence of a new generation of economists inspired by Keynesianism.

References

Andersen, Ellen and Niels-Henrik Topp, 1982, The first Danish empirical model, in: Economic essays in honour of Jørgen H. Gelting (Copenhagen).
Andersen, Peder, 1983, On rent of fishing grounds: A translation of Jens Warming's 1911 article, with an introduction, History of Political Economy 13, 391–396.
Betænkning om foranstaltninger mod inflation, afgivet af finansministeriets udvalg af 30. Januar 1943 (Copenhagen).
Cain, Neville, 1979, Cambridge and its revolution: A perspective on the multiplier and effective demand, Economic Record 55, 108–117.
Gelting, Jørgen, 1941 (1975), Nogle bemærkninger om finansieringen af offentlig virksomhed, Nationaløkonomisk Tidsskrift 79, 293–299. Translated as: Some observations on the financing of public activity, History of Political Economy 7, 36–42.
Gelting, Jørgen, 1948, Finansprocessen i det økonomiske kredsløb (Copenhagen).
Hansen, Alvin H., 1941, Fiscal policy and business cycles (New York).
Hansen, Bent, 1975, Introduction to Jørgen Gelting's 'Some observations on the financing of public activity', History of Political Economy 7, 32–35.
Kahn, R.F., 1931, The relation of home investment to unemployment, Economic Journal 41, 173–198.
Kærgård, Niels, 1984, The earliest history of econometrics: Some neglected Danish contributions, History of Political Economy 14, 437–444.
Lerner, A.P., 1943, Functional finance and the federal debt, Social Research 10, 38–51.
Meddelelser fra Generalsekretariatet IV, 1945, Referat af William Beveridge: Fuld beskæftigelse i et frit samfund (Copenhagen).
Myrdal, Gunnar, 1934, Finanspolitikens ekonomiska verkningar (Stockholm).
Pedersen, Jørgen, 1935, Review of Hugh Dalton e.a.: Unbalanced Budgets, London 1934, Economica, 468–471.
Pedersen, Jørgen, 1937 (1975), Einige probleme der finanzwirtschaft, Weltwirtschaftliches Archiv 45, 467–492. Translated by Karsten Laursen in: Jørgen Pedersen, Essays in monetary theory and related subjects (Copenhagen).
Philip, Kjeld, 1942, Bidrag til læren om forbindelsen mellem det offentliges finanspolitik og den økonomiske aktivitet (Copenhagen).
Topp, Niels-Henrik, 1981, A nineteenth-century multiplier and its fate: Julius Wulff and the multiplier theory in Denmark 1986–1932, History of Political Economy 13, 824–845.
Topp, Niels-Henrik, 1987, Udviklingen i de finanspolitiske ideer i Danmark 1930–1945 (Copenhagen).
Warming, Jens, 1928, Beskæftigelsesproblemet, Gads danske Magasin 22, 609–721.
Warming, Jens, 1931, Tilpasning, Gads danske Magasin 25, 481–505.
Warming, Jens, 1932, International difficulties arising out of the financing of public works during depression, Economic Journal 42, 211–224.
Warming, Jens, 1933, Den økonomiske usikkerhed and likvid kapital, Nationaløkonomisk Tidsskrift 71, 89–126, 221–251 and 337–358.
Wulff, Julius, 1896, Have en nations forbrugere og producenter modsatte interesser?, Tidsskrift for Industri og Haandværk 5, 41–99.
Zeuthen, Fr., 1935, Arbejdsløsheden som kronisk samfundsonde, Nationaløkonomisk Tidsskrift 73, 145–164.

[15]

A Note on the Present Slump and the Depression in the 1930's

Hans E. Zeuthen

In a survey concerning the Danish balance of payments 1872 to 1972 professor Gelting states the opinion that in the context of the survey the period between the two world wars was "of greater interest from a psychopathological than from an economic point of view".[1] When one looks at the period after 1972, however, a comparison with the thirties may be of interest.

Figure 1. Gross domestic product at factor cost in Denmark 1930-1938 (1929 prices) and 1973-1981 (1975 prices).

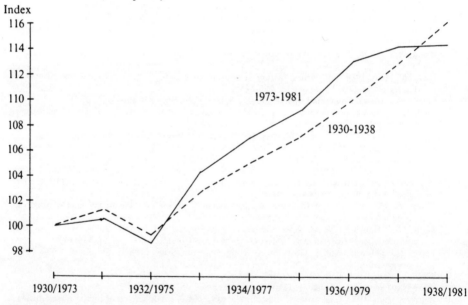

Sources: 1930-1938: Hansen (1974). 1973-1981: Danmarks Statistik (1981) and Danmarks Statistik (1982).
Note: Adjustments have been made for the inclusion of maintenance and repairs of fixed assets for the period 1930-1938 in Hansen (1974).

---

1. Gelting (1972) p. 401.

As seen from figure 1 the growth of real gross domestic product at factor cost from 1973 to 1981 has been very similar to the development during the 8 year-period from 1930 to 1938. The smoother growth during the 1930's is probably to some extent due to the more primitive national income statistics of the 1930's. For instance changes in stocks outside agriculture have not explicitly been taken into account. However, it seems rather clear – as could be expected – that the growth 1935 to 1938 was more accentuated than 1979 to 1981. (Although the international crisis started in 1929, the development 1929 to 1930 was very satisfactory in Denmark. Export prices fell, but the drop in import prices was even stronger, and real GDP increased by almost 7%).

The stagnation tendencies 1979 to 1981 are more evident when only GDP in the private sector is examined (see figure 2). The real increase in total GDP 1973 to 1981 was to a very large degree due to the continued growth of the public sector. The real growth of the public gross domestic product averaged 4.2% during the period 1973 to 1981, and also government consumption expenditure for commodities increased considerably more than the 1.7% annual growth of total GDP.

In the 1930's the increase in public gross domestic product was only moderately faster than that of total GDP (just under 3% whereas total GDP increased by little less than 2% p.a.). And which is, of course, far more important, the share of the public sector was much smaller in the 1930's. In 1977 public GDP at current prices amounted to 20.8% of total GDP, while the public share of GDP was only 6.3% in 1934.[2]

The more unfavourable conditions for the private sector 1973 to 1981 than 1930 to 1938 also had consequences for investments, and are reinforced through these consequences. This is illustrated in figure 3. The relative fall in investments 1930 to 1932 was stronger than that from 1973 to 1975, but real investments in the second half of the 1930's were almost as high as in 1930. Also in relation to GDP investments regained strength in the second half of the 1930's. From 1934 and onwards the investment ratio was higher than in the good year of 1929. (It should also be noted that the composition of investments changed during the 1930's. Whereas investments in agriculture constituted 30% of the total gross investments in 1930, this share was below 10% in most of the following years – in 1933 even negative due to stock changes. Investments outside agriculture therefore increased considerably during the 1930's).

---

2. Cf. Hansen (1974) for the period 1930 to 1938, and Danmarks Statistik (1981) and Danmarks Statistik (1982) for the period 1973 to 1981. The public share for the 1930's includes repairs and maintenance in the GDP-data. The share would almost increase to 6.8% if repairs and maintenance could be omitted.

Investments also recovered notably in 1976 but then they decreased in real terms. The fall during the two years 1979 to 1981 was even stronger (in relative as well as absolute terms) than the decline from 1973 to 1975.

It is worth noting that the fall in the share of GDP in the present slump is considerably stronger than experienced during the 1930's. From 1930 to 1932 the investments ratio fell by 4.7% (see figure 3). The decline 1973 to 1975 was 6.4% and 1979 to 1981 6.7%. The total decrease in the share of investments 1973 to 1981 was 12.2%. The impact on the economic activity of the fall in investments has thus been much stronger during the present slump than in the 1930's.

This very deep wound in the economy is due to many factors. The level of investments in relation to GDP in 1973 was much higher than in 1930. Therefore, a drop in investments by a given percentage has a stronger impact on the economy than before. Even in 1981 the investment ratio is higher than in the peak year of 1930. This high level probably first of all reflects a changed composition of

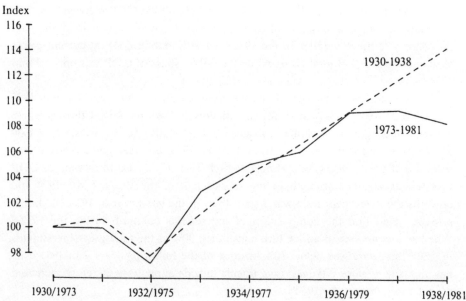

Figure 2. *Private gross domestic product at factor cost 1930-1938 (1929 prices) and 1973-1981 (1975 prices).*

Sources: Same as figure 1.
Note: Due to lack of data no adjustments are made for the inclusion of repairs and maintenance in Hansen (1974). (The stronger decrease 1931-1932 in figure 2 than in figure 1 is no doubt caused by the inclusion of repairs and maintenance).

real capital. It might also be due to a shortening of the economic lifetime of real capital.³

The extremely high starting level in 1973 was not only connected with the high rate of real growth in previous years but was also due to the fact that investments in residential buildings were unusually high (among other things the results of a firm belief in steadily growing incomes and a negative after tax real rate of interest on mortgage loans).

The very strong increase in interest rates in the years after 1973 and the continued debate about a future fall in inflation rates have clearly contributed to the very weak development of investments. But it is worth mentioning that the development in investments is still consistent with the development in production.⁴

Considering the above-mentioned drop in the investment ratio of more than 12% of the gross domestic product it is in a way remarkable that GDP in 1981 was higher than in 1973. A main reason for that, of course, is the growth of real government consumption expenditure and the existence (and growth) of the built-in-stabilizers. In spite of an increasing tax-burden (and in spite of falling real government investments) the public sector has neutralized a considerable part of the fall in investments. Measured in constant prices government consumption expenditure increased almost as much as total investments declined.⁵ (The differences amounting to 2.2% of GDP in 1981).

However, the increase in transfer incomes 1973 to 1981 due to rising unemployment and higher levels of support etc. could not completely offset the increase in direct and indirect taxes and the effect of the deterioration in the terms of trade during the same period. In spite of a falling propensity to save – due mainly to a change in income distribution⁶, growth in consumption therefore was slightly slower than that of gross domestic product at factor cost (1.2 and 1.7% respectively).

---

3. The depreciations in the national accounts statistics are also relatively larger than previously.
4. Cf. Det økonomiske Råd (1982) p. 76.
5. 1973 to 1981 the price developments for government consumption and for total investments were almost identical. Ignoring differences regarding indirect taxes and subsidies the fall in autonomous demand due to the decline in investments therefore was by and large offset by the increase in government demand. But naturally even a constant sum of investments and government consumption expenditure implies stagnation.
6. As productivity increases are generally higher for private consumption goods than for total GDP (especially if the public sector is relatively large) a faster real growth in private consumption than in GDP at factor cost would under more normal circumstances occur if the net tax-burden was not increased. A faster increase in import prices than in domestic costs as experienced 1973 to 1981, however, will have a counterbalancing effect.

Figure 3. *Investments 1930-1938 (1929 prices) and 1973-1981 (1975 prices). The share of investments in GDP (Current prices).*

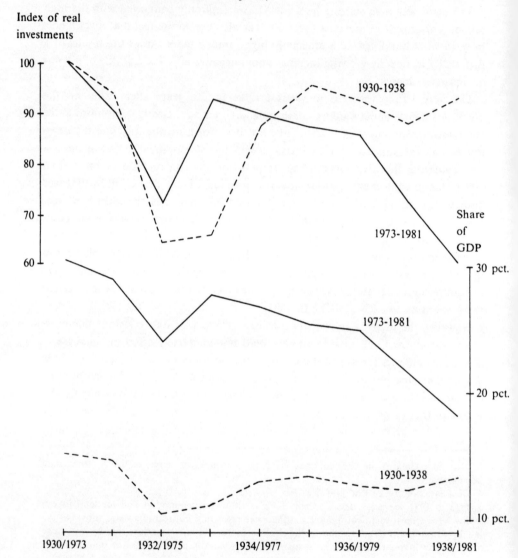

In the 1930's this was different. The real growth of private consumption and gross domestic product at factor cost 1930 to 1938 seems to have been identical

(1.9% p.a.)[7], despite the fact that the principle of keeping the budget balanced apparently was maintained during the 1930's[8], whereas a government budget surplus in 1973 was turned into a large deficit in 1981. This shift in the government budget, however, roughly corresponds to the increase in government consumption and is therefore of no direct importance to the relationship between consumption and GDP.

Terms of trade also deteriorated 1930 to 1938 (though for the period as a whole less than 1973 to 1981). The price development for consumption, however, was parallel to that for GDP probably due to the fact that the terms of trade deterioration unlike 1973 to 1981 reflected a strong decline in export prices and not an excess increase in import prices, and therefore being of greatest importance to incomes in export industries. Productivity differences in the various sectors may also have been of importance. The effect of the moderate increase in the tax-burden in the 1930's apparently has been absorbed by changes in the income distribution or saving behaviour. The shakiness of the data should, of course, also be taken into consideration. (However, there is no doubt that private consumption 1930 to 1938 increased considerably. According to the national accounts statistics per capita consumption increased by 1% p.a. and the evidence of a rising standard of living is supported by statistics on consumption of food, fuel, etc. (cf. Henriksen 1960)).

It is a characteristic feature of the 1930's as well of the present slump that internal "exogenous" demand is weak. In the 1930's the sum of investments and government consumption expenditure in constant prices did increase, but only by barely 1% p.a. from 1930 to 1938. During the period 1973 to 1981 the sum of real investments and government demand on an average declined by ½% p.a.. And furthermore – as has also been mentioned – consumption as a proportion of GDP fell slightly during that period when measured in constant prices. (In current prices the share of private consumption increased a little. The difference is due to the deterioration of the terms of trade as well as the increase in the share of indirect taxes (and other factors)).

In spite of the fact that 1930 to 1938 as well as 1973 to 1981 are periods when economic growth internationally was low, foreign trade has been an important growth factor in Denmark in both periods.

---

7. Estimated on the assumption of the same price development for government consumption minus GDP in the public sector as for total comsumption minus GDP in the public sector. (In Hansen (1974) there are only data on total consumption in constant prices).
8. Cf. H. C. Johansen in Dybdahl (1973), p. 64 ff.

1973 to 1981 exports of goods and services in constant prices showed an average annual increase of 4.2%. (Commodities 4.7% and services 2.7% p.a.). And in the same period imports went up by .6% p.a. only, which is less than the rate of growth of private GDP. (Commodity imports hardly increased at all). The improvement of the balance of goods and services in constant prices 1973 to 1981 amounted to as much as 10% of GDP in 1981.

Obviously, this is not the complete impact of the foreign transactions. The stronger increase in import prices than in internal prices (and export prices) has – as mentioned above – contributed considerably to the very weak development in private consumption. Also the steadily growing interest payments on foreign debt have reduced the consumption possibilities. By and large, however, these negative impacts would have existed also without the improvement in the balance of goods and services in constant prices (the interest payments would have been even higher, and the deterioration of the terms of trade probably somewhat smaller).

The vigorous improvement of the balance of payment in constant prices is to a great extent a relatively automatic reaction. Higher import prices (e.g. higher oil prices) reduce the propensity to import and the very moderate growth in the private sector implies a modest increase in imports. It is very difficult to estimate the underlying increase in the international division of labour, but unless this tendency is very strong, the development in imports can to a large extent be explained by the above-mentioned rather automatic factors.

Also the export development is primarily automatic. The international growth has generally been stronger than that of Denmark, and the growth in export markets has (with the exception of recent years) been of roughly the same magnitude as the real increase of the Danish export markets.[9]

The improvement of Denmark's competitive position during recent years has contributed to the large improvement of the balance of goods and services in constant prices, but substantially it has been an automatic reaction.

The balance of payments in constant prices also improved somewhat from 1930 to 1938. Thus the commodity trade balance 1930 to 1938 was improved by 3.5% of GDP in 1938.[10]

But this was a result of a development rather different from what happened 1973 to 1981. 1930 to 1938 commodity exports in constant prices declined by 1% p.a. (though with considerable fluctuations). But the fall in imports amounted to 2.5% p.a.

---

9. Cf. Det økonomiske Råd (1982).
10. Figures for commodity exports and imports in constant prices are calculated on the basis of prices from Ølgaard (1966) p. 242 and amounts from Bjerke (1958) p. 153.

Figure 4. *Commodity exports and -imports as percentage of GDP 1930-1938. Terms of trade 1930-1938.*

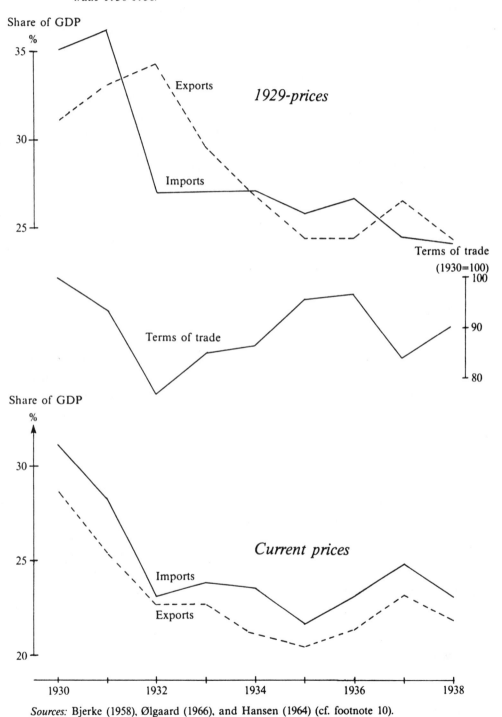

Sources: Bjerke (1958), Ølgaard (1966), and Hansen (1964) (cf. footnote 10).

A NOTE ON THE PRESENT SLUMP AND THE DEPRESSION IN THE 1930's

As world trade was generally falling in the beginning of the 1930's the decline in Danish exports was by no means unusual. (Actually Danish export quantities peaked as late as 1932 due to a large export of agricultural products at very unsatisfactory prices 1931 and 1932). The considerable reduction of imports with slow but still positive growth in production was more remarkable.

This process was partly the result of a substantial devaluation and of import control. In the 1930's and the following decades great importance was attached to the import control. The devaluation was mostly regarded as a measure to improve income conditions in agriculture. But obviously devaluation made the import control a much easier task. (It is also worth mentioning that although some production fell when trade was eventually liberalized, most of the production proved competitive).

The "de-internationalization" of the Danish economy 1930 to 1938 is illustrated in figure 4 where also the development in the terms of trade is shown. In figure 5 the corresponding figures for the period 1973 to 1981 are given.

Whereas Denmark in the 1930's became a more closed economy the opposite has been the case during recent years. This is especially clear when the shares of commodity exports and imports are measured in current prices (which also seems most reasonable in this context).

In the 1930's there were several incidents which were labelled exchange crises and as a matter of fact the net foreign balance of the National Bank was negative during several periods[11], but there were no huge deficits on current accounts and for the period as a whole there was a small surplus (especially in 1937 and 1938)[12].

1973 to 1981 the opposite was the case. The foreign balance of the National Bank has generally been favourable during that period, but current accounts have constantly been in deficit. (In 1976 and 1979 amounting to more than 5% of GDP).

The more effective part of the economic policy during the 1930's, however, was directed against the current accounts. It would be a too sweeping generalization to argue that it has been the other way round 1973 to 1981. The increase in tax rates and the exchange rate changes obviously have had an effect on current accounts. But the relatively comfortable size of the foreign exchange reserves and thus the lack of manifest exchange crisis may have made it more difficult to implement a policy effectively improving the competitiveness (which is of course necessary if a simultaneous improvement is wanted in employment, current accounts and real income).

---

11. Cf. Hoffmeyer (1968) p. 160 ff.
12. Cf. Bjerke (1958) p. 153.

Figure 5. *Commodity exports and -imports as percentage of GDP 1973-1981. Terms of trade 1973-1981.*

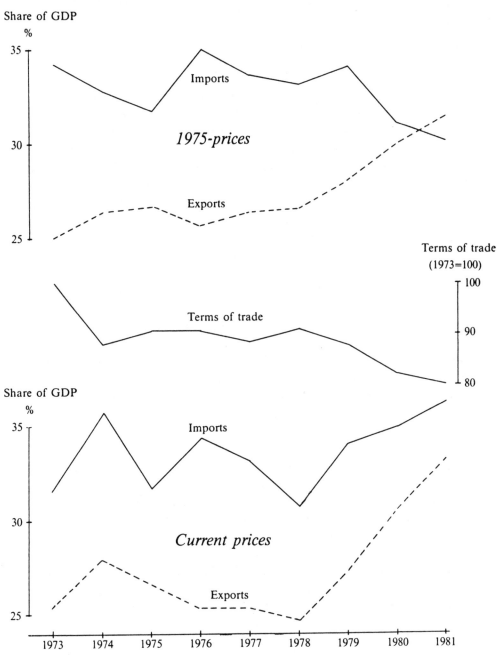

Sources: Danmarks Statistik (1981) and Danmarks Statistik (1982).
Note: Terms of trade are calculated as the proportion between implicit prices for exports and imports of commodities.

The labour force 1973 to 1981 increased by 1.3% p.a.[13] 1930 to 1938 the rate of growth of the labour force has been estimated by Hansen (1974) to be of almost the same magnitude, viz. 1.1% p.a. But whereas employment 1973 to 1981 (measured in persons) increased by barely .2% p.a. the growth 1930 to 1938 apparently was considerably higher. According to Hansen (1974) employment increased by .6% p.a. But the figures for total unemployment (and therefore also for employment) for the 1930's are very dubious. In 1930 less than 16% of the labour force were members of recognized unemployment insurance schemes. In 1938 this percentage had increased to close to 23%. The figures in Hansen (1974) are based on the assumption that the unemployment ratio for the *total* labour force is equal to half the ratio of members of unemployment insurance schemes. As already mentioned the proportion of insured increased considerably during the 1930's. Furthermore, the registration efficiency seems to have increased.[14] The increase in employment may therefore have been stronger than estimated by Hansen. Thus, if it is assumed that the rise in the total number of unemployed equals the increase in the registered number[15] (including uinsured persons registered at the employment exchange offices), the increase in employment becomes somewhat larger. Also the figures regarding the labour force are uncertain.

From other – independent – sources it seems clear, however, that employment increased considerably in several non-farm industries.[16] Agricultural employment declined moderately (approximately 30,000 during the period) and the increase in the number of persons in the public sector was probably of the same magnitude. The growth in private non-farm industries therefore equalled the total increase in employment. It seems plausible to assume that non-farm private employment increased around 1% p.a. 1930 to 1938. In contrast private employment generally declined strongly during the period 1973 to 1981 (on average 1.4% p.a.).[17]

The official percentage of unemployment was very high in the 1930's, rising from 14% in 1930 to 32% in 1932 and still 21% in 1938. But these figures only concern unemployment as regards members of unemployment insurance schemes, as previously mentioned at that time only representing a minor fraction of the labour force. The total number of registered unemployed persons (including uninsured registered at the employment exchange offices) only amounted to 6.8% of the total labour force in 1932 (and 2.2% and 5.6% in 1930 and 1938 respec-

---

13. Unemplished material in the secretariat of Det økonomiske Råd.
14. Cf. Dich (1939).
15. Cf. Zeuthen (1939) p. 246.
16. Cf. Ole Hyltoft in Dybdahl (1975).
17. Cf. footnote 13.

tively). These figures, however, clearly underestimate the unemployment. Probably a considerable number of persons was not registered as unemployed, but nevertheless wanting a job at the prevailing wage-rate.

The "true" unemployment of the present slump may well be higher than the 9.1% of the total labour force in 1981 (and the estimated 9.7% for 1982), but probably not substantially higher. (There is no doubt that some of the unemployed in 1981 preferred uenemployment *with* unemployment relief to work, but most of these persons would probably prefer work with pay to unemployment without relief. On the other hand, there is also disguised unemployment to-day).

On balance it is very difficult to settle whether unemployment at present is higher than in 1932. It is not only a matter of figures but also of definition and interpretation. However, there is no doubt that the increase 1973 to 1982 is larger than that from 1930 to 1932 as the employment situation 1973 was much better than in 1930.

The productivity growth during the period 1973 to 1981 has been considerably smaller than in the previous decade. The same was the case 1930 to 1938. According to the official statistics for manufacturing industries, there was no productivity growth at all 1930 to 1938 in these industries. The import control no doubt gave rise to some low-productivity industries. However, many new products were manufactured in the 1930's (due to the higher degree of self-sufficiency and the technological development), and this may easily have disturbed the statistics. The "real" productivity development may very well have been positive.[18]

Compared to many other countries the economic development in Denmark during the 1930's was reasonably satisfactory (though with a huge dispersion between different groups in society). In the U.S. GNP fell by 30% from 1929 to 1933.[19] The 1929-level was not regained until 1939. Also in Germany and France the slump was very deep – with a very different time pattern, however.[20]

Although the dip lasted longer in the United Kingdom than in Denmark, the development in the U.K. was rather similar to the Danish one.[21] Obviously this was one of the reasons why Denmark managed relatively well, as U.K. was far the most important country for Danish foreign trade in the 1930's. Also the development in the other Scandinavian countries was reasonably good.[22]

It has often been pointed out that the countries doing relatively well in the

---

18. Cf. Hyltoft in Dybdahl (1975).
19. Cf. Department of Commerce (1966).
20. Cf. appendix in Maddison (1964).
21. Cf. Feinstein (1974).
22. Cf. Appendix in Maddison (1964).

1930's did so through incapsulation and beggar-my-neighbor policies. But it is worth noting that the initial openness of these countries often was considerable. Better competitiveness (sometimes in strange forms) may also have played a central role, maybe the most important one. (As most trade became bilateral also ability to negotiate became of great importance).

During the period 1973 to 1981 the Danish performance has been relatively poor compared to other countries. Economic growth and especially the development in private consumption has been much weaker in Denmark than the OECD average.[23]

There are several reasons for that. Thus the oil price explosion has hit Denmark harder than many other countries because of the relatively large energy imports. The productivity development for the total economy has also been relatively weak due to the strong increase in the public sector where productivity is below average. (Also the mere size of the public sector is of importance in this connection as (registered) productivity is constant in the production of government services). As previously mentioned investments in residential buildings were also unusually high in 1973 (more than 11% of GDP in current prices) which of course has strengthened the impact of the collapse in the housebuilding sector. (The fall in residential construction 1973 to 1981 amounts to 6.8% of GDP in current prices).[24] Finally, also the very rapid growth of the interest payments on foreign debts obviously has been a greater problem for Denmark than for most other countries.

The improvement of the competitiveness has not been sufficient to counterbalance the above-mentioned factors. Although the balance of payments, as already mentioned, has been the most expansive element 1973 to 1981 a further strengthening is the only feasible way if the Danish performance regarding production, private consumption and unemployment is to be improved – especially if also current account has to be bettered.

---

23. Cf. Det økonomiske Råd (1982).
24. It also has to be mentioned that growth of the labour force has been above average. The impact of that on GDP is no doubt positive since increase in the labour force will imply rising unemployment payments and thus increased demand. But in an open economy unemployment will in the short run nevertheless increase.

References

Bjerke, Kjeld og Niels Ussing. 1958. *Studier over Danmarks Nationalprodukt 1870-1950.*

Danmarks Statistik. 1981. *Statistiske Efterretninger.* A 1981, 30.

Danmarks Statistik. 1982. *Nyt fra Danmarks Statistik* Nr. 80, 28. april.

Department of Commerce. 1966. *The National Income and Product Accounts of the United States 1929-1965.*

Dich, Jørgen S. 1939. *Arbejdsløshedsproblemet i Danmark 1930-38.*

Dybdahl, Vagn et. al. 1975. *Krise i Danmark.*

Feinstein, C. H. 1974. *National Income and Output of The United Kingdom 1835-1965.*

Gelting, Jørgen H. 1972. Den danske betalingsbalance 1872-1972, *Nationaløkonomisk Tidsskrift,* vol. 110 no. 5-6.

Hansen, Svend Aage. 1974. *Økonomisk vækst i Danmark, Bind II: 1914-1970.*

Henriksen, Ole Buus og Anders Ølgaard. 1960. *Danmarks Udenrigshandel 1874-1958.*

Hoffmeyer, Erik. 1968. Perioden 1931-1960. In *Dansk Pengehistorie* by Knud Erik Svendsen et. al. vol. 2, pp. 155-332.

Maddison, Angus. 1964. *Economic Growth of the West.*

Zeuthen, Frederik. 1939. *Arbejdsløn og Arbejdsløshed.*

Ølgaard, Anders. 1966. *Growth, Productivity and Relative Prices.* Amsterdam.

[16]

Excerpt from Anders Ølgaard, *The Danish Economy*, 9–34.

Chapter I

STRUCTURAL PROBLEMS OF THE DANISH ECONOMY

INTRODUCTION

1. Rather frequently, the Danish economy is referred to as one based mainly on agriculture. It is, indeed, true that agricultural produce dominated export earnings until a few decades ago. During the last quarter of the 19th century, the Danish economy - like the Dutch - adjusted to the international decline in prices of grain, etc. by rapidly increasing the production of animal products such as bacon, beef, and butter. This structural change was greatly helped by the new cooperative movement. While output of grain continued to increase, it was now mainly used as input for animal products, providing the base for increasing exports of these products to the more industrialized economies of the UK, Germany, and others. From 1890 onwards, the terms of trade of agriculture improved, and just before 1930 agricultural exports accounted for 75 per cent of total exports, while well over 20 per cent of gross domestic product (GDP) was attributable to agriculture.

Before the First World War, Danish manufacturing industry started to develop slowly, mainly in the field of small-scale import substitution, following the pattern typical of the first phases of industrialization. However, a few export industries did emerge, one of which was ship-building.

2. During the 1930s, declining export possibilities mainly hit agriculture, the largest exporting sector, and from the early 1930s onwards, the share of agriculture in exports - and employment - started to decline, the latter even in absolute terms.

As in other European countries, quantitative import restrictions were introduced in order to stimulate employment in manufacturing, the unemployment rate being substantial - reaching a peak of 32 per cent (average) in 1932. With the benefit of hindsight, it is doubtful whether this policy formed part of an industrial strategy designed to shift the basis of the economy from primary to secondary industries. Be this as it may, the outcome was very much along these lines. At the beginning of the 1950s, manufacturing industry was ready for, and able to accomplish, a major expansion of industrial exports, covering a wide range of products.

- 10 -

It has been argued that the development of manufacturing industry from the early 1930s onwards represents an example of a successful 'infant industry' policy. The fact that the reconstruction problems after the German occupation during the Second World War were rather small, at least compared with those of most of our neighbouring countries, probably contributed to this success. Thus, Danish exporters of manufactured goods had an earlier start than their foreign competitors. Furthermore, non-agricultural money wages were comparatively low after the Second World War, as the distribution of income changed rather drastically during the war in favour of agriculture and to the disadvantage of urban workers. Finally, the Danish Krone was devalued in line with Sterling in 1949.

3. One of the arguments against the infant industry strategy is that once introduced, protection is very difficult to eliminate. In the case of Denmark, this problem was solved from abroad. Like other Western European countries, Denmark received Marshall aid from the US - totalling 1.7 billion kroner corresponding to one third of one year's export earnings. But the aid was given on the usual condition that imports of manufactures etc. should be liberalized within the OEEC framework. Whereas - contrary to developments in most other Western European countries - liberalist thinking during the early 1950s was mainly expressed by the spokesmen for Danish agriculture, representatives of manufacturing industry still argued along protectionist lines. But with enforced liberalization of Danish imports in these fields, the protectionists in manufacturing industry had to give in.

Hence the 1950s are often referred to as the period of the second industrial revolution, with manufacturing exports increasing sharply - mainly light industries covering a large number of products in very different fields. In 1960, exports of manufactured goods exceeded those of agricultural products.

During the first half of the 1950s, the major problem of economic policy was considered to be that of the balance of payments. During the late 1940s, this problem was expected to be solved by increased agricultural exports. With minimum international liquidity - and an almost total shortage of dollars - Denmark could not afford a balance of payments deficit, hence total domestic demand had to be reduced in order to keep imports down.

However, from 1957 onwards the new majority government took a more active hand in promoting foreign borrowing. At the same time, the terms of trade were improving, and more generous rules on depreciation allowances (based on net depreciated value) were introduced.

These factors all contributed to an unprecedented boom, and in the early 1960s, urban unemployment vanished for the first time.

4. From this period onwards, economic development became more like that in neighbouring countries. While still contributing substantially - although with a declining share - to total exports, agriculture was increasingly subsidized with respect to domestic sales. The system according to which domestic prices of agricultural produce were fixed was changed from the British system (prices corresponding to world market prices) to the Continental system (prices reflecting the cost of domestic production). At the same time, the labour force engaged in agriculture declined substantially, by far the major part of the non-owners moving to urban industries.

- 11 -

If the 1950s could properly be labelled the second industrial revolution, the 1960s might be called the years of (uncontrolled) revolution in the size of the government sector. From 1960 to 1973, total taxes as a percentage of GDP increased from 28 per cent to well over 50 per cent. The increase in public expenditure (government and municipal) was equally strong both for purchases of goods and services and for transfers. While the public share of GDP around 1960 was not extremely high by Western European standards (low post-war reconstruction costs and modest defence expenditure), by the 1970s it was among the highest in Europe. The fact that, from the late 1960s onwards, the increase was mainly financed by higher income taxes, added substantially to political tensions, caused perhaps not so much by the high level of overall taxation as by the composition of taxes and their rapid rate of increase.

The increase in public purchases of goods and services during the 1960s took place at a time of rapidly increasing activity in the field of building and construction. The number of new dwelling units per year was doubled, leading to a very high average standard of housing as compared to that in other countries. The building boom reflected both a rapid increase of private income, and the substantial direct and indirect subsidies available in the field of housing.

The 1960s were expected to be the decade of a rapidly increasing urban labour force, partly reflecting the large number of children born during the 1940s, and partly because of the decline in rural employment, and this caused great concern about the expected rate of unemployment. Experience proved these worries to be unfounded. The rapid increase of the building and construction sector, and the even faster increase of employment in the public sector, led to labour shortages, although these sectors were able to compete successfully for the available labour resources. But the exporting industries and those competing with imports found it difficult to offer equally high increases in pay, and wages as well as profits in the balance of payments industries were squeezed.

Against this background, it was hardly surprising that the balance of payments became the predominant problem of economic policy and the question of unemployment became insignificant during most of the period 1960-73. In 1960, Denmark's foreign debts were approximately equal to its foreign assets. By 1973, net outstanding foreign debt had increased to nearly 20 billion kroner.

During the early 1960s, the balance of payments problem was mainly considered to result from domestic savings being insufficient to finance private investment. A high level of private sector investment was required in order both to increase output in manufacturing industry and to introduce more capital intensive means of production in agriculture, so as to maintain output in spite of a declining labour force.

However, it gradually became evident that the balance of payments deficit had become a more permanent aspect of the functioning of the Danish economy, and that the share of total resources employed in the balance of payments industries had become too small to provide the output necessary for any improvement. The low share of resources in these industries in turn reflected the booming demand from 'domestic industries', in particular from the public sector, and the housing industry. Hence in order to improve the balance of payments, a reallocation of resources was required.

- 12 -

It was hoped that the entry of Denmark into the EEC would contribute substantially to solving the balance of payments problem by improving the terms of trade, mainly because of higher agricultural export prices. The terms of trade did improve, but economic policy immediately after the EEC entry was not kept sufficiently tight to counter the effects of the increase in real income caused by the improvement of the terms of trade. Furthermore, the reallocation process started too late to take advantage of the 1972-73 boom in world trade. Hence the economy was very badly prepared to meet the serious consequences of the rapid increase in oil prices as well as the general weakening of world demand which occurred from late 1973 onwards.

5. To summarize, developments in the Danish economy from the end of the post-war reconstruction period may be divided into four sub-periods:

a) <u>1950-58</u>: Substantial unemployment, low growth rates of output, low rates of inflation, balance of payments equilibrium.

b) <u>1958-66</u>: Sharply declining unemployment, high growth rates of output, increasing - but still rather modest - rates of inflation, but balance of payments deficits.

c) <u>1966-73</u>: Full employment, slightly lower rates of growth than in the preceding period, accelerating rates of inflation, persistent balance of payments deficits.

d) <u>1973-77</u>[1]: Increasing unemployment, low rates of growth, high - although declining - rates of inflation and substantial balance of payments deficits.

However, before these sub-periods are studied in more detail using national accounts statistics, the growth and composition of the population and labour force will be analysed.

POPULATION

6. Following the First World War, a referendum was held in the southern part of Jutland (Slesvig). In accordance with its outcome, the northern part of Slesvig returned to Denmark in 1920, adding 160 000 persons to the population, which in 1921 amounted to 3 270 000 inhabitants. The 4 million mark was passed in 1945, and in 1973 the population for the first time exceeded 5 million persons.

7. Changes in the age distribution of the population are shown in table I.1. The pattern is rather similar to that of many other Western European countries. On the whole, the share of children (aged below 18) has declined, except for the effect of a substantial temporary increase in the number of births during the late 1940s. With a time lag, this temporary increase also affected the proportion of young people (aged 18-24), producing a temporary increase around 1970.

---

[1] Developments since 1973 are summarized in chapter XI.

- 13 -

Table I.1

Age distribution of the population of Denmark

	1921	1930	1940	1950	1960	1970
Age (both sexes): 0-17	37.0	33.0	29.1	30.5	30.5	27.8
18-24	12.5	12.7	11.8	9.6	9.6	11.3
25-59	40.2	43.5	47.2	46.5	44.3	43.2
60-69	6.1	6.2	7.2	7.8	8.9	9.8
70-	4.2	4.6	4.7	5.6	6.7	7.9
TOTAL, per cent	100.0	100.0	100.0	100.0	100.0	100.0
Total population, 1 000 persons	3 268	3 551	3 844	4 281	4 585	4 938

Source: Danmarks Statistik: Befolkningsudvikling og sundhedsforhold 1901-60, S.U. No 19 and supplementary information.

At the other end of the age-scale, the proportion of people aged 60 or over has increased substantially, from 10 per cent in 1921 to no less than 18 per cent in 1970. Before the Second World War, the tendency for the proportion of children to decline exceeded that of the old to increase, hence the proportion of those contributing most to the labour force (people aged 25-59 years) was increasing. However, over the last decades, this trend has been reversed.

8. Additional key figures which help to explain changes in the population by appropriate 'flows' are shown in table I.2. The average annual increase of the population of Denmark has on the whole been about 30-40 000 persons, representing a declining percentage rate of growth as the total size of the population increases. By far the major part of the changes in the growth rate of the population is explained by the birth rate. The absolute number of deaths has been steadily increasing, the accelerating rate during the 1960s mainly reflecting the change in the age composition of the population.

The net reproduction rate has shown marked fluctuations. It exceeded that corresponding to a stationary population during most of the 1920s, but declined during the next decade. It increased subsequently and reached a peak of 1 370 during the mid 1940s. During the 1950s and 1960s it remained above 1 000, but since 1969 its level has suggested a tendency for the population of Denmark to decline in the long term.[1]

---

[1] The lack of stability of the net reproduction rate suggests that alternative models might preferably be used for purposes of forecasting, e.g. the cohort method. Here the basic variable is the number of children born during the fertile period of a certain woman. This figure has been declining over time, but apparently according to a more predictable pattern. However, the profile of 'spacing' varies; it may, for instance, be postponed by economic recessions, improved methods of contraception, etc.

Table I.2

Births, deaths, immigration: annual averages by decades

	Increase of tot. pop.		Births	Deaths	Net immigration	Net reproduction rate
	per cent	1 000	1 000 persons			
1921/30	0.89	31.3	71.2	38.3	-1.6	1 104
1931/40	0.79	28.8	66.2	39.6	2.2	941
1941/50	1.12	44.2	85.3	39.4	-1.7	1 217
1951/60	0.70	31.6	76.2	40.4	-4.2	1 191
1961/70	0.75	34.9	79.2	47.0	2.7	1 135

Source: Danmarks Statistik: **Statistisk Årborg** 1976 and supplementary information.

9. Perhaps the most interesting figures of table I.2 are those of net immigration. Compared with other countries, the net figures are surprisingly small, only a few thousand persons per year. This order of magnitude was maintained even during most of the 1960s in spite of the high rate of growth of the economy and labour shortages. It was only from 1969 onwards that net immigration became sizeable, reaching a peak of 12 000 in 1973.

The explanation of this delayed response can probably be found partly in the attitude of the trade unions. During the 1930s, unemployment in manufacturing industry was substantial, and the situation was similar, although to a lesser extent, in the 1950s. Hence the trade unions were reluctant to let foreigners compete with domestic workers for the limited number of jobs. It was only after a period of several years of full-employment that this attitude became more relaxed.[1]

THE LABOUR FORCE AND PARTICIPATION RATES

10. Labour force statistics prior to the 1970s are mainly based on figures from population censuses held every five years. However, employment surveys were introduced in 1967 and have been made frequently since 1969. In table I.3, 1970 figures from both sources are shown, but it should be pointed out that the definitions used differ slightly between the two sources.

11. The total labour force has increased roughly at the same rate as that of the population aged 15-74 years. Hence total participation rates have remained stable, and the changes in the published figures mainly reflect definitional changes.

---

[1] However, from 1958 onwards, free labour mobility existed in the Nordic countries (Scandinavia and Finland).

Table I.3

Danish labour force by occupation

	Census figures			Employment surveys[a]	
	1950	1960	1970	1970	1973
	1 000 persons				
Agriculture etc.	518	367	244	267	233
Trade and industry	551	613	660	687	652
Build. and construc.	134	150	211	200	202
Distribution, banking, etc.	263	294	356	381	384
Transport	132	145	153	157	167
Private services	209	197	203	216	204
Government services	169	236	416	441	564
Others	48	62	67	31	40
TOTAL LABOUR FORCE	2 024	2 064	2 310	2 380	2 446
	per cent				
Agriculture etc.	25.6	17.8	10.6	11.2	9.5
Trade and industry	27.2	29.7	28.6	28.9	26.7
Build. and construc.	6.6	7.3	9.1	8.4	8.3
Distribution, banking, etc.	13.0	14.3	15.4	16.0	15.7
Transport	6.5	7.0	6.6	6.6	6.8
Private services	10.3	9.5	8.8	9.1	8.3
Government services	8.3	11.4	18.0	18.5	23.1
Others	2.5	3.0	2.9	1.3	1.6
TOTAL	100.0	100.0	100.0	100.0	100.0
Population age 15-74, 1 000 persons	3 029	3 266	3 572	3 559	3 628
Participation rate	(66.8)[b]	63.2	64.7	66.9	67.4

[a] Spring survey in 1970, autumn survey in 1973. In 1970, no autumn survey was made. However, seasonal fluctuations are not very pronounced.
[b] Due to changes of definitions, this figure should be reduced before being comparable with corresponding figures for later years.
Source: Danmarks Statistik: Statistisk tiårsoversigt 1973 and 1974.

Table I.3 shows a break-down of the labour force by industries. The number of employed in agriculture has been reduced by more than half between 1950 and 1973, leaving less then ten per cent of the labour force in the agricultural sector at the end of the period. The share of employment in trade and industry has remained roughly stable at 26-29 per cent, while the substantial increase in the activities of the building and construction sector during the 1960s is reflected in an increasing share of the labour force being employed in this industry.

The most interesting part of the table, however, is that showing persons employed by the government sector. The absolute number increased from 170 000 persons in 1950 to no less than 565 000 persons in 1973. While agriculture employed a quarter of the labour force in 1950 and slightly below ten per cent in 1973, the figures for the share of government employees show almost exactly the opposite development. This dramatic expansion of the proportion of the total labour force engaged in government activities will be discussed further in chapter VI.

12. The composition of the total labour force with respect to occupational status has changed considerably since 1950. Admittedly, the proportion of skilled workers has remained at 12-14 per cent and that of unskilled workers has only declined moderately, from about 33 per cent to 29 per cent. But the proportion of self-employed (including employers) has shown a marked decline from around 22 per cent to about 13 per cent, which is more than made up for by the change in the proportion of salaried employees, which increased from 21 per cent in 1950 to 40 per cent in 1973.

13. As pointed out above, the total participation rate of the population aged 15-74 years has remained roughly constant. But behind this apparent stability are some substantial changes within groups according to age, sex etc. Table I.4 shows that the participation rate of men has declined, while that of women has increased. The increase of 7.4 percentage points for women exceeds the corresponding decline for men, but since the larger part of the labour force consists of men, the two changes result in a roughly unchanged total participation rate.

14. The decline in the participation rate of young men was not unexpected due to generalized and extended education. However, the decline for males aged 25-59 years - representing roughly two thirds of the total male labour force - has taken most experts by surprise. A partial explanation can probably be found in increased early retirement. The same may partly explain the reduced participation rate for those over 60 years old. For this group, in particular, an additional factor may be important. The process of overall growth implies structural shifts, leaving people unemployed at least temporarily. It is obviously more difficult for older people to find alternative jobs, hence early retirement is often forced upon them.

15. The increased participation rate of _women_ as a whole is exclusively due to the trend among married women. The rate for _unmarried_ women remained unchanged. For those aged 15-24, the participation rate declined, corresponding to the trend for men, but this was offset by an increase for the large group aged 25-59.

The participation rate for _married_ women increased substantially between 1967 and 1973 for all groups below the age of 60 years. Any detailed analysis of

Table I.4

Participation rates, 1967 and 1973

	Men		Women		Unmarried women		Married women	
	1967	1973	1967	1973	1967	1973	1967	1973
Labour force:[1]								
15 - 19	123.2	96.9	81.9	72.3	78.8	70.3	3.1	2.0
20 - 24	163.5	135.7	123.9	128.7	77.4	79.6	46.5	49.1
25 - 59	998.9	1038.5	453.0	614.1	141.2	149.8	311.8	464.3
60 - 74	170.4	159.3	39.3	48.4	22.7	25.3	16.6	23.1
	1456.0	1430.4	698.1	863.5	320.1	325.0	378.0	538.5
Participation rates:								
15 - 19	65.2	50.4	44.8	40.1	45.4	39.8	34.1	55.0
20 - 24	77.5	70.4	61.5	69.6	79.3	73.0	44.7	64.6
25 - 59	96.5	93.8	43.4	56.0	71.0	73.3	36.9	52.1
60 - 74	60.0	50.7	12.0	13.2	12.7	15.2	11.2	11.5
	84.7	79.2	39.8	47.2	49.3	49.5	34.2	45.9

[1] 1 000 persons. Military conscripts, domestic servants and 'assisting housewives' are excluded. Part-time employees are included in the figures without reducing their weight.

Source: Employment surveys, autumns. For some of the figures, see William Scharling, Tendenser for udbudet af arbejdskraft 1973-1988, Copenhagen 1973 (unpublished).

this change would have to take into account a number of aspects, such as the distinction between married and unmarried women which is changing due to changes in family patterns. But in the present context attention will only be given to one particular aspect. As will be further discussed in chapter VI, for government employees the rate of increase has been much faster for married women than for men and unmarried women. What has probably happened is a process corresponding to that in the food processing industry. An increasing proportion of activities in both fields has moved from the home to an outside 'work place'. This in turn has permitted women to work outside their homes (something most men would do anyway), but at the same time increased participation rates presuppose facilities for taking care of children, just as they presuppose industries for producing canned food and refrigerators.[1]

---

[1] The implicit consequences for using the size of GNP as an expression of the standard of living of a given population, if this hypothesis holds, should be kept in mind, but will not be elaborated here.

GROWTH RATES AND INDUSTRIAL STRUCTURE, 1950-73

16. In the final part of the introduction above, three sub-periods with different patterns of growth were distinguished: 1950-58, 1958-66 and 1966-73. In the following, differences between these sub-periods will be analysed on the basis of national accounts data for 1950, 1958, 1966 and 1973. In all these years, economic activity was high compared with neighbouring years. Supplementary year-by-year figures are shown in appendix tables I.1 and I.2.

To some extent, the techniques applied in handling the national accounts data will differ from usual procedures, and some concepts will be introduced which differ from those used in traditional analysis. This is partly due to the fact that Danish national accounts data for 1950-73 at constant prices are calculated and presented on the basis of 1955-prices. Hence for the early 1970s, the weights applied in the constant-price figures are more than 15 years old. The implied index-number problems are therefore quite substantial. A detailed treatment of these problems can be found in the appendix (see pp. 35-44).

Table I.5

Gross domestic product at factor cost, current prices

DKR 1 000 million

	1950	1958	1966	1973
Agriculture etc.	4.6	5.5	7.7	12.5
Manuf., handicraft etc.	6.3	10.1	22.8	46.2
of which: manufacturing	4.1	6.4	14.4	30.9
handicraft	1.9	3.0	7.0	13.1
electr., gas, etc.	0.3	0.7	1.4	2.2
Building and construction	1.4	2.4	6.8	15.1
Distribution, banking, hotels etc.	4.3	6.4	14.0	28.3
Transport	1.8	3.4	7.3	14.9
Private services, incl. use dwellings	1.6	2.9	6.2	11.8
Government services	1.6	3.3	9.9	30.3
Total GDP at factor cost	21.6	34.0	74.7	159.1
- net interest payments, etc.	0.1	0.0	0.1	1.0
Total GNI at factor cost	21.5	34.0	74.6	158.1
- repair, maintenance, depreciat.	2.7	5.5	12.8	27.5
TOTAL NNI AT FACTOR COST	18.8	28.5	61.8	130.6

Sources: See sources to appendix table I.1.

Table I.6

Gross domestic product at factor cost, at constant
1955-prices (= real product)

	1950		1958		1966		1973	
	DKR 1 000 million	per cent	DKR 1 000 million	per cent	DKR 1 000 million	per cent	DKR 1 000 million	per cent
Agricult. etc.	5.2	20.1	5.9	18.7	6.3	13.5	6.2	9.9
Trade and Industry	7.5	29.1	9.0	28.4	15.1	32.4	22.1	35.3
of which: manufact.	4.8	18.5	5.9	18.6	10.2	22.0	15.8	25.3
handicraft	2.4	9.4	2.6	8.3	3.8	8.1	4.2	6.7
el, gas, etc.	0.3	1.2	0.5	1.5	1.1	2.3	2.1	3.3
Building and construction	1.8	7.1	2.2	6.9	3.8	8.3	5.0	7.9
Commerce, banking, hotel etc.	4.9	18.9	6.9	19.1	9.3	19.9	12.7	20.2
Transport	2.2	8.7	3.1	10.1	4.6	9.9	6.4	10.3
Priv. services, incl. use of dwellings	2.1	8.0	2.5	7.9	3.0	6.6	3.5	5.6
Government services	2.1	8.1	2.8	8.9	4.4	9.4	6.8	10.8
Total real GDP = real prod.	25.8	100.0	31.5	100.0	46.5	100.0	62.7	100.0

Note: Percentages are calculated before rounding of the basic data.
Sources: See sources to appendix table I.1.

17. Table I.5 shows usual[1] figures for gross domestic product at factor cost by industry at current prices. However, the figures are of course affected by inflation. In order to remedy this distortion, similar figures are shown in table I.6, calculated at 1955-prices according to the technique used by the

---

[1] Repair and maintenance are included in the gross figures. This inflates the 'level' of the Danish figures somewhat, as compared with the similar figures for other EEC countries.

Table I.7

Real income by industries, 1955-prices

	1950		1958		1966		1973	
	DKR 1 000 million	per cent	DKR 1 000 million	per cent	DKR 1 000 million	per cent	DKR 1 000 million	per cent
Agricult. ect.	5.4	21.2	5.1	16.2	5.0	10.3	5.1	7.8
Trade and industry	7.5	29.2	9.4	29.7	14.8	30.6	19.2	29.1
of which:								
manufact.	4.9	19.0	6.0	19.0	9.3	19.3	12.8	19.4
handicraft	2.2	8.7	2.8	8.8	4.6	9.5	5.5	8.3
el., gas, etc.	0.4	1.5	0.6	1.9	0.9	1.8	0.9	1.4
Building and construction	1.7	6.6	2.2	7.0	4.4	9.1	6.3	9.5
Distribution, banking, hotels etc.	5.1	19.8	5.9	18.7	9.0	18.7	11.8	17.8
Transport	2.1	8.3	3.2	10.1	4.7	9.7	6.2	9.4
Priv. services, incl. use of dwellings	2.0	7.6	2.7	8.5	4.0	8.3	4.9	7.4
Government services	1.9	7.3	3.1	9.8	6.4	13.3	12.6	19.0
Total real income	25.7	100.0	31.6	100.0	48.3	100.0	66.1	100.0

Sources: See sources to appendix table I.1.

Danmarks Statistik (The Danish Statistical Office). These figures will, in future, be referred to as real product figures. They are estimated on the assumption that all inputs and outputs in each year during the whole period are valued at 1955-prices, and hence relative prices are implicitly assumed to have remained constant over the whole period.

According to table I.6, the share of agriculture in total real product declined from 20 per cent in 1950 to 10 per cent in 1973, the main adjustment taking place during the period of urban expansion from 1958 onwards. The share of trade and industry remained slightly below 30 per cent during the 1950s, but subsequently increased to 35 per cent, whilst that of building and construction increased substantially from 1958 to 1966. Finally, the share of government services in total real product showed a steady, although apparently not very substantial, increase from 8.1 per cent in 1950 to 10.8 per cent in 1973.

18. Some of these findings, based on traditional procedures of deflation, are somewhat surprising. Furthermore, they are to some extent misleading because of the implied assumption of constant relative prices over the period shown.

An obvious alternative would be to retain the figures for total real GDP of the various years and subsequently use the implied deflator for total GDP to deflate figures for individual industries in a particular year. According to this procedure, the percentage distribution of real GDP by industry will of course correspond exactly to the distribution at current prices (cf. table I.5), because the same deflator is used for all industries in a given year.

In table I.7, such estimates have been made, and are labelled figures of real income of the various industries. In brief, these figures could be described as illustrating actual trends, but on the assumption that no general price increase had taken place. On the other hand, the real income figures do reflect the changes in relative prices between the various industries which have actually occurred.

One immediate conclusion from the above calculations could be that while figures of real product and real income for a certain industry in a certain year could differ a great deal because of the different methods of price deflation, the time series of total real product and total real income would be identical. When figures in the bottom rows to tables I.6 and I.7 are compared, it will be seen that this is not exactly the case. The explanation of this discrepancy is related to changes of the terms of foreign trade. Obviously, when traditional procedures of deflation are applied (cf. table I.6), such terms of trade changes cannot possibly be reflected in the figures, because relative prices are implicitly assumed to have remained constant. This issue is elaborated in the appendix.

19. Although the percentage distribution of real income by industries (cf. table I.7) is identical to that of GDP at current prices (cf. table I.5), the growth pattern of real income by industry differs substantially from that of real product (cf. table I.6). From 1950 to 1973, the share of agriculture in total real income declined at a faster rate than that of real product, whilst the share of trade and industry in total real income remained roughly constant. However, the most significant change occurs with respect to government services. From 1950 to 1973, their share of real product, only increased moderately. However, their share in total real income increased from 7.3 per cent in 1950 to 19.0 per cent in 1973 (reflecting a similar increase based on figures at current prices). According to an opportunity-cost interpretation, the figures imply that while the economy in 1950 sacrificed 7.3 per cent of alternative total output in order to obtain government services, the corresponding figure in 1973 was 19 per cent.[1]

---

[1] As in other countries, Danish figures on contribution to GDP by government services are estimated from the input side, because no market price is obtained for such services. In this connection, no productivity increases have been assumed to take place. Many of the problems relating to GDP figures for government services are particularly difficult to solve in relation to real product estimates. In this connection it should be recalled that the figures of shares of GDP can also be obtained from national accounts at current prices.

Table I.8

Annual growth rates of real product and real income

	1950-58		1958-66		1966-73	
	Real prod.	Real inc.	Real prod.	Real inc.	Real prod.	Real inc.
Agriculture, etc.	1.6	-0.8	0.8	-0.3	-0.2	0.3
Trade and industry	2.3	2.8	6.7	5.8	5.8	3.7
of which: manufacturing	2.6	2.6	7.2	5.6	6.5	4.5
trade	1.0	2.7	4.6	6.5	1.5	2.5
el, gas, ect.	6.1	5.4	10.6	4.8	10.0	0.5
Building and construction	2.2	3.5	7.3	8.9	4.2	5.5
Distribution, banking, hotels etc.	2.6	1.9	5.6	5.4	4.5	4.0
Transport	4.4	5.1	4.8	5.0	4.8	4.3
Private services, inc. use of dwellings	2.3	4.1	2.6	5.1	2.0	3.0
Government services	3.6	6.5	5.7	9.5	6.8	10.0
TOTAL	2.5	2.6	5.0	5.4	4.4	4.6
Implicit price deflator of total	3.2	3.1	5.1	4.7	6.8	6.6

Sources: See sources to appendix table I.1.

20. In table I.8, findings according to tables I.5 - I.7 are summarized, expressed in terms of percentage rates of growth per year. In terms of overall growth rates, the bottom part of the table confirms the suggestions made in the final part of the introduction above. In the period 1950-58, the average overall growth rate only amounted to roughly 2.5 per cent, in 1958-66 - with declining rates of unemployment - it reached 5-5 1/2 per cent, and in the third sub-period, viz. from 1966 to 1973, the overall growth rate declined to 4 1/2 per cent, partly because as full employment had been reached in the mid-1960s, the possibilities of increasing total employment became more limited.

The bottom row of the table shows that the rate of inflation as expressed by the implicit GDP deflator was only slightly above 3 per cent per year during the period 1950-58. In the second sub-period, it increased to roughly 5 per cent and from 1966 to 1973, averaged nearly 7 per cent, maintaining an accelerating trend, (cf. the year-by-year figures of growth rates and price increases in appendix table I.1).

21. The growth rates of individual industries will be dealt with in later chapters.

Table I.9

Shares of GDP by main groups of industries

(per cent)

	1950	1958	1966	1973
Shares of real product				
Balance of payments industries (agric., manuf. ect.)	49.2	47.1	45.9	45.2
Domestic industries (building and constr., gov.t services)	15.2	15.8	17.7	18.7
Other industries	35.6	37.1	36.4	36.1
Shares of GDP at current prices = shares of real income				
Balance of payments industries (agric., manuf. etc.)	50.4	45.9	40.9	36.9
Domestic industries (building and constr., gov.t services)	13.9	16.8	22.4	28.5
Other industries	35.7	37.3	36.7	34.6
TOTAL	100.0	100.0	100.0	100.0

Sources: Tables I.6 and I.7.

22. Before concluding this section on the structure of industry, an important distinction should be mentioned, i.e. that between 'balance of payments industries', 'domestic industries' and 'other industries'. The persistent balance of payments deficit since 1960 suggests that the industrial pattern has not been consistent with external equilibrium. Resources employed in industries which compete with foreign firms either abroad (exports) or on the home market (mainly agriculture and manufacturing industries), have been too limited. On the other hand, domestic industries (building and construction, government services) have been able to expand too fast from the viewpoint of external equilibrium. This problem has been particularly urgent in periods of full employment. With total resources fully utilized, a dampening of the growth of domestic industries is obviously a necessary condition for the expansion of the balance of payments industries.

Table I.9 includes the additional group of 'Other industries', covering distribution, transport and private services, etc. In a more detailed analysis, some of these industries ought to be placed in the two other groups of the table.[1] However, the pattern according to table I.9 would largely remain

---

[1] E.g., foreign shipping, tourist industries etc. should be considered balance of payments industries whereas banking should be grouped with domestic industries.

Table I.10

GDP and domestic demand, current prices

(DKR 1 000 million)

	1950	1958	1966	1973
GDP, factor cost	21.6	34.0	74.7	159.1
+ indir. taxes, net	1.5	3.2	9.0	21.9
GDP, market prices	23.1	37.2	83.7	181.0
+ imp. goods and services	6.8	10.9	23.9	55.9
Total	29.9	48.1	107.6	236.9
- exp. goods and services	6.0	11.9	22.9	52.9
Domestic demand	23.9	36.2	84.7	184.0
of which: consumption	18.0	27.7	61.1	130.9
fixed investm.	3.4	5.9	16.6	38.1
stockbuilding	0.9	-0.2	0.5	1.4
repair and maint.	1.6	2.8	6.5	13.6

Sources: See sources to appendix table I.1.

unaffected by such adjustments, and the share of 'Other industries' would remain stable anyway.

The upper part of the table shows that, the share of the balance of payments industries, measured on a real-product basis, declined slightly from 1950 to 1973, while that of domestic industries increased correspondingly. However, in order to illustrate the problem of resource allocation, shares of real income (equal to shares of GDP at current prices) provide the proper background, and such figures are shown in the lower part of the table. According to these figures, resource allocation has changed substantially from 1950 to 1973, the share of balance of payments industries having declined from 50 to 37 per cent and that of domestic industries having increased from 14 per cent to no less than 28 per cent. Against this background, it is hardly surprising that there have been persistent balance of payments deficits.

THE STRUCTURE OF DOMESTIC DEMAND, 1950-73

23. In this section, patterns of growth and structural changes of domestic demand will be analysed on the basis of national accounts data, applying techniques similar to those which were used in the preceding section in connection with the supply side.

Table I.11

Domestic demand, 1955-prices (constant relative prices over time)

	1950		1958		1966		1973	
	DKR 1 000 million	per cent	DKR 1 000 million	per cent	DKR 1 000 million	per cent	DKR 1 000 million	per cent
Consumption								
private	16.3	66.7	18.9	67.3	27.9	60.6	36.3	56.3
public	2.9	11.7	3.9	13.8	6.0	13.2	9.6	14.8
TOTAL	19.2	78.4	22.8	81.1	33.9	73.8	45.9	71.1
Fixed invest.								
housing	0.8	3.1	0.8	2.9	1.9	4.1	3.5	5.4
other priv.	2.3	9.5	3.4	11.9	7.0	15.2	10.9	16.8
public	1.0	4.0	1.3	4.8	2.7	6.0	3.4	5.3
TOTAL	4.1	16.6	5.5	19.6	11.6	25.3	17.8	27.5
Stockbuilding	1.2	5.0	-0.2	-0.7	0.4	0.9	0.9	1.4
TOTAL DOMESTIC DEMAND	24.5	100.0	28.1	100.0	45.9	100.0	64.6	100.0
of which:								
public	3.8	15.7	5.2	18.6	8.7	19.2	13.0	20.1
housing inv.	0.8	3.1	0.8	2.9	1.9	4.1	3.5	5.4
public + housing	4.6	18.8	6.0	21.5	10.6	23.3	16.5	25.5

Note: Techniques of deflation correspond to those applied in table I.6.
Sources: See sources to appendix table I.1.

24. Standard[1] national accounts data at current prices are shown in table I.10, but the figures are to a large extent affected by accelerating rates of inflation.

---

[1] Contrary to what could be done when figures for GDP by industries were shown above, it is possible to separate figures on repair and maintenance when demand components are illustrated. In the following, this has been done, and in tables I.11 and I.12 this item is completely disregarded. The purpose has been to provide for better comparability with similar figures for other EEC countries.

(cont'd on page 26)

Table I.12

Domestic demand, 1955-prices

(same deflator of all components in a given year)

	1950		1958		1966		1973	
	DKR 1 000 million	per cent	DKR 1 000 million	per cent	DKR 1 000 million	per cent	DKR 1 000 million	per cent
Consumption								
private	16.8	68.6	18.6	66.1	26.3	57.3	31.6	49.6
public	2.6	10.6	4.2	14.8	8.3	18.0	15.8	24.4
TOTAL	19.4	79.2	22.8	80.9	34.6	75.3	47.4	73.4
Fixed inv.								
housing	0.7	2.9	0.8	2.9	2.1	4.5	4.5	7.0
other priv.	2.3	9.6	3.4	11.9	6.0	13.1	8.1	12.6
public	1.0	3.8	1.3	4.8	2.9	6.4	4.0	6.1
TOTAL	4.0	16.3	5.5	19.6	11.0	24.0	16.6	25.7
Stockbuilding	1.1	4.5	-0.2	-0.5	0.3	0.7	0.6	0.9
TOTAL DOMESTIC DEMAND	24.5	100.0	28.1	100.0	45.9	100.0	64.6	100.0
of which:								
public	3.6	14.4	5.5	19.6	11.2	24.4	19.8	30.5
housing inv.	0.7	2.9	0.8	2.9	2.1	4.5	4.5	7.0
public + housing	4.3	17.3	6.3	22.5	13.3	28.9	24.3	37.5

Note: Techniques of deflation are similar to those applied in table I.7.
Sources: See sources to appendix table I.1.

In table I.11, demand components at constant prices are presented, assuming that relative prices have remained constant over the period 1950 to 1973.

(cont'd of note 1 on page 25)
Furthermore, all figures at 1955-prices are indicated at factor cost. In this way, the effects of indirect taxation are excluded. The adjustment has been made on the assumption that net indirect taxes affect prices of private consumption only. While this is not completely true, the discrepancies are insignificant and do not affect the main pattern according to the figures.

According to the table, the share of total consumption (at factor cost) in total domestic demand has declined from roughly 80 per cent during the 1950s to slightly above 70 per cent during the last part of the period, while the share of total fixed investment has increased correspondingly. Furthermore, the composition of total consumption has changed. While the share of private consumption has shown a substantial decline, that of public consumption has increased, although only moderately - from 11.7 per cent in 1950 to 14.8 per cent in 1973.

25. In table I.12, a different method of deflation is used, applying the same deflator for all demand components in a given year. Hence the percentage distribution according to table I.12 is identical to a percentage distribution based on corresponding figures at current prices.[1]

26. The shares of total consumption and total investment in total domestic demand are very similar according to the two tables, but this is not true for the components of each of these totals. The share of private consumption in total domestic demand according to table I.12 declines even more than that in table I.11. At the same time, the share of public consumption in table I.12 shows a more dramatic increase, from 10.6 per cent in 1950 to 24.4 per cent in 1973. The discrepancy between the two tables with respect to the share of public consumption mainly reflects the fact that public consumption is very labour intensive and, furthermore, not subject to significant increases in labour productivity. Hence costs in this field, largely reflecting wage rates for government employees, have tended to show a faster rate of increase than most other costs and prices. For private consumption, the implication is that prices have shown a comparative decline, probably partly due to increases in productivity.

27. Turning to the components of total investment, the share of 'other private investment' (excluding residential investment) in total domestic demand shows a smaller increase in table I.12 than in table I.11. As with private consumption, goods incorporated in 'other private investment' have become comparatively less expensive over time, probably due also to substantial increases in productivity.

Apparently, the opposite has been true for residential investment and public investment. On the whole, the shares of both show a significant increase, measured at constant relative prices (cf. table I.11), but the increase is even larger according to table I.12.

28. The share of total public demand for goods and services including total investment in housing is shown separately in the bottom part of tables I.11 and I.12. The reason for including residential investment at this point is partly that this demand is primarily directed towards 'domestic industries', and partly that private residential investment has been subject to direct government regulations, restrictions, and subsidies to such an extent as may

---

[1] In order not to complicate the presentation too much, the deflator applied in table I.12 is simply the deflator of total domestic demand. Therefore, the figures of <u>total</u> domestic demand in DKR 1 000 million are identical in table I.11 and I.12. Thus, the technique in the present context is simpler than the corresponding one applied in table I.7.

justify it being treated in the same way as direct public purchases of goods and services.

According to the bottom row of table I.11, the share of public demand including residential investment increased from below 20 per cent in 1950 to slightly above 25 per cent in 1973. However, including the effect of changes in relative prices, the increase becomes much more pronounced: from 17.3 per cent to no less than 37.5 per cent (cf. the bottom row of table I.12). These figures imply that the total share of private consumption and business investment in total domestic demand has fallen from well over 75 per cent in 1950 to 60 per cent in 1973.

29. In brief, one of the main results of the above analysis is that the share of total demand which is under (direct) government control has increased substantially, partly because of increased levels of activity, and partly because of increases in relative prices, especially in the field of public consumption.

In this connection, an additional comment should be made on the demand management by government with respect to public expenditures and residential investment. As has been pointed out, overall real growth rates declined from the second to the third sub-period, viz. from 1958-66 to 1966-73, the main reason being that full employment was reached in the mid 1960s. However, in spite of scarcities of resources and lower overall growth rates during the third sub-period, the growth of public demand in real terms continued at about 10 per cent per year. The consequences of this policy for the balance of payments hardly need elaboration.

UNEMPLOYMENT

30. As stated previously, unemployment was substantial during most of the 1950s. From the late 1950s to the mid 1960s, it declined and, subsequently, almost disappeared. During most of the period from 1966 to 1973, full employment prevailed.

In the following section, this summary will be elaborated, based on figures for 1950, 1958, 1966 and 1973 (cf. table I.13). Supplementary year-by-year figures for the overall rate of unemployment are given in appendix table I.2.

31. From 1950 to 1973, the number of employees covered by the unemployment-insurance scheme, under which the major part of unemployment-relief payments is financed by government transfers and only a minor part by contributions from members, increased from 630 000 to 830 000. Thus only one third of the labour force was covered by the scheme. Even when the self-employed (including owners) are deducted from the labour force, only half of the total number of employees were insured, and percentages of unemployment according to table I.13 only refer to this group. As unemployment among the non-insured employees has, at least until recently, been insignificant, the percentages shown in the table should be reduced substantially to make them comparable with corresponding figures for most other countries.

32. During most of the 1950s, the overall rate of unemployment among insured employees remained at a level of roughly ten per cent (cf. also appendix ta-

ble I.2). Although unemployment rates had been even higher during the 1930s, such a level was clearly not acceptable. However, during most of the 1950s a shortage of foreign exchange was an important problem, and expansionist policies in order to reduce unemployment would necessarily have aggravated the balance of payments problem, the more so because quantitative import restrictions were being dismantled within the OEEC framework.

Table I.13

Unemployment

	1950	1958	1966	1973
	1 000 persons			
Total labour force (cf. table I.3)	2 024	–	–	2 446
Number of persons with unemployment insurance	633	709	797	833
of which: men	504	555	595	652
women	129	154	202	181
	per cent			
Unemployment as % of insured employees				
Men	9.7	10.9	2.7	2.4
Women	4.6	5.5	1.0	2.4
TOTAL	8.7	9.6	2.3	2.4
February ⎫	14.7	17.8	6.3	3.6
June ⎬ Not seasonally adjusted	3.9	4.1	0.5	1.2
November ⎭	7.6	6.7	1.7	2.2
Trade and industry	5.7	6.8	1.8	1.9
Building and construction	15.2	19.8	6.0	5.0
Unskilled workers	14.4	16.9	4.8	3.4
Northern Jutland, all industries	16.6	16.9	6.5	5.8

Note: For coverage, see text.
Sources: Danmarks Statistik: **Statistisk tiårsoversigt** 1950-60, 1970 and 1975.

However, these high average annual rates of unemployment conceal substantial seasonal variations (cf. the figures for February, June and November in table I.13). During the 1960s and the first part of the 1970s, seasonal unemployment was reduced substantially, partly because of the declining importance of some industries with large seasonal variations (e.g. agriculture), and partly because of new techniques allowing activities to continue throughout the winter months (e.g. in building and construction). From the mid

1960s onwards, overall unemployment became insignificant, at least when short term unemployment, e.g. in connection with change of job, is disregarded.

33. In addition, regional unemployment problems were reduced. Being a small country with reasonably good means of transportation, regional problems are small compared with those of most other countries.[1] But of course regional differences do exist. Thus a high share of the population - roughly 25 per cent - lives in the area around Copenhagen, on the eastern outskirts of Denmark. In Jutland most activities take place along the east coast, but western Jutland is less densely populated. Finally, unemployment rates are usually highest in northern Jutland, although, as is shown in table I.13, progress was made in the 1960s in this area.

THE BALANCE OF PAYMENTS

34. As shown in the previous section, economic growth during the main part of the 1960s contributed substantially to solving the unemployment problem of the 1950s. A price for this achievement was, however, paid in the form of a persistent and increasing balance of payments deficit. This issue will be more fully discussed in chapter X, and the main figures are presented in table X.1. However, a chapter on the structural problems of the economy cannot avoid at least mentioning this subject.

Whereas the external goods and services account showed surpluses during most of the 1950s, a series of increasing deficits has been recorded since 1960 (cf. appendix table I.2). Consequently, foreign debt has been increasing, and so have foreign interest payments. Hence the deficits on the current account as a whole have increasingly exceeded those for goods and services.

SUMMARY

35. In brief, Danish basic economic problems from 1950 to 1973 may be summarized as follows:

a) During the main part of the 1950s the important constraint for economic policy was related to shortages of foreign exchange. Balance of payments deficits had to be avoided - and so they were. Manufacturing industries expanded in spite of increasing foreign competition. In particular, exports of manufactured goods increased rapidly. But unemployment remained substantial.

b) From the late 1950s to the mid 1960s, unemployment was declining and full employment was subsequently achieved. However, rates of inflation increased, and became higher than in many neighbouring countries. Balance of payments deficits became a persistent feature of the Danish economy.

---

[1] However, it has become increasingly difficult for the smaller Danish islands to retain their inhabitants. This problem is partly industrial, but is also related to difficulties with respect to social facilities, e.g. schools.

- 31 -

c) From the mid 1960s to 1973, full employment was largely maintained, but problems with respect to inflation and the balance of payments were aggravated. As shown in the analysis above, one of the most important factors behind this development is to be found in changes in the structure of total demand, with domestic industries being allowed to expand too fast. This policy in the field of public expenditure etc. gave rise to serious problems for the balance of payments industries.

36. Against this general background, the most important Danish industries will be examined in the following chapters.

- 32 -

Appendix table I.1

Total GDP, real product, real income etc., 1949-1973

	GDP, current prices, DKR 1000 million	GDP deflator 1955 = 100	Terms of trade, 1955 = 100	Real product, 1955-prices		Real income, 1955-prices	
				DKR 1000 million	per cent increase	DKR 1000 million	per cent increase
1949	18.9	78.6	107	24.0		24.4	
1950	21.6	83.6	98	25.8	7.6	25.7	5.3
1951	23.4	90.2	89	25.9	0.4	25.1	- 2.3
1952	25.0	95.1	94	26.3	1.2	25.8	2.9
1953	26.5	95.3	97	27.8	5.9	27.6	6.8
1954	27.6	96.8	99	28.5	2.5	28.5	3.3
1955	28.7	100.0	100	28.7	0.1	28.7	0.8
1956	30.6	104.7	101	29.3	1.9	29.4	2.4
1957	32.7	106.0	98	30.8	5.4	30.6	4.2
1958	34.0	107.8	100	31.5	2.3	31.6	3.1
1959	37.4	111.9	106	33.4	6.1	34.2	8.4
1960	40.5	113.8	103	35.6	6.5	36.1	5.4
1961	45.4	120.7	102	37.6	5.6	37.8	4.8
1962	50.8	127.9	104	39.7	5.6	40.3	6.6
1963	53.5	134.2	105	39.9	0.4	40.6	0.9
1964	61.1	140.9	107	43.4	8.8	44.6	9.7
1965	68.3	150.0	107	45.5	5.0	47.0	5.3
1966	74.7	160.7	109	46.5	2.2	48.3	2.8
1967	81.9	169.1	107	48.4	4.1	49.8	3.2
1968	89.3	176.4	104	50.6	4.5	51.6	3.6
1969	101.1	184.5	106	54.8	8.2	56.3	9.1
1970	112.6	200.2	106	56.3	2.6	57.9	2.8
1971	123.5	211.9	106	58.3	3.6	60.0	3.6
1972	138.9	227.7	109	61.0	4.6	63.9	6.4
1973	159.1	253.7	110	62.7	2.8	66.1	3.5

Note: The terms of trade figures in the third column are calculated from the implicit deflators of exports and imports of goods and services according to the national accounting data. On the whole, they are very similar to the unit-value indices, published by Danmarks Statistik, the latter covering trade of goods only. The main exception is that the figures above show a smaller deterioration from 1949 to 1951 (from 107 to 89) than figures derived from the unit-value data (from 112 to 86). It should be added that real-income figures are calculated before rounding of the terms of trade figures above. In fact the terms of trade improved slightly in 1965 and in 1970.

Sources: Danmarks Statistik: Nationalregnskabsstatistik 1947-1960, S.U. No 7 and Statistisk tiårsoversigt 1970 and 1975.

Appendix table I.2

External balance, GDP, unemployment, 1949-1973

	Exports	Imports	Export surplus	Domestic demand	GDP market prices	Indirect taxes net	GDP factor cost	Percentage rate of unemployment[1]
	Goods and services							
	DKR 1 000 million, current prices			DKR 1 000 million, current prices				
1949	4.7	4.9	-0.2	20.4	20.2	1.3	18.9	9.6
1950	6.0	6.8	-0.8	23.9	23.1	1.5	21.6	8.7
1951	7.8	8.0	-0.2	25.3	25.1	1.7	23.4	9.7
1952	8.0	7.8	0.2	26.5	26.7	1.7	25.0	12.5
1953	8.2	8.0	0.2	28.4	28.6	2.1	26.5	9.2
1954	8.8	9.2	-0.4	30.3	29.9	2.3	27.6	8.0
1955	9.8	9.5	0.3	31.0	31.3	2.6	28.7	9.7
1956	10.5	10.5	0.0	33.4	33.4	2.8	30.6	11.1
1957	11.4	11.1	0.3	35.2	35.5	2.8	32.7	10.2
1958	11.9	10.9	1.0	36.2	37.2	3.2	34.0	9.6
1959	12.9	12.7	0.2	40.9	41.1	3.7	37.4	5.9
1960	13.8	14.2	-0.4	44.8	44.4	3.9	40.5	4.2
1961	14.3	14.9	-0.6	50.0	49.4	4.0	45.4	3.3
1962	15.3	16.8	-1.5	57.2	55.7	4.9	50.8	3.0
1963	17.3	17.0	0.3	58.9	59.2	5.7	53.5	4.2
1964	19.4	20.5	-1.1	68.8	67.7	6.6	61.1	2.4
1965	21.4	22.3	-0.9	77.0	76.1	7.8	68.3	2.0
1966	22.9	23.9	-1.0	84.7	83.7	9.0	74.7	2.3
1967	24.2	25.7	-1.5	93.3	91.8	9.9	81.9	2.7
1968	27.2	28.3	-1.1	102.3	101.2	11.9	89.3	5.0
1969	30.7	32.9	-2.2	117.4	115.2	14.1	101.1	3.9
1970	34.6	37.8	-3.2	131.1	127.9	15.3	112.6	2.9
1971	39.2	41.0	-1.8	142.4	140.5	17.0	123.5	3.7
1972	44.1	42.7	1.4	157.3	158.7	19.8	138.9	3.6
1973	52.9	55.9	-3.0	184.0	181.0	21.9	159.1	2.4

[1] Calculation techniques were slightly changed in 1959. The effect on the figures is, however, not substantial.
Sources: See sources to appendix table I.1 supplemented by additional information (cf. sources to table I.13).

Appendix table I.3

Indice of real income, real product etc. by industry;
1958, 1966 and 1973 (1950 = 100)

	1950	1958	1966	1973
Agriculture, etc.				
real income	100	94	92	95
real product	100	114	121	120
real inc./real product	100	83	76	79
Manufacturing				
real income	100	123	191	263
real product	100	123	215	332
real inc./real product	100	100	89	79
Handicraft				
real income	100	124	205	245
real product	100	108	155	174
real inc./real product	100	115	132	140
Electricity, gas, ect.				
real income	100	152	221	228
real product	100	160	360	680
real inc./real product	100	95	62	34
Building and construction				
real income	100	131	259	369
real product	100	119	209	272
real inc./real product	100	110	124	136
Distribution, banking, etc.				
real income	100	116	178	231
real product	100	123	190	259
real inc./real product	100	95	94	89
Transport				
real income	100	148	220	289
real product	100	141	204	285
real inc./real product	100	106	108	101
Private services				
real income	100	137	205	252
real product	100	120	147	168
real inc./real product	100	115	140	149
Government services				
real income	100	166	343	670
real product	100	133	208	322
real inc./real product	100	125	165	208
Total value added				
real income	100	123	188	257
real product	100	122	180	243
real inc./real product	100	101	104	106

Note: All figures are calculated before rounding of the basic data. For comments, see final part of appendix to chapter I.
Sources: See sources to appendix table I.1.

[17]
Danish Industry 1964-1979

Ebbe Yndgaard

1. Introduction

This paper tries to describe the development of Danish Industry 1964-1979 by a simple macro-sectoral model.[1]

The idea of the paper is to accept a traditional framework at face value, give it a maximum chance of success, including a calibration of parameters, to see how well it is able to track observed phenomena. At the same time we try to approach real life by letting decision makers react to *expected* signals only, by assuming that firms expect to be quantity-rationed on the selling side; implicitly, their equalization of realized production with expected sales builds on the assumption that for industry as a whole such a procedure is profitable.

The unknown parameters *and* capital figures are not estimated in the usual sense; instead we have calibrated both so that a properly defined penalty function is minimized, in principle enabling us to avoid the non-meaningful symmetric treatment of residuals in e.g. the production function.

As a consequence of our procedure, no test statistics etc. are reported – or available – except for the primitive, but powerful reports on the model's ability to track actual development.

It should be emphasized in advance that *all implications of the paper hinge on all assumptions as one composite set, including relevance of data applied*; this may be a drawback. However, a powerful characteristic of our results is that they rely on the internal consistency of the neoclassical model.

2. Production Assumptions

2.1. Technology

ASSUMPTION 1: *The aggregate production function of Danish industry in period t is assumed to be*

$$X_t = Ae^{\beta v t}(K_{t-1}(1-\delta_t)+I_t e^{\theta t})^{\alpha}(L_t)^{\beta} \qquad (1)$$

---

1. It is my hope, that the provocative approach will give rise to a serious debate. As to methodology, I can think of no criticism, which cannot equally forcefully be raised against conventional methods. No matter how the economist/econometrician behaves, some arbitrariness and subjective preferences affect his results.

where X_t is a production index, K_t capital, I_t investment and L_t the number of man hours used. While v represents the rate of disembodied technical progress, θ is an embodied technical progress parameter. δ_t is an endogenously determined rate of depreciation.

2.2. Parameters α & β

ASSUMPTION 2: $\alpha = 0.45$ & $\beta = 0.55$.

We do not estimate the parameters α and β,[2] but postulate their values in accordance with the functional distribution of income of Danish industry. In fact it is impossible to achieve unbiased estimates of the parameters, if sectoral data do not reflect full employment of factor inputs. In consideration of the irreversibility of investment we accept the possibility of underutilization of capacity for capital and hoarding of labour.

2.3. Capital K_t

ASSUMPTION 3: *There exists a unique capital stock of machinery, measurable in one dimension, viz. efficiency units in old techniques.*

We disregard all aggregation problems etc. and neglect other factor inputs by considering them limitational to machinery and labour (buildings, transport equipment, etc.)

2.4. Depreciation and Capital

ASSUMPTION 4: *The rate of depreciation δ_t is constructed so that a high or low utilization degree in the past leads to an increase or a decrease of δ_t respectively.* Actually δ_t is calculated by formula (2)

$$\delta_t = \delta_0 U_{t-1} \tag{2}$$

where U_t is the utilization rate, defined as actual production/calibrated production capacity according to (1). However, δ_t is limited to the interval $(0.20 \leq \delta_t \leq 0.50)$ for all t.

To construct capital figures, we must postulate some initial capital value K_1 followed by insertion in the first parenthesis in (1). Both δ_0 and K_1 are determined iteratively by the calibration algorithm.

---

2. Trying to do so leads to meaningless results as is usual in analogous situations, e.g. $(\hat{\alpha} + \hat{\beta}) \geq 3.00$.

3. Behavioural Assumptions

ASSUMPTION 5: *Industry is quantity-rationed on the selling side. It minimizes expected costs w.r.t. inputs of capital and labour, implicitly assuming that profit is positive to the representative firm of industry.*

ASSUMPTION 6: *User costs for capital u_t are represented by the long-term interest rate multiplied by an index for the price of capital goods (machinery etc.)*

ASSUMPTION 7: *Firms produce the expected sales volume at minimum expected costs.*

The calibration procedure has revealed that a distributed lag model for formation of expectations is acceptable. For an arbitrary variable, y, the distributed lag model (3), estimated by OLS

$$\hat{y}_t = \hat{a}_1 + \hat{a}_2 y_{t-1} + \hat{a}_3 y_{t-2} + \hat{a}_4 y_{t-3} \tag{3}$$

produces the expected values for y_t.

The problem is *not* to establish a close relationship between observations and estimated values, *but* to establish an acceptable reproduction of the *decision makers' conception* of the future development of the variable in question. Some other procedure might therefore work even more satisfactorily. Using an asterisk to indicate the expected value of a variable, the cost minimizing problem of the firm amounts to minimizing (4) for each t

$$C_t = u_t^* I_t + w_t^* L_t \tag{4}$$

subject to

$$X_t^* = A e^{\beta v t} (K_{t-1}(1-\delta_t) + I_t e^{\theta t})^\alpha (L_t)^\beta \tag{5}$$

with respect to L_t and I_t; u_t^* and w_t^* are the expected user costs and wage rate respectively.

Minimizing the proper Lagrangean we get the following planned 'optimal' values for I_t and L_t

$$I_t^\Delta = \left\{ \left[X_t^* \Big/ \left[(A e^{\beta v t}) \left(\frac{\beta}{\alpha} \frac{u_t^*}{w_t^* e^{\theta t}} \right)^\beta \right] \right]^{\frac{1}{\alpha+\beta}} - (K_{t-1}(1-\delta_t)) \right\} e^{-\theta t} \tag{6}$$

and

$$L_t^\Delta = \left\{ \frac{\beta}{\alpha} \frac{u_t^*}{w_t^* e^{\theta t}} (K_{t-1}(1-\delta_t) + I_t^\Delta e^{\theta t}) \right\} e^{-\theta t} \tag{7}$$

where $u_t^* = p_{Q,t}^* \cdot r_t^* \cdot q$

r_t being the long-term interest rate, p_{Qt} the price (index) of machinery and q a scaling parameter, adapted and calibrated to harmonize user costs and the investment units, including limitational capital goods.

4. Calibration and data

The data used for our exercises, which are reproduced in the appendix, only deserve the usual general remark. Under ideal circumstances more appropriate data might have been found; especially, the data for user costs are dubious, because they neglect taxes, capital gains etc. Therefore in some sense data are part of the composite hypothesis.

The calibration algorithm shall not be presented in detail here.[3] The parameters to be calibrated are: A, θ, v, (α), (β) from the production function, δ_0 and K_1 for the capital construction segment and finally q for pure scaling purposes, i.e. in our presentation, where α and β are preset, the vector to be determined is

$$V = \{A, \theta, v, \delta_0, K_1, q\} \qquad (8)$$

To do so we minimize a penalty function with partly asymmetric weights, viz. so that the residuals from the production function are raised to the fourth power if positive and to the second power only if negative; thus we penalize heavily overutilization of capacity. If residuals are less than one, the weights are reversed.

The other elements in the criterion function include the sum of the squared deviations between the following pairs of time series.

1'. {actual/optimal investment}

2'. {actual/optimal man hours}

3'. {'actual'/optimal capital stock}

4'. {planned capital/capital needed to produce actual output if actually used man hours were input}

The last item is included to guarantee/support the calibrated level of the capital stock, including K_1.

The algorithm is initiated by postulating an initial set of values for the vector V (8); after calculating the corresponding penalty value, the algorithm searches by a

---

3. A copy of the computer program applied is available on request from the author.

steepest descent method for the most efficient direction of change. The algorithm stops, when improvement of the penalty function becomes negligeable.[4]

5. Results

Table 1 exhibits the observed and calculated values for production, labour, and capital respectively. The corresponding deviations, measured in per cent are reproduced in table 2, while the appendix contains the calculated expected values. Table 3 collects the calibrated parameters V, cfr. (8).

Table 1

	Output from Danish industry (X) and its calibrated value ($\hat{X}$) (capacity)		Man Hours Used in Danish industry (1000.000 per year) (L) and the calibrated optimal value (L^d).		Constructed capital in machinery ($\hat{K}$), optimal capital (K^d), observed (I) and optimal investment (I^d).			
Year	X	$\hat{X}$	L	L^d	$\hat{K}$	K^d	I	I^d
1960	67.00	73.68						
1961	71.00	76.30						
1962	76.00	82.78						
1963	77.00	84.89						
1964	86.00	93.29	647.80	466.07	4636.58	4900.12	1319.54	1511.50
1965	90.00	101.26	654.40	504.91	5405.15	5556.28	1434.44	1537.65
1966	91.00	104.25	629.30	458.80	5951.61	6029.63	1309.68	1359.63
1967	94.00	104.90	588.50	455.57	6443.48	6500.77	1269.79	1304.07
1968	100.00	105.07	570.50	467.70	6608.94	6727.24	1109.00	1175.70
1969	116.00	112.13	589.10	440.50	7224.08	7688.26	1365.38	1611.88
1970	117.00	117.02	578.50	489.40	7991.19	8410.45	1541.07	1750.01
1971	119.00	120.83	554.10	438.75	8898.26	8792.70	1587.39	1537.58
1972	130.00	125.40	548.50	445.46	9627.48	10138.01	1517.69	1742.01
1973	138.00	132.39	540.20	466.52	10885.72	10821.30	1799.27	1772.29
1974	133.00	138.44	526.50	433.51	12204.77	12024.30	1877.22	1806.85
1975	128.00	131.42	455.10	407.69	12782.34	12234.87	1535.20	1335.55
1976	145.00	139.36	464.00	386.21	13993.47	13204.37	1734.55	1464.55
1977	153.00	141.10	456.60	432.30	14434.25	13761.17	1591.35	1375.03
1978	157.00	140.84	448.00	394.15	14475.17	14097.81	1475.56	1361.51
1979	163.00	147.02	453.70	406.63	15426.15	15088.42	1685.06	1589.20

The values of α and β were – as already mentioned above – preset at levels, which quarantee both homogeneity of degree one and according to the observed functional income distribution an alibi for a marginal factor remunerating construction.

---

[4]. As is usual for numerical methods, uniqueness is not quaranteed. Therefore inspection of results for reasonableness is required.

Table 2. Residuals in percent between pairs of variables

Year	$X/\hat{X}$	I/I^Δ	L/L^Δ	$\hat{K}/K^\Delta$
1964	− 7.82	14.55	−28.05	5.68
1965	−11.12	7.19	−22.84	2.80
1966	−12.71	3.81	−27.09	1.31
1967	−10.39	2.70	−22.59	.89
1968	− 4.83	6.01	−18.02	1.79
1969	3.45	18.05	−25.22	6.43
1970	− .02	13.56	−15.40	5.25
1971	− 1.51	− 3.14	−20.82	− 1.19
1972	3.66	14.78	−18.79	5.30
1973	4.24	− 1.50	−13.64	− .59
1974	− 3.93	− 3.75	−17.66	− 1.48
1975	− 2.60	−13.00	−10.42	− 4.28
1976	4.05	−15.57	−16.77	− 5.64
1977	8.43	−13.59	− 5.32	− 4.66
1978	11.47	− 7.73	−12.02	− 2.61
1979	10.87	− 5.69	−10.37	− 2.19

Table 3. Calibrated parameter values

Production function	Capital construction	Scale parameter
A: 0.05767	K_1: 2990	q: .008382
α: 0.45	δ_0: 0.3104	
β: 0.55		
v: 0.0133		
θ: 0.0632		

The calibrated values for θ and v seem reasonable; a technical progress rate of 6 per cent per year should lead to an annual capital-labour ratio change of approximately 7.5%; the estimated value, cfr. figure 5, from our model is slightly below 10 percent. The overestimated value of the K/L-trend is connected with the "shake-out" effect of labour, cfr. below. It is not possible to identify the progress parameter v with either labour input or firms' organization of the production process.

Under steady state conditions with no changes of relative factor prices, a permanent increase of I by 5 percent, say, per year would lead to an annual increase of output for a given labour input by 6.5 per cent per year.[5] This number is

---

5. Viz. $v + \alpha(\theta + 0.05)$.

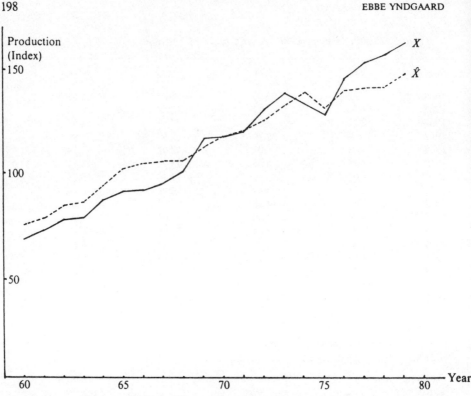

Figure 1. Actual (X) calibrated $(\hat{X})$ production

interesting, because it reflects the non-inflationary part of wage increases; as the average annual growth of I for Danish industry was approximately 1.5 per cent per year, the non-inflationary wage increase including labour input reductions per year was 5 per cent; in comparison to this the actual average annual increase of the wage rate was about 13 per cent in the period 1964-1980.

δ_0, the value of which was calibrated to 0.31 seems reasonable also taking into consideration the K_1-value of 2990. After 9 years a machine has been practically written off at this rate; the average stock of a constant investment stream of 1000 units would be approx. 3200, which seems acceptably close to our K_1-figure.

The tracking ability of the production function is acceptable except for some periods where production "exceeds" capacity; a final scaling mechanism of the algorithm could remove this.[6] Instead of doing so, we might postulate that under "normal" conditions, industry is working approx. 10 per cent below maximum capacity, cfr. figure 6.

---

6. It's only a question of sufficient computer time; the program is a bit expensive to run.

DANISH INDUSTRY 1964-1979

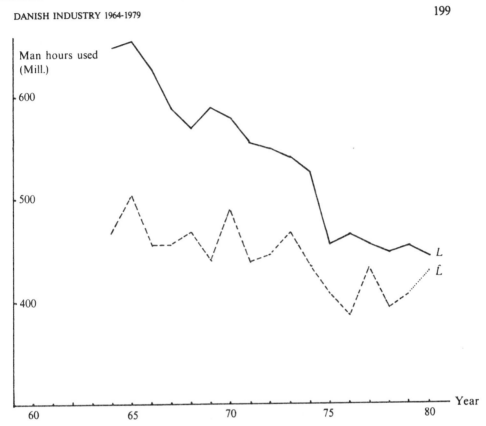

Figure 2. Actual (L) and optimal ($\hat{L}$) man hours used.

6. Some tentative conclusions and implications

With the reservation given in the introduction we may draw some tentative conclusions, the most general one being that it is possible to calibrate parameters in a neoclassical model so that its reproduction of observations, based on well-known cost-minimizing assumptions, looks reasonable.

The signals of the decision maker may be *expected* values, as created by a simple distributed lag model.[7] A macro-production function approach, even though it builds on a calibrated capital stock, works reasonably well. However, in spite of the apparent success of our approach, we are not able to reject the hypothesis that competing approaches might work as well, if they were given as favourable a chance.

---

7. For cost considerations we have not tried to use a perfect foresight approach, setting expected values equal to observed values; anyway, to do so would be in conflict with real life phenomena.

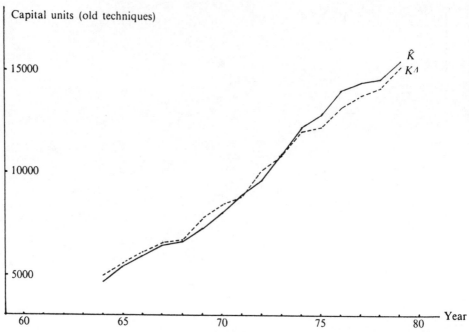

Figure 3. Calibrated ($\hat{K}$) and optimal (K^A) capital.

The applicability of our results for forecasting purposes is reflected as the dotted lines for 1980 in the figures 2 and 4.

As to the specific sector analyzed, some observations are significant.

Firstly, the reproduction of the development of investment is astonishingly precise, cfr. figure 4.

However, given the parameters of the production function of the sector, in the beginning of the period, i.e. until about 1973 firms have underinvested, perhaps due to lagged response to investment orders or other institutional obstacles. On the other hand from 1974, the optimal capital stock has been lower than actual capital equipment of Danish industry. Naturally, irreversibility of investment prevents firms from disinvesting; however, realized investment was in fact growing relatively fast in this period in comparison to the optimal investment scheme.

In retrospect, the steady labour saving investment development is surprising; at face value, the relative factor prices do not motivate this increase of the capital-labour ratio. If exogenous forces to the model have brought about this result is an open question.

Secondly, the development of actual and optimal labour inputs is significant;

DANISH INDUSTRY 1964-1979

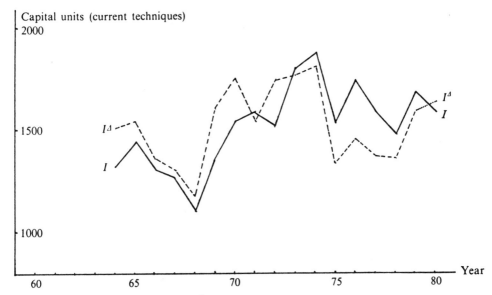

Figure 4. Actual (I) and optimal (I^A) investment.

apparently, the general overestimation of labour productivity, characteristic to primarily the beginning of the period, has been reduced drastically during the period 1964-1979.

While the general level of overemployment of labour was in the neighbourhood of 25 per cent at the beginning of the period, the same number has been reduced to about 10 per cent in the later part of the period.[8] Stated differently, if overemployment had been at the same level in 1979 as it were in 1964, industry in 1979 would have employed 15 per cent more persons, i.e. approximately 15,000 blue collar or 45,000 persons including white collar workers.

Even though the long-term rate of interest has increased drastically during the period 1964-1979, the ratio between user costs and wage costs has been steadily falling, leading to an optimal K/L-ratio that is increasing over time, cfr. figure 5. A solid piece of evidence in favour of the neoclassical investment theory is reflected in the relatively precise tracking ability of the optimal K/L-ratio to the actual ratio; the hoarding of labour is reflected in the lower *level* of $\hat{K}/L$ in comparison to K^A/L^A.

---

8. The same phenomenon, denoted the shake-out has been observed in the *UK* also, cfr. e.g. J. Taylor & D. Gujarati, *The Behaviour of Unemployment and Unfilled Vacancies: An Interchange. The Economic Journal* 1972, pp. 1352 ff.

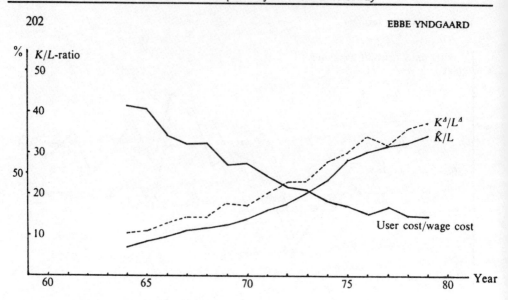

Figure 5. Actual ($\hat{K}/L$) and optimal (K^d/L^d) capital-labour ratio. User cost/wage costs.

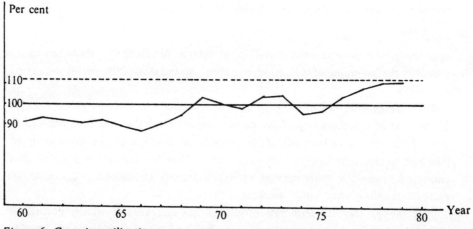

Figure 6. Capacity utilization.

The same characteristic is presented in figure 7, where the ratio between the optimal and actual labour inputs is seen gradually to approach one hundred per cent.

With the calibrated parameters at our disposal we are able to point at further interesting implications.

Even though the annual average increase of the long-term interest rate has been 5 per cent and the price of machinery has risen by approximately 7.5 per cent per year,

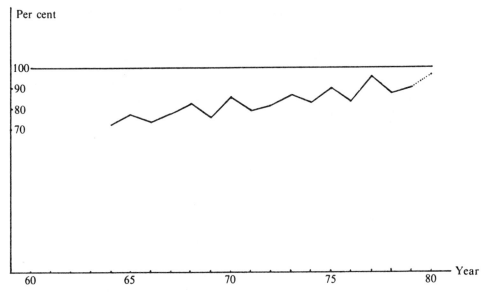

Figure 7. Optimal/actual input of labour.

the technical progress rate θ of about 6 per cent has led to an annual increase of user costs per efficiency unit of about only 6 per cent, i.e. about half the annual increase in wage rates. On that background the substitution of labour by capital was to be expected, cfr. figure 5.

We are also able to give an impression of the magnitude of the reactions to relative changes of user costs and wage rates.

In table 4 we present the partial elasticities between investment and labour inputs to the rates of interest and wages.

Table 4. *Elasticities between investment (I^A) and optimal labour input (L^A) to rate of interest (r) and wage rates (w). Level: 1979.*

	Investment	Labour input
User cost	$\dfrac{\dot{I}^A}{I^A} \bigg/ \dfrac{\dot{r}}{r}$: -1.37	$\dfrac{\dot{L}^A}{L^A} \bigg/ \dfrac{\dot{r}}{r}$: 0.454
Wage rate	$\dfrac{\dot{I}^A}{I^A} \bigg/ \dfrac{\dot{w}}{w}$: 1.63	$\dfrac{\dot{L}^A}{L^A} \bigg/ \dfrac{\dot{w}}{w}$: -0.401

The level of employment in Danish industry in 1979 was 275,000 blue collar and 103,000 white collar workers, i.e. approx. 380,000 persons in all. Thus one percent represents about 3800 persons, so that an increase of the rate of interest[9] by 1 per cent would lead to an increase of industrial employment by about 10,000 persons; conversely achievement of the same increase of imployment by wage reductions would require a wage cut of about 6 per cent. Strictly speaking these calculations could only be performed for blue collar workers, unless there exists a fixed ratio between blue and white collar worker inputs.

Also our calculations rely on the assumption that production could be sold at a positive profit. If the plausibility of this assumption is dubious – as is the case presently – sales can only be increased by a lowering of costs; so to increase employment significantly, the rate of interest should not be decreased; instead a substantial reduction of wage rates should take place to bring about a general increase of employment. As the model is constructed the total wage *share* will not change, but its distribution on wage earners will differ; employed persons may demonstrate their solidarity with formerly unemployed persons, by sharing the total and via increased production greater wage bill with them, via firms and not via public transfer payments.

---

9. If the level of the rate of interest is 20, one percent corresponds to a reaction of approximately 5* .454.

Appendix

Data
Indices for production, wage rates per hour etc. 1960-1980

	$X_t(^a)$	$L_t(^b)$	$r_t(^c)$	$w_t(^d)$	$p_{Qt}(^e)$	$p_t(^f)$	$I_t(^g)$
1960	67.00	636.90	102.00	549.00	80.00	100.00	887.50
1961	71.00	630.90	119.00	616.00	82.00	105.00	1017.07
1962	76.00	648.80	115.00	679.00	85.00	111.00	1197.65
1963	77.00	632.40	102.00	733.00	86.00	113.00	1093.02
1964	86.00	647.80	122.00	796.00	87.00	116.00	1319.54
1965	90.00	654.40	141.00	890.00	90.00	122.00	1434.44
1966	91.00	629.30	148.00	1010.00	93.00	128.00	1309.68
1967	94.00	588.40	158.00	1120.00	96.00	132.00	1269.79
1968	100.00	570.50	143.00	1240.00	100.00	136.00	1109.00
1969	116.00	589.10	173.00	1393.00	104.00	136.00	1365.38
1970	117.00	578.50	186.00	1567.00	112.00	144.00	1541.07
1971	119.00	554.10	174.00	1795.00	119.00	152.00	1587.39
1972	130.00	548.50	171.00	2018.00	130.00	158.00	1517.69
1973	138.00	540.20	204.00	2394.00	137.00	173.00	1799.27
1974	133.00	526.50	230.00	2913.00	158.00	193.00	1877.22
1975	128.00	455.10	200.00	3470.00	179.00	220.00	1535.20
1976	145.00	464.00	219.00	3911.00	191.00	227.00	1734.55
1977	153.00	456.60	243.00	4313.00	208.00	241.00	1591.35
1978	157.00	448.00	260.00	4755.00	225.00	254.00	1475.56
1979	163.00	453.70	267.00	5296.00	241.00	274.00	1685.06
1980	163.00	444.00	275.00	5872.00	265.00	296.00	1586.04

Notes: (^{a}) Value added in industry, fixed prices; index 1968 = 100. (^{b}) No. of hours used in industry. (^{c}) Index for the long-term interest rate. (^{d}) Total wage rate per hour in industry. (^{e}) Prices of factors of production, machines; index 1968 = 100. (^{f}) Implicit GDP-deflator for industry. (^{g}) Investments in machines, etc.; fixed prices, constructed by current price value, deflated by p_{Qt}.
Source: Statistisk Tiårsoversigt, various years.

Expected values of production volume (X), long-term interest rate (index) (r), wage rate per hour (w), price of machinery (p_Q)

Year	X	X*	Deviation per cent	r	$\hat{r}$	Deviation per cent	w	$\hat{w}$	Deviation per cent	p_Q	$\hat{p}_Q$	Deviation per cent
1964	86.00	83.38	3.14	122.00	124.03	−1.64	796.00	817.37	−2.61	87.00	89.68	−2.99
1965	90.00	93.56	−3.81	141.00	138.92	1.50	890.00	899.33	−1.04	90.00	90.85	−.94
1966	91.00	93.45	−2.62	148.00	137.89	7.33	1010.00	1028.03	−1.75	93.00	94.57	−1.66
1967	94.00	97.71	−3.79	158.00	150.19	5.20	1120.00	1164.78	−3.84	96.00	97.81	−1.85
1968	100.00	102.15	−2.11	143.00	167.34	−14.55	1240.00	1252.80	−1.02	100.00	101.11	−1.10
1969	116.00	106.51	8.91	173.00	158.69	9.02	1393.00	1396.34	−.24	104.00	105.73	−1.63
1970	117.00	119.24	−1.88	186.00	190.07	−2.14	1567.00	1588.63	−1.36	112.00	110.10	1.73
1971	119.00	116.25	2.37	174.00	180.76	−3.74	1795.00	1775.08	1.12	119.00	119.74	−.62
1972	130.00	126.82	2.51	171.00	188.16	−9.12	2018.00	2063.43	−2.20	130.00	127.10	2.28
1973	138.00	135.93	1.52	204.00	197.92	3.07	2394.00	2258.60	5.99	137.00	140.08	−2.20
1974	133.00	138.91	−4.26	230.00	213.73	7.61	2913.00	2831.80	2.87	158.00	146.82	7.61
1975	128.00	137.35	−6.81	200.00	220.26	−9.20	3470.00	3446.81	.68	179.00	173.01	3.46
1976	145.00	140.01	3.57	219.00	213.50	2.58	3911.00	3987.13	−1.91	191.00	195.63	−2.37
1977	153.00	153.99	−.65	243.00	251.93	−3.54	4313.00	4293.52	.45	208.00	206.99	.49
1978	157.00	150.15	4.56	260.00	243.64	6.71	4755.00	4741.78	.28	225.00	227.09	−.92
1979	163.00	159.80	2.00	267.00	260.75	2.40	5296.00	5275.44	.39	241.00	245.63	−1.89
1980	163.00	167.78	−2.85	275.00	276.21	−.44	5872.00	5932.24	−1.02	265.00	263.05	.74
$\hat{a}_1$	10.8228				9.8603			24.8255			−5.1719	
$\hat{a}_2$	.8589				.6881			2.1968			1.3090	
$\hat{a}_3$	−.4593				−.2856			−1.7687			.2438	
$\hat{a}_4$	.5821				.6457			.6133			.0366	

[18]
The Decline of Social Democracy*

*Karl Ove Moene
and Michael Wallerstein*

Introduction

Social democracy today faces a troubled future. Electoral support is falling, the system of collective bargaining is in disarray, pressure is mounting to reduce welfare expenditures, income inequality is rising again and, most strikingly, the major social democratic parties are rapidly abandoning social democracy and embracing market liberalism. During the height of social democratic influence in the late 1960s and early 1970s, much of the debate over social democracy centered on the prospects for advancing toward socialism.[1] It is indicative of the current troubles of social democracy that the contemporary debate concerns the durability of social democracy's past achievements. Instead of profiting from the political collapse of communism, their traditional competitor on the left, social democrats today fear their own collapse will follow.

The essence of the political strategy of social democracy centered on the cumulative nature of political mobilization and legislative reforms (Esping-Andersen 1985: 3–38; Przeworski 1985: 239–48). The more workers were organized in unions and mobilized as voters, the less employers and governments would be able to resist workers' demands. Each victory in parliament or at the bargaining table, in turn, increased workers' strength and laid the groundwork for the next advance. No reform was revolutionary in itself, but the cumulative impact of incremental increases in workers' power would transform society in the long run. Moreover, the flexibility of capitalism seemed to allow social democrats to finesse the one major demand that defied compromise with non-socialist parties: the elimination of private concentrations of wealth. Never having sufficient political power to challenge private ownership of capital, social democrats sought instead to construct a system of incentives that would lead private businesses to allocate their capital in socially desirable ways without altering formal property rights. The Swedish social democrats adopted the term 'functional socialism' to denote the programme of 'divesting' capitalists of the functions of ownership without challenging ownership per se (Adler-Karlsson 1967).

Skeptics have doubted the long-term feasibility of the social democratic strategy from the beginning. In 1899 Rosa Luxemburg described trade unions and, by extension reformists in the party, as engaged in 'a sort of a labour of Sisyphus' (1970: 43) in which partial victories would be continually eroded by market forces. Contemporary conservative critics make the reverse argument that market forces have been steadily eroded by social democratic achievements with deleterious consequences for economic performance. For example, a recent review of the Swedish model by Erik Lundberg (1985) begins with the assertion that four decades of social democratic governments have produced a 'cumulative rise in state intervention and in selective regulation of the economy, implying distortions of markets and of the price system...[and a] weakening of incentives to work, invest and save, as well as to start new enterprises'.

Does social democracy represent a potentially stable organization of advanced industrial societies, or a precarious compromise that is impossible to sustain over the long run? Our purpose in this paper is to provide what answers we can based upon an assessment of the difficulties that have emerged in the social democratic strongholds of Norway and Sweden.[2]

Social democracy can be characterized in many ways. In political terms, social democracy represents the building of workers' power through strong unions. The unions represent workers directly vis-a-vis employers and exert a strong influence over the party. The party, in turn, is (or used to be) the dominant actor in parliament. Institutionally, social democracy is distinguished by a large welfare state, encompassing and centralizing trade unions and a system of routinized consultation and cooperation between government, union and employer representatives that has been given the label of 'corporatism'. In terms of policy, social democracy in Northern Europe is characterized by a commitment to wage levelling through solidaristic bargaining, the provision of basic goods and services to all as a right of citizenship, and full employment as the primary objective of macroeconomic policy. In the discussion that follows, we primarily address the viability of social democracy as a social and economic system rather than as a political movement, even though some of the most visible signs of distress are political. But before we consider the long-term feasibility of social democracy, we briefly review both its past achievements and its current difficulties.

Past Achievements

A discussion of the current state of disarray of social democracy in Norway and Sweden must begin with its past success. Superficially, at least, there is little reason to say there was anything wrong with social democracy. By most comparative measures, social democratic governments in the two countries have done remarkably well in obtaining their objectives while maintaining conditions conducive to continual private investment and economic growth.

The primary goals of social democracy in Northern Europe have been to reduce the insecurity and inequality of income for wage-earners in a capitalist society. Insecurity has been reduced, above all, by the gamut of programmes that constitute the welfare state, most notably public pensions and health care. Sweden is well known as having one of the largest welfare states in the world, as measured by government expenditures as a share of GDP: 61.3 per cent in 1988 (OECD 1989: 20). The 54 per cent of GDP that is spent by all levels of government in Norway is low only in comparison to Sweden, Denmark and the Netherlands (OECD 1991a: 159) A significant share of the housing stock was built by municipal governments in Sweden and by state-subsidized cooperatives in Norway. A public day care system provides care for almost all children in Sweden; around half in Norway. Elderly are guaranteed a basic pension that is independent of their lifetime earnings or contributions to the pension system. Good health care is available to all. Adam Przeworski and Jeong-Hwa Lee (1990) estimate that a Swede with no participation in the labour force received the equivalent of $3,360 (1980 US dollars) from the government in 1981. A Norwegian in the same position received $2,930. In contrast, an American received $1,971 while a Japanese received only $1,164.

Insecurity was also reduced by a strong commitment to the maintenance of full employment. The most innovative policy was the active labour market policy, pioneered by the Swedes in the 1950s and copied by the Norwegians in the 1970s. The active labour market policy consists of a variety of measures designed to improve labour mobility: information to workers about vacancies and to employers about applicants, subsidies for relocation and, above all, vocational retraining. In the 1980s, Sweden was spending close to two per cent of GDP on active labour market policies, much more than any other country. But since Sweden was spending less on unemployment benefits, total expenditures on labour market policies were close to the European average (Layard, Nickell and Jackman 1991).

The active labour market policy kept open unemployment down by sending the unemployed back to school for vocational training.[3] The other part of the social democratic employment strategy was the use of macroeconomic policies to maintain full employment. The emphasis on employment reflected the trade union base of the social democratic movement. Full employment was valued because it increased both workers' security and workers' influence. The way to maximize workers' power inside the factory, the thinking went, was to maintain conditions where workers could always quit and obtain another job across the street if they were dissatisfied. In a comparative context, the Swedish and Norwegian commitment to full employment was extraordinary. Norway and Sweden kept unemployment below 2.5 per cent throughout the period when unemployment rates were rising above 10 per cent in much of Europe. Of the advanced industrial societies, the only other countries with as small an increase in unemployment during the decade following the first oil price shock of 1973/74 were Austria, Switzerland and Japan (Bean, Layard and Nickell 1986).

Inequality of income has been reduced through both fiscal policies and solidaristic wage bargaining (Strøm, Stølen and Torp 1988, Hibbs and Locking 1991, Bojer 1992). Fiscal policy has reduced income inequality largely through expenditures in universalistic programmes, rather than through progressive taxation or means tested programmes. Nevertheless, the impact has been substantial.[4] In addition, the union commitment to the reduction of wage inequalities through collective bargaining has had a strong impact on pre-tax wage dispersion, particularly in the public sector. According to Richard Freeman (1988), Sweden had the most egalitarian wage structure of any advanced industrial society. Norway and Denmark were tied for second place.

Finally, it should be observed that economic performance along other dimensions was not notably worse than elsewhere in Europe until the 1980s. Economic growth in Sweden has been lower than the European average through much of the postwar period, but Sweden began the period with a relatively high level of GDP per capita. Economic growth in the richer US was even slower. Norway has grown exceptionally rapidly, surpassing the US and all other advanced industrial societies in GDP per capita by 1985 (Summers and Heston 1988). In the early 1980s, much of the growth of income in Norway was due to rising revenues from exports of North Sea oil. Yet Norway grew rapidly prior to the discovery of oil. Moreover, Norway managed to escape the rise in unemployment (the Dutch disease) that accompanied the oil boom in the Netherlands and Great Britain.

Current Difficulties

It is easy to praise Scandinavian social democracy. If social democracy is so successful, one might retort, why is it in such disarray? Electoral support for the social democratic parties has fallen in both Norway and Sweden from its postwar peak. The Norwegian Labour Party received 46 per cent of the vote in 1969, but only 34 per cent in 1989. In 1968 the Swedish Social Democrats obtained 50 per cent of the vote. In 1991, votes for the Swedish Social Democratic Party fell below 38 per cent. The decline of votes for the Norwegian Labour Party has been partially, albeit not entirely, offset by growing votes for the greenish Left Socialist Party. In Sweden the decline in votes for the Social Democratic Party was amplified in 1991 by similar losses for the other, smaller parties on the left. In both countries, the biggest gainers have been the most rightwing of the bourgeois parties. Moreover, the youngest voters are the most likely to vote for the right.

As social democracy has declined at the polls, the social democratic model of industrial relations characterized by highly centralized bargaining and a general absence of industrial conflict has completely disappeared in Sweden. The mortal blow to the Swedish centralized bargaining system appears to have been the withdrawal of the metal workers from the central negotiations in 1983. In the second half of the 1980s, centralized bargaining was resurrected, but without any obligation to refrain from industrial conflict in supplementary bargaining at the industry and local level. In 1990, the national association of Swedish employers (SAF) eliminated the possibility of centralized bargaining by disbanding its bargaining unit (Myrdal 1991).

In Norway centralized bargaining continues, albeit tentatively. Throughout the 1980s, locally bargained wage increases constituted a rising share of aggregate wage growth (Rødseth and Holden 1990). In 1988 and 1989, wages were frozen by an act of parliament. The first 1990 central agreement was rejected by the union membership in a ratification vote forcing the union leadership back to the bargaining table to renegotiate a new contract. By 1991, leaders of the Norwegian employers' association (NHO) were discussing withdrawing from all government committees concerned with centralized wage negotiations (Nordby 1991). The sharpest evidence of the decline of social democracy is to be found in the current policies of the social democratic parties. Tax reform modelled after the Reagan tax reform in Sweden,[5] deregulation of the housing market in Norway, deregulation of financial markets in both countries, all testify to the increased support for free market policies in social democratic cabinets. The most dramatic deviations from past practices, however, are in macroeconomic policy and the question of entry into the European Community.

The commitment to full employment has gone. In 1988 unemployment in Norway jumped sharply to around 4.5 per cent. Three years later, the Norwegian unemployment rate had risen to 5.6 per cent (Central Bureau of Statistics 1991). Rather than stimulate demand in response, the Labour government has tied the Norwegian kroner to the ecu. In 1990, the Swedish Social Democratic government declared for the first time since coming to power in 1932 that price stability would henceforth be given priority over full employment *(Economist,* Nov. 17, 1990: 95). Between 1990 and 1991, Swedish unemployment doubled from 1.5 per cent to 3.0 per cent. Current forecasts are for unemployment in Sweden to continue to climb as high as 4.5–5.5 per cent (Central Bureau of Statistics 1991).[6] Such levels of unemployment may seem mild compared to most countries, but they are exceptionally high for countries whose unemployment rate scarcely exceeded two per cent for four decades. Politically, it is devastating. The promise of full employment was one of the pillars of social democratic electoral support. For the first time since the Norwegian Labour Party came to power in 1935, public opinion polls reveal that voters no longer think the Labour Party can do a better job than the bourgeois parties in fighting unemployment.

The second dramatic policy reversal concerns membership in the European Community. On July 1, 1991 the Swedish Social Democratic government submitted an application to join the EC. The Norwegian Labour Party is proceeding with caution, having fought and lost a bitter election over joining the EC in 1972. Most of the party leaders, however, are in favour of applying for membership. The costs and benefits of membership for different groups within Norway and Sweden are too complex and controversial to review here. Suffice to say that membership is likely to force a reduction of some of the most important taxes in terms of revenue collection, notably the value-added tax. Membership may also accelerate the recent trend toward greater income inequality. It is sometimes said that one of the competitive advantages of both Norway and Sweden is the relatively low price of highly skilled technical and scientific labour. With open labour markets and much higher wages abroad, can the wages of multi-lingual engineers be kept from rising?

As Przeworski (1985: 239-43) observed, social democratic achievements are not irreversible. Past gains can be lost as a consequence of reversals at the ballot box, or declines in union strength. Of course, a society does not change radically just because the bourgeois parties manage to form the government or the social democratic parties adopt liberal economic policies. The decline of social democracy is likely to be gradual but cumulative in a way that mirrors its step-by-step rise. What went wrong?

The Long-Run Viability of Social Democracy

We divide our discussion into problems with welfare policy, wage determination and unemployment, centralized bargaining, capital controls and productivity growth.

Welfare Policy

The welfare state may prove to be the most durable social democratic achievement. Welfare policies remain politically popular. Moreover, welfare programmes seem to have proven to be effective instruments for achieving the twin social democratic objectives of greater security and less inequality of income. That welfare policies have effectively reduced poverty and increased security for all citizens is uncontroversial. (The contrast with the US in this regard is bracing.) That welfare policies have also increased the equality of income is less so. It is certainly true that the benefits citizens receive bear little relation to the taxes they contribute. Many have argued, however, that the direct redistributive impact of taxes and welfare expenditures is offset by a more inegalitarian pre-tax distribution of income. Yet, in a system where most wages are set through collective bargaining, the likely net effect of redistributive policies is to increase the equality of income because of the way that welfare programmes improve the bargaining position of the lowest paid groups.

To see this, consider a model of social democracy as an n-person bargaining game. Leif Johansen (1979) argued that social democracy is best understood as a 'bargaining society' where the allocation of income is determined through centralized negotiations among the major social groups. Thus, the bargaining framework is a natural one to use. Let the gains from bargaining be represented by a standard superadditive characteristic function with transferable utility, where $v(S)$ represents the total that could be obtained by coalition S without a central agreement and $v(N)$ represents the total payoff obtainable by the grand coalition of all groups. To keep things simple, we assume the core exists.

We model welfare programmes as providing income and services received independently of employment, such as national health care, family allowances, subsidized housing, and so on. We ignore those welfare benefits that are received in place of employment. We also ignore the impact of taxes and transfers on aggregate production in order to focus on redistribution. The payoffs (after tax) for each individual are denoted x_i. Let x^* be the social wage that is guaranteed for all, t be the uniform tax rate on market income and s be the number of members of S. Then the core of the game with taxes and the social wage would be defined to be an allocation of payoffs to individuals $x_1, x_2, \ldots, x_n$ that satisfies

$$\sum_{i \in N} (x_i + x^*) = v(N), \text{ and}$$

$$\sum_{i \in S} (x_i + x^*) \geq (1-t)v(S) + sx^* \equiv Q(S) \text{ for all } S \subset N.$$

The tax rate needed to finance transfer payments of nx^* depends on the particular coalitions that form. Since the game is superadditive, a division of the grand coalition into a large number of small coalitions may imply lower aggregate income and a higher necessary tax rate. We will assume that all possible coalitions S act on the basis of optimistic expectations in the sense that each believes that members of N not in S, written N/S will stick together. (Other assumptions regarding conjectures would serve equally well.) Then the average tax rate is $t = nx^*/[v(S) + v(N\backslash S)]$. Inserting this expression for t in the definition of $Q(S)$ and rearranging terms, we have

$$Q(S) = v(S) + \frac{s(n-s)}{v(N\backslash S) + v(S)} \left[\frac{v(N\backslash S)}{n-s} - \frac{v(S)}{s} \right] x^*.$$

Thus the minimal payoff a coalition must obtain is an increasing function of x^* for any group that can guarantee itself less per capita in the market $v(S)/s$ than the per capita income of their complement $v(N\backslash S)/(n-s)$. Conversely, the constraint is reduced as x^* rises for a group with $v(S)/s > v(N\backslash S)/(n-s)$. By improving the outside option for low income groups, a uniform tax on income together with welfare benefits distributed equally to all pushes the final allocation in a more egalitarian direction.[7]

Yet all is not well with the welfare state. The cost of maintaining existing levels of benefits is growing faster than the economy. One reason is simply demographic and shared by all advanced industrial societies: the growing share of pensioners in the population. But it is not only the elderly who have placed increasing demands on the welfare system. In Scandinavia, like in the US, the number of single-parent families has increased sharply. The surge in women's participation in the labour force has led to a new and expensive demand for public provision of child care. Moreover, productivity gains are hard to obtain in the public sector and solidaristic bargaining has raised wages in the relatively low-paid public sector more rapidly than elsewhere in the economy.

At the same time, it is no longer feasible to raise taxes significantly. Taxes as a share of GDP in the Nordic countries seemed to have reached their political, if not their economic, ceiling during the early 1980s. In fact, Swedish taxes have been reduced substantially in the past decade. Therefore, the rising cost of maintaining existing benefits has meant increasingly visible declines in quality and lower government investment. In terms of the model, the situation has changed from a world where x^* was chosen and t was adjusted accordingly, to a world where t is given and x^* adjusts. As x^* falls, the final distribution of income becomes less egalitarian. Moreover, as the quality of public services decline, people with sufficient wealth demand access to private alternatives. There is much discussion of whether or not private hospitals or private schools should be permitted. The danger, as Hirschman (1970) argued, is that once people exit the public system, they will no longer fight for better public services, nor vote in support of high taxes.

The increasing cost of welfare benefits and the declining quality of public services raises anew the question of universalistic versus means-tested programmes. In sharp contrast to welfare policy in the US, social democrats have traditionally chosen universalistic benefits, i.e. benefits that go to all by virtue of citizenship, rather than benefits that go only to those in need. Universalistic programmes have good features from both economic and political perspectives. From the economic viewpoint, universalistic programmes avoid the bad incentive effects of policies which subsidize certain choices and punish others. The only way to protect children without discouraging two-parent households, for example, is to give child support to all parents regardless of marital status. From a political viewpoint, universalistic programmes obtain levels of popular support that far exceed the support for programmes whose benefits go only to relatively small groups. Consider the difference in political support for social security in the US, as compared to support for means-tested welfare programmes. Universalistic programmes are expensive, however. As the pressure to limit costs increases, so does the pressure to limit benefits to those in greatest need. But as welfare programmes come to consist of benefits targeted for particular groups, public support declines.

A different type of problem with the welfare system stems from dissatisfaction with the way in which benefits are distributed. Welfare benefits have to be rationed, since demand exceeds supply. Some benefits, such as pensions, are distributed on the basis of clearly defined rules. Others, like non-emergency medical procedures, are distributed with a large component of administrative discretion. Discretion is inevitable when an attempt is made to give priority to those in greatest need, since rules for every contingency are impossible to write. Discretion, however, easily appears to be arbitrary. Prospective hospital patients can jump to the head of the queue by finding a doctor willing to help. Parents can get their children put first in line for day care by convincing a municipal employee that their need is particularly acute. As it becomes common knowledge that the welfare system is capable of being manipulated, everyone feels that they must seek to manipulate the system as well to receive as much as the others.

Increased dissatisfaction with the cost and quality of welfare services has led to demands for reforms that introduce greater competition in the public sector. However, changes in the system of welfare provision that threaten to reduce the wages of welfare providers, increase their workload or remove their job security are fought by the public sector unions. Thus the bourgeois parties have an easier time championing welfare reform than the social democratic parties with their trade union base.

Nevertheless, the welfare state remains an achievement social democrats are justly proud of. While there is much controversy over the way in which welfare services are provided and whether welfare benefits ought to be maintained at their current levels, the core programmes of the welfare state remain popular. Indeed, the threat that the political programmes of the non-socialist parties pose to the funding of welfare services has become the most effective campaign issue for social democratic parties today.

Wage Determination and Unemployment

The central position of the trade unions in the social democratic movement is one of the most distinctive characteristics of Scandinavian social democracy. Many critics have argued that a market economy dominated by powerful unions is bound for trouble. To the extent that unions obtain monopoly rents by curtailing output and raising the price, allocative efficiency is impaired. If unions capture a share of the quasi-rents associated with sunk investments in plant and equipment, firms will invest less (Grout 1984, Moene 1990). If the unions' political influence leads to policies that maintain employment by accommodating union wage demands, the result will be accelerating inflation and possible lower employment (Calmfors and Horn 1985).

Yet the Nordic experience speaks against the view that the stronger the unions, the worse the economy. Precisely because the unions in Norway and Sweden were strong institutions in the sense of being large relative to the work force, highly centralized and closely allied with a party that was often (in the Swedish case always) in government, they accepted much responsibility for national economic performance. National-level bargaining reduces the ability of industrial unions to raise the relative price of output through wage increases (Calmfors and Driffill 1988). Centralized bargaining increases the willingness of unions to restrain wage growth in order to obtain investment, since the benefits of investment are typically received by members of more than one union (Wallerstein 1990). Institutional stability and centralization may increase the unions' time horizon, leading to a greater willingness to make short-term sacrifices for long-term gains (Przeworski and Wallerstein 1982, Rødseth 1986). Solidaristic bargaining encourages the building of new plants while it forces less efficient plants to close (Moene and Wallerstein 1992). Finally, the close alliance between the unions and a party either in government or soon to be in government leads as much to self-discipline on the part of the unions as it does to accommodating policies on the part of the government (Lange and Garrett 1985).

The past success of the social democratic system of wage determination in reconciling strong unions with macroeconomic stability and full employment presents a sharp contrast with the current disarray. The problem can be seen as one of equilibrium between the government and the institutions of collective bargaining. The system of collective bargaining worked as well as it did because it was supported by macroeconomic policies to maintain international competitiveness and full employment. Similarly, government macroeconomic policy depended for its effectiveness on the unions' ability to restrain wages through centralized bargaining.

According to the Aukrust model (sometimes called the Scandinavian model) of wage-driven inflation in an open economy, the long-term rate of wage growth in the traded-goods sector is determined by the rate of productivity growth and the rate of change of the home country price of tradeables (Aukrust 1970, 1977). If there are constant returns to scale and international capital mobility, wage growth higher than the sum of productivity and price growth will cause capital flight and a reduction in employment in the traded-goods sector. If wage growth is lower than the growth of productivity and traded-goods prices, there will be a capital inflow, an increase in employment in the traded-goods sector and, eventually, labour shortages. Thus, the stability of employment in the traded-goods sector demands equality between wage increases and the sum of productivity growth and price changes. Equilibrium in the national labour market implies that wages in the rest of the economy grow at the same rate as wages in the traded-goods sector. In fact, according to Rødseth and Holden (1990), if one looks at aggregate wage growth over a period of, say, ten years, the Aukrust relationship fits the Norwegian data very closely.

In spite of the high level of centralization, the collective bargaining systems in Norway and Sweden did not provide self-regulating mechanisms for keeping wage growth in line with productivity plus foreign price growth under conditions of full employment.[8] While the central negotiators were sensitive to the need to maintain international competitiveness, much of wage growth in both countries occurred in supplementary negotiations at the local level. The union locals were forbidden to strike after the central agreement was signed, but other threats such as go-slow or work-to-rule actions remained available. In fact, the close collaboration between firms and unions at the local level in Scandinavia gives workers significant control over the work process that can easily be used to obtain local increases.

Locally bargained wage increases, or wage drift, is thus an important component of the Scandinavian system of wage determination, accounting for around half of the increase in total wages in the 1950s and 1960s. Steinar Holden (1991) has found that the amount added to wages at the local level is independent of both the wage increase obtained earlier through centralized bargaining central agreement and the rate of unemployment (within the limited range that unemployment varied prior to 1988). As wage increases negotiated at the central level declined in Norway in the 1980s, the share of drift in total wage growth has risen above 80 per cent (Rødseth and Holden 1990). This in itself has led to increasing conflicts between those unions whose members obtain drift and do not mind wage restraint at the central level and those unions whose members receive no drift and want compensation.[9] Studies of wage drift in Sweden by Bertil Holmlund and Per Skedinger (1990) and Douglas Hibbs and Håkan Locking (1991) conclude that drift partially offsets changes in the central agreement. As the centrally negotiated wage increase declines, wage drift increases. Since the LO cannot accept a negative wage increase in the national agreement, local bargaining sets a floor on nominal wage increases.

The preservation of international competitiveness, therefore, depends on sufficiently rapid productivity and foreign price growth to cover the wage drift plus some room for a centrally negotiated increase. When those external conditions failed, the maintenance of international balance required government intervention. The two most important instruments have been income policies (in Norway) and devaluations (in both). Reducing wage growth by government decree is politically acceptable in Norway only when used infrequently. Setting wages in parliament has never been accepted in Sweden. The attempt by the Swedish Social Democrats to impose wage controls in the winter of 1990 resulted in a parliamentary defeat and the resignation of the government. In addition, social democratic governments in both countries have tied the kroner to the ecu and declared that devaluations will no longer be employed to rescue firms when costs rise faster at home than abroad.

The new exchange rate regime is, in part, a consequence of the deregulation of domestic financial markets and the elimination of border controls on capital movement that have increased the cost of discretionary policies. But, of course, the liberalization of financial markets is not an exogenous event. A deeper reason, perhaps, lies with the weakening (Norway) or collapse (Sweden) of the collective bargaining institutions. Devaluations are effective only as long as wages do not rise as fast as the price of tradeable goods. Underlying the successful use of monetary policy was the ability and willingness of the unions to restrain the centrally negotiated part of wage increases. In addition, since central bargainers generally demand a nominal wage increase which is then followed by additional increases negotiated at the local level, real wage restraint requires a moderate amount of inflation in the absence of sufficient productivity growth (Calmfors 1991). With the abandonment of an independent monetary policy, the entire burden of preserving full employment is placed directly on the unions. In practice, the self-discipline of the unions has been at least partially replaced by the harsher discipline of layoffs.

The Breakdown of Centralized Bargaining

Underneath the abandonment of the traditional social democratic promise of full employment lies the fragmentation of an increasingly heterogeneous union movement. Throughout Scandinavia, the unions have been successful in breaking out of their traditional strongholds and organizing in all industries and occupations. In the old days, (the 1950s and 1960s), the union movement was dominated by the confederation of blue-collar workers with close ties to the social democratic parties (known in both countries as the LO). Moreover, the LO was itself dominated by private sector workers in exporting industries, the metalworkers in particular.

The situation is quite different today. While total union membership has grown (in Sweden) or remained constant (in Norway) as a share of the labour force, the relative size of the LO has shrunk. Only 60–65 per cent of union members in Norway and Sweden belong to the LO, down from 80–90 per cent in the early postwar period (Hernes and

Marøen 1985: 10, Esping-Andersen 1985: 64, Strøm, Stølen and Torp 1988: 91-2). The fastest growing parts of the labour movement are the unions of white-collar and professional workers outside the LO. Moreover, the composition of the LO has changed, with public sector workers growing relative to private sector workers. In both countries, the metalworkers' union had been replaced by the union of municipal employees as the largest union in the country.

As the LO has declined in relative terms, so has the centralized bargaining pattern associated with it. Centralized bargaining, in which wage determination throughout the economy took place within a framework negotiated by the LO and the national employers' confederation, allowed the unions to accomplish two goals. The first was to restrain overall wage increases in line with the requirements of the government's economic policy. The second goal was to reduce wage differentials.

Wage restraint and wage equality are controversial goals for a union to pursue, especially a union like the metalworkers whose core membership consists of highly skilled workers whose wages are being held back on both accounts. It is even harder when unions who represent higher-paid white collar and technical workers and support higher wage differentials start competing successfully for members among the upper echelon of blue collar workers at the expense of the LO (Lash 1985). Yet the LO's ability to negotiate wage contracts that allow greater wage dispersion is constrained by the growing weight within the LO of public sector unions who represent relatively low-paid workers.

Consider again Johansen's (1979) image of social democracy as a 'bargaining society', represented by a characteristic function with transferable utility, this time without a social wage. In a subsequent article, Johansen (1982) argued that the concept of the core required excessively acquiesent behaviour. As before, let N be the grand coalition, S any subset of N and $(N\setminus S)$ the members of N not in S. An imputation (an allocation of $v(N)$) is in the core as long as no subset of actors can do better by withdrawing. More typically, Johansen argued, actors demand what they could obtain outside the grand coalition plus a share of the surplus that they create by joining. Thus, what we will call the Johansen core is defined to be an allocation of payoffs to individuals $x_1, x_2, \ldots, x_n$ that satisfies

$$\sum_{i \in N} x_i = v(N), \text{ and} \qquad (1)$$

$$\sum_{i \in S} x_i \geq v(S) + \lambda_S [v(N) - v(S) - v(N\setminus S)] \text{ for all } S \subset N \qquad (2)$$

According to the second equation, each group S demands what it could get outside the grand coalition, $v(S)$, plus the fraction λ_s of the surplus it brings to the coalition by joining, $[v(N) - v(S) - v(N\setminus S)]$. Note that the ordinary core is defined by equations (1) and (2) with $\lambda_s = 0$. It is clear that as the aggressiveness of the actors increases, that is as λ_s rises, the Johansen core may be reduced. Indeed, the Johansen core cannot possibly exist unless $\lambda_s + \lambda_{N\setminus S} \leq 1$. Otherwise the demands for a share of the surplus are incompatible.

How should the weights λ_s be determined? One possibility is to consider the λ_s's as being the product of bargaining between the coalition S and its complement $(N\setminus S)$ over sharing the surplus. That is, coalition S threatens to leave the bargaining table and bargains with the remaining players over how to share the surplus should it remain. In this case, we would have $\lambda_s + \lambda_{N\setminus S} = 1$. But under these conditions, the Johansen core is almost always empty. Equations (1) and (2) imply

$$\sum_{i \in N\setminus S} x_i \leq v(N\setminus S) + (1 - \lambda_s)[v(N) - v(S) - v(N\setminus S)]. \tag{3}$$

But if $(1 - \lambda_s) = \lambda_{N\setminus S}$, then equations (2) and (3) imply that the inequality signs must be replaced by strict equality:

$$\sum_{i \in S} x_i = v(S) + \lambda_s [v(N) - v(S) - v(N\setminus S)] \text{ for all } S \subset N. \tag{4}$$

Equations (1) and (4) constitute a set of $2^n - 1$ equations to determine n variables $x_1, x_2, \ldots, x_n$. A solution will not exist except in very special circumstances. In general, it is impossible to obtain a centralized agreement that is 'renegotiation proof'. All possible allocations leave some group worse off than they could be if they withdrew from the grand coalition and bargained over the terms of rejoining.

Such a multilateral bargaining model has become more applicable to Norway and Sweden as the number of actors on the union side has increased and as relations among the unions have grown increasingly competitive. In earlier periods, wage bargaining was dominated by the LO and the national employers' confederation. Conflicts of interest among unions were tempered by a common political allegiance to the social democratic party. As new union growth has occurred outside the LO, and as the LO itself has become increasingly divided between private and public sector workers, these conditions no longer hold. The new unions are not political allies with the LO. They are often strenuously opposed to the LO's egalitarian goals and they compete with the LO for members. The unions have always argued with each other. Increasingly, however, they seem to bargain with each other in the same spirit as they bargain with employers. Under such conditions, no allocation is stable.

In sum, the union movement has become more heterogeneous and internally divided as union membership has grown at both tails of the wage distribution. In Sweden, centralized bargaining collapsed when the union and the employers' association in the metalworking industry withdrew from the centralized negotiations. Norwegian employers are internally divided over whether they should follow the Swedish example. The labour peace that Scandinavia has been known for since the 1930s has vanished. The number of industrial disputes has increased sharply as unions fight with each other as much as with management over their relative wage share. As centralized bargaining has declined, wage dispersion has increased, and the capacity of the unions to restrain wages in conditions of full employment has dwindled (Hibbs and Locking 1991).

Control Over Investment

Lack of control over investment is often seen as the Achilles heel of social democracy. Strong unions may be able to set wages, hiring and firing may be regulated by both the government and union contracts, but as long as capital formation depends on private investment, the argument goes, the ability of social democrats to create a more equal and more secure society is sharply restricted.

In fact, social democratic governments in both Sweden and Norway have employed an extensive array of policies to influence the quantity, timing, and sectoral allocation of private investment. During most of the postwar period, interest rates in Norway were kept below the market-clearing level and credit was rationed. There were special quotas as well as different interest rates for investment in housing, agriculture, fishing and in factories located outside the major cities. The Swedish approach relied more on the tax system. Swedish firms could escape all taxes on as much as 40 per cent of pre-tax profits by depositing the funds in special closed accounts. Money in the funds could then be withdrawn only upon approval of the government (Esping-Andersen 1985: 233). In Norway too, tax incentives for investment have been generous up till now.

In some respects, social democratic investment policies worked well. Aggregate capital formation was high, in spite of the extensive redistribution of income. In addition, government controls worked well in terms of counter-cyclical policy. The Swedish governments timed the release of funds to avoid overheating during upturns and to increase aggregate demand during recessions. In Norway, the counter-cyclical policy worked automatically. With credit rationing, fluctuations in demand resulted in changes in the length of the queue rather than changes in the quantity of investment.

Credit controls have worked less well in terms of the efficiency of investment however. Norway is distinctive in Western Europe for both the large share of investment in GDP and the low productivity of that investment. According to OECD figures, Norway ranked 19th of 19 advanced capitalist economies in terms of the growth of the productivity of capital in the business sector from 1960 to 1989 (OECD 1991a: 120). In part, this is a reflection of the high rate of capital formation since the higher the capital-labour ratio, the lower the productivity of capital. If Norway had experienced an exceptionally rapid growth of labour productivity (which goes up as the capital-output ratio rises), one might attribute all of the low growth of capital productivity to capital deepening. However, the growth of labour productivity in Norway was close to the OECD average from 1960–1973, and below average since 1973. Thus, it is likely that the low productivity growth of capital in Norway reflects the extensive use of capital controls. In Sweden, policies to influence the allocation of private investment were far less ambitious, and the growth of the productivity of capital in Sweden was closer to the OECD average.

The relatively low productivity of investment in Norway was a natural result of the government's use of investment controls to subsidize house construction and economic activities in rural areas, particularly agriculture and fishing. Governments intervene in credit markets because they have other goals than simply maximizing the efficiency of investment. Thus, the fact that government intervention reduced the aggregate productivity of capital does not indicate a policy failure, provided the political goal achieved was worth the foregone output. Nevertheless, the subsidization of capital inputs is an expensive way to maintain the rural population. To subsidize rural labour directly would be cheaper. Moreover, when credit is rationed, two groups are advantaged. The first are the most creditworthy borrowers. With a fixed price of credit, banks maximize the safety of their loans. The second group that benefits are those with good personal or business connections with the banks' managers. Such a system does not maximize the allocative efficiency of capital.

The most serious problem with discretionary capital controls is the impetus it gives to rent-seeking behaviour. In both Norway and Sweden, the threat of plant closures in the

1970s and 1980s generated demands for subsidies. Since the demands were often satisfied, they also contributed to a decline in the productivity of investment. Discretionary capital controls represent a clear case of concentrated benefits and diffuse costs. A union local will fight hard for a subsidy to keep its plant open. Workers elsewhere in the economy are unlikely to worry much about the marginal difference one bail-out represents. Public control over investment easily degenerates into public subsidies for unproductive plants.

The Decline of Labor Productivity Growth

Perhaps the most important but least understood reason for the multitude of current problems is decline in the growth of the productivity of labour that occurred after the mid-1970s. From 1960 to 1973, output per employed person in the business sector increased by 4.1 per cent per year in both Norway and Sweden (Table 1). In the period 1973–1989, average productivity growth was only 1.6 per cent in Sweden and 0.5 per cent in Norway. In the long run, wage growth is determined by labour productivity growth. Everything else is secondary. Thus, if Przeworski and Lee (1990) are right in their conclusion that if social democratic rule reduces productivity growth, then the long run prospects of social democracy are dim.

Comparisons of productivity growth are complicated, however. Productivity declined everywhere after 1973, not just in Norway and Sweden. Table 1 presents some benchmarks to judge the relative performance of Norway and Sweden. Both Norway and Sweden have had lower labour productivity growth than the other European OECD countries since 1960. Yet Sweden has maintained a rate of productivity growth close to the OECD average both before and after 1973. Even Norway's low productivity growth since 1973 is not worse than productivity growth in the US in the same period.

Table 1: Average annual growth of output per employee in the business sector

	1960–73	1973–89
Norway	4.0	0.5
Sweden	4.1	1.6
OECD Europe	5.0	2.3
OECD	4.1	1.5
United States	2.2	0.5

Source: OECD 1991a, Table 43. The business sector in Norway excludes oil production.

Moreover, there are a number of potentially mitigating factors that are relevant in assessing the relative productivity performance of Norway and Sweden. Output per worker generally increases as unemployment rises, since firms shut down their least productive plants or lay off their least productive workers. Freeman (1988) presents data showing an inverse relationship between the rate of employment growth and the rate of productivity growth among OECD countries after 1973. Thus, at least part of the low productivity growth of Norway and Sweden (as well as the US) since 1973 can be explained by the relatively large increase in employment during the same period. The Nordic countries of Norway, Sweden and Finland were the only countries in Western Europe to maintain positive employment growth in the period 1973–1984 (Freeman 1988: 70).

The second factor that may account for a significant part of the productivity growth differential between Norway and Sweden (and the US) with the rest of Europe since 1973 is that these countries began the period with above average productivity. Countries with lower levels of productivity can grow faster by copying or importing the technology already in use in countries that have higher levels of productivity. Dowrick and Nguyen (1989) present evidence of a stable negative relationship between initial per capita income and total factor productivity growth since 1950, both among the OECD countries and among larger samples. Dowrick and Nguyen estimate that Sweden's initial high level of per capita income reduced income growth in Sweden by 0.7 per cent per year between 1973 and 1985. The amount of 0.7 per cent per year represents the entire gap between the Swedish productivity growth and the average for European OECD members since 1973.

Thus, whether or not social democracies have experienced lower productivity growth remains an open question. Productivity has been unambiguously low in Norway if oil production is excluded. Yet per capita income (including oil revenues) rose faster in Norway between 1973 and 1985 than any other OECD country (Dowrick and Nguyen 1989). Swedish per capita income growth has lagged behind the rest of Europe, but the difference may be explained by such factors as Sweden's initial wealth and full employment policies. Nevertheless, voters do not control initial levels of wealth or the growth of employment when comparing real wage growth at home and abroad. The popularity of social democracy has suffered from stagnant real wages, whether or not social democratic policies are to blame. Nowadays, when employers complain that high taxes, welfare benefits and the egalitarian wage scale have curtailed productivity growth by undermining workers' incentives to work, they get a sympathetic hearing.

Conclusion

Social democracy in Norway and Sweden can be credited with a number of achievements, and some of them may prove to be permanent. The elimination of severe poverty and the granting of health care, housing and a modest but decent income as a right of all citizens stand out as important accomplishments. The contrast between the poor neighbourhoods of any large city in the US with the poorest urban areas of Norway or Sweden is dramatic. The welfare state may be trimmed, but it is unlikely to be cut to American levels. The active labour market policies that were developed in the 1950s in Sweden and adopted in the 1980s in Norway remain popular. The social democrats were perhaps the first to assert that the most important economic resource of a country is the health and training of its work force, and that part of their programme endures. Nevertheless, social democracy is in retreat. Both the egalitarian distribution of income and the security of income that distinguished social democratic societies from other advanced capitalist democracies are declining.

Social democracy flourished for decades. Why is it so fragile today? Most explanations of social democracy's decline focus on exogenous changes common to most advanced industrial societies, such as the decline in blue-collar industrial workers as a share of the electorate (Przeworski and Sprague 1986), the decline of mass production (Pontusson 1991b) or increased international capital mobility (Steinmo 1990). The most direct exogenous change, however, is the creation of a single market within the EC. Both Swedish and Norwegian firms fear that closer internal integration within the EC will lead to higher trade barriers against outsiders. Already accustomed to foreign investment, Swedish firms rushed to protect themselves by buying plants inside the EC. The resulting massive capital flight out of Sweden provides the most compelling explanation for the abrupt decision of the social democratic government to apply for membership. Once Sweden joins, it is difficult for Norway to remain outside. Almost 25 per cent of Norway's trade is with Sweden, and most of the rest is with other European countries (OECD 1991b: 461–2). Membership in the EC, however, requires that Norway and Sweden abandon central elements of their social and economic policy, such as industrial subsidies (Norway), high value-added taxes and discretionary monetary policy.

Yet, the decline of social democracy is not entirely due to external causes. The collapse of the centralized bargaining system in Sweden happened before Sweden applied to join the EC and tied its currency to the ecu. The abandonment of full employment as the overriding macroeconomic policy goal in both Norway and Sweden may be as much a consequence as a cause of the decline of centralized bargaining.

Social democracy is, in part, a victim of its own success. The children of workers who get university educations and professional jobs do not have the same loyalty to the social democratic party, nor the same interest in redistributive policies, as their parents. When the society is wealthier and people have greater material security, they value social insurance programmes less.

Finally, when the unions succeed in organizing workers in all occupations and sectors of the economy, the union movement becomes as divided as the entire society. With unions less able to hold down wages in line with macroeconomic stability, governments of both the right and the left increasingly rely on unemployment to restrain wage growth. The fundamental bargain whereby the unions provided real wage restraint in exchange for government policies to prevent unemployment has broken down. The result is a decline of the institutions and policies that made social democracy distinctive.

Notes

* An earlier version of this paper was presented at the conference on Perspectives on Market Socialism held at the University of California, Berkeley, May 16–19, 1991. We thank Lloyd Ulman, Steinar Strøm, Atle Seierstad, Adam Przeworski, Bjørn-Erik Rasch and Hege Torp for helpful comments.
1. See, for example, John Stephens (1980), Walter Korpi (1978,1983) or Gøsta Esping-Andersen (1985).
2. Other recent studies of social democratic decline include Hernes (forthcoming), Fagerberg, Cappelen, Mjøset and Skarstein (1990), Pontusson (1991a) and Swenson (1991). Moreover, Sandmo (1991) provides an overview of the changing attitudes of economists towards the welfare state with an emphasis on experiences from the Scandinavian countries.
3. Some studies have questioned the extent to which active labour market policies affect unemployment. It is argued that the direct effect of reducing unemployment is offset by an indirect

effect of encouraging higher wage demands. See Calmfors (1991) for a review of the literature.
4. Data collected around 1970 indicate that taxes and transfer payments reduced the Gini coefficient by 36 per cent in Sweden and 23 per cent in Norway (Hicks and Swank 1984). In contrast, fiscal policy reduced the Gini coefficient by 4 per cent in Germany, 9 per cent in France and 14 per cent in the US.
5. A similar but less radical tax reform was proposed by the Labour government in Norway in Spring 1991.
6. The unemployment figures for Norway and Sweden do not include laid off workers who are enrolled in the various labour market training programmes.
7. Hibbs (1987) derives a similar result from a different mechanism. He constructs a model in which redistributive increases in taxes and transfers reduce the unions' shadow price of equality and therefore promote relatively equal pre-tax wage settlements.
8. Useful discussions of wage determination in Norway and Sweden can be found in Flanagan, Soskice and Ulman (1983) and in the papers on Norway and Sweden in Calmfors (1990).
9. In the latest bargaining rounds in Norway (1990–1991), a two-tier centrally negotiated wage increase was introduced. Those unions that normally obtain drift got roughly half of the increase given to unions that receive no drift.

References

Adler-Karlsson, G. (1967), *Funktionssocialism*, Lund: Prisma.
Aukrust, O. (1970), PRIM 1: A Model of the Price and Income Distribution Mechanism in an Open Economy. Oslo: Article 35 from the Central Bureau of Statistics.
Aukrust, O. (1977), Inflation in the Open Economy: A Norwegian Model. Oslo: Article 96 from the Central Bureau of Statistics.
Bean, Charles, Richard Layard and Stephen Nickell (1986), The Rise in Unemployment: A Multi-Country Study, *Economica*, 53: S1–S22.
Bojer, Hilde (1992), Occupational Status, Sex and Individual Income in Norway, unpublished paper, Oslo: University of Oslo, Department of Economics.
Calmfors, Lars (ed.)(1990), *Wage Formation and Macroeconomic Policy in the Nordic Countries*, Oxford: Oxford University Press.
Calmfors, Lars (1991), What Can We Learn from the Macroeconomic Experience of Sweden, Paper presented to Symposium on Unemployment, Haag, Dec. 13.
Calmfors, Lars and John Driffill (1988), Bargaining Structure, Corporatism and Macroeconomic Performance, *Economic Policy*, 3: 13–61.
Calmfors, Lars and Henrik Horn (1985), Classical Unemployment, Accommodation Policies and the Adjustment of Real Wages, *Scandinavian Journal of Economics*, 87: 234–61.
Central Bureau of Statistics (1991), *Økonomiske Analyser*, 9/91, Oslo: SSB.
Dowrick, Steve and Duc-Tho Nguyen (1989), OECD Comparative Economic Growth 1950–85: Catch-Up and Convergence, *American Economic Review*, 78: 1010–30.
Esping-Andersen, Gøsta (1985), *Politics Against Markets: The Social Democratic Road to Power*, Princeton: Princeton University Press.
Fagerberg, Jan, Ådne Cappelen, Lars Mjøset and Rune Skarstein (1990), The Decline of Social-Democratic State Capitalism in Norway, *New Left Review*, 181.
Flanagan, Robert J., David W. Soskice and Lloyd Ulman (1983), *Unionism, Economic Stabilization and Incomes Policies: European Experience*, Washington DC: Brookings.
Freeman, Richard B. (1988), Labour Market Institutions and Economic Performance, *Economic Policy*, 3: 64–80.
Grout, Paul A. (1984), Investment and Wages in the Absence of Legally Binding Labour Contracts, *Econometrica*, 52: 449–60.
Hernes, Gudmund (Forthcoming), Karl Marx and the Dilemmas of Social Democracies: the Case of

Norway and Sweden, in Philippe Schmitter (ed.), *Experimenting with Scale*, Cambridge: Cambridge University Press.

Hernes, Gudmund and Atle Marøen (1985), *Fagbevegelsen og Arbeidslivet*, Oslo: FAFO.

Hibbs, Douglas A. Jr. (1987), Fiscal Influences on Trends in Wage Dispersion in Sweden, Paper presented at the European Public Choice Society Meeting, Reggio Calabria, Italy, April 22–25.

Hibbs, Douglas A. Jr. and Håkan Locking (1991), Wage Compression, Wage Drift, and Wage Inflation in Sweden, FIEF Working Paper No. 87, Stockholm: Trade Union Institute for Economic Research (FIEF).

Hicks, Alexander and Swank, Duane (1984), Governmental Redistribution in Rich Capitalist Democracies, *Policy Studies Journal*, 13: 265–86.

Hirschman, Albert O. (1970), *Exit, Voice and Loyalty*, Cambridge, Mass.: Harvard University Press.

Holden, Steinar (1991), Wage Drift and Bargaining: Evidence from Norway, *Economica*, forthcoming.

Holmlund, Bertil and Per Skedinger (1990), Wage Bargaining and Wage Drift: Evidence from the Swedish Wood Industry, in Lars Calmfors (ed.), *Wage Formation and Macroeconomic Policy in the Nordic Countries*, Oxford: Oxford University Press.

Johansen, Leif (1979), The Bargaining Society and the Inefficiency of Bargaining, *Kyklos*, 32: 497–522.

Johansen, Leif (1982), Cores, Aggressiveness and the Breakdown of Cooperation in Economic Games, *Journal of Economic Behavior and Organization*, 3: 1–37.

Korpi, Walter (1978), *The Working Class in Welfare Capitalism: Work, Unions and Politics in Sweden*, London: Routledge and Kegan Paul.

Korpi, Walter (1983), *The Democratic Class Struggle*, London: Routledge and Kegan Paul.

Lange, Peter and Geoffrey Garrett (1985), The Politics of Growth, *Journal of Politics*, 47: 792–827.

Lash, Scott (1985), The End of Neo-Corporatism?: The Breakdown of Centralized Bargaining in Sweden, *British Journal of Industrial Relations*, 23: 215–39.

Layard, Richard, Stephen Nickell and Richard Jackman (1991), *Unemployment, Macroeconomic Performance and the Labour Market*, Oxford: Oxford University Press.

Lundberg, Erik (1985), The Rise and Fall of the Swedish Model, *Journal of Economic Literature*, 23: 1–36.

Luxemburg, Rosa (1970), *Reform or Revolution*, New York: Pathfinder Press.

Moene, Karl Ove (1990), Union Militancy and Plant Design, in M. Aoki, B. Gustafsson and O. Williamson (eds), *The Firm as a Nexus of Treaties*, Beverly Hills: Sage Publications.

Moene, Karl Ove and Michael Wallerstein (1992), Bargaining Structure and Economic Performance, *FIEF Studies in Labor Markets and Economic Policy*.

Myrdal, Hans-Göran (1991), The Hard Way from a Centralized to a Decentralized Industrial Relations System: The Case of Sweden and the SAF, in Otto Jakobi and Dieter Sadowski (eds), *Employers' Associations in Europe: Policy and Organization*, Baden: Nomos Verlag Baden.

Nordby, Trond (1991), Korporatismens Sammenbrudd, *Dagens Næringsliv*, Nov. 30: 47.

Organization for Economic Cooperation and Development (1989), *OECD Economic Surveys: Sweden 1988/1989*, Paris: OECD.

Organization for Economic Cooperation and Development (1991a), *OECD Economic Outlook*, No. 497, Paris: OECD.

Organization for Economic Cooperation and Development (1991b), *Taxing Profits in a Global Economy*, Paris: OECD.

Pontusson, Jonas (1991a), The Crisis of Swedish Social Democracy, paper presented at the Center for Social Theory and Comparative History, UCLA, 1991.

Pontusson, Jonas (1991b), Fordism and Social Democracy: Towards a Comparative Analysis, paper presented at the Annual Meetings of the American Political Science Association, Washington DC.

Przeworski, Adam (1985), *Capitalism and Social Democracy*, Cambridge: Cambridge University Press.

Przeworski, Adam and Jeong-Hwa Lee (1990), Cui Bono? Corporatism and Welfare, University of Chicago: Manuscript.

Przeworski, Adam and John Sprague (1986) *Paper Stones: A History of Electoral Socialism*, Chicago: University of Chicago Press.

Przeworski, Adam and Michael Wallerstein (1982), The Structure of Class Conflict in Democratic Capitalist Societies, *The American Political Science Review*, 76: 215-36.

Rødseth, Asbjørn (1986) Trade Unions, Investments and the Possibility for Full Employment, memorandum from the Department of Economics, University of Oslo, No. 3.

Rødseth, Asbjørn and Steinar Holden (1990), Wage Formation in Norway, in Lars Calmfors (ed.), *Wage Formation in the Nordic Countries*, Oxford: Oxford University Press.

Sandmo, Agnar (1991), Economists and the Welfare State, *European Economic Review*, 35, 213-39.

Steinmo, Sven (1990), The End of Redistributive Taxation? Tax Reform in a Globalizing World Economy, paper presented at the annual meeting of the American Political Science Association, San Francisco.

Stephens, John D. (1980), *The Transition from Capitalism to Socialism*, Atlantic Highlands NJ: Humanities Press.

Strøm, Steinar, Nils Martin Stølen and Hege Torp (1988), *Inntektsdannelsen i Norge;* Oslo: NOU 1988: 24.

Summers, Robert and Alan Heston (1988), A New Set of International Comparisons of Real Product and Price Levels: Estimates for 130 Countries, 1950-1985, *Review of Income and Wealth*, 34: 1-25.

Swenson, Peter (1991), Labor and the Limits of the Welfare State: The Politics of Intraclass Conflict and Cross-Class Alliances in Sweden and West Germany, *Comparative Politics*, 23: 379-99.

Wallerstein, Michael (1990), Centralized Bargaining and Wage Restraint, *American Journal of Political Science*, 34: 982-1004.

Part III
Innovation and Technological Change

The
SCANDINAVIAN ECONOMIC HISTORY REVIEW

VOLUME XXVIII:2, 1980

The Transition from Sail to Steam in the Danish Merchant Fleet, 1865—1910

By OVE HORNBY and CARL-AXEL NILSSON *

I

The most recent authoritative work on the modern economic history of Denmark gives a survey in broad outline of the development of the Danish merchant fleet and shipping industry in the nineteenth and early twentieth centuries.[1] According to this account there was a traffic revolution during the 1860s taking the form, as far as the merchant fleet was concerned, of a substantial increase in steam-tonnage. The faster and more regular conveyance provided by steamship is emphasised and the steady extension of the route network during the second half of the century is regarded as a consequence of it. The expansion of the merchant fleet was accompanied by a separation between the shipowning and trading sides of the business, and the capital requirements of regular traffic meant that steamship companies were usually formed on a joint-stock basis.[2] The 1890s brought a new turning-point for Danish shipping: the rise in freight rates caused tonnage to double in a single decade, and steamships were now wholly predominant. Prosperity was accompanied by the founding of numerous companies and a notable redeployment of ships towards the international freight market.[3] However, the work in question devotes most of its attention to the contribution made by shipping to the growth of Denmark's gross national income, and in this respect the conversion of the Danish merchant fleet from sail to steam is declared to be a growth-promoting factor.

---

* Ove Hornby, born 1942, and Carl-Axel Nilsson, born 1931, are senior lecturers at the Institute of Economic History, University of Copenhagen. Ove Hornby takes a special interest in the Danish economy and economic policy of the 19th century, whereas Carl-Axel Nilsson mainly has concerned himself with structural changes in the Swedish economy during the last century.

[1] S. A. Hansen, *Økonomisk vækst i Danmark*, I—II, Copenhagen 1972—75.
[2] *ibid.*, I, 180 f.
[3] *ibid.*, I, 305 f.

The conversion itself is taken as a more or less given fact, and the statistical basis of this part of the exposition is somewhat shaky.[4] However, the background for making a synthesis is not of the best; the literature on the topic tends to be of the *Festschrift* type, concentrating on the history of individual persons, ships or companies, and even in scholarly studies a solid statistical foundation is usually lacking.[5]

Thus the present study can be regarded in many ways as a step into deep (and virgin) waters. The main objective is to carry out an empirical analysis of the actual course of the transition from sail to steam in order to establish a firmer foundation for further research. But even an objective as limited as this does of course require some preliminary discussion of principles and theoretical approaches.

Internationally economic historians have taken some interest during the last couple of decades in the shipping technology of recent times, and in the second half of the 1950s two articles were published which can each be said to have established schools in this field.[6]

Douglas C. North uses models derived from neo-classical theory to try to discover the causes of changes in productivity. His broad aim is to arrive at an understanding of the factors that contribute to economic growth and to measure their comparative significance. The conclusion of the study is that the role of technical innovation is reduced. 'While downward shifts in the supply curve, reflecting innovations in shipping, have received the lion's share of the credit for the decline in freight rates, the credit actually should be distributed more widely... The shift from sail to steam, therefore, was not the major determinant of the decline in ocean freight rates.'[7] North himself has continued to pursue this line of research in his subsequent writings and has also acquired a number of followers.[8] A typical conclusion is the following: 'The introduction of steam power had important initial

---

[4] *ibid.*, II, 312. We may merely note here the use of a constant conversion factor for converting sail- and steam-tonnage to a common measure of transport capacity, cf. note 15. Moreover an error is present throughout in the conversion from Danube to British rule — multiplication by 1.1 instead of 0.91.

[5] Particular attention may be drawn to *Danmarks søfart og søhandel fra de ældste tider til vore dage*, I—II, ed. B. Liisberg, Copenhagen 1941; K. Klem, *De danskes vej. Rids af dansk søhistorie*, Copenhagen 1941; H. P. Carl, *Træk af dansk skibsfarts historie*, Copenhagen 1949; K. Koch, *Danske dampskibsselskabers historie*, Copenhagen 1929; J. Schovelin, *Det Forenede Dampskibs Selskab. 40 års udvikling*, Copenhagen 1906; P.G. Ernst, *Det store eventyr om H.N. Andersen og Ø. K.*, Copenhagen 1937; E. Mægaard & J. Vestberg, *Dansk Dampskibsrederiforening 1884—17. Januar — 1934*, Copenhagen 1934; H. Fode, *Småskibsfarten på Arhusbugten 1865—1914*, Arhus 1971.

[6] G.S. Graham, 'The Ascendancy of the Sailing Ships 1850—85', *Economic History Review*, Sec.Ser. IX:1, Aug. 1956. D.C. North, 'Ocean Freight Rates and Economic Development 1750—1913', *Journal of Economic History*, XVII, Dec. 1958.

[7] North, *loc.cit.*, p. 541.

[8] D.C. North, 'Sources of Productivity Changes in Ocean Shipping 1600—1850', *Journal of Political Economy*, 76, Sept.-Oct. 1968; J. Mak and G. Walton, 'Steamboats and the Great Productivity Surge in River Transportation', *Journal of Economic History*, XXXII, Sept. 1972; J. Mak & G. Walton, 'The Persistence of Old Technologies: The Case of Flatboats', *Journal of Economic History*, XXXIII, June 1973; E. F. Haites & j. Mak, 'Economies of Scale in Western River Steamboating', *Journal of Economic History*, XXXVI, Sept. 1976.

effects, but most of the reduction of costs came from subsequent improvements after the introduction of steam ... the result of learning by doing.'[9]

Gerald S. Graham's article, on the other hand, is a study of the process of the diffusion of a new technology and thus has the aim of exploring more directly the changeover from sail to steam technology. He emphasises the leisurely pace at which change proceeded. As early as the 1860s 'higher pressures had become the means of winning vital economies in fuel consumption and of adding cargo space', but something else was still missing before steamships could win the battle, and 'this last step could only be accomplished with the aid of the metallurgist'.[10] The development of the rolling-mill technique was of particular significance, and by the beginning of the 1880s the contest had already been decided in principle in favour of the ocean-going steamship.

Since then Charles K. Harley too has dealt with the problem of diffusion, but using a more explicitly theoretical approach.[11] He adopts a position directly opposed, for example, to Joseph Schumpeter's stress on discontinuities and believes that the most important factor in the process is 'the more or less continuous improvement that occurred in the fuel consumption of the marine engines', whereas 'the improvements in the machinery were marginal' and also were introduced gradually.[12] Harley's view derives logically from the neo-classical theory, for he writes that his model is based on 'the assumption that shipping and shipbuilding markets were generally in long-run competitive equilibrium', and that the choice between sail and steam was thus governed by shifts in the relative prices of ships and other inputs.[13]

The sail versus steam problem has been dealt with in a more general way by Nathan R. Rosenberg, who at a number of points subscribes to the theoretical approaches of North and Harley.[14] The innovation structure is presented 'as occurring along a gradual downward slope of real costs rather than as a Schumpeterian gale of creative destruction'.[15] But Rosenberg also opposes North —

---

[9] Mak and Walton, 'Steamboats and the Great Productivity Surge', p. 635. — Ramon Knauerhase also takes the productivity aspect as his starting-point in 'The Compound Steam Engine and Productivity Changes in the German Merchant Marine Fleet 1871—1887', *Journal of Economic History*, XXVII, Sept. 1968. His conclusion that steam technology was the main source of advancing productivity was heavily criticised by Walton in *Journal of Economic History*, XXX, June 1970.

[10] Graham, *loc.cit.*, p. 86.

[11] C. K. Harley, 'The Shift from Sailing Ships to Steamships 1850—1890: A Study in Technological Change and its Diffusion' in *Essays on a Mature Economy: Britain after 1840*, ed. D.N. McCloskey, Princeton, New Jersey 1971.

[12] Harley, *loc.cit.*, p. 216. In Harley's opinion sailing-ships were still fully competitive on several ocean-going routes even at the beginning of the 20th century.

[13] *ibid.*, p. 216. — For an example of the type of explanation in which market imperfections play the biggest role instead, see G.R. Henning & K. Trace, 'Britain and the Motorship. A Case of the Delayed Adoption of New Technology?', *Journal of Economic History*, XXXV, June 1975. These scholars believe that British shipowners were slow in changing to diesel-engined ships and that the shipowners would have gained by going over more quickly to the new technique, but that even so it cannot be concluded that they were unduly slow. The authors emphasise 'the strength of the coal lobby and pro-coal sentiment in Britain' and 'the overoptimistic performance claims by builders of steam-turbine machinery', *loc.cit.*, p. 385.

[14] N. R. Rosenberg, 'Factors Affecting the Diffusion of Technology', *Explorations in Economic History*, Fall 1972.

[15] *ibid.*, p. 33.

and therefore Robert Fogel and Stanley Engerman too, both of whom endorse North's views — notably by ascribing to technological change a crucial impact upon the development of productivity. It is important to have a different starting point besides changed relative factors and commodity prices, viz. that 'the speed at which new technologies replace old ones will depend upon the speed with which it is possible to overcome an array of supply side problems'.[16]

There has been a tendency among the scholars cited to concentrate upon ocean shipping, and often, moreover, only upon the earlier phases of the transition from sail to steam. Furthermore the main emphasis is generally laid upon analysis based on theoretical models and not on systematic quantitative studies of variations and dissimilarities. However, the declared purpose of the present article is to analyse the changeover of the Danish merchant fleet from sail to steam in its entirety; also it is doubtful whether the employing of theoretical models in productivity studies will get us very far in trying to explain a process of *historical* change. Moreover it is by no means certain that the equilibrium model has the highest explanatory value; at all events the possibility cannot be excluded that explanations of the Schumpeter type, which make a principle of stressing the discontinuous elements, may still offer advantages as explanations in the historical analysis.

When Rosenberg criticises those who heavily play down the significance of technology by pointing out that other factors are not independent of technological change, he lays himself equally open to criticism for rejecting the discontinuous element and asserting instead that 'the process of diffusion necessarily must be slow'. Even within the framework of a process which may perhaps be gradual when viewed in its entirety, there *can* be discontinuities present which actually constitute the strategic elements.

However, Rosenberg's closing remarks may be regarded as an excellent starting point for the study that follows. Having pointed out that he has not answered the question 'How slow is slow?' he adds that little harm is done 'so long as we can advance our understanding of the reasons for the *actual* historical pace of technological diffusion'.[17]

One of the objectives of the present study is to look for the answers to a number of questions that appear relevant in regard to analyses of the Rosenberg type. A broad mapping-out of patterns of growth and cyclical fluctuations is followed by three case-studies: the first of these deals with the speed with which the merchant fleet was being renewed; the second explores the question of continuity or discontinuity by disaggregating the total inventory of ships into four categories of size; and finally, an attempt is made in the third study to distinguish the outlines of a possible specialisation of functions between steam and sail in the actual performance of the task of conveying goods.

[16] *ibid.*, p. 6.
[17] *ibid.*, p. 33.

II

The study concentrates upon the shift of the Danish merchant fleet from sail to steam during the period 1865—1910. The placing of the starting point after the war of 1864 with Prussia and Austria enables the area covered by the national territory of Denmark to remain the same throughout the period, and even though the first Danish-owned steamship began sailing in home waters as early as 1819, steamships still accounted for little more than 3 % of aggregate Danish merchant tonnage as late as 1865. By the end of the period selected the figure was almost 80 %, so that the bulk of the transition to steam must have taken place during the intervening years. The period selected offers a further advantage inasmuch as there are copious and continuous published statistics permitting year-by-year comparisons to be made after a few adjustments and conversions.[18]

---

[18] It is true throughout that source-material for the tables and figures cited in this article is culled from the official publication *Statistisk Tabelværk*, (Tabeller over den danske handelsflåde, over skibsfarten mellem danske og fremmede havne samt over skibsfarten mellem danske havne indbyrdes). The raw tables are not published here but are available in the Copenhagen University Institute of Economic History, Njalsgade 102, DK-2300 Copenhagen S. Until 1874 the year used was the financial year (1/4—31/3): thereafter it was the calendar year. — The tonnage was not measured according to the same principles all the way through the period 1865/66—1910, since there was a change-over from the original German rule to British rule, then to Danube rule and finally back to British rule again. The last of these changes, which took place in 1895 and of which the *Statistisk Tabelværk* figures give an accurate account, does not raise any special problems. On the other hand, however, it is not entirely clear when the change to Danube rule occurred. For example, according to C. Hage, *Haandbog i Handelsvidenskab*, Copenhagen 1894, p. 776, the decision to effect this change was made in 1878. But conversions to Danube rule from 1879 onwards produce certain oddities. Despite the fact that the number of ships in the merchant fleet increased between 1878 and 1879, there is a fall in total tonnage. This applies even to ships in the > 500 NRT size-category, which shows a rise in the number of ships from 37 to 38 but a fall in tonnage from 29,650 to 28,428 NRT. Moreover this involves a discrepancy with data on acquisitions and disposals given in the tables. It is impossible to avoid contradictions of this sort by choosing some other year than the one cited. Nevertheless in later volumes of *Statistisk Tabelværk* conversion has been effected from 1879 onwards in the publication of historical series, and it was accordingly decided in spite of everything to make the conversion from 1879 for the purposes of the present study. In consequence the year 1879 shows a modest decline in Fig. 1 but a rise in Fig. 2. Even more of a problem is presented by the changeover from German to British rule early on in the period. The switch was to be made in accordance with the Laws on Ship Measurement of 13 March 1867 and 15 May 1868, and according to Hage was so implemented. However, it has proved impossible to find any year in which conversion does not produce totally unacceptable oddities in the statistical series as a result. Neither is any sign of conversion to be found in the shipping lists, which showed all steamships, published in every annual volume of *Statistisk Tabelværk* up to and including 1869/70. Only a more detailed scrutiny of the source-material for *Statistisk Tabelværk* volumes will be able to disclose the procedure employed by the authorities in implementing the provisions of the law. — It should be observed that motorships were first distinguished in *Statistisk Tabelværk* as a separate category in 1908. In the present study, therefore, they count in the sailing-ship category. See further in note 27.

Diagram 1. Tonnages in the Danish merchant fleet 1865—1910 (NRT)

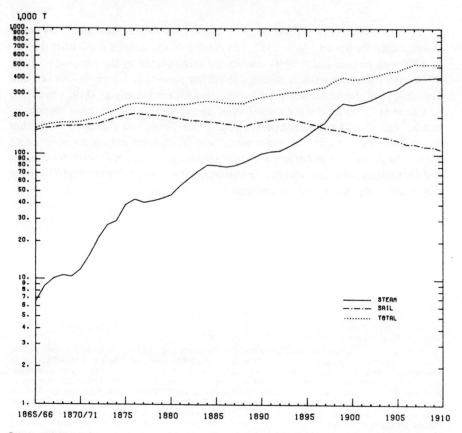

Source: See Note 18

As already noted, the period is characterised by a very vigorous growth of steamship tonnage, which rose between 1865 and 1910 from less than 7,000 net register tons to about 400,000 (Diagram 1). In broad terms this represents a rate of growth of about 8—10 % per annum, even though direct falls in tonnage consequent upon cyclical business conditions are observable in the years 1878, 1885—86 and 1900, and a considerable slowing-down of progress in 1869, 1891—92 and the years subsequent to 1907. The cyclical peaks occur in 1877, 1884, 1890, 1899 and 1907.

Differences in the rate of growth during the individual six or seven-year periods stand out clearly: steam-tonnage doubled in the periods 1870—75 and 1879—84, while in 1893—99 the increase was 150 %. Growth was slower in 1901—07, tonnage rising by only 60 %, and the business boom of 1887—90, during which the tonnage of the steamship fleet went up by a mere 30 % or so, seems to have been particularly short-lived and feeble.

Sail-tonnage generally exhibits the opposite tendency. Over the period as a whole it fell from about 150,000 to 110,000 NRT, but it was still moving upwards during the business boom of the 1870s. The decline did not begin until 1877, and even then was succeeded by further growth in 1888—93, a period when the rise in steamship tonnage was proceeding at a particularly slow pace. After that the decline of sail-tonnage was resumed and continued for the remainder of the period save for a brief respite in 1902. Steam-tonnage overtook sail in the mid-1890s.

The overall result of these two patterns of growth was that the tonnage of the Danish merchant fleet grew fairly slowly. This applies particularly to the first part of the period; the twelve years that followed the growth of 1870—76 were characterised mostly by stagnation. The years 1889—1907, however, show another picture with a fairly steady rate of growth and a total increase in tonnage of about 70 %.[19]

By looking at the annual net changes in the tonnage (Diagram 2) it becomes possible to fill in more of the detail in our picture of the pattern of events. The watershed of 1877 is shown in sharp relief: before then the annual increase of sail and steam had been fairly uniform, although the expansion of sail tonnage had still been at a higher level in the second half of the 1860s. The disparity was smaller during the boom of 1870—75, but sail-tonnage was still increasing more than steam with a growth of 36,500 NRT compared with 29,000.

After this it was steamships alone that accounted for the rise in merchant fleet tonnage, though there was a sudden, remarkable but short-lived interruption of the trend in 1889—93, when sail showed an increase of a similar order of magnitude to steam, viz. 28,000 NRT as against 30,000.

---

[19] The pure tonnage figures given here are obviously not an ideal basis of measurement. In particular the higher potential speed of steamships means that their effective capacity is heavily undervalued compared with sail, if tonnage figures alone are utilised. A conversion equivalent is often employed in statistics and scholarly literature to permit direct effective comparisons. The procedure has not been applied in the present context, since it seems improbable that the equivalent would be the same throughout the period. Steamship technology was undergoing rapid development, and there are great difficulties involved for example in undertaking direct comparisons between the large vessels at the beginning of the 1900s and the biggest steamships in the merchant fleet of the seventies and eighties, which were not much larger than 1,000 NRT — not to mention earlier periods still, when steamships seldom exceeded 500 NRT. A correct measurement of the effective carrying capacity of steamships would show a bigger rise over the period than would the tonnage figures, but since immediately available information with regard to the technical progress of the Danish steamships fleet is lacking, the attempt to compute some kind of accurate conversion factors is precluded for the time being; as will be evident from the case-studies, what we have done instead is to make approaches from a variety of angles in an attempt to form some idea of the real competitive situations and carrying capacities of wind- and steam-propelled vessels respectively.

Diagram 2. Annual acquisitions and disposals in the Danish merchant fleet 1865—1910 (NRT)

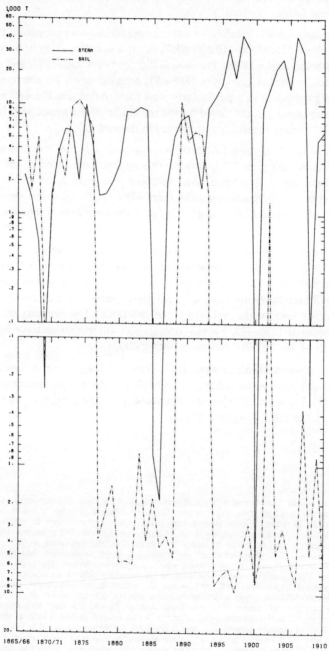

Source: See Note 18

Table 1. Acquisitions and disposals in the Danish merchant fleet 1870—1907
Annual averages for the boom periods ascertained.

Period	1. Acquisitions			2. Disposals			3.[1] Rate of renewal		4.[2] Rate of disposal	
	Number	Aggregate tonnage	Average size of ships	Number	Aggregate tonnage	Average size of ships	Number (%)	Tonnage (%)	Number (%)	Tonnage (%)
A. Entire Merchant fleet										
1870/75	147	19,235	131	125	11,913	95	28.6	47.3	22.2	33.9
1879/84	110	15,200	138	120	13,021	109	21.0	34.5	22.6	31.6
1887/90	98	21,229	216	95	14,219	150	11.2	29.9	12.0	18.6
1893/99	105	33,396	319	119	16,389	137	20.7	57.0	24.1	38.1
1901/07	115	39,284	342	105	19,919	190	20.6	44.7	20.9	35.4
B. Sailing-ship fleet										
1870/75[3]	134	14,930	112	104	9,927	95	27.6	43.8	23.0	35.4
1879/84	91	7,975	88	115	12,021	105	19.1	26.3	23.1	35.3
1887/90	80	13,206	165	89	11,909	134	10.5	29.0	12.3	27.7
1893/99	73	8,774	120	109	12,790	118	16.7	29.4	24.3	46.4
1901/07	77	5,332	69	90	8,930	100	16.6	30.8	20.8	42.6
C. Steamship fleet										
1870/75[3]	13	4,304	331	..	..	..	46.7	65.6	..	..
1879/84	19	7,225	380	4.5	1,000	222	41.6	52.5	14.1	13.5
1887/90	18	8,023	446	6	2,310	385	22.7	31.4	8.6	11.6
1893/99	32	24,653	770	11	3,599	327	45.3	67.6	22.1	23.3
1901/07	38	33,952	893	15	10,989	733	41.2	59.1	21.9	31.1

Notes: 1 Acquisitions in each period as a proportion of the number of ships or of tonnage at the end of the period.
2 Total disposals during each period as % of the number of ships or of tonnage at the beginning of the period.
3 For the period 1870/75 there are only data for 1873/75 divided between steam and sail. Disposals of steamships were negligible in these years. It may therefore be presumed that for this period all disposals consisted of sailing-ships. Consequently there will be no difference between gross and net acquisitions of steamships.

Source: See Note 18.

The figure reflects clearly the cyclical variations. When the intervals between the various slump years are determined, five complete cycles of increase of steamship tonnage emerge:

1869 — 1875 — 1877 = 8 years
1877 — 1883 — 1886 = 9 years
1886 — 1890 — 1892 = 6 years
1892 — 1898 — 1900 = 8 years
1900 — 1906 — 1908 = 8 years

Two levels of expansion can be distinguished. During the first three cyclical phases (i.e., between 1870 and 1892) tonnage rose annually by 5,000—6,000 NRT, whereas the annual increase during the last two phases amounted to about 20,000 NRT. In this respect the 1890s brought a clear breach with the earlier pattern.

III

In the first of the case-studies the objective has been to determine the speed of renewal of the Danish merchant fleet and especially to clarify the extent to which the process was characterised by continuity or discontinuity. The primary focus of interest is the transition from sailing-ship to steamship technology but attention is also paid to renewal within each category regarded on its own. It has to be underlined, however, that direct technological variables are not used, but in the present context it was considered justifiable to use the average size of ship as a proxy variable.

As Table 1 shows, wide fluctuations both of expansion and of contraction are concealed behind the net change depicted in Diagram 2.[20] All the periods of expansion adduced show figures of both acquisitions and disposals amounting to about 100 ships per annum or more. Although the number of ships disposed of exceeded acquisitions in certain years, the ships brought into service were invariably so much larger than those retired that the average tonnage added in each period was bigger than that deducted.

The average size of ships acquired increased in each period. However, two notable jumps can be discerned: in 1887/90 the average increased by 56 % simultaneously with an extraordinarily modest turnover of ships and again by 48 % in 1893/99 when, by contrast, the turnover was very brisk.

As regards the number of ships the 'rate of renewal' and 'rate of disposal' vary between 20.6 % and 28.6 %, the period 1887/90 being the sole exception. The tonnage figures disclose both higher renewal and higher liquidation in percentage terms. Almost 50 % of the total tonnage of the merchant fleet at the end of 1875 had been acquired during the preceding five-year period, and one third of the tonnage existing at the start of the five-year period had been retired by its end. The next two

[20] For the division into part-periods see page 114. It was decided to assign the years 1884, 1889 and 1907 to the boom periods because of their high absolute levels of acquisition.

periods show falling figures, but 1893/99 repeats the pattern of 1870/75 with a 'rate of renewal' of 58 % and a 'rate of disposal' of 38 %. The figures drop again during the subsequent period but nevertheless remain at a high level.

If the acquisition and disposal figures for sailing-ships and steamships are regarded separately, it becomes obvious that they cannot be explained purely in terms of the transition from sail to steam. The trend in the sail category is rather irregular, but new ships were being acquired all the time — even, as will be shown, over and above what was needed to keep the fleet intact after allowing for losses by shipwreck. The number of sailing-ships added admittedly exceeded those lost only during the period 1870/75, but both during this period and in 1887/90 there was a net increase measured by tonnage, and the newly-acquired ships both in 1887/90 and in 1893/99 were bigger on average than they had been in 1870/75. Furthermore it is equally evident that the big rise in the average size of newly-acquired sailing-vessels in 1887/90 is the explanation of the jump in the corresponding figure for the combined merchant fleet.

The renewal of the sailing-ship fleet was manifestly at its maximum in 1870/75, but the figures do not show a uniformly downward tendency, and both 1893/99 and 1901/07 manifest a higher rate of renewal than the 1880s. However, the most interesting period seems to be 1887/90, when the turnover was admittedly rather modest but renewals, even at this relatively late point in time, exceeded disposals.

Not surprisingly, the trend is clearer in the case of steamships. Broadly speaking there is substantial growth in the numbers of ships acquired each year and in their average size. At the same time disposals were quite modest and consisted of considerably smaller ships. It was not until the later periods that disposals became of major significance.

With regard to the annual acquisitions of ships and tonnage it seems the most natural procedure to work at two levels separated by a boundary placed at some point in the early 1890s. While 1893/99 shows a rise of 60 % in the average tonnage of ships, the other periods before and after show a rate of increase of only between 17 and 26 %. There is a fair degree of continuity with regard to numbers of newly-acquired steamships: 41—47 % of them were replaced in each part-period but in 1887/90 only 23 %. In terms of tonnage there was a wider disparity in the rate of renewal; the figures are particularly high in 1870/75 and 1893/99, when renewals amounted to about two-thirds.

It is evident that it was the steamship situation that constituted the prime determinant of the development of the entire merchant fleet. The pace of renewal is generally distinctly higher in the steamship than in the sailing-ship fleet in terms both of numbers of vessels and of tonnage; the exception is 1887/90 when the sailing-ship fleet enjoyed about the same rate of renewal as steamships. The rate of disposal was lower for the steamship fleet with the exception of the last period, when relatively more steamships than sailing-ships were being disposed of and the rate of disposal of steamships approached that of sailing-ships even in terms of tonnage, since no less than one third of the steamship tonnage was struck off from the merchant fleet over a period of only seven years.

Table 2. Purchase of Danish and foreign ships and wrecks, scrapping and sales of secondhand ships abroad. Percentage Distribution

		Acquisitions						Disposals					
		Newly-built Danish ships		Newly-built foreign ships[2]		Secondhand foreign ships[2]		Shipwrecks		Ships scrapped		Ships sold abroad	
Period		Proportion of tonnages %	Average size of ships	Proportion of tonnages %	Average size of ships	Proportion of tonnages %	Average size of ships	Proportion of tonnages %	Average size of ships	Proportion of tonnages %	Average size of ships	Proportion of tonnages %	Average size of ships
A. Sailing-ships													
1870/75[1]		37.5	84	62.5	138			67.1	107	2.3	17	30.6	105
79/84		28.6	52	71.4	122			53.6	105	6.0	35	40.3	149
87/90		11.6	62	88.4	211			54.2	136	5.8	58	40.0	163
93/99		27.2	78	9.2	145	63.6	152	54.9	124	2.9	34	42.2	123
1901/07		66.6	77	7.0	78	26.4	59	42.0	96	3.7	22	54.3	135
B. Steamships													
1870/75		52.8	545	47.2	230			..	..	..	..	..	..
79/84		38.0	614	62.0	310			86.9	435	7.6	57	5.5	47
87/90		51.0	584	49.0	349			82.7	764	1.0	73	16.3	151
93/99		14.0	493	54.1	972	31.9	689	40.0	438	1.5	97	58.5	327
1901/07		21.3	632	45.3	1089	33.4	933	35.1	871	0.7	169	64.2	687

Notes: [1] Re 1870/75 cf. Table 1, note 3. The distribution of sailing-ships acquired in the same period is based upon data from 1873/75 with the distribution of steamship acquisitions as residual items.

[2] Foreign ships are specified as new or secondhand for the first time in 1889.

Source: See Note 18.

The shipping statistics also make it possible to study more closely the extent to which acquisitions of ships are attributable to purchases in Denmark or abroad, and how disposals were distributed between shipwreck, scrapping and sales to other countries (Table 2).

In the case of sailing-ships it is generally true that only a minor part of the additional tonnage came from Danish yards; moreover, Danish-built vessels were of a relatively modest average size which remained fairly constant. The average size of vessels purchased from abroad, on the other hand, fell considerably after the turn of the century.[21]

As far as disposals are concerned, losses by shipwreck were of predominant importance. Scrapping, on the other hand, played a subordinate role throughout the period, and the vessels broken up were always small. Sales to foreign countries were limited in volume during the expansive period 1870/75, but the proportion did increase after that, especially during the general expansion of the sailing-ship fleet about 1890. The explanation is probably that to a certain extent the shipowning companies were simultaneously selling older tonnage and buying new larger vessels, whereas during the expansion of the 1870s they were making purchases without selling off very much of their older tonnage. Again as far as disposals are concerned the situation changed greatly after the turn of the century with sales of ships to foreign countries increasing rapidly.

The situation with the steamship fleet was quite different. Shipwreck was the paramount cause of disposals until the 1880s, since of course the fleet was still decidedly in the building-up phase from a very low base. During this period Danish shipyards were of more importance to the steamship fleet than to sailing-ships; about half the tonnage acquired was newly-built in Denmark, and Danish ships were twice as big on average as those from abroad. However, this situation underwent a crucial change in 1893/99 and 1901/07. The proportion of new tonnage represented by Danish-built ships fell heavily, and the average size of the latter increased only slightly. The bulk of new tonnage now consisted of new ships from abroad, and big ones at that, averaging about 1,000 NRT. Almost as important was the acquisition of used ships from abroad, these too being bigger than the Danish-built ships and in 1901/07 of almost the same average size as the newly-built ships being purchased from abroad. At the same time a considerable export trade was being done in older ships, and as time went on this grew to embrace about 60 % of all disposals. Since the average size of vessel being sold was fairly large, this may indicate that renewal of the steamship fleet, after the turn of the century at any rate, was effected in the form of the exporting of older, relatively large Danish-built ships and the importing of new, still bigger ships.

It is possible, finally, to offer an overall view of production at Danish shipyards; we may note that it was not until 1889 that Danish export of newly-built ships became worth mentioning.

---

[21] The division into periods in Table 2 only affords an incomplete impression of the great expansion of the sailing-ship fleet around the year 1890, of which a notable feature was the purchase of large secondhand ships from abroad.

	Danish production for home market			Danish production for export			Proportion of production exported
Sailing-ships:	No. of ships	Aggregate tonnage	Average size of ships	No. of ships	Aggregate tonnage	Average size of ships	
1889—99	22	4,273	194	361	30,271	84	12.4
1900—08	27	647	24	399	28,325	71	2.2
Steamships:							
1889—99	28	19,229	687	90	44,427	494	30.2
1900—08	40	40,611	1,015	93	54,868	590	42.5

Thus sailing-ships were produced with an eye almost exclusively to the home market while Danish steamship yards enjoyed substantial foreign sales. Exports of steamships during the period 1900—08, which included some very large vessels, are particularly noteworthy; the average size was similar to that of the steamships imported. This indicates that the Danish economy was marked by a high level of specialisation after the turn of the century. Vessels of 1,000 NRT and over were sold by Danish shipyards to foreign shipowners and were bought by Danish shipowners from abroad. Presumably the Danes were also buying vessels of this size to a more limited extent from Danish shipyards.

We may sum up by saying that this part of the study suggests an answer to Rosenberg's question 'How slow is slow?' It is difficult to regard rates of renewal of over 40 % by numbers of vessels and over 45 % by tonnage as reflecting a particularly slow pace of change. In the eyes of contemporaries at least this sort of tardiness must have seemed rapid enough.

It is also possible to perceive certain tendencies towards discontinuity. More will be said about this below, however, where some attempt will be made to elucidate the question of the extent to which sail and steam did in fact compete with one another.

IV

The statistical material available permits the classification of the merchant fleet according to size, although the boundaries do shift as the period proceeds. From the end of the 1860s onwards, however, the categories 4—20, 21—50, 51—100, 101—300, 301—500 and >500 NRT can be employed, while from the second half of the 1880s it is possible in addition to specify the bigger vessels a little more closely.

We may begin by noting fairly sharp differences in the orders of size of the sailing- and steamship fleets respectively, as these are disclosed by examining the situations in two selected years at the beginning and end of the period (percentage distribution):

DANISH MERCHANT FLEET

1875 Sailing-ships	4—20 (NRT)	21—50 (NRT)	51—100 (NRT)	101—300 (NRT)	301—500 (NRT)	>500 (NRT)	Total
No. of ships	39.8	19.5	14.8	23.3	2.0	0.6	100.0
Aggregate tonnage	5.7	8.6	16.2	52.8	10.1	6.5	100.0
Steamships							
No. of ships	21.6	10.8	15.0	26.8	7.8	18.0	100.0
Aggregate tonnage	1.0	1.5	4.6	20.1	13.3	59.5	100.0
1900 *Sailing-ships*							
No. of ships	61.5	19.9	5.4	10.8	1.1	1.3	100.0
Aggregate tonnage	11.5	12.9	8.4	36.7	8.1	22.4	100.0
Steamships							
No. of ships	20.9	8.7	5.8	17.0	9.5	38.1	100.0
Aggregate tonnage	0.4	0.5	0.9	5.8	7.4	85.0	100.0

The sailing-ship fleet is characterised by the large proportion of quite small vessels; in tonnage terms the main weight falls in the 101—300 NRT category. The average size of all sailing-ships was 70 NRT in 1875 and 49 in 1900. The steamship fleet shows a somewhat more even distribution of vessels between the different size-categories; the largest number of vessels is to be found in the 101—300 NRT category in 1875 but in the >500 NRT category in 1900. In terms of tonnage it was the very biggest ships that were dominant: they represented 60 % of the total tonnage of the steamship fleet in 1875 and 85 % in 1900.

In order to arrive at a more manageable system of classification for further analysis of the size-structure it seems reasonable to set the 'small sailing-ship' limit at 50 NRT and the 'small steamship' limit at 100. The 'medium-size' limits can be put at 51—300 NRT for sailing-ships and 101—500 NRT for steamships. The average size of ships in these classes did not change very much during the course of the period under review and was somewhere around the mid-point of the respective classes.

However, the very biggest ships present considerable difficulties; the average size of steamships of over 500 tons and of sailing-ships of over 300 NRT moved as follows:

| | Sailing-ships >300 NRT | | Steamships >500 NRT | |
Year	Number	Average size	Number	Average size
1870	56	430	5	574
75	75	452	30	780
80	77	451	42	735
85	69	428	70	815
90	90	482	86	845
95	108	572	111	865
1900	70	641	184	1,141
05	41	866	255	1,142
10	21	755	323	1,136

The average size of these big sailing-ships was quite stable until about 1890. A rise of about 12—15 % then ensued in the next two five-year periods, culminated in a 35 % increase in 1900-05 and was then followed by a fall. It should be noted that the number of ships expanded considerably as well in 1885—95, whereas the subsequent rise in average size coincided with a sharp drop in the number of ships. This calls for placing sailing-ships in three categories (< 50, 51—300 and >300 NRT) up to the end of the eighties but adding a 'very large' category of ship thereafter.

Steamships, on the other hand, show a substantial rise amounting to 36 and 32 % in the first half of the seventies and the second half of the nineties respectively. And in the case of steamships likewise it seems inexpedient to apply only a single system of classification: a threefold division (< 100, 101—500 and >500 NRT) works well enough until the mid-nineties, but thereafter a further category of 'very large ships' — i.e., >1,000 NRT — has to be added.[22]

It seems clear that the pattern of development of large steamships was marked by discontinuities. There were two brief periods when vessels of a different order of size were being bought in large numbers; these were followed by a somewhat longer period when large purchases continued but with a slower rate of increase in the average size of vessel. These circumstances may be interpreted as indicating that in the two brief periods mentioned there was a swift introduction of new technology. In both cases this qualitative change was followed by a less dramatic succession of events, chiefly of a quantitative character.

Sailing-vessels, too, experienced a short period of sudden growth in the years around 1890. However, discontinuity is not quite so much in evidence; the rise is attributable chiefly to an increase in the number of ships in the size-category 501—1,000 NRT, which does not necessarily imply a qualitative change of the same

---

[22] Prior to 1870 the size-structure of the steamship fleet does not seem to differ essentially from that of the sailing-ship fleet, but in the first half of the seventies the average size of large Danish steamships clearly increased substantially. However, this fact does not justify changing the classification, since the *Statistisk Tabelværk* classification in the period prior to 1869 differs so widely from subsequent practice that it cannot be used in the present context.

Diagrams 3a and b. Tonnages in the Danish merchant fleet 1865—1910 (NRT) Size-categories: small and medium-size ships

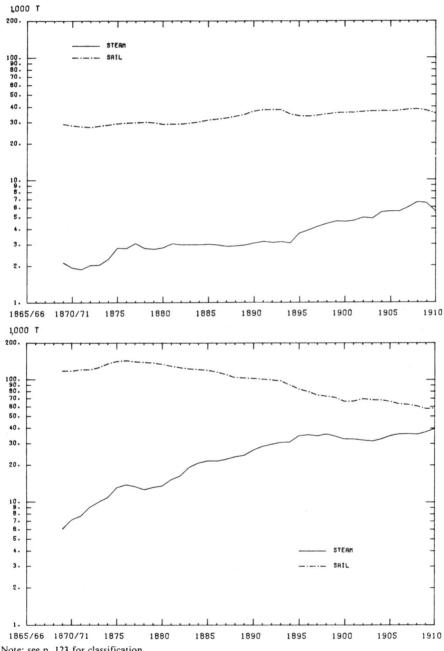

Note: see p. 123 for classification
Source: See Note 18

type as in the case of steam vessels. However, an entirely new type of sailing-ship also appeared on the scene.[23] In 1888 there were only two sailing-ships in the Danish merchant fleet of over 1,000 NRT, but by 1893 there were nine, and the number went on to reach a peak of 13 in 1897. After the turn of the century there was a decline to seven in 1910; at this point, moreover, all the sailing-ships in the 501— 1,000 NRT category had been sold. It is to be presumed that in the case of sailing-ships, too, some qualitative technological innovation must have been introduced in the course of the brief period mentioned, but in contrast to what happened with steamships the change did not produce any significant quantitative repercussions.

The general trend of tonnages in the various size-categories is shown by Diagram 3. There are obvious differences in the sail/steam ratio within the various classes, and it is generally true that the larger the vessel, the greater the degree of steam dominance. In the 'small' and 'medium-sized' categories of vessels, sail-tonnage still exceeded steam at the end of the period, and indeed small sailing-vessels were increasing throughout the period. These vessels particularly must have been operating in a sector of the transport industry — probably coastal traffic between Danish ports for the most part — where the shift from sail to steam technology was very limited.

There is an obvious tendency in the 'large' and 'very large' categories for sailing-ships to disappear from the picture completely towards the end of the period. The line of demarcation can be discerned clearly in the second half of the 1890s; before then the aggregate tonnage of large sailing-ships was declining slowly, and around 1890 there came the short-lived but almost explosive rise in numbers of very large sailing-ships. But in 1895, or some years later in the case of very large sailing-ships, the turning-point came in the shape of rapid and persistent decline.

Our analysis has thus shown that the real transition from sail to steam was completed in the second half of the 1890s. But it has likewise shown that sailing-ship technology offered scope for development for a long time and that the conditions of competition were complex. It would therefore seem natural to try in the last case-study to form a clearer impression of the nature of the competitive situation actually prevailing between sail and steam on various maritime trade routes.

V

The transition from sail to steam is clearly reflected in the figures of tonnage engaged in shipping. For example, if one looks at the aggregate tonnage under the Danish flag departing from Denmark for foreign destinations, the trend for sailing-vessels is seen to be stagnant and eventually downward, whereas steam-tonnage steadily rises (Diagram 4). Perhaps the most notable deviation from Diagram 1 is that the immensely increased rate of growth of steam-tonnage in the merchant fleet from the mid-nineties has no counterpart in any equivalent increase of direct Danish

---

[23] What is particularly in mind here is the introduction of iron- and steel-hulled sailing-ships after 1886, cf. e.g. *Statistisk Tabelværk*, 4 ser. letter D, no. 29 (1897), introduction, p. 11*.

Diagrams 3c and d. Tonnages in the Danish merchant fleet 1865—1910 (NRT) Size-categories: large and very large ships.

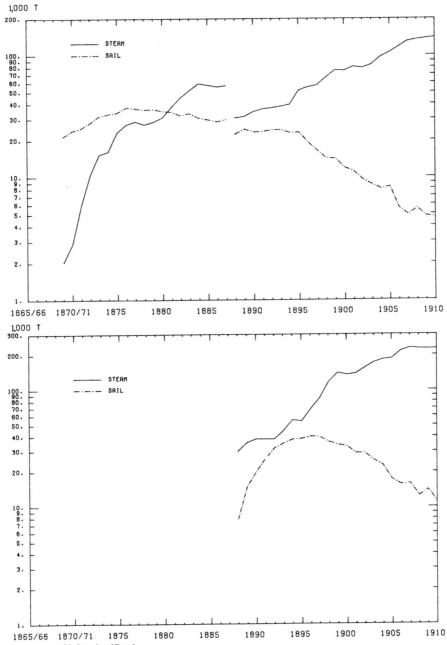

Note: see p. 123 for classification
Source: See Note 18

traffic between Denmark and other countries (nor in coastal traffic either), so that it may be regarded more as a manifestation of a growing Danish involvement in the steamship traffic between foreign ports.[24]

The overall trend of tonnage in the shipping industry, however, will not be pursued in the present context, where the main objective is a preliminary identification of the respective functions of sail- and steam-vessels. The usefulness of the tonnage criterion is reduced by the imperfections of the statistics of steamship tonnage in service up to 1874—75 and by the difficulties involved in employing common conversion factors in order to equate the effective sail and steam tonnages. If instead of this we turn our attention to the transport services performed by the two categories of ship, it lays near at hand to test possibilities afforded by shipping statistics for tracing the trend of the volume of goods traffic, the more so since it is known that on average the degree of stowage capacity utilisation was considerably higher in sailing ships than in steamships.[25] On the other hand the steadily increasing importance of steamships with regard to passenger and postal traffic will not be gone into here.

Five three-year periods at ten-year intervals have been selected with a view to illustrating the long-term structural changes in the ratio between sail and steam and to revealing the contours of a possible specialisation of functions. What has been studied for these years is the ratio between the effective transport of goods under the Danish flag by sailing- and steamships respectively in the traffic between Denmark and its most important trading partners, the total share taken by Danish ships in the traffic between Denmark and each of the other countries individually, and finally the volume of goods exchanged with the individual countries as a proportion of Denmark's aggregate seaward trade in the years in question. (Table 3).

Outward cargoes for the three-year period 1865—66/1867—68 averaged 353,000 register tons. If this figure is taken as 100, then the quantities for the subsequent four selected periods are respectively 114.7, 146.1, 181.8 and 329.1. The corresponding inward cargoes for the three-year period 1865—66/1867—68 averaged 716,000 register tons, and the index figures for the subsequent periods are respectively 157.5, 236.6, 337.7 and 517.2. It should be observed that the figures — especially for steamship traffic — probably underestimate the trend. The cargo figures reported will often be too small, since the cargo stowed aboard fully-laden

---

[24] Until 1905 Danish consuls in foreign ports had to send in annual reports of Danish ships calling at the ports in question. However, both the collection and the processing of these data were so defective that the published shipping statistics do not offer scope for any sort of reliable estimate of the transport services provided in these years by Danish ships in traffic between foreign ports. From 1905 onwards shipping companies were obliged to submit statistics of vessels of 20 GRT and over involved in foreign traffic, and according to the returns based on these (which are still far from reliable) no less than 64 % of the volume of goods carried in Danish ships in 1905 consisted of cargoes moving between foreign ports; of this quantity sailing-ships accounted for 14 %. In these circumstances the results of the present study cannot of course be regarded as conclusive with respect to the development of Danish shipping during the period; however, it must again be underlined that the main objective here is to shed light on the *technological transition*. Cf. *Statistisk Tabelværk*, V D, 17, pp. 19* and 29* ff.

[25] See the introductions to *Statistisk Tabelværk* for the years concerned.

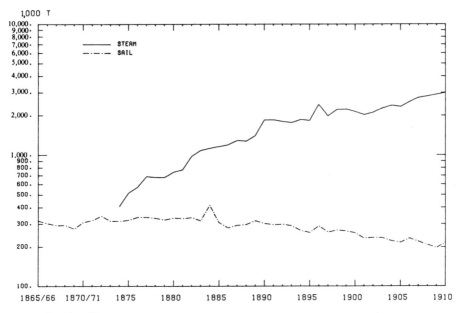

Diagram 4. *Danish sail and steam tonnage in traffic between Danish and foreign ports. Ship departures (NRT)*

Source: See Note 18

ships is recorded as equivalent to the ship's net tonnage, although the quantity of merchandise actually taken on board could be up to twice as much. This applies particularly to steamship cargoes.[26]

Another factor possibly contributing to an understating of the importance of steamship traffic is the fact that although barges and lighters were often towed by steam tugs, they were consistently assigned to the sailing-ship category as long as they were equipped with oars, mast and sails. Finally, it should be remarked that the 'sailing-ship' category in shipping statistics includes motor vessels, which in the period studied, however, were used principally in fishing.[27]

Table 3 generally confirms the conception of a steadily increasing share of freights to and from Denmark being accounted for by steamships, but it also discloses notable differences between the trades with individual towns and countries as regards the tempo and to some extent the tendency of the transition. Even during the first three-year period studied Danish steamships were responsible for a vital share of the goods traffic with western and southern Swedish ports and German

---

[26] cf. e.g. *Statistisk Tabelværk*, V D, 27, p. 21*.
[27] Motor vessels at the end of 1910 formed 25.1 % of the number and 7.8 % of the tonnage of the aggregate Danish sail and motor fleet; the largest motorship was of 153 NRT. See also note 18.

Table 3. *Traffic between Denmark and abroad 1865-66/67-68—1905/07*

A. Stowage of ships arrived. Percentages of three-year averages.
 1. Share of sailing-ships in traffic under Danish flag with country of departure.
 2. Share of Danish sailing- and steamships in total traffic with country of departure.
 3. Traffic with country of departure as a proportion of aggregate inward traffic.

Country of departure	1865-66/67-68			1875/77			1885/87			1895/97[1]			1905/07		
	1	2	3	1	2	3	1	2	3	1	2	3	1	2	3
Schleswig-Holstein	74.4	77.4	7.8	48.5	81.1	4.1	55.8	77.2	3.1	74.6	73.0	2.0	77.6	60.4	0.9
Lübeck	57.4	46.6	1.4	48.5	26.7	1.1	24.3	27.1	1.3	20.3	29.3	1.2	41.7	25.7	1.0
Hamburg	100	14.1	0.5	100	5.0	0.7	6.1	54.7	0.9	3.5	65.0	2.9	5.2	48.2	4.8
Rest of Germany[2]	79.8	20.4	5.1	49.5	39.4	5.7	29.7	48.4	8.0	30.4	44.3	7.3	20.0	49.7	9.0
Norway	88.2	19.9	12.2	55.0	29.6	5.5	29.0	39.1	2.7	21.7	36.0	1.5	13.1	28.6	1.5
Sweden	57.0	15.1	16.9	42.6	27.2	21.6	37.9	36.4	18.3	25.1	43.7	16.3	15.1	49.0	17.1
Russia[3]	99.6	18.6	4.4	79.2	28.6	4.9	23.9	38.3	6.2	25.0	28.5	9.1	11.2	28.1	6.3
Great Britain	93.7	49.6	43.9	66.1	50.8	49.6	35.9	46.4	48.8	18.0	46.4	47.1	6.6	59.8	42.0
Holland	92.8	18.9	1.3	73.3	23.6	1.2	93.8	15.1	1.1	59.6	12.0	0.7	7.2	7.5	1.4
USA	100	52.4	0.1	100	12.3	1.7	0.9	42.2	4.4	2.4	43.2	6.1	0.0	53.0	12.0
Overseas regions[4]	100	67.6	2.3	98.5	48.2	1.1	100	24.8	0.9	80.9	8.6	0.9	5.8	17.9	0.5
Nordic dependencies[5]	98.2	100	0.8	97.2	99.7	0.7	76.7	96.3	0.5	46.0	80.0	0.5	7.2	83.3	0.6
Total			96.7			97.9			96.2			95.6			97.1

Notes: [1] In 1894—96 the Copenhagen Freeport was regarded as abroad for statistical purposes inasmuch as the traffic between customs-dutiable territory (including Copenhagen) and the Freeport was included in the traffic between Danish and foreign ports, while at the same time traffic between the Freeport and true foreign ports was not recorded. From 1897 onwards the Freeport is treated in the statistics like any other Danish port. As a result the impression of direct imports into Denmark from overseas regions may possibly be undervalued a little.
[2] Here reckoned as corresponding to Prussia in the periods 1865—66/67—68 and 1875/77.
[3] Including Finland.
[4] Comprises non-European regions with the exception of the United States but including the Danish West Indies.
[5] Comprises the Faroes, Iceland and Greenland, which were part of the Danish realm.

Source: See Note 18.

B. Stowage of ships departed. Percentages of three-year averages.

1. Share of sailing-ships in traffic under Danish flag with country of destination.
2. Share of Danish sailing- and steamships in total traffic with country of destination.
3. Traffic with country of destination as a proportion of aggregate outward traffic.

Country of destination	1865-66/67-68			1875/77			1885/87			1895/97[1]			1905/07		
	1	2	3	1	2	3	1	2	3	1	2	3	1	2	3
Schleswig-Holstein	73.8	69.6	19.3	57.7	76.1	14.4	24.4	87.3	10.2	38.5	67.0	9.2	70.2	25.9	7.0
Lübeck	58.2	54.8	2.2	62.2	56.6	1.9	31.8	40.8	1.6	26.9	36.4	2.1	18.8	37.8	1.5
Hamburg	100	11.2	0.4	94.1	6.0	0.4	3.2	52.4	1.1	1.4	86.0	5.5	3.7	73.7	3.9
Rest of Germany[2]	64.3	26.1	2.8	59.4	46.1	6.7	24.5	60.3	9.5	32.4	50.0	14.0	17.4	61.4	15.5
Norway	88.5	54.6	12.1	43.8	68.2	10.6	25.1	77.2	5.8	42.4	72.3	4.4	25.1	65.3	4.1
Sweden	50.3	18.6	9.0	15.9	37.6	16.6	24.3	54.9	18.4	17.1	55.2	15.2	10.7	49.8	17.8
Russia[3]	98.4	15.6	1.1	71.7	54.6	1.7	28.8	69.9	3.7	20.2	68.6	8.6	5.7	51.2	9.6
Great Britain	93.2	72.4	42.3	38.0	67.6	40.9	11.7	80.6	35.9	2.7	75.7	29.7	1.0	78.1	24.3
Holland	98.9	45.8	3.5	78.0	32.7	1.0	84.2	39.2	0.8	27.3	19.2	0.6	63.6	35.4	0.4
USA	—	0.0	0.1	100	1.7	0.1	—	13.4	4.5	0.6	90.3	3.6	—	99.7	8.7
Overseas regions[4]	100	99.9	0.8	100	74.1	0.4	100	95.8	0.3	92.6	98.2	0.2	3.3	80.3	1.7
Nordic dependencies[5]	99.6	99.5	3.3	90.1	99.5	3.3	10.3	98.8	3.0	52.6	85.7	2.9	11.6	85.3	3.0
Total			96.9			98.0			94.8			96.0			97.5

Note: See notes to Table 3A.
Source: See Note 18.

Baltic ports. In the following ten-year period steamships gained much ground in the traffic with the neighbouring countries of Norway and Sweden, and something of the same can be said of the traffic with Great Britain, especially in the outward direction. The latter is undoubtedly to be viewed in the context of the orientation of Danish agricultural exports towards livestock products shipped directly to Great Britain and the opening of the port of Esbjerg on the west coast of Jutland in 1874 as the increasingly important gateway for the trade.[28]

During the interval between 1875/77 and 1885/87 sailing-ships lost ground heavily in the traffic between Denmark and Russia, Hamburg and the United States, while at the same time regular steamship services were being established on those same routes.[29] In the next decade, however, there was a slowing-down of the switch-over from sail to steam, apparently related in part to the development of bigger and technologically more advanced sailing-ships coinciding with a reduced demand for transport on the established steamship routes.[30]

Finally, the table shows that Danish shipping traffic with the Nordic dependencies and overseas regions in the years around the turn of the century underwent a drastic shift from sail to steam. It may be noted that the traffic between Denmark and Holland, which constituted only a minor part of the total business, displays wide fluctuations throughout the period of study.

The overall trend accords well in its main features, but with variations of tempo, with the internationally accepted picture in which 'steamships gradually displaced sail first on the short trades and then on the long'.[31] Nevertheless Table 3 also bears witness to another tendency working in the opposite direction. Even if we ignore the figures for the less important trading partners where the situation, as in the case of Holland, is often characterised by wide and possibly fortuitous fluctuations, there remain nonetheless a number of instances where a temporary or even persistent return from steam to sail is observable. The inward trade from Schleswig-Holstein shows a marked trend in this direction as early as 1875/77—1885/87, followed by the outward trade from 1885/87—1895/97 and on to the end of our period of study. During the period 1885/87—95/97 likewise, sail accounted for an increasing share of cargoes shipped to 'the rest of Germany', of inward traffic from Russia and outward traffic to Norway. A similar trend developed in the Hamburg trade and in the inward trade from Lübeck during the period around the turn of the century, while the tendency already present in the Schleswig-Holstein traffic, especially in the outward traffic, was reinforced.

---

[28] See B. N. Thomsen & B. Thomas, *Dansk-engelsk samhandel 1661—1963*, Århus 1966, p. 130 f. *et passim*.
[29] J. Schovelin, *op.cit.*, p. 13 ff.
[30] K. Klem, *op.cit.*, p. 148 and J. Schovelin, *op.cit.*, p. 30.
[31] C. Harley, *loc.cit.*, p. 225.

We can establish that where an increased share of Danish shipping traffic with the countries and cities in question was accounted for by sailing vessels, this was accompanied by a diminution of the Danish share of the aggregate traffic with the locality concerned and — usually — a decline in the proportion of Denmark's total shipping traffic for which the trade in question was responsible. There are exceptions to this, however, the most striking being the outward traffic to Sweden in the period 1875/77—1885/87. The explanation is probably to be found in the vastly increased Danish exports to Sweden of heavy goods such as coal, corn and bricks during this period: sailing-ships at this time were often extremely competitive where the transport of these types of goods were concerned.[32]

Danish coastal shipping generally repeated the broad pattern of the foreign trades. As early as 1865/67 36.5 % of domestic seaborne goods were carried in steamships, almost all of them Danish, whereas both Danish and foreign steamships together still took at this time only 17.1 % of inward and outward cargoes between Danish and foreign ports. The share taken by steam rose steadily but not particularly rapidly in the next decades, until a definite stagnation supervened in 1895/97—1905/07. This is shown clearly by the following averages for inward and outward cargoes in the trade between Danish ports (percentage figures of three-year averages):

	1865/67	1875/77	1885/87	1895/97	1905/07
Sail	63.5	51.1	43.4	33.9	32.8
Steam	36.5	48.9	56.6	66.1	67.2

In evaluating these figures, however, account must be taken of the fact that steam ferry traffic, not included here, grew in importance throughout the period and in 1905/07 was conveying about half the goods moving in domestic traffic. The increase in the transport of goods between Danish ports was significantly slower than that between Danish and foreign ports; if the average for inward and outward cargoes in the trade between Danish ports in 1865/67 (563,000 register tons) is put at 100, then the figures for the next four selected three-year periods become 115.5, 134.8, 198.4 and 237.9, to which must be added the quantities of goods carried by steamferries. Steamships particularly became more and more aware of the at times heavy-handed competition of the railway network, and from the 1890s onwards there was a gradual reduction of regular domestic steamship services, with the general result that traffic became concentrated upon the bigger internal ports.

---

[32] *Statistisk Tabelværk* (Handels- og Skibsfartsstatistikken) for the years concerned; K. Klem, op.cit., p. 195.

This summary thus demonstrates that even after the last overseas bastions fell about and also after the turn of the century, sail still had its strongholds in domestic trade and in the traffic with the Swedish and Norwegian ports of the Kattegat and the Sound as well as with the western Baltic.[33] Steamships had spread themselves like rings of water, but it is evident that in the original centre smooth water could be found for an 'old' technology. As the average size, capacity and operational radius of steamships increased, so was the attention of the shipowning companies drawn away from some of the nearer destinations, which were simultaneously declining in importance relative to Danish shipping as a whole. The big money was to be made in the big ports, and it was on these latter that the interest of the steamship companies became concentrated for a time.

VI

The present study must be regarded primarily as a necessary staking-out of territory for subsequent exploration. The account given of the pace and scope of the transition (especially the emphasis laid on a number of short and apparently crucial periods), and the rudimentary explanations in terms of functional analysis, are offered as points of departure for future and more detailed studies.

It seems a particularly attractive prospect to seek some clarification of the question to what extent the pattern of events in Denmark is attributable to direct technological substitution in a competitive situation where the falling costs of the new means of transport permitted it to take over in a continuous run large parts of the existing transport market — and how far the victory of the steamships resulted from the fact that new transport technology, closely allied with other changes of the same type in the production processes, was alone capable of meeting the new transport needs, while at the same time the old technology melted away because its secure field of operations increasingly lost importance in step with the modernisation of the economy.

---

[33] cf. p. 126.

[20]

The SCANDINAVIAN ECONOMIC HISTORY REVIEW
and
ECONOMY AND HISTORY

VOL. XXXIII, NO: 2 1985

Technological Transformation in the Norwegian Whaling Industry in the Interwar Period

by

BJØRN L. BASBERG*

Introduction
Inventions, innovations and technological changes in the broadest sense are often treated as an independent process and are not subjected to any detailed attempts at explanation. It is scarcely anything exceptional, for example, that Sigurd Risting, the first historian of the whaling industry in Norway, explains the development of whaling as follows:

> 'Thus there has been a large stock of finback whales along the coast of Norway for hundreds of years without their having been an object of regular profitable hunting. The reason for this has been nothing more than lack of tackle and methods capable of making hunting possible. The moment these become available, whaling as a rational business will arise by itself out of natural necessity, so to speak.'[1]

---

* Bjørn L. Basberg, b. 1952, is a research fellow in economic history at the Norwegian School of Economic and Business Administration. The article is based on a thesis of 1980 titled: *Innovasjons-teori, patenter og teknologisk utvikling i norsk hvalfangst ca. 1860–1968.*

1. S. Risting, *Av hvalfangstens historie,* Kristiania 1922, p. 103.

No attempt is made to say anything about the mechanisms which led to the invention, application and dissemination of the tackle. Neither are any questions posed over inventions having been made at one point in time and not at another. Such questions form the starting point of this article, however.

We begin with a description of the technological development of the modern Norwegian whaling industry from about 1880 to 1968 as far as this is disclosed by the patent statistics. The use of this type of data generally suffers from a number of well-known weaknesses which may be difficult to overcome by the use of aggregated data.[2] With regard to patents associated with the Norwegian whaling industry, studies indicate that the picture of developments given by the aggregated figures agrees to a large extent with the picture produced by other measures of technological change.

The intervals between invention, patent, innovation and diffusion also appear to have been particularly brief in this industry. It looks as though a basic innovation tends to be located in time somewhere near the centre of a cluster of patents linked with it. Further on in the present article we shall cite a few indications of such conformity.[3]

After having offered a presentation of the patent data, we shall compare the fluctuations of the patents over time with measures of investment activity, whale oil production and prices in the form of correlation and regression calculations for the period from 1880 to 1968. The discussion will be aimed primarily at elucidating and suggesting answers to the question of how variations in technological development are to be explained. Is the direction of causality *from* technological change *to* change in economic variables or the reverse? Can technological changes be related in any way to fluctuations in business conditions?[4]

The time-span from 1880 to 1968 will be divided into three periods. It is customary to speak in terms of a single period up to about 1905, when catching on the coast of Finnmark was prohibited (1904) and whaling in the Antarctic gradually began. The year 1923 may also be regarded as the point of transition to a new period: the pelagic, when whaling became independent of land stations based upon British concessions. The division into periods thus becomes a) 1880–1905, b) 1906–1922 and c) 1923–1968.

---

2. The most exhaustive study of patents used as a technology indicator is still J. Schmookler, *Invention and Economic Growth*, Cambridge, Mass. 1966, which also examines critically the usefulness of the data. A review of the commonest arguments for and against this method of measuring technological change is to be found in L.J. Harris et al., *The Meaning of Patent Statistics*, (National Science Foundation), Washington D.C. 1978, p. 39 ff. A survey of this field of research and a discussion of the collected Norwegian patent material may be found in B.L. Basberg, *Patenter og teknologisk endring i Norge 1840–1980. En metodediskusjon om patentdata anvendt som teknologi-indikator*, (Norwegian School of Economics and Business Administration), Bergen 1984.

3. For an explicit discussion of the usefulness of patent statistics as a technology indicator in this industry, see B.L. Basberg, 'Technological Change in the Norwegian Whaling Industry. A Case Study in the use of Patent Statistics as a Technology indicator', *Research Policy*, XI, 1982, p. 163 ff.

4. The discussion thereby touches on the theoretical problems that have been posed in the literature on explanations of technological change. See F. Sejersted, 'Økonomisk transformasjon. Randkommentarer til et forskningsprosjekt om krisen i 30-årene', in Sejersted (ed.), *Vekst gjennom krise. Studier i norsk teknologi-historie*, Oslo 1982, p. 270 ff.

The analysis of the patent data and relationships with economic variables will point to the 1920s and 1930s as being particularly interesting with regard to technological change. We shall therefore analyse this period in detail. In recognition that patents can hardly embrace all the phenomena relevant to forming a picture of inventive activity and innovations, technological development in the interwar period will be illustrated by other indicators as well. These are cost reductions and improved efficiency of catching, growth of tonnage, rate of renewal of material, company formation and capital deepening.

Patents

Figure 1 (a) shows numbers of whaling-related patents reported in Norway between 1880 and 1968. The curve displays wide fluctuations from year to year and well-defined peaks in the 1920s and 1930s. The curve for a ten-year moving average reveals this with extra clarity. We shall argue below that this peak gives a good indication of a crucial technological transformation. Around 1935 the industry had already attained a high level of technological maturity and perfection. The technological development that

Figure 1(a). Whaling-related patents granted in Norway 1880–1968

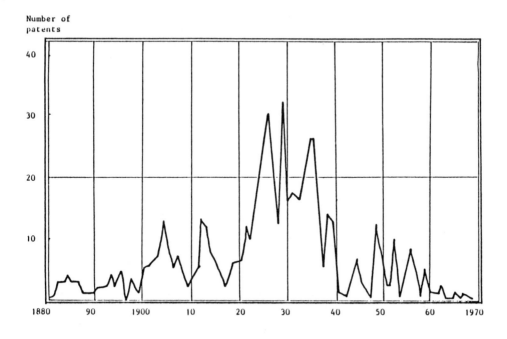

Source: Arne Odd Johnsen, *Norwegian Patents Relating to Whaling and the Whaling Industry,* Oslo 1947 and J.N. Tønnessen, unpublished works.

occured from then until the cessation of Norwegian whaling in 1968 was moderate by comparison. There is little to suggest that any lower proportion of inventions was patented during the later period such as would reflect declining inventive and innovative activity rather than a declining interest in taking out patents. The curve displays local peaks both in 1904 and in 1912. It is customary to credit both these periods with significant technological breakthroughs. Thus, the first experiments in pelagic whaling were made around 1904, and numerous technological problems were solved by patented inventions. A number of other important technical problems in the field of refining technology were solved around 1912.

Patents and investment
The first of the variables with which patents will be compared is investment. Investment is an interesting measure in itself, but it can also be an example of an endogenous economic variable and may thus be typical of the character of economic changes in the whaling industry.[5]

The measure of investment utilised here is the number of newlybuilt whaling vessels in Norway and the number of whaling vessels in Norway employed in the industry. This is obviously a more imprecise measure than total investment expressed in fixed prices. Such a measure is much more difficult to arrive at, however, and I have to assume that whaling vessel construction and whaling vessels in service constitute an acceptable substitute. This assumption may be regarded as justifiable because in the present context it is the fluctuations and changes over time that are of primary interest: total magnitudes are of less significance.

Variations in new construction from year to year were very large. The first well-defined peak occured in the 1911/12 season. This coincided with the first expansion in Antarctica and also with heavy incursions into the areas along the coasts of Australia and Africa. There followed a swift decline, then a complete halt in investment during the First World War, then afterwards the great Antarctic expansion of the 1920s. The last year of high-level investment was 1930, after which there was another fall in the early 1930s. Whaling vessel construction in Norway never thereafter reached such high levels as in 1912 and 1930. This is not in conformity with the numbers of whaling vessels in service, which are shown in figure 1(b). Here a peak likewise appears about 1950, and it also clearly reflects an investment peak. For expansion after the Second World War was based primarily on capital equipment built abroad. For example, about 50 corvettes constructed in Canada during the war were converted to whalers in the course of this postwar expansion.[6] However, the fluctuations around 1912 and 1930 are shown in both curves and support the view that the number of whaling vessels in service reflects the fluctuations in investment to a degree sufficient for this purpose.

5. See Schmookler, *op.cit.*, whose comparisons have formed the model for this section.
6. J.A. Tønnessen and A.O. Johnsen, *Den moderne hvalfangsts historie*, Sandefjord/Oslo 1959-1967, vol. IV, p. 209. Abbreviated hereafter as DMHvH.

Figure 1(b). Norwegian whaling vessels in service in all areas

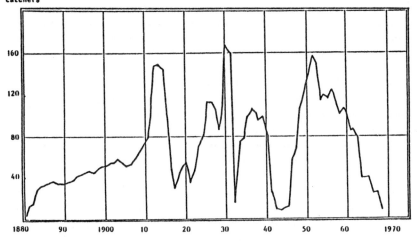

Source: IWS, II, DMHvH, p. 540, Hvf. reg. 1928, Hist. stat. tab. 128., 1968.

The correlation coefficient (r) for the whole period 1880 to 1968 between numbers of whaling-related patents taken out in Norway and numbers of whaling vessels in service is 0.42. If we break down the calculations we find that r = 0.52 in the period 1880–1905, r = 0.46 in the period 1906–1922 and r = 0.31 for the period 1923–1968. This applies to comparisons for the same year, viz. patents taken out in a particular year correlated with whaling vessels in service the same year. However, the correlation coefficient is somewhat higher when the patents for the year are compared with whaling vessels a year later: r = 0.48 for the entire period and 0.63, 0.31 and 0.4 respectively for the three part-periods. Two reasons can be adduced for this. Firstly, whaling vessels in service in the 1929/30 season, for example, are plotted in 1930. This explains some of the timeshift. Another cause is that a peak in the number of whaling vessels in service will follow after a peak in investment. If one assumes that the link between patenting activity and investment is not fortuitous, this too will result in a time-shift.

A comparison of whaling vessels in service with patents taken out two years previously likewise gives correlations of over 0.4. Correlation calculations have also been made between patents and new construction of whaling vessels. For the whole period from 1880 to 1968, r = 0.47. In the first and the third period, r = 0.63 and 0.68. In the second period (1906–1922), r = 0.07.[7]

A question mark can be placed over whether it is correct to make a correlation between patents and investments in the same year. One can assume alternative hypotheses which are based both on the supposition that patents in several preceding years will affect the behaviour of investment and on its reverse, viz. that investment during several previous years will affect patenting activity. Thus, both patents and investment can be selected as

7. The extremely low correlation in the time around the expansion after 1910 can also be seen in the first calculation. For whaling vessels in service compared with patents taken out two years previously in the period 1906–1922, r = 0.09. This is markedly lower than for the other part-periods.

the independent variable. Correlation calculations with one-, two- and three-year time-shifts are made, but r never becomes as high as when comparison is made in the same year.

Furthermore it may be queried whether instead of the year of construction (year of delivery) of whaling vessels it would be more correct to use the year of contract (the time of decision) in the comparison with patents. Contracts for whaling vessels could easily be placed from one to three years prior to delivery. Nor does such a correlation calculation give r values similar to those produced by calculations in the same year.

Thus it is impossible to draw from these calculations any conclusions about the causal relationships between the two variables patents and investment (measured in terms of whaling vessels in service and whaling vessel construction). The most that can be said is that a certain degree of co-variation appears to be present. However, a correlation coefficient that broadly speaking varies between 0.4 and 0.5 does not furnish a basis for firm conclusions.

Neither does it appear possible from this to say anything about causal relationships.

Visual inspection of figure 1(b) suggests that other variables must be brought in as explanatory factors and that investment and patents must be explained different. The heavy investment in materiel in the years 1912-1914 and in the early 1950s finds no counterpart in sharply increased patent figures: there is some increase, but not of the same order. As far as the first expansion is concerned, an explanation of the deviation can be advanced in the lack of any challenge to the whaling industry during this period to rationalise and improve its catching gear and methods. For the changeover to whaling in Antarctica represented no difficulties or novelties compared with whaling off Finnmark. Hunting was conducted from land stations according to exactly the same principles as from Finnmark. There was only a brief period around 1905 when, exceptionally, pelagic hunting took place (off Bjørnøya and Spitsbergen), and Johnsen suggests this as a possible cause of the slight rise in patenting activity in the years around 1905.[8] The investment theme was a factor, however: the price of whale oil was rising almost throughout the period up to 1920. Most of the companies were expanding and new ones emerging until the First World War.

A similar explanation can be adduced for the expansion of capital equipment up to 1950. After the Second World War there was a need for the renewal of equipment coinciding with rising prices and an atmosphere of optimism. This expansion likewise failed to offer any technological challenges.

Only in the 1920s and 1930s can it be said that the fluctuations in patents and investments followed each other to a very marked degree, and the next section will attempt to explain in detail how and why this period seems to mark itself off from the rest of the history of the whaling industry.

Patents and production

The need and demand for the products of the whaling industry may be regarded as a central quantity in attempting to explain technological development. Production can be

---

8. A.O. Johnsen, *Norwegian Patents Relating to the Whaling and the Whaling Industry*, Oslo 1947, p. 33 and 36.

viewed as an expression of realised demand and will be compared with patents in this section.

Oil production is shown in figure 1(c). The figures go back only to 1900, so that whaling off Finnmark falls outside their scope. As the curve demonstrates, oil production was level at first, then rose quickly until the peak season of 1912/13. Production then fell until the end of the First World War, after which it rose sharply and almost without interruption all through the 1920s.[9]

Figure 1(c).   Patents and whale oil production

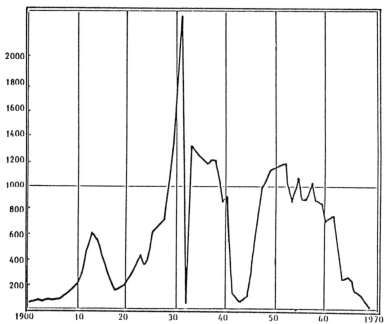

Source: For production
1900-1909: DMHvH, II, p. 585,
1910-1968: Historisk statistikk, tab. 128.

Note: Production figures for 1900-1909 are for all companies in all areas. Subsequent data are for Norwegian companies in all areas.

9. The 1923/24 season was the only one to show a slight decline attributable to specially severe weather and ice conditions. *The Norwegian Whaling Gazette* (abbreviated below to NWG), no. 5, 1924.

After the laying-up season of 1931/32 production reached only a little more than half of its peak of 1931 and went into a sharp decline until the Second World War, when whaling virtually ceased. There was then a marked expansion from 1946 to 1952. Production held up through the 1950s, then fell off dramatically in the 1960s.

The up- and downswings of catching and production are the factors that generally constitute the background for speaking of expansion and crisis in the industry. Tønnesen, for example, uses the following scheme, which can be viewed in conjunction with the production figures:

Expansion 1906-14
Crisis after the First World War
Expansion 1927-31
Crisis 1931-34
Crisis 1937-39
The penultimate expansion 1946-52
The final expansion 1955-61
Collapse 1962-68[10]

A connection with patent variations can be seen directly from the figure. In the 1920s and early 1930s both curves reach their highest levels. On the other hand the postwar period shows differing levels. Both curves move upward around 1950, but the increase in production is much more pronounced. Here too the comparison with patent variations is made by correlation calculations. For the period 1900 to 1968 as a whole the correlation is strongest if the production of a particular year is compared with the patents reported two years earlier, $r = 0.54$. When compared with patents taken out in the same year, $r = 0.39$.

The same applies to the individual periods. The correlation is strongest when a 'time-lag' is introduced. During the period 1900 to 1905, which obviously is too short for special weight to be attached to it, $r = 0.90$ for production compared with patents one year in advance. The same applies to the period 1906-1922. The highest figure for r is 0.59. For the final period 1923-1968 the connection is strongest for production and patents reported two years earlier, $r = 0.52$.

Thus the calculations show that patent activity seems to fluctuate in advance of production by one and two years. This is also the result one arrives at if one attempts to compare the turning points of the curves.[11] This appears to point in the same direction as the correlation calculations, with reservations for the uncertainties involved in such a mode of measurement. Broadly speaking the patent curve turns between one and three years prior to the curve for production.

10. DMHvH, II, p. 494, III pp. 179, 339, 384 and IV pp. 35, 230, 328, 472.
11. The use of curve turning point analysis is inspired by Schmookler, *op.cit.*

A correlation coefficient of only a little over 0.5 cannot be considered to evidence any strong co-variation, and again conclusions must be drawn with caution. The result appears to point in the opposite direction to J. Schmookler's studies in other industries, for example, which conclude that production fluctuates before patents. He cites this as supporting the view that variations in patenting activity follow in consequence of changed production and demand.[12]

Johnsen holds a view similar to Schmookler's and he interprets the relationship between the fluctuations of patents and production before 1935 in the following terms:

'...the patents-activity – which in our days is practically identical with inventive activity – in this sphere has been produced by and has been greatly dependent on the catch conditions. These have in their turn been dependent on certain material conditions, such as the size of the stocks of whales on the various whaling grounds and of the prevailing demand for fats.'[13]

He generalises further:

'This result is of general interest. (...) We should be able to establish something substantial concerning the relation between matter and idea, i.e. between the material conditions and the inventive activity, namely that the latter when it appears intensively is a direct consequence of the former. Such a result would undeniably be a weighty argument in favour of a materialistic view of history. It would take away something of the halo attaching to the idea, to the individual invention, but at the same time would bear powerful witness to the elasticity and perfectibility of the human spirit, to its phenomenal power of adapting itself to the ever changing material conditions.'[14]

The correlation calculations are unable to offer support to such a view. It appears rather that technological development measured by patents helps at times to make the good catch results possible.

K. Brandt has offered such an explanation:

'Through the centuries there has always been demand for whale oil. This demand changed in intensity and in volume according to a variety of different factors and their relative weight. The potential demand depends first of all on the technical usefulness of the commodity. Remarkable changes in its technical utility have taken place during the past two decades, as new inventions in the processing and further utilisation of whale oil have opened up the demand on a broader scale for new purposes.'[15]

12. *Ibid.*
13. Johnsen, *op.cit.* p. 35.
14. *Ibid.* p. 36.
15. K. Brandt, *Whale Oil – An Economic Analysis*, Stanford 1940, p. 133.

The deviation between the curves for oil production and patents in the 1950s also contradicts Johnsen's conclusions. Despite the fact that the correlation is in excess of 0.5, the levels are extremely dissimilar, as has been noted. The same explanation as was adduced in the last section for the deviation between patent activity and investment can be invoked here. Again it tends to suggest that an explanation of the patents' variations must be sought in terms of relationships with other variables. In the next section the prices of whale oil will be brought in so as to be able perhaps to say something more detailed about this.

Patents and prices

Prices of whale oil from 1880 to 1968 are given in figure 1 (d). The main fluctuations consist of a fall from the beginning of the period until 1905. There is than a rise until 1920, when prices fall drastically until 1922 in conjunction with the international crisis. Thereafter they tend to vary and sag right through to 1934. The main trend after that is a rising one until about 1950. The fluctuations are wide through the 1950s and 1960s, but the tendency is downward.

Figure 1(d)   Whale oil prices. Average no. 1, London

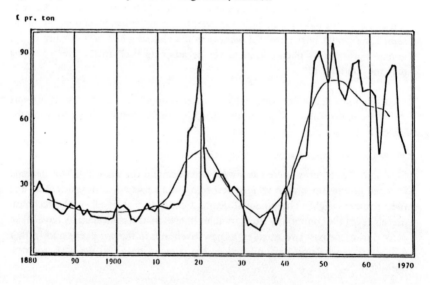

Source: K. Brandt, *Whale oil – An Economic Analysis,* Stanford 1940. D. Geddes & Son Selling Agents, *Main catch reports,* London 1946. DMHvH, I, p. 505 and IV, p. 636.

Note: The smoothed-out curve is the 10-year moving average.

It may be as well to examine prices in the 1920s a little more closely, since they will form the most important basis for the subsequent discussion of the technological tranformation in these years. It is contended that whale oil prices remained fairly stable from 1922 to 1929, and that the heavy price fall did not accur until 1930–31. Prices rose from 1922 to 1924 and from 1927 to 1928, and the dramatic decline from 1920 to 1921 did not continue. It can also be contended that the price peak of 1920 was extraordinary because of the war and that the 'ordinary' trend was thus a rising one from before the war and far on into the 1920s. Such an interpretation is hardly satisfactory. True enough there were periods when prices were rising, as the figure shows, but it is characteristic that these did not offset the heavier falls of longer duration. The overall trend from 1920 to 1934, therefore, was clearly a downward one.

It would also be unnatural to single out 1930 as the first year with a heavy price fall, even though the price curve does waver a little at that point. It would be possible to speak of a sharp decline at any rate as early as 1926. The annual report of A/S Sydhavet for the 1925/26 season expresses this: 'Thus the strain has been great, and one must go back to 1920/21, when the price of whale oil fell from £90 per ton in 1920 to £31-5-0 in 1921, to find a more difficult year.'[16]

These fluctuations must be viewed in close conjunction with prices on the rest of the market for edible oil and fat.

Whale oil prices follow the prices of the competing types of fat almost completely.[17] The important and interesting feature of this relationship is that it is whale oil prices that are determined by prices on the rest of the market, i.e. by the prices of the substitutive products.[18]

It would be wrong to ascribe no significance at all to supply and demand conditions in the industry,[19] but whale oil constituted only a small portion of total supply, and it is therefore natural that any change in the prices 'of other fats carried the price of whale oil with it'.[20]

Whale oil prices will be used as a measure of business conditions,[21] and the whaling industry shows no specially deviant features compared with other business conditions.[22] Whale oil prices attained a peak about 1870 and then went into a decline until about 1905. A new high was reached about 1920, and it is this latter and the subsequent price

---

16. Cited after NWG no. 10, 1926.
17. International Whaling Statistics no. 16, Oslo 1942, p. 56.
18. K. Brandt, *op.cit.* pp. 175, 230, 231 and NWG no. 6, 1941.
19. See DMHvH III p. 421.
20. Brandt, *op.cit.* p. 174.
21. For a general discussion of this: R.S. Hartmann and D.R. Wheeler, 'Schumpeterian waves of innovation and infrastructure development in Great Britain and the United States: The Kondratieff cycle revisited', in *Research in Economic History*, vol. 4, 1979, p. 45 ff.
22. See e.g. J. Randers, 'Om den økonomiske utvikling på 10-15 års sikt', in *Bergen Bank Kvartalsskrift* no. 4, 1978.

fall that we shall focus upon here. The minor fluctuations throughout the 1920s followed the general movements of the trade cycle. Germoe observes that it is

> '...evident that the trade cycle affected whaling in the same way as other industries. It shows a peak in 1920 (1919/20 season), a trough in 1921 (1920/21), a peak in 1925 (1924/25), a through in 1927 (1926/27), a peak in 1929 (1928/29), a trough in 1932 (1931/32) and a peak in 1936 (1935/36) or 1937 (1936/37)'. [23]

We can compare the changes in patenting activity with the movement of prices.

The period that attracts attention immediately at an intuitive glance is the 1920s and early 1930s. In a time of steeply falling prices inventive activity attains its peak. If one also considers the corresponding peak in investment, Eilif Gjermoe's remark appears very apt: 'Over a few years enterprises expanded apparently in sheer defiance of inflation.'[24]

The correlation is negative ($r = -0.28$) throughout the time-span covered by the study. In the first period, 1880–1905, there is a slight visual tendency towards falling prices and increasing patenting activity, but the correlation is only $r = -0.19$. In the middle period, 1906–22, the picture is more obscure. Prices rise monotonously while patents vary, seemingly independently. The correlation is $r = -0.15$, i.e. a very weak negative co-variation. Only during the third period, from 1923 to 1968, is there a strong negative co-variation between prices and patents. The correlation coefficient is $r = 0.63$. In the 1920s and through to 1934 prices were falling. Patenting activity, which reached a peak in 1929, certainly fell off noticeably twice, in 1927 and 1930, but it attained its final peak in 1934.

Prices then rose until 1948 (except for a couple of minor falls), which coincides with a downward phase of the patent figures. From about 1950 onwards the movement of prices was downward. This was the broad tendency for patents as well, apart from a rise around 1950 just as prices were turning.

These results too must be interpreted with caution. It is true enough that there was a negative co-variation between patents and prices over the entire period from 1880 to 1968, but only the last part-period, from 1923 to 1968, when $r = 0.63$, can reliably be attributed with explanatory power. It is this period which will be subjected below to the most detailed analysis proceeding from the assumption that it was price pressure and depressed business conditions that were crucial cause of the vigorous technological transformation (measured in terms of patents) of the 1920s.

Transformation and expansion

We shall sum up the foregoing comparisons. Prior to 1905 the trend was upward for most of the variables examined. The patent figures were generally low, but they did rise a

---

23. Gjermoe, *op.cit.* p. 59.
24. *Ibid.* p. 56.

little from 1900 to a peak in 1904. Investment followed the same pattern but did not peak in 1905: the rise simply continued. The same applied to whale oil production. The data for oil production go back only to 1900, but it is hardly plausible that production before then will have been any higher. Only prices had an opposite tendency: they were clearly in decline until 1905.

The picture from 1905 onwards is much more obscure. Patents declined, though they achieved a minor peak in 1912. They then fell off again somewhat until 1917, when a rise began and continued until the high peak of the middle 1920s.

Investment continued its rising tendency that had begun before 1905 and reached a peak after very vigorous growth from 1909 to 1912. A rapid drop followed, with a lull during the First World War and tend further vigorous growth in the early 1920s. Production followed the same pattern as investment in this period also, with a peak in 1912, then decline and new growth after the First World War. Prices reached a trough in 1905, subsequently climbing steadily until 1915 and then vigorously until 1920. After that they fell sharply, then more moderately during the 1920s. Thus it was again prices that behaved contrary to the other variable. The very large investment figures of 1912 stand out as well. These occurred without any similar vigorous growth in other variable.

This picture is maintained in the 1920s also. While prices showed a decline lasting until 1934 (admittedly marked by some degreee of stability in the middle 1920s), the other variables attained very high levels.

Patents attained their high point in 1929, dropped to a lower level for three years around the laying-up year, then went on to a final peak in 1934/35, when prices turned. Investment followed the pattern of patents until 1930 but failed to achieve a similar vigorous rise again around 1935. Production reached its peak in 1931 and by 1933 had recovered to the level of 1929. It then declined until the Second World War. The other variables too, apart from prices, went down.

After 1945 prices continued to rise until about 1950. Production was going up as well during the same period, reaching a peak in 1952. Patents rose until 1947, then fell until 1951.

From about 1950 onwards the trend of prices was downward, although year-to-year fluctuations were wide.

Production, patenting activity and investment also declined.

As has been argued above, patenting activity may be regarded as an expression of technological transformation. Investment growth, on the other hand, can be viewed as an expression of quantitative expansion. The correlation calculations and the foregoing argument express the fact that expansion and transformation are to some extent interlinked. An example is provided by the way in which the patent figures show a marked decline simultaneously with a fall in production and investment during the laying-up season of 1931/32.

But reservations must be made. The patent figures do not reflect the high investment peak of 1912 to any notable degree, nor to any marked extent the uppswing that occured around 1950.

This tends to suggest that transformation (patents) and expansion (investment) must explained separately. Demand can then ble introduced as a factor explaining expansion. If oil production is used as a measure of realised demand, there is a very high correlation between demand and investment. The peaks of 1912, the 1920s and 1950 all coincide.

On the other hand the patents showed a marked peak only in the 1920s, with only minor increases around 1912 and 1950. It is therefore evident that there must be some other explanation of the peaking of patents in the 1920s than the fact that demand and expansion also peaked. It has been hinted several times already that it is prices that are being cited as the explanation here. There was no price pressure during either expansion after the First and Second World Wars. It was good market conditions that led to high investment, and rising prices did not generate any pressure for hunting to become more efficient.

During the expansion of the 1920s, on the other hand, falling prices were an important characteristic, and the vigorous technological transformation can be seen as having been powered by the need that was then created to make production and hunting more rational and efficient in order to reduce costs. Obviously this transformation also made higher production levels possible. This accords with the correlation calculation between production and patents, where patents appear to change before production. A statement such as the following taken from a report on the 1927/28 season in the *Norsk Hvalfangst Tidende* must therefore be regarded at most as an explanation of some, but not the most fundamental, of the causes of the transformation:

> 'The good catch results of last season have rightly or wrongly played a large part in stimulating development – firstly in the direction of the formation of new companies and secondly in the direction of increasing and improving the tackle and equipment of existing companies.'[25]

Here both expansion ('increasing') and transformation ('improving') are being explained in terms of good catch results.

From what has been said here about the importance of prices (business conditions) to transformation one could have expected a new upswing in patents throughout the 1950s resulting from a new price fall. This did not happen.

The explanation here may be found in the general decline of the industry and what has previously been written concerning a possible technological life-cycle. This was after the Second World War entered its final phase. The decline can thus be said to have taken place unaffected by external stimuli. Such a picture can also help to explain why patents increased only moderately around 1910: the stimuli needed to trigger off a decisive transformation (metaphorically at the vigorous growthphase of the life-cycle curve) were lacking. Price pressure and crisis symptoms in the 1920s and 1930s were what was needed and are thus part of the explanation of the patenting peak of that era.

K. Brandt believed it possible to discern such a culmination and in 1940 launched a hypothesis of the 'exhaustion of efficiency reserves'.[26] He elaborated it as follows:

25. NWG no. 8, 1928, p. 161.
26. K. Brandt, *op.cit.* p. 129.

'Refinements in equipment, operation and utilization are probably still possible. But nautical engineers, engineers in the fat-rendering and refining industries, and all the miscellaneous accessory industries have succeeded in reducing costs of whaling and processing the carcasses so far as to leave only slight opportunities for further refinement.'[27]

The next section will concentrate more particularly on the 1920s and 1930s and will endeavour to substantiate further the attempts made here to explain transformation.

The 1920s – good years or bad?
We have proceeded from the assumption that it was mainly the general fall in prices from 1920 to 1934 that provided the incentive to innovation and technological change. However, it is clear that despite this steady price fall there was no 'crisis atmosphere' prevailing in the whaling industry or among investors during the 1920s. One reason may be that the price fall was so effectively met by rationalisation, innovation and technological renewal: production was very high and, as will appear below, costs were effectively pruned. Capital expansion and rationalisation occurred.

It is also clear, moreover, that there were intervals of rising prices during the period. Both from 1922 to 1924 and from 1927 to 1928 there were minor recoveries in prices. Whether it was years such as these that kept optimism alive or whether it was the universal expectation of a continuance of falling prices that influenced decisions and therefore technological transformation is difficult to discern from aggregate statistics. If one assumes a growth-led explanation, for example, it would be natural to regard the peak year of 1920 as a year that influenced investment and innovation favourably in subsequent years despite the swift decline in prices that followed. A/S Ørnen's annual report for 1920, for instance, contained the following: '...now, when the company is so strongly placed financially, (it) must undertake an improvement of catching gear in order to ensure profitable operation in future...'[28] New whaling vessels were bought, and 'Furthermore it is proposed that the whale factory ship 'Bombay' should be replaced by a bigger and newer ship.'[29]

But A/S Ørnen also responded positively to the crisis impulses. In one and the same section of the report on the 1930/31 season the shareholders were advised on the one hand of a proposal to equip one of the factory ships with a slipway *and* on the other of the poor market conditions that were to lead to the laying-up of the fleet for the next season.[30]

Other companies responded negatively and considered liquidation. One hypothesis is that all companies were stimulated to make new investment and replace equipment when

27. *Ibid.*
28. A/S Ørnen annual report 1919–20.
29. *Ibid.*
30. A/S Ørnen annual report 1930–31.

times were good, while those which survived the crisis also responded positively to its impulses. This will be enlarged upon below.

The favourable demand situation along with the price pressure brought elements of both crisis and growth to the 1920s and 1930s.

It is not difficult to find several indications that the 1920s were a prosperous era in many ways. Firstly, the difficult price situation in certain years at the beginning of the 1920s was offset by the high exchange rate of the pound sterling. Almost all whale oil was sold in terms of sterling, and 'the *krone* exchange rate was just as important as the oil price during these years'.[31] However, this advantage was shortlived because of Norwegian parity policy, and in 1926 the value of the *krone* went up and the companies obtained lower profits for the same volume of production sold at the same price.[32]

Secondly, any assessment of the relative profitability of the whaling industry compared with other industries has to conclude that it bore the marks of prosperity. Comparison with shipping, for example, reveals that dividends of under ten per cent were more uncommon in the whaling industry in the interwar period. In relative terms rates of this order occurred six times more frequently in the shipping industry.[33]

All the same this makes no difference to the fact that this period was one when the whaling industry too was under pressure. Dividends in the 1920s and 1930s were very low in relation to what had been customary during the previous decade, and net profits fluctuated widely from year to year. The number of years showing a breakeven balance or deficit was larger in the interwar years.[34] The whaling industry has traditionally been regarded as a very lucrative business during this period. Many companies showed profits and returns far in excess of the norm. There was also much activity in the establishing of new companies. But the picture is hardly a satisfactory one. In the period 1924 to 1938 about forty Norwegian companies went into liquidation as a result of financial problems. 'The whaling industry at the close of the 1920s was not the kind of goldmine it was imagined to be,' is Tønnessen's comment.[35]

Cost-cutting and efficiency improvement
One of the industry's most noticeable reactions to hard times consisted of attempts to reduce costs and improve the efficiency of production. In this process one may see in the most direct way the negative correlation between prices and patents referred to previously.[36] For very many of the patents taken out during this period concerned the

31. Hans Bogen, *Linjer i Den moderne Hvalfangsts historie*, Oslo 1933, p. 116.
32. DMHvH III, p. 184.
33. Gjermoe, *op.cit.* p. 62.
34. See e.g. Figures for A/S Ørnen in annual reports and in *Aktieselskabet Ørnen – 25 års fangst i Sydishavet*, Oslo 1930, and H.I. Bogen, *Aktieselskabet Ørnen 1903–1953*, Sandefjord 1953. A/S Ørnen appears to represent an average company as regards results in this period, see DMHvH III, p. 568.
35. Joh. N. Tønnessen, 'Noen problemer i den moderne hvalfangsts historie', in *Vestfoldminne*, 1964, p. 72.
36. Such a reaction to economic crises is not unique to the whaling industry and can be noticed elsewhere. Some observers even believe that inventive activity is directly *determined* by expected reductions in costs. See R.R. Nelson, 'The Economics of Invention. A survey of the literature', in *The Journal of Business*, 2, 1959, p. 107.

extraction of oil and the rationalisation of this process. The endavours were successful: costs were curtailed in step with the decline of prices throughout the 1920s and offset its effects to some extent.³⁷ Only in one year (1931) did costs per ton exceed price per ton.

A citation from the *Norsk Hvalfangst Tidende* in 1916 is illustrative in this regard. An editorial reference is being made to a patent taken out on equipment for outboard flensing in the open sea, so that whaling could be made independent of contact with land, following the whale on their migrations instead. This proposal for a form of pelagic whaling is dicussed in the following terms:

> '...the practical difficulties have time and again thrown all speculation away, and it may be regarded as virtually proven that at the normal price on which it has become customary to reckon, hunting activity on the lines indicated above will certainly be unremunerative. (...) On the other hand it should also perhaps be regarded as proven that it is impossible to undertake this on a sufficiently large scale for the catch – We are still thinking here about ordinary oil prices – to be profitable.'³⁸

Whale oil prices in 1916 were at the same level as in the middle of the 1920s when pelagic hunting *was* introduced. And it was introduced despite the fact that prices were no higher then in 1916. Something must have changed then. An obvious factor is the technological changes that occurred during the 1920s. As well as overcoming practical barriers they represented necessary rationalisation and improvement of efficiency.

Some of the cost reductions manifestly were due simply to falling prices of factors of production, which followed the same trend as oil prices. But it can be seen that this represented only a part of the reason for declining costs, e.g. in 1927, when the exceptionally low price was not followed by corresponding cuts in costs. On the contrary, there were rises at certain points. This, combined with a sharply rising *krone*, made the 1926/27 season 'the most difficult period for a long time'.³⁹

The reaction to this pressure is illuminating:

> 'On the one hand, then, the most urgent task for the companies is to curtail their expenditure further. And this is being achieved to some extent in the autumn equipment programmes for the new whaling season. But another task is to continue the work already begun on raising the quality of production so that whale oil can command the best possible price.'⁴⁰

The effects did not fail to appear. Transformation measured in patents attained its maximum in 1929, and the following description was applied to the 1929/30 season:

37. Tønnesen, *op.cit.* p. 72 and Brandt, *op.cit.* p. 125.
38. NWG, no. 2, 1916.
39. NWG, no. 5, 1927.
40. NWG, no. 10, 1927.

'The size of whaling vessels is increasing, horsepowers are rising, range of operation, seaworthiness and towing capacity are all improving. New Hartmann apparatuses are being introduced, more and larger boilers, and the number of barrels produced per calculated blue whale is rising constantly. We cannot afford to allow any usable raw material to go to waste.'[41]

The Hartmann system of boiling apparatus may be mentioned here. 1929 was a peak year for new installations in Norwegian whale factory ships, but from then on the Hartmann apparatuses were rapidly replaced by a new system, viz. the Kvaerner boiler. This transition took place during the difficult years around 1930, and it is characteristic that the only point at which the two systems differed was that the Kvaerner apparatus was able to make better use of bones and knucklebones, so that utilisation of raw material became as high and effective as possible.[42]

Growth in tonnage

Figure 2 shows the size of a selection of Norwegian whale factory ships arranged according to the year they were put into service. Each dot represents one such ship, showing its tonnage and its first year of operation. The changes over time thus show the trend of factory ship size.

Figure 2. Selected Norwegian whale factory ships according to size and first catching year

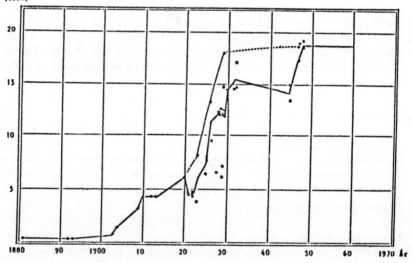

Source: DMHvH, III, p. 609 and Hvalfangstregister 1928 and 1936.

Note: The curve shows the annual average. The stippled curve shows the largest whale factory ship taken into operation at any one time.

41. NWG, no. 6, 1930.
42. See K. Anker-Olsen, *Kvaerner Brug gjennom 100 år*, Oslo 1953 and NWG, 1929-31 and nos. 9. and 10, 1938.

The curve that has been drawn represents the average size of new whale factory ships every year and can give a picture of technological development. The rise is almost nil until about 1900, whereafter there is a steeper rise lasting until 1920. The first sharp rise occurring just prior to 1905 was related to the early pelagic trials ('Admiralen'), then there was another jump about 1910. The factory ships then brought into service 'stood for a number of years as a kind of standard of what was required of a well-equipped whale factory ship for the southern seas'.[43]

It was with this type of factory ship that the first expansion took place immediately after 1920, but the increase was very pronounced all through the 1920s and was associated with the introduction of pelagic whaling and other aspects of technological transformation in this period. Of the 'C.A. Larsen', which went into service in 1926, it was written:

> 'It is the biggest vessel ever to have been fitted out as a whale factory ship and also the biggest ship ever taken into the service of the whaling industry and the probabilities are that the upper limit has now been reached.'[44]

The 'C.A. Larsen' was of 13246 gross registered tons. The 'Kosmos', 17801 gross registered tons, was built only three years later.

In the 1930s the curve flattens out, then makes a final upswing corresponding to the newly-built postwar factory ships.[45] As can be seen, however, the factory ships of the postwar era were not much bigger than the largest ones that had been built around 1930. Thus the 1920s were the period when the most radical remodelling occurred. Again the transformation can be depicted by the shape of the curve. It is S-shaped in character, which accords well with customary assumptions concerning the development and maturation of a technology.[46] The shape of the curve also gives further reason for regarding technological change and development as variable and uneven over time.

The difference between the quantitative expansion peaking in 1913 and the expansion of the 1920s has already been dealt with, but can be illustrated further from the development of the factory ship. The trend of ship size compared with the number of Norwegian whale factory ships hunting in Antarctica every season reveals differences between the two periods of expansion.[47] The number of factory ships, like the number of whaling vessels and the production of whale oil, shows clear peaks in 1913, 1925 and 1929. Around 1913, however, ship size manifests no particular trend. It is only the expansion at the close of the 1920s that also coincides with vigorous growth in the size of whale factory ships. This supports the explanation advanced earlier for the divergencies

---

43. NWG no.'9, 1926.
44. Ibid.
45. 'Thorshavet', 'Thorshøvdi', 'Kosmos III' and 'Kosmos V'.
46. See e.g. E.M. Rogers, Diffusion of Innovation, N.Y. 1983, (3 edn.), p. 11.
47. Statistisk Sentralbyrå, Historisk statistikk, Oslo 1978, p. 187.

between patents and investments around 1910, viz. that investment occured when capital was being extended. Capital was being extended in the 1920s too, but in contrast to the earlier expansionary era, that period did contain a strong element of transformation and capital expansion. This can be seen from the patent variations and also from the marked growth in ship size.

It has been asserted that 'circumstances along with the development of the industry as a whole more or less compelled size to increase'.[48] The particularly marked growth in size in the 1920s suggest that this is correct. The pressure to improve equipment was then greater than ever. It was a matter of installing as much extraction equipment as possible within a single hull. More storage space for fuel and finished products had to be crowded in, since the hunting season was extended and more distant grounds were exploited.

Changes in business structure

In general, the establishment of new firms can be a sign of transformation, both because new firms avail themselves of the best technology and because established firms tend to stick to old technology, products or markets.[49] What will be considered below is the business structure of the whaling industry in the 1920s and 1930s, its modification over time, and possible connections with the transformation that occurred during the period.

The favourable market conditions and outlook throughout the 1920s caused a number of new companies to be established in the same way as during earlier expansionary periods off Spitzbergen and the African coast. The peak year was 1928, when six new Norwegian companies were founded. But companies were formed almost every single year from 1920 to 1931,[50] in contrast to the previous decade when hardly any new establishments were made at all. Figure 3 gives a breakdown of Norwegian whaling companies in Antarctica in the 1920s and 1930s. The numbers of companies engaged in hunting each season are compared according to the period in which they were established. Establishments between 1910 and 1920 were negligible and are not included.

---

48. NWG no. 9, 1926.
49. A classic study showing this is W.R. MacLauren, *Invention and Innovation in the Radio Industry*, N.Y. 1949, p. 243.
   In Norway the so-called '1930's study' has made use of data on the establishment of firms as a measure of transformation. See Sejersted (ed.), *op.cit.*
50. DMHvH III, p. 589.

Figure 3. Norwegian companies hunting in the Antarctic according to season and year of establishment

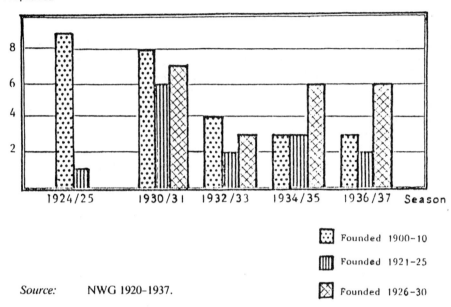

Source: NWG 1920-1937.

As will be seen, the established companies were totally dominant right up to the end of the 1920s. In the first hunting year after the laying-up year the number of companies was reduced, but the figure then rose again somewhat, although the number of companies hunting never attained the same level as prior to the laying-up year. It was now no longer the established companies formed between 1900 and 1910 that predominated, but new companies formed after pelagic hunting had begun and for the purpose of conducting pelagic operations. Even companies formed in the early 1920s largely fell out of the game after the laying-up year. This suggests that the older companies did not surmount the hurdles of the transformation and the conversion to new equipment required in order to conduct pelagic operations and to meet the standards of efficiency necessary for participation in whaling in the 1930s. The transition to pelagic hunting and especially the crisis of 1931/32 brought substantial changes of structure. One example is the introduction and diffusion of the slipway from 1925 onwards. For the most part it was newlyfounded companies that led the way in this development. A/S Globus, which was the first, was started for the very purpose of bringing Sörlle's patented slipway into service.[51]

51. Ø. Naess, *Hvalfangstselskabet Globus A/S*, Larvik 1951, p. 111 ff.

H. Bogen remarks with regard to this transition to pelagic whaling: 'It brought its consequences, especially for the respected older companies, some of which did not survive.'⁵² The citation is taken from a commemorative volume on A/S Ørnen, and it added that Ørnen was one of the few established companies to survive the 1920s and 1930s. This company responded positively to the impulses of the crisis. One example of this is furnished by the Thor Dahl companies' experiments with the electrical harpooning of whales from 1930 onwards.⁵³ Even in the most difficult years funds were made available for A.J. Foyn's experiments despite very uncertain results, uncertain prospects for this method of catching, heavy costs entailed in the experiments and a marked aversion on the part of whaling personnel. True enough it was Foyn who was pressing all the time to continue the experiments, but they did continue even during the laying-up season of 1931/32.⁵⁴ Such receptiveness to new ideas during hard times provides some explanation of the longevity of this company.

Despite this example, the picture remains one in which it was the newest companies that led the way. For instance, possibly the most active company in the experimentation with electrical slaughtering of whales was A/S Rosshavet, which was founded in 1923.⁵⁵

The following data, culled from the annual reports and account of 37 whaling companies for the 1919/20, 1924/25, 1929/30 and 1934/35 seasons, bear witness that there really did occur a technological transformation in conjunction with the change in the business structure.⁵⁶

The hypothesis has been that an expansion of capital and a transition to better and more rational technology occurred in the course of the 1920s and 1930s, and that the companies that survived the pressure of competition and crisis differed from those that went under by virtue of more vigorous technological renewal. The measures utilised are firstly a measure of capital deepening (C/L), secondly a measure of productive efficiency (barrels per ton deadweight), and finally a measure of the age of the whale factory ship.⁵⁷

---

52. H.I. Bogen, *Aktieselskabet 'Ørnen', 1903-1953*, Sandefjord 1953, p. 54.
53. The Thor Dahl companies were Ørnen, Odd and Bryde & Dahls hvalfangstselskab.
54. Correspondence between A/S Thor Dahl and the engineer A.J. Foyn 1930-1935. Lodged in the Chr. Christensen Whaling Museum, Sandefjord.
55. DMHvH IV, p. 534.
56. From C. Kierulf & Co. A/S, *Håndbok over norske obligationer og aktier*, Oslo 1920-1935.
57. C/L is an abbreviation for a measure of capital deepening viz. the capital/labour-ratio. It shows the amount of capital per worker. If the capital factor and the labour factor increase at the same rate this is called capital widening, whereas if the capital factor increases more rapidly than the labour factor, this is called capital deepening. The latter is often associated with technological progress. The operational measure here is a company's total capital measured by the total sum in the balance divided by the annual wages costs. Barrels per ton means more precisely the number of barrels of oil produced in a season by a whale factory ship divided by the ship's tonnage (tonnage deadweight). There is plainly room for doubt as to the accuracy (reliability) of C/L especially. Obviously the content of wages accounts would vary over time and from one company to another, and the size of the total capital depended upon modes of depreciation which could create a book value somewhat removed from the real value. But as far as explanatory power (validity) is concerned, I am prepared to believe that the three variables employed together at least offer a serviceable measure of technological level and technological differences.

As can be seen from Table 1, the relationships are very clear. The companies that survived the crisis and the laying-up year both enjoyed a higher capital/labour-ratio, produced more barrels per ton deadweight, and generally had newer equipment. This was the case from as early as the 1919/20 season onwards. The companies which subsequently survived the crisis of 1931/32 already had on average a higher technological level.

Table 1. Technological differences between companies which wound up and those which survived the crisis of 1931/32 (average)

	Whaling companies which		
	wound up in the 1920s	wound up in the 1930s	survived the crisis
Season 1919/20:			
Age of whale factory ship (years)	31	26	22
C/L	6.6	8	20
Barrels/ton	(no data)	3.7	3.1
Season 1924/25:			
Age of whale factory ship	32	29	23
C/L	7	9.2	9.9
Barrels/ton	1.6	3.6	4.3
Season 1929/30:			
Age of Whale factory ship		29	21
C/L		4.5	5.4
Barrels/ton		4.6	4.8
Season 1934/35:			
Age of Whale factory ship		23	23
C/L		6	7.2
Barrels/ton		3	5.9

Source: 37 annual reports and accounts of Norwegian whaling companies. C. Kierulf & Co. A/S, *Håndbok over norske obligationer og aktier*, 1920–1935.

Note: Norwegian companies which went over to English ownership after the laying-up year are counted among those surviving the crisis. Their winding-up as Norwegian companies was not caused by technological factors.

The companies which survived tend to have been the ones with the newest equipment, but the age of the factory ships was generally extremely high for all companies. This gives a somewhat misleading picture of the character of the equipment. For the majority of whale factory ships were purchased as secondhand tankers or passenger ships and then refitted. Even an old vessel could thus be fitted out with completely modern boiling equipment etc. The pioneer whale factory ship 'Lancing', for example, which came into service in 1925, was built in 1898, and while the average age of factory ships operating during the 1934/35 season was 23 years, they had been in service as factory ships for an average of only six years.

Nevertheless the total age of ships does furnish a picture of the technological level. Size was determined entirely by age, and size largely set the limits for the layout and equipment that could be selected. For example, the factory ship needed a certain size to enable a slipway to be brought into use.

When one knows that the companies which survived were mainly the newer companies, the conclusion that must be drawn is that transformation was largely associated with these.

As has appeared from the foregoing, the laying-up year of 1931/32, when the entire Norwegian whaling fleet stayed at home, had a particularly strong impact upon transformation and the waning dominance of the older companies.

E. Dahmén, who has studied the establishment of Swedish companies during this period, called the crisis of 1920 a peaceful crisis in which there was no struggle going on between old and new. Not until after the 1920s and into the 1930s does it become possible, in his view, to perceive a structural crisis in which such a struggle becomes intensified, victory goes to the new, and innovations become diffused.[58] One derives the same impression in the whaling industry. A structural crisis sets in during the 1920s as a result of price pressure, competition, shortage of resources and institutional retrenchment. Its ultimate consummation was reached in the laying-up year. After the laying-up year all catching was quota-regulated, and efficient equipment was one of the factors that determined the quotas. For some of the older factory ships the only solution was the breaker's yard, and a number of companies surrendered their quotas to those with the newest and best equipment.[59] The consequence was that in the 1932/33 season it was '...exclusively material that was first class in every way that will be used in the forthcoming season...'[60] Of more than 40 whale factory ships hunting in 1930/31, 21 of the older ones were taken out of service in the first years of the crisis. Offsetting this, 13 new and rebuilt factory ships became operational between 1932 and 1938, and these had a capacity getting on for three times as great as that of the 21 ships scrapped.[61]

58. E. Dahmén, *Svensk industriell företagarverksamhet*, Stockholm 1950, p. 366 ff.
59. NWG no. 10, 34 p. 166.
60. NWG no. 8, 1932.
61. DMHvH III p. 423.

Conclusion

This article has attempted to explain invention, innovation and technological change in the Norwegian whaling industry primarily by comparing patenting data with several economic variables.

The patent figures between 1880 and 1968 display wide annual fluctuations but also a clear pattern, with a concentration of patenting activity in the 1920s and 1930s. Regarded in isolation the patents appear to describe a technological life-cycle for an entire industry.

While both patents, investment and production show simultaneous high levels in the 1920s and 1930s, only investment and production also have well-defined peaks immediately after 1910 and around 1950. This is considered to be an indication that patenting may to some extent have to be explained in terms other than as a phenomenon varying in step with these quantities. In this connection whale oil prices are introduced as a possible variable of explanation. The co-variation is negative, and the interwar period particularly stands out as an era of substantial technological transformation and heavily falling prices. It appears that price pressure and depressed business conditions had a decisive influence on technological development in that more effective and rational production methods were introduced in reaction to the pressure. Thus the whaling industry forms an example of a crisis-led transformation in the Schumpeterian sense.

We have studied the interwar period in somewhat greater detail. Firstly we have shown that these years were difficult ones for the industry and that cost-cutting and improved efficiency formed the response to price pressure. Use is also made of data additional to patents showing that the 1920s and 1930s were the central transformation period. The curve representing the trend of whale factory ship size is S-shaped. Changes in the business structure in the form of the establishment of new companies also displayed a concentration in this period. It was mainly the new companies that survived the difficult years at the beginning of the 1930s, and there are numerous indications that these were the very companies that were responsible for technological transformation.

Part IV
Wages, Unions and the Labour Market

[21]

Wage Formation in the Norwegian Industry 1840 - 1985

Arne Kiel and Lars Mjøset

Introduction

Is there a common logic to wage formation in a market economy, no matter what institutions are affecting the labour market? Neoclassical economics would opt for a qualified yes: The labour market should in principle be analysed as any other market, regarding observed differences in labour-market performance as resulting from the influence of various factors on the ever-present forces of supply and demand. There are at least two ways of assessing the *gehalt* of this proposition. One may start out with some kind of Phillips-curve relation and then try to estimate its parameters for various historical periods.[1]

Alternatively, one may argue that institutional settings crucially influence supply and demand. After all, it is human beings that are demanded and supplied in the labour market, and they are capable of acting and forming institutions. Since the early days of 19th century liberal capitalism, the attempt to restructure the labour market according to the atomistic, competitive ideal type has been countered by waves of protest and collective organization. Since institutional patterns are shifting both with the balance of social forces and with other factors, a study of their impact must necessarily focus on specified periods. In this article, we shall study the phases of the Norwegian labour market.

Our main point of departure is the regulation approach, an interdisciplinary venture involving economics, sociology and history. We start with a critical presentation of this approach, with special reference to the regulationists' analysis of the wage relation. Our study is limited to the manufacturing sector of Norwegian industry, and the second section provides some basic information on this sector. We then analyse Norwegian wage formation in three periods: the last half of the 19th century (including the first decade of the 20th century), the inter-war period and three post-war subperiods. Our major focus is on the two earliest periods, since very few studies of this kind are available for the pre-1945-era. As for the post-war period, we mainly survey the results of other studies, contrasting this phase to the earlier period. A concluding section sums up our results and suggests directions for further research.

---

[1] Cf. e.g. Sumner, M.T. & Ward, R., "The reappearing Phillips curve", *Oxford Economic Papers*, 1983: Supplement.

Scandinavian Economic History Review

Macroeconomic patterns, institutions and periods

The label "regulation school" is applied to the writings of a group of Paris economists (Aglietta, Boyer, Coriat, Mistral, Mazier, Lipietz, a.o.).[2] Its inspiration is drawn from "heretic", that is non-neo-classical economists, combining "Marxian intuitions and Kaleckian or Keynesian macroeconomics in order to revive institutionalist or historicist studies".[3] While certainly dealing with fundamental problems, the main emphasis of the regulation school is on "intermediary concepts". Shuttling between partial models, qualitative historical information, time series, typologies and periodisations, the school's emphasis is to the inductive side, at least compared to the heavily deductive neo-classical approach.

In the broadest definition, *regulation* denotes "the conjunction of economic mechanisms associated with a given set of social relationships, of institutional forms and structures".[4] Boyer and Mistral have later claimed that the English term "regulation" is misleading because of its administrative connotations.[5] As an alternative, they propose to translate the French term régulation by "socio-economic tuning", which "covers the whole set of institutions, of private behaviors and of actual functioning of various markets which channel the long-term dynamics and determine the cyclical properties of the economy during an historical period and for a given society." This term was not maintained, however, so the accepted term is now régulation.[6]

The emphasis on periodisation is important. In his early study of French wage formation, Boyer emphasized the necessity to "isolate a certain number of periods which are more or less homogeneous so far as the social, institutional and legal factors governing the determination of wages are concerned".[7] The main idea is that the

---

[2] For a recent critical summary, see Boyer, R., *La theorie de la régulation: Une analyse critique*, Paris: La Decouverte 1986 (U.S. translation forthcoming, New York: Columbia U.P. 1990). The approach has received international acclaim during the last decade: For the U.S., see Davis, M., "Fordism in Crisis", *Review*, 1978:2. For Germany, see Hübner, K., *Theorie der Regulation*, Berlin (West): Edition Sigma 1989. For Europe in general, see De Vroey, M., "A regulation approach interpretation of the contemporary crisis", *Capital & Class*, 1984:23. For Scandinavia, see Mjøset, L., "Regulation and the institutional tradition", in Mjøset, L. & Bohlin, J., editors, *Introduksjon til reguleringskolen, Nordic Summer-University: Working Papers*, Vol. 21, Aalborg, Denmark 1985.

[3] Boyer, R., "Régulation", in Eatwell, J. et. al., editors, *The New Palgrave*, Vol. 4, London: Macmillan 1987, p. 127.

[4] Boyer, R., "Wage formation in historical perspective: The French experience", *Cambridge Journal of Economics*, 1979:3, p. 100; Boyer, R., "La Crise actuelle: une mise en perspective historique", *Critiques de l'économie politique*, 1979:7-8.

[5] Boyer, R & Mistral, J., "The present crisis: from an historical interpretation to a prospective outlook", *European Federation for Economic Research, Working Papers* 1984 (translated from *Annales* 1983:3/4).

[6] Boyer, "Régulation", p. 126 f.

[7] Boyer, "Wage formation in historical perspective", p. 104.

Wage Formation in the Norwegian Industry 1840-1985

most relevant laws and regularities which economists and economic historians deal with, must be traced within specific periods.[8]

The roughest and earliest periodisation presented was between old, competitive and monopolistic regulation. We shall here survey the definition of these ideal types as applied to the labour market (Figure 1). The "old" - *ancienne* - regulation is defined as a parallell movement in production and nominal wages, with a reverse movement in the cost of living. This reflects the pre-capitalist situation where agricultural crises cut production dramatically, and employment is reduced directly. Those who were still in work, would see their wages falling and the cost of living would rise, mainly as a reflection of the price of grain. In such situations, famine and starvation would often occur.

Competitive regulation is defined as the situation where "it is falls in the cost of living imposed by the market which are the means via which productivity movements affect workers' standards of living; while money wages reflect labour market conditions, real wages register the favourable effects of price reductions, particularly in recessions."[9] Compared to the old regulation, there is a strengthening of the link between money wages and economic activity, and a major change is that now prices too tend to move in line with production. Typically, money wages become the main source of income for labourers, but workers' consumption is not large enough to have any major impact on production. Nominal wages are determined in a decentralised fashion with no collective organisation, neither on the supply, nor on the demand side. The fairly irregular increases in productivity create a downward pressure on the prices which define the cost of living, thus boosting real wages in these specific periods.

In monopolist regulation, productivity gains (now more regular than before) are not mediated through price-changes, they "are associated with an increase in money wages, without any *ex ante* change in prices. The growth in demand caused by these wage increases is associated with growth in productive capacity without the need for large downward adjustments in prices or wages".[10] Product markets are now linked to labour markets, and money wages no longer stand in a unique relation to the pressure of demand in the labour market.

At the roots of these different constellations lie different types of labour processes. Competitive regulation involves a sluggish development of productivity, based more on addition of new workers than on continuous productivity changes through labour process organization and institutionalized r&d-activity. These latter features marks monopolist regulation. In the labour process of competitive regulation, craft workers control the pace of production, but reduction of working hours, as well as hiring and

---

[8] This idea looms large also in the quite advanced institutionalism of Johan Åkerman, cf. Åkerman, J., *Ekonomisk teori*, Vol.2, Lund: Gleerups 1944; Mjøset, L., "Johan Åkermans distinksjon - kalkyle og kausalanalyse", *Sosiologi i dag*, 1988:4 (with bibliography).

[9] Boyer, "Wage formation in historical perspective", p. 111.

[10] Ibid., p. 111f.

Scandinavian Economic History Review

Figure 1 Four patterns of regulation related to macro-economic aggregates.

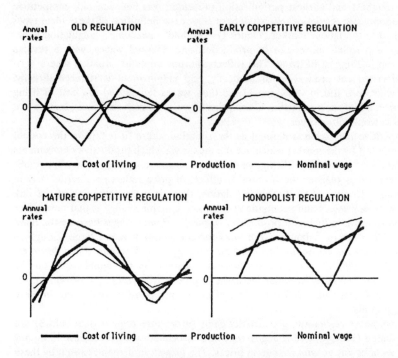

Sources: Boyer, R., "Les salaires en longue période", *Economie et Statistique*, 1978, p. 103, Graph IX; Boyer, R., "Technical change and the theory of 'regulation'", in Dosi, G./Freeman, C./Nelson, R./Silverberg, G./Soete, L., editors, *Technical Change and Economic Theory*, London: Pinter Publishers 1988.

firing is easy, since there are large (often hidden) supplies of labour and only very primitive legal and institutional defenses connected to the work contract.

The monopolist case involves continuous technical change, Taylorist and Fordist methods of work organization imposed by a large middle management, and above all, real wage growth which is linked to productivity. These features interact with increasingly oligopolistic price-formation and state interventionist management of the domestic credit system.[11] In this case, labour gains from productivity increases by explicitly recognizing them at the level of shop floor bargaining, whereby wages become directly linked to the productivity growth. Hence, deflationary movements are not necessary to give workers a share of the productivity gains. In addition there

---

[11] It should be noted that the definition of monopolist regulation is not the same as more traditional definitions of "monopoly capitalism" in orthodox Marxist theories. The latter theories only consider monopoly in the relation between firms. As should be clear from the discussion above, the regulation approach rather holds that oligopolistic competition prevails, and they also strongly emphasize the tendential "monopolization" of the supply of labour power by the union movement.

Wage Formation in the Norwegian Industry 1840-1985

is a linkage (for all wage-earners, not only for workers in the manufacturing industry) to the consumer price index. And in this case, mass consumption of consumer durables produced by manufacturing industry is growing, while the importance of traditional sector products in the household budgets are diminishing.[12] But the traditional sector may still be important as a source of newcomers to the labour force.[13]

While this seems fairly straightforward, a closer look at Boyer's analysis shows that he refers to "regulation" in three different senses: (i) as the patterns of economic indices of crucial labour market variables at a very aggregated level (cost of living, nominal wages, employment/activity level, productivity); (ii) as a set of labour market institutions (in particular institutions related to collective bargaining); (iii) and as the total constellation of institutions, private behavior, and market mechanisms which defines a period.

These three distinct meanings may account for some of the ambiguities in Boyer's early study of French wage formation: He finds competitive regulation (i) in France for the whole period 1850-1940, but notes a number of institutional shifts (from legal codes imposing liberal labour market mechanisms to collective agreements) through this 90 year period, indicating several regulations (ii). Thus, his analysis often slips into the language of "gradual change" and "slow drift" (a terminology not really consistent with the idea of defining homogenous periods, as in the (iii)-definition): Already in the *ancienne regime* there is a "gradual altering" towards competitive regulation, a "long period of transition" following the 1791 Loi Le Chapelier, involving "a coming together of certain elements of the *ancienne régulation* (conjunctural movements in opposite directions of wage levels and the cost of living) and new developments connected with the development of capitalist relationships".[14]

Turning to regulation (iii), he argues that "the competitive régulation can be seen partly as a continuation of the previous régulation, to the extent that the degree of dependence of movements in money wage levels in comparison with the rate of economic activity is strengthened. The major change was the appearance of some synchronisation between wage levels and the cost of living; prices tended to develop in the same direction as production."[15] Then he finds that this syncronization was stronger in 1852-70 and 1900-1914 than in 1870-1900. Boyer stylizes this as an "alteration" of competitive regulation,[16] and argues that 1900-1914 saw a "slow drift" away from competitive regulation. He finds a change in regulation (ii), with more collec-

---

[12] Cf. Aglietta, M., *Régulation et crises du capitalisme*, Paris: Calman-Levy 1976, where this constellation was dubbed "Fordism", referring to Gramsci's visionary analysis written in the inter-war period, cf. Gramsci, A., "Americanism and Fordism", in Gramsci, A., *Prison Notebooks*, New York: International Publishers 1971.

[13] Cornwall, J., *Modern Capitalism*. Oxford: Martin Robertson 1977; Kindleberger, C.P., *Europe's Postwar Growth. The Role of Labor Supply*, Cambridge, Mass.: Harvard U.P. 1967.

[14] Ibid., p. 106.

[15] Ibid., p. 106.

[16] Boyer, R., "Les salaires en longue période", *Economie et Statistique*, 1978: 103, p. 55. The two versions of competitive regulation are found in Figure 1, the latter has a higher elasticity - actually close to 1 - of the nominal wage with respect to the cost of living.

tive agreements and early state interventionism, e.g. paternalist social insurance arrangements. Here, it seems, he is close to a synthesis, treating regulation (iii) as a combination of regulations (i) and (ii).

In the early inter-war period Boyer finds an important change in private investment behavior, as a new mass production mode of accumulation gives rise to considerable productivity gains. But he claims that the institutional changes which took place at the same time did not lead to patterns which could stabilize this type of industrial growth. He concludes that there was an incoherence between the mode of accumulation (the "social and economic structure") and the "pattern of wage determination", dubbed "regulation" - obviously (ii). Hence, regulation (i) had not really changed: "Thus once the crisis became apparent collective agreements declined rapidly, further strengthening the negative influence of a high level of unemployment on money wages. The pre-eminence of competitive mechanisms therefore explains both the slight growth in real wages during the boom and the continuation of this growth during the years 1930 to 1933".[17] Only in the post-war period, the structure of accumulation is matched by monopolist regulation, creating the coherent growth pattern of Western Europe's "Golden age" of the 1960s.

The problem seems to be that there are no clearcut relations between the aggregate patterns of regulation (i), and the institutional changes indicated by regulation (ii). In addition, Boyer also introduces the notion of accumulation regimes into his analysis. This notion is necessary because his arguments about the relationships between the aggregate variables of regulation (i), must be related to some model of the impact of productivity trends, technological change, development of demand and the reproduction of the productive structure. Above, some of these features were introduced as "roots" of competitive and monopolist regulation, but in an unsystematic manner.

In the most general definition, the regime of accumulation is "a mode of systematic reallocation of surplus, serving to guarantee, during a prolonged period, a certain adequation between the transformations of the conditions of production and the transformations of the conditions of consumption. Such a regime of accumulation is summarized by a given scheme of reproduction, describing the allocation of social labour and the distribution of products between the different sectors of production from period to period".[18]

In many contexts, the regime of accumulation is presented as a "growth model". The regulation school originally analysed two accumulation regimes: an extensive and an intensive one. Whereas the earliest presentations were coached in Marxist

---

[17] Boyer, "Wage formation in historical perspective", p. 113.

[18] Lipietz, A., "De la nouvelle division internationale du travail a la crise du fordisme périphérique", *CEPREMAP*, Working Paper, No. 5225, Paris 1982, p. 4; Boyer, R., "La Crise actuelle", p. 2.

Wage Formation in the Norwegian Industry 1840-1985

terms, it seems that attempts at specifications relates mainly to Neo-Keynesian growth models and Schumpeterian long wave chronologies.[19]

According to the definition above, a regime of accumulation is a stable relationship between the two departments of production. Boyer's later definition, however, reads: "a regime of accumulation is defined by the whole set of regularities which allow a general and more or less consistent evolution for capital formation, i.e. which dampen and spread over time the imbalances which permanently arise from the process itself".[20] This latter definition seems to overlap with the definition of regulation as such.[21] Another ambiguity may also be noted: A Keynesian growth model may be constructed for periods of the development of a national economy. But if we define e.g. a post-war "Fordist" mass production model, such a model would transcend the borders of a small, open economy like Norway. Because of these ambiguities, and also because data (e.g. on productivity) are lacking for our earliest period, we shall not use the notion of accumulation regimes below.

The regulationists are partly aware of such ambiguities, and argue that since the approach is actually a "research programme", definitions must be refined and adjusted as empirical and theoretical results accumulate. It seems that the ambiguities create particular problems for the regulationists' analysis of the inter-war period. In fact, there is not much agreement on this period. Boyer has tried to utilize the conceptual distinction between regulation and regime of accumulation, classifying the inter-war period as "intensive accumulation without mass consumption". In this way, he is able to stylize "three major patterns of growth": in the pre-World War I-period, extensive accumulation combines with competitive regulation, in the inter-war period, intensive accumulation combines with competitive regulation, and in the post-war period, intensive accumulation combines with monopolist regulation.[22] This rather grand generalisation has been challenged. National experiences seem to differ significantly. Mazier et.al. have instead offered a typology of different inter-war models.[23] They emphasize that despite the strong international turmoil of the 1930s,

---

[19] Cf. for instance Boyer, R., "Formalizing growth regimes", in Dosi, G., Freeman, C., Nelson, R., Silverberg, G. & Soete, L., editors, *Technical Change and Economic Theory*, London: Pinter Publishers 1988.

[20] Boyer, R. "Technical change and the theory of 'regulation'", in Dosi, G., Freeman, C., Nelson, R., Silverberg, G. & Soete, L., editors, *Technical Change and Economic Theory*, London: Pinter Publishers 1988, p. 71.

[21] Boyer, "Technical change and the theory of 'regulation'", p. 71-75, discusses institutional regulations which ensure the stability of the accumulation regime and the mode of regulation respectively. It turns out that these institutional regularities are partially overlapping. On the other hand, Boyer, "Régulation", p. 127 comes up with a third notion - "mode of development" - which is defined as "the conjunction of the mode of *régulation* and the accumulation regime".

[22] Boyer, "Technical change and the theory of 'regulation'", p. 79.

[23] Mazier, J., Basle, M. & Vidal, J.-F., *Quand les crises durent...*, Paris: Economica 1984, pp.176-179, claim that the U.S. roaring twenties was a case of intensive accumulation combined with middle class mass consumption. If that is right, Boyer, "Technical change and the theory of 'regulation'", p. 87, is not correct when he indicates that Ford's problems in 1927 was probably the first crisis of Fordism. That crisis, as analysed by Hounshell, D. A. *From the American System to Mass Production 1800-1932*, Baltimore: Johns Hopkins University Press 1984, was an internal crisis of the Ford

the nature of the crises was basically national, with international events making things even more complicated.[24] In contrast, they hold that the crisis of the 1970s was of a genuinely international nature.[25]

In the rest of this paper, we restrict ourselves to an investigation of whether macroeconomic patterns of regulation (i) can be traced in the major phases of the Norwegian labour market development. The appendix gives a brief description of our time-series, which are surely scarce for the earliest periods. On the basis of these data, we explore the econometric relations[26] studied in Boyer's analysis of French wage formation. Unlike Boyer we do not consider all the variables at the aggregate national level.[27] Instead we concentrate on manufacturing industry. Actually, this is the only sector for which some data are readily available. For the earliest period, we are forced to deal only with textile industry. For the other periods, however, we can rely on more aggregate data - with all their blessings and pitfalls. In the next section,

---

Company, reflecting its extremely rigid tooling of the production line, relying on special machinery only. As Hounshell shows, already at that time, General Motors (under Sloan) had arrived on more flexible production arrangements which allowed yearly model changes. The combination of heavy public relations work and yearly cosmetic design changes was "Sloanism", not "Fordism". But Aglietta, *Régulation et crises du capitalisme*, in his original discussion of Fordism fuses the characteristics of Sloanism and Fordism. But while the 1927 crisis was above all a firm-specific crisis, one may argue with Mazier, Basle & Vidal, *Quand les crises durent...* that the 1930s crisis in the U.S. was a crisis for intensive accumulation based on middle class mass consumption. This middle class also included many farmers. Lutz, B., *Der kurze Traum immerwährender Prosperität*, Frankfurt a.M.: Campus, p. 140, points out that the traditional sector was much weaker in the U.S. than in Europe. The U.S. had no inherent family tradition in agriculture. Its labour force was largely recruited from immigrants leaving the traditional sectors of their home countries. The U.S. lacked many of the European legal and institutional defenses of the traditional sector, and U.S. agriculture was much more dependent on modern forms of trade and credit, farms were larger and the agricultural structure had developed not before, but simultaneously with the extension of the railroad network.

[24] Among the many unsolved questions relating to the inter-war period are the following: To what extent must the new Taylorist/Fordist types of labour process organization spread before the economy confirms to a model of intensive accumulation? To what extent may the persistence of a traditional sector barr the development of intensive accumulation? How large a section of the manufacturing industry labour force must bargain collectively before we can conclude that mass consumption is institutionalized? What is the role of social legislation and implementation of minimum wage levels? Are there functional equivalents to working class mass consumption? Is there an inherent connection between collective bargaining and productivity-related real wage growth, or can these features be disconnected? The role of external pressure must also be investigated, as the case of Germany and its war reparations surely makes clear.

[25] Mazier, Basle & Vidal, *Quand les crises durent...*, pp. 169-191.

[26] The general lack of satisfactory time series up to the 1920s makes econometric specification look exceedingly makeshift. The most pressing problem is not lack of data as such, but of comparable series for the same time-span. A way of avoiding this problem is to utilize a standard Box-Jenkins approach to time-series analysis, which concentrates on analysing one data-string at a time, but this method is not so well suited for tracing out relationships between variables as it is for prediction. See e.g. Harvey, A. C., *The Econometric Analysis of Time Series*, London: Phillip Allan 1981; Harvey, A. C., *Time Series Models*, London: Phillip Allan 1981. Another snag of this technique is that one easily looses touch with the economic theory that ideally should be guiding the statistical work; the 'best' specification seems to come out of nowhere. Thus, we prefer to rely on more traditional regression techniques.

[27] Cf. Boyer, "Wage formation in historical perspective", p. 109 for some reflections on a more disaggregated approach.

Wage Formation in the Norwegian Industry 1840-1985

we comment on these limitations, and give a quick bird's eye view of the development of Norwegian manufacturing industry.

Manufacturing industry in the Norwegian economy

The manufacturing sector is the core of the process of industrialization. Here, for the first time in history, we find workers relying solely on money incomes. Hence, the construction of real-wage series is meaningful. Furthermore, industrial conflict, class struggle and trade union activity started and spread from this sector.

Table 1 Number of workers employed in various industries (excluding mining), union members, unemployment rates, 1850-1985, selected years.

	Textiles[1]	Metals Machinery	Foods Beverages	Wood[2] Pulp,etc	Industry total	Union members LO[3] total	metal- workers	Unem- ploy- ment[4]
1850	1481 [12]	1368 [11]	2792 [23]	632 [5]	12279			
1865	3359 [14]	4999 [20]	4072 [17]	914 [4]	24431			
1875	5128 [11]	10927 [24]	6010 [13]	1945 [4]	45657			
1885	6037 [13]	9570 [21]	6478 [14]	3443 [8]	45313	1600		
1890	8153 [13]	13663 [22]	7827 [13]	6235 [10]	60956	4800		
1900	9265 [12]	16790 [22]	9882 [13]	8443 [10]	76326	1909		
1905	9153 [11]	18295 [22]	11162 [14]	10641 [13]	81379	15600	4779	4.4
1909	10776 [11]	23406 [24]	14471 [15]	12148 [12]	99581	44518	7708	2.9
1920	9667 [6]	36023 [23]	22820 [15]	17187 [11]	154211	142642	20937	2.3
1925	10326 [8]	20494 [26]	20494 [16]	17073 [13]	129127	95961	12009	13.2
1930	10536 [9]	27019 [23]	12691 [11]	24992 [22]	115733	139591	15057	16.2
1939	13449 [9]	38403 [26]	16267 [11]	28211 [19]	146956	352479	32605	23.1
1945	10585 [8]	45811 [33]	13062 [10]	10558 [8]	136893	407029[5]	445075[5]	3.6[5]
1950	18547 [6]	41532 [14]	18570 [6]	18298 [6]	307000	488442	53573	1.7
1960	14965 [5]	44414 [13]	29158 [9]	21882 [7]	330000	541519	68573	2.5
1970	11878 [3]	68942 [18]	46642 [12]	19354 [5]	378000	594359	89538	1.4[6]
1980	11874 [3]	85415 [23]	54871 [15]	17449 [5]	375000	748040	106779	
1985	7956 [2]	85782 [24]	52047 [15]	13641 [4]	353000	768778	101630	

1 Excluding clothing. 2 Including leather and rubber industries up to 1920. 3 Pensioneers included. 4 Unemployed union members, all branches. 5 1946. 6 End of this time series.

Notes: Workers employed: percentages of total in brackets. Number of workers employed has functionaries included up to 1920.

Sources: Workers employed: 1850-1909: Norwegian Central Bureau of Statistics (NCBS), Statistiske oversikter, Oslo 1914; 1920-1985: NCBS, Statistical Yearbook, Oslo, various years. Union members: 1890, 1905; Bain, G. S. & Price, R., Profiles of Union Growth, Oxford: Basil Blackwell 1980. The rest: The Labour Union Federation of Norway (LO), LO-yearbook, Oslo, various volumes. Unemployment: NCBS, Historical Statistics, Oslo 1978, Table 47.

Finally, in the 20th century, this sector has been a "wage-leader", as unions in other sectors have claimed the same wage-increase as the manufacturing sector.[28] Table 1 provides some basic information on the Norwegian industrial workforce; its distribution on sectors, as well as information on unionization and unemployment.

In 1830, about 90 percent of the workforce was still employed in the non-manufacturing sectors. Apart from the odd craftsman going mechanic, there was hardly any manufacturing production in Norway until the 1840s (the exception being saw mills), when textile-industry and a few mechanical workshops were started in the Kristiania (Oslo) area, producing goods for the home market. The most important ones were Hjula (weaving, established 1849), Nydalen and Graah's Vøien (spinning, established 1845/46). The founding dates of these firms are obviously connected to the fact that Britain lifted the ban on machinery exports in 1842.[29] Altogether, in 1855 and 1865 respectively, Norway had 20/32 mechanical workshops, 15/21 spinning factories and 16/16 weaving shops.[30]

Norway's main export-incomes in the 19th century stemmed from rural activities, often conducted by farmers as side-activities on small farms. In 1869, eight items included in the foreign trade statistics (wood and timber, salted herring, salted and dried cod, stockfish, fish-oil, roe, ice and oats) accounted for 86.6 per cent of the total value of Norwegian merchandize exports.[31] Towards the end of the century, also canned fish became important, and the forest industry extended its activities to manufacturing not only of planed wood, but also pulp and paper. Originally, this production for exports was conducted in connection with agriculture. Fishing was a strictly seasonal activity, and particularly in the North, the men would periodically go fishing leaving the women to take care of the small farm. As for forestry, timber would be cut in the winter in the large woods of the central area. The timber would be left on the icy rivers being floated down the rivers in the spring to some factory. Alternatively, the timber would be sawed in the spring or summer at local saws. It has been claimed that these possibilities of combining different activities in the Norwegian countryside explains the absence of disastrous famines and other kinds of rural problems well known from early modern European history:

> They were all free men, even serfs experienced increasingly secure conditions, and by the end of the period [1800-1850] most farmers were self-owners. Within this institutional framework, the natural resources were exploited by means of combined occupational activities [yrkeskombinasjon]. Full employment coincided with savings, invest-

---

[28] Certainly, our limitation is not without problems: Our focus on the industrial sector means that the further we look back into the 19th century, the smaller is the share of the workforce we shall be dealing with. In fact, the dominant export-activities of the 19th century will be left out of our analysis, as only a small percentage of Norwegian manufacturing output at that time was produced for export.

[29] Pryser, T., *Norsk historie 1800-1870*, Oslo: Det norske samlaget 1985, p. 198; Bruland, K., *British Technology and European Industrialization. The Norwegian textile industry in the mid nineteenth century*, Cambridge: Cambridge University Press, 1989.

[30] Pryser, *Norsk historie 1800-1870*, p. 198.

[31] Klovland, J. T. "A chronology of cycles in real economic activity for Norway, 1867-1914", Norwegian School of Economics and Business Administration, *Discussion Paper*, 1987: 2, p. 6.

ments and growth of production. With such a secure basis in the primary sector, external markets could be exploited. There was a concentration of income in the interface between foreign trade and primary sectors, giving rise to external expansion. Generally, however, the distribution of income was egalitarian. This spurred increasing production. The egalitarian distribution of income went hand in hand with a safe way of life for most people. Economic development was *balanced*, both between sectors and between social groups. Society was in equilibrium. Most likely, not only Norwegians will agree that at that time, Norwegian society was a good society to belong to.[32]

This picture is maybe too idyllic, but at least, it is likely that Norwegian early modern history was not marked to any large degree by the vicissitudes of the "old regulation" as Boyer defines it.

Returning to manufacturing industry, it is clear that only the final stage of the forest and fish production chain would count as manufacturing industry. Fish processing and canning developed on the eastern and northern shorelines and paper/pulp-factories around the Oslo and Trondheim fjords. A complete study of the late 19th century industrial wage relation should have included these sectors, but in our analysis of the first period, the focus is even more restricted: we deal with wages only in the most urbanized area at that time, the capital city of Oslo (Kristiania). Lacking wage-data from metalworking shops, we are left with the textile plants.

During the two main periods of the 20th century, new layers were added to the industrial structure: In the first decades of the century a number of large plants producing chemical products as well as semi-finished products were buildt. Producing fertilizers, aluminium, and other semi-finished products, these plants utilized the huge resources of hydro-electric power that the new electricity-generating techniques enabled Norway to produce from the many waterfalls. In the 1930s, a number of smaller shops grew up, producing simple durable consumer goods (e.g. furniture), doing repair work, and relating in many ways to the domestic market. Finally, in the post-war era, the Norwegian industrial structure still basically relied on the capital-intensive heavy industry which produced raw materials and semi-finished goods (and this aspect was actually strengthened with the discovery of oil off the Norwegian coast in the early 1970s). But also a new layer of medium sized producers of more advanced means of consumption and production (e.g. electronics) developed, in train with the post-war "Fordist" mass-consumption model.

1840-1907: The era of liberal capitalism

Boyer's macro-economic model of wage formation under competitive capitalism seems to consist of two mechanisms: In the product market, good times create increasing demand, and there is a certain inflation. Boyer refers to movements in production as an indicator of the activity level. As for the labour market, increasing production increases general economic activity, and when the labour market becomes tighter, nominal wages tend to rise as a consequence of strong demand for labour.

---

[32] Dyrvik, S. et al., *Norsk Økonomisk historie*, Oslo: Universitetsforlaget 1979, p. 251 (chapter by S. Tveite).

Scandinavian Economic History Review

Figure 2 The relation between money wages, cost of living and production 1850-1910. Selected wage series.

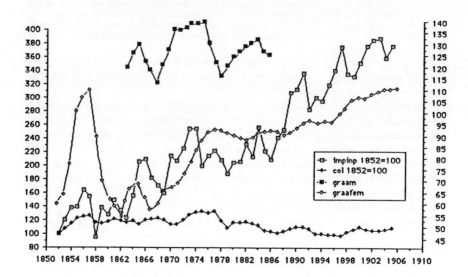

Note: All series are 3 year moving averages. *Col* is the Cost of living index, the two wage series are male (*graamale*) and female (*graafem*) wages at Graa textile works in Oslo, while *impinp* is our index of imported textile production inputs. *Col* and *impinp* are indeces, measured on the left-hand scale. The wage series are measured in monetary units (øre per day), indicated on the right-hand scale.

Sources: See Appendix 3, 1, 6.

Figure 2 plots Ramstad's cost of living index with nominal wage-series from one of the major Oslo textile plants. As for the cost of living, we can detect five year inflation/deflation cycles between 1852 and 1874, then there is a downward trend 1874-89 (a national incarnation of the late 19th century worldwide great depression), then the index is quite stable at the turn of the century.

Relating to Boyer's stylized schemes, we can make only one firm conclusion: the secular rise in the price level, characteristic of monopolistic regulation, is absent. Apart from that, it is very hard to find a clearcut pattern of competitive regulation as in Figure 1. Studying only the relation between the growth rates of the cost of living index and production (indicated by imported inputs), the pattern conforms roughly to competitive regulation in the periods 1855-1863, and 1875-98.[33] Including also the nominal wages of female workers (at Vøien/Graah), the impression of a competitive situation is confirmed for 1875-1883, and for the period after 1890. There are no data before 1864. The relation between those three variables in the 1864-73 period - somewhat surprisingly - looks more like Boyer's "old regulation". In that case how-

---

[33] These figures are not reproduced in this essay.

Wage Formation in the Norwegian Industry 1840-1985

ever, it is highly unlikely that the pattern is generated by the mechanisms pointed out by Boyer.

Even if money wages show a quite steady upward trend, in some years they fell substantially. Comparing selected real-wage series with the corresponding money wages[34], we find the standard deviation of the former being in all cases the smallest, but even these have a high degree of variability.[35] Below, we shall discuss two alternative explanations of this variability: bottlenecks in the supply of labour (meaning that there is not unlimited supply of labour), and profitability. But since visual scrutiny of curves may sometimes be delusive, we shall first give a more formal statistical analysis of our time series for the 1863-1907-period.

Table 2 Determinants of money-wage inflation in textile industry, Kristiania, 1863-1907

	Graah textile plant		Christiania canvas factory	
	Males	Females	Weavers	Spinners
Regr.no.	1	2	3	4
Method	OLS	CO(1)	CO(1)	CO(1)
Constant	-0.004	-0.001	0.179	0.0
	(-0.2291)	(-0.821)	(1.177)	(1.201)
PR	-0.359	0.500	0.419	0.706
	(-1.057)	(1.376)	(1.156)	(2.870)
PR_{-1}	-	-	0.486	-
			(1.384)	
XR	0.551	0.640	0.041	0.158
	(2.885)	(3.108)	(0.265)	(1.311)
XR_{-1}	0.389	-	-	-
	(2.262)			
R^2	0.3119	0.232	0.106	0.264
SER	0.081	0.094	0.085	0.721
DW	1.938	2.049	1.903	2.1022
N	45	44	51	51

Notes: Dependent variable: Nominal hourly wages. PR: Ramstad's consumer price index, XR: volume of production (index of imports of textile production inputs: *impinp*). Estimation methods: OLS - ordinary least squares; C/O - Cohrane/Orcutt method. t-values in brackets. All variables are growth rates.

Sources: See Appendix: 6, 1, 3.

---

[34] See Appendix, the Ramstad index is used as deflator.

[35] Boyer, "Wage formation in historical perspective", p. 102, claims that a "pronounced flexibility of money wages" represents "*a priori* evidence of the predominance of competitive adjustments".

Table 2 shows a regression of the growth of money wages on the growth rates for the cost of living and industrial production. The fit is quite poor, but in the series from the Vøien/Graah textile factory, the price variable seems uncorrelated with wage movements. In one of the series from the canvas factory, however, there is a significant correlation between these variables. This exception apart, the difference from the close correlation in the inter- and post-war periods is striking. The link between production and money wages is clear in the case of the textile plant, but again the other factory deviates. Since canvas was an important input to the flourishing Norwegian merchant shipping fleet, one may speculate as to whether external factors like booms and slumps in the international freight market may have been more influential here than in other lines of textile production.[36]

In sum, a formal statistical analysis does not bring us much closer to a firm conclusion. We are not able to find a clearcut pattern of competitive regulation in the data we have used so far. The Graah-series fit as to the nominal wage/production-relation, while the canvas-factory-series fit as to the nominal wage/cost of living-relation.

Returning to the question of why money wages show considerable variation, we shall attempt a more qualitative analysis of the supply of labour. If there was an unlimited supply of labour, the eager entrepreneur would be ensured a massive supply of unskilled labour, willing to work at wage-rates close to the subsistence level. Employment in the agrarian sector would be residually determined as people would leave for towns whenever there was an opportunity. In neo-classical terminology, this would mean that the marginal (agricultural) productivity of labour was close to zero, and in any case lower than the real wage. In such a case, the most likely explanation of the variability in wages would be variations in the cost of living. Table 2, however, rejects this.

Thus, one possible explanation of this variability is that supplies of labour were not unlimited, that there was in some sense bottlenecks. One argument supports such an hypothesis: It seems that the supply of labour from rural areas did not go straight into manufacturing industry. Recent research has pointed out that there was kind of an "internal labour market" in the Kristiania area, the only really urban area. Immigrants from rural areas were generally confined to the lowest-paid work. Industrial wages being higher than the wages of other urban labourers (e.g. servants), this meant that as rural immigration caught on, urban labourers moved into manufacturing work.[37] Many industrial workers were recruited from an urban background.[38]

If significant bottlenecks emerged in the Kristiania labour market, wages would be pushed upwards whenever the situation approached full employment, and downwards when there was much unemployment. It is, however, hard to study this empirically, since our data on urban unemployment starts at the turn of the century.

---

[36] To investigate this further, we would need not only a Norwegian price index, but also a comparable one for the world market.

[37] Seierstad, S., *Hvordan fagbevegelsen formet arbeidslivet*, Oslo: Pax 1982, p. 22.

[38] Pryser, *Norsk historie 1800-1870*, p. 208-210.

Wage Formation in the Norwegian Industry 1840-1985

However, the possible proxy of poor relief recipients shows no significant correlation with any of the wage series we have examined.[39] This fact supports the hypothesis of an effective reserve army, a kind of "unlimited supply of labour". There may have been an "internal labour market" in Kristiania, but it still seems that the supply of labour at the bottom of the hierarchy was sufficient to ensure a permanent surplus of labour willing to work in the new industries.

Traditionally, historians have emphasized that workers were to a large extent recruited to Kristiania from the large class of cotters and day-labourers in the agricultural sector.[40] According to Bull[41], living conditions among rural labourers were dreadful, with an ever-present possibility of hunger. The size of this group was rising sharply. Partly as a result of exceptionally high birth rates in the years after 1814, the number of land-holding cotters went up from 48,000 in 1825, to 65,000 in 1855, when the complete group of cotters (including families) comprised between a fifth and a fourth of the total population.[42] The wage-series we have for day-labourers do not indicate any dramatic leaps in the real wage, but (in the few circumstances where series are directly comparable) states a substantially higher wage-level in urban than in rural areas.[43] This also supports the view that there was a steady flow of labour into urban areas.

It is true that large-scale emigration to the U.S. until the 1920s relieved some of the labour surplus. In 1863-77, an average of 0.52 percent of the population emigrated each year, in 1877-97 this figure was 0.7, and in 1897-1918 it was 0.53. Nearly all emigrated to the U.S. In the 1881-1920-period, an average of between 66 and 70 percent of the emigrants emigrated from rural areas. Earlier, the percentage was even higher.[44] There seems to be an inverse relationship between overseas emigration and net migration to Kristiania (Oslo). In 1879-83, 1886-88, 1890-92, 1898-1903 and 1919-21, migration to Kristiania fell off while emigration to the U.S. rose. In 1875-79, 1883-84, 1888-90, 1893-98, 1903-08, 1914-17 and 1927-36, it was the other

---

[39] Textile workers, workers employed in road-construction, sawmill workers. All these wage series were taken from Ramstad, J., *Kvinnelønn og pengeøkonomi. En studie av kvinners lønn i tekstilindustrien i Kristiania ca. 1850-1910*, Master's thesis, Norwegian School of Economics and Business Administration, Bergen 1982.

[40] Bull, E., *Arbeiderklassen i norsk historie*, Oslo: Tiden 1947, estimated that 2/3s of the labour supply to manufacturing industry originated from the lower strata in agriculture.

[41] Bull, E., *Norsk fagbevegelse*, 2.ed, Oslo: Tiden 1968, p. 31.

[42] Hodne, F., *Norges økonomiske historie, 1815-1970*, Oslo: Cappelen 1981, p. 59. (The first, preliminary edition of this book, is in English: *An Economic History of Norway 1815-1970*, Trondheim: Tapir 1979.)

[43] Norwegian Central Bureau of Statistics (NCBS), *Statistiske Oversikter*, Oslo 1948, Table 193; Gjølberg, O. *Reallønnsutvikling og levekår for jordbruksarbeidere ca. 1830-1880*, Master thesis, The Norwegian School of Economics and Business Administration, Bergen 1974, Tables 25 and 33. For a general survey, see Minde, K. B. & Ramstad, J., "The development of real wages in Norway about 1730-1910", *Scandinavian Economic History Review*, 1986:2, pp. 90-121.

[44] Moe, T., *Demographic developments and economic growth in Norway 1740-1940: An econometric study*, Ph.D.-dissertation, Stanford University, 1970, p. 119.

way around.⁴⁵ These movements may be an important factor in explaining the political tranquillity of the rural transformations in Norway. But emigration in no way emptied the rural labour reservoar.

Doubting that bottlenecks in the labour market can explain the variability in wages, we must seek for an explanation which is consistent with the existence of unlimited supply of labour. It seems to us that profitability may provide an explanation. Of course, it is virtually impossible to construct an indicator of profitability at the micro level. Very detailed price indices for outputs and inputs at the sector or even firm level is probably impossible to get even today. Thus, all we can offer are some tentative and qualitative arguments.

If profitability is an important explanatory factor behind the variation in wages, it seems that the employer for some reason grants his workers higher wages when profitability is good. One possibility is that the employer simply needs to grant wage increases to speed up productivity. Another possibility is that when times are good, the employer, because of paternalist attitudes, shares his increased profits with the workers. Let us look at these two possibilities in turn.

We indicated in our first section that in the predominantly artisanal type of labour process of the late 19th century, craft workers were able to determine the pace of production. This was so, although one would believe that new workers could easily be trained, that the costs of hiring and firing were low, and there was no labour hoarding in the slump. Given narrow possibilities of productivity-increases, employers would have to bid up wages to get the few productivity increases which could be gained. Unfortunately, it is not possible to investigate this quantitatively, since time series showing short-term fluctuations in productivity are not available.⁴⁶

The question of whether artisanal control of the labour process mattered or not, may be related to some interesting comparative studies of the textile industry labour process in England and the U.S. in the early 19th century. There were two technologies of spinning: the mule (later the selfacting mule), and the throstle. Put very simply, the throstle implied deskilling, while the mule could only be handled by skilled workers. Cohen's comparative studies show that the mule lost out completely in America, but retained a dominant position in British textile industry.⁴⁷ The throstle was typically operated by female workers, paid according to piece rates. The reason why the mule was maintained in England, was not only the stronger collective traditions (artisans' "friendly societies", which developed into unions) of Lancashire textile craftsmen. The mule used less energy than the throstle, and since Lancashire lacked cheap waterpower, expensive steam from coal had to be used. Furthermore, the mule produced more varied and finer yarns.

We know that the early Norwegian textile plants were set up by people (for instance Knut Graah) who had aquired technical knowledge in England, and they

---

⁴⁵ Moe, *Demographic developments and economic growth in Norway*, pp. 122-131.

⁴⁶ This would require a detailed time series of production, and such a series has not so far been constructed for this period.

⁴⁷ Cohen, I., "Industrial Capitalism, Technology, and Labor Relations: The Early Cotton Industry in Lancashire (1770-1840) and New England (1790-1870)", *Political Power and Social Theory*, 1985:5.

Wage Formation in the Norwegian Industry 1840-1985

also often hired British factory foremen.[48] But it turns out that in Norwegian spinning, the throstle quite soon came to dominate over the mule, like in the U.S.[49] The majority of permanent textile workers (70 percent) were female. Women did the spinning and weaving, relying on skills acquired in the household. The male workers were mainly involved in maintainance, repairs, artisanal work, and acted as guards and foremen.[50] As Figure 2 indicates, their wage-level was higher. The textile plants were located around Akerselva, since they quickly found that the waterpower from the waterfalls provided cheaper energy than steam. Steam was later only used for heating. The female workers were payed piece rates.[51] The fact that Norwegian textile industry (at least in spinning) used the deskilling throstle process, indicates that there was not much craft control of the labour process.

We therefore turn to the other possibility, namely that there was some kind of paternalism, meaning that the family firm employers would let their workers benefit from the good times. Bull shows that paternalism was fairly common.[52] He describes the textile plants as relatively closed, dense factory societies, marked by "the combination of factory and a place to live (...), by employers who arrange celebrations, parties and other arrangements outside working hours, who take part in the education of children by contributing to schooling, and who to a limited extent also provided for the safety of the workers' households by sickness and pension insurance arrangements, as well as in other ways."[53] Even such arrangements, like the technologies themselves, emulated a "British model".

The existence of paternalist patterns may so far be the most credible hypothesis. But it is not hard to find conflicting evidence. Despite our doubts as to supply bottlenecks, historical accounts tell us that turnover in the textile industry was quite high, and that employers wanted to avoid loosing too many of their best workers.[54] Many statements indicate that employers found it hard to recruit workers, some plants even imported female labour from Sweden.[55] On the other hand, in the case of the cotton famine 1861-65, employment of spinners was halved, as there was a

---

[48] Bruland, *British Technology and European Industrialization*.

[49] Parmer, T. "Hvordan industriteknologien først kom til Norge", i Sejersted, F., editor, *Vekst gjennom krise*, Oslo: Universitetsforlaget 1982, p. 25.

[50] Bull, E., *Arbeiderklassen blir til*, Vol. 1 of *Arbeiderbevegelsens historie i Norge*, Oslo: Tiden 1985, p. 259.

[51] Pryser, *Norsk historie 1800-1870*, p. 195-7, p. 203.

[52] Bull, *Arbeiderklassen blir til*, p. 258.

[53] Ibid., p. 264.

[54] Pryser, *Norsk historie 1800-1870*, p. 208.

[55] Bruland, *British Technology and European Industrialization*, p. 85, indicates a general lack of qualified workers, and on p. 130 provides evidence of a lack of qualified weavers. But Bruland's investigation mainly focuses on lack of know-how at the entrepreneurial level, i.e. the need to import foremen and skilled workers from England. This concerns set up, maintainance and repair of machines, and tells us little about skill requirements of workers themselves.

cutoff during the American Civil war of raw cotton from the U.S. South.[56] It is also told that young, unmarried women had to use connections (family or friends) to get a job in a textile factory.[57] It may of course be, that these accounts lump together information from different phases of the business cycle. In sum, the idea that paternalism generated some kind of "profit sharing" may at least be worthy of further research. As noted, our discussion is quite tentative, unrelated both to closer quantitative studies and to concrete case-studies. Since we deal only with the textile sector, it is also difficult to judge whether the results of such a sectoral analysis can be generalized. There is evidence of correlation between seamen and road workers for this period.[58] But these were quite mobile workers, and did not work in a factory setting.

1907-1940: The era of organized capitalism

As the number of industrial workers increased, unionsation gained pace, and the 1880s saw the formation of a strong labour movement. Existing unions created umbrella organisations, and new unions were formed until most branches were covered. The Labour Party was officially formed in 1887, one year after its Danish and Swedish counterparts. Initially, this had little influence on the labour market as such. Whereas craftsmen went on strike as early as the beginning of the 1870s (during high times), most unskilled workers, enjoying a higher standard of living than in the rural area they had moved in from, were unwilling to face the risk of being sacked. Not until the early 20th century did the unions successfully organize major strikes, but in 1907, the metalworkers' union, by threatening to go on strike, achieved the right to negotiate wages on behalf of their members. This was probably the first case in which the employers accepted collective bargaining.

We may tentatively conclude that from now on, the industrial workforce had become so large, both in total numbers and at the level of single plants, that the power of those workers could no longer be contained by bringing in poor, rural labourers. Organized workers were probably less receptive to paternalism. If this is correct, we should at this time be able to discover some new patterns. First of all, we expect to find a correlation between cost of living and wage development. Secondly, productivity growth, being a major argument in tariff negotiations, may turn out to be an influential factor, whereas the link between wages and the activity level is broken. Although we were not able to reach any firm conclusions on the competitive

---

[56] Our index of textile industry imports (*inpimp* in Figure 2, above), does not reflect this drop in imports, since it includes also different types of yarns. It seems that the weavers changed from Norwegian spun yarn to imported yarn. But in the basic data on cotton imports, the effects of the cotton famines are clearly visible.

[57] Pryser, *Norsk historie 1800-1870*, p. 202-3.

[58] Hodne, F. & Gjølberg, O., "Market integration during the period of industrialization in Norway", in Bairoch, P. & Lévy-Leboyer, M., editors, *Disparities in economic development since the industrial revolution*, London: Macmillan 1981; Fischer, L.R. & Nordvik, H.W., "From Namsos to Halden: Myths and realities in the history of Norwegian seamen's wages, 1850-1914", *Scandinavian Economic History Review*, 1987: 35.

Wage Formation in the Norwegian Industry 1840-1985

wage relation in Norway, these developments would mean a move away from the competitive ideal type.

Unionisation implies negotiations. This implies some degree of controllability, as well as an area for government intervention. Not surprisingly, we find the government entering this arena as early as 1911, as mediator in a conflict affecting 32 000 men.[59] However, no government before the Second World War seems to have attempted outright incomes policies. The tariff negotiations did not seem to involve discussions of tax-rates or other factors affecting the net disposable income of wage-earners.

The war in Europe never reached Norwegian territory, and did not have any strong negative effect on the economy as a whole. On the contrary, the important shipping sector prospered. Indeed, the outbreak of World War 1 may be seen to mark a consolidation of the new phase. Between 1904 and 1914 the number of industrial workers increased by 50 per cent, and LO-membership quadrupled (Table 1). Trade union density jumped from 7.6 in 1910 to 20.4 in 1920.[60] As industrialization caught on, production became more geographically differentiated, and the structure of industry more varied, so too was recruitment to the organized labour movement. At this time the new layer of energy- and capital-intensive plants began to transform the Norwegian industrial structure. This era - named the "jobbing era" - gave many Norwegians the impression of major social change: "Coming at a time when almost half of all economically active men worked out of their own households as self-employed, on a (small) farm, in a shop, or as independent craftsmen, the establishment of many new and large factories, employing hundreds of workers, changed the picture of the future for many".[61]

The troubled 1920-1940 period started with a dramatic increase in unemployment in 1921. As in other European countries, organized labour gained some major reforms in the last half of the 1910s (social legislation was initiated, the length of the work-day being regulated for the first time in 1915), but in the 1920s there were setbacks and very dramatic conflicts in the labour market. Like Sweden, Norway was among the most conflict-ridden countries at that time. From the 1920 peak, trade union density actually declined to 18.3 in 1929, then rising rapidly to 34.3 in 1936.[62] The 1920s contrasts with the late 1930s which had relatively more peaceful labour relations.[63] This has to do with the Labour party's turn to reformism. The party had a (very) brief stint in government in 1928, but held this position permanently from 1935. Of course, the employers had reacted to the increased unionisation by forming their own organisations, and by the start of the 1930s, the opposing parties had become so large that major conflicts necessarily implied heavy costs on both sides.

---

[59] Bull, *Norsk fagbevegelse*, p. 118.

[60] Bain, G. S. & Price, R. *Profiles of Union Growth*, Oxford: Basil Blackwell 1980.

[61] Rogoff Ramsøy, N., "From Necessity to Choice: Social Change in Norway 1930-1980", in Erikson, R. et.al., editors, *The Scandinavian Model*, Armonk, New York: M. E. Sharpe 1987, p. 77.

[62] Bain & Price, *Profiles of Union Growth*, p. 158.

[63] Korpi, W., *The Democratic Class Struggle*, London: Routledge & Kegan Paul 1983.

Figure 3 The relation between money wages, cost of living and production 1910-1940. Selected wage series.

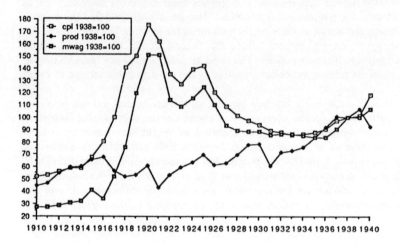

Sources: See appendix: 1, 3, 6.

Figure 4 Real wages. Unemployment. 1910-1940.

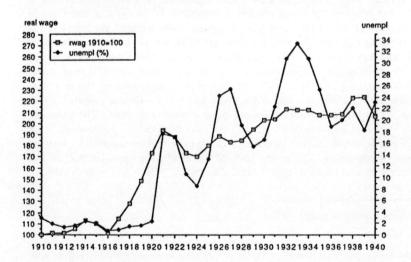

Sources: See appendix: 6, 5.

Wage Formation in the Norwegian Industry 1840-1985

However, in this case mutual deterrence did not have the alleged effect of truce, and more regulated agreements were needed. "Hovedavtalen" (literally: "The Main Agreement") between the LO and the Employers' Federation (NAF), setting the formalities of bi-annual wage negotiations, was signed in 1935. The common phenomenon of the 1970s, the *wage-drift* (meaning local wage changes agreed on at the local level inbetween central re-negotiations), was probably present to some extent from now on.

We may regard labour market performance in the 1920s and 1930s as a result of two opposing forces: on the one hand, the increasing bargaining power of the labour-organizations, and on the other hand the fact that these unions had to cope with the severe economic crisis. The combined effect on wages is naturally not clear, and the results given in Table 3 indicates several factors at work. Disregarding simultaneity problems, our results are remarkably strong; even though a good fit is quite common when regressing time-series, both the t-values and the r-squares are very high. Following Table 3 then, we see that changes in the cost of living is by far the most important variable.[64] This supports the assumption of trade-union influence at an early stage, but such a conclusion has an obvious problem: it is equally true for positive as for negative price changes. In 14 out of the 28 years included prices fell, sometimes dramatically, and this went in train with wage-cuts. No trade union would support such a symmetry.

The symmetry indicates a complex situation in which those workers who are lucky enough to be employed, get a real wage increase thanks to strong deflation, as was the case in Norway 1925-26 and 1927-32 (Figure 4). Only in 1921-24 and in 1926-7, employers succeeded in reducing nominal wage growth enough to diminish the real wage. But the real wage increases followed from the deflationary movements, a trait typical of competitive regulation. Deflation was obviously also influenced by the monetary policies which brough the Norwegian Krone to the prewar parity between 1928-31. The 1933 level of real wages was nearly maintained, with some improvements in 1937/38. Both 1924-26 and 1929-32, real wages increased at the same time as unemployment soared. (Real wages may increase, but aggregate demand may not pick up if unemployment is still high.)

Since the early decades of this century contain some very strong leaps in our time series (most dramatically the rise in unemployment from 1920 to 1921), we have run a number of regressions with different starting and ending points. The conclusion from this excercise is that the results obtained for the full 1910-39 period are strengthened when we concentrate on the middle period, i.e. approximately the years

---

[64] Such an increasing elasticity of nominal wages to prices is also found in French data, and it is also a stylized fact for the U.S. and England. Boyer, "Wage formation in historical perspective" argues that when this elasticity is close to 1, real wages - which influence the rate of profits through the wage/profit-share - will only change by more pronounced fluctuations in the cost of living. Boyer claims that this is only a break with competitive regulation if changes in the activity level has a counteracting effect. But Boyer finds a strong correlation between the volume of industrial production and nominal wages. Given that Boyer uses industrial production as an indicator, it is surprising that he has not used unemployment data instead, since for the inter-war period, such data must be available for France. This is especially surprising, since Boyer finishes off by doubting the index he is using, arguing that what seems like a strengthening of the competitive mechanism may instead be due to a change in the construction of the index.

Scandinavian Economic History Review

from 1916 and 1928. Evaluating the periods 1910-16 and 1929-39 separately, the correlations seem to break down, but the number of observations is so low that no firm conclusions should be drawn from this.

Table 3 The relationship between money wage inflation, cost of living, productivity and unemployment in manufacturing industry 1910-1940

Regr. no.	1	2	3	4
Period	1911-39	1910-39	1910-39	1916-28
Constant	-0.002	0.014	-0.013	0.0573
	(-0.151)	(1.201)	(-0.904)	(0.347)
WR_{-1}	-1.136	0.305	-	-
	(-0.827)	(4.256)		
PR	0.936	1.144	0.856	0.966
	(10.067)	(10.261)	(9.039)	(16.145)
PR_{-1}	0.459	-	0.237	0.33
	(2.070)		(2.915)	(5.749)
ZR	0.639	0.146	0.678	0.889
	(3.125)	(0.596)	(3.405)	(5.428)
ZR_{-1}	0.119	-	-	-
	(0.628)			
$(1/U)^2$	-0.090	-0.042		
	(-3.092)	(-1.023)		
$(1/U)^2_{-1}$	0.158	-	0.148	0.185
	(5.390)		(4.176)	(7.643)
R^2	0.967	0.921	0.949	0.995
SER	0.035	0.049	0.039	0.024
DW	2.050	2.018	1.949	2.034
N	29	30	30	13

Notes: Dependent variable: Nominal hourly wages. PR: Consumer price index; ZR: Productivity, Production per man-hour; U: Unemployment rate (trade union members). t-values in brackets. Estimation method: Cochrane-Orcutt iteration. All variables except unemployment are growth rates.

Sources: See Appendix: 6, 1, 4, 5.

A strong influence of unemployment would be another indication of the presence of traditional competitive forces. In 1920-21 unemployment exploded and nominal wages dropped. A similar pattern is seen in 1925-27. But in the third major slump for industrial production, 1930-33, unemployment reached record levels while nominal wages remained constant. Unemployment among unionized workers was re-

Wage Formation in the Norwegian Industry 1840-1985

duced in the late 1930s, but was only down to 18 percent, still above the 1921-peak, in 1939.[65]

One might hypothesize that the strong dependence on prices is due to price-changes being an indicator of variation in profitability. Firms facing sluggish demand are "forced" to cut wages, and growth in demand boosts wages. It seems that in the 1921-crisis, unemployment first occurred in the export-oriented parts of manufacturing industry, and the explosive unemployment would then cause a weakening of demand.

If profitability determine the variation in nominal wages, then product prices is the relevant variable. Thus, we replaced the Consumer Price Index with an indicator of product prices.[66] This gave no major changes. If, however, both the consumer price index and product prices are included, the impact of the latter is explained by the former (that is, imported inflation has an impact through domestic inflation). In sum, it seems that profitability cannot explain the symmetry which implies "indexation" of wages to the cost of living with no downward rigidity. The picture is somewhat like Boyer's case of "mature competitive regulation". The sole trace of a specific influence of trade unions may be the element of productivity-related wage inflation (but the coefficient here is rather small).

Concerning the inter-war crisis, Boyer claims that in France institutional changes made wages fluctuate with the prices, and that this maintained the purchasing power. But another major aspect in monopolist regulation, namely an institutionalized productivity indexation was still absent. Norway differs from France in World War I of course. Norwegian industry had about the same pace of productivity growth in the 1910-20 as in the 1922-30-period, but while real wages in the first period seemed to outpace productivity, real wage growth was below productivity growth in 1922-30 (Table 4).

Boyer regards the high productivity growth as an indication of an intensive regime of accumulation, pointing to the introduction of Taylorist and Fordist production methods in French industry. This judgement have been questioned. Mazier, for instance, argues that productivity growth reflected catching up after the war, that dualism and craft production still persisted, and that the degree to which "Americanist" production methods spread was very limited.[67] We would hold that the same points are even more relevant to Norway. What occurred, as already mentioned, was the growth of some large new industrial sectors (like the energy-, import- and capital-intensive furnace sector), rather than a turn to intensive accumulation. Of course, there was some degree of "homogenization", meaning replacement of craft workers by semi-skilled workers in the core sectors of manufacturing industry, but there are few historical studies of such labour process

---

[65] Note however, that the activity level is measured by $1/U^2$, with U fluctuating between 1 and 35 percent. Hence, the large coefficients for $1/U^2$ cannot be compared to those relating to the growth of prices and productivity.

[66] See Appendix: 7.

[67] Mazier, et.al., *Quand les crises durent...*, p. 172-173.

transformations in Norway. Hence, the formula "intensive accumulation without mass consumption" must be doubted.

Table 4 Real wages and productivity. Annual average rates of change.

	Production per man-hour	Hourly real wages	Productivity/ Real wages
1910-20	2.58	5.64	-3.06
1922-30	2.72	0.98	1.74
1930-37	0.50	0.37	0.13

Sources: See Appendix: 4, 6.

Boyer argues that "the conditions at which wages were determined were incompatible with the new mode of accumulation at the end of the First World War"[68], and furthermore that economic policies, an export boom and accomodating credit creation could only for a period (the late 1920s) conceal "the disequilibrium between the growth of productive capacity and overall demand".[69] At least for Norway, we would propose another conclusion: collective organization of the workers implied a defense against heavy real wage losses in the 1920s, but the real wage did not become linked to productivity. The productivity increases may have been linked to the high unemployment, but in that case, the sluggish productivity growth of the 1930s is hard to understand. Unemployment had declined even before the Labour party came into office, but in the late 1930s, it persisted at around 20 percent of all unionized workers and generally, there seems to have been little demand management by the Labour government before the war.

While the 1880-1920-period had seen an increasing flow of labour from agriculture to industry and services, this trend was reversed in the late 1920s and 1930s. There was an increasing number of small farms which provided housing and food, but where the money income had to come from other activities (e.g. fishing, forest work). Fewer young people left the countryside. Referring to the population census of 1930, Rogoff Ramsøy[70] finds that 33.2 percent of men between the age of 31-40 worked in industry, while only 28.7 percent of those between 26-30 did and only 25.3 percent of those between 21-25. While more people stayed on in agriculture, the primary sector became overpopulated and productivity slumped. There was no

---

[68] Boyer, "Wage formation in historical perspective", p. 112.

[69] Ibid., p. 112.

[70] Rogoff Ramsøy, "From Necessity to Choice", p. 78.

Wage Formation in the Norwegian Industry 1840-1985

secondary schooling available in rural areas, and in the cities such schooling was so expensive that few from the lower classes could afford to attend.

Industrial production began to grow more steadily after 1933 (see Figure 3). Schumpeterian economic historians[71] have argued that this trend was basically due to the development of small scale industrial activity in rural areas and small towns. As it was difficult to find employment, many young entrepreneurs, using the new technologies of small combustion engines, started production of simple durable consumer goods (furniture), repair shops, etc. One should, however, remember that the Norwegian devaluation connected to the breakdown of the gold standard brought about a favourable development of terms of trade, which moved from 100 in 1928 and 1930, to 84 in 1932, 91 in 1935, 80 in 1937 and down to 80 in 1939/40.[72] In this situation, Norwegian producers won market shares both in home and export markets.

The postwar economy: Monopolistic regulation in an open economy.

The 1945-52-period was a reconstruction phase. During the war, a group of Norwegian economists, led by the pioneer of mathematical economics, Ragnar Frisch, worked on what was to be known as the National Accounting System. This conceptual framework, closely connected to Keynesian economic theory, was used as the basis for an annual National Budget (the first came in 1947) and spurred the idea of government intervention. The first cohorts of Frisch's candidates quickly filled central positions in the bureaucracy (Treasury, Bank of Norway, The Central Bureau of Statistics), becoming, in this sense, the "organic intellectuals" of the reformist Labour party.[73] Thus, the administration of the war economy found its echo in an increased interest in, and possibility of, a planned economy.

Reconstruction was indeed characterized by detailed central planning. "Temporary" wartime laws turned out to be quite handy - and permanent. The economic historian Fritz Hodne[74] claims that Norway in this period had "a more extensive and more detailed permanent system of price controls than any other democratic country". Rationing of consumer goods was in general maintained up to a phase of liberalization in 1949-1952, the end of which marks the start of the 20-year long "Golden Age". This periodization is not, however, reflected by the traditional macro-economic variables, which show a steady growth from 1945 onwards. Pre-war levels of production and employment were in most sectors reached as early

---

[71] Sejersted, editor, *Vekst gjennom krise.*

[72] NCBS, *Historical Statistics*, HS 1978, Fig. 43, which uses 1961 = 100. With 1928 = 100, the major improvements are concentrated in 1932-1936. See Table 1:12 in Nordiska Historikermøtet i Uppsala 1974, *Kriser och krispolitik i Norden under mellankrigstiden*, Uppsala: Almqvist & Wiksell 1974. The same applies to the other Nordic countries, and this has been mentioned as one of the reasons why the social democratic governments could claim success for their economic policies.

[73] Bergh, T. & Hanisch, T. J. 1984. *Vitenskap og politikk. Linjer i norsk sosialøkonomi gjennom 150 år*, Oslo: Aschehoug, pp. 185-189.

[74] Hodne, *Norges økonomiske historie, 1815-1970*, p. 559.

Scandinavian Economic History Review

as 1947.[75] Between 1946 and 1973 the annual economic growth was on average 4.7 per cent.

The Government's number one priority was to avoid the massive inflation that might have incurred as rationning was abandoned, and stalling wage inflation became central in order to achieve this. Appealing to overriding national goals might have been easier than nowadays, but even at that time had to be supported by firmer means. A law prohibiting wage increases was passed in 1950. The regulation of the wage relation was generally an "administered" one.

The atmosphere of cooperation left by the years of occupation, together with the generally favourable economic development, all but erased industrial conflicts from the agenda of the late 1940s and early 1950s.[76] Knutsen reports a complete shift in the attitudes towards strike activity.[77] Before the war, "blacklegs" had been heavily condemned, but now a similar anger was directed against strikers. In the 1945-49-period, an average of 76 000 workdays were lost in strikes per year; for the 1950-54-period the figure was down to 70 000. This relative tranquility is remarkable when compared with even the most peaceful years of the inter-war time: an average of 600 000 workdays were lost per year between 1935 and 1939.[78]

Almost twenty years of Labour governments sealed a commitment to full employment, but a tight labour market combined with modest inflationary pressure gave little need for short-term intervention. Between 1952 and 1962 real wages were almost exclusively determined through labour-capital negotiations. In this period, wages were either set locally, branchwise, or by centralized negotiations of the umbrella organizations on both sides: the NAF and the LO. In the fifties, branchwise negotiations dominated, while the central organizations took over in the sixties. However, at several times in the sixties and seventies, the Government took an active part in central negotiations.[79]

Irrespective of organizational level, the bi-annual agreements set forth in the 1935 treaty has been a persistent phenomenon. Post-war data reflects this, by making the distinction between wage changes determined through negotiations, and changes taking place in a more uncontrolled manner ("wage-drift", or market-induced wage inflation). A common feature of empirical studies on wage formation is an attempt to find different mechanisms behind the two. Brunstad and Aarestad estimate the negotiated and the drift-part of the total wage formation separately, using data for

---

[75] Norwegian Central Bureau of Statistics, *Norges økonomi etter krigen*, Social Economic Studies (SES), No. 12, Oslo: NCBS 1965, p. 36 ff; and Hodne, *Norges økonomiske historie, 1815-1970*, p. 563 for growth rate figures.

[76] A comprehensive description of the Norwegian post-war economy is available in NCBS, *Norges økonomi etter krigen*, cf. also Hodne, F., *The Norwegian Economy 1920-1980*, London: Croom Helm, 1983.

[77] Knutsen, P., "Statsbærende og opposisjonell reformisme", *Tidsskrift for arbeiderbevegelsens historie*, 1977:2, p. 14.

[78] Bull, *Norsk fagbevegelse*, p. 155.

[79] Cappelen, Å., "Inntektspolitikken i Norge i etterkrigstiden",*Vardøger*, 1981: 11, pp. 178-210.

Wage Formation in the Norwegian Industry 1840-1985

the 1940-1969-period.[80] One would assume the tightness of the labour market to have a stronger influence on the drift-part, but on the whole their results are rather inconclusive. The sign of the coefficiats are sometimes wrong, the fit is poor and the coefficients seldom significant. The same goes for productivity; the only variables with consistently significant coefficients are cost-of-living and lagged changes in the real wage, both influencing negotiated changes only.

Isachsen takes the former study as his starting point, and attempts a better specification of the wage-drift.[81] His main argument is that labour-demand is not a function of cost of living, but of product prices, and that this is the relevant price variable behind wage-drift. His regressions (1953-1971) confirm this hypothesis; of the other variables he includes, none are significant, even though the coefficient for unemployment has the right sign and its size is fairly constant throughout the analysis. And again, productivity carries no significance. Isachsen also provides a survey of seven empirical studies of wage-drift, with the two we have mentioned included. To sum up, the conclusion is that the product prices and unemployment probably has some effect on the wage-drift, but results for other variables are at best ambiguous. The more recent studies in this field we know of confirms this conclusion.[82] Recent calculations on the 1965-83-period at the NCBS, however, have found a certain long term influence of productivity.[83]

The already close ties between the Labour Party and the LO became even stronger in this period, and a final purge of communists was successful as the cold war made any group negative to NATO-membership an easy target.[84] As for incomes policies, the Labour Party and LO held forth the possibility of redistribution within the wage-earning class, but subscribed to a freeze of the profit/wage ratio, in order to secure full employment and increase production through sufficient private investment. This would appear in the statistics as a close fit between wages and productivity and a weakening of the relation between wage inflation and unemployment. However, there might have been an increase in labour's share of factor income due to various indexation clauses. Automatic indexation had temporatily been introduced in the autumn of 1950, providing almost 90 per cent compensation for inflation.[85] Wage increases for some time surpassed growth in productivity and real wages started to display the now familiar pattern of downward rigidity.

The fixed income distribution between labour and capital is an explicit feature of a "Scandinavian Inflation Model", alternatively named the "Aukrust-model", a simple

---

[80] Brunstad, R. & Aarestad, J., "Lønns- og prisutviklinga i Norge 1950-1969: ein empirisk studie på årsdata", *Sosialøkonomen*, 1972: 7, pp. 11-22.

[81] Isachsen, A. J., "Lønnsglidningshypoteser: En test med norske data", *Sosialøkonomen*, 1976:3, pp. 15-24.

[82] Isachsen, A. J. & Raaum, O., "Solidarisk lønnspolitikk. Hvor effektiv er den egentlig?", *Sosialøkonomen*, 1978: 3, pp. 14-20; Hersoug, T., "Tarifftillegg, lønnsglidning og samlet lønnsøkning i Norge 1946-1981", Department of Economics, University of Oslo: *Memorandum*, 1983: 21.

[83] Stølen, N. M., "Faktorer bak lønnsveksten", NCBS, *Økonomiske analyser*, 1985:9, p. 40, Table 7.

[84] Knutsen, "Statsbærende og opposisjonell reformisme".

[85] Cappelen, "Inntektspolitikken i Norge i etterkrigstiden", p. 185.

model for inflation in a small, open economy.[86] This model makes a distinction between two sectors of the economy, one in direct confrontation with world markets, another sheltered from foreign competition. In the "open" sector, a fixed factor income distribution implies that growth in wages must follow the sum of increases in (import) prices and productivity. Wages in the sheltered sector is assumed to follow developments in the open sector. Hersoug analyses the period as a whole in this perspective.[87] It is somewhat tricky to sort the impact of import-price rises from pure cost-of-living indexation (this amounts to drawing the line between the Aukrust model and a "pure" monopolistic regulation!), but his study seems to support the influence of the world market. This is supported by the findings of a recent project on income determination in Norway in the 1970s and the 1980s.[88]

In what way were the institutional forces altered as an effect of the economic crisis of the early seventies?[89] The wage-price spiral was set in motion by increased inflation, and government intervention into central bargaining greatly increased. In sum we observe a shift away from the productivity-link towards a closer link between wage- and price-inflation. This may be studied more closely by tracing changes in factor income shares. The increasing number of public employees makes productivity less important in tariff negotiations, as productivity in the service sector is notoriously difficult to measure. The central labour union organization, the LO, is in a defensive position, as it has not been able to organize large enough shares of the new middle classes. Hence, their share of unionized wage-earners has been declining since the 1960s and other "yellow" central organizations are growing in importance.[90] How this interacts with segmentation of the labour markets and technological change is a crucial question, but one which we cannot pursue here.

Conclusions

We have been able to trace some contrasts between a largely competitive labour market in the 19th century, and the more organized patterns of the 20th century. Our concluding remarks relate to the 19th century only, since the analysis here gave somewhat vague results.

There may also be problems involved in the definition of competitive regulation. First, one may question the isolation of the labour market and the wage relation from on the one hand techno-economic factors, on the other hand, institutional

---

[86] Aukrust, O., "Inflation in the open economy", in Krause, L.B. & Salant, W.B., *Worldwide inflation*, Washington D.C.: Brookings 1977.

[87] Hersoug, "Tarifftillegg, lønnsglidning og samlet lønnsøkning i Norge 1946-1981".

[88] NOU (Norwegian Public Reports) 1988:24, *Inntektsdannelsen i Norge*, Oslo 1988.

[89] For a more general analysis of the Norwegian economy in this period, see Mjøset, L., "Norway's full employment oil economy - flexible adjustment or paralysing rigidities?" *Scandinavian Political Studies*, 1989: 4, pp. 1-29; Fagerberg, J., Cappelen, Å., Mjøset, L. & Skarstein, R., "The break-up of social democratic state capitalism in Norway", in Camiller, P., ed., *The Left in Western Europe*, London: Verso 1990 (forthcoming).

[90] Fennefoss, A., *Lønnstaker-organisering*, Oslo: FAFO, 1988.

patterns related to the inter-firm structure and to monetary relations. Integrating these fields into the analysis is in fact a part of the regulationist programme. As for the relation between firms, we can assume that the competitive conditions were fulfilled: family firms prevailed and even the largest ones lacked the managerial hierarchies which are typical of the modern corporation.[91] As for the monetary system, however, monetary policies may have influenced prices, while Boyer in his original analysis seems to assume that monetary policies are accommodating. This goes also for monopolist regulation: It is not evident that this labour market pattern as such explains the secular post-war inflation (rising cost of living), since in addition, we must note the possibility that factors linked to price formation and domestic credit-management have some impact on their own. A more comprehensive study should investigate this further.

Our discussion of the Norwegian 19th century labour market, brought us into quite complex considerations concerning the supply of labour. A closer study should deal more thoroughly with the impact of dualism, a factor which is insufficiently dealt with in Boyer's original analysis. In competitive regulation, workers' consumption mainly consists of housing and non-durable consumer goods. If we define the traditional sector in a broad sense (including also household labourers who are family members, not earning a market wage[92]), it seems that most of the consumer goods and services were supplied from this sector. In this respect, the definition quoted in our first section, according to which workers in competitive regulation benefit from productivity increases through price-reductions in the product markets, becomes vague, since most of their consumption is not produced in the sectors where they work.

In sum, it seems important to study other factors which may have influenced the cost of living. Some of these factors were probably internal to the traditional sector (for instance, its exposure to competition from imported foodstuffs), but others may have been related to the domestic credit system (for instance the degree to which the supply of credit was restrained by rigid gold-standard rules).

For the 19th century, data are scattered. Our attempt to trace what we defined as regulation (i), did not lead to any clearcut understanding of periods in Norwegian labour market development during the era of liberal capitalism. We have pointed to some difficulties inherent in the regulationist research programme. But it should be emphasised that we still think that this programme is a promising one. A more comprehensive study would need to combine regulation (i) and regulation (ii), arriving at a full understanding of regulation (iii) in different socio-economic periods.

---

[91] Chandler, A. D., *The Visible Hand*, Boston: Harvard University Press 1977.

[92] Cf. Lutz, *Der kurze Traum immerwährender Prosperität*.

Scandinavian Economic History Review

Data Appendix

This paper reports some findings from the project "The Norwegian Model. Studies in the Political Economy of Norway 1814-1985" at the Institute for Social Research, Oslo. It has been financed by the Norwegian Research Council for Science and the Humanities. A first version of the paper was presented to the "International conference on the theory of regulation", Barcelona, June 16-18, 1988. It was last revised in January 1990.

Historical Statistics, published by the NCBS (The Central Bureau of Statistics), with its last edition in 1978, is the starting point for anyone interested in a more detailed description. Unless otherwise stated, our data are drawn from this source. We use the abbreviation HS78 for the 1978-edition, and HS68 for the 1968-edition, with table numbers added.

1. *Cost-of-living indexes*. Ramstad's cost of living index for female textile workers in Kristiania (Oslo) 1850-1910 is by far the best Norwegian CPI for this period: Minde, K. B. & Ramstad, J., "The development of real wages in Norway about 1730-1910", *Scandinavian Economic History Review*, 1986:2, pp. 90-121. Two studies indicate that the Ramstad-index is representative for large parts of Southern Norway, cf. Hodne, F. & Gjølberg, O., "Market integration during the period of industrialization in Norway", in P. Bairoch and Lévy-Leboyer, M., editors, *Disparities in economic development since the industrial revolution*, London: Macmillan 1981; Fischer, L.R. & Nordvik, H.W., "From Namsos to Halden: Myths and realities in the history of Norwegian seamen's wages, 1850-1914", *Scandinavian Economic History Review*, 1987:1. The only competing index is the one computed by Juul Bjerke from estimated National Account figures, 1865 onwards, but this index is very poorly documented. Bjerke, J., *Langtidslinjer i norsk økonomi 1865-1960*, Social Economic Studies (SES), No. 16, Oslo: NCBS 1966. After 1910 we rely on the consumer-price index of NCBS (HS78, Tab. 286).

2. *Employment*. From every 5th year from 1850 to 1900, we have reports on employment (number of workers) in mining and industry, cf. NCBS, *Statistiske oversikter*, Oslo 1914. After this we have annual figures (number of workers and man-hours), but definitions of the categories in use vary. Data on the period 1900-1927 is not readily available, but may be extracted from various editions of the Norwegian *Statistical Yearbook*, which was first published (by the NCBS) in 1880. Table 1 above contains a selection of these data.

3. *Production*. Public statistics on production do not appear until 1909, after which we have an annual volume series (HS78, Table 135). However, foreign trade figures appear already in 1866, and some of the posts here may be taken as (admittedly rough) proxies for production levels. We have computed an index for the textile industry, consisting of (the sum of) wool, cotton, linen, hemp, tow, as well as yarns made of these materials. Tons of imports of these inputs were reported in several volumes of *Norwegian Public Statistics*, cf. *Tabeller vedkommende Norges handel*, NOS, C, No. 3, various volumes 1866-1906.

4. *Productivity*. Before 1909, we have no reliable data on productivity. Problems continue for the next two decades, primarily because the data for production and employment seldom are directly comparable. (We have used HS78, Table 135, Column 1, on HS78, Table 129.)

5. *Unemployment*. Unemployment figures from the 19th century are notoriously hard to come by, but may tentatively be inferred from available poor-relief statistics (HS68, Table 316). Boyer, as we have seen above, takes variations in the activity level as an indicator. Another possible proxy is the level of *emigration*. From 1905 we have two series: registered enemployment and percentage of union members out of work. The latter may be extracted from the annual Statistical Yearbook.

6. *Wages*. Before 1900, the Wederwang-archive in Bergen (located at The Norwegian School of Economics and Business Administration, NSE) provides wage series for some industries, in particular the textile industry (cf. Minde & Ramstad, "The development of real wages in Norway about 1730-1910", for further references). In our analysis of the 19th century, we have used wage series from three Oslo textile plants, reported in Ramstad, J., *Kvinnelønn*

Wage Formation in the Norwegian Industry 1840-1985

og pengeøkonomi. En studie av kvinners lønn i tekstilindustrien i Kristiania ca. 1850-1910, Master's thesis, Norwegian School of Economics and Business Administration, Bergen 1982, p. 353 for the Graa series and p. 509 for Chr. Seilduksfabrikk. After 1910, we have reasonable data for most sectors. We have used an index of manufacturing industry [verkstedsindustri] wages (HS68, Table 295). An index of real hourly real wages 1900-1950 is provided in a study from 1955: Stoltz, G., *Økonomisk utsyn* 1900-1950, Social Economic Studies (SES), No. 3, Oslo: NCBS 1955, Table 89. We have used this index.

7. *Profitability*. To indicate profitability in the inter-war period, we have used an indicator of product prices (the export price index plus the import price index (HS78, Table 171) divided by 2).

8 A Counterfactual Study of Economic Impacts of Norwegian Emigration and Capital Imports

Christian Riis and Tore Thonstad*

1 INTRODUCTION

The economic history of Norway has been characterised by periods of large factor flows to and from other countries. In the latter part of the nineteenth century and the early parts of this century, a large share of the Norwegian population (and labour force) migrated overseas. In Europe, only Ireland had higher emigration rates. From the 1890s up to the First World War, capital imports covered a fairly large part of gross domestic investment, and in the 1920s and the 1970s, capital imports were again substantial. Compared with most other developed countries (cf. Kuznets, 1966, tables 5.3 and 5.5) Norway has financed a larger part of its gross domestic capital formation by capital imports. In fact, Canada and Australia had even higher shares of foreign financing but, as Marris (1985) notes, these countries share with Norway the characteristics of sparse population and large unexploited natural resources.

Economic historians have discussed the impacts of these large factor flows upon the economic development of Norway, but to our knowledge, none has tried to produce any quantitative estimates of the impacts. This chapter reports on the early stages of a project which aims, first, at describing aggregate inflows and outflows of labour and capital over the period 1865–85, and then assesses the impacts of aggregate factor flows upon total factor supply and economic growth, using a 'counterfactual' type of approach. Of particular interest is the impact of emigration on the ratio between the labour force and the total population, and how this influenced growth in net domestic product per capita.

Some historians have questioned the value of a counterfactual approach. Ingrid Semmingsen (1950), for example, says in her pioneering study of

---

*We thank Professor P. Geary, Maynooth, for useful comments on an earlier version of this chapter. A fuller version including some details of the factor flows and the bases of estimation is available from the authors.

Norwegian emigration to America from 1865 to 1915: 'The speculations of what would have happened if emigration had been larger, smaller or if it had not at all taken place, can never constitute a realistic problem formulation. We cannot remove or change any chain in the sequence of historical events without changing all other elements in the sequence' (p. 445; translated from Norwegian).

However, other researchers have taken a different stand, for example Gjølberg (1979, pp. 302–6), while the Emigration Committee of 1912–1913, reflecting on how economic development in Norway would have been between 1885 and 1910 if there had been no emigration, says:

> From an economic point of view, one has reasons to ask how during these 25 years we could have managed to supply work and subsistence for a population increase of 336 670 persons in Norway. Would it have led to depressed conditions by and large and thus have reduced the 'standard of life'? Even the good years in the 90's with their use of labour for enterprises in the towns did not halt emigration, but only reduce it for some time. [ibid. annex 1, p. 216, translated from Norwegian]

More generally, in writings by historians, one often finds statements of the type 'emigration led to ...'. This implies a counterfactual approach. In our opinion, any study trying to trace causes and effects must necessarily be counterfactual. Our study is based on the belief that it is possible to gain interesting insights by experimenting with counterfactual studies of factor flows. A limitation of the analysis is that we do not discuss the circumstances which might have produced this counterfactual outcome of zero net migration – for example, immigration barriers abroad or emigration control in Norway – and any other effects these might have had on the Norwegian economy.

The paper is arranged as follows: section 2 assembles, for the period 1866–1985, the available estimates of net emigration from Norway, and projects how the population of Norway and the labour force would have developed if there had been no net emigration. Section 3 presents the available data on net capital inflows to Norway and estimates their effects on the development of aggregate real capital. Section 4 combines our counterfactual estimates of real capital and the labour force, and compares observed with hypothetical capital–labour ratios. Section 5 presents estimates of a macroproduction function for Norway and uses it to simulate the contributions of factor flows to economic growth in Norway. Finally, in section 6, a savings function is estimated and applied, together with the production function, in a neoclassical simulation model for the Norwegian economy.

2 THE EFFECTS OF EMIGRATION ON GROWTH IN LABOUR SUPPLY

Norwegian population statistics give annual data on emigration to overseas countries back to 1825. Since 1869, age- and sex-specific data on emigration are available due to the supervision of transportation of emigrants, which was introduced by law. Emigration to European countries and immigration from abroad were, however, not registered systematically prior to 1947. The net population outflow has thus to be estimated as the difference between natural increase (births minus deaths) and observed growth in the population.

Before 1866 net migration from Norway was small. It peaked in the period 1851–5 when net emigration amounted to 18 per cent of natural increase. About 51 000 people (net) left Norway between 1825 and 1866, whereas our estimates indicate that almost 69 000 (net) emigrated in the following five years. Over the whole period 1825–1980 net emigration is estimated at nearly 650 000, representing the balance between 920 000 emigrants to overseas countries *plus* an unknown volume of emigration to European countries *minus* return migration (estimated by Backer (1965) at 155 000 in the period 1891–1940 alone) and an unknown volume of foreign immigration to Norway.

Virtually all this net emigration occurred in the period up to 1930, since when only modest net inflows and outflows have been experienced. The highest rates of net emigration were in the years 1866–1910, during which time it averaged 0.6 per cent of the population per annum and offset nearly half the effects of natural increase. Within this time a number of separate waves of migration are evident, with peaks in 1866–70, 1880–90 (including a 1½ per cent loss in 1882 alone) and 1901–5 – while there was a subsequent, much lower peak in 1921–30. Moe (1977) has offered a statistical analysis of how these fluctuations may be related to developments in the Norwegian and American economies. Our concern in this chapter, however, is with the effects rather than the causes of Norwegian emigration.

The *total* effects of migration on population and labour force growth have been estimated by projecting forward the Norwegian population from 1865 using observed age-specific fertility and mortality rates in each period, and comparing these hypothetical populations with those observed in subsequent years. The choice of base year was based on the fact that emigration from Norway was modest before 1865, and that according to Drake (1969), the 1865 census was of higher quality than those for earlier years. The projection procedure was that of Arriaga *et al.* (1976), with mortality rates from Borgan (1983) and fertility rates estimated by H. Brunborg (1988). The labour force projections were based on *average* participation rates by age and sex (as in Bjerke, 1966), rather than the more volatile marginal rates used by Lettenstrøm and Skancka (1964).

These projections indicate that in the absence of net emigration abroad, both population and labour force growth in the period 1865–1910 would have been more than doubled. By 1910 the hypothetical population is 35 per cent above the observed level, subsequently rising to 40 per cent above in 1930, and falling slowly to 34 per cent above in 1985. However, the hypothetical and observed labour forces differ even more. In 1930, the labour force is 45 per cent higher in the hypothetical case. Emigration reduced population as a productive resource more than it reduced population as consumers. For example, without emigration, labour force as a proportion of population would have increased by 5.6 per cent in the period 1865–90, compared with an observed increase of 1.2 per cent.

3 THE EFFECTS OF NET CAPITAL IMPORTS ON FIXED CAPITAL FORMATION

Estimates of net capital inflows have been calculated for the entire period 1865–1984 by equating net capital imports with the deficit on current account:

$$Q_t = X_t + R_t + T_t \tag{8.1}$$

where, for year t, Q_t is the deficit on current account, X_t is the import surplus, R_t is net interests and dividends paid to other countries, and T_t is net transfers to other countries. This definition involves some problems, particularly in the treatment of different kinds of transfer, while as Bjerke (1966, pp. 66–7) points out the data, especially for the last century, are rather uncertain. Comparison with Skånland's (1967) financial flow estimates shows no serious inconsistencies in the period between 1926 and 1952, but the latter suggest a rather smaller inflow in the period from 1952 to 1963.

The level and direction of net capital flows has shown considerable fluctuations but in seventeen of the twenty-three five-year periods for which we have estimates there were net capital imports into Norway. In the first quarter century from 1865 there were actually some small capital exports and the first wave of large-scale capital imports occurred in the following twenty-five years up to the outbreak of the First World War. During this period the inflow represented around 4 per cent of GDP and about a quarter of gross investment in Norway. During the war there were again capital exports as debts were repaid and foreign investments repatriated, but from 1919 to 1924 there were renewed capital imports amounting to about 9 per cent of GDP. Between 1925 and 1939 flows were more or less balanced, but in the reconstruction period after the Second World War capital imports again reached high levels. Without large foreign aid through the Marshall plan capital imports *on our definition* would have been still higher. Imports persisted until 1979, generally on a more modest scale, but with a leap up to 8 per cent of GDP in 1975–9 (due to countercyclical policy and large investments in the petroleum sector).

To approach the problem of analysing the impacts of capital imports on the accumulation of real capital, we now have to estimate *hypothetical gross investment* in each year, i.e. the volume to be expected in the absence of capital imports. A proper investigation of this would require a complete macroeconomic model of the Norwegian economy (cf. section 6). In the absence of such a model, we shall make the heroic assumption that the whole of positive net capital imports went to real investment in fixed capital, with net capital exports being wholly at the expense of real investment, and no impact at all on domestic savings. Existing evidence on this issue is inconclusive (cf. Mikesell and Zinser, 1973, p. 12 ff), but our tentative explorations in Section 6 of this chapter suggest that Norwegian capital imports may indeed have led to a reduction in domestic savings. Consideration of the effects of capital inflow on future domestic savings through its impact on incomes will also be deferred until section 6.

A current account deficit of Q_t, measured in current prices, gives room for an investment in fixed capital (in 1938 prices) of:

$$\hat{J}_t = \frac{Q_t}{P_t} \tag{8.2}$$

where

$\hat{J}$ = gross investment in fixed capital, in 1938 prices, due to capital imports.
P = price index for investment in fixed capital, with $P_{1938} = 1$.

The growth in the stock of 'foreign' fixed capital is determined by capital imports and depreciation:

$$F_{t+1} - F_t = \hat{J}_t - d_t F_t \tag{8.3}$$

where

d = depreciation rate for real capital.
F_t = stock of 'foreign' fixed capital (at the end of year t), in 1938 prices, due to previous capital imports.

In the calculations, we disregarded capital imports before 1865, and calculated the hypothetical growth in real capital year by year 1865–1939, by subtracting the foreign capital from the observed stocks. The results indicate that net capital exports between 1865 and 1890 lowered the stock of real capital in 1890 by 3 per cent. However, the first wave of large-scale capital imports, in the period 1890–1910, added about 21 per cent to aggregate capital in 1910. Capital exports during the First World War led to a fall of about 7 per cent in the 'foreign' capital stock, which was regained due to large current account deficits in the period 1920–5. Thereafter up to 1939, when there were some years with net capital imports, and some with net capital exports, the relative difference between observed and hypothetical real capital declined. By 1939 then the level of fixed capital was only 5–6 per cent higher than it would have been likely to be without net capital flows in the previous seventy-five years.

Our macro approach hides the widely different patterns of development in different sectors of the economy, which Bergh *et al.* (1980, pp. 101 ff) describe, and may not bring out fully how dependent the expansion of the manufacturing sector was on capital inflow. Of particular relevance for the approach of this chapter is their discussion of the linking of direct foreign investments in Norway with imports of technology – in particular in the first decades of this century. This points in the direction of treating direct foreign investments and foreign borrowing differently in a model trying to explain the relationships between capital inflows and economic growth. Stonehill (1965) emphasises the importance of direct investment in foreign owned firms – which may have occurred even when there were net capital exports – even in cases where ownership was later repatriated. On this basis, including all corporations whose existence could be attributed to present or past foreign ownership, he finds a much larger proportion of the capital stock to be the result of foreign investments (23.7 per cent in 1962). Obviously, however, his approach is very different from ours.

4 OBSERVED AND HYPOTHETICAL CAPITAL–LABOUR RATIOS

The extent to which the outflow of migrants and inflow of capital has tended to increase the capital–labour ratio in the Norwegian economy is indicated in Table 8.1, which compares observed values of this ratio with time-series estimates based on zero net flows of capital and/or labour.

For the three periods 1865–90, 1890–1915, and 1915–39, it can be seen that the observed C/L ratio grew by 1.1–1.3 per cent per year in each period, and most rapidly in the middle period. However, without capital imports, but with observed labour migration (column 2), the growth in C/L would have been much slower in this period. On the other hand, with observed capital flows, and assuming zero emigration (column 3), the C/L ratio would have been almost stagnant in the period 1865–90. The key finding, however, is that in the absence of either capital imports or emigration (column 4), C/L would have grown from 5.9 to 6.5, i.e. only 10 per cent in the fifty-year period 1865–

Table 8.1 Observed and hypothetical capital–labour ratios (Fixed capital in 1000 1938 crowns (C) per person in the labour force (L))

	(1) Observed	Calculated using		
		(2) Observed L, hypothetical C	(3) Observed C, hypothetical L	(4) Hypothetical L and C
1865	5.9	5.9	5.9	5.9
1890	7.7	7.9	6.1	6.3
1900	8.5	7.9	6.5	6.0
1915	10.7	9.3	7.5	6.5
1930	12.9	11.3	8.9	7.7
1939	14.4	13.6	10.2	9.6
Percentage yearly growth				
1865–1890	1.1	1.2	0.1	0.3
1890–1915	1.3	0.7	0.8	0.1
1915–1939	1.2	1.6	1.3	1.6

1915, compared with the actual 81 per cent growth (from 5.9 to 10.7). Of the two sets of flows, it was labour migration which accounted for the larger part of the boost to the C/L ratio.

By contrast in the period 1915–39, emigration had no significant effect while the observed growth in the C/L ratio was lower than would have been the case with zero net capital flows, reflecting the net capital exports during the First World War.

The results in this section are based on a very partial approach, incorporating only the direct effects of factor flows, ignoring any repercussions in the domestic economy. In particular, the calculations do not take into account that savings might have been different if there had been no emigration or capital imports. The two following sections extend the analysis to allow for such changes by reference to a more complete economic model.

5 INCOME AND OUTPUT EFFECTS OF FACTOR FLOWS

For a counterfactual analysis of the impacts upon net domestic product of inflows and outflows of labour and capital, we need first to estimate a macroproduction function. Aukrust and Bjerke (1958) used the following production function:

$$Y_t = A C_t^a L_t^b e^{gt} \qquad (8.4)$$

where, for year t, Y_t is net domestic product, C_t is aggregate fixed capital (both in 1938 prices) and L_t is aggregate employment, in man-years. They obtained the following estimates of the coefficients:

Period	$\hat{A}$	$\hat{a}$	$\hat{b}$	$\hat{g}$
1900–55	2.262	0.203	0.763	0.0181
1917–39	0.045	0.719	0.619	0.0118

Unfortunately, their estimates are strongly dependent on the time period used in the estimation, and the standard errors are large. We note in particular that using data for the entire period 1900–55 yields an elasticity with respect to scale $(a+b)$ slightly below unity, whereas the estimates for 1917–39 yield 1.338. Furthermore, it is somewhat unsatisfactory that so much of the growth is 'explained' by a trend factor.

Using the same production function to analyse growth over the period 1865–1956, Bjerke (1966, pp. 50–1) found that the proportion of the total growth rate which could not be explained by means of growth in labour and capital increased over time (cf. Moe, 1977, p. 48). Obviously, this model does not take into account that new technology is often embodied in new capital, and the model may therefore underestimate the importance of investment for growth.

We have followed up the Aukrust–Bjerke analysis by making a large number of attempts to estimate a macroproduction function of the Cobb–Douglas type for Norway, using different observation periods, different types of time trends, and by estimating both average and 'frontier' production functions. The idea behind experimenting with frontier production functions was that it would be a way of taking into account that in some years, a large part of labour and capital was underutilised. Unfortunately, it turned out that the estimates varied a great deal according to which time period was selected for analysis. The method is extremely sensitive to measurement errors, since outlying observations have a strong impact upon the coefficient estimates. We have therefore concluded that we cannot rely upon the results in our simulations.

In most of the experiments with an average production function, we introduced no restriction on the coefficients for returns to scale. In some of these experiments, we obtained extremely high returns to scale, and a negative time trend. In other experiments, the returns to scale turned out to be well below unity, combined with a strong positive trend factor. We conclude that due to multicollinearity in the explanatory variables, we are not able to distinguish properly between returns to scale and the trend factor – or indeed between the impacts of labour and capital upon NDP, since the elasticities vary a great deal – sometimes involving meaningless values (even negative or above unity. This is unfortunate since the returns-to-scale parameter is crucial to production function analysis. The limited availability of some natural resources, in particular agricultural land, pulls in the

124   Norwegian Emigration and Capital Imports

direction of decreasing returns to scale. On the other hand, the tendency towards larger enterprises, combined with increasing returns within each enterprise, pulls in the opposite direction. Furthermore, there may have been increasing returns in the infrastructure. It would therefore have been highly desirable to obtain an estimate of the returns to scale at the macro level.

But due to lack of reliable evidence we have been forced to adopt the conventional *a priori* assumption of constant returns.

Following Bjerke's (1966) results we did, however, allow the unexplained residual factor to vary over time in the macroproduction function which was estimated:

$$Y_t = AC_t^a L_t^{1-a} e^{(u+vt)t} \qquad (8.5)$$

We have fitted this function by ordinary least squares to data for 1865–1939. Obviously, this may introduce a simultaneity bias, as well as a bias because of measurement errors. Data for Y_t and C_t in 1938 prices were obtained from the National Accounts 1865–1960, and for L_t we used estimates of the labour force since satisfactory employment data are not available before 1930. Among the major weaknesses of using labour force data as proxies for employment are of course that the daily working time has declined, and that unemployment has varied over time. A similar objection can also be raised against using available capital instead of utilised capital.

Besides estimating equation (8.5), we also tried putting u and v, respectively, equal to zero. Putting $v=0$ yielded meaningless results ($a>1$), probably due to multicollinearity. The other estimates were (with standard errors in parentheses):

	a	$1-a$	u	v
(8.5a)	0.199	0.801	0.00195	0.00012
	(0.291)	(0.291)	(0.00339)	(0.000013)
(8.5b)	0.360	0.640	0	0.00012
	(0.080)	(0.080)		(0.000013)

The squared correlation coefficient was in both cases 0.992. In (8.5a), the standard errors are large, in particular for u, probably due to multicollinearity. (8.5b) has well-determined coefficients. Unfortunately, it can be shown that the estimates in that regression are not independent of the choice of origin for time (we have used 1864). On the other hand, the elasticity with respect to labour has a reasonable magnitude. Bjerke (1972, p. 11) estimates the share of wages and other labour incomes as ranging between 0.61 and 0.68 in the period 1865–1930, with an average of 0.645. Thus, we choose (8.5b) as the basis for stimulation of the counterfactual situation. One may perhaps feel uneasy about the progressively growing trend factor in (8.5b). However, it implies a trend rate of growth in 1865 of 0.02 per cent, and in 1939 of 1.77 per cent, still less than in the Aukrust–Bjerke estimates for 1900–55.

In the simulations based on this production function we retain the assumption that savings are unaffected by emigration and capital imports (which will be examined in section 6). We also ignore the possible impacts of emigration on labour force participation and unemployment in Norway, although these could have been large in the periods when large cohorts of youths entered the labour market. A possible way of approaching this problem would have been to try to estimate the relationship between labour force participation rates and the growth in population in working ages. In a simple counterfactual study of growth in NDP per capita 1865–1910, Gjølberg (1979, p. 304) assumed that NDP would have remained unchanged if emigration had not taken place. However, in our opinion, this assumption is much less realistic than our approach. A further possibility which we ignore is that emigration reduced the average quality of the labour force, so that productivity would have been higher in the absence of emigration (cf. Emigration Committee 1912–1913, pp. 24–5). This factor pulls in the opposite direction to the effects of emigration on participation and unemployment.

For various reasons, therefore, our simulations are very tentative, but we still believe that the results presented in Table 8.2 illustrate some important implications of factor flows. From a comparison of columns (2) and (3) in this table, it can be seen that the growth of NDP was not much affected by capital imports, apart from the period 1890–1915. In 1915, NDP would have been 5 per cent lower in the absence of capital imports. Comparison of

Table 8.2 Observed and hypothetical net domestic product (Mill. crowns, 1938 prices)

	(1) Observed[1]	Calculated using the production function (8.5b)[2]			
		(2) Observed C and L	(3) Observed L, hypothetical C	(4) Observed C, hypothetical L	(5) Hypothetical C and L
1865	922	958	958	958	958
1890	1410	1359	1375	1581	1598
1900	1718	1717	1671	2033	1978
1915	2597	2436	2312	3066	2910
1930	4148	3764	3580	4782	4548
1939	5310	5122	5022	6400	6276

[1]*Source*: National Accounts, 1865–1960.
[2]C = fixed capital, L = labour force.

columns (2) and (4) shows that emigration reduced the growth of NDP substantially, in particular in the period 1865–1915. In 1915, NDP would have been 26 per cent higher in the absence of emigration, and in 1939, 25 per cent higher.

When the results are expressed on a per capita basis, in Table 8.3, we find that without emigration, the growth in NDP per capita would have been significantly reduced, due to a reduction in the marginal productivity of labour. However, this effect is partly offset by the fact that emigration led to a smaller reduction in the growth rate of population than in the growth rate of the labour force. Thus, according to this calculation, without emigration, NDP per capita would have been reduced by 8 per cent in 1915 and by 10 per cent in 1939.

Let us finally analyse the growth in NDP per capita by causes. Taking into account that NDP per capita (Y/N) equals NDP per member of the labour force (Y/L) times the ratio between the labour force and population (L/N), we obtain from equation (8.5):

$$\frac{Y_t}{N_t} = A \left(\frac{C_t}{L_t}\right)^a e^{(u+vt)t} \cdot \frac{L_t}{N_t} \tag{8.6}$$

Thus, we can split the causes of growth in NDP per head into growth caused by increase in the capital–labour ratio, by increase in the labour–population ratio and a residual. We shall here only give results for the period 1865–90, when emigration was very large, see Table 8.4.

Thus in the observed case, 53 per cent of the growth in NDP per capita was due to increase in the capital/labour ratio, against 6 per cent in the case

Table 8.3 Observed and hypothetical net domestic product per capita (Crowns, 1938 prices)

	(1) Observed[1]	Calculated using the production function (8.5b)[2]	
		(2) Observed C, L and N	(3) Observed C, hypothetical L and N
1865	542	563	563
1890	704	678	650
1900	766	766	724
1915	1035	971	896
1930	1474	1337	1215
1939	1781	1717	1551

[1]*Source*: National Accounts, 1865–1960 and population data.
[2]C = fixed capital, L = labour force, N = population.

Table 8.4 Growth in net domestic product per capita by sources, 1865–90

	Percentage growth in NDP per cap.	Proportion of growth due to		
		Growth in C/L	Growth in L/N	Residual factor
Observed C, L and N	20.4	0.53	0.06	0.41
Observed C, hypothetical L and N	15.5	0.06	0.36	0.58

without emigration (where C/L would have grown very little). However, an interesting feature is that in the latter case, 36 per cent of the growth would have been due to an increase in the ratio between labour force and population, which was largely negated in practice because emigration reduced the labour force relatively more than population.

6 SIMULATING IMPACTS VIA SAVINGS

In all the simulations so far, we have assumed that savings are unaffected by factor flows. We shall try here to investigate how our conclusions would be modified if we took into account the endogenous determination of savings.

Suitable previous estimates of total savings functions (covering total savings) for Norway are lacking. Bjerke's (1972) estimates of private consumption functions for 1865–1968 fail to separate out the effect of population increase, while Biørn's (1974) analyses of per capita private consumption only cover the post-war period.

Real net saving is defined as real disposable income minus real consumption. Thus:

$$\frac{S_t}{N_t} = \frac{Z_t}{N_t} - \frac{H_t}{N_t} \tag{8.7}$$

Here, S_t is real net saving (private and public), N_t is total population, Z_t is real disposable income, and H_t is real total consumption. We introduce the consumption function:

$$\frac{H_t}{N_t} = A \left(\frac{Z_t}{N_t}\right)^\alpha \tag{8.8}$$

Real disposable income is here defined as net domestic product in current prices deflated by a price index for domestic consumption and investment (current value divided by value in 1938 prices). In this way, terms of trade

128   *Norwegian Emigration and Capital Imports*

effects are implicitly taken into account. Net interest payments and transfers are disregarded.

This equation was fitted to data for 1865–1939 – using simple least squares, thus neglecting the simultaneity problem – with the following results (standard errors are in parentheses):

$$\ln\frac{H_t}{N_t} = 0.4222 + 0.9270 \ln\frac{Z_t}{N_t} \quad R^2 = 0.9797 \tag{8.8a}$$
$$\phantom{\ln\frac{H_t}{N_t} =\ } (0.1060)\ (0.0156)$$

There was serial correlation in the residuals (Durbin–Watson statistic 0.47). Alternative regressions with net interest payments and net transfers included in disposable income yielded very similar results.

Simulations were undertaken with the production function (8.5b), the savings function corresponding to (8.8a), and alternative assumptions about capital imports. Real net savings were assumed to be converted into net investments in fixed capital, and investments in year t to be added to fixed capital in year $t+1$. Relative prices of the components of GDP are assumed to be the same in all simulations, equal to observed relative prices.

Table 8.5 presents our results for observed and simulated aggregate fixed capital. Comparison of columns (1) and (2) shows that the model does not simulate the observed outcome well. This could partially reflect large deviations in particular years from the fitted production and savings functions, discrepancies between the relative price indexes for savings and for investment, or inconsistencies in the national accounts between fixed capital growth and investment less depreciation. However, it is clear that the model systematically underestimates capital accumulation. Nevertheless it may serve as a basis for comparison of the effects of different factor flow situations.

Comparing columns (2) and (3), we find that capital imports led to a stock

Table 8.5 Observed and simulated aggregate fixed capital (Mill. crowns, 1938 prices)

	(1) Observed	Simulated using			
		(2) Observed L and cap. imp.	(3) Observed L, no cap. imp.	(4) Hypothetical observed cap. imp.	(5) Hypothetical L, no cap. imp.
1865	3 890	3 890	3 890	3 890	3 890
1890	6 030	5 033	5 230	5 081	5 279
1915	10 649	9 580	7 915	10 114	8 404
1930	15 054	14 205	11 563	15 076	12 919
1939	18 872	17 149	15 076	19 683	17 380

Note: L = labour force.

of capital in 1915 and 1939 above what it would otherwise have been, by 21 and 14 per cent respectively. The impacts are stronger than those estimated in section 3, because they allow for the boost that capital imports gave to domestic savings as a result of faster growth in incomes. Comparing columns (2) and (4) shows, however, that, for given capital imports, savings would have been higher in the absence of emigration, leading to 15 per cent higher capital in 1939.

In section 5, we found that in the absence of emigration, and taking observed capital accumulation as given, NDP per capita would have been 10 per cent lower in 1939. Here, where we include impacts upon savings, we find that the reduction is only 5 per cent (compare columns (2) and (4) of Table 8.6). Thus increased capital accumulation reduced the tendency towards lower NDP per capita.

Comparing columns (2) and (3) indicates that without capital imports, NDP per capita would have been about 5 per cent lower in 1939. Comparing finally columns (2) and (5), we find that without capital imports and emigration, NDP per capita would have been about 9 per cent lower in 1939.

Our tentative conclusion is, therefore, that *emigration as well as capital imports contributed towards growth in NDP per head*. However, given the drastic assumptions used in this study, and the unreliability of some of our data, our results are not much more than a hypothesis which can be used as a basis for further analysis.

In order to test the robustness of these conclusions we have carried out some alternative simulations with different parameters for the production function, and also examined alternative specifications of the savings function.

In the first case we tried both increasing the output elasticity with respect to labour (from 0.64 to 0.8), while retaining constant returns, and also allowing for increasing returns (by raising the sum of the elasticities to 1.1),

Table 8.6 Observed and simulated net domestic product per capita (Crowns, 1938 prices)

	(1) Observed	Simulated using			
		(2) Observed L, N and cap. imp.	(3) Observed L, N, no cap. imp.	(4) Hyp. L, N, obs. cap. imp.	(5) Hyp. L, N, no cap. imp.
1865	542	563	563	563	563
1890	704	636	645	612	620
1915	1035	935	872	880	823
1930	1474	1309	1216	1233	1149
1939	1784	1662	1586	1575	1506

Note: L = labour force, N = population.

while retaining the original elasticity with respect to labour. Both changes had the effect of closing the gap between observed changes and those hypothesised for the zero migration situations: with the higher elasticity on labour NDP per head was virtually the same in the two situations, while with increasing returns it would have been 3 per cent lower in the hypothetical situation, rather than 5 per cent as in the original estimates. It is doubtful, however, whether increasing returns would have obtained, particularly in the last century when Norway was largely an agricultural society.

Secondly, we have considered the question of whether savings are independent of capital flows. To do this we have introduced deflated capital imports per head (cf. equation (8.2)) as explanatory variable in an alternative savings function. Ordinary least squares regression yields:

$$\frac{S_t}{N_t} = -78.4 + 0.176 \frac{Z_t}{N_t} - 0.766 \frac{\hat{J}_t}{N_t} \quad R^2 = 0.87 \qquad (8.9)$$
$$\phantom{\frac{S_t}{N_t} = -}(9.76) \;\; (0.01) \phantom{\frac{Z_t}{N_t}} (0.07)$$

If (8.9) gives a true description of reality, capital imports contributed very little to capital accumulation, because they reduced domestic savings substantially. We are, however, for a number of reasons, reluctant to accept the estimation results. First of all, savings are estimated as a residual in the national accounts. If, for example, imports are overestimated, leading to an overestimate of capital imports, this leads to a corresponding underestimate of savings (cf. Bjerke, 1966, p. 71). Thus an error-in-variables approach is called for. Secondly, the direction of causality in the observed relationship between savings and capital imports is not clear. If savings for some reasons are low in a given year, this may lead to a need for capital inflow. The alternative hypothesis is that if capital inflow is high, e.g. the public sector borrows heavily abroad, it leads to less public savings. There is thus a need for further investigation, disaggregating the capital flows. In the meantime, we have not dared to rely upon equation (8.9) in our simulations, despite the fact that it fits the data well.

10 CONCLUSIONS

The approach presented in this paper has a number of obvious limitations and the analysis could be improved in a number of directions. In particular it would be desirable to distinguish between at least the primary and manufacturing sectors, to look more closely at how capital imports affect savings, and at capital transfers and later remittances directly associated with emigration (cf. Semmingsen, 1950, p. 454 ff).

However, these provisional results suffice to show both the scale of factor flows affecting the Norwegian economy in the late nineteenth and early twentieth century and, in the context of a supply-oriented model, the likelihood of these flows having significantly raised the capital–labour ratio, and thereby average incomes in Norway.

References

Arriaga, E., Anderson, P. and Heligman, L. (1976) *Computer Programs for Demographic Analysis* (Washington: US Department of Commerce, Bureau of the Census).

Aukrust, Odd and Bjerke, Juul (1958) 'Real Capital and Economic Growth, 1900–1956', *Artikler*, no. 4 (Oslo: Central Bureau of Statistics of Norway). In Norwegian with English summary. Also printed in R. Goldsmith and C. Saunders (eds) *The Measurement of National Wealth*, International Association for Research in Income and Wealth (London: Bowes and Bowes, 1959) pp. 80–118.

Backer, Julie E. (1965) *Marriages, Births and Migrations in Norway 1856–1960*, Samfunnsøkonomiske Studier, no. 13 (Oslo: Central Bureau of Statistics of Norway). In Norwegian with English summary.

Bergh, T., Hanisch, T. J., Lange, E. and Pharo, H. Ø. (1980) *Growth and Development: The Norwegian Experience, 1830–1980* (Oslo: Norwegian Institute of International Affairs).

Biørn, Erik (1974) 'Estimating Aggregate Consumption Functions for the Post-War Period: Methodological Problems and Empirical Results', *Artikler*, no. 63 (Oslo: Central Bureau of Statistics of Norway). In Norwegian with English summary.

Bjerke, Juul (1966) *Trends in Norwegian Economy, 1865–1960*, Samfunnsøkonomiske Studier, no. 16 (Oslo: Central Bureau of Statistics of Norway). In Norwegian with English summary.

Bjerke, Juul (1972) 'Estimating Consumption Functions from National Accounts Data', *Artikler*, no. 53 (Oslo: Central Bureau of Statistics of Norway). In Norwegian with English summary.

Borgan, Jens-Kristian (1983) *Cohort Mortality in Norway, 1846–1980*, Rapporter 83/28 (Oslo: Central Bureau of Statistics of Norway). In Norwegian with English summary.

Brunborg, Helge (1988) *Cohort and Period Fertility for Norway 1845–1985*, Rapporter 88/4. (Oslo: Central Bureau of Statistics of Norway). In Norwegian with English summary.

Drake, Michael (1969) *Population and Society in Norway, 1735–1865* (Cambridge: Cambridge University Press).

Emigration Committee 1912–1913 (1915) (Indstilling fra Utvandringskomiteen II, Lov om utvandring m.v.), Kristiania. In Norwegian.

Gjølberg, Ole (1979) *Økonomi, teknologi og historie* (Economics, technology and history), Bergen. Unpublished.

Kuznets, Simon (1966) *Modern Economic Growth: Rate, Structure, and Spread* (New Haven: Yale University Press).

Lettenstrøm, Gerd Skoe and Skancke, Gisle (1964) 'The Economically Active Population in Norway 1875–1960 and Forecasts up to 1970', *Artikler*, no. 10 (Oslo: Central Bureau of Statistics of Norway). In Norwegian with English summary.

Marris, Stephen (1985) *Deficits and the Dollar: The World Economy at Risk* (Washington: Institute for International Economics).

Mikesell, Raymond F. and Zinser, James E. (1973) 'The Nature of the Savings Function in the Developing Countries: A Survey of the Theoretical and Empirical Literature', *Journal of Economic Literature*, March, vol. II, no. 1, pp. 1–26.

Moe, Thorvald (1977) *Demographic Developments and Economic Growth in Norway, 1740–1940* (New York: Arno Press).

Semmingsen, Ingrid (1950) *Veien mot Vest* (The Road towards the West): Part 2, *Utvandringen fra Norge, 1865–1915* (Emigration from Norway, 1865–1915) (Oslo: Aschehoug).

Skånland, Hermod (1967) *The Norwegian Credit Market Since 1900*, Samfunnsøkonomiske Studier, no. 19 (Oslo: Central Bureau of Statistics of Norway). In Norwegian with English summary.

Stonehill, Arthur (1965) *Foreign Ownership in Norwegian Enterprises*, Samfunnsøkonomiske Studier, no. 14 (Oslo: Central Bureau of Statistics of Norway).

The
SCANDINAVIAN ECONOMIC HISTORY REVIEW
and
ECONOMY AND HISTORY

VOLUME XXX: 2, 1982

A Quantitative Study of Emigration from Denmark to the United States, 1870—1913

By ULLA MARGRETHE LARSEN*

1. Introduction

A comprehensive investigation of migration in the nineteenth and early twentieth centuries was carried out in Scandinavia during the 1960s and 1970s. The work was undertaken partly in association with the Institute of American History at the University of Uppsala, partly at a series of seminars and conferences[1] and partly in the form of independent projects.[2]

Thus in the last two decades a multi-faceted and basic core of material has been assembled and organised,[3] while at the same time several local studies have been

---

* Ulla Margrethe Larsen, born 1953. Cand. phil. Odense 1979.

[1] The Institute of American History was established in Uppsala in 1962, and the Emigration Institute was founded in Växjö in 1965. Collaboration in the field of migration problems was enlarged in 1967 when representatives of the Nordic countries and the United States took part in a seminar arranged by the Emigration Institute in Växjö. A seminar on migration, with participants from Iceland and Great Britain as well, was held in Uppsala in 1969, and the joint endeavour was carried further in 1971 at the Congress of Nordic Historians in Copenhagen. The groundwork for the actual Nordic research project on 'Nordic Emigration' at Uppsala was laid at the seminar of 1969, although it was not completed until 1977. S. Åkerman, 'A Brief History of a Research Project', *American Studies in Scandinavia*, IX, 1977, pp. 5—9; *From Sweden to America: A History of the Migration,* eds. H. Runblom & H. Norman, Uppsala 1976, pp. 11—19.

[2] For example Kr. Hvidt, *Flugten til Amerika: Drivkræfter i masseudvandringen fra Danmark 1868—1914,* Århus 1971.

[3] L.-G. Tedebrand, 'Sources for the History of Swedish Emigration', in Runblom & Norman, *op.cit.*, pp. 76—94.

undertaken[4] and an intensive theoretical discussion has been pursued.[5] The micro level has been the usual point of departure for these researches, and in Scandinavia itself not a single econometric study has been carried out at the macro level.[6] Such studies have been made in America, however, where Maurice Wilkinson[7] and John Quigley[8] have analysed the Swedish and Thorvald Moe the Norwegian emigration to the United States during the period between the Civil War and the First World War.

As far as Denmark is concerned, no econometric studies of emigration to the United States have been published. In fact only one study of total emigration has been published,[10] and this has been criticised both for being based upon inadequate sources and for employing too superficial methods of analysis.[11]

This is the background to the following econometric analysis of emigration from Denmark to the United States during the period 1870—1913. The econometric studies of Swedish and Norwegian emigration mentioned above are discussed by way of introduction, and the material that is to form the basis of the analysis is then presented and commented on. An attempt is made in the light of the studies cited and of the nature of the proxy measurements of economic development to show which economic and demographic forces influenced Danish emigrants. First the mass of emigrants is studied as a whole. Then it is broken down by sex so as to try to establish whether men or women were the decision makers in group emigration. Finally are sketched some of the conditions and guidelines for carrying out a comparative analysis of emigration from Denmark, Norway and Sweden to the United States during the period 1870—1913.

The emigrants are grouped by sex to see whether men and women were prompted to emigrate by the same causes and whether a better explanation presents itself when the mass of emigrants is broken down into smaller units. At the same time it becomes possible to study whether one of Edward Ravenstein's laws,[12] which says that long-distance migrants comprise mostly men and short-distance ones mostly women, is applicable to the Danish pattern of emigration, and also to show whether there are any changes over time in the proportion of migration by sex.

---

[4] For example F. Nilsson, *Emigrationen från Stockholm till Nordamerika 1880—1893: En studie i urbanutvandring*, Stockholm 1970.

[5] S. Åkerman, 'Theories and Methods of Migration Research', in Runblom and Norman, *op.cit.*, pp. 19—76.

[6] E. M. Hamberg, *Studier i Internationell Migration*, Stockholm 1976. It is true that an econometric study of Swedish emigration to the United States in the period 1871—1900 is made in this dissertation. However, Hans Chr. Johansen has shown, in *Historisk Tidskrift*, Stockholm 1977, pp. 108—13, that the equations presented on pp. 26—9 cannot be given any explanatory value.

[7] M. Wilkinson, 'Evidences of Long Swings in the Growth of Swedish Population and Related Economic Variables, 1860—1965', *Journal of Economic History*, XXVII, 1967, pp. 17—39.

[8] J. Quigley, 'An Economic Model of Swedish Emigration', *Quarterly Journal of Economics*, LXXXVI, 1972, pp. 111—27.

[9] T. Moe, *Demographic Developments and Economic Growth in Norway, 1740—1940: An Econometric Study*, Michigan 1970.

[10] Hvidt, *op.cit.*

[11] H. Chr. Johansen, 'Danish Emigration Prior to 1914', *Scandinavian Economic History Review*, XX, 1972, pp. 113-17; L.-G. Tedebrand, 'Dansk massutvandring', *Historisk Tidskrift*, Stockholm 1973, pp. 275—85.

[12] E. Ravenstein, 'The Laws of Migration', *Journal of the Royal Statistical Society*, XLVIII, 1885, pp. 198—200.

Some of the factors of explanation tested have been chosen arbitrarily, although in such a way that the economic factors involved are related to the labour market, e.g. real wages and occupation, and the demographic motives to population increase, e.g. annual population growth. An emigrant is defined in this discussion as a person who settles abroad for at least one year while the term 'Dane' is used of persons who have resided in Denmark for at least one year.

An Emigration Act was passed in 1868 under which was established the official registration of persons leaving Denmark in order to settle abroad.[13] The year 1870, rather than 1869, has been selected as a starting point because a certain degree of inefficiency in administration and in the compilation of statistics is to be assumed in the initial period.

The Emigration Act of 1868 was not changed until 1914 apart from an amendment in 1872. However, the effect of the change made in 1914 was that the passively paternal emigration policy was supplanted by more active governmental intervention.[14] Opportunities for emigration were thereby altered in crucial respects, and it is for this reason that 1913 is selected as the terminating point of the present study. The outbreak of the First World War should also be noted in this regard since the war affected Danish emigration to a considerable extent.

The mass of data is broken down by years, which means that for the period 1870—1913 there are 44 cases and the population studied is thus of a size that makes possible an econometric analysis. In addition the intensity of emigration was greater in this period than in the preceding and succeeding periods,[15] and the studies of Swedish and Norwegian emigration mentioned earlier fall within the same period.

2. Econometric Studies of Swedish and Norwegian Emigration to the United States

The econometric studies of Swedish and Norwegian emigration mentioned earlier attempt to explain various manifestations of emigration by means of multiple regression. The explanatory variables employed in the regression equations are given in the schedule below.

---

[13] Law of 1 May 1868.
[14] Hvidt, *op.cit.*, p. 43.
[15] *Statistisk Årbog*, Copenhagen 1922, pp. 16—17; *Statistisk Årbog*, 1896 ff; *Sammendrag af Statistiske Oplysninger angaaende Kongeriget Danmark*, Copenhagen 1874, 1876, 1880, 1885, 1889 and 1893, abbreviated hereafter as *Statistiske Sammendrag*.

EXPLANATORY VARIABLE	MEASURE USED BY		
	Wilkinson	Quigley	Moe
Wages in USA	Not included	Real wages in industry and agriculture	Net national product
Wages in country of emigration	Not included	Real wages in industry and agriculture	Net national product
Unemployment in USA	Production index	Not included	Frickey's index
Unemployment in country of emigration	Production index	Not included	Unemployment index
Flow of information	Emigration in previous year	Emigration in previous year	Not included
Overpopulation	Not included	Birth rate 26 years previously	20—29 year-olds in previous year

As will be seen from the schedule, the official statistics contain only a few of the time-series which the authors wanted to use. They therefore had to construct certain figures which they considered to be acceptable proxies; but how useful these constructions are for the purpose for which they have been employed is open to discussion. It is uncertain, for example, whether the indirect measures of unemployment utilised by Wilkinson[16] are on the whole applicable to those labour markets which may have had an influence on the decision to emigrate.[17] Because of these problems of source-criticism Quigley has introduced data relating to wage-levels in place of manifestations of employment conditions,[18] but it is doubtful whether these are affected by short-term economic fluctuations. Quigley has also been compelled to interpolate and compound data from several sources in order to produce annual data on the wages of agricultural workers in the United States, and other things being equal, this further impairs the evidential value of the time-series.

[16] Wilkinson, loc.cit., p. 34.
[17] These problems are discussed by Hans Chr. Johansen in his 'Sverige i internationell migration', Historisk Tidskrift, Stockholm 1977, p. 109.
[18] Quigley, loc.cit., pp. 115—17.

Finally, Wilkinson[19] and Quigley[20] have both utilised official Swedish emigration statistics at face value. This seems highly problematical, since a number of critical studies of the sources have shown that this time-series is incomplete.[21] Indeed Ingrid Eriksson has even suggested that unrecorded emigration to North America amounted to at least 40 per cent of the recorded.[22] Moe likewise has omitted to carry out any critical analysis of the sources of Norwegian emigration statistics,[23] presumably because such a study has already been made by Ingrid Semmingsen.[24]

As an expression of the differences in wages (living standards) between the United States and Norway, Moe has used the mean value of the difference between the two countries' gross national product per person of working age in the last five years prior to emigration.[25] Sune Åkerman criticises this proxy measurement for not including the psychological reasoning that may illustrate how the emigrant perceived his situation.[26] He feels that in general Moe shows insufficient appreciation of the theoretical problems involved in transforming the concept to a measurable quantity: he believes that even the variable mentioned can be considerably improved if the income-differential is related to the number of households and their average size, not to each individual emigrant. Whether such a modification would be an improvement is open to discussion.

Åkerman goes on to remark that it is an open question whether the distribution of income is the same in the two countries and that account ought to be taken of the ages of emigrants and of the time remaining to them on the labour market. In other words, potential emigrants will have made some sort of calculations of wage-differentials over a lifetime. It is a common feature of these objections that they require the introduction of factors for which it is very difficult to construct time-series. For example, on the basis of the information available it does not seem possible to construct any better expression of the difference in wages (living standards) between the United States and Norway, even though the average productivity of labour does not necessarily reflect wages (the standard of living) and no account is taken of sudden changes in economic activity when mean values for the last five years are employed.

Over the entire period studied by Moe there are no annual statements of unemployment in the United States. A production index is therefore introduced, made up from factors in the business and transport sectors,[27] while the official unemployment statistics in the industrial sector are used as far as Norway is

---

[19] Wilkinson, *loc.cit.*, pp. 21, 34.
[20] Quigley, *loc.cit.*, p. 119.
[21] L.-G. Tedebrand in Runblom and Norman, *op.cit.*, pp. 88—91.
[22] I. Eriksson, 'Passenger Lists and Annual Parish Reports as Sources for the Study of Emigration from Sweden', *Nordic Emigration. Research Conference in Uppsala September 1969*, Emigrationsforskningsgruppen vid historiska institutionen i Uppsala 1970, p. 3.
[23] Moe, *op.cit.*, pp. 163—4.
[24] I. Semmingsen, *Veien mot vest*, I—II, Oslo 1942, 1950.
[25] Moe, *op.cit.*, pp. 164—7.
[26] S. Åkerman, 'Migrationen — ett tvärvetenskapligt forskningsområde', in *Utvandring: Den svenska emigrationen till Amerika i historisk perspektiv*, ed. Ann-Sofie Kälvemark, Stockholm 1973, pp. 32—40.
[27] Moe, *op.cit.*, pp. 167—8.

concerned.[28] In this connection Åkerman remarks that Moe has not investigated the evidential value of the Norwegian unemployment statistics.[29] Nor are any grounds offered, indeed, for thinking that a direct and an indirect measure can be applied to the same set of circumstances or that the figures employed cover the short-term economic fluctuations at all. For example, it is doubtful how faithfully a production index reflects the employment situation, since a rise in production can be caused both by increased employment and by expanded technology and automation.

Åkerman sums up by suggesting that to employ expressions within the same model to explain both long-term (wage-differentials) and short-term (employment in the United States and unemployment in Norway) fluctuations of the migration curve is a theoretically dubious proceeding, though his argument for this view is not convincing. On the other hand, Åkerman rightly points out that the gaps in the source-material impair the explanatory value of the model presented.

In the econometric study[30] on which this exposition is based, Moe's model has been used for Danish emigration. The independent variables have been determined in accordance with Danish conditions but adapted to express the same facts as the independent variables embodied in Moe's model. The result of this analysis shows that 76 per cent of Danish emigration to the United States in 1870—1913 can be explained in terms of economic developments in the United States and that the percentage of explanation can be brought up to 83 per cent when factors expressing Danish conditions are introduced. Since neither multicollinearity nor autocorrelation occur and since all factors are significant, it must be concluded that this result substantiates the general value of the model and reduces the effect of the criticism adduced by Åkerman. It should be emphasised in this regard that the same forces were not necessarily operative in different countries and that therefore it will not do, perhaps, to measure the explanatory value of the model by its general value, although both Åkerman[32] and Moe[33] mention this criterion.

In the three studies mentioned a multiple regression analysis embodying various forms of time-lag is carried out to determine how good an explanation of emigration can be offered by the factors adduced. In fact it is characteristic of Wilkinson's and Quigley's analyses that in the published results they have not tested whether multicollinearity occurs. Indeed Quigley has not even looked for autocorrelation, whereas a significance test has been made in all three instances.

After the analyses all three authors give a picture of the observed and estimated values, which reveals possible gaps in the estimated values. For example, Moe's model turns out to lack sufficient elasticity to register local maxima and minima.[34]

[28] ibid., p. 168.
[29] cf. note 26.
[30] U. Larsen, 'En kvantitativ undersøgelse af udvandringen fra Danmark til USA i tiden 1870—1913', unpublished special study, Odense 1979.
[31] Hamberg, op.cit. A model very like Moe's is used in this dissertation. However, the analysis suffers from such crucial defects (no account being taken of multicollinearity, for example) that no value can be attached to the findings. See further in note 6.
[32] S. Åkerman in Kälvemark, op.cit., p. 37.
[33] Moe, op.cit., p. 182. However, Moe is more interested in investigating the explanatory power of the model with regard to sub-groups than in demonstrating its general value.
[34] ibid., p. 174.

Åkerman explains this by saying that the model does not include comprehensive variables for the short-term fluctuations, for instance in ticket-prices, and that the model does not incorporate sociological and psychological factors.[35] It is very difficult to find time-series to measure these factors, however, and Åkerman does not offer any suggestions for solving this problem, which diminishes the force of his criticisms.

It appears from the correlation coefficients computed in the regression analyses that 75—90 per cent of the annual emigration can be explained by the models constructed. At the same time, it is confirmed that conditions in both the receiving and the donor countries influenced the volume of emigration because, broadly speaking, pull and push forces exercised equal influence. A similar result emerges when Swedish emigrants are broken down according to whether the districts they came from were agricultural or not, since Quigley demonstrates that these two groups both reacted in more or less the same way.[36]

With regard to Norwegian emigration, Moe finds that both economic and demographic factors played a part but that no structural changes took place in the period 1870—1913.[37] He also examines Norwegian emigration broken down by age (15—29 years and 30—34 years) and by sex, firstly in order to ascertain whether the model constructed has general explanatory power and secondly to see whether different groups of the Norwegian population have been similarly affected by the same factors.[38] It emerges that the model is suitable for use in studies of disaggregated groups because the regression equations constructed are capable of explaining 85—88 per cent of emigration while at the same time there is no autocorrelation or multicollinearity and all factors are statistically significant.[39]

The 15—29 age-group was most affected by the wage-differential between the United States and Norway, while conditions of employment had more or less the same significance for the two groups although the 15—29 age-group was more influenced by conditions in the United States, whereas that of 30—34 was most affected by economic conditions in Norway.[40] On the other hand Moe does not find any noticeable differences between men's and women's motives in emigrating. As it is impossible from the material available to group emigrants according to civil status, Moe believes that any divergencies that existed could have been cloaked by the fact that married women will have tended to react in the same way as their husbands.[41]

It is a crucial shortcoming of the three studies that none of them has shown how large an effect each independent variable separately exercised on the correlation coefficient. It is therefore impossible to offer a precise opinion concerning the relation between the push and pull forces and the effect of demographic conditions.

[35] S. Åkerman in Kälvemark, *op.cit.*, pp. 38, 46.
[36] Quigley, *loc.cit.*, pp. 122—5.
[37] Moe, *op.cit.*, pp 179—82.
[38] *ibid.*, p. 182.
[39] *ibid.*, pp. 184, 186.
[40] *ibid.*, pp. 183—5.
[41] *ibid.*, pp. 185—8.

In general terms it can be said of the econometric studies cited that they show that forces in both receiving and donor countries played a part in emigration. The conclusions arrived at are based on sound statistical findings, while it is less certain whether the underlying time-series measure what they purport to measure. Taking the deficiencies of source-criticism as the starting point, Åkerman levels vigorous criticism against Moe's study and against econometric models in general.[42] He does not believe it to be theoretically possible to combine in the same model both expressions of short-term fluctuations and expressions of trends of economic development, and he further declares that Moe has not paid sufficient regard to sociological and psychological factors.

Working jointly with participants in the Uppsala project, Åkerman has constructed a model which would take account of these defects.[43] However, no studies prepared in accordance with this model have yet been published, even though the Uppsala project has now been concluded — which could be interpreted as a sign that the model is of no practical use, in the same way that suggestions adduced for improvement of Moe's model cannot be put into effect because of lack of source-material.

3. Source-material for Danish Emigration

The Emigration Act of 1868 required a written contract to be effected between an emigration agent and the emigrant and to be officially approved. The object of the Act was to ensure that the traveller received the victuals promised and to keep a check on the quality of the ship used.[44] At the same time, however, it furnished raw material for three time-series — registers maintained by the Copenhagen police,[45] an appendix to the Copenhagen police commissioner's annual report,[46] and the official statistics[47] — covering emigration from Denmark to the United States during the period 1870—1913.

The procedure was for the contract to be stamped and signed by the police in the police district where the journey was to commence. At this point the Copenhagen police entered the contents of the contract into a separate register[48] and these registers are still in existence.[49] From 1869 onwards the registers were arranged on a uniform system, and the information entered is stated so precisely and unambiguously that it can be processed mechanically without any major problems. Kristian Hvidt has exploited the opportunity thus presented by coding certain selected data for the period 1869—99 on magnetic tape.[50]

---

[42] S. Åkerman in Kälvemark, *op.cit.*, pp. 32—40; S. Åkerman in Runblom and Norman, *op.cit.*, pp. 51—6.
[43] S. Åkerman in Runblom and Norman, *op.cit.*, pp. 71—5.
[44] Law of 1 May 1868.
[45] Københavns politis udvandringssager. Tillæg A. Københavnske Politi- og Domsmyndigheder I. Landsarkivet for Sjælland etc., Copenhagen 1975, pp. 205—9.
[46] See preceding note.
[47] *Statistisk Årbog*, Copenhagen 1896 ff; *Statistiske Sammendrag*, Copenhagen 1874, 1876, 1880, 1885, 1889 and 1893.
[48] Hvidt, *op.cit.*, p. 67.
[49] cf. note 45.
[50] Hvidt, *op.cit.*, pp. 75—80.

In addition, the Copenhagen police compiled an annual statement of the emigration applications dealt with during the year and appended it to the Copenhagen police commissioner's annual report.[51] It was generally assumed that the bulk of Danish emigration was recorded by the Copenhagen police, but all police commissioners throughout Denmark were ordered in a circular[52] to send the contracts issued during the previous year to the Department of Statistics.[53] In this way is was formally ensured that the time-series compiled for use in official statistics were complete.[54]

The three time-series supplement one another in certain aspects, and in the study[55] on which the present article is based it has been established that they can be utilised in conjunction with one another in analysing Danish emigration because they show similar fluctuations of the overall trend and only a relatively limited difference in absolute figures.

The Copenhagen police registers provide details of the emigrant's name, occupation, age, destination, form of emigration, year, month and day of emigration, last place of residence, and (after 1899) place of birth.[56] Hvidt has processed this material so as to encode information on where in the registers an individual emigrant can be found, the first letter of his surname, the form of emigration, the year and month, the size of the emigrant group and the individual emigrant's placing in it, along with the emigrant's sex, occupation and age, last place of residence before departure, and destination.[57]

By way of supplementary information, the appendix to the Copenhagen police commissioner's annual report states the company with which the emigrant travelled and whether he used a pre-paid ticket.[58] There is no more detailed information in the official statistics, but these are notable for being published and for including all registered emigrants.[59] As regards the reliability of the individual data, the normative framework is very likely to have acted as a form of control. For example, a standard contract was used, but if nevertheless some dispute arose when a contract was being issued, it was possible to seek the advice of a consultant.[60] Furthermore all contracts had to be certified,[61] and if any errors came to light it was the principal agent who was responsible for the oversight. It may therefore be presumed that the agents were wary of accepting incorrect contracts. The control tests carried out by comparing random samples taken from Hvidt's computer-recorded material with other independent time-series such as population census-lists and parish registers all

---

[51] cf. note 45.
[52] Circular of 28 April 1869. *Departementstidende*, 1869, p. 435.
[53] Term used in this study. Between 1849 and 1895 the office was called *Det statistiske Bureau* and for the rest of the period under review *Statens statistiske Bureau*.
[54] cf. note 47.
[55] Larsen, *loc.cit.*, pp. 50—2.
[56] cf. note 45.
[57] For further details regarding the translation of the figures from the magnetic tape to verbal information, reference may be made to 'Kodeinstruks til udvandringsundersøgelse', (dated 12 May 1966), and to Hvidt, *op.cit.*, pp. 75—80.
[58] cf. note 45.
[59] cf. note 47.
[60] Hvidt, *op.cit.*, p. 71.
[61] *Ministerialtidende* 1873, p. 115.

indicate that Hvidt's material is usable as far as age, occupation and sex distribution are concerned, but very unreliable with regard to the geographical data.

Finally, it should be mentioned that American immigration statistics are in existence. However, the information about Danish immigrants in this time-series is subject to so many factors of uncertainty that it is not really justifiable to employ them for purposes of detailed analysis.[63]

Economic Conditions in the United States

As is explained in greater detail in the two studies of Swedish and Norwegian emigration cited in Section 2, for the period 1870—1913 there are no contemporary statistics of economic conditions capable of yielding time-series for use in an econometric analysis of the pull-effect from the United States. It is therefore necessary to look for proxy measurements that can be presumed to move in step with the trend of business conditions and economic growth.

Employment in the United States

The numbers of unemployed in the United States are not recorded annually throughout the period 1870—1913.[64] An estimated production index[65] is therefore used as a proxy measurement of employment for the purposes of the detailed analysis. The individual data in this index are stated as percentages of the trend, which is calculated by means of a quadratic equation.

As a test of how well this expression measures employment, a comparison has been made with Stanley Lebergott's[66] estimated values for unemployment in years of economic depression during the period 1870—1889 and with the annual data of registered unemployment 1890—1913.

The two time-series fluctuate in opposite directions, and for the years 1890—1913 the co-variation is $R = -0.83$. This leads to the conclusion that Edwin Frickey's production index constitutes a tolerably close measure of employment in the United States prior to the First World War and covers short-term economic fluctuations.

[62] Larsen, *loc.cit.*, pp. 52—7; H. Højgaard, 'Studier i vandringsforholdene omkring en dansk provinsby i slutningen af 1800 tallet', unpublished special study, Odense 1977, pp. 13—16; A. D. Holt, 'Udvandringen til Amerika fra Humble sogn' in *Studier i dansk befolkningshistorie 1750—1890*, ed. H. Chr. Johansen, Odense 1976, pp. 76—82; L. Havelund and J. Thomsen, 'Nordisk emigrationsforskning og lægdsrullernes udvandringsoplysninger. Et studium i etapevandringernes problematik, belyst for Svendborg Amt 1875—90', unpublished paper, Odense 1973, pp. 54—63.
[63] Larsen, *loc.cit.*, pp. 58—60.
[64] S. Lebergott, *Manpower in Economic Growth*, New York 1964, pp. 43, 187—8.
[65] E. Frickey, *Production in the United States 1860—1914*, Massachusetts 1974, pp. 118—19. In Appendix D, pp. 224—40, Frickey describes how the index is constructed, how the time-series (income and expenditure with diverse forms of transport etc.) are weighted, and how the calculations are carried out.
[66] Lebergott, *op.cit.*, pp. 43, 187—8.

Wages in the United States

Simon Kuznets's estimate of the national product per head of the United States labour force, expressed in dollars at 1929 prices with a five-year moving average,[67] is utilised as a measure of the level of incomes in the United States. A moving average is used in order to make this variable measure the long-term trend as far as possible.

Economic Activity in the United States

The growth of the railway by 1,000-mile sections[68] is brought in as a measure of both long-term and short-term fluctuations in economic conditions, since the construction of a railway network is both a political decision with effects over several years and a possible field of employment for immigrants. These data are utilised first as absolute figures and secondly as a percentage of the trend calculated by means of a quadratic equation.

Summary

The same criticism can be raised against the material that will be used to illustrate economic conditions in the United States as against Moe's sources,[69] — that not enough is done to verify that the expressions involved really measure what they are supposed to measure. However, it is impossible to procure figures with greater comprehensiveness and there is no alternative to the variables employed despite the unreliability associated with them.

Economic Conditions in Denmark

In the case of Denmark there are no direct figures on economic conditions during the period under review, so that proxy time-series have to be used instead.

Employment in Denmark

Annual statements of unemployment in Denmark[70] do not exist for the whole period 1870—1913, and in their place gross investments in Denmark, calculated at 1929 prices,[71] are used to express employment.[72]

---

[67] S. Kuznets, *Capital in the American Economy. Its Formation and Financing*, Princeton University Press 1961, pp. 633—4.

[68] B. Thomas, *Migration and Economic Growth. A Study in Great Britain and the Atlantic Economy*, Cambridge 1973, p. 402.

[69] See this paper pp.105—6.

[70] P. Boje, *Det industrielle miljø 1840—1940. Kilder og litteratur*, Copenhagen 1976, pp. 64—6.

[71] S. A. Hansen, *Økonomisk vækst i Danmark*, Copenhagen 1974, pp. 236—7.

[72] E. Olsen, *Danmarks økonomiske historie siden 1750*, Copenhagen 1967, p. 214. In the above-mentioned work the average percentage unemployment is given for members of the unemployment benefit societies from 1903 onwards. If the changes in this time-series are compared with the annual fluctuations of gross investment in Denmark at 1929 prices, a reverse movement is revealed for most years — which increases confidence that gross investment in Denmark at 1929 prices does reflect short-term economic fluctuations.

The deviation from the trend is similarly computed by means of a quadratic equation[73] so as to isolate the short-term fluctuations in economic activity.

Wages in Denmark

A number of conversions have been made in order to obtain an expression capable of being compared with the measurement established for wages in the United States.

The net factor income at 1929 prices[74] is compared with the labour force in Denmark,[75] a five-year moving average is then constructed, and finally conversion is made to dollars (1 *krone* = 0.266 dollars).[76]

The difference in wages (living standards) between the United States and Denmark then emerges as the difference between the two time-series expressing wages in the United States and Denmark respectively, and this should produce figures representative of the long-term trend of wage-differentials between the United States and Demark.

Demographic Conditions in Denmark

As a factor indicating demographic conditions in Denmark, population growth is calculated on the basis of the total population on 1 July each year.[77] The annual number of marriages per 1,000 inhabitants in Denmark is also included.[78]

Summary

In assembling data relating to economic conditions in Denmark, efforts have been made to ensure that these express the same thing as the proxy measurements employed for these factors in the United States. In the case of both Denmark and the United States attempts have been made to introduce material reflecting both the short-term (Frickey's production index and gross investments in Denmark) and the long-term fluctuations (wage differentials between the United States and Denmark).

4. An Econometric Study of Danish Emigration to the United States

Commencing with the above-mentioned time-series, an attempt has been made to discover with the aid of multiple regression the best forms of co-variation between different expressions of emigration and the proxy measurements described for economic and demographic developments. A number of different aspects have been studied and the best results are cited below.

[73] The trend is computed from the equation $y = (323.2)(1.038^x)$ $x = 1891 = 0$.
[74] K. Bjerke and N. Ussing, *Studier over Danmarks Nationalprodukt 1870—1950*, Copenhagen 1958, pp. 144—5.
[75] Hansen, *op.cit.*, pp. 202—3.
[76] *Statistisk Årbog*, Copenhagen 1930, p. 97.
[77] *Statistisk Årbog*, Copenhagen 1922, pp. 16—17.
[78] *ibid.*

Total Emigration from Denmark to the United States, 1870—1913

The best explanation of total emigration from Denmark to the United States is expressed in Equation 1.

Equation 1.

$$y = (-2.96) + 1.57 \log x_1 + 0.01 x_2$$
$$(7.24) (3.21)$$

$$+ 3.06 \log x_3 - 0.47 \log x_4$$
$$ (6.05) (5.73)$$

$$+ 0.93 \log x_5 - 3.02 \log x_6$$
$$ (5.38) (5.40)$$

$$R^2 = 0.95 \quad d = 1.69$$

y = aggregate emigration from Denmark to the United States.[79]

x_1 = the wage-differential between the United States and Denmark measured as the difference between national product per head of the United States labour force expressed in dollars at 1929 prices with five-year moving average[80] and net factor income[81] per head of the Danish labour force[82] expressed in dollars at 1929 prices with five-year moving average, two years prior to y.

x_2 = the absolute data as a percentage of the trend of growth of railways in 1,000-mile sections in the United States, one year prior to y.[83]

x_3 = employment in the United States measured in terms of an estimated production index, 0 years prior to y.[84]

x_4 = gross investments in Denmark, 0 years prior to y.[85]

x_5 = population growth percentage in Denmark, five years prior to y.[86]

x_6 = number of marriages in Denmark per 1,000 inhabitants, one year prior to y.[87]

---

[79] *Statistisk Årbog*, Copenhagen 1896 ff; *Statistiske Sammendrag*, Copenhagen 1874, 1876, 1880, 1885, 1889 and 1893.
[80] Kuznets, *op.cit.*, pp. 633—4.
[81] Bjerke and Ussing, *op.cit.*, pp. 144—5.
[82] Hansen, *op.cit.*, pp. 202—3.
[83] Thomas, *op.cit.*, p. 402. Thomas has computed the trend from the equation: $\log y = 2.5135 + 0.0170x - 0.0004x^2$. $x = 1872 = 0$.
[84] Frickey, *op.cit.*, p. 119.
[85] Hansen, *op.cit.*, pp. 236—7.
[86] *Statistisk Årbog*, Copenhagen 1922, pp. 16—17.
[87] *ibid.*

Expressing the constituent variables as decimal logarithms makes R larger than in a non-logarithmic presentation, and better significance is obtained inasmuch as the best explanation is still achieved when the growth of railway sections in the United States (x_2) is not stated as a decimal logarithm.

Presentation in logarithmic form means that an absolute growth in value of an independent variable brings a corresponding percentage growth in value of the dependent variable.

Table 1. *The effect on variables of the correlation coefficient R*

Variable	R	R^2	R^2 Growth
log x_3	0.76	0.57	0.57
log x_1	0.89	0.79	0.22
log x_4	0.93	0.86	0.07
log x_5	0.95	0.90	0.04
log x_6	0.96	0.93	0.03
x_2	0.97	0.95	0.02

95 per cent of total emigration from Denmark to the United States during the period 1870—1913 can be explained by the expression in Equation 1, and $d = 1.69$ confirms that the co-variation is satisfactory. A correlation matrix, shown in Table 2, has been calculated with a view to discovering whether two or more of the independent variables are mutually dependent.

Table 2. *Correlation matrix*

	log x_1	log x_2	log x_3	log x_4	log x_5	log x_6
log x_1	1.00	0.08	0.13	0.74	0.42	—0.52
x_2	0.08	1.00	0.47	—0.21	0.21	—0.04
log x_3	0.13	0.47	1.00	0.01	0.54	—0.35
log x_4	0.74	—0.21	0.01	1.00	0.45	—0.29
log x_5	0.42	0.21	0.54	0.45	1.00	—0.24
log x_6	—0.52	—0.04	—0.35	—0.29	—0.24	1.00

It is evident from Table 2, that there is considerable mutual dependence of the wage-differential between the United States and Denmark (log x_1) on the one hand and gross investments in Denmark (log x_4) on the other. Thus it is difficult to decide whether changes in the number of emigrants are caused by the one or the other of these two factors.

In an attempt to eliminate this element of uncertainty, the formula for the wage-differential between the United States and Denmark (log x_1) has been resolved into two variables giving, respectively, real wages in the United States in terms of Phelps Brown's real-wage index[88] and real wages in Denmark in terms of net factor income per head of the Danish labour force expressed at 1929 prices in dollars with a five-year moving average.[89] This reveals merely that there is considerable dependence between both the two expressions for real wages in the United States and Denmark and between each of these and gross investments in Denmark. Tests were also made to determine whether there were time-shifts between emigration and the causal factors mentioned, the findings being negative; likewise, to express one or more of these variables as natural numbers does not produce a better result.

Finally, the relationship between the United States/Denmark wage-differential (log x_1) and the deviation from the trend of gross investments in Denmark[90] has been worked out, since gross investment in Denmark indicates the long-term and the deviation from the trend the short-term economic fluctuations. In this case the correlation between the two explanatory factors studied ceases; but at the same time the correlation with Danish emigrants diminishes.

The variables in Equation 1 show all the signs that could be expected. Furthermore Table 1 reveals that Frickey's production index (log x_3) exercised the most important motive force, followed by the wage-differential between the United States and Denmark (log x_1), i.e. the proxy measurements of economic conditions in the United States. For the Danish emigrants the pull-effect was thus stronger than the push-effect, while demographic conditions in Denmark (log x_5, log x_6) played the smallest role.

It is difficult to make any general statement about the demographic factors over the whole period 1870—1913 because of the transition that took place from group to individual emigration. However, a certain co-variation does reveal itself between the number of emigrants and population growth (log x_5), a co-variation which is biggest when population growth also is big five years prior to emigration. This time-shift may be due to emigrants having hesitated until their children emerged from infancy before making the move, and finally, marriage and family may have tied potential emigrants to the homeland a couple of years longer. That this was the case is borne out by the variable log x_6, which has a negative sign and measures the number of marriages per 1,000 inhabitants in Denmark during the previous year.

On the other hand it is impossible to prove any effect arising from there having been particularly large numbers in the emigration-intensive ages between 18 and 30 years. For example, an attempt has been made to bring in the 20—29 Danish age-group as an independent variable. This age-group manifests — probably quite fortuitously — a high co-variation with the wage-differential between the United

---

[88] E. Phelps Brown, *A Century of Pay*, New York 1968, pp. 448—9. Methods and sources are referred to on pp. 420—2 of the work cited, since the index of real wages employed consists of the difference between a weighted index of monthly wages in the United States and a weighted index of living costs in the United States 1860—1914.

[89] Bjerke and Ussing, *op.cit.*, pp. 144—5.

[90] Hansen, *op.cit.*, pp. 236—7. The trend is computed from the equation $y = (323.2)(1.038)^x$ $x = 1891 = 0$.

Diagram 1. Total Emigration from Denmark to the United States, 1870–1913

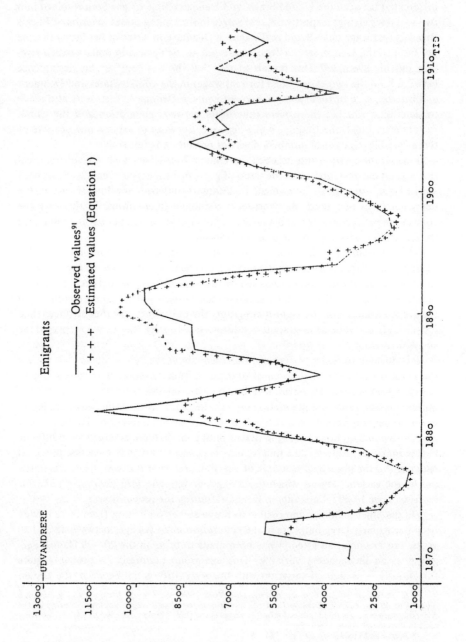

[91] *Statistisk Årbog*, Copenhagen 1896 ff; *Statistiske Sammendrag*, Copenhagen 1874, 1876, 1880, 1885, 1889 and 1893.

States and Denmark (log x_1), while it affects total emigration to only quite a small extent. It might also be thought that earlier emigrants stimulated potential emigrants by means of letters and the like, but it is impossible to prove such a link between emigration one year and emigration the previous year.

The significance test shows that each individual coefficient is significant. A general view of the relationship between the observed and estimated values can be obtained by means of a graphic representation. It will be seen from Diagram 1 that it is with the local maxima especially that the estimated values are poor, which may be a sign that the factors measuring economic conditions in the United States are not comprehensive enough.

Against this background an attempt has been made to replace x_2 (the absolute data as a percentage of the trend of growth of railways in 1,000-mile sections in the United States one year prior to y) first with an expression for coal production in the United States[92] and second with an index of the annual total of building permits in the United States.[93] Both the absolute figures and those showing a percentage of the trend have been utilised as well as various time-lags, but without any success in improving the explanatory value of the model constructed.

The same defect discloses itself, as already noted, in Moe's model, and Åkerman asserts that this is because insufficient account has been taken of short-term fluctuations in emigration.[94] Åkerman further postulates that if, for example, a time-series for ticket-prices were introduced, this would improve Moe's model.

However, it has been found impossible to construct a coherent time-series for ticket-prices over the entire period 1870—1913. An analysis made by Hvidt covering a shorter period suggests that it is doubtful whether there was a link between ticket-prices and numbers of emigrants.[95] A better explanation of total emigration from Denmark to the United States might be established perhaps if the period 1870—1913 were broken down, for example into the sub-periods 1870—1899 and 1890—1913. Account could then be taken of the shift from group to individual emigration. Such a study has not been undertaken here, however, because the period studied amounts to only 44 years. If the population is divided up, while at the same time up to seven variables are employed, the factor of uncertainty becomes too big. But tests were made to discover whether the explanatory factors adduced have shifted the time-lags along through the period and whether a better explanation could be arrived at by taking account of possible shifts. This was found not to be so.

Thus, Equation 1 is unable to account for about 5 per cent of Danish emigration to the United States in 1870—1913. This residual group may partly have been influenced by non-measurable motives such as thirst for adventure and the like, may partly be attributable to defective statistics (errors of measurement), and may partly

---

[92] Thomas, *op.cit.*, p. 401. Thomas has computed the trend from a quadratic equation. log y = 1.55694—0.03705x—0.00015x^2. x = 1877 = 0.

[93] *ibid.*, p. 112. Thomas has computed the trend from a quadratic equation. y = 29.8172 + 0.096x + 0.0022x^2. x = 1872 = 0.

[94] Further details on pp. 105—7.

[95] Hvidt, *op.cit.*, pp. 452—61.

have been caused by the fact that emigration was a phenomenon that appeared not only on the Danish scene in the period 1870—1913 but all over Europe,[96] so that it must be regarded as a flow over time affected by causes whose ramifications extended beyond the boundaries of individual nations. Finally, the model is found to offer the poorest explanation in the years when those travelling to overseas countries other than the United States were relatively numerous, and especially in the years around 1890. It is therefore conceivable that there may have been a degree of competition between receiving countries in attracting immigrants and that this fact exercised a certain amount of influence on the Danish emigration pattern.

Total Emigration from Denmark to the United States Distributed by Sex, 1870—1913

The official statistics do not distinguish emigration to the United States from total emigration overseas in the time-series that are broken down by sex.[97] However, the study on which the present account is based shows that it is possible to use Danish emigration overseas broken down by sex as a measure of Danish emigration to the United States in the period 1870—1913 by virtue of the fact that emigration to the United States was the dominant component of total emigration throughout the entire period.

The best explanation of female emigration from Denmark to the United States during the period 1870—1913 is given in Equation 2.

Equation 2.

$$y = 3.3234 + 0.0012\ x_1 + 0.1474 \log x_2 + 0.0119\ x_3$$
$$(6.67) \quad (2.24) \quad\quad (5.78)$$

$$-0.0004\ x_4 + 0.5893 \log x_5 - 2.0184 \log x_6 + 0.00001\ x_7$$
$$(4.00) \quad\quad (3.82) \quad\quad\quad (4.43) \quad\quad\quad (1.00)$$

$R^2 = 0.95 \quad d = 1.71$

y = female emigration from Denmark to the United States.[99]

x_1 = wage-differential between the United States and Denmark, measured as the difference between the national product per head of the United States labour force expressed in dollars at 1929 prices with five-year moving average[100] and the net factor income[101] per head of the Danish labour force[102] expressed in dollars at 1929 prices with five-year moving average, two years prior to y.

[96] Thomas, *op.cit.*, pp. 399—400.
[97] *Statistisk Årbog*, Copenhagen 1896 ff; *Statistiske Sammendrag*, Copenhagen 1874, 1876, 1880, 1885, 1889 and 1893.
[98] Larsen, *loc.cit.*, pp. 75, 77—8, 81—2.
[99] *Statistisk Årbog*, Copenhagen 1896 ff; *Statistiske Sammendrag*, Copenhagen 1874, 1876, 1880, 1885, 1889 and 1893.
[100] Kuznets, *op.cit.*, pp. 633—4.
[101] Bjerke and Ussing, *op.cit.*, pp. 144—5.
[102] Hansen, *op.cit.*, pp. 202—3.

x_2 = absolute data of growth of railways in the United States by 1,000-mile sections, one year prior to y.[103]

x_3 = employment in the United States measured as an estimated production index, 0 years prior to y.[104]

x_4 = gross investments in Denmark, 0 years prior to y.[105]

x_5 = population growth percentage in Denmark, five years prior to y.[106]

x_6 = number of marriages per 1,000 inhabitants in Denmark, one year prior to y.[107]

x_7 = deviation from the trend of total emigration from Denmark to the United States, one year prior to y.[108]

The best explanation of male emigration from Denmark to the United States during the period 1870—1913 is given in Equation 3.

Equation 3.

$$y = -4.00 + 1.40 \log x_1 + 0.22 \log x_2 + 3.07 \log x_3$$
$$(5.76) (2.72) (4.95)$$

$$-0.35 \log x_4 + 0.87 \log x_5 - 2.00 \log x_6$$
$$(3.68) (4.22) (3.22)$$

$R^2 = 0.93 \quad d = 1.35$

y = total male emigration from Denmark to the United States.[109]

x_1 = wage-differential between the United States and Denmark measured as the difference between the national product per head of the United States labour force expressed in dollars at 1929 prices with five-year moving average[110] and the net factor income[111] per head of the Danish labour force[112] expressed in dollars at 1929 prices with five-year moving average, two years prior to y.

x_2 = absolute data of growth of railways in the United States by 1,000-mile sections, one year prior to y.[113]

x_3 = employment in the United States measured as an estimated production index,[114] 0 years prior to y.

[103] Thomas, *op.cit.*, p. 402.
[104] Frickey, *op.cit.*, p. 119.
[105] Hansen, *op.cit.*, pp. 236—7.
[106] *Statistisk Årbog*, Copenhagen 1922, pp. 16—17.
[107] ibid.
[108] *Statistisk Årbog*, Copenhagen 1896 ff; *Statistiske Sammendrag*, Copenhagen 1874, 1876, 1880, 1885, 1889 and 1893.
[109] ibid.
[110] Kuznets, *op.cit.*, pp. 633—4.
[111] Bjerke and Ussing, *op.cit.*, pp. 144—5.
[112] Hansen, *op.cit.*, pp. 202—3.
[113] Thomas, *op.cit.*, p. 402.
[114] Frickey, *op.cit.*, p. 119.

x_4 = gross investments in Denmark, 0 years prior to y.[115]
x_5 = population growth percentage in Denmark, five years prior to y.[116]
x_6 = number of marriages per 1,000 inhabitants in Denmark, one year prior to y.[117]

Table 3. *The effect of the correlation coefficient R on the variable*

	Equation 3			Equation 4	
Variable	R	R^2	Variable	R	R^2
x_3	0.77	0.60	log x_3	0.78	0.60
x_1	0.89	0.80	log x_1	0.90	0.81
x_4	0.94	0.88	log x_2	0.93	0.86
log x_5	0.95	0.91	log x_6	0.94	0.88
log x_6	0.97	0.94	log x_5	0.95	0.90
log x_2	0.97	0.95	log x_4	0.96	0.93
x_7	0.97	0.95			

It will be seen from Table 3 that in the case of male emigrants the three variables representing economic conditions in the United States first enter into the calculation with a total growth of R^2 = 0.86, while x_3 and x_1 alone enter into it in the case of women with a contribution of R^2 = 0.80. On the other hand conditions at home mean more to female than to male emigrants. This is likewise reflected in the effect of R^2, which attains a value of 0.95 for women compared with 0.93 for men.

The explanation of female emigration takes in the additional variable x_7, which express a stock effect. This variable does not add so much growth to R^2 as to influence the second decimal, but it does become significant, which is not the case with the analysis of total emigration or of male emigration. Thus female emigrants seem to have been more affected by earlier emigrants than were men.

Regressions 2 and 3 show that breaking down according to sex does not produce any better explanation of Danish emigration. That the co-variation is otherwise satisfactory is confirmed by the fact that there is no autocorrelation and that all factors are significant and have the signs that might be expected.

The reason why the percentage of explanation is highest for female emigrants is probably that the variables which measure demographic conditions are more correct than those measuring economic conditions in the United States and Denmark, while at the same time women are in fact most influenced by the former and men by the latter factors.

---

[115] Hansen, *op.cit.*, pp. 236—7.
[116] *Statistisk Årbog*, Copenhagen 1922, pp. 16—17.
[117] *ibid.*

Diagram 2. Total Female and Male Emigration from Denmark to the United States, 1872—1913

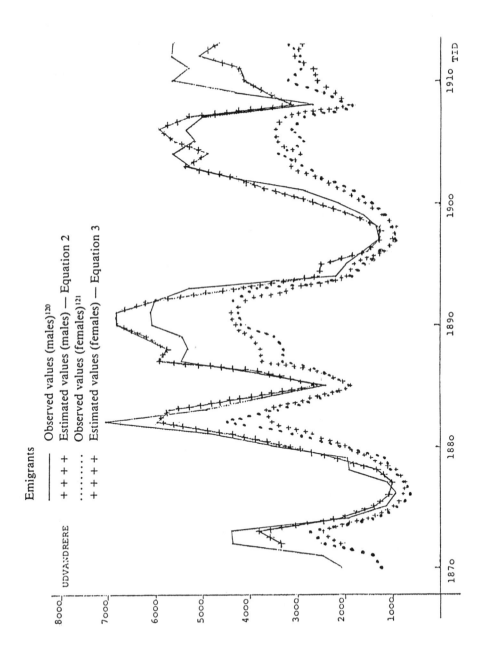

The fact that there are no time-series for unemployment in both the United States and Denmark presents a problem inasmuch as the proxy measurements probably do not sufficiently express short-term trade-cycle fluctuations. This defect is reflected in the statistical calculations, in the shape firstly of a mutual relationship ($R = 0.74$) between the proxy measurements of the wage-differential between the United States and Denmark ($\log x_1$) — the long-term fluctuations in economic conditions — and gross investments in Denmark ($\log x_4$) — the short-term fluctuation in economic conditions — and secondly of too low a correlation with the group of emigrants studied.

Parallel with the study of total emigration, the graphical representation in Diagram 2 likewise shows the biggest divergency between observed and estimated values in years of heavy emigration. Diagram 2 further shows that more men emigrated than women and that the disparity widens in step with the increase of total emigration — a structural phenomenon also observed by Hvidt[118] and expressed in one of Ravenstein's laws.[119]

Group or Individual Emigration from Denmark to the United States, 1870—1899

Were Men or Women the Decision-makers in Group Emigration?

It has already been demonstrated above that female emigrants were little influenced by earlier emigrants. This fact can be interpreted partly in the way in which women went out later than their spouses and partly as a sign that men reached the decision to move more independently.

With this in mind the question has been studied whether it can be proved that the man was more likely than the woman to be the decision-making party in group emigration. The analysis was made on the basis of Hvidt's emigration statistics,[122] which are broken down by sex, and also according to whether the journey was made alone or in groups during the period 1870—1899.

Three regression equations, D1, D2 and D3, have been constructed. The dependent variable y expresses, respectively, total male emigration to the United States,[123] lone male emigrants and group male emigrants,[124] while the independent variables from x_1 to x_7 are the same in the three equations.

---

[118] Hvidt, *op.cit.*, pp. 175—6.
[119] Ravenstein, *loc.cit.*, pp. 198—9.
[120] *Statistisk Årbog*, Copenhagen 1896 ff; *Statistiske Sammendrag*, Copenhagen 1874, 1876, 1880, 1885, 1889 and 1893.
[121] *ibid.*
[122] Hvidt, *op.cit., p. 542.*
[123] *Statistisk Årbog*, Copenhagen 1896 ff; *Statistiske Sammendrag*, Copenhagen 1874, 1876, 1880, 1885, 1889 and 1893.
[124] Hvidt, *op.cit.*, p. 542.

x_1 = wage-differential between the United States and Denmark, measured as the difference between the national product per head of the United States labour force expressed in dollars at 1929 prices with moving five-year average[125] and the net factor income[126] per head of the Danish labour force[127] expressed in dollars at 1929 prices with five-year moving average, two years prior to y.

x_3 = employment in the United States measured by an estimated production index, 0 years prior to y.[128]

x_4 = gross investments in Denmark, 0 years prior to y.[129]

x_5 = population growth percentage in Denmark, five years prior to y.[130]

x_6 = number of marriages per 1,000 inhabitants in Denmark, one year prior to y.[131]

x_7 = deviation from the trend of total emigration from Denmark to the United States, one year prior to y.[132]

Equation D1.

$$y = -3.86 + 1.41 \log x_1 + 3.61 \log x_3 - 0.62 \log x_4$$
$$(4.23)(3.97)(3.67)$$

$$+ 0.92 \log x_5 - 2.47 \log x_6$$
$$(2.68)(.300)$$

$R^2 = .93 \quad d = 1.56$

Equation D2.

$$y = -3.18 + 1.37 \log x_1 + 3.41 \log{}_3 - 0.58 \log x_4$$
$$(4.14)(3.63)\phantom{\log{}_3 - }(3.01)$$

$$+ 0.77 \log x_5 - 2.99 \log x_6$$
$$(1.95)(3.10)$$

$R^2 = 0.89 \quad d = 1.37$

---

[125] Kuznets, *op.cit.*, pp. 633—4.
[126] Bjerke and Ussing, *op.cit.*, pp. 144—5.
[127] Hansen, *op.cit.*, pp. 202—3.
[128] Frickey, *op.cit.*, p. 119.
[129] Hansen, *op.cit.*, pp. 236—7.
[130] *Statistisk Årbog*, Copenhagen 1922, pp. 16—17.
[131] ibid.
[132] *Statistisk Årbog*, Copenhagen 1896 ff; *Statistiske Sammendrag*, Copenhagen 1874, 1876, 1880, 1885, 1889 and 1893.

Equation D3.

$$y = -9.53 + 1.56 \log x_1 + 4.73 \log x_3 - 1.24 \log x_4$$
$$(4.01) \quad\quad (4.29) \quad\quad (5.46)$$

$$+ 1.03 \log x_5 + 1.67 \log x_6$$
$$(2.22) \quad\quad (1.47)$$

$R^2 = 0.89 \quad d = 0.98$

Table 4. *The effect of the correlation coefficient R on the variables*

	D1			D2			D3		
Variable	R	R^2	Variable	R	R^2	Variable	R	R^2
$\log x_3$	0.80	0.64	$\log x_3$	0.77	0.59	$\log x_3$	0.78	0.61
$\log x_1$	0.91	0.83	$\log x_1$	0.89	0.79	$\log x_4$	0.86	0.74
$\log x_4$	0.94	0.88	$\log x_4$	0.91	0.83	$\log x_1$	0.92	0.84
$\log x_6$	0.95	0.90	$\log x_6$	0.93	0.87	$\log x_5$	0.94	0.88
$\log x_5$	0.96	0.93	$\log x_5$	0.94	0.89	$\log x_6$	0.94	0.89

Comparison of D1 and D2 discloses that each individual variable enters into the same series with almost the same growth of R^2, and that the coefficients b1 to b6 broadly speaking assume values of similar magnitude.

On the other hand the independent variables enter into D3 quite differently, while at the same time the numerical value of the coefficients diverges somewhat from D1 and D2, and finally, x_6 is not significant. Thus it can be seen that men who emigrated alone were influenced by the same factors and with the same force as those who went in groups. But men who travelled in groups did react in a different manner to the same impulses. That is to say, these men were not alone in taking the decision to make the move, or else men who acted in groups were receptive to other factors.

Next a study was made of the question whether the total number of female emigrants[133] in Equation E1, lone women in Equation E2 and female participants in group emigration[134] in Equation E3 were affected by the same motivating forces.

[133] *ibid.*
[134] Hvidt, *op.cit.*, p. 542.

Equation E1.

$$y = 3.21 + 0.00114\, x_1 + 0.01433\, x_3 - 0.00043\, x_4$$
$$(4.96)(4.91)(2.53)$$

$$+ 0.6673 \log x_5 - 2.038884 \log x_6 + 0.00001\, x_7$$
$$(2.67)(3.40)(1.00)$$

$R^2 = 0.96 \quad d = 1.76$

Equation E2.

$$y = 3.92 + 0.00096\, x_1 + 0.0139\, x_3 + 0.00005\, x_4 - 0.06403 \log x_5$$
$$(3.69)(5.21)(0.26)(0.23)$$

$$- 3.31262 \log x_6 + 0.00002\, x_7$$
$$(3.36)(1.00)$$

$R^2 = 0.94 \quad d = 1.99$

Equation E3.

$$y = 0.20 + 0.00117\, x_1 + 0.01727\, x_3 - 0.00136\, x_4 + 0.72833 \log x_5$$
$$(3.16)(3.65)(t=5.04)(t=1.80)$$

$$0.68872 \log x_6 + 0.00001\, x_7$$
$$(0.71)(1.00)$$

$R^2 = 0.91 \quad d = 1.05$

Table 5. The effect of the correlation coefficient R on the variables

Variable	R	R^2	Variable	R	R^2	Variable	R	R^2
	E1			E2			E3	
x_7	0.84	0.71	x_7	0.78	0.62	x_3	0.81	0.65
$\log x_6$	0.90	0.81	$\log x_6$	0.94	0.87	x_7	0.87	0.75
x_3	0.94	0.88	x_3	0.95	0.90	x_4	0.92	0.84
x_1	0.96	0.92	x_1	0.97	0.94	x_1	0.94	0.89
$\log x_5$	0.97	0.94	x_4	0.97	0.94	$\log x_5$	0.95	0.90
x_4	0.98	0.96	$\log x_5$	0.97	0.94	$\log x_6$	0.95	0.91

It is evident from the regression analysis that the causes underlying the decision of a lone female to emigrate are different from those influencing the total group of female emigrants, since x_4 and x_5 in Equation E2 have the wrong sign, while at the same time x_5 is not significant.

In Equation E3, x_6 is of no use, and the variables included enter in an order different from that of Equation E1 and E2. That is to say, women travelling alone were motivated by factors other than those which influenced women in groups. Furthermore the reasons moving men who emigrated in groups were almost identical to those underlying total male and female emigration. In other words the man was the dominant partner in the decision making-process that resulted in the emigration of a group.

Finally, it appreas that x_6 is without significance for both men and women travelling in groups but an important factor for women emigrating alone. Thus, emigration may have been regarded as an alternative to marriage as far as certain women were concerned.

Perhaps the man did exercise the biggest influence, but he was decidedly not alone in taking the decision that the family should emigrate. This is shown by letting the dependent variable y represent the ratio between male and female emigration, while the independent variables (x_1 to x_6) are the same as in Equation 3. For a correlation coefficient of only $R^2 = 0.52$ is obtained, while at the same time there is autocorrelation, and several factors are not insignificant.

5. Conclusion

In the course of the work involved in studying Danish emigration to the United States it became apparent that the unearthing of information about the pull-effect from the United States generally presents a problem. There are no contemporary statistics on business conditions, and the time-series constructed are only proxy measurements. Wilkinson and Quigley, for example, in studying Swedish emigration made use respectively of a production index and a composite set of figures for real wages, while Moe, in a dissertation on the Norwegian emigration pattern, introduced a production index for trade-cycle fluctuations and estimated figures to represent the difference in wages (standard of living) between Norway and the United States as measures of the trend of economic events.

In the light of the excellent results achieved by Moe, and since the figures introduced by him seem on the face of it to cover the actual facts best, an effort has been made in the present study to establish corresponding time-series for the pull-effect. In the econometric studies of Swedish and Norwegian emigration which have been mentioned and in the analysis of Danish emigration itself what has been used to represent economic conditions in the donor country has mostly been a variety of expressions of national income.

Åkerman has criticised Moe for not having taken account of the problems involved in transforming a concept to a set of specific figures — and on the grounds that it is doubtful in general whether the time-series introduced measure what they purport to measure. Åkerman further believes that Moe's model would have explained emigration better if figures more representative of short-term economic fluctuations in the United States had been included and some account ought to have been taken of sociological and psychological conditions.

Since to a certain extent the same sources are used in the present analysis as in Moe's and the model constructed for all emigrants is a development of Moe's, the criticism adduced by Åkerman could equally be applied to this study. Åkerman is right in saying that the source-material employed is subject to a certain amount of uncertainty and that it would have been desirable for short-term fluctuations in the pull-effect to be better represented; but up to now it has been impossible to establish more adequate expressions for the entire period 1870—1913.

With regard to the inclusion of sociological and psychological factors Åkerman offers no concrete suggestions as to how these can be expressed in terms of measurable figures on the macro-plane. On the other hand Åkerman reasons that the individual should be taken as the starting point, for he believes that in this way it would become possible to take account of both the short- and the long-term fluctuations of economic events as well as of the sociological and psychological arguments that have been raised. In collaboration with other scholars associated with the Uppsala project, Åkerman has constructed a model for such an analysis, but no studies based on this model have yet been carried out, which weakens the criticisms made by Åkerman. The studies of Swedish emigration establish that both push- and pull-effects were operative and that there were no notable differences underlying emigration from country and town respectively. Moe's study of emigration from Norway reveals the same pattern, both for all emigrants and for subgroups broken down by sex and age. However, it emerges that the 15—29 year-old category was more affected by economic conditions in the United States than was the 30—44 year-old. It is not indicated in these regression analyses how much each separate independent variable affected the correlation coefficient, which means that it is impossible to state exactly what significance each separate factor has had.

In the actual analysis of emigration from Denmark to the United States in 1870—1913 it is confirmed that economic conditions in the United States exercised a greater influence than did conditions at home, where the demographic influence in particular played a negligible role. Thus it has been impossible to prove either a stock effect or a cohort effect. If the emigrant group is broken down by sex, it emerges that men were more influenced by conditions in the United States than were women, who on the other hand were more strongly influenced by push-effects, although it has been possible to demonstrate a weak stock effect among female emigrants. In the case of group emigration, in fact, it appears that wives did not exert the same influence over the decision to make the move as did husbands.

Lastly, it should be remarked that no success was achieved in devising a better explanation by breaking down the Danish emigrant category by sex or according to whether emigration occurred by groups or by lone individuals. Moreover it has been impossible to deduce possible differences and similarities in emigration from the

Scandinavian countries, since the studies existing do not cover the same period, do not employ the same measures of pull- and push-effects, and have not gone into the question whether the emigration statistics of the individual countries cover the same population.

6. Proposals for a Comparative Study of Emigration from Sweden, Norway and Denmark to the United States, 1870—1913

If it is desired to make a comparative study on the macro-plane of emigration from the Scandinavian countries to the United States it can be done in at least two ways. One can either carry out three parallel analyses and compare the results obtained or one can examine emigration from Sweden, Norway and Denmark combined.

Before it is possible to begin a comparison across the Scandinavian frontiers, however, the question of whether the information in the emigration statistics of the three countries has acceptable evidential value must be studied, including whether they cover the same population and whether it is possible to break down the emigrant mass into sub-groups.

If three separate studies are carried out, the procedure to employ can be to introduce the same quantities for the pull-effect while an effort is made at the same time to establish adequate measurements of conditions in Sweden, Norway and Denmark respectively. Three multiple regression analyses can be carried out on this basis, and by comparing the estimated statistical correlations a picture can be derived of differences and similarities in the emigration patterns of the three Scandinavian countries.

If it is desired to study emigration from Sweden, Norway and Denmark simultaneously, a time-series cross-section regression analysis can be carried out.[135] By using this method it is possible in a single model to explain differences and similarities in the role played by a series of independent variables for emigrants in each of the three countries.

---

[135] D. J. Drummond and A. R. Gallant, 'The Tscsreg Procedure', in *SAS Supplemental Library User's Guide*, ed. J. T. Helwig, North Carolina 1977, pp. 155—68.

Union Growth in Denmark, 1911–39*

Peder J. Pedersen
University of Aarhus, Denmark

Abstract

The years up to 1939 constitute the penetration phase of unions in Denmark. Models of the Ashenfelter-Pencavel or Bain-Elsheikh type are not able to explain the development in the degree of unionization. A model with special emphasis on the narrow relationship between union membership and unemployment insurance in Denmark gives a much more satisfactory explanation. The benefit wage ratio and real payments to unemployment insurance contribute significantly in explaining union growth. In addition the rate of inflation has a significantly positive effect.

I. Introduction

The years between the outbreak of the First and Second World Wars were decisive in the development of Danish trade unions. From 1911 to 1939, unionization increased from 23.1% to 57.2% among blue-collar workers. In-between there were periods with drastic decreases in the degree of unionization followed by new upswings. At the turn of the century unions were still fighting for formal recognition. At the end of the period under review they formed part of the establishment. The purpose of this paper is to examine whether this development can be explained by economic factors.

Union growth is described in Section II. Then, Section III contains a model with special emphasis on the narrow relationship between union membership and unemployment insurance which has been characteristic of the Danish labor market.[1] Finally, a summary and some conclusions are presented in Section IV.

II. Description

Between 1911 and 1939, we find two periods with rapid increases in the degree of unionization: from the outbreak of World War I to 1919/20 and the 1930s. Immediately after 1920, there was a drastic reduction in the degree of unionization, which is also found in a number of other countries; cf. e.g. Bain & Elsheikh (1976).

---

* Comments from two anonymous referees are gratefully acknowledged.
[1] The same narrow relationship has existed in Sweden.

In Warming (1930), Marstrand (1934) and Galenson (1952), the development during and immediately following World War I is explained by three factors. The first is a reaction to the violent inflation which, in the first years of the war, led to serious erosion of the real wage. The second factor was union drives among hitherto weakly organized groups, e.g. rural and female workers. Third, the terms for entering the unemployment insurance system were made much more easy, especially in 1917 and 1918, and the institutional arrangements were (and are) such that entering unemployment insurance normally meant simultaneous entry into a union.

The drastic fall in the degree of unionization in 1921/22 is explained by different factors. In 1920/21, the conditions for entering unemployment insurance were tightened significantly. The severe post-war depression may have contributed to the explanation. Warming (1930, p. 511) and Galenson (1952, p. 29) argue that a depression could induce an increase in union growth in an attempt to protect real wages, but that this could be more than outweighed by people leaving unions due to financial stress, which would make them unable to pay their contributions.

The increasing degree of unionization in the 1930s is explained by Galenson (1952, p. 30) as a reaction to the falling real wage, i.e. the same mechanism as during World War I. Institutionally, the 1930s are characterized by improvements in unemployment insurance schemes that might have stimulated the propensity to unionize in a period with high unemployment risk; cf. Dich (1967) and Kallestrup (1946).

The hypotheses found in the literature are all of an aggregate nature. One reason for this is a lack of data on union density on a sectoral basis. Nor do we have data on unemployment and wages for union and nonunion members. When the development in average wages is compared e.g. between industry and agriculture, it is found that real wages were stabilized during the 1930s in the more highly organized industrial sector. Agricultural wages, on the other hand, were sharply depressed. Unfortunately, the overall lack of data has made it necessary to keep the analysis on an aggregate level, both in the contemporary literature and in this study.

This brief review of the sporadic comments in the literature indictates that three factors are emphasized to explain differences in the speed with which unionization proceeded: the rate of inflation, the development of real wages and changes in the laws and regulations concerning unemployment insurance.

III. An Economic Model

In the literature, economic factors have always played a vital role in models of union growth. Political and institutional factors are often mentioned as

Table 1. *Union growth in Denmark, 1911-39. Economic variables*

Regression	1	2	3	4	5	6	7
R^2	0.37	0.37	0.38	0.36	0.45	0.70	0.46
$\bar{R}^2$	0.32	0.32	0.30	0.31	0.37	0.63	0.34
DW	1.56	1.65	1.73	1.67	1.85	2.04	1.72
Dependent variable	DC	DC	DC	TC	TC	TC	TC
Constant	3.22 (1.63)	−0.99 (1.50)	−1.01 (1.66)	0.75 (3.58)	1.05 (3.72)	13.05 (5.75)	14.67 (9.09)
D_{t-1}	−0.06 (0.06)					−0.35 (0.20)	−0.29 (0.30)
PC_t	0.21 (0.06)	0.25 (0.07)	0.26 (0.07)	0.59 (0.16)	0.64 (0.16)	0.60 (0.12)	0.46 (0.28)
UM_t		0.22 (0.20)	0.40 (0.33)	0.44 (0.48)	1.53 (0.74)	2.30 (0.67)	
UM_{t-1}			−0.19 (0.30)		−1.23 (0.66)	−1.38 (0.67)	1.11 (0.76)
UM_{t-2}							−0.92 (0.85)
EC_t						−3.17 (1.28)	
WC_t							0.03 (0.16)

Notes: Dependent variables: DC=change in percentage points in the degree of unionization D, TC=relative change in the number of blue-collar union members. PC=rate of change in prices, UM=rate of unemployment, EC=relative change in the number of blue-collar workers in the labor force, WC=rate of change in hourly earnings in manufacturing. For further details see the Data Appendix and Pedersen (1979). Standard deviations in parentheses.

important, but are seldom used in empirical work. Presumably, one reason is that purely economic variables are easier to quantify.

In the well-known models of Hines (1964), Ashenfelter & Pencavel (1969) and Bain & Elsheikh (1976), the variables used to explain union growth are: the rate of inflation, the rate of change in nominal or real wages, the level or rate of change in unemployment, and the rate of change in employment (potential union membership).[2] Generally these models explain union growth with a reasonably good fit, even over long periods of time. Their stability over time, however, seems dubious; cf. e.g. Moore and Pearce (1976) and Pedersen (1978).

Models which make use of purely macroeconomic variables are clearly unsatisfactory in explaining union growth in Denmark in the period under review. The results for a number of specifications are given in Table 1. The

---

[2] Ashenfelter & Pencavel also use a political variable, i.e. the share of Democrats in the House of Representatives.

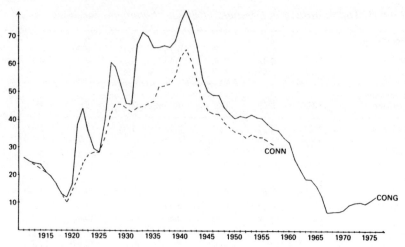

Fig. 1. The ratio between average unemployment benefits and average earnings 1911–1976.

degree of explanation is low except for regression 6, inspired by the Ashenfelter-Pencavel model. However, the coefficient of one of the central variables, the rate of change in potential union membership EC, is significant but with the wrong sign.[3] Overall, the rate of inflation is the only variable with a rather stable significant coefficient. Otherwise, significant coefficients with different signs are found in regressions 5 and 6 when both the current and lagged unemployment rates are entered, indicating a positive effect from *changes* in unemployment. The results from a number of other specifications using purely macroeconomic variables are reported in Pedersen (1979). The main findings are low R^2's, a significantly positive coefficient for the rate of inflation and, for some specifications, a significantly positive coefficient for the first difference in the rate of unemployment.

It was mentioned above that a characteristic feature of the Danish labor market has been the narrow relationship between union membership and unemployment insurance. This fact is taken as a point of departure for a model where the crucial explanatory variables are measures of the benefits and costs of unemployment insurance. The ratio between average unemployment benefits paid out per week and average weekly earnings in industry was chosen as a measure of the benefits. In the following, this measure is called the degree of compensation (COMP).[4] As a measure of

---

[3] The series EC is dubious, as it is calculated by interpolation between census years.
[4] Note that benefits actually paid out were used in the calculation. Consequently, changes in the rules governing eligibility, waiting periods and maximum benefit duration are more or less perfectly reflected in this variable. An alternative would be to model these changes in rules directly. The result of a simple attempt in this direction is found in Table 3 below.

Fig. 2. Real unemployment insurance contributions, gross and net 1911–1976.

the costs of unemployment insurance we use the ratio between members' average yearly payments (gross and net) and the average earnings per hour in industry, i.e. the cost of being insured measured in hours (denoted CONG for gross and CONN for net payments measured in hours).[5] As union membership and unemployment insurance practically coincide, contributions to the union might be added to the insurance contribution as a measure of total costs. Based on information in Warming (1930) and Galenson (1953) on average union contributions in 1914, 1927 and 1948, contributions for these years ranged between 0.9% and 1.1% relative to average yearly income. As it would be quite laborious to find data on union contributions for intervening years and as relative union costs seem to be approximately constant, it was decided to use insurance contributions as a proxy variable for total costs.

The measures of benefits and costs have changed significantly during the period. Figure 1 illustrates the development in the degree of compensation, showing dramatic shifts during and immediately after World War I and a significant increase in the 1930s. For purposes of comparison, the figure shows the development for the entire period 1911–76. Average payments in hours, gross and net, are shown in Figure 2. A fall during World War I is followed by an increasing trend. The development after 1940 is again included in the figure. Until 1939, unemployment insurance appears as a genuine insurance system. Afterwards, it moves definitely into the field of social policy.

---

[5] The difference between gross and net contributions consists of payments to "crisis funds" (a kind of imperfect, experience-rated contribution levied on individual unions).

P. J. Pedersen

Table 2. *Changes in the degree of unionization for blue-collar workers, Denmark, 1912–39 and 1940–76*

Regression	1	2	3	4	5
Period	1912–39	1912–39	1912–39	1940–76	1940–76
R^2	0.75	0.79	0.78	0.17	0.18
$\bar{R}^2$	0.69	0.74	0.73	0.04	0.05
DW	1.59	1.53	1.65	1.16	1.22
Constant	1.40	0.82	1.95	−4.53	−3.93
	(1.83)	(1.71)	(1.72)	(2.33)	(2.45)
D_{t-1}	−0.02	0.004	−0.04	0.08	0.07
	(0.04)	(0.04)	(0.04)	(0.03)	(0.04)
	(0.04)	(0.04)	(0.04)	(0.03)	(0.04)
ΔCOMP	54.23	59.76		3.89	
	(11.69)	(10.10)		(4.67)	
ΔCONG	−0.10		−0.09		−0.02
	(0.07)		(0.06)		(0.07)
ΔCONN		−0.40		0.004	
		(0.16)		(0.09)	
ΔUM×COMP			0.58		0.15
			(1.32)		(0.30)
UM×ΔCOMP			7.55		−0.62
			(1.61)		(1.10)
PC	0.19	0.13	0.17	−0.01	−0.01
	(0.04)	(0.05)	(0.04)	(0.05)	(0.05)
ΔUM	0.12	−0.22		−0.01	
	(0.26)	(0.19)		(0.15)	

Notes: COMP denotes the ratio between average weekly unemployment compensation and average weekly earnings, ΔCONG and ΔCONN are changes in gross and net real payments from members to unemployment insurance funds. Legend for the other variables, see notes to Table 1. Standard deviations in parentheses.

First, we test whether changes in the degree of compensation and in real payments to unemployment insurance contribute to the explanation of union growth. Second, we go on to test a simple hypothesis that changes in the degree of unionization are induced by changes in the expected net economic benefits from unemployment insurance. Current costs are given by the real insurance contribution. As a measure of expected benefits, we use $p(U) \times \text{COMP}$, where $p(U)$ indicates the probability of becoming unemployed in a given period. The changes in expected benefits are approximated by:

$$\Delta p(U) \times \text{COMP} + p(U) \times \Delta \text{COMP}. \qquad (1)$$

The probability of becoming unemployed is approximated by the rate of unemployment, U. In addition to measures of expected net economic benefits from joining a union, it is assumed that purely macroeconomic variables may also contribute to the explanation of union growth. Table 2 lists the results from a number of regressions with the change in the degree of unionization in percentage points as the dependent variable. (The same form of dependent variable as in Hines' (1964) model.) The degree of explanation is satisfactory and more than twice as high as when e.g. the Hines model is estimated using Danish data. Regressions 1 and 2 indicate that changes in the degree of compensation have a very significant positive impact on unionization, while changes in real payments to unemployment insurance funds have a negative impact. It is only when net payments are used that the coefficient is significant at the 5% level. The rate of inflation has a significant positive influence on changes in the degree of unionization, while changes in unemployment seem to be without importance. The rate of unemployment multiplied by changes in the degree of compensation has a highly significant positive impact on unionization; cf. regression 3.[6] Otherwise only the rate of inflation has a significant coefficient. Re-estimation of regressions 1–3 with the exclusion of insignificant variables leads to the following "best" regression, with changes in the degree of unionization in percentage points as the dependent variable:

$$DC = 0.74 - 0.36\Delta CONN + 7.85(UM \times \Delta COMP) + 0.14PC \qquad (2)$$
$$\quad (0.40) \quad (0.13) \qquad\qquad (1.20) \qquad\qquad\qquad (0.04)$$
$$R^2 = 0.80; \quad \bar{R}^2 = 0.77; \quad DW = 1.75.$$

The results are extremely poor for the period 1940 to 1976, as shown in regressions 4 and 5. The shift away from agriculture proceeded much faster during this period than in the years 1911–39. Sectoral unionization data are available for the year 1948; see Galenson (1953), p. 30. These data can be used to calculate that about 40% of the increase in the aggregate degree of unionization is due to the shift away from agriculture. The aggregate degree of unionization up to about 1970 lies on a smoothly increasing trend, uncorrelated with both purely macroeconomic variables and insurance variables.

In the models by Ashenfelter–Pencavel and Bain–Elsheikh, the dependent variable is the percentage change in the number of union members. The outcome from changing to this version of the dependent variable are shown in Table 3. The results are qualitatively unchanged. The variable $\Delta UM \times COMP$ still has an insignificant coefficient. It does become significant in a regression on the longer period 1911–76, but the regression itself is not stable over this length of time. Separate regressions on the period 1940–76 give the same poor results as in Table 2.

---

[6] As mentioned above, unemployment data on nonunion members are not available. If unions manage to stabilize real wages, one conceivable consequence would be higher unemployment in depression periods in the unionized sector. Consequently, a simultaneity bias might result from the impact running from the dependent variable DC to the explanatory variable UM.

Table 3. *Percentage change in the number of blue-collar union members, Denmark, 1912–39*

Regression	1	2	3	4
R^2	0.85	0.86	0.85	0.91
$\bar{R}^2$	0.81	0.83	0.83	0.88
DW	1.61	1.72	1.68	1.80
Constant	6.16	7.64	4.49	8.15
	(3.43)	(3.27)	(0.82)	(2.64)
D_{t-1}	−0.04	−0.08		−0.11
	(0.08)	(0.08)		(0.06)
ΔCOMP	135.24			
	(20.28)			
ΔCONN	−0.90	−0.83	−1.01	
	(0.31)	(0.30)	(0.27)	
ΔUM×COMP		1.53		
		(2.07)		
UM×ΔCOMP		18.05	19.00	
		(2.80)	(2.47)	
PC	0.36	0.32	0.29	0.31
	(0.10)	(0.09)	(0.09)	(0.07)
ΔUM	0.22			0.86
	(0.38)			(0.36)
L1				25.55
				(3.42)
L2				−16.55
				(3.51)
L3				6.37
				(2.88)

Notes: Legend, see notes to Tables 1 and 2. $L1$, $L2$ and $L3$ are dumy variables for legal changes. Standard deviations in parentheses.

So far, the insurance system has been represented by measures of actual benefits and costs. Benefits actually paid out are to some degree influenced by the rules governing eligibility, etc. Consequently, our estimates are affected by simultaneity, as paid-out benefits are influenced by the rate of change in the number of union members. A preferable approach would be to model the insurance system explicitly. Unfortunately this is hardly possible because the number of changes in rules is very large. As an attempt in this direction, the three most dramatic changes in the system have been represented by dummy variables. The result is shown in regression 4. The dummy variable $L1$ takes the value 1 in 1918 (zero elsewhere) when the waiting period for benefit eligibility was reduced considerably. $L2$ is set at 1 in 1921 (zero elsewhere) when conditions for entering and remaining a member of the insurance system were tightened to a very large

Data Appendix

	T	D	COMP	CONG	CONN	PC	UM
1911	117 417	23.1	0.128	26.1	26.1	0.53	2.20
1912	125 921	24.5	0.140	24.9	24.9	4.75	1.88
1913	137 333	26.4	0.149	24.1	23.6	3.03	1.93
1914	141 847	27.1	0.157	23.8	22.2	5.06	2.56
1915	155 998	29.4	0.161	21.0	20.9	16.00	1.99
1916	171 272	32.0	0.138	19.4	19.3	16.38	1.68
1917	200 227	36.9	0.121	16.5	16.5	14.81	3.36
1918	276 475	50.4	0.267	13.0	12.9	15.48	7.41
1919	298 677	54.0	0.197	11.8	10.0	20.11	5.45
1920	305 086	54.5	0.193	16.5	14.1	21.40	3.38
1921	265 107	44.4	0.150	38.1	18.6	−11.11	8.54
1922	260 338	42.9	0.158	43.8	24.2	−13.79	7.39
1923	255 126	41.5	0.150	35.1	27.1	3.00	4.82
1924	261 716	42.0	0.154	29.4	28.0	4.85	4.13
1925	269 258	42.7	0.147	28.1	28.0	− 2.31	5.61
1926	270 924	42.3	0.173	39.3	33.4	−12.80	7.77
1927	270 709	41.9	0.167	60.4	41.2	− 3.80	8.32
1928	275 982	42.3	0.155	58.8	45.4	− 1.13	6.73
1929	284 234	43.2	0.156	52.1	45.4	− 1.14	5.70
1930	295 237	44.4	0.144	45.8	44.1	− 4.62	5.22
1931	308 284	45.4	0.160	45.6	42.7	− 6.06	6.74
1932	323 172	46.2	0.165	66.9	44.3	0	12.09
1933	355 456	49.7	0.191	71.3	44.8	− 2.58	11.55
1934	371 899	50.7	0.211	69.8	45.8	4.40	9.46
1935	385 472	51.3	0.181	65.8	46.6	3.01	8.63
1936	406 325	52.8	0.218	65.9	51.8	1.75	8.74
1937	432 609	54.9	0.261	66.6	52.2	3.45	10.27
1938	447 139	55.6	0.261	66.0	52.8	1.67	10.25
1939	471 966	57.2	0.269	68.3	55.7	2.19	8.92

T=number of blue-collar union members. D=degree of unionization for workers. COMP= average unemployment benefits in percent of average weekly earnings in industry. The series for average unemployment benefits has kindly been supplied by N. Kærgård, Institute of Economics, University of Copenhagen. CONG=average total contribution per member to unemployment insurance funds (ordinary+extraordinary contribution to "crisis funds") divided by average hourly earnings in industry. CONN=average ordinary contributions per member to unemployment insurance funds divided by average hourly earnings in industry. PC=rate of change in consumer prices. UM=rate of unemployment calculated as the ratio between an estimated total number of unemployed and an estimate of the total number of wage-earners.

extent. Finally, $L3$ is set at 1 in 1933 (zero elsewhere) when the maximum duration of benefits was increased significantly. The coefficients of the dummy variables are all significant and on the whole, regression 4 is marginally superior to the other specifications.

IV. Summary and Conclusion

The well-known models of union growth using purely macroeconomic variables do not explain the penetration phase of Danish unions in a satisfactory way. Instead, a model with variables taken from the unemployment insurance system was tested. It is shown that a high degree of explanation is found when variables related to insurance benefits and costs or to major changes in rules are used in combination with the rate of inflation. The model is not able to explain union growth in the years after World War II.

References

Ashenfelter, O. & Pencavel, J. H. American trade-union growth: 1900–1960. *Quarterly Journal of Economics:* 434–48, 1969.

Bain, G. S. & Elsheikh, F.: *Union growth and the business cycle. An econometric analysis.* Oxford, 1976.

Dich, J. S.: *Kompendium i socialpolitikkens historie.* 2nd ed. Aarhus, 1967.

Galenson, W.: *The Danish system of labor relations.* Cambridge, Mass, 1952.

Hines, A. G.: Trade unions and wage inflation in the United Kingdom, 1893–1961. *Review of Economic Studies:* 221–52, 1964.

Kallestrup, L.: *Arbejdsanvisning og arbejdsløshedsforsikring.* Copenhagen, 1946.

Marstrand, E.: *Arbejderorganisation og arbejderkaar i Danmark fra 1848 til nutiden.* Copenhagen, 1934.

Moore, W. J. & Pearce, D. K.: Union growth: a test of the Ashenfelter–Pencavel model. *Industrial Relations:* 244–47, 1976.

Pedersen, P. J.: Union growth and the business cycle: a note on the Bain–Elsheikh model. *British Journal of Industrial Relations:* 373–377, 1978.

Pedersen, P. J.: Aspekter af fagbevægelsens vækst i Danmark, 1911–76. Memo 1979–5. Institute of Economics, University of Aarhus, Denmark, 1979.

Warming, J.: *Danmarks erhvervs- og samfundsliv.* Copenhagen, 1930.

First version submitted June 1981;
final version received August 1982.

Resource Boom, Wages and Unemployment: Theory and Evidence from the Norwegian Petroleum Experience

*Jan Morten Dyrstad**
University of Bergen, Norway

Abstract

The effects of Norwegian petroleum activities on nominal wages and the rate of unemployment are analyzed in this paper. The theoretical model is based on standard theory of segmented labor markets. Increased nominal wages in the petroleum sector will unambiguously increase the wage level and the rate of unemployment. Increased petroleum employment will under realistic assumptions also raise the wage level. The effect on the rate of unemployment in this case is ambiguous. The empirical model is embedded in reduced forms of the theoretical model and the estimated parameters are consistent with the theoretical results.

I. Introduction

Norwegian petroleum production affects the domestic economy through two principal channels. The economy is affected directly by the sector's own demand for domestic resources (the resource-movement effect), and indirectly by use of the additional national revenue created by this production (the spending effect).[1] The purpose of this paper is to analyze theoretically and empirically how Norwegian petroleum activities affect domestic wages and the unemployment rate through the resource-movement effect.

To our knowledge, there are relatively few studies concerning the Norwegian petroleum sector's impact on the labor market. Surveys by

---

*I am grateful to A. E. Risa, E. R. Steffensen, I. H. Thorsen, B.-A. Wickström and J. Aarrestad for helpful comments and discussions. Comments from two anonymous referees have improved the article considerably. I am solely responsible for any remaining errors. Financial support from the Norwegian Research Council for Science and the Humanities is gratefully acknowledged.

[1] For a discussion of these effects in general, see e.g. Cordon and Neary (1982).

126   J. M. Dyrstad

Holm (1982) and *Gruppen for Ressursstudier* (The Resource Policy Group; GRS, 1982) conclude that growth in the petroleum sector has increased competition for special types of labor in particular regions of the country. Furthermore, both studies indicate clearly that this increased competition has had a positive effect on wage policies of the firms in question. Steigum (1983) conjectures that the direct effect seems to have been more important, especially in the labor market, "than what many felt was desireable or even possible ten years ago".[2] Even though we apply a different approach to the problem, the above studies form an important basis for our analysis.

In section II, we point out three distinctive features of the petroleum sector in relation to the labor market. This serves as a background for the theoretical model, which is presented in Section III. The comparative statics results are outlined and discussed in Section IV. The empirical model, data and interpretation of the results are given in Section V. Finally, Section VI summarizes the main conclusions.

II. The Petroleum Sector and the Labor Market

The petroleum sector is usually divided into primary and secondary activities. Primary activities comprise firms directly engaged in oil and/or gas production. Other industries produce goods and services partly for primary activities and partly for other markets. Those areas which produce for primary activities are defined as secondary activities. In the following, primary activities are referred to as the petroleum sector.

In the context of this paper, three important features should be kept in mind regarding the Norwegian petroleum sector and the labor market. First, this sector is concentrated geographically to particular regions of the country. As an illustration, in 1984, about 55 per cent[3] of employment in the petroleum sector was concentrated in Rogaland county.[4] Second, the share of skilled workers is considerably higher in the petroleum sector than in other sectors.[5] Since the markets for this kind of labor were already characterized by excess demand before petroleum production began, the growth in this sector has intensified

---
[2] Steigum (1984, p. 39).
[3] Directorate of Labor (1984).
[4] This concentration is, of course, due to the fact that the Norwegian authorities first gave permission to start petroleum production on the southern part of the Norwegian continental shelf and that the Stavanger area in particular became a natural center for these activities.
[5] GRS (1982, p. 41).

demand pressure.⁶ Third, wage rates in the petroleum sector are very high as compared to other sectors.⁷ In addition, income tax laws are relatively more favorable for some off-shore workers.⁸

III. The Model

Occupational and geographical mobility obstacles make it unrealistic to regard the labor market as a single national market. Hence the framework of the model is that the labor market is divided into a large number of submarkets according to occupational and geographical criteria.

The model distinguishes between six groups of submarkets. The groups are determined on the basis of whether the submarkets included are occupationally and geographically close to or distant from the petroleum sector. The division of the market groups may be illustrated as follows:

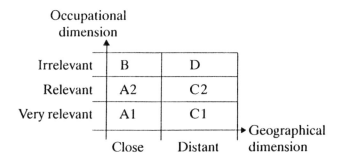

Groups A1, A2 and B contain submarkets which are geographically close to the petroleum sector, while the markets contained in C1, C2 and D are distant in this respect. Labor in groups B and D are irrelevant for the petroleum sector. Groups A2 and C2 comprise labor relevant for the petroleum sector, but not to the same extent as in A1 and C1. The distinction between A1 and C1, and A2 and C2 is that the

---

⁶ This aspect of the petroleum sector's impact on the labor market is discussed in *ibid.* and Holm (1982).
⁷ For instance, average hourly earnings (nominal) for petroleum workers in general were approximately NOK 99 in 1982. The corresponding figure for skilled workers in manufacture of fabricated metal products, machinery and equipment was NOK 58. Source: The Norwegian Employers' Confederation; see Section V.
⁸ See GRS (1982, p. 124).

128 J. M. Dyrstad

petroleum sector is rationed on the demand side in the A1 and C1 market groups, while in A2 and C2 the supply side is rationed vis-à-vis the petroleum sector. We introduce this distinction in order to capture the second feature of the relation between the labor market and the petroleum sector mentioned in the preceding section.

The petroleum sector is exogenous in relation to the market groups and is therefore not included in any of them. We assume that all submarkets can unambiguously be assigned to one of these six market groups. Furthermore, we assume that all submarkets in a market group can be represented by aggregate supply and demand functions.

The structural form of the model is as follows:

$$N_i^S = N_i^S(w_i^c, w_i^o) \qquad i = A1, C1 \qquad (1),(2)$$

$$N_j^S = N_j^S(w_j^c, \tilde{N}^o) \qquad j = A2, C2 \qquad (3),(4)$$

$$N_k^S = N_k^S(w_k^c) \qquad k = B, D \qquad (5),(6)$$

$$N_l^D = N_l^D(w_l^p) \qquad l = i + j + k \qquad (7)-(12)$$

$$w_l^c = W_l/P_l^c \qquad (13)-(18)$$

$$w_l^p = W_l/P_l^p \qquad (19)-(24)$$

$$w_i^o = W^o/P_i^c \qquad (25),(26)$$

$$P_l^c = g_l(N^o) + P^c \qquad g_l(0) = 0 \qquad (27)-(32)$$

$$\qquad g'_{A1} = g'_{A2} = g'_B > g'_{C1} = g'_{C2} = g'_D = 0$$

$$P_l^p = h_l(N^o) + P^p \qquad h_l(0) = 0 \qquad (33)-(38)$$

$$\qquad h'_{A1}, h'_{A2}, h'_B > h'_{C1} = h'_{C2} = h'_D = 0$$

$$W_m = e_m(\bar{W}) \qquad m = j + k \qquad (39)-(42)$$

$$\qquad 1 \geqslant e'_{A2} \geqslant e'_{C2} > e'_B \geqslant e'_D \geqslant 0$$

$$\bar{W} = \sum_i v_i W_i \qquad \sum_i v_i = 1 \qquad (43)$$

$$\tilde{N}^o = \lambda N^o \qquad 0 < \lambda < 1 \qquad (44)$$

$$N_i^S = N_i^D \qquad (45),(46)$$

$$U_m = N_m^S - N_m^D \qquad (47)-(50)$$

$$U = \sum_m U_m \qquad (51)$$

Scand. J. of Economics 1987

$$W=\sum_m n_m W_m + \bar{n}\bar{W} + n^\circ W^\circ \qquad \sum_m n_m + \bar{n} + n^\circ = 1 \qquad (52)$$

$$N=\sum_l N_l^D + N^\circ. \qquad (53)$$

The $+/-$ signs under the arguments in (1)–(12) indicate the sign of the partial derivative with respect to that argument. All of the variables are listed in Appendix 1. The model has a total of 57 variables in 53 equations. Since P^c, P^p, W^o and N^o are treated as exogenous, the model is complete.

Before presenting the comparative statics results, we motivate the structural relations of the model.

The *labor supply* in all market groups [(1)–(6)] is standard in the sense that it is a function of the real wage rate. However, for market groups A1 and C1, the real wage rate in the petroleum sector, w_i^o, forms part of the labor supply. This wage rate is included because other studies indicate that at least parts of the petroleum sector have been rationed in some submarkets.[9] A1 and C1 comprise submarkets with such labor.

In a study by the Norwegian Dirctorate of Labor (1982), the excess demand for welders was estimated to be 10.4 per cent, plumbers 9.0 per cent, material inspectors 7.2 per cent, scaffold workers 6.6 per cent and sheet-metal workers 5.0 per cent. However, these figures should be interpreted with caution for two reasons. The definition of the petroleum sector used in the Directorate's study differs from ours in that it includes both primary and secondary activities. In other words, the underlying situation could have been excess demand in secondary activities and balance, or near balance, in primary activities. Second, temporary rigidities in the labor market might explain some of the relatively large figures referred to above. On the other hand, if the petroleum sector is rationed, it can set high wage rates in order to obtain the labor demanded. The sector's ability to pay high wages implies that it can choose such a strategy. The studies by Holm (1982) and GRS (1982) indicate that parts of the petroleum sector have chosen this strategy.[10]

---

[9] See *ibid.* and Holm (1982).
[10] This does not exclude the possibility of rationing. One important restriction which faces at least some firms in the petroleum sector is that they more or less have to adapt to the wage policies set by the employers' federations. Other firms are restricted by profitability.

130 J. M. Dyrstad

Even though the studies referred to above indicate some degree of demand-side rationing in the petroleum sector, there are good reasons for believing that other types of labor are rationed on the supply side.[11] This kind of labor is included in A2 and C2. As petroleum wages are much higher than in alternative industries, there is a queue to obtain jobs in the petroleum sector. If this is the case, then there must be another explanation for the high wages paid by the sector. Strong and influential trade unions could be one important reason. Another, but not contradictory, reason is that the petroleum sector sets wages so high that it will always have a queue of labor and will thus obtain the labor demanded at any point in time. Consequently, the amount of this kind of labor in the petroleum sector, $\tilde{N}^o$, is an argument in (3) and (4). $\tilde{N}^o$ affects the labor supply in market groups A2 and C2 negatively. From (44) it follows that this part of petroleum employment is assumed to be a constant fraction of total petroleum employment, N^o.

One objection to the formulation of (1) and (2) is that the real wage rate in market group A1 should be an argument in (2) and vice versa. A corresponding objection could be made in relation to (3) and (4). Since the model assumes that labor can move from these markets to the petroleum sector, why is it that the same labor cannot move between relevant market groups? The implicit assumption here is that the wage differences between groups A1 and C1, and between groups A2 and C2 are so small that incentives for this type of mobility are lacking.[12]

The *demand for labor*, (7)–(12), has a standard formulation as a function of the real wage rate.

The consumer and producer *price indices*, P_i^c, P_i^p, for market groups C1, C2 and D are equal to P^c and P^p, respectively. P^c and P^p are assumed to be determined exogenously. However, the indices for market groups A1, A2 and B are determined partly by the size of the petroleum sector, measured by N^o. This formulation indicates that the establishment of these activities in limited geographical regions entails pressure on resources which cannot be supplied from outside the region. High housing prices in the Stavanger area, where approximately half of all petroleum activities are located, can serve as an example of this kind of price effect. Since groups A1, A2 and B cover the same geographical regions, it follows that $P_{A1}^c = P_{A2}^c = P_B^c$. The realism of

---

[11] See Norman (1983, p. 124).
[12] This assumption is in accordance with the arguments behind the formulation of (39)–(42); see below.

taking all other prices as exogenously determined can be justified in the long run because the Norwegian economy is very open and exchange rates are fixed.

Wages are set through collective bargaining and the organizations involved in wage settlements play an important role. One of the trade unions' important goals is to minimize *geographical* wage differences, and to some extent also wage differences *between* industries. This assumption is a slightly different version of the solidary trade union policy underlying the so-called Aukrust inflation model.[13] The concept of *comparison mechanism* is crucial. According to this mechanism, when preparing their demands in wage negotiations, trade unions make comparisons with those occupational groups in a given industry that receive the highest wages. Such a comparison is necessary in order to work towards the goals mentioned above. The formulation of (39)–(42) is a simple way of incorporating this mechanism into the model.[14] Equations (39)–(42) express nominal wage rates in the m markets as functions of the average wage rate in the A1 and C1 markets, $\bar{W}$; cf. (43).

These markets comprise the occupational groups which have experienced the highest wage growth in recent years.[15] The relationships between the derivatives, e'_m, express the goals of the trade unions, i.e. that the comparisons are made first and foremost *within* the same industry and, to a lesser extent, *between* industries.

The model is closed by assuming market clearing in the A1 and C1 markets,[16] while this is not assumed in the other markets; cf. (45)–(50). Equations (51)–(53) define the number of unemployed, U, the average nominal wage level, W, and the number of employed in the economy, N, respectively.

IV. Comparative Statics Results

The model may now be used to discuss how the petroleum sector affects the nominal wage rate and the unemployment rate. In order to

---

[13] See Aukrust (1977, p. 113).
[14] This part of the model could be motivated by competition between the different market groups, i.e., a competition mechanism could be used instead of a comparison mechanism. However, in a Norwegian institutional context, the comparison concept seems important and realistic.
[15] See Dyrstad (1986).
[16] This corresponds to the second feature mentioned in Section II.

simplify the expressions somewhat, let

$$\alpha_i = \frac{\partial N_i^s}{\partial w_i^c}\frac{\partial w_i^c}{\partial W_i} - \frac{\partial N_i^D}{\partial w_i^p}\frac{\partial w_i^p}{\partial W_i} > 0 \qquad \Theta_i = \frac{\partial N_i^s}{\partial w_i^c}\frac{\partial w_i^c}{\partial P_i^c} + \frac{\partial N_i^s}{\partial w_i^o}\frac{\partial w_i^o}{\partial P_i^c}$$

$$\gamma_i = \frac{\partial N_i^D}{\partial w_i^p}\frac{\partial w_i^p}{\partial P_i^p} > 0 \qquad \rho_j = \frac{\partial N_j^s}{\partial \tilde{N}^o} < 0 \qquad \sigma_i = \frac{\partial N_i^s}{\partial w_i^o}\frac{\partial w_i^o}{\partial W^o} < 0.$$

Differentiation of (45) and (46), using (43), yields

$$d\tilde{W} = -\sum_i v_i \alpha_i^{-1} \sigma_i dW^o + v_{A1}\alpha_{A1}^{-1}(\gamma_{A1} h'_{A1} - \Theta_{A1} g'_{A1}) dN^o$$
$$+ \sum_i v_i \alpha_i^{-1} \gamma_i dP^p - \sum_i v_i \alpha_i^{-1} \Theta_i dP^c. \tag{54}$$

Furthermore, combining (54) with (39)–(42) and (52), the comparative statics results for W are

$$\frac{\partial W}{\partial W^o} = -\pi \sum_i v_i \alpha_i^{-1} \sigma_i + n^o > 0 \tag{55}$$

$$\frac{\partial W}{\partial N^o} = \pi v_{A1} \alpha_{A1}^{-1}(\gamma_{A1} h'_{A1} - \Theta_{A1} g'_{A1}) > 0 \text{ if } \Theta_{A1} \leq 0 \tag{56}$$

$$\frac{\partial W}{\partial P^c} = -\pi \sum_i v_i \alpha_i^{-1} \Theta_i \geq 0 \text{ if } \Theta_i \leq 0 \tag{57}$$

$$\frac{\partial W}{\partial P^p} = \pi \sum_i v_i \alpha_i^{-1} \gamma_i > 0, \tag{58}$$

where

$$\pi = \sum_m n_m e'_m + \tilde{n} > 0.$$

The only unambiguous results are (55) and (58). The reason for $\partial W/\partial W^o > 0$ is, of course, that higher nominal wages in the petroleum sector increase w_i^o, so that workers move from the A1 and C1 markets to the petroleum sector and, through excess demand, push W_i upward. The reason for $\partial W/\partial P^p > 0$ is that increased producer prices reduce w_{A1}^p and thereby increase the demand for labor. These two wage effects are spread to the other markets via the comparison mechanisms.

Scand. J. of Economics 1987

Resource boom, wages and unemployment 133

Equations (56) and (57) contain terms which work in opposite directions. First, the interpretation of (56) is that higher N^o increases P_{A1}^c and thereby reduces w_{A1}^c and w_{A1}^o. Lower w_{A1}^o implies increased supply in the A1 markets and downward pressure on W_{A1}. However, lower w_{A1}^c implies reduced supply and pushes W_{A1} upward. These two effects are contained in Θ_{A1}, so theoretically the sign of Θ_{A1} cannot be determined. Second, higher N^o also has a positive impact on P_{A1}^p, so we obtain the same effect on W here as mentioned in connection with (58). Furthermore, we see that (57) is also ambiguous because of Θ_i. Therefore, if $\Theta_i<0$, we can obviously conclude that both (56) and (57) are positive. $\Theta_i>0$ implies that workers move from the petroleum sector to the i markets when consumer prices increase, and that this effect dominates. In our opinion it seems theoretically doubtful to accept $\Theta_i>0$, because wages in the petroleum sector are considerably higher than in alternative sectors; cf. Section II. A more plausible assumption is that the net effect is reduced supply, i.e., $\Theta_i<0$.

The rate of unemployment, u, is defined by dividing (51) by (53). Differentiation of u then yields

$$du = \left(-u \sum_i \eta_i \, dW_i + \phi \, d\bar{W} + \chi \, dN^o + \psi \, dP^c - \omega \, dP^p \right) N^{-1} \quad (59)$$

where

$$\eta_1 = \frac{\partial N_l^D}{\partial w_l^p} \frac{\partial w_l^p}{\partial W_l} < 0 \qquad \phi = \sum_m (\alpha_m - \eta_m u) \, e_m' > 0$$

$$\chi = \sum_z \frac{\partial N_z^S}{\partial w_z^c} \frac{\partial w_z^c}{\partial P_z^c} g_z' - (1+u) \sum_z \gamma_z \, h_z' - u\gamma_{A1} \, h_{A1}' + \lambda \sum_j \rho_j - u < 0,$$

$$z = A2, B$$

$$\psi = \sum_m \frac{\partial N_m^S}{\partial w_m^c} \frac{\partial w_m^c}{\partial P_m^c} < 0 \qquad \omega = u \sum_l \gamma_l + \sum_m \gamma_m > 0.$$

The comparative statics results for the unemployment rate are then obtained by substituting for dW_i from (45) and (46) and by using (54):

$$\frac{\partial u}{\partial W^o} = N^{-1} \left[-\phi \sum_i \nu_i \alpha_i^{-1} \sigma_i + u \sum_i \eta_i \alpha_i^{-1} \sigma_i \right] > 0 \quad (60)$$

134 J. M. Dyrstad

$$\frac{\partial u}{\partial N^o} = N^{-1}\left[\chi + \alpha_{A1}^{-1}(\phi v_A - u\eta_{A1})(\gamma_{A1} h'_{A1} - \Theta_{A1} g'_{A1})\right] \quad (61)$$

$$\frac{\partial u}{\partial P^c} = N^{-1}\left[\psi - \phi\sum_i v_i \alpha_i^{-1}\Theta_i + u\sum_i \eta_i \alpha_i^{-1}\Theta_i\right] \quad (62)$$

$$\frac{\partial u}{\partial P^p} = N^{-1}\left[-\omega + \phi\sum_i v_i \alpha_i^{-1}\gamma_i - u\sum_i \eta_i \alpha_i^{-1}\gamma_i\right]. \quad (63)$$

The signs of these partial derivatives are ambiguous, except for (60).

The interpretation of (60) is as follows. ϕ represents wage effects resulting from increased wages in the A1 and C1 markets via the comparison mechanism. The standard positive correlation between wages and unemployment explains $\phi > 0$. From (54) we saw that $\partial \bar{W}/\partial W^o > 0$, because reduced supply in the i markets generates positive wage pressure there. Thus, the first term in (60) contains effects which raise the rate of unemployment.

The second term in (60) is also positive. Because higher W^o reduces supply in the i markets, employment in these markets is reduced through increased W_i. This, by itself, will increase the rate of unemployment.

In regard to (61), we see that $\chi < 0$. The first three terms in χ comprise price effects generated directly by the petroleum sector in the A1, A2 and B markets. Since higher prices reduce real wages, labor demand increases and supply decreases, thus reducing the number of unemployed workers in the A2 and B2 markets. In the A1 markets, this effect reduces the rate of unemployment because N^D_{A1} decreases. The last two terms, $\lambda\Sigma\rho_j - u$, are also negative. If the suppliers in the A2 and C2 markets are rationed, higher N^o will reduce supply through ρ_j. Of course, the effect depends on the share of total employment in the sector, λ. Higher petroleum employment directly increases the denominator in the definition of u, so that u is reduced.

The two effects contained in the final term in (61) are generated from both producer and consumer price effects in the A1 markets due to changes in petroleum employment; cf. the last parenthesis in (61). From the discussion of (56), it seemed reasonable to assume that this parenthesis is positive, i.e., $\Theta_{A1} \leq 0$, which is assumed in the following.

Increased producer and consumer prices in the A1 markets raise W_{A1} and consequently $\bar{W}$. Therefore, the first of these two effects works through the comparison mechanisms included in ϕ and is, of course, positive. The second effect refers to wage effects caused by reduced real wage rates on both the supply and demand sides in the A1 markets. These shifts in the supply and demand functions will increase W_{A1} and thus reduce employment in the A1 markets. Hence the unemployment rate will increase. It then follows that the effect on u due to changes in N^o is ambiguous.

We see that (62) and (63) contain the same two types of effects as those discussed above; the difference is that they originate from changes in other variables. ψ in (62) is negative because an increase in consumer prices reduces the supply in the A2, C2, B and D markets. But since the other effects in (62) have opposite signs, we cannot determine the sign of $\partial u/\partial P^c$.

As for (63), higher producer prices increase the demand for labor in all submarkets, thereby increasing employment and reducing the rate of unemployment. This effect is contained in the first term in ω. The second term contains the effect that increased demand will directly reduce unemployment in the A2, C2, B and D markets, because we have not assumed market clearing in these markets. Therefore $-\omega < 0$. But since the other effects in (63) work in the opposite direction, $\partial u/\partial P^p$ is also ambiguous.

In the next section we present an empirical model embedded in reduced forms of the theoretical model. The primary target is to estimate the parameters which correspond to the comparative statics results.

V. Empirical Analysis

The Empirical Model

$$W_{ht} = a_0 + a_1 W^o_t + a_2 N^o_{ht} + a_3 P^c_t + a_4 P^p_t + \sum_{r=2}^{4} a_{3+r} KV_r + V_1 \qquad (64)$$

$$u_{ht} = b_0 + b_1 W^o_t + b_2 N^o_{ht} + b_3 P^c_t + b_4 P^p_t + b_5 KV_1 + b_6 KV_4$$

$$+ \sum_{h=1}^{9} b_{6+h} F_h + V_2. \qquad (65)$$

The variables are defined as follows:

W_{ht} = average hourly earnings (nominal) for workers in region h in period t

W_t^o = average hourly earnings (nominal) for workers in primary activities of the petroleum sector in period t

N_{ht}^o = number of persons directly engaged in oil activities in region h in period t, measured in 1,000 persons

P_t^c = national consumer price index in period t

P_t^p = national producer price index in period t

u_{ht} = rate of unemployment in region h in period t

KV_r = 1 if the observation belongs to quarter r, 0 otherwise

F_h = 1 if the observation belongs to region h, 0 otherwise

V_1, V_2 = error terms.

Assuming linearity in the theoretical model, the expressions from that model corresponding to $a_1 - a_4$ and $b_1 - b_4$ above are (55)–(58) and (60)–(63), respectively.

Data

The parameters in (64) and (65) are estimated by OLS[17] on panel data[18] (pooled cross-section and time-series data) from the ten counties

---

[17] Since u_t and W_t are determined simultaneously, an objection to the use of OLS is that the error terms in (64) and (65) are correlated. Even though this is the case, it does not imply any contradiction to the BLUE property of OLS in a single equation. On the other hand, a gain in efficiency can be obtained by viewing the equations as part of a system, i.e., seemingly unrelated regression equations (SURE). However, the correlation between the error terms in the corresponding three versions of (64) and (65) is 0.064 [(64)–(65)], −0.032 [(64*)–(65*)] and −0.015 [(64**)–(65**)]. See Table 1. This suggests that only a small gain in efficiency can be obtained by using a SURE method; see Harvey (1982, p. 67).

[18] Use of OLS to estimate the parameters in (64) is based on the assumption that a_0–a_7 are constant both over time and over cross-section units. Institutional arrangements have played — and are still playing — an important role in wage settlements in Norway. Since there seem to be small geographical variations in this respect, this assumption appears acceptable. However, in regard to (65) we assume that the parameters are constant over time, but not over cross-section units. This is because the industrial structure varies over counties, thereby influencing the unemployment rate. We have thus introduced dummy variables which allow the intercept term to vary over counties.

The dummy variables KV_1 and KV_4 in (65) are used as seasonal corrections for high unemployment rates during winter. The dummy variables in (64) are intended to capture the effects of wage negotiations. These negotiations usually start in the second quarter, but it may take up to three quarters before agreements are reached and take effect. Thus, full seasonal correction is used in (64).

with the highest rate of petroleum employed during the period 1971–82.[19] Thus the geographical unit is a county and the data are quarterly.

The wage data are estimated directly from quarterly statistics of the Norwegian Employers' Confederation (NEC), which are anonymous regarding firms.[20]

The petroleum employment figures are estimated from the Directorate of Labor (1973–82). A consequence of this is that N^o_{ht} comprises both the primary and secondary activities of the petroleum sector, while N^o in the theoretical model comprises only primary activities. This difference between the theoretical and empirical model is due to the fact that available data sources provide limited information as to how petroleum employment is distributed over these two types of activities. From an econometric point of view, we think it is correct to treat petroleum employment in the country as an exogenously determined variable, since it is derived directly from the authorities' program for petroleum extraction. On the other hand, the regional distribution of some amount of petroleum employment is perhaps determined endogenously.

The unemployment rates are estimated from NOS (1973–83) and NOS (1970, 1980). The consumer and producer price indices are given in NOS (1984) and NOS (1978, 1981, 1983),[21] respectively. It should be noted that these price indices differ from those used in the theoretical model in that the theoretical indices express only exogenously given prices, while the empirical indices also comprise the endogenous element. However, the indices used in the regressions are acceptable approximations of the correct theoretical ones.[22] The period of estimation is third quarter 1976–fourth quarter 1982.[23]

---

[19] The ten counties are Oslo, Akershus, Vestfold, Telemark, Vest-Agder, Rogaland, Hordaland, Møre og Romsdal, Sør-Trøndelag and Nord-Trøndelag.
[20] This data base is described in Dyrstad (1986).
[21] Observations on the producer price index for the third and fourth quarters of 1976 are not available. But since this variable exhibits a clear-cut upward trend, these observations are constructed by linear extrapolation.
[22] We were unable to obtain price data from Stavanger which would have yielded price indices more in accordance with the variables in the theoretical model.
[23] The length of this period is determined by the fact that data on W^o_t cannot be obtained for a longer period.

Table 1. *Parameter estimates of three versions of equations (64) and (65). Absolute t-ratios in parentheses*

Variables†	(64)	(64*)	(64**)	(65)	(65*)	(65**)
W_t^o	0.112 (7.41)	0.085 (5.01)	0.108 (8.58)	0.018 (2.83)	0.014 (2.55)	0.014 (4.58)
W_{t-1}^o	—	0.057 (3.45)	—	—	0.014 (2.70)	—
N_t^o	0.392 (3.74)	0.556 (1.91)	0.286 (3.45)	−0.047 (1.35)	−0.080 (0.89)	−0.028 (1.88)
N_{t-1}^o	—	−0.123 (0.44)	—	—	0.032 (0.36)	—
P_t^r	0.237 (6.98)	0.133 (1.66)	0.138 (4.18)	0.049 (5.54)	−0.002 (0.08)	0.045 (5.93)
P_{t-1}^r	—	0.068 (0.94)	—	— (4.56)	0.109	—
P_t^p	−0.006 (0.17)	0.0002 (0.002)	0.027 (0.94)	−0.050 (6.24)	0.062 (3.38)	−0.052 (6.61)
P_{t-1}^p	—	0.030 (0.45)	—	—	−0.183 (7.08)	—
DEP_{t-1}	—	—	0.292 (5.09)	—	—	0.695 (14.53)
Statistics††						
$\bar{R}^2$	0.58	0.60	0.71	0.68	0.79	0.92
SEE	0.92	0.91	0.88	0.28	0.24	0.23
d	1.89	1.93	(1.93)	2.15	2.11	(2.00)
h	—	—	0.84	—	—	−0.02
F (MLM)	9.76	10.08	10.10	10.26	3.53	2.02
F	39.58	26.37	60.75	31.03	39.83	152.36
d.f.	190	177	189	183	170	182

†The estimates refer to these variables. DEP = dependent variable.
†† $\bar{R}^2$ = adjusted R square, SEE = standard error of estimation, d = Durbin-Watson's d statistic, h = Durbin's h statistic, F (MLM) = F statistics for the modified Lagrange Multiplier test, F = F statistics for the regression, d.f. = degrees of freedom.

Results

Estimates $\hat{a}_1-\hat{a}_4$ and $\hat{b}_1-\hat{b}_4$, which are the most interesting parameters in our context, are shown in Table 1.[24] The table also contains estimates from versions of (64) and (65) where the time aspect of the adjustment process has been taken into consideration. Since our data are quarterly, this seems particularly relevant.

The difference between (64) and (65) on the one hand, and (64*) and (65*) on the other, is that (64*) and (65*) also include lagged values

---

[24] The other estimates can be obtained from the author on request.

($t-1$) of those variables which correspond to a_1-a_4 and b_1-b_4. Lagged values ($t-1$) of the dependent variable are included in (64**) and (65**). In the formulation of (64*) and (65*), we implicitly assume that the adjustment process takes two quarters, while the formulation of (64**) and (65**) implies that the lag coefficients decline geometrically.

The estimations are based on data organized as added time series per cross-section unit. When the equations are estimated on the original data set, the d and h statistics yield significant first-order autocorrelation.[25] As our data are quarterly, we might expect to find up to fourth-order autocorrelation in the error terms. We therefore used a modified Lagrange Multiplier (MLM) procedure[26] to test the null hypothesis of zero autocorrelation against the alternative hypothesis that the error terms are generated by an AR(4) process.[27] Except for (64**), we reject the null hypothesis even at the 1 per cent level of significance. In the case of (64**), the null hypothesis is accepted at this level of significance, but not at the 5 per cent level.[28] The estimates and statistics presented in Table 1 are thus obtained from transformed data. The transformation is carried out on the assumption that the pattern of the autoregressive structure is AR(4).[29] As shown in the table, both the d and h statistics indicate that the first-order autocorrelation is removed. According to the MLM test, we cannot reject the null hypothesis at the 1 per cent [(64), (64*), (64**), (65)] and the 5 per cent [(65*), (65**)] level of significance.[30]

---

[25] The d statistics are 0.27 (64), 0.26 (64*), 1.01 (65) and 1.13 (65*). The h statistics in this case are -2.95 (64**) and 3.21 (65**).
[26] This test is described in Harvey (1981, pp. 167 and 277). The test consists of regressing the OLS residuals v_t on the set of explanatory variables (including DEP_{t-1}) and $v_{t-1}... v_{t-4}$, and then testing the joint significance of the lagged estimated residuals by the F statistics.
[27] The alternative hypothesis is:

$$V_t = \rho_1 V_{t-1} + ... + \rho_4 V_{t-4} + \varepsilon_t, \qquad \varepsilon_t \sim N(0, \sigma^2).$$

[28] The F statistics corresponding to (64)–(65**) are 360.93, 335.65, 9.22, 28.08, 22.69 and 20.63. Critical F values are 13.54 (1 per cent level) and 5.66 (5 per cent level).
[29] For (64), (64*), (65) and (65*), the data are transformed by using the two-step Cochrane–Orcutt method, i.e., estimating the autocorrelation coefficients from the OLS residuals and then applying GLS; see Johnston (1972, p. 259). In the case of (64**) and (65**), we transformed the data according to the instrumental variable method proposed by Wallis, described in *ibid.* (p. 319).
[30] In the case of (64**), the MLM test yields a larger F value after this transformation as compared with the value based on the original data set; see footnote 27. Since the null hypothesis was accepted at the 1 per cent level, the data were first transformed in order to remove the significant first-order autocorrelation. However, when (64**) was estimated on that data set, the MLM test rejected the null hypothesis at the 1 per cent level ($F = 30.31$). We thus carried out a transformation based on an AR(4) structure.

140 J. M. Dyrstad

Before discussing the results in relation to the theoretical model, we should comment on the dynamic specifications of (64) and (65). The estimates referring to the lagged dependent variable in (64**) and (65**) yield relatively large adjustment coefficients. Consequently, both the wage rate and the unemployment rate adjust rapidly. The adjustment coefficients are 0.708 $(=1-0.292)$ and 0.305 $(=1-0.695)$, which indicate that the wage and unemployment rates adjust over approximately $1\frac{1}{2}$ and $3\frac{1}{4}$ quarters, respectively. It follows from (64**) that the long-run estimates of a_1-a_4 are 0.153, 0.404, 0.195 and 0.038, respectively.[31] Comparing these estimates with the two-quarter estimates from (64*) and the estimates from (64), we see that they are nearly identical. This also confirms that the adjustment period is short and that (64)–(64**) are mutually consistent. In the same type of comparison for (65)–(65**), we see that the long-run estimates from (65**)[32] are larger (absolute values) than the two-quarter estimates from (65*), which again are larger than the estimates from (65). This indicates a longer adjustment period and mutual consistency.

The standard error of estimation (SEE) in Table 1 decreases from (65) to (65**), thus indicating that (65**) is a better specification than the other two. The same conclusion may be drawn for (64)–(64**).

Given this background, we decided to use the estimates from (64**) and (65**) when commenting on the results.

$\hat{a}_1$ is significantly greater than zero.[33] This result is in accordance with our theoretical expectations, cf. (55), and indicates that at least some parts of the petroleum sector have been rationed in the labor market.

We found from (57) that increased prices affect both w_i^c and w_i^o, and that these two effects work in opposite directions with respect to W. The implication of $\hat{a}_3$ significantly greater than zero is that the effect from reduced w_i^c is stronger than that from w_i^o or, alternatively, that $\Theta_i < 0$. This result and the estimate of a_4 are important when discussing $\hat{a}_2$, because the theoretical counterparts of these parameters, (57) and (58), are partly included in the theoretical counterpart of a_2, (56).

---

[31] The 95 per cent confidence intervals for these estimates are (0.11, 0.20) (a_1), (0.17, 0.66) (a_2), (0.11, 0.27) (a_3) and (−0.04, 0.12) (a_4); see Pindyck and Rubinfeld (1981, p. 270).
[32] The long run estimates corresponding to b_1-b_4 are 0.046 (0.03, 0.07), −0.092 (−0.20, 0.01), 0.148 (0.10, 0.22) and −0.170 (−0.25, −0.12).
[33] Subsequent statements concerning statistical significance refer to a 5 per cent level of significance unless otherwise stated explicitly.

Scand. J. of Economics 1987

Table 1 shows that $\hat{a}_2 = 0.286$ and significantly different from zero, while $\hat{a}_4$ is not. However, the sign of $\hat{a}_4$ is in accordance with (58). Comparing these three estimates with the theoretical framework, we find that the estimated values yield consistent predictions. The estimate of a_4 not significantly different from zero, which indicates that the γ_i's are small. And since $\hat{a}_2 > 0$, this indicates $\Theta_{A1} \leq 0$, which does not contradict $\Theta_i < 0$, implied by $\hat{a}_3$ statistically greater than zero.

Turning to the $\hat{b}$'s, we see that $\hat{b}_1$ is significantly positive. This estimate is therefore in accordance with our expectations, since (60) comprises effects working in the same direction. $\hat{b}_2$ is negative at a 6 per cent level of significance. The implication of this is that the negative effects contained in (61) dominate the positive effects, so that increased petroleum employment reduces the total unemployment rate. $\hat{b}_3$ is significantly greater than zero, which is in accordance with $\hat{a}_3$, since this indicates $\Theta_i < 0$. The theoretical counterpart of b_4 is (63). From the discussion of (63) we know that $-\omega < 0$. The interpretation of $\hat{a}_4$ indicates that the γ_i's are small. Consequently, $\hat{b}_4$ significantly negative is in accordance with the other empirical results and the theoretical model.

VI. Concluding Remarks

At first glance, the estimated parameters — and their underlying effects — seem to be of little importance. One way of illustrating their magnitude is to multiply the long-run estimates from (64**) and (65**) by the change in the corresponding variable over the estimation period.[34] We then see that approximately 20 per cent of the nominal wage growth in the most petroleum-relevant county, Rogaland, can be explained by the growth in petroleum employment. The average percentage for all ten counties is nearly 4.5.

As for the impact of petroleum employment on the unemployment rate, we find that it is reduced by 1.4 per cent in Rogaland, but by only 0.3 per cent on average.

The nominal wage rate in the petroleum sector, W^0_p, increased by NOK 56.00 during the period 1976–82. Based on the long-run estimate of $\hat{a}_1$, this indicates that W_{ht} on average increases by NOK 8.60, or 33.6 per cent.

---

[34] Strictly speaking, the estimates are valid only for small changes in the variables. But we allow use of this method for illustrative purposes.

Using b_1, this increase in W_t^o changes the unemployment rate by 2.6 per cent, which is considerable in the Norwegian context.

It is therefore quite obvious that the growth in petroleum employment has had a clear impact on nominal wages in petroleum-relevant regions. In regions more distant to petroleum activities, the effects seem to have been relatively small. The impact of employment in the petroleum sector on the unemployment rate is, of coure, also largest in the most petroleum-relevant regions.

Our results show that the effect on nominal wages due to increased wages in the petroleum sector is considerable. This indicates that the petroleum sector is, or has been, rationed in the labor market. Finally, the effect on the unemployment rate due to growth in W_t^o is very large.

To the extent that it is possible to compare our analysis with those of Holm (1982) and GRS (1982), it appears that their findings are confirmed by our study.

Appendix 1. List of Variables

N_l^S = supply of labor in submarket group l
N_l^D = demand for labor in submarket group l
w_l^c = real wage rate facing the supply side of submarket group l
w_l^p = real wage rate facing the demand side of submarket group l
w_i^o = real wage rate of the petroleum sector facing the supply side of market group i
N^o = total number of workers in the petroleum sector
$\tilde{N}^o$ = number of workers in the petroleum sector who are rationed on the supply side
W_l = nominal wage rate in market group l
W^o = average nominal wage rate in the petroleum sector
P_l^c = consumer price index in market group l
P_l^p = producer price index in market group l
P^c = exogenously determined consumer price index
P^p = exogenously determined producer price index
U_m = number of unemployed workers in market group m
U = total number of unemployed workers in the economy
W = average nominal wage rate in the economy
N = total number of employed workers in the economy.

References

Aukrust, O.: Inflation in the open economy: A Norwegian model. Article no. 96, Central Bureau of Statistics, Oslo, 1977.
Cordon, W. M. and Neary, J. P.: Booming sector and de-industrialization in a small open economy. *The Economic Journal 92*, 825–48, 1982.
Directorate of Labor: Sysselsettingen ved oljeaktivitetene 1973,...,1984. Arbeidsdirektoratet, Oslo, 1973–84.
Dyrstad, J. M.: *Oljevirksomhetens innvirkning på lønnsdannelsen*. Department of Economics, University of Bergen, Bergen, 1986.
GRS (*Gruppen for Ressursstudier*): Vekst og vansker. Oljens betydning for arbeids- og kapitalmarked mot 2010. Report no. 474, Oslo, 1982.
Harvey, A. C.: *The Econometric Analysis of Time Series*. Philip Allan, Oxford, 1981.
Holm, T.: Virkninger for industrien av oljesektorens rekruttering av teknisk peronell. Working Paper no. 45, Institute of Industrial Economics, Bergen, 1982.
Johnston, J.: *Econometric Methods*. McGraw-Hill, 2nd ed., 1972.
Norman, V. D.: *En Liten, åpen økonomi*. Universitetsforlaget, Oslo, 1983.
NOS (Norway's Official Statistics): *Population and Housing Census, 1970, 1980*. Central Bureau of Statistics, Oslo, 1970, 1980.
NOS: *Labor Market Statistics*, 1973,...,1983. Central Bureau of Statistics, Oslo, 1973–83.
NOS: *Monthly Bulletin of Statistics*, no. 7, 1978, 1981, 1983. Central Bureau of Statistics, Oslo, 1978, 1981, 1983.
NOS: *Statistical Yearbook 1984*. Central Bureau of Statistics, Oslo, 1984.
Pindyck, R. S. and Rubinfeld, D. L.: *Econometric Models and Economic Forecasts*. McGraw-Hill, 2nd ed., 1981.
Steigum, E.: Oil and structural change — a Norwegian perspective. In *Oil and Industry — Are They Compatible?* Bergen Conference on Oil and Economics, Bergen, 1983.

First version submitted February 1986;
final version received December 1986.

Part V
Foreign Trade

[26]

Excerpt from Anders Ølgaard, *Growth, Productivity and Relative Prices*, 221–43.

CHAPTER 12

The Danish Terms of Trade in Foreign Trade, 1875—1963

Introduction.
1. In the present chapter, the development of the Danish terms of trade in foreign trade over the last century will be studied. During this period, relative prices have changed considerably, and the same holds for the commodity composition of Danish foreign trade. Hence the traditional index-number problems arise. However, instead of neglecting these problems, the approach of the following remarks is to make alternative computations, based on different sets of weights corresponding to the composition of foreign trade in different years. A comparison of these different indices illustrates the importance of the index-number problem; in particular it brings out to what extent quantities imported and exported have been adjusted to shifts in relative prices.

The basic data required for these computations are *consistent price series* for the goods entering into the Danish imports and exports. These price series have been calculated from Danish foreign trade statistics. The difficulties that arise in this field are well known. Quality changes and the introduction of new goods represent one type of obstacles to satisfactory measurement, changes in the methods of collecting and presenting trade statistics represent another.

In the following, no attempt has been made in order to solve the quality problem for all commodity groups. Instead, the analysis has been limited to *exports of agricultural products* and to *imports of raw materials etc.* Of course, quality changes have also taken place in these fields, but the changes have probably been less pronounced than for manufactures and capital goods.

A basic improvement of Danish trade statistics took place in 1910. In order to take advantage of the more detailed commodity specification

222 TERMS OF TRADE

available from this year onwards, the century covered by the analysis has been divided into two periods, before and after 1910 (or, more precisely, before and after 1912/13, cf. below)[1].

2. Price series are available for all years since 1874; in an appendix to the present chapter yearly indices for export prices, import prices and the terms of trade are indicated. However, the main purpose of the analysis has been to illustrate structural changes rather than short-term fluctuations of the terms of trade; hence more detailed computations have only been made for selected years. In order to make these years as comparable as possible, years with a relatively high level of employment have been chosen.

A priori, one might expect this procedure to lead to poor results, because the inflationary pressure has varied in intensity between the different peaks. However, a closer analysis of the basic price material confirms that this factor has not been of decisive importance, at least when two-year averages are used. This procedure has therefore been adopted, except for 1949.

The years included in the analysis are indicated in table 12.1[2]. Obviously, all prices of the analysis are expressed in Danish kroner. In order to allow a conversion to other currencies, the table indicates the Danish exchange rate for sterling. On the whole, this rate has been rather stable, the most important exception being a sharp decline in the value of the krone in terms of sterling in the early 1920's. However, in the mid-1920's the krone was brought back to the gold parity which had prevailed before the First World War[3].

The composition of Danish foreign trade since 1875.

3. In the following sections, a summary of the commodity composition of Danish foreign trade since 1875 is given with particular reference to the

1. A preliminary version of the present chapter was published in Danish in 1958, cf. "Det danske bytteforhold i udenrigshandelen 1875–1955", *Festskrift til Frederik Zeuthen*, København 1958. Price series for individual commodities were extended and published in Ole Bus Henriksen og Anders Ølgaard, *Danmarks Udenrigshandel* (Danish Foreign Trade) *1874–1958*, København 1960. Reference is made to this volume for a further discussion of the reliability of the data etc. (The volume contains an English introduction; all headings of tables etc. are translated into English).
2. Throughout part III, "1923/24" indicates the *average* of 1923 and 1924 – and not fiscal years etc.
3. When the United Kingdom suspended the gold standard in 1931, Denmark took a similar step. In 1933, the krone was devalued. The new exchange rate was maintained until the Second World War; in 1942 the krone was revalued. Since then, the sterling rate has remained unchanged, except for minor fluctuations.

Table 12.1. The Sterling rate of the Danish krone in the years included in the analysis.

	Danish kroner per pound sterling
1875/76 1883/84 1890/91 1899/1900 1912/13	18.16[a]
1923/24	25.74
1928/29	18.16[a]
1937/38	22.40
1949 1954/55 1962/63	19.34

[a] Par value, gold standard.

commodities analysed in the present study[1]. The choice of 1875 as a starting point for the study is mainly due to the fact that foreign trade statistics were definitely improved in the first part of the 1870's. From an analytical point of view, it would have been desirable to include a few additional decades. Admittedly, the expansion of exports of animal agricultural products and the development of Danish industry took place mainly in the last quarter of the nineteenth century, but the foundations were laid in the preceding decades.

4. *Exports.* The structure of Danish exports has changed considerably during the last century, cf. table 12.2. Up to the First World War exports originated mainly from agriculture. Within this group, the share of animal products was increasing. At the same time, exports of grain declined and an import surplus developed, providing the basis for a rapid increase in output of pork and bacon. Non-agricultural exports represented only 10-15 per cent of total exports.

During the inter-war years and, in particular, after the Second World War, exports of industrial products etc. increased considerably, and the share of agricultural products declined to about half of total exports. Consequently, the share of total exports included in the present analysis fell

1. A more detailed break-down of yearly exports and imports by commodity groups is presented in tables 3 and 5 in *Danmarks Udenrigshandel 1874-1958*.

Table 12.2. Exports by commodity groups for selected peak years.

Percentage distribution	1875/76	1883/84	1890/91	1912/13[a])	1928/29	1937/38	1954/55	1962/63
Covered by the analysis:								
Butter	21	20	39	31 (31)	31	24	13	6
Cheese	—	—	—	— (—)	1	1	4	3
Eggs	1	2	3	5 (5)	5	9	7	1
Cattle, beef and veal.	16	16	11	11 (10)	5	4	7	7
Bacon, pork and pigs.	12	21	18	25 (25)	31	25	19	14
Grain, meal and flour[b])	29	14	7	2 (—)	—	—	—	—
Total covered	79	73	78	74 (71)	73	63	50	31
Not covered by the analysis:								
Other agricultural products	8	14	9	12 (15)	6	8	10	9
Other exports (mainly industrial products)	13	13	13	14 (14)	21	29	40	60
Total	100	100	100	100 (100)	100	100	100	100
Value of total exports, million kroner, current prices	156	159	202	617	1581	1538	6874	11785

[a]) The figures in parentheses should be used for comparisons with later years, the other figures should be used for comparisons backwards.

[b]) Exports of grain after 1912/13 have been rather unimportant and have not been included.

from 70–80 per cent before 1914 to 50 per cent in the middle of the 1950's, and this trend has continued during the last decade.

5. *Imports.* The price analysis covers 45–60 per cent of total imports, cf. table 12.3. However, it should be kept in mind that for some of the raw materials, the figures understate total imports of the goods concerned. For instance, imports of textile fibres, yarns and fabrics refer only to wool and cotton. This limitation has been made in order to obtain relatively homogeneous commodity groups; on the whole, additional weights have not been used.

The increase in coverage from 45 to 60 per cent in the period up to the First World War is partly due to an increase in imports of grain, oil-cakes and – in the last part of the period – fertilizers. In addition, the developing Danish industry was able to supply an increasing share of the domestic market for final goods. This tendency was strengthened by the Danish import restrictions during the 1930's.

DANISH FOREIGN TRADE 1875 - 1963

Table 12.3. *Imports by commodity groups for selected peak years.*

Percentage distribution	1875/76	1883/84	1890/91	1912/13	1928/29	1937/38	1954/55
Covered by the analysis:							
Grain, meal and flour...	5	11	12	14	11	8	5
Oil-cakes, fertilizers....	4	3	5	16	18	15	9
Iron and steel	3	3	3	4	3	7	6
Timber	7	5	4	4	3	3	3
Paper, etc.	—	—	1	1	2	3	3
Textile fibres, yarns and fabrics	14	11	11	7	7	8	6
Fuels, solid	6	5	7	9	6	10	10
Fuels, liquid...........	1	1	2	1	3	4	7
Coffee, tobacco, etc.....	5	4	4	4	4	3	5
Total covered	45	43	49	60	57	61	54
Not covered	55	57	51	40	43	39	46
Total	100	100	100	100	100	100	100
Value of total imports, million kroner, current prices[a]).........	210	252	283	758	1681	1637	8066
Imports as percentage of net domestic product[b])	31	34	32	38	34	25	34

[a]) According to *Danmarks Udenrigshandel 1874-1958*, table 1.
[b]) Net domestic product according to Kjeld Bjerke and Niels Ussing, *Studier over Danmarks Nationalprodukt 1870-1950*, København 1958, pp. 144-45.

After 1945 international specialization has increased the share of final goods in Danish imports, hence the coverage has been shrinking; a decline in imports of raw materials for agriculture has strengthened this tendency.

For most of the century total imports have amounted to roughly one third of net domestic product, cf. the bottom line of table 12.3. This means that about one fourth of total demand has been met by foreign suppliers. This share was slightly increasing up to the First World War. The depression in the 1930's led to a sharp reduction, but after 1945 the share of foreign suppliers has recovered.

Procedure of the analysis.

6. Before the results of the price index computations are presented, a few words on the procedure may be appropriate. Price indices for imports as well as exports have been computed for each of the subperiods 1875/76–1912/13 and 1912/13–1962/63. For each of these four groups of indices,

the quantities of each peak have been evaluated, alternatively applying the prices of all the peaks. Denoting the various peaks (base years) by subscripts $1, 2, \ldots t$, this means that the following values have been computed:

$$
(12.1) \quad
\begin{array}{cccc}
\sum p_1 q_1, & \sum p_2 q_1, & \sum p_3 q_1 & \cdots & \sum p_t q_1 \\
\sum p_1 q_2, & \sum p_2 q_2, & \sum p_3 q_2 & \cdots & \sum p_t q_2 \\
\sum p_1 q_3, & \sum p_2 q_3, & \sum p_3 q_3 & \cdots & \sum p_t q_3 \\
\cdot & \cdot & \cdot & & \cdot \\
\cdot & \cdot & \cdot & & \cdot \\
\cdot & \cdot & \cdot & & \cdot \\
\sum p_1 q_t, & \sum p_2 q_t, & \sum p_3 q_t & \cdots & \sum p_t q_t
\end{array}
$$

Dividing the elements of each row by its first element gives rows of price indices with fixed weights, the weights corresponding to each of the base years[1]. Such fixed weight indices with alternative weights are presented in the following. The time series of Paasche indices follow immediately as the indices on the north-west – south-east diagonal.

In addition, Laspeyres chains and Paasche chains are found. Here the weights are adjusted successively. At t, the Laspeyres chain index is

$$
(12.2) \quad \frac{\sum p_2 q_1 \sum p_3 q_2 \cdots \sum p_t q_{(t-1)}}{\sum p_1 q_1 \sum p_2 q_2 \cdots \sum p_{(t-1)} q_{(t-1)}}
$$

and the corresponding Paasche chain index is defined as

$$
(12.3) \quad \frac{\sum p_2 q_2 \sum p_3 q_3 \cdots \sum p_t q_t}{\sum p_1 q_2 \sum p_2 q_3 \cdots \sum p_{(t-1)} q_t}
$$

If purchases (or sales) have been adjusted from year 1 to year t in such a way that quantities have increased most where the relative decline in prices has been largest, then the Laspeyres price index will exceed the Paasche price index, and vice versa. Hence if purchases are adjusted in accordance with an indifference map of the usual shape and with income elasticities equal to unity, then the Laspeyres price index will always exceed the Paa-

---

1. Obviously, if the elements of each *column* had been divided by its first element, columns of quantity indices would be obtained.

sche price index[2], the indifference determined price index being situated somewhere in between. If, instead, Laspeyres and Paasche chain indices were used, one might expect to obtain narrower limits for the indifference determined price index, because the weights are adjusted successively. In this sense, chain indices might be claimed to be superior to direct indices.

However, this conclusion does not hold generally. It requires that relative prices during the subperiods from year 1 to year t have persistently changed in the same direction. If relative prices have oscillated between 1 and t, then the difference between the chain indices at t may well exceed that between the direct Laspeyres and Paasche indices. This can easily happen for year-to-year indices, in particular if marked business cycles fluctuations take place. However, in the present computations only peak years are compared, hence chain indices may, a priori, be expected to provide the narrowest limits.

Indices of export prices.

7. In table 12.4, prices indices for exports from 1875/76 to 1912/13 are indicated as alternative fixed weight indices; in addition, the implied Paasche index and the two series of chain indices are shown.

Table 12.4. Price indices of exports from 1875/76 to 1912/13.

		Indices for the years:				
		1875/76	1883/84	1890/91	1899/1900	1912/13
Fixed weight indices:						
Weights:						
quantities in	1875/76	100	84	79	74	96
	1883/84	100	84	78	76	101
	1890/91	100	84	79	81	103
	1899/1900	100	83	79	83	105
	1912/13	100	83	79	82	105
Paasche index:						
basis	1875/76	100	84	79	83	105
Chain indices:						
Laspeyres		100	84	78	80	101
Paasche		100	84	78	82	105

It should be recalled that the data refer only to agricultural exports, cf. table 12.2 above.

2. If sales (output) are adjusted in accordance with a given transformation curve of the usual shape, then the Paasche price index will always exceed the Laspeyres price index. On the similar problem for quantity indices, see section 9 of chapter 10 above.

TERMS OF TRADE

As appears from the table, the newer the weights, the higher the indices; this is in accordance with what should be expected if the shift of the transformation curve had been neutral, cf. chapter 9 above. The difference is rather insignificant, at least when the indices with 1875/76-weights are excluded. This is mainly due to the fact that the prices of the various animal products developed in very much the same way[1].

Table 12.5. Price indices of exports from 1912/13 to 1962/63.

		\multicolumn{7}{c}{Indices for the years:}						
		1912/13	1923/24	1928/29	1937/38	1949	1954/55	1962/63
Fixed weight indices:								
Weights:								
quantities in	1912/13	100	211	141	130	317	348	346
	1923/24	100	214	143	133	320	350	347
	1928/29	100	213	143	133	320	350	349
	1937/38	100	217	144	129	318	348	340
	1949	100	221	146	127	323	351	339
	1954/55	100	214	143	137	333	368	369
	1962/63	100	209	141	144	342	378	389
Paasche index:								
basis	1912/13	100	214	143	129	323	368	389
Chain indices:								
Laspeyres		100	211	141	132	325	353	354
Paasche		100	214	144	128	326	360	371

Table 12.5 indicates price indices from 1912/13 to 1962/63; these figures refer only to exports of *animal* agricultural products, cf. table 12.2. On the whole, the pattern according to table 12.4 is repeated, except when 1937/38- and 1949-weights are used; in these years, market conditions were abnormal[2]. There are, however, other exceptions; in particular, price indices for 1923/24 and for 1928/29 are lower when 1962/63-weights are used than when 1954/55-weights are applied. The reason is not that the composition of output has not been adjusted to changes in relative prices. Instead, the explanation is that relative prices have not changed persistently in the same direction.

1. Except egg prices, but the weight of eggs in the indices is small.
2. In 1937/38, restrictions were imposed on production of pigs. Exports of bacon to the United Kingdom declined, while bacon prices increased, cf. table 12.6.

Table 12.6. *Price and quantity indices for exports of some Danish agricultural products.*

		Indices for the years:						
		1912/13	1923/24	1928/29	1937/38	1949	1954/55	1962/63
Butter	p	100	223	145	106	293	309	282
	q	100	133	174	177	157	154	123
Cattle, beef	p	100	158	98	114	329	391	437
and veal	q	100	91	137	98	57	213	315
Bacon, pork	p	100	212	150	167	342	374	394
and pigs	q	100	155	208	151	85	224	280
Eggs	p	100	236	149	118	320	374	335
	q	100	194	187	379	318	420	176

p = price indices, q = quantity indices.

In particular, this holds for beef and butter, cf. table 12.6. From 1912/13 to 1928/29, beef prices declined compared with prices of other agricultural products, but after the Second World War they have shown a marked increase. On the other hand, butter prices were relatively favourable during the 1920's but fell during the 1950's. And when relative prices oscillate, the pattern according to table 12.4 does not appear, even if the composition of output is adjusted to changes in relative prices.

Indices of import prices.

8. Indices of import prices, covering the two subperiods 1875/76–1912/13 and 1912/13–1962/63, are indicated in tables 12.7 and 12.8. Here,

Table 12.7. *Price indices of imports from 1875/76 to 1912/13.*

		Indices for the years:				
		1875/76	1883/84	1890/91	1899/1900	1912/13
Fixed weight indices:						
Weights:						
quantities in	1875/76	100	77	84	82	94
	1883/84	100	76	82	79	91
	1890/91	100	76	81	77	90
	1899/1900	100	77	79	74	87
	1912/13	100	76	78	74	84
Paasche index:						
basis	1875/76	100	76	81	74	84
Chain indices:						
Laspeyres			100	77	83	78	91
Paasche			100	76	82	77	87

TERMS OF TRADE

Table 12.8. Price indices of imports from 1912/13 to 1962/63.

		Indices for the years:						
		1912/13	1923/24	1928/29	1937/38	1949	1954/55	1962/63
Fixed weight indices:								
Weights:								
quantities in	1912/13	100	206	134	133	378	509	464
	1923/24	100	198	128	125	356	471	429
	1928/29	100	196	124	123	349	458	419
	1937/38	100	193	120	118	334	442	401
	1949	100	187	115	117	313	415	391
	1954/55	100	180	110	113	292	378	357
	1962/63	100	174	107	106	276	365	337
Paasche index:								
basis	1912/13	100	198	124	118	313	378	337
Chain indices:								
Laspeyres		100	206	133	132	374	496	468
Paasche		100	198	125	123	329	425	393

one might expect a priori that the higher the relative price of a good, the smaller the purchases. At least, this holds when expenditure proportionality can be assumed. Hence the older the weights, the higher the resulting indices. This argument may hold not only for final goods, cf. the indifference maps of chapter 9, but also for current inputs of intermediate goods. Such goods were assumed away in chapter 9, but this was obviously an unrealistic assumption. And if intermediate goods are specified as inputs in the production functions and the latter allow for substitution, then – given the isoquant maps – a similar pattern of adjustment would be expected to take place.

The figures indicated in tables 12.7 and 12.8 actually behave according to this hypothesis; in both tables the indices are higher, the older the weights. Furthermore, the results depend more heavily on the weights than in the case of exports, in particular for the period since 1912/13, cf. table 12.8. In this period, the pattern of relative prices must have changed constantly in the same direction and, in addition, Danish foreign purchases have been adjusted to these changes. At least, this must have been the case for a considerable part of the goods under study.

In table 12.9, further details have been indicated for commodity groups whose prices have shown a trend which has persistently differed from the general price trend. This has been illustrated by indicating for each

Table 12.9. "Relative"a) price and quantity indices for six commodity groups of Danish imports.

		\multicolumn{9}{c}{Indices for the years:}									
		1875/76	1883/84	1890/91	1899/1900	1912/13	1923/24	1928/29	1937/38	1954/55	1962/63
Fertilizers	p	135	135	97	94	100	69	67	63	46	47
	q	34	21	30	38	100	161	204	199	284	265
Paper	p	178	179	160	115	100	96	103	99	94	100
	q	39	38	65	74	100	130	141	183	202	253
Rubber	p	b)	b)	b)	b)	100	23	20	21	13	13
	q	b)	b)	b)	b)	100	317	411	1361	2560	1530
Liquid fuel	p	315	240	235	125	100	88	84	78	53	56
	q	54	77	100	96	100	240	344	588	1325	1825
Timber	p	77	74	87	100	100	113	118	125	166	185
	q	224	188	151	114	100	69	56	40	31	33
Tobacco	p	60	78	76	67	100	101	133	130	172	228
	q	302	248	228	159	100	74	71	101	87	73

p = price indices, q = quantity indices.
a) The indices are deflated by over-all price and quantity indices; see text.
b) Imports are so insignificant that they provide no basis for computations.

good a "relative" price index instead of the usual one. This index has been obtained by dividing the individual price indices by a price index of total imports[1]. A similar procedure has been followed with respect to the quantity indices.

For six commodity groups price changes have had the same direction throughout the period. For fertilizers, paper, rubber and liquid fuel, prices have declined continually relatively to average import prices, while prices of timber and tobacco have risen more or declined less than average import prices. A more detailed analysis must, inter alia, include a study of the constancy of qualities over time. However, at first glance the results appear to be reasonable: It is fairly certain that the production of goods with declining relative prices has become more efficient throughout the last century while, on the other hand, such a development has hardly taken place in the case of timber.

Comparing the price and quantity indices of table 12.9, it appears that there has been a relative increase in the volume of all those commodities

1. Fixed weight indices with 1912/13-weights have been used for the price index of total imports as well as for the price indices of commodity groups.

TERMS OF TRADE

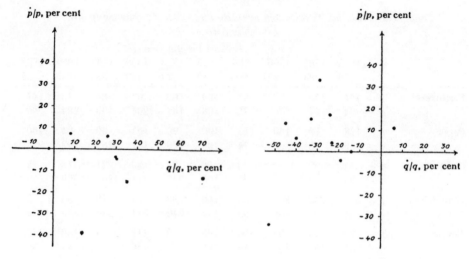

Diagram 12.1. Paper. Diagram 12.2. Timber.
Corresponding rates of growth of quantities and prices for sub-periods, cf. table 12.9 and text.

whose prices have shown a relative decline, and vice versa. For each good one can draw a diagram with percentage[1] increase of prices between two successive base years (peaks) along the vertical axis and of quantities along the horizontal. In such a diagram, the development between two successive base years can be indicated by a dot. When this is done for the first four goods in table 12.9 most of the dots will lie in the south-east quadrant, cf. diagram 12.1, which illustrates the development for paper. For the last two goods, most of the dots will lie in the north-west quadrant, cf. diagram 12.2 for timber.

Obviously, similar diagrams could also be drawn for the remaining commodities, cf. table 12.3. For the same reasons as indicated above, one might immediately have expected the dots to lie in the north-west and south-east quadrants. Actually, such a result does not come out. Many reasons for this can be indicated: Grain prices should rather be related to prices of bacon, since imports of grain are used mainly as fodder; in addition, harvest results should be taken into account. Prices of a certain input, e.g. solid fuel, should rather be compared to prices of near substitutes[2], e.g. liquid

1. Percentages are always computed relatively to the numerically lower figure. 1949-data are omitted, otherwise all subperiods are shown in the diagrams, cf. table 12.9.
2. The sharp decline in imports of rubber from 1954/55 to 1962/63, cf. table 12.9, is due to the introduction of synthetic rubber.

fuel, than to the general price level etc. Hence more specified hypotheses are required before an attempt to estimate price elasticities can be made. In particular, the basic question whether the figures refer to a demand function as implied above or to a supply function ought to be raised. The fact that Danish importers have bought more of the relatively cheaper goods, cf. table 12.9, obviously must imply that foreign suppliers have increased output of those goods. These problems will be reconsidered in chapter 16 below.

9. The indices of import prices may be subdivided into an index of raw materials for agriculture and an index of raw materials for industry.

Table 12.10. *Price indices of imports of raw materials for agriculture and for industry, 1912/13–1962/63.*

		Indices for the years:						
		1912/13	1923/24	1928/29	1937/38	1949	1954/55	1962/63
Agriculture.[a]								
Fixed weight indices:								
Weights:								
quantities in	1912/13	100	191	132	117	315	399	375
	1937/38	100	180	120	104	300	367	328
	1962/63	100	170	114	98	261	316	289
Industry.[b]								
Fixed weight indices:								
Weights:								
quantities in	1912/13	100	223	138	162	471	656	648
	1937/38	100	213	127	150	422	562	568
	1962/63	100	193	119	135	362	479	486

a) Grain, oil-cakes and fertilizers.
b) Iron and steel, timber, paper, wool and cotton (and wool and cotton yarn but not piece goods) and one fourth of the total imports of fuel. This share of the imports of fuel corresponds largely to the conditions prevailing at the end of the period, cf. The Statistical Department, *Danmarks Energiforsyning 1900-1958*, København 1959.

At least, such a split-up can be made for the period after the improvement of the basic data in 1910, cf. table 12.10. It appears that the prices of raw materials used in agriculture have increased less than the price index of raw materials used in industry. While the prices of grain, oil-cakes and fertilizers have increased three or four times from 1912/13 to 1962/63 (depending on the weights used), the prices of raw materials used in industry have increased even more sharply. This is mainly due to a considerable

TERMS OF TRADE

increase of the prices of timber and iron and steel; thus the price of timber increased more than eight times from 1912/13 to 1962/63.

Estimates of the terms of trade in foreign trade.

10. The results of the preceding sections immediately lead to terms of trade indices. A terms of trade index is defined as an index of export prices divided by an index of import prices; in the following, the same system of weights is always used for the export and import indices entering into a certain terms of trade index. In addition, the limited range of goods covered by the two sets of indices should be recalled, cf. tables 12.2 and 12.3.

The terms of trade indices appear in tables 12.11 and 12.12 and in diagram 12.3. Up to 1890/91, it is difficult to detect any clear trend[1], but subsequently an improvement takes place; it continues up to about 1930. After 1930, the terms of trade show a marked deterioration until the beginning of the 1950's. During the last decade a stabilization and an improvement has taken place.

Although this general conclusion holds independently of the weights used[2], the estimate of these shifts does to a great extent depend on the

Table 12.11. The terms of trade in Danish foreign trade from 1875/76 to 1912/13.

		\multicolumn{5}{c}{Indices for the years:}
		1875/76	1883/84	1890/91	1899/1900	1912/13
Fixed weight indices:						
Weights:						
quantities in	1875/76	100	110	94	91	102
	1883/84	100	109	95	97	112
	1890/91	100	111	97	105	115
	1899/1900	100	107	100	112	121
	1912/13	100	109	101	110	126
Paasche index:						
basis	1875/76	100	109	97	112	126
Chain indices:						
Laspeyres		100	110	95	103	111
Paasche		100	109	96	107	122

1. This conclusion is confirmed by a series of year-to-year indices, cf. the appendix to the present chapter.
2. There is one exception; from 1928/29 to 1937/38 the terms of trade improve, based on 1962/63-weights, while they deteriorate according to the other indices. The reason is that the prices of butter and eggs declined sharply in this period, cf. table 12.6, and the share in agricultural exports of these products in 1962/63 is small, cf. table 12.2.

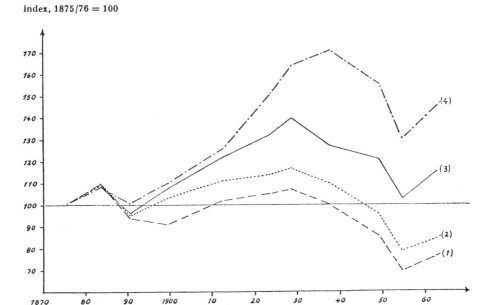

Diagram 12.3. The Danish terms of trade in foreign trade 1875-1963 (1875/76 = 100).

(1) *Fixed weight index with old weights.* 1875/76-weights are used for the period 1875/76 — 1912/13; 1912/13-weights are used from 1912/13 onwards, cf. the first rows of tables 12.11 and 12.12. A linking has been made in 1912/13.
(2) *Laspeyres chain*, cf. data in tables 12.11 and 12.12.
(3) *Paasche chain*, cf. the bottom lines of tables 12.11 and 12.12.
(4) *Fixed weight index with new weights.* 1912/13-weights are used up to 1912/13; 1962/63-weights are used in the remaining part of the period, cf. the fifth line of table 12.11 and the seventh line of table 12.12.

weights. In the preceding sections it was found that, on the whole, the export price indices showed a higher increase, the newer the weights, and that the import price indices followed the opposite pattern. In a terms-of-trade index, these two effects will reinforce each other, and hence the indices show a more favourable development, the newer the weights. Furthermore, the difference between the Laspeyres and Paasche chains is much smaller than that between fixed weight indices reflecting quantities at the beginning and at the end of the period, cf. diagram 12.3.

The dependence of the quantitative expressions of the terms of trade on the weights chosen points towards the conclusion that, while in a long-run

TERMS OF TRADE

Table 12.12. The terms of trade in Danish foreign trade from 1912/13 to 1962/63.

Indices for the years:

		1912/13	1923/24	1928/29	1937/38	1949	1954/55	1962/63
Fixed weight indices:								
Weights:								
quantities in	1912/13	100	102	105	98	84	68	75
	1923/24	100	108	112	106	90	74	81
	1928/29	100	109	115	109	92	77	83
	1937/38	100	113	120	109	95	79	85
	1949	100	118	127	109	103	85	87
	1954/55	100	119	130	122	114	97	103
	1962/63	100	120	131	136	124	104	116
Paasche index:								
basis	1912/13	100	108	115	109	103	97	116
Chain indices:								
Laspeyres		100	102	106	100	87	71	76
Paasche		100	108	115	104	99	85	94

analysis one might be able to detect trends in the terms of trade, caution is required when this development is quantified[1].

11. For the period since the mid-1930's, the yearly detailed statistical surveys of foreign trade, published by the Statistical Department, contain volume indices by commodity groups for the *total* foreign trade and hence allow a comparison with the results obtained above. These volume indices are fixed weight indices, hence the resulting unit values will be of the Paasche type. These figures are found without taking possible quality changes into consideration and are therefore based on prices per ton of watches, machines etc. Consequently, they should not be interpreted uncritically[2].

In table 12.13, the two sets of results are compared. According to the figures on total foreign trade by the Statistical Department, the terms of trade were unchanged from 1937/38 to 1949, but declined by 20 per cent from 1949 to 1954/55.

The commodity break-down used by the Statistical Department is the

1. The 1962/63-index of terms of trade is equal to 76 (1875/76 = 100), when "old" weights are used, cf. curve (1) in diagram 12.3. If, instead, "new" weights are used, cf. curve (4), the corresponding index is equal to 145 (1875/76 still = 100).
2. This mechanical procedure is usually used to compute unit-value indices. A study along these lines has been undertaken by C. P. Kindleberger, cf. *The Terms of Trade. A European Case Study*, New York 1956.

Table 12.13. A comparison of foreign trade price indices published by the Statistical Department and the results of the present study.

Indices	1949 (1937/38 = 100)	1954/55 (1949 = 100)
Present Study:[a]		
Imports	266	130
Exports	254	110
Terms of trade	95	85
The Statistical Department:[b]		
Imports	232	121
of which:		
unprocessed goods	270	128
less processed goods	235	124
processed goods	218	114
Exports	250	109
of which:		
less processed food etc.	268	104
Terms of trade, total	105	90
of which:		
exports of less processed food divided by imports of unprocessed goods	99	81

a) Since the indices of the Statistical Department are of the Paasche type, weights have been chosen from the ends of the two periods: in the first column, 1949-weights are used; in the second, weights of 1954/55 are applied.

b) The volume indices behind the figures of the first column have 1935-weights up to 1947; from 1947 to 1949, 1947-weights are used. Hence the indices have to be linked in 1947; this does not improve the quality of the figures, because the structure of foreign trade was rather untypical in 1947. – From 1949 onwards, the volumn indices are based on 1949-weights, and hence no problem arises.

Source: The indices based on the data of the Statistical Department are found from *Danmarks Vareindførsel og -udførsel*, Statistisk Tabelværk, 5. række, for the years 1938, 1947, 1949 and 1955. Here, the weights of the various commodity groups can also be found.

same for imports and exports and is unchanged over the period 1937/38–1954/55; it originates from a document by the League of Nations[1]. Goods are classified according to how far they are processed. On the side of imports, the goods covered by the present study would correspond to "un-

1. Communiqué de la Société des Nations C. 268. M. 136. 1935. II A.

238 TERMS OF TRADE

processed goods" plus part of "less processed goods". Actually, for both subperiods the import price indices of the present study correspond fairly well to the indices referring to these commodity groups, cf. the table.

On the side of exports, the goods covered by the present study would roughly correspond to the subgroup "less processed food". Again, the corresponding indices are very similar. Hence the terms of trade of "less processed food" in exports over "unprocessed goods" in imports would correspond to the concept of the present study and actually the results are very similar: The terms of trade of these groups for the two periods are 99 and 81 respectively, while the corresponding results of the present study are 95 and 85 [1].

12. A comparison of the two sets of figures in table 12.13 is also interesting from another point of view. The figures of the Statistical Department cover all foreign trade, while the present analysis excludes industrial goods, i.e. manufactures and final goods. Although different industrial goods are traded in imports and exports, one might, on the whole, expect prices to have followed a similar trend for the two groups. This would imply that this part of foreign trade exerts a stabilizing influence on the terms of trade (although not necessarily on the price indices of imports and exports, taken per se): tables 12.11 and 12.12 give an acceptable impression of the direction of the changes in total terms of trade in foreign trade, but the quantitative results overstate the strength of the shifts.

This hypothesis is confirmed by the figures of the Statistical Department, cf. table 12.13. For the period from 1937/38 to 1949, the price index of the remaining exports would be approximately 230; this is not very far from the import price indices of "less processed" and "processed" goods. And for the period from 1949 to 1954/55, the price index of the remaining exports would be 115–120, again corresponding to a price index of the remaining imports.

For the period 1937/38–1949 the inclusion of the remaining commodity groups could not be expected to give rise to any stabilization, since the terms of trade are already stable according to the figures of the present analysis, but for the following period the present analysis leads to a terms-of-trade index of 85, while the terms-of-trade index of total foreign trade computed by the Statistical Department is equal to 90.

1. Obviously, the similarity should not give rise to too much comfort. After all, the basic data of the two sets of computations are identical.

13. When the results are interpreted, the limited range of goods covered by the present analysis must be kept in mind. Furthermore, attention should be drawn to the price development of invisibles on the current account of the balance of payment. The most important item on this part of the Danish balance of payments is the earnings by Danish shipping. A preliminary study of the development of the international freight rates [1] seems to indicate that in the 1920's they declined relative to export prices. On the other hand, they may have shown a greater increase than export prices in the following period. If this description is correct, it implies that the inclusion of the freight rates will lead to a further dampening of the changes of the terms of trade according to the present analysis.

Conclusions.

14. The results of the preceding analysis may be summarized as follows:
(a) The terms of trade in Danish foreign trade improved from the later part of the nineteenth century to about 1930. Subsequently, a deterioration took place; on the whole it continued until the mid-1950's. However, the figures in tables 12.11 and 12.12 tend to overstate the strength of the deterioration (and perhaps the strength of the improvement, too). This is due to the limited range of goods covered by of the present analysis.
(b) This conclusion holds, no matter what weights are used in the computation of the indices. However, the weights determine the strength of the changes, the development being more favourable, the newer the weights used. This result is caused both by the fact that export price indices show a higher increase, the newer the weights, and by the fact that import price indices are higher, the older the weights.
(c) This dependence on the weights, which is particularly pronounced for the import indices, seems to indicate that throughout the period under review there have been systematic changes in relative prices. Furthermore, the pattern of adjustment is not inconsistent with the result to be expected if (1) relative prices were exogenous, (2) *purchases* had been adjusted to these prices in accordance with indifference maps and isoquant maps, both being subject to expenditure proportionality, and (3) *sales* had been adjusted to prices in accordance with transformation curves, the latter showing neutral shifts.

---

1. For further details, see pp. 388-389 in my article on the Danish terms of trade, mentioned in the footnote in section 1 above.

TERMS OF TRADE

15. From a short-run point of view, one might say that an improvement of the terms of trade in foreign trade involves a gain in the sense that a given amount of exports finances increased quantities of imports. A more precise statement of and comparison between alternative gain concepts is given in the following chapter.

APPENDIX TO CHAPTER 12

Yearly Figures for the Terms of Trade in Danish Foreign Trade

In chapter 12, attention was concentrated on the *trend* of the terms of trade in foreign trade, the trend being expressed by pairs of peak years. In order to illustrate the magnitude of short-term fluctuations, series of year-to-year figures of export prices, import prices and the terms of trade are indicated in table 12.14; they are all based on 1912/13-weights. These figures provide a very incomplete description of the strength of the trend; on this point reference should be made to tables 12.11 and 12.12 and to the comments to these tables in the text. However, the figures in table 12.14 may give a satisfactory impression of the short-term fluctuations, although the limited range of goods covered by the analysis should be kept in mind.[1]

Export and import prices as well as the corresponding terms-of-trade series according to table 12.14 are shown in diagram 12.4. The diagram has log-scales along the vertical axes, the same units of measurement being applied in the upper and the lower part.

---

1. In particular, the figures of the Second World War may be somewhat misleading — quite apart from the fact that they are not very interesting. The figures of this period differ considerably from the price indices implied in the computations of the Statistical Department, covering total foreign trade, cf. table 12.13.

242 TERMS OF TRADE

Table 12.14. *The terms of trade in Danish foreign trade. Yearly figures, 1912/13-weights.*

1912/13 = 100	Export prices	Import prices	Terms of trade		Export prices	Import prices	Terms of trade
1875	97	123	79	1920	327	479	68
76	94	116	81				
77	79	109	73	1921	259	247	105
78	73	100	73	22	195	176	111
79	69	93	73	23	200	198	101
80	81	99	82	24	222	214	104
				25	207	192	108
1881	82	100	82	26	153	141	108
82	88	96	91	27	136	134	101
83	81	93	87	28	138	136	102
84	77	89	87	29	143	132	109
85	73	84	87	30	122	109	112
86	69	79	87				
87	70	80	88	1931	94	89	105
88	73	85	86	32	80	94	86
89	76	91	83	33	95	100	95
90	74	92	80	34	103	105	97
				35	113	106	107
1891	75	93	81	36	121	112	108
92	78	86	91	37	127	135	94
93	74	82	89	38	133	131	101
94	69	78	88	39	135	130	104
95	66	75	88	40	153	215	71
96	66	75	88				
97	76	75	102	1941	210	333	63
98	73	79	92	42	215	381	56
99	74	84	88	43	230	401	57
1900	80	94	86	44	229	412	56
				45	224	332	67
1901	83	85	97	46	215	318	68
02	82	86	96	47	253	416	61
03	81	83	97	48	316	445	71
04	78	82	95	49	317	378	84
05	84	84	99	50	307	444	69
06	88	89	98				
07	85	96	88	1951	331	584	57
08	84	92	91	52	360	591	61
09	88	93	95	53	346	522	66
10	93	92	102	54	345	504	68
				55	351	515	68
1911	92	93	99	56	365	537	68
12	98	101	97	57	332	534	62
13	102	99	103	58	310	466	67
14	101	100	101	59	349	445	78
15	135	135	100	60	332	456	73
16	160	183	88				
17	175	292	60	1961	321	452	71
18	285	342	83	62	328	456	72
19	307	361	85	63	365	473	77

Terms-of-trade figures are computed before rounding of the export and import price indices.

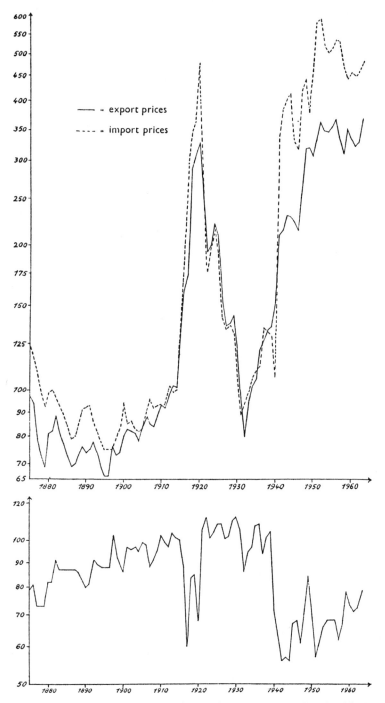

Diagram 12.4. Export prices, import prices and the terms of trade, cf. table 12.14.

Part VI
The Public Sector

[27]

The
SCANDINAVIAN ECONOMIC HISTORY REVIEW
and
ECONOMY AND HISTORY

VOL. XXXV, NO: 2, 1987

Public Infrastructure,
Its Indispensability for Economic Growth:
The Case of Norwegian Public Health Measures 1850-1940*

by
FRITZ HODNE and BJØRN BASBERG**

'To a great extent, the growth and development of civilized societies has been predicated on the development of infrastructure and institutions designed to separate what we eat from what we excrete. When such institutions and infrastructure have deteriorated under cultural and economic collapse, the result has been epidemics of disease which accompanied the dénouement of that society.'

John Grauerholz, M.D.
Executive Intelligence Review, June 27, 1986.

* The authors would like to thank Maureen Roycroft and Lewis Ross Fischer for valuable comments. Also Helge Nordvik, Kris Inwood, Donald N. Steinnes, and Albright G. Zimmerman, who participated in a seminar in Berne, Switzerland, August 1986, where the paper was presented, also offered comments that have helped improve the contents of the paper.

** Fritz Hodne, born 1932, dr.oecon., associate professor at the Norwegian School of Economics and Business Administration.
Bjørn L. Basberg, born 1952, dr.oecon., research associate at the Department of Economics, University of Trondheim.

INTRODUCTION

The aim of the paper

This paper explores the issue whether public infrastructure influences the course of economic growth in any way. Specifically, by using public health measures from Norway in the 19th and 20th centuries as representative cases of public infrastructure, the paper seeks to determine its role in the recent health revolution, including its impact on the decline of average mortality and infant mortality rates 1865-1929. This is done by using regression analysis. It should be understood that other methods might yield other results. The results of the quantitative method used here suggest that on balance health investments have been a permissive factor, while economic factors, expressed by average per capita income, have been decisive for the outcome.

Section I introduces the ideas and arguments that by the 1960s resulted in a consensus in economics to the effect that health care should be a public task, since health should be regarded as a public rather than private good. Cognizance is taken of the present rising criticism of this consensus.

Sections II and III offer brief sketches of the rise and development of a public health system in Norway 1815-1940. The period is divided into two sub-periods, viz. an initial period 1815-1860, and the transition period 1860-1940. In the first period a medicinal police system was set up, in the latter the system by degrees gained control of the environment. Notes are offered on the institutions, the personnel, the costs, and the health gains obtained from the expenditures. These notes are offered as a necessary introduction to the regression analysis presented in the following section.

Section IV reports on the data, methods and results achieved from a regression analysis of the possible causal links between government health investments and improvements in the health situation reached in the period 1865-1929, for which period we have been able to assemble continuous data.

Section V contains some summary remarks on the findings.

I. Public infrastructure and economic growth in general.

Definitons

Infrastructure is here taken to be synonymous with social overhead capital (SOC). Usually the terms, both originating in the 1950s, include three categories of government investment: education, health measures, and transport & communications, though some authors add energy, dams, irrigation, and similar items. Interest in these particular areas of investments arose after World War II when Western experts went out to former colonies to formulate and implement plans for rapid economic growth and modernization. One of them, Albert Hirschman, pronounced social overhead capital to comprise ... 'those basic services without which productive activities in primary, secondary and tertiary activities cannot take place'.[1] SOC, in other words, was declared a necessary condition for economic

---

1. Albert O. Hirschman, *The Strategy of Economic Development*, Yale UP, New Haven & Oxford UP, London 1958.

growth. The view was popularized by Nurkse, Lewis, Bauer and Rostow, and widely accepted in the economic growth literature e.g. Musgrave, that proliferated in the 1960s.[2] According to majority opinion among economists in the 1950s and 1960s, once a basic framework of social overhead capital was in place, sustained, self-reinforcing economic growth was assured. In other words, capital was the essence of the growth arithmetic. In the 1960s the human capital school convinced the scientific community that expenditures on health and education should be viewed as additions to the capital stock.[3]

Why government? Why not leave social overhead capital to private agents? Rostow, Musgrave, and others, harking back to historical precedents in the capitalist Western countries, pointed to the lack of private capital in the early stages, also the initial lack of expertise in the private sector. The *ad hoc* explanation was strengthened by the theory of public goods, developed in the 1960s, and brought to bear on the growth issue in the 1970s (Peston, Mueller).[4] Public infrastructure was classified as collective goods, as opposed to private goods. The distinction originated in fact with Adam Smith, who in *Wealth of Nations* declared that it is

> 'the duty of the sovereign or commonwealth to erect and maintain those public institutions and those public works, which, though they may be in the highest degree advantageous to a great society, are, however, of such nature, that the profit would never repay the expence to any individual or small number of individuals, and which it, therefore, cannot be expected that any individual or small number of individuals should erect or maintain.' (Book V, part 2.)

2. Ragnar Nurkse, *Problems of Capital Formation in underdeveloped Countries*, Oxford UP, London 1953.
   Arthur W. Lewis, *The Theory of Economic Growth*, London 1955.
   P.T. Bauer & B.S. Yamey, *The Economics of underdeveloped Countries*, Cambridge UP 1957.
   Walt Whitman Rostow, *The Stages of economic Growth: A Non-Communist Manifesto*, Cambridge Univ.Press, Cambridge 1960, 2. ed., 1972.
   Walt Whitman Rostow, *The Economics of Take-off into sustained Growth*, London 1963.
   Richard A. Musgrave, *Fiscal Systems*, New Haven & London, Yale UP 1969.

3. Gary Becker, *Human Capital. A theoretical and empirical analysis with special reference to education*, New York 1975.
   Theodore W. Schultz, *Investment in human Capital*, New York 1971.
   B.A. Weisbrod, 'Education and Investment in Human Capital', *The Journal of Political Economy*, vol. 70, 1962.
   René L: Frey, 'Probleme der statistischen Erfassung der Infrastruktur,' *Schweitzerische Zeitschrift für Volkswirtschaft u. Statistik*, Bern, 103, 1967.
   R.L. Frey, 'Infrastruktur und Wirtschaftswachstum', *Konjunkturpolitik*, Berlin, 15, 1969.
   R.L. Frey, *Infrastruktur. Grundlagen der Planung öffentlicher Investitionen*, Tübingen-Zürich 1970, 1972.
   R.L. Frey, 'Infrastruktur', *Handwörterbuch der Wirtschaftswissenschaft*, 1978, vol. IV.
   R. Jochimsen, 'Über 'Infrastrukturen' als Voraussetzungen einer funktions-fähigen Volkswirtschaft', Gottfried-Karl Kindermann, ed., *Kulturen im Umbruch*, Freiburg 1962.
   R. Jochimsen, *Theorie der Infrastruktur. Grundlagen der marktwirtschaftlichen Entwicklung*, Tübingen 1966.
   R. Jochimsen & Udo E. Simonis, eds., *Theorie und Praxis der Infrastrukturpolitik*, Berlin 1970.
   R. Jochimsen & K. Gustafsson, eds., 'Infrastruktur', *Handwörterbuch der Raumforschung und Raumordnung*, Hannover 1970.

4. Maurice Peston, *Public Goods and the Public Sector*, London 1972.
   Dennis Mueller, 'Public Choice: A Survey', *Journal of Economic Literature*, vol. XIV, 1976.

The distinction drawn by Adam Smith parades in the current theory of public goods under a series of related key words, including externalities, free riding, non-excludability, non-rivalry, and jointness of supply and consumption, all of which offer suggestions why public goods will not be produced in optimal amounts in private markets. They are cases of market imperfection, by virtue of their 'nature'; occasionally no alternative to collective action exists:

1) Technically, infrastructural investments are characterized by a certain indivisibility, long periods of duration, interdependence between parts, and they tend to provide general, non-discriminatory services for the rest of the economy, e.g. roads, bridges, harbours, and piers.

2) Economically, infrastructural investments are characterized by economies of scale, high fixed costs relative to variable costs, high capital coefficients, strong externalities with the attendant incentives to free riding. Examples include roads and other transport facilities, health systems, education and telecommunication, most of which tend to be natural monopolies by virtue of the nature of their cost structure.

3) Institutionally, infrastructural investments accordingly involve most often public institutions, financed over public budgets, in a setting providing insufficient market signals or no market pricing at all, e.g. railways, education or preventive hygiene. Public ownhership is preferred, since the public, faced with a monopoly anyway, prefer a public to a private solution as a guarantee against private abuse of power.

The role of infrastructure

In sum, infrastructural investments or SOC, according to orthodox belief in the 1960s and 1970s, are necessary conditions for economic growth; hence their indispensability, hence their significance. Since they will not be forthcoming in satisfactory amounts as market goods, they must be undertaken by government, local and central. In the 1980s, this orthodoxy is being questioned; indeed, how sharp is the dichotomy between 'private' and 'collective' goods?

Admittedly, few goods fall exclusively into the public goods-category. For example, the greater part of higher education, curative medicine (as opposed to preventive hygiene), transportation, and communication, clearly fall into the category of mixed goods. They allow market pricing; they involve rivalry in consumption; they permit exclusion of non-payers. Moreover, this is borne out historically, in the USA, and in West-European countries. By and large up to World War II, only elementary education, preventive health measures and some transportation were provided by government, while most higher and specialized education, the greater part of individual curative medicine, and transportation were bought and sold as private services. They still are in the United States, but less so in the West European countries. Moreover, recent experience in Asian countries, Taiwan and Singapore among them, would suggest that economic growth, in *per capita*-terms, has depended less on government infrastructure than on the private market sector. Conversely, economic progress has been sluggish in countries and areas most committed to public provision of infrastructure, public planning and central control. Cuba under Fidel Castro, though offering free public education through university levels, has scored poorly in the international competition for *per capita* income growth. A similar conclusion could be drawn from recent experience in some East European countries of the Comecon bloc.

Summarizing, we are bound to say that government infrastructure at best appears to be a necessary condition rather than a sufficient cause of economic growth. This would hold both for historical experience and current contemporary evidence. Indeed, whether economic growth is causally connected with government infrastructure at all appears on balance an open issue, despite the widespread declarations and programmes to the contrary. At any rate, on the level of aggregation touched on above, the issue of the causal relationships between government infrastructure and economic growth cannot satisfactorily be settled. The problem of possible causal connections cannot be confirmed or refuted in those terms. We therefore turn to a concrete case. We want to see if testable propositions can be developed by studying one particular set of infrastructural investments, and turn to a review of Norwegian public health measures 1850-1940.

II. Economic growth and government health measures in Norway: The initial period 1815 -1860

The system
Antedating in part the break-up of the Danish-Norwegian monarchy in 1814, the rudiments of a government health system were in place when after 1814 Norway set out to establish its own government. In the area of health the nation by the 1820s boasted the following: Sundheds-kollegiet (The Health Collegium) a central administrative office, though not manned by doctors or medical servants, a corps of about 25 medical servants in the counties, called the district doctors, a training hospital for the kingdom, (Rikshospitalet) located in Christiania, the capital, both for midwives and medical students, and a string of 'hospitals' in the towns, operating with charity funds and local and central government money.

The organizational network was steadily up-dated, diversified, and given new tasks in line with a growing corpus of medical knowledge, and the shocks of cholera epidemics that recurred seven times in Western Europe in the 19th century. The ambition was inherited from an earlier 18th century mercantilist era. That is, the goal of the public health police was to create a healthier, stronger population, to the benefit of individual and public happiness. The economic motive was obvious, and at times voiced directly. Better health, it was argued, meant better and stronger workers, that is, more work and less absenteeism. In other words, the health expenditures were conceived to be

investments in human capital. Attempting to measure the economic returns is merely to honour the system's paternalistic intentions.

Among the early activities, not yet entirely co-ordinated, assumed by the new central government of Norway, we observe the following tasks:

- monitoring the quarantine regulations of 1791 and 1805, inherited from the Danish period, designed to prevent the spread of epidemic disease,

- overseeing the work of midwives, statutes for whom were also inherited from the Danish period,

- training medical students at Rikshospitalet, a new task undertaken after 1815,

- overseeing the government medical servants, the district doctors, charged with the general job of monitoring health conditions in their districts, and specifically,

- providing vaccination against smallpox for the entire population as ordered by the decree of April 3, 1810. Though antedating 1814, the decree was put into effect by degrees until by the 1880s the entire population could be said to have been vaccinated, including infants, children, and adults.

The costs

Central government accounts, including health outlays, exist from the initial budget year of the modern constitutional era, viz. from 1815/16. Municipal and county accounts, however, provide coherent information only from the 1880s, in the rural districts. Town budgets and accounts are such as to permit detailed information on the diverse expenditures already from the 1830s, following the Municipality Act of 1837. In addition to public health expenditures there was the private health consumption. We do not have estimates of the size of the doctor's bill for the 19th century. By the early 1940s estimates by the Central Bureau of Statistics have set the private health consumption at three times those paid out by the public authorities. A detailed review of the figures is not called for in our context, however. A cursory glance at table 1 yields the conclusion that health expenditures ranged from 0.7 to 2.7 per cent of central government budgetary outlays 1825-1860. The costs were not directly for medical services. What indeed did curative medicine have to offer before 1860?

The costs in this period covered mainly salaries and hospital care, including maternity care, for poor and destitute citizens, including public prostitutes at the Rikshospital in Christiania; from the 1850s also the insane, and the lepra pasients, as had the charity work carried out by the church and monasteries of an earlier age. The results should be judged accordingly. As we know, the bacteriological age did not begin till the 1880s.

Table 1. Central government expenditures on health and total budgetary outlays 1825-1940, current kroner.

Year	Central government medical expenditures 1000 kroner	Total central government outlays 1000 kroner	Medical outlays in per cent of total
1825	127	8.805	1.4
1830	74	9.158	0.8
1835	83	9.996	0.8
1840	94	12.744	0.7
1845	156	11.356	1.3
1850	266	13.135	2.0
1855	467	17.191	2.7
1860	567	23.346	2.4
1865	668	20.057	3.3
1870	716	20.238	3.5
1875	1.023	38.253	2.7
1880	1.595	44.400	3.6
1885	1.548	42.500	3.6
1890	1.968	52.900	3.7
1895	2.534	71.400	3.5
1900	3.161	110.400	2.9
1905	3.301	101.300	3.3
1910	3.808	120.900	3.1
1915	4.300	158.100	2.7
1920	23.600	653.400	3.6
1925	20.000	444.900	4.5
1930	14.500	373.700	3.9
1935	14.200	384.000	3.7
1940	22.500	1.132.200	2.0

Sources: Government accounts, printed in *Stortingets Forhandlinger*, a multi-volume publication from 1815: from 1879 extracts in *Statistical Yearbooks*. From 1915 the figures here are from *Historical Statistics 1968*, CBS, tables 233, 234.

The results

The contours and contents of the demographic transition in Europe 1800-1930 is by now widely disseminated, figure 1. The conclusions as to the role of causal factors, however, are still a matter of international debate.[5] The findings reported here in general support the views of the McKeown school, whose proponents, following the originator, professor Thomas McKeown, of Birmingham, England, argue that improved nutrition is the central causal factor in the recent health revolution.[6] Omitting detailed documentation here, it seems on balance fair to say that the health gains 1815-1860 also in Norway were mainly due to improved dietary status and other income determinants. Curative medicine, apart possibly from smallpox vaccination, had at best a minor effect on the health situation; and preventive medicine, as seen from the outbreaks and lethality of three major cholera epidemics 1832-1853, can be ignored in an explanation of the reported health gains. The following three sections review in summary form the evidence for the above conclusions.

Briefly, the health gains in the period 1815-1860 were as follows: Directly following the end of the Napoleonic Wars 1815, the mortality rate, that had gyrated wildly during the previous century, fig. 2, dropped 20% up to 1826/30, and 25% by 1851/55. The base is here the average rate 1811/15. Infant mortality rates, 0-1 year, available from 1836, also improved, down from 134 per thousand in 1836 to 102 per thousand in 1860, a gain of 24%. Expectation of life at selected years is at hand from 1821/30. For men the average expectation at birth increased from 45.0 to 47.4 years between 1821/30 and 1856/65, a gain of 5.3 per cent. For women the gain was similarly two years, up from 48.0 to 50.0 years in the period, a gain of 4.2 per cent. The drop in mortality rates proved permanent, and the rate continued to fall evenly throughout the century. See fig. 2 for the longterm view for all the Scandinavian countries. We move on from description to explanation.

Vaccination against smallpox

As to the role of the public medicinal police for the reported health gains at the time, the government doctors in this period could in principle have influenced the health conditions in the case of smallpox and cholera. Smallpox was regarded a particular danger. The tradition lingers on in our textbooks still. Now, two independent death lists have recently been uncovered, with breakdowns of the causes of death, which offer the first precise information on the role of smallpox in national mortality figures over the crucial years 1785-1815.[7] The one list from Jarlsberg county, along the west bank of the Oslofjord, comprised 1230 deaths 1785-1801. The other list contained 356 deaths from Akershus county, just north of the Oslofjord 1801-1815. Smallpox accounted for 7.1 per cent in the first, nine per cent in the second case, or an average of about eight per cent.

---

5. Robert Fogel, 'Nutrition and the Decline in Mortality since 1700', NBER, *Working Paper*, 1402, Cambridge, Mass. 1984.
6. Thomas McKeown, *The Modern Rise of Population*, London 1976.
   Thomas McKeown, 'Food, Infection and Population', *Journal of Interdisciplinary History*, vol. XIV, 1983. p. 229 ff.
7. Sölvi Sogner, *Folkevekst og flytting*, Universitetsforlaget, Oslo 1979.

Figure 1. The demographic Transition: Births and Deaths per 1000 in the Nordic countries 1750-1950.

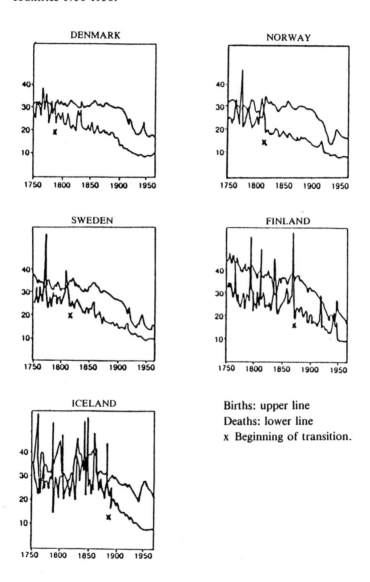

Births: upper line
Deaths: lower line
x Beginning of transition.

Source:Ståle Dyrvik's article in Fifth Scandinavian Symposium, *The Scandinavian Demographic Society,* Oslo 1979, p. 99.

Figure 2. Mortality Rate per 1000 in Norway, Denmark and Sweden 1735-1980.

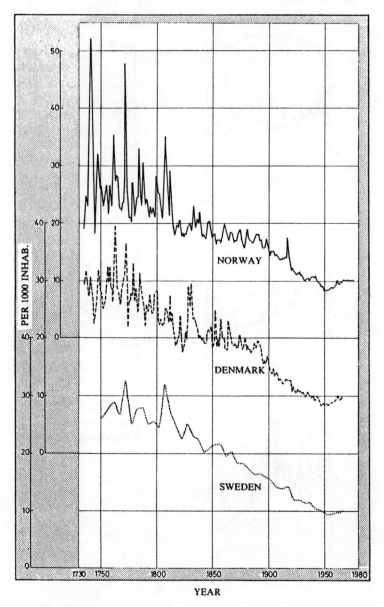

Sources: See Figure 1.

Similar results in the same period have been reported from Sweden.[8] Hypothetically then, if all smallpox infections were removed, and granted that Jarlsberg and Akershus were representative, the national mortality levels would still fall only about eight per cent. True, we also assume unchanged lethality among those infected.

We just observed, however, that within ten years after the Napoleonic Wars 1815, the mortality rate dropped, not eight, but 20 per cent. Moreover, as late as 1860 a mere three per cent of the total population had in fact been vaccinated with the cow serum, the immunizing agent against the real smallpox pathogen.[9] The vaccination programme so far had not been a success. Ignorance and fear kept rural folk away from doctors and their vaccination assistants, despite the fact that the vaccination was free of charge, as was the vaccination document, and the doctors travel expenses were covered by the central government. Still, a growing percentage of the new-born were in fact vaccinated: 31% during the decade 1811-20 as against 82% in the decade 1851-60. This may have prevented the recurrence of the dreaded smallpox epidemics of an earlier era, in that the virulence of the bacteria stock could have been reduced, but this is a mere conjecture.[10] In sum, even if the government vaccination campaign against smallpox had been a success by 1860, directly, or indirectly, by creating a milder epidemical climate, the endeavour still falls far short of explaining the decline in mortality rates observed between 1815 and 1860.[11]

Cholera epidemics 1832-53

Next, consider the effectiveness of the public hygiene net in this period in containing the cholera threat, the new epidemic threat in the 19th century in Europe. The bacteria 'Vibrio comma cholerae', was identified in 1883 by Robert Koch during expeditions to Egypt and India, and reported by him the following year. From Asia, where the cholera is endemic, hence 'Asiatic cholera', seven pandemics spread all over Europe between 1817 and 1896. In Norway there were repeated cholera epidemics in the forty years between 1832 and 1873. In a severe outbreak in the capital and environs 1832/34 altogether 1896 cholera patients died.[12] During another severe attack 1848-50 there were 1853 deaths from cholera. In the third major attack in 1853 in Christiania, the capital, cholera struck 2453 persons within a few months, of which 1597 died. At that time Christiania had 30 000 inhabitants. Lethality was as high as 65%. The epidemic spread to nearby towns and townships along the Oslofjord. According to Lise Knarberg-Hansen altogether 3803 persons were taken ill with diarrhea and about 2500 died in that year from cholera.[13] The

8. G. Utterström, 'Some Population Problems in Pre-Industrial Sweden', *Scandinavian Economic History Review*, vol. 2, 1954, pp. 160-165.
9. Ole Olsen Malm, *Kopper og vaccinationen i Norge*, Kristiania 1915.
10. Ståle Dyrvik, 'Poteta, dødsrata og demografien', *Historisk Tidsskrift*, 1978, p. 272.
11. Michael Drake, 'Norway', in *European Demography and Economic Growth*, ed. W.R. Lee, London 1979, pp. 248-318.
12. Ole Jacob Broch, *Kongeriget Norge og det norske Folk*, Christiania 1878, pp. 50-51.
13. Lise Knarberg-Hansen, 'Koleraen i Christiania i 1853', Doctoral Thesis, University of Oslo 1986, Institute of Medical History.

1853-pandemic turned out to be the last major cholera attack in Norway. During the pandemics 1863-73 and 1881-96 only minor cholera outbreaks were reported, viz. in 1866 and 1873.

Against the evidence above one must conclude that the public hygiene net against cholera was a failure till the 1860s, despite repeated and growing government efforts to stem the epidemics.[14]

Birth weights

The absence of medical factors in the reported health gains up to 1860, suggests that the gains as argued by the McKeown school, should instead be ascribed to dietary factors. A new, relevant piece of evidence, pointing to the role of dietary improvements, are birth weights, recently uncovered from the Rikshospitalet in Oslo and from public maternity hospitals in Bergen and Trondheim, the other major towns. It turned out that the bound, handwritten midwife reports at Rikshospitalet, Oslo, the earliest of which go back to the year 1837, contained fairly coherent birth weights for the year 1845, 51 out of a total of 276 births for that year. For the previous years only scattered weights were found. Not till the late 1850s are the figures again systematic.[15] The arithmetic average for 1845 was found to be 3392 (i.e. 3400) grammes, despite the fact that many of the mothers in the reports were marked p.p., or *puellae publicae,* i.e. prostitutes. The figure of 3392 g ties in with the average figures found by Rosenberg and Wallöe in their recent study of the midwife journals at the public hospitals of Oslo, Bergen, and Trondheim for the period 1860-1980.[16]

That is, already by 1845 the Norwegian birth weights had reached the level of our own contemporary birth weights of 3400-3600 grammes, see fig. 3. Incidentally, the figure is in dramatic contrast to those reported from similar London mothers, at a slightly earlier period. According to Robert Fogel the average weight of babies born to poor, young London mothers 1800-1810, some of whom were prostitutes, was only 2276 grammes.[17] The difference underscores in an unexpected manner the dietary factor in the health gains achieved by the Norwegian population in this period. Other interpretations of the Norwegian birthweights in the 1840's cannot be excluded, though, since the sample above is small, and direct comparison of birthweights in Christiania 1845 and London ca. 1810 may be unwarranted.

14. *Ibid.,* pp. 9, 11-13, 17, 48.
15. Fritz Hodne, 'Medisin og miljø – nye synspunkter', in Ø. Larsen, O. Berg & F. Hodne, *Legene og samfunnet,* Oslo 1986. Part 1, pp. 76-108.
16. Margit Rosenberg & Lars Wallöe, 'Infant birth weight, menarcheal age, and nutrition', Suppl. No. 1, *Annals of Human Biology,* vol. 12, 1985, p. 60 ff.
17. R. Fogel, *op.cit.,* p. 63.

Figure 3. Birth Weights in three Norwegian Cities 1860-1980.

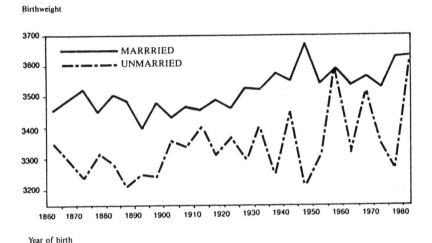

Source: Margit Rosenberg, *Birth weights in three Norwegian cities 1860-1980. Secular trends and influence factors,* University of Oslo, Institute of Informatics, 1985.

Assessment to 1860
Summarizing, we may say that in the first half of the 19th century the central government of Norway spent 0.7-2.7 per cent of its budget expenditures on a national system of preventive medicine. The health gains from the system up to 1860, however, appear in retrospect nil or negligible. This is not to say that the system, in a long term perspective, offered no positive health gains; indeed, the doctors may have helped disseminate a new definition of health and behaviour appropriate to individual and public health. The verdict for the period up to 1860, fragmentary as the evidence is, rests in particular on evidence of the smallpox vaccination programme and the course and outcome of three cholera epidemics 1832-1853. The 25% drop observed in the mortality rate up to 1855 is instead ascribed to improvements in the dietary status of the population and similar income-determined factors, e.g. better housing, which, by increasing human resistance to infectious disease, helped reduce the incidence and lethality of both infectious diseases and epidemics. Relevant evidence here are also the birth weights. Already from 1845 they had apparently reached the modern levels of high income countries, 3400-3600 grammes, for unmarried and married mothers respectively, though this conclusion on the strength of the evidence, should be regarded provisional.

III. The transition period 1865-1940

Organization and activities

The cholera epidemic of 1853 precipitated a legislative overhaul of the health system in Norway. By act of May 16, 1860, Sundhedskommissioner, (local health boards), headed by an authorized physician, were set up in each municipality, urban and rural alike. From 1874 the local health boards were subjected to far stronger central control. This occurred when a separate directorate of health was organized in Christiania in the year mentioned. A special office of director of health (Medicinal- direktören) was set up 1894. The new health authorities were given more powers to intervene in health matters and their tasks were specified in far greater detail. Clearly, 1860 is a landmark year in public health history.

Next, the number of district doctors in government pay increased from 60 in 1848 to 126 in 1869 and 152 by 1900. In 1910 the country boasted 1249 authorized doctors (physicians), 64 of which worked in the USA, and the number reached 2472 physicians by 1940. In relative terms there were 4800 inhabitants per physician in 1860 as against 1261 by 1940.[18]

The number of midwives with authorization also increased from 438 in the first census taken in 1857 to 1364 in 1910 and 1469 in 1940. By 1900 they handled 80% of all births. There were 360 midwives in public employ in 1857 and 671 in 1896.[19] During this time they received a salary from the municipalities, supplemented by socially graded fees from their customers. However, new legislation 1898 gave them back a legal monopoly, which they had enjoyed 1810-1839, and their salary was henceforth shared equally by state and municipality.

The country's physicians united in a national professional organization in 1886, Den norske Lægeforening (The Norwegian Medical Association). In contrast to most other European doctors, all physicians in Norway settled under one single umbrella. The unity reflected the egalitarian structure of the Norwegian society. On an average 90-92 per cent of all physicians have held membership in their association (DNL) throughout the hundred years of its existence.[20] Dentists and veterinarians trace their origins back to the 1850s, their professions rising to competence around the turn of the century. Nurses trace their beginnings to the 1870s, when religious organizations took the initiative to help poor

---

18. Fritz Hodne, *Stortingssalen som markedsplass. Statens grunnlagsinvesteringer 1840-1914*, Oslo 1984, p. 125.
    S. Laache, *Norsk medicin i hundrede Aar*, Kristiania 1911, p. 253.
    Central Bureau of Statistics of Norway, *Historical Statistics 1978*, Oslo 1978, NOS XII, 291, table 34.

19. Kristina Kjærheim, *Mellom kloke koner og hvitkledde menn: Det norske jordmorvesenet på 1800-tallet*, Univ. of Oslo, Dept. of Medical History, Oslo 1980; p. 96. (The Norwegian Midwives in the 19th century.)

20. Ole Berg, 'Verdier og interesser – Den Norske Lægeforenings fremvekst og utvikling', Part 3 in Ø. Larsen, O. Berg & F. Hodne, *Legene og samfunnet*, Oslo 1986, pp. 151-330.

and destitute individuals in towns. A national organization for nurses was set up around 1910.

Tuberculosis according to public health statistics was the greatest killer in Norway in the 19th century, as elsewhere; alone it accounted for 15 – 18% of all deaths past 1910. For a while the old miasma-philosophy continued to dominate. Increasingly, however, medicial opinion swung in favour of microbes and their transportation as the causal agents and channels of dissemination. Robert Koch scored victory for the view in 1882 when he identified the tubercle-bacillus. Immediately there arose in Norway a campaign – a state hygiene campaign - for more effective measures against tuberculosis. The physicians took the lead. They agitated high and low, printed leaflets, formulated legislation and were even invited to argue their case from the high bench of Parliament. The resultant Act against Tuberculosis of May 8, 1900, introduced strong preventive measures, among them the duty of visiting physicians to report all cases of tuberculosis discovered, a mandatory registry of all tb-patients to be kept by the local health boards, a ban against tb-patients working with children and foodstuffs, and other measures to restrict their movements, and ensure their isolation from the rest of the population. No triumph of curative medcine, but a triumph of public hygiene, for by 1940 deaths from tuberculosis, measured per 100 000, tumbled from 299 in 1900 for men to 84 in 1941/45. In forty years tuberculosis for all age groups dropped about 72% even before modern effective chemotheraphy had been introduced. The period 1900 – 1940 was the era of public sanatoriums, which combined individual care and isolation of the infected patients, but also entailed obvious infringements of the individual liberty of the victims.

Costs

The public health system from the 1880s, was increasingly financed by urban municipalities while the central government carried the responsibility for the outlying rural areas. Of the total costs the central government paid 51% in 1884 and 37% in 1913. Conversely the towns' share rose from 49% to 63% in the period, in line with industrialization and the rapid growth of towns and urban living. Health care represented 3.6% of total central government expenditures in 1880, up from 2.4% twenty years earlier, but as late as 1920 the share was still 3.6%. In macro- economic terms total public health costs, including government, counties and municipalities, represented 0.2% of gross national product in 1884, and 0.5% by 1913.[21] Relative to gross domestic capital formation (GDCF) the health costs in so far as they represented investments, were 1.3% in 1884 and 2.5% by 1913. By contrast investments in ships averaged about 22% of GDCF in the period 1865-1910.[22] As late as 1931 public health still represented a mere 0.8% of gross national product and 3.1% of gross domestic capital formation. Yet in terms of rates of growth health care was a growth sector from the 1880s. This is revealed by comparing the growth rate for public health expenditures with the rate of growth of the national product; table 2:

21. F. Hodne, 'Tabeller over helseutgifter mv.', in Ø. Larsen, O. Berg & F. Hodne, *op.cit.*, pp. 487, 488.
22. F. Hodne, *Norges økonomiske historie*, Oslo 1981, p. 168.

Table 2. Rates of growth of public health expenditures, gross national product, both in fixed 1910-prices, and the elasticity (ε) of public health expenditures with regard to GNP 1885-1924.

Decade	Public Health Expenditures	Gross Domestic Product	ε ($\varepsilon = 1:2$)
	(1)	(2)	(3)
1885-94	5.5	1.9	2.9
1895-04	1.9	1.7	1.1
1905-14	8.6	3.4	2.5
1915-24	5.2	1.5	3.5

Sources: Col. 1: F. Hodne, *Stortingssalen som markedsplass. Statens grunnlagsinvesteringer 1840-1914,* Universitetsforlaget, Oslo 1984, pp. 302-305. (State Infrastructure 1840-1914.) Central government accounts, local government accounts. *Statistical Yearbook* 1879. Col. 2: *National Accounts 1865-1960,* CBS, Oslo 1965, table 51.

A comment on the figures in table 2 could be that public health expenditures in Norway 1885 – 1925 increased more than twice as fast as gross national product. This yields an income elasticity for health expenditures of 2.4. The latter figure indicates that when total value creation grew by one per cent, public health expenditures increased by 2.4 per cent. Yet in a European setting Norwegian physicians in the public sector earned less than most of their colleagues abroad. They still do.[23]

In the interwar period costs for public health stagnated. Instead, while lepra patients disappeared, the money was transferred to tuberculosis prevention. By 1920 the expenditures on anti-tuberculosis measures were the biggest single cost item. We have worked out the elasticity figures for the interwar period. For the years 1920-1939 the figure was found to have been $\varepsilon = 1.1$. The figure 1.1 means that the rate of growth of the public health expenditures in this period just kept pace with the rate of growth of the gross national product.

---

23. OECD, *Public Expenditure on Health,* Paris 1977, p. 28.
Jean Pierre Poullier, *Public Expenditures on Health,* Paris 1985, prel.fig., Central Bureau of Statistics, Oslo.

Health gains 1860-1940

Table 3 below offers information on the changes in key health indicators for various periods between 1856 and 1940.

Table 3. Key health indicators 1860-1940 and observed changes.

	1856/60	1896/1900	1916/20	1936/40
Infant mortality				
0 – 1 years per 1000	101.2	95.7	61.9	39.4
Mortality rate per 1000	16.9	15.7	14.2	10.3
Average life expectancy (years)				
Men	47.4	50.4	55.6	64.1
Women	50.0	54.1	58.7	67.6
Per cent change between periods				
Infant mortality		- 5.4	- 35.3	- 36.3
Mortality rate		- 7.1	- 9.6	- 27.5
Average life expectancy				
Men		+ 6.3	+ 10.3	+ 15.3
Women		+ 8.2	+ 8.5	+ 15.2

Source: *Historical Statistics 1968,* NOS XII, 245, CBS, Oslo 1969, Tables 20, 32.

The figures indicate that the population experienced substantial progress in the general health situation. Infant mortality tumbled from an average of 101.2 in the 1850s to 39.4 in the years 1936/40, a gain of 61%. There was a clear acceleration downwards around the turn of the century. This is brought out more dramatically in fig. 4. Average mortality also came down, but more evenly. Over a ninety-year period the mortality rate fell by 39%, down from 16.9 to 10.3 per thousand between 1856/60 and 1936/40. Life expectancy at birth improved at an accelerating rate, for women up from 50 years to 67.6 years between 1856/60 and 1936/40, and for men up from 47.4 to 64.1 years in the same period.

Figure 4. Infant mortality per 1000 live births by age of child during first year of life 1876-1955.

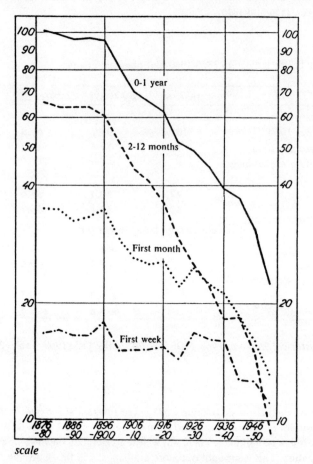

Source: Julie Backer, *Dødeligheten og dens årsaker i Norge 1856-1955,* CBS, Oslo 1961, p. 59.

Epidemiological Transition

Moving closer to the realities behind the statistical figures, we find that the health gains, reported above, followed the gradual reduction of all sorts of epidemics, above all cholera and infectious diseases, notably tuberculosis. This is echoed elsewhere.[24] Indeed, nearly all the gains in health status in the 19th century were due to the elimination or reduction of infectious disease and epidemics, hence the term the epidemiological

24. Britt Inger Puranen, *Tuberkulos. En sjukdomsförekomst och dess orsaker. Sverige 1750-1980,* Umeå Studies in Eonomic History no. 7, Umeå University, Umeå 1984.

transition, in line with the ordered pattern observed in the demographic transition 1800-1930. The entire disease panorama changed. To illustrate only, tuberculosis caused 127 deaths per thousand in 1878. A hundred years later tuberculosis is just about extinct. So is leprosy, smallpox and cholera. Infectious diseases, including tuberculosis, measles, diptheria, scarlet fever, whooping cough and polio accounted for 149 deaths per thousand in 1876 against four 1966/ 70, a hundred years later.

On the other hand cardiovascular diseases, that killed 43 persons per thousand in 1878, killed 499 per thousand 1966/70, a tenfold increase. Violent deaths, earlier a negligible death factor in the national figures (though drowning was common in the coastal districts) have shown a dramatic increase, following the recent spread of the automobile and travel in general.

Not only has the disease panorama changed; in an environment of less virulent pathogens, the infectious diseases, pneumonia, influenza or polio, no longer strike as hard as they used to. Though still endemic, they no longer kill. Again, unpasteurized milk, a classic risk factor behind typhoid or paratyphoid fevers during summers, is a thing of the past.

Since chemotherapy made its entry only after the turn of the century, and sulphonamides and antibiotics were introduced on a large scale only after World War II, it would seem that the roll-back of epidemics must be ascribed largely to preventive rather than curative medicine in conjunction with the other income-determined factors touched on earlier. Preventive medicine would include public hygienic measures. They took on real urgency with the bacteriological revolution of the 1880s. Hygiene was the main topic at several international medical congresses between 1870 and 1920. Beginning in 1891, the government paid the travel money and expenses for Norwegian participants to all these international hygiene congresses. At the congress in Budapest September 1-9, 1894, hygiene cropped up directly in 350 papers presented under 19 diverse hygiene categories, among them ethiology, bacteriology, the prevention of epidemics, child hygiene, school hygiene, town hygiene, hygiene of foodstuffs, housing hygiene, tropical hygiene, military hygiene, and state hygiene. It was the public sanitation decades, when town veterinarians cried out against unsanitary slaughter houses, when town chemists called for the closedown of dairies and shops selling unpasteurized milk and physicians warned against the dangers of city waste, garbage and pollution. It was the era of factory inspection, sewers, water works, sand filtration, free meals for poor school children,and ban on child labour.[25]

By now we see that preventive medicine, indicated above, would also embrace social medicine. After all, it was hardly sensational in the 1880s to argue that human disease was caused as much by a filthy environment as by personal negligence. The view that disease had social rather than individual origins, however, did harbour radical consequences. For by the same token poverty was less an individual than a social disease, responsibility for

---

25. Anne Lise Seip, *Sosialhjelpstaten blir til. Norsk sosialpolitikk 1740-1920*, Oslo 1984, pp. 217-257.

which should rest with society. Equally, good health would be a social gain as much as an individual blessing, since good health improved the productivity of the workers. Medicine was politics.

The implication of these summary remarks is to call attention to the role of economic factors in attempts at explaining the epidemiological transition 1880s-1940s. This is justified, for the physicians in charge of decisions at the time, argued the case for public health care expenditures by pointing at economic benefits, public and private, to be harvested now and in the future.

A new accounting mentality arose around the turn of the century. The pioneering figure Klaus Hansen, the architect behind the tuberculosis act of 1900, and a brother of Armauer Hansen, who discovered the lepra bacillus, made a strikingly modern estimate in 1895 of the annual costs to the Norwegian economy caused by tuberculosis. The value of lost production for the age groups 16-60 years and other expenditures due directly and indirectly to tuberculosis each year was 28 million Nkr, or ten times the annual sum paid out in public health money in the 1890s.[26] Figures like that did make an impression on a cost-conscious parliament. At any rate the state-supported hygiene campaign against tuberculosis dates from about 1900.

IV. Causal factors of the health gains 1860-1940

We have now reported the major health gains achieved 1860-1940, sketched the government efforts to build an efficient health net round the population, and offered figures on the costs. Does the causality run from government infrastructure to better health? Or do both the health gains and public infrastructure reflect an underlying trend, for example, economic growth?

Several American studies have raised the question, but have despaired for lack of public health expenditure estimates.[27] For Norway such figures are available, for central government back to 1816, for municipalities from 1884. National accounts figures are available from 1865. This means that we have sufficient data to test statistically to what extent the health gains were related to the general economic development and to what extent they were related to increased public health care. We use infant mortality i.e. number of deaths per thousand in the first year of life as a proxy for health improvement. We use gross national product *per capita* in fixed 1910-prices as indicator of the overall

---

26. F. Hodne, 'Økonomisk vekst og helse', in Ø. Larsen, O. Berg & F. Hodne, *Legene og samfunnet*, Oslo 1986, p. 121.
27. E. Meeker, 'The improving Health of the United States', *Explorations in Economic History*, vol. 9, 1971-72, pp. 353-373.
   Robert Higgs, 'Mortality in rural America 1870-1920: estimates and conjectures', *Explorations in Economic History*. vol. 10, 1973, pp. 177-195.
   Robert Higgs, 'Cycles and trends of mortality in 18 large American cities 1871-1900', *Explorations in Economic History*, vol. 16, 1979, 381 ff.
   G.A. Condran & Eileen Crimmins-Gardner, 'Public Health Measures and Mortality in US-Cities in the late Nineteenth Century', *Human Ecology*, vol. 6, 1978, pp. 27-54.
   G.A. Condran & Rose A. Cheney, 'Mortality Trends in Philadelphia: Age and Cause – specific Death Rates 1870-1930', *Demography*, vol. 19, 1982, pp. 97-123.

economic development, and finally government outlays for health care *per capita* (in 1910-prices) as proxy for investments in health infrastructure. Continuous data have been assembled for the period 1865 – 1929, table 4.

If changes in gross national product and government health expenditures influenced infant mortality rates, such changes obviously would take time to materialize. We have therefore calculated a five-year moving average of both the data for gross national product and the government health expenditure series. These averages are then compared with the annual infant mortality rates. We will test a simple linear relationship of the form $Y = f(X_1, X_2)$
where $Y =$ the number of deaths per thousand in the first year of life in year t (1869-1929)
$X_1 =$ average gross national product *per capita* in year t-4...t (1865-1929)
$X_2 =$ average public health expenditures *per capita* in year t-4...t (1865-1929)

There are obviously strong relationships between the three variables. Correlation analysis done separately between Y and the two independent variables shows $r = -0.92$ between Y and X_1 and $r = -0.84$ between Y and X_2. The estimated regression equation is the following:

$$Y = 160 - 0.142 X_1 - 0.0084 X_2$$
$$(-7.22) \quad (-0.32)$$

R-squared adjusted for the degrees of freedom is 84.3%, and the Durbin Watson statistic is 1.01. Only the relationship between infant mortality and gross national product is significant; at a 0.5% level. The results indicate that the reduced infant mortality rates depended more on general economic progress, as measured by *per capita* income gains, than on public expenditures for health care. Caution is called for. For one thing, the Durbin-Watson statistic is low, 1.01, which suggests auto-correlation, also the desirability of introducing additional explanatory variables. Secondly, there is evidence of strong multi-colinearity between the two explanatory variables ($r = 0.85$). For these reasons the regression results reported above should be taken as suggestive rather than conclusive. Nevertheless the evidence does point strongly towards the importance of nutrition as a causal factor in the decline of mortality, i.e. economic factors. Not surprisingly, government incomes did vary with the ups and downs of the business cycle throughout the period 1860-1940. That is, economic progress influenced health in two ways, directly through gains in *per capita* incomes, indirectly through permitting more government revenue, hence increased outlays on government health programmes. Even popular expectations of health changed. A symptom of the new expectations would be life insurance, the break-through for which on a broader front occurred in the 1880s, though life insurance traces its origin in Norway to the 1840s.

The reason why mortality and health expenditures are not more significantly related, deserves a little more digging. Investigating the data in a little more detail, we

Table 4. Gross national product per capita, central government health expenditures per capita, five-year averages 1865-1929 in fixed 1910-kroner, and annual infant mortality rates 1869-1929.

1865-1929	GNP per capita kroner 5-year average	Central government health expenditures øre 5-year average	Annual infant mortality 0-1 year
1	364	50.4	111.4
2	368	50.0	100.7
3	372	52.3	98.7
4	379	51.4	102.5
5	388	48.6	105.9
6	396	45.4	112.7
7	406	46.3	114.9
8	417	46.3	108.1
9	433	51.0	107.2
10	423	57.4	103.1
11	421	64.2	91.7
12	420	71.3	95.3
13	417	79.8	96.6
14	415	86.4	111.0
15	417	90.0	96.6
16	421	93.8	96.3
17	422	94.8	93.1
18	422	96.0	90.6
19	423	97.0	87.5
20	428	100.0	97.3
21	436	102.8	96.9
22	445	107.0	110.0
23	445	108.0	97.2
24	465	113.0	103.8
25	473	119.8	89.1
26	478	128.6	103.8
27	481	134.0	95.5
28	485	144.7	96.5
29	492	150.2	95.6
30	496	153.8	89.4
31	502	154.2	106.7
32	508	154.0	90.5
33	515	154.0	91.1
34	518	153.4	73.8
35	521	153.0	77.9
36	521	154.0	74.8
37	522	156.2	81.5
38	525	156.2	69.1
39	532	155.0	65.8
40	543	165.0	75.0
41	556	166.4	69.5
42	572	166.6	67.2
43	588	171.4	64.5
44	605	178.6	67.2
45	625	171.2	64.3
46	644	181.2	67.6
47	665	187.8	67.3
48	685	186.4	64.0
49	686	183.2	64.0
50	675	178.8	62.9
51	682	176.8	61.7
52	692	187.2	57.5
53	682	214.6	53.8
54	700	257.0	54.5
55	726	311.0	49.5
56	732	348.2	50.0
57	740	370.0	50.2
58	764	391.2	47.9
59	781	397.4	50.7
60	801	394.0	49.0
61	838	405.8	54.4

Sources: Col 1: CBS, *National Accounts*, Oslo 1965, Table 51.
Col 2: F. Hodne, *Stortingssalen som markedsplass*, Oslo 1984, pp. 302-305.
Col 3: CBS, *Historical Statistics 1978,* Oslo 1978, Table 9.

PUBLIC INFRASTRUCTURE

have in figure 5 plotted our infant mortality data (Y) against *per capita* GDP-data (X_1). Similarly, in figure 6 the infant mortality data have been plotted against government health expenditure (X_2). While the first plot shows a fairly uniform negative relationship, the second plot displays a decreasing relationship.[28] The discrepancy between the two results is probably due to the fact that while there was an increase in government health expenditures after 1920 up till 1930, the decline in infant mortality in that period decreased at an unchanged rate (see fig. 4). This is an illustration of decreasing marginal returns on public investment in health care and would explain the weak statistical relationship.[29]

Knut Liestöl in a slightly different area used menarcheal age for Norwegian school girls and GNP-figures to see how far the menarche was affected by changes in the social situation.[30] Though the foundation of his data is shaky, his findings are clearly reconcilable with our own regression results, see fig. 7. Both point to the far-reaching effects of economic circumstances on health and physical growth.

V. Summary

No single cause explains the entire course of the demographic transition 1815-1940. Diet improvements would seem to have been the most important factor in the initial period 1815-1860 in bringing down the incidence and lethality of disease. The government health system at the time can be written off as a negligible factor. In the following period 1860-1940 curative medicine, though of growing psychological importance to patients, was a minor factor in explaining the health gains. By contrast, diet and other income related factors appear to have been decisive. Both diverse statistical tests and detailed investigation on the course of the demographic variables in the period point to this conclusion. The economic improvement, represented by GDP - *per capita* affected the health status directly through dietary improvements, and indirectly through expanded programmes of government preventive hygiene. The role of public hygiene was particularly evident 1900 - 1940 in combating perinatal and infant mortality, and above all, in almost eliminating tuberculosis. Finally, curative medicine, by contrast, has had a decisive impact in the post World-War II-period.

---

28. As an illustration we have plotted the least square lines in figure 5 and 6 as linear and exponential respectively. However, we have not worked out estimations based on a non-linear regression model.
29. The conclusion gains credence from the following: A regression analysis on the period up to 1920 on our data improves the relationship between infant mortality and government health investments. It is significant, but still only at a 10% level. R-squared is 77.3, and D.W.statistic is slightly higher; 1.12.
30. Knut Liestöl, 'Social Conditions and Menarcheal Age,' *Annals of Human Biology*, vol. 9, 1982, p. 529 ff.

Figure 5. Infant mortality per 1000 and Gross national product *per capita* 1865-1929 (fixed 1910 Nkr).

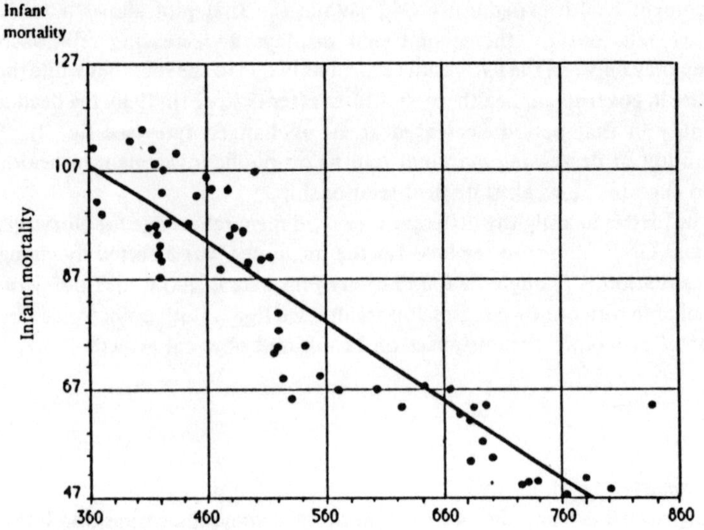

Average GNP per capita (1910 Nkr)

Figure 6. Infant mortality per 1000 and government *per capita*-outlays on health care 1865-1929 (fixed 1910 Nkr)

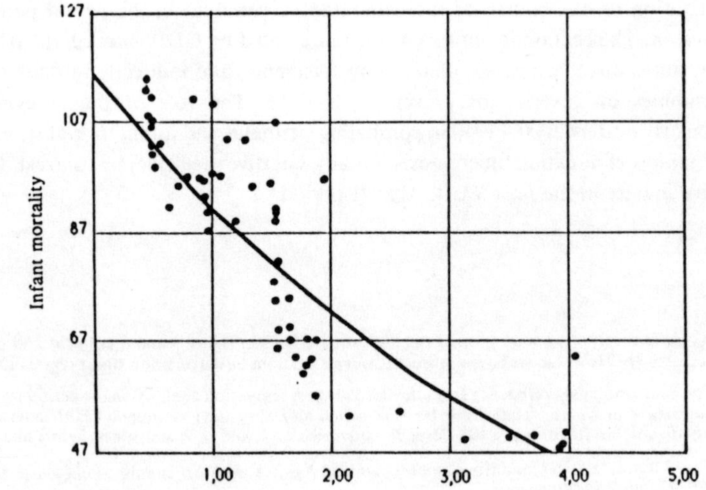

Central Government per capita expenditures on health (1910 Nkr).

Figure 7. Social conditions and menarcheal age.

———: GDP for Norway
……..: Smoothed values for menarcheal age in Oslo, Norway

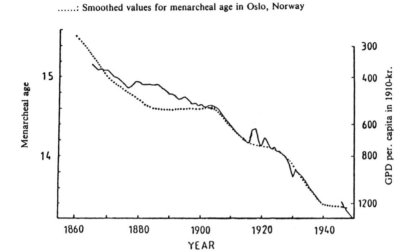

Source: Knut Liestöl, "Social Conditions and Menarcheal age: The importance of early years of life", *Annals of Human Biology,* 1982, vol. 9, 529.

To return to the problem posed in the introduction, government infrastructure in health does affect the course of modern economic growth. Indeed, as far as the elimination of epidemics, as distinct from curative medicine, is concerned, government hygienic and health programmes 1895-1940s were arguably the sufficient cause. The virtual extermination of traditional infectious diseases, notably tuberculosis, reflected, not only private income increases, but also the role of medical knowledge and medicinal police, brought to bear by legislation and government expenditures. In conclusion, the intricate connections between different factors at diverse levels of aggregations, affecting the modern revolution in health, can, it would seem, best be studied at the level of individual countries.

[28]

THE SCANDINAVIAN WELFARE STATE :

ANATOMY, LOGIC AND SOME PROBLEMS

Gunnar Persson
University of Copenhagen
and
London School of Economics

Contents

Editorial Note

1. The Anatomy of the Scandinavian Welfare State (SWS)
   1.1 Health
   1.2 Housing
   1.3 Family Policy
   1.4 Education and Culture
   1.5 Labour Market
   1.6 Risks and Income Maintenance
   1.7 Services for Elderly
   1.8 Redistribution in the SWS
   1.9 Conclusion

2. The Logic of the SWS

3. Problems in the SWS
   3.1 Disincentives and Crowding Out
   3.2 Will there be a Demographic Impasse for the Welfare State?
   3.3 Break-up of the Welfare State Coalition?

References

Discussion Paper
No.7
March 1986

The Welfare State Programme
Suntory-Toyota International
Centre for Economics and
Related Disciplines
London School of Economics
10 Portugal St
London WC2A 2HD
Tel : 01-405 7686

1. THE ANATOMY OF THE SCANDINAVIAN WELFARE STATE*

The Scandinavian Welfare State (henceforward SWS) is considered throughout the world to be a specific Scandinavian achievement. It is necessary to stress, however, that the design of the SWS shares many similarities with welfare programmes in the rest of Europe and especially in the UK.

Although Scandinavian social scientists such as Gunnar Myrdal and Frederik Zeuthen devoted their talent to the development of the principles of the welfare state an equally important intellectual stimulus in the formative years of the SWS was Lord Beveridge.

The specificity of the SWS becomes more evident when the quantitative aspects are scrutinised. Some 40-50% of GNP is now devoted to welfare spending evenly divided between welfare public consumption and income transfers. The share of public sector spending approaches as high a proportion as 65% in Sweden. (The figures are lower for Norway.)

The SWS is a post-World War II phenomenon. In the 1930s, welfare spending in Scandinavia was proportionally smaller than in continential Europe, but some initiatives were taken in that era away from the residual (ie. poor relief) type of welfare towards a much more universalistic approach.

That strategy - an evolution towards the _institutional_ welfare model, using Titmuss terminology - has been followed in the post-war era and has received a broad support from a coalition of the working and middle classes as well as rurally-based parties. Social democratic parties - based on the working and lower middle classes - have, no doubt, played a leading role in the build up of the welfare state but except for the occasional conflict there has been a sort of consensus around the main targets of welfare

---
* I have benefitted from corrections, ideas and suggestions proposed by Søren Geckler, Julian Le Grand, Gunnar Olofsson and Sven E Olsson. Mich Tvede assisted me in doing some of the tables. The views expressed are mine and so are remaining errors.

policy. The introduction of state earnings-related pension schemes, for example, caused political conflict in Sweden in the late fifties and early sixties but later became consensus politics in Norway.

The general historical trend has been to reduce means-testing and to provide services and transfers on fairly general grounds through simple administrative routines. Social assistance, ie. cash transfers that are provided after close inspection of personal economic conditions, consequently play an insignificant role, accounting for a few per cent of total welfare spending at present, although it is now tending to increase again. Only recently has there been an articulate critique based on libertarian principles against the welfare state. Although right-wing political parties have adopted a more critical attitude towards the welfare state they have neither instituted radical changes of its structure nor significantly diminished welfare spending when in power, presently in Denmark and Norway and between 1976 and 1982 in Sweden. The long-run increase in the proportion of taxes out of income has come to a halt, however. A consensus seems to have evolved that the tax share cannot increase above its present level at some 45-50% of GNP, highest in Sweden and lowest in Norway. The evolution of welfare spending, here broadly defined as the sum of public consumption (exclusive of pure public goods) and social security transfers, is presented in Table 1 below.

TABLE 1

Share of welfare spending in GNP

	Percentage of GNP				
	1950	1960	1970	1975	1981
Denmark					
Current transfers to households	5.8	7.4	11.4	13.9	18.2
Welfare public consumption	8.7	10.1	17.2	23.2	25.8
Norway					
Current transfers to households	4.9	7.0	13.7	13.7	15.0
Welfare public consumption	9.0	11.3	13.5	16.3	16.5
Sweden					
Current transfers to households	6.3	8.5	10.2	13.4	18.1
Welfare public consumption	9.9	12.0	18.1	20.5	26.6

Note : The share of welfare transfers is somewhat underestimated because not all relevant transfers are included such as subsidies encouraging household consumption of goods and services.

Source : OECD NATIONAL ACCOUNTS

The growth in public consumption has of course been associated with an increase in public employment, especially local government services. In recent decades public employment has increased at a faster rate than total employment which is documented in Table 2.

4

TABLE 2

Growth of employment by sector

	Percentage growth per year			
	Denmark		Norway	Sweden
	1972-78	1979-81	1972-80	1970-81
Total employment	0.7	-1.5	2.0	0.9
Public sector, total	4.7	5.0	6.9	4.8
Administration and defence	2.6	4.3	4.7	2.3
Health services	4.1	8.3	8.5	7.3
Education	5.3	3.1	6.4	5.8
Social services (mainly for children and elderly)	8.1	4.8	16.3	9.9

Source : Kruse (1984)

Public employment has primarily affected the labour market participation rates of women which is higher in Scandinavia than in most other industrial economies. No less than 60-70% of public employment consists of women in Scandinavia, although a considerable number only work part-time. Manufacturing employment stagnated or diminished in the seventies but there has been a recovery in industrial job creating during the first half of the eighties. At present some 25% (Norway) to 35% (Sweden) of the labour force is employed in the public sector, most of them by local governments.

Let us now turn to a brief overview of the main areas of welfare policy.

1.1 Health

Health Services including drugs are 'free' or heavily subsidised. Production of health services is predominantly public, more specifically under the authority of local government on county level. GPs are either public employees or contracted by local governments. Health services provided by large-scale hospitals have been expanding faster than GP services in recent decades. Some 10-15% of GNP is spent on health consumption and transfers related to sick leave.

1.2 Housing

The public (local government) and cooperative housing sectors dominate post-war new housing projects apart from owner-occupiers. Housing consumption is encouraged primarily by

a) housing benefits to households
b) loans with below market interest rates provided to developers and owner-occupiers
c) tax-deductions for owner-occupiers

In Sweden, for example, about 2% of GNP is spent on housing benefits and interest subsidies. Another 2% represents taxes foregone through generous tax deductions related to owner-occupation.

1.3 Family Policy

The main family-related transfers are paternity and maternity pay of up to 12 months and child benefits, means tested in Denmark.

Maternity/paternity pay is partly earnings related and administered as a part of the sick leave insurance, covering some 80-90% of normal income.

Child care services are subsidised by centraland local governments and predominantly provided by local government but there is rationing of existing services because of excess demand. Some 30-50% of eligible children get publicly provided care.

Around 5% of GNP is spent on family related transfers and services.

1.4 Education and Culture

Most educational services are publicly produced, with a subsidised private sector in Denmark. As a rule there are no fees paid, not even at university level. Furthermore, for higher education, there are various state subsidised borrowing schemes for students. Cultural production is heavily subsidised including public grants to newspapers and publishing, film and theatres, public libraries and to sport.

1.5 Labour Market

There is a much firmer commitment to low unemployment in Norway and Sweden than in the rest of Western Europe. Open unemployment rarely surpasses a 3.5% level in Norway and Sweden, but it is on a continental level in Denmark. The, comparatively speaking, low unemployment in Sweden and Norway reflects a concern with other ways of handling unemployment manifested in an extensive use of (wage-) subsidies and large scale retraining programmes.

1.6 Risks and Income Maintenance

As already mentioned the SWS is built around the institutional welfare model wilth an extensive system of predominantly compulsory public insurance schemes covering sickness, accidents, unemployment and old age. There are state earnings related pension schemes in Norway and Sweden covering some 50-60% of normal earnings in addition to a basic state pension. In Denmark there is a variety of private or trade-union implemented pension schemes covering some 40% of the eligible population. Income is maintained at a 70-85% level through unemployment and somewhat higher in sickness insurance. Approximately half of all welfare transfers are related to income-maintenance at old age.

1.7 Services for the Elderly

There is a wide variety of services provided, primarily by local government for the elderly such as residential apartments, homes with various facilities, old age homes and wards for chronically weak or ill pensioners. There is an intention to provide services through professional helpers in the ordinary homes of pensioners, however, both for economic and social reasons. But some 10% of pensioners are still in different sorts of institutional care, mainly those above the age of 80.

The allocation of welfare resources between different uses can be seen in Table 3 below. It is based on the social expenditure concept used by OECD. In comparison with the welfare spending used in Table 1, this one excludes certain types of public consumption, such as higher education and some services provided by local governments. Welfare transfers are also restricted to social security benefits which excludes subsidies for household consumption widely used especially in Sweden. Nonetheless the relative distribution of welfare spending as between different areas is not significantly altered by these conceptual differences.

TABLE 3

Social expenditure by area 1960-1981

Percentage of total social expenditure

	Denmark		Norway			Sweden		
	1970	1981	1960	1970	1981	1960	1970	1981
Education (consumption)	27	23	33	28	23	30	27	20
Health (consumption)	20	17	24	17	24	22	27	26
Pensions	28	33	24	32	29	29	27	35
Unemployment	2	10	1	1	1	1	1	2
Other social expenditures (consumption and transfers)	23	26	18	19	23	18	17	17

Source : OECD (1985)

1.8 Redistribution in the SWS

As has been demonstrated in the preceding pages the SWS constitutes a system of cash transfers and non-market production and distribution of services such as education, cultural services, health and child care.

There are observed redistributional effects in Scandinavia of both transfers and public provision of services. Two inter-related approaches to the redistributional problem will be presented. First we will investigate the redistribution between income-groups at a specific point of time and then look at the redistributional effects over the lifecycle, or more accurately, between age-groups at a given point of time.

A recent study by Björn Gustavsson (1984) based on Swedish household survey data confirms the results found in other nations that the redistributional effect in an egalitarian direction stems from transfers, rather than taxes. Gustavsson compares before and after taxes and transfers. Income is measured in units of "material standard", one unit being the officially approved minimum income for an individual. The results from Gustavsson's analysis are illustrated in Figure 1 below. The thin curve describes the material standard before taxes and transfers while the thickly drawn curve denotes the material standard after taxes and transfers.

FIGURE 1

Distribution of material standard before and after taxes and transfers, Sweden 1981

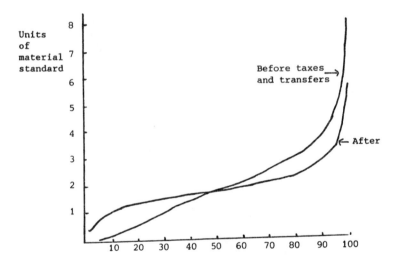

Per cent of individuals

Source : Gustavsson (1985)

The considerable redistributional effect is also demonstrated with the familiar Lorenz-curves as in Figure 2 with the straight 45° showing a perfectly egalitarian distribution of material standard.

10

Now the thin curve - that denotes the cumulated per cent of material standard of the cumulated deciles of all individuals - is closer to the straight 45° line than the thick pre tax and transfer curve. That consequently implies an egalitarian effect of taxes and transfers. The Gini coefficient are 0.404 (before) and 0.212 (after taxes and transfers).

FIGURE 2

Lorenz curves of material standard before and after taxes and transfers, Sweden 1981

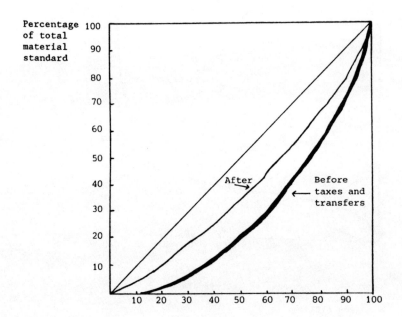

Percentage of all individuals

Source : Gustavsson (1984)

11

Finn Kenneth Hansen (1981, 1985) at the Danish Institute for Social Research, also using household survey data, has measured redistributional effects of transfers as well as of consumption of public services. As far as the pure tax and transfer effects are concerned he was able to show a pattern in Denmark similar to that just described for Sweden. Including effects of welfare services he was able to detect a slight additional redistributional towards the less rich but most of the redistributional effects stem from the transfer payments. Finn Kenneth Hansen also showed that the redistributional effect of services and transfers diminished somewhat from the middle of the seventies to the early eighties, probably due to increasing unemployment.

Another way of looking at redistribution is of course to approach it as a redistribution over the life-cycle. Below, in part two, I present some arguments for making that redistribution through a welfare state rather than through credit and insurance markets. Here I intend to illustrate the life-cycle approach by showing what individuals of different age groups receive (at a given point of time) in terms of transfers and services on the one hand and what they contribute in terms of taxes and social security contributions tied to the wage-bill. Basically there is a redistribution between inactive age-groups and active ones.

Although the specific data I use for Figure 3 below is from Sweden and expressed in Swedish kr. (£1 ≈ 10 Skr.) the pattern that emerges is fairly typical for the SWS as a whole. Above the age line the curve denotes the value of transfers and welfare services. Before entrance into the labour market public consumption consists of education and child care services and there are transfers such as child benefits.

Public consumption in the active ages consists mainly of health services increasing with age. Health consumption increases dramatically with age as well as other services and transfers (pensions).

FIGURE 3

The intergenerational redistribution profile, Sweden

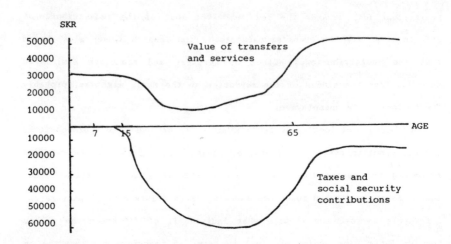

Source : SCB (1985)

1.9 Conclusion

The basic characteristics of the SWS can be summarised as follows :

a) a predominantly public production of educational and health services, child care and services for the elderly.

b) comprehensive and (mostly) compulsory insurance schemes in health, unemployment and pensions.

c) redistribution of income primarily through cash transfers related to age, number of children and housing consumption to households.

We will now turn to an inquiry as to why the SWS to such an overwhelming extent has eschewed market solutions and market institutions.

2. THE LOGIC OF THE SWS

As can be understood from the description presented above the SWS is built around a diversity of institutions and activities covering a wide variety of social and economic probelms. Is there an inner logic or some unified principle behind the developed welfare state? I will argue that there is.

The procedure establishing this claim will not, however, be one in which the ideological motives of politicians are discussed or for that matter official welfare ideology. In my view such a procedure would leave too many contradictory suggestions to be of any explanatory value. The main emphasis of the approach suggested here is that the welfare state responds to universalistic rather than sectional (class) interests. Now this is not a view currently favoured in the academic discussion on the welfare state in Scandinavia. In that discussion the development of the welfare state has been viewed as a matter of class politics in which welfare institutions have been interpreted as responding to the interests of the working-class specifically. This argument seems to imply that welfare policy primarily is concerned with redistribution between classes in society (cf. Esping-Andersen and Korpi, forthcoming, and Therborn, 1984). The approach I favour points out - on the other hand - that redistribution in the SWS is between risk-groups, types of households, and over the life-cycle of households and that the public provision of services responds to potential or real market failures. This does not (necessarily) contradict the observed (cross-section) redistribution from rich to poor (cf. above) because households typically experience periods of both affluence and lack of resources over time. Furthermore, my approach will be based on the hypothesis that if an institution is fairly stable and has a long duration then we should try to find some rational or general efficiency characteristic as an explanation of its exitence. That is the implicit assumption in much economic theorising about the market institution. It is argued that markets might be efficient and it is believed that they do exist just because they are efficient. I will transpose that argument somewhat arguing that if non-market institutions do exist it might be because market institutions in these specific areas are inefficient or would be inefficient and for that reason non-market institutions are invented. The structure of the argument is a familiar one in many different branches of the social sciences and it has a strong functionalist flavour.[1] I will not try to give a full account of the methodological requirements for a well-behaved functionalist theory, ie. an argument that an item exists _because_ it has some beneficial effect or consequence. My aim is the more modest one of trying to show that the areas of economic and social life in which the SWS has replaced the market typically are areas where you might suspect markets of failing and to be inefficient. And if that is true it would be reasonable to conjecture that this is the very reason behind the appearance of welfare state institutions.

I have developed a typology of welfare institutions inspired by the Scandinavian experience based on these conjectures and hypotheses which will be discussed and presented in Table 4 below.

Insofar as economists admit the need for a visible hand they usually ascribe that need to the existence of public goods. But few welfare state activities are pure public goods, although L Thurow (1971) and others have suggested that you can interpret the distribution of income as a pure public good. That means, in this context, that all citizens get some sort of satisfaction from a certain, presumably less unequal, distribution. Being a pure public good no one could be excluded from the said

15

TABLE 4

A typology of the developed Welfare State

Characteristics of households, goods and services	Areas of economic and social life	Varieties of institutional solutions
Type 1 Uncertainties about properties of goods and services, because infrequent transactions impede learning; goods and services are non-standardised; inefficient market production of information; producers have market power due to asymmetries in information.	Health services. Education.	Non-profit (non-selfish) ethos among producers. Relations of trust rather than mutual benefit between producer and consumer. Public supervision of production and marketing. Public production. Private but non-profit production.
Information about a service cannot be separated from its consumption.	Education.	Compulsory arrangements.
Irreversible effects of household action or non-action and/or of goods and services under uncertainty.	Some health services, complicated products.	Licensing of and control of professional standards and/or products. Non-deterrent (subsidized) prices. Compulsory arrangements, e.g. health insurance.
Addiction as a special case of irreversibility.	Drugs, alcohol.	Prohibition, regulation of sales. Deterrent prices.
Type 2 'Learning-by-living' infers uncertainty about future preferences. Irreversibility is sometimes present.	Household lifecycle distribution of income flows.	Tax and transfer programmes affecting lifecycle distribution based on implicit contracts between generations, i.e. pension schemes, child benefits.
Type 3 Altruism, more specifically: conditional solidarity.	Risks of low income, poor health and un-employment; non-selfinflicted risks. Redistribution of income.	Non-discrimination of risks in insurance, e.g. un-employment or sick leave insurance costs independent of risks.
Type 4 'Household externalities' Decisions of household head affect other household members without adequately reflecting their preferences, present or future. Irreversible effects sometimes present.	Education. Housing. Nutrition. Life-cycle distribution of income flows.	Subsidised or non-fee education, health service, child benefits - "There-is-no-such-thing..." but anyway: free meals - Pension schemes for dependents. - Housing benefits encouraging high standards. - Compulsory arrangements, e.g. child health, education.

satisfaction. This stimulates free rider behaviour that eventually would call for state action to bring about the desired outcome.

Imaginative as this solution is, it is of doubtful validity because it introduces a sort of moral double-talk. It is somewhat implausible that man could enjoy satisfaction from a "fair" distribution but also act "unfairly" through free rider behaviour. A solution to this puzzle can, however, be found along the lines suggested in Sen's 'assurance game' (Sen, 1967). Assume that most citizens can express altruism in some social matters, mostly - as it seems - in cases of wholly or partly non-self-inflicted risks of low income, unemployment and poor health. (It is noteworthy that recent attempts in Scandinavia to change sick leave insurance to reduce benefit for those with repeated sick leave spells have been met with a moral outrage while no one seems to question the fact that car insurance costs reflect individual risks. What seems to be the heart of the matter is - I conjecture - that the latter problem is considered as a matter of self-inflicted risks.) In the particular case of unemployment and health, such altruism implies that individual insurance costs should not reflect individual risks.

Now it is well established that competitive insurance markets with egoistic agents easily cause adverse selection resulting in prohibitively high insurance policies for those with high risks. But what _if_ citizens really are altruistic? Wouldn't they buy insurance contracts on a competitive market that have the desired redistributive effect in favour of those with high risks? Even if it is perfectly possible that competitive firms could offer such insurance contracts, there is little hope that uncoordinated market behaviour of altruistic individuals would ensure that a number of citizens sufficiently large to inhibit adverse selection actually signed for that particular risk-neutral insurance. This is so because it is perfectly rational for an altruistic person to argue in the following way : "Lacking adequate information about what others will do, I prefer to be cautious and act egoistically, because it is no use acting altruistically alone." No-one wants to be a "sucker". So what we in fact are dealing with is a sort of conditional solidarity, which means that any individual is willing to act altruistically if others do it as well. Markets do not have the capacity of giving individuals either this kind of information or the assurance of what others will do. My conjecture is that morals, ideology and compulsory arrangements such as comprehensive (risk neutral) health insurance all represent varieties of institutional solutions to the problem of information and assurance of what others will do, when such knowledge is necessary for the choice of preferred action by an individual. For similar reasons voluntary philanthropy will be less efficient than redistribution through state agencies which is the proposed reason as to why redistribution is arranged through taxes and transfers rather than by gifts in modern society.

This is the very reverse of a free rider problem. The free rider acts egoistically independently of what others do, but altruistic man acts egoistically only when lacking appropriate information and assurance of that others act altruistically as well.

To sum up, the fact that markets are inefficient when citizens express solidarity or altruism is an important source of market failure that might account for welfare state institutions. The argument is presented in a digested form under type 3 in Table 4. Going back to type 1 in Table 4 we encounter the problem of imperfect information and more seriously perhaps asymmetries in information between producer and consumer. Since most people gain their information by experience and trial and error we can expect serious problems of information if goods or services are non-frequently traded. Markets for information might also be imperfect because it is difficult to protect property rights which give producers insufficient incentives to produce it. Furthermore many products, for example health services, are not always sufficiently standardised for production of information. In the extreme case information cannot in fact be captured until the good is consumed or until a considerable time <u>after</u> consumption of it, as is the case with a full evaluation of the quality of education and some health services. Imperfect information creates several other problems. If producers have superior information it will give them a sort of market power which we - following the traditional behavioural assumption in economics on market behaviour - must assume producers exploit to their own advantage. Now this is clearly a source of inefficiency. Imperfect information also is problematic if there are irreversible effects of a non-trivial nature, for example consumption of harmful products or treatment by incompetent medical producers.

Several institutional alternatives to markets can be seen as responses to the problems just discussed. For example, the licensing of products or control of professional standards give imperfectly informed consumers the assurance of not becoming victims of irreversible effects. The market power of producers with superior information can be checked by the existence of a non-profit or non-selfish ethos or by the de-privatisation of such production. Public production or public supervision of quality standards in production of health or education considerably reduce the transaction and information search costs involved in taking appropriate decisions. Believing that publicly enforced standard are upheld and satisfy reasonable requirements, the citizen can dispense with the time-consuming information search and choice problem. The role of politics would then be to supervise quality standards on behalf of the rest of society when the self-policing of perfect markets does not work.[2] Turning to the related problem under type 2 in Table 4 we here face the problem of "imperfect" preferences. For several reasons most people change preferences during their life-cycle. They tend to "learn by living", new information is gained through trial and error in consumption and in life generally. And changes in the environment and social status tend to cause changes in preferences.

Most of these changes are trivial although it might take a couple of years to develop a taste for the best whiskey or toothpaste (or both). Non-trivial cases occur when irreversibilities are involved, however. It is not easy to predict, for example, the needs and preferences at old age, and you could easily save too little. In a sense you have to live your life twice to make the appropriate decisions on how to allocate the income flow over the life-cycle since it will depend on such unpredictable factors as household size, length of life and changes in preferences. For reasons already discussed, you would not trust bankers or insurance agents to do these decisions for you because they must be expected to exploit your uncertainty to their own advantage.

The political process has the advantage of introducing an institution of inter-generational bargaining here. At different stages in the life-cycle citizens can voice their needs and preferences as they presently perceive them. The outcome of this bargaining cannot be predicted in a detailed manner and it need not because there is a sort of implicit contract that ensures stability in the commitments that the different generations owe each other.

Finally, I will turn to type 4 in the table which deals with what I have called household externalities. This simply means the many cases in which head(s) of households make decisions that do not adequately reflect the present or future preferences of dependent members of households.

Compulsory schooling or free child health can be seen as protection for dependent children in case the head of household believes that children do not need or deserve education or in case the household head has allocated income in such a way that it excludes appropriate consumption of paid health care. (Compulsory schooling might be motivated also by the fact :
1) that education has certain public good effects, such as being a precondition for a democracy.

2) that you really cannot appreciate your need for education until you have got at least some basic training and knowledge.)

Now, this typology summarised in Table 4 evidently invites accepting the basic premise that welfare state institutions do have some efficiency properties that markets would not have under the given circumstances. This is a rather controversial argument. Most Scandinavian critics of the welfare state as elsewhere seem to be preoccupied with the disincentive effects of the financing of the welfare state rather than by the functions of the welfare state institutions as such. Some of these problems will be dealt with in the next section.

3. PROBLEMS IN THE SWS

3.1 Disincentives and crowding out

In the sixties and seventies - the period of rapid build-up of the SWS - growth of public consumption was a couple of percentage points above real growth rates in GNP and growth in transfers doubled that of growth in GNP. The result has been a high level of taxation, 45-50% of GNP, which is now generally considered in Scandinavia as a maximum in the sense that it is not feasible to try to push it even higher. So the rate of growth of revenue for the public sector cannot depart significantly from the rate of real growth in the private sector which has slowed down during the last ten years. There are, however, some semi-automatic increases in public spending stemming from demographic changes as well as a tendency of wages - which amount for 80-90% of costs of public consumption - in the public sector to grow at the same rate as wages in the private sector. With productivity in the public sector presumably growing at a slower rate public sector services are becoming more expensive relatively speaking. With no signs of an immediate upturn of economic activity welfare state development has come to a temporary standstill. There are consequently no new reforms on the agenda.

While there is an agreement on the fact that sluggish economic growth and the existing level of taxes are constraints for welfare spending some will make the much more controversial claim that the growth of the welfare state is responsible for the slowing down of growth rates in recent decades. There has been a slow down, no doubt, especially in Denmark and Sweden, with growth rates at 3-5% in the sixties and half of that in the seventies and eighties. (Norway has shown persistently high growth rates throughout the seventies and early eighties, ie. 3.5-4% annually.)

Most of the critical arguments are echoes of the Anglo-Saxon debate, which is remarkable bearing in mind that welfare state growth has been much more advanced at an early date in Scandinavia. Economists in Scandinavia express the familiar view about de-industrialisation due to growth of welfare state services, financial and labour market crowding out and disincentive effects of the high level of taxation (Lindbeck, 1981). Although strong views are presented, there are still few systematic inquiries into these matters and no conclusive results have been presented (cf. Kruse, 1984). Discussing labour supply, for example, there are very weak disincentive effects of taxes shown in the few Swedish investigations made on this subject (SOU, 1984, pp.290-291).

Labour supply changes are, however, open to conflicting interpretations. Scandinavian economists tend to interpret the long-run trend visible since the sixties of a decline in aggregated hours worked as a disincentive effect of taxes (Stuart, 1981). But with the regeneration of economic activity in the early nineteen eighties that trend has been broken and hours worked increase again without any changes in tax pressure. One unintended (?) effect of the tax system is, however, that paid work has become of a more equal length as among man and woman of the typical household. The high marginal taxes on overtime work have created incentives for women to increase their labour force participation.

Although their gross wages in general are lower than that of their husbands, their "take-home pay" might be higher than the "take-home pay" of their husbands on marginal hours.

It is true that industrial employment stagnates in Scandinavia as was shown in Table 2 above (there has been a resurgence in recent years, however). Part of that reflects a change in the pattern of demand towards services as income per capita increases. Critics argue, however, that trade deficits in industrial goods still reflect a de-industrialisation. Others point out that there is a profound restructuring of the industrial sector caused by changes in the international economy. Again critics of the welfare state tend to argue that the adaption to a changed economic environment has become much slower than before. It is further argued that the rapid expansion of public sector employment has imposed an upward trend in wages for the private sector and that high marginal taxes have disincentive effects on labour mobilityi. It seems, however, as if the declining labour mobility is caused by a decrease in job openings following the downturn in economic activity in the seventies (SOU, 1974, p.295). And with most new employees in the public sector being comparatively low-paid females the effect on industrial wages is not self-evident.

The commitment to low unemployment (in Sweden) and the generous unemployment benefits (in Denmark) have made these economies operate with high budget and balance of payment deficits in recent years. There was a tendency at the end of the seventies of a mounting structural budget deficit as well, ie., a deficit that would persist also at full employment. It seems as if this structural deficit has disappeared in recent years, however, disproving the claim that welfare state expansions necessarily lead to permanent deficits (Jespersen, 1984).

The budget deficit has of course attracted much interst being the alleged cause of a financial crowding out of the private sector. Now this argument is based on an assumption of a close link between the size of the budget deficit and the level of interest rates, that is far from conclusively corroborated. The decline in growth rates from the seventies and onwards is not a phenomenon restricted to Scandinavia but part of an international recession. So it is obviously a somewhat premature conclusion to ascribe the decline in growth to the level of welfare; for thse differ considerably among nations. Korpi (1985), in a comparative study covering the OECD countries, takes the long view and detects a <u>positive</u> relationship between productivity growth and grwoth of GNP on the one hand and various welfare state indicators - including relative share of welfare spending - on the other hand for most of the period 1950 to 1982. That does not prove a causal link but, more modestly, suggests that a high rate of growth of GNP and wages, that is not explained as such, permits an advanced welfare state.

At the present stage of knowledge, unfortunately, not very much more can be said.

3.2 <u>Will there be a demographic impasse for the welfare state?</u>

Scandinavia faces similar demographic changes to the rest of the advanced industrial world. In particular, the key problem is that of the increase in the elderly as a proportion of the population.

Since most age-related transfers are based upon the principle of (intergenerational) redistribution, it is believed that the future will see political conflicts between the gainfully employed generations and the elderly. This presumption is based on the idea that the burden of transfers and services for the elderly will be very heavy for the active generations. Is that really the case?

A couple of recent Scandinavian studies do address themselves to this very question. Karsten Albæk (1982) constructs and uses a method of estimating costs to active generations of the demographic changes in Denmark. The argument is built upon the assumption that the 'unit cost' of a dependent (young or old non-active) individual changes at the same rate as the real income of the active generation. So in a sense a pure demographic effect is the subject of the analysis. The results based on expected demographic trends in Denmark show that there are negligible effects up to the year 2010 but, after that, about 20% of a yearly growth rate of 2% will be captured automatically by the increased costs of dependents due to demographic changes. At higher growth rates the relative proportion of productivity growth covering the increased costs will decline.

Valuable as these measurements are, they are (as pointed out by the author) based on simplifying assumptions. For example, the demographic changes in the active generations might diminish the adaptability and mobility of the labour force which probably will have negative effects on productivity growth. Furthermore, there is a problem in the assumption that 'unit costs' of dependents will grow at the same rate as income of the active generation. It seems as if unit costs have growth faster than that in recent decades.

Ann-Charlotte Ståhlberg (1984) has studied the Swedish pension system and other age-related transfers and her conclusions are broadly similar. Again of course the effects will be heavily dependent on the growth of real income. With low real growth of wages (1% per year) the transfers to elderly will increase from some 17% of aggregated wages in the middle of the eighties to 23% in the year 2025. But that proportion will be fairly stable in the whole period at some 16-17% if the wages grow moderately, ie. 1% to the year 1990 and 2% per year thereafter.

But transfers are only one part of the costs of the elderly. Increased demand for health services and care is equally costly. With the reasonable assumption that these costs will be growing at a rate double that of real wages the share of transfers plus services for the elderly will amount to some 15% of GNP by the end of this century, a slight increase. There will predictably be some strains put on the welfare system caused by the demographic changes, but they are not as severe as often believed. The question, of course, remains open whether an electoral system in which the elderly are becoming more and more decisive will be flexible enough to solve the intergenerational redistribution. What has been proposed is to diminish the burden for the active generations by making some of the services for the elderly accessible on payment. Since a larger portion of the elderly will be covered by earnings-related pensions in the future their ability to pay for these services will increase. Politically, however, this is quite a problematic issue.

The costs of the pension system can also be diminished somewhat by changing the rules for eligibility of pension with different coverage.

So, on balance, there are problems with the ageing of the population - especially if growth rates in the economy are sluggish - but not to the extent that the foundations of the welfare state are threatened.

3.3 Break-up of the welfare state coalition?

It has been argued here that the SWS by and large was initiated and supported by a broad working- and middle-class party coalition in which social democrats played and play a leading role. Liberal and right-wing parties have increasingly articulated a critique of the high level of taxation necessarily associated with the Welfare State. But with the modest claims that marginal tax rates should not exceed 50% this is not a tax revolt of a kind seen elsewhere. Furthermore, there is a certain unease typically in the middle-class towards the public (semi)monopolies in education and health which does not imply, however, that education and health services are not generally believed to be provided on the principle of need rather than economic entitlements.

Recent public opinion polls seem to register an increasing unease with the bureaucratic tendencies in the Welfare State and perhaps especially in tax collection methods. Some 80% of a representative sample of Swedes do agree to the following statement : "The state has become increasingly despotic at the expense of individual rights." But there is still a solid support for a welfare state of an advanced type, but not necessarily taking such a high share of total resources as at present. Two out of three believe that tax pressure is too high. On the other hand there is a majority (1984) agreeing to the following statement : "The public sector must be retained at its present level and even expanded." Liberals and socialists being most favourable to that assertion as can be expected (Olsson, 1985). There is also a considerable stability in the opinions expressed as can be seen from Table 5 below.

TABLE 5

Swedish attitudes towards social policy, 1955, 1964 and 1978

	1955* %	1964 %	1978 %
Social policy is generally worth what it costs, but certain features ought to be expanded	17	19	14
Social policy is generally satisfactory as it is, but means-tests ought to apply to more benefits	46	45	45
Social policy has gone too far; reliance on welfare and a poor sense of responsibility follow in its tracks	31	33	36
Hesitant, don't know	6	2	6
	100	100	100

* Approximations of fairly similar questions.

Source : Zetterberg (1979)

Although there have been political movements in Scandinavia that have articulated a radical break with the SWS they have not been electorally

27

successful in recent years. In fact those parties have experienced setbacks in recent elections. As has been pointed out above conservative and centre parties have - when in power - not been willing (or able) to institute anything but marginal changes in the SWS. For the future I believe we can expect a greater institutional flexibility implying a break-up of some public (semi-monopolies) in welfare state production. We will perhaps also see a reduced concern with an egalitarian distribution of income as well as welfare cuts. But there are no signs that Scandinavia will abandon its commitment to the institutional and comprehensive welfare model.

FOOTNOTES

1 K J Arrow (1963) suggested an interpretation of non-market institutions along these lines.

2 In perfect markets there is self-policing in the sense that producers do not cheat consumers. This is so, not because producers are soulful or moral but because it would be irrational to do so. Well-informed consumers would discover and abandon a cheating producer and therefore the producer abstains from such behaviour by pure self-interest.

REFERENCES

Albæk, K (1982), Fødseltal, forsørgergerburder og økonomisk vækst, Nationaløkonomisk tidskrift, 120, pp.310-320

Arrow, K J (1963), Uncertainty and the Welfare Economics of Medical Care, The American Economic Review, 53, pp.941-973

Esping-Andersen, G and Korpi, W (forthcoming), Social Policy as Class Politics in Postwar Capitalism : Scandinavia, Austria and Germany, Stockholm : Swedish Institute for Social Research (mimeo)

Gustavsson, B (1984), Transfereringar och inkomstskatt samt hushållens materiella standard, Stockholm : Ministry of Finance

Hansen, F K (1981), Forbrugsmuligheder og omfordelingen over den offentlige sektor, Copenhagen : Lavtindkomstkommissionens sekretariat

Hansen, F K (1985), Fordelingspolitiken og dens virkninger, Copenhagen : Danish Institute for Social Research

Jespersen, J (1984), Statsgældspolitik i de nordiske lande, Copenhagen : Nordisk Forlag

Korpi, W (1985), Economic Growth and the Welfare State : Leaky Bucket or Irrigations System? , Stockholm : Swedish Institute for Social Research (mimeo)

Kruse, A (1984), Den offentliga sektorns effekter på sysselsättningen, Stockholm : Nordic Council of Ministers

Lindbeck, A (1981), Work Disincentives in the Welfare State, National-ökonomische Gesellschaft Lecture 1979-80, Vienna : Austrian Economic Association

OECD (1985), Social Expenditures 1960-1990, Paris

Olsson, S-E (1985), The Swedish Welfare State, Recent Changes and Future Developments, Stockholm : Swedish Institute for Social Research (mimeo)

Sen, A K (1967), Isolation, assurance and the social rate of discount, Quarterly Journal of Economics, 81, pp.112-124

SCB (1985), Offentlig sektor, Stockholm : Central Bureau of Statistics

SOU (1984), Arbetsmarknadspolitik under omprövning, No.31, Stockholm : Ministry of Labour

Stuart, G E (1981), Swedish Tax Rates, Labour Supply and Tax Revenues, Journal of Political Economy, 89, pp.1020-1038

Ståhlberg, A-C (1984), Överföringar från förvärvsarbetande till den äldre generation, Stockholm : Swedish Institute for Social Research

Therborn, G (1984), The Prospects of Labour and the Transformation of Advanced Capitalism, New Left Review, No.145, pp.5-38

Thurow, L C (1971), The Income Distribution as a Pure Public Good, Quarterly Journal of Economics, 85, pp.327-336

30

Zetterberg, H S (1979), En politik för åttiotalet, in Westholm, C-J, <u>Skapande eller bevakande Sverige?</u>, Vol.II, Stockholm : Confederation of Swedish Employers

Name Index

Aall, Jacob 55, 79
Aarestad, J. 486
Adler-Karlsson, G. 385
Aghevli, Bijan B. 260
Aglietta, M. 462
Akerman, Sune 513–16, 525, 534–5
Albæk, Karsten 643
Andersen, Ellen 327
Anker, Christian 104
Arriaga, E. 494
Aschehoug, Torkel H. 97, 113, 124
Aschenfelter, O. 537, 539–40, 543
Astrup, Hans R. 101
Aukrust, O. 393, 488, 498–9, 501, 553

Backer, Julie E. 494
Bain, G.S. 537, 539, 543
Bairoch, P. 490
Balassa, B. 297
Bauer, P.T. 597
Bean, Charles 387
Beckerman, W. 286
Berend, T. 76, 88
Bergh, T. 76, 497
Beveridge, Lord 327, 621
Bíórn, Erik 503
Bismarck, Otto E.L. 156
Bjerke, Juul 53, 69–70, 106, 166, 490, 494–5,
  498–501, 503, 506
Bjerke, Kjeld 264
Bjórn, Claus 162, 169–70, 172
Bogen, H. 454
Bojer, Hilde 387
Bordo, Michael D. 240, 260
Borgan, Jens-Kristian 494
Boserup, Ester 156
Boyer, R. 462, 465–8, 471–3, 483–4, 489–90
Brandt, K. 441, 446
Broch, Jacob 97
Brug, Kværner 104
Bruland, Kristine 76–7, 91–2
Brunborg, H. 494
Brunstad, R. 486
Bull, E. 475

Calmfors, Lars 392, 394
Cameron, Rondo 6–7, 40, 302, 316

Carlson, John A. 249
Caspersen, Sven 264
Castro, Fidel 599
Chayanov 165
Chenery-Syrquin 153
Choi, K. 279, 286
Chow, Gregory C. 238, 242
Christensen, Jens P. 40, 153, 157, 163–4,
  169–70
Clapham, J.H. 171
Cobb, C.W. 205
Cohen, I. 476
Cohn, E. 143
Cooley, Thomas F. 242
Coriat 462
Cornwall, J. 286–9, 297
Cox 246
Crafts, N.F.R. 153

Dahl, Thor 454
Dahmén, E. 456
Davidson, Russell 246
Deaton, A.S. 246
Dich, Jórgensen 265, 276, 538
Douglas, P.H. 205
Dowrick, Steve 399
Drake, Michael 494
Driffill, John 392
Dybdahl, Vagn 162

Easton, S.T. 131
Egeberg, Westye 94
Egmose, Sven 264, 272
Einarsen, E. 120, 124
Einarsen, J. 112–13
Elsheikh, F. 537, 539, 543
Engerman, Stanley 410
Eriksson, Ingrid 513
Ernle, Lord 153
Esping-Anderson, G. 385, 395, 397, 633

Falbe-Hansen, V. 143
Fei, John C.H. 46
Fischer, L.R. 490
Fisher, Douglas 251–2
Fogel, Robert 410, 606
Foyn, A.J. 454

Freeman, C. 278
Freeman, Richard 387, 398–9
Frew, James R. 249
Frickey, Edwin 518, 520, 523
Fridlizius, G. 237
Friedman, Milton 238, 240, 251–3, 260
Frisch, Ragnar 111–12, 485
Frølich, Fritz H. 84

Galenson, W. 538, 541, 543
Garrett, Geoffrey 393
Gelting, Jørgen 327, 330
Gerschenkron, A. 77, 85, 89, 91–2
Gjermoe, E. 112, 444
Gjølberg, Ole 490, 493, 501
Goldfeld, S.M. 136, 255
Graah, Knut 90, 92–3, 476
Graham, Gerald 409
Grauerholz, John 595
Graves, Philip E. 260
Grout, Paul A. 392
Gustavsson, Björn 628–9
Gutzeit, Hans 101

Hanisch, T.J. 76
Hannover, H.I. 23
Hansa 48
Hansen 104
Hansen, Alvin H. 326
Hansen, Armauer 614
Hansen, Finn K. 276, 631
Hansen, Klaus 614
Hansen, Svend Aage 25, 27–43, 132, 144, 157, 161–3, 166, 236, 340
Harley, Charles K. 409
Hauge, Hans N. 89
Hausman, J.A. 255
Heller, H. Robert 251
Hendry, David F. 254
Henriksen, O.B. 159, 343
Hernes, Gudmund 394
Hersoug, T. 488
Hertzberg, Ebbe 97
Heston, Alan 388
Heyerdahl 104
Hibbs, Douglas A. Jr 387, 393, 396
Hines, A.G. 539, 543
Hiorth, Adam 90, 92–3
Hirsch, S. 288
Hirschman, Albert O. 391, 596
Hodne, Fritz 75–7, 81–2, 88, 96, 280, 485, 490
Holden, Steinar 388, 393
Holm, T. 548, 551, 564

Holmlund, Bertil 393
Horn, Henrik 392
Hvidt, Kristian 164, 516–17, 525, 530
Hyldtoft, Ole 25, 28, 30–31, 35, 37, 39–40, 132, 136, 139–40, 143

Isachsen, A.J. 487

Jackman, Richard 387
Jacobsen, Carsten 101
Jebsen, Peder 90–92
Jensen, Einar 153, 174
Jensen, Jens 101
Jensen, S.P 159–61, 169
Jespersen, J. 642
Johannsen, F. 324
Johansen, H.C. 34, 37, 40
Johansen, Leif 390, 395–6
Johansson, 'O' 236–7
Johnsen, A.O. 438, 441–2
Johnston, J. 136
Jonung, Lars 240, 260
Jörberg, L. 88, 120, 126, 220–21, 232
Jorgensen, Dale 46

Kaldor, N. 286, 327
Kallestrup, L. 538
Kampmann, V. 275
Keilhau, W. 130
Keynes, John M. 257, 324–6
Khan, Mohsin, S. 251
Kindleberger, Charles P. 49, 121, 153, 171
Klein, Benjamin 249–50, 260–61
Klovland, Jan T. 240–41
Knarberg-Hansen, Lise 605
Knutsen, P. 486
Koch, Robert 605, 609
Kondratieff 140, 143, 151
Koopmans, T.C. 112
Korpi, W. 633, 643
Koutsoyiannis, A. 144
Kruse, A. 641
Kuznets, S. 222, 492, 519

Laidler, David 238, 241
Lamfalussy, A. 286
Lange, E. 76
Lange, P. 393
Lash, Scott 395
Layard, Richard 387
Lebergott, Stanley 518
Lee, Jeong-Hwa 387, 398
Lerner, A.P. 326
Lettenstrøm, Gerd S. 494

Levy, Moritz 307
Lévy-Leboyer, M. 490
Lewis, Arthur W. 597
Lewis, Sir Arthur 46, 49–50
Lieberman, Charles 242
Liestöl, Knut 617
Lindbeck, A. 641
Linder, S.B. 280, 287–9, 297
Lipietz, A. 462
List, Friedrich 77
Locking, Håkan 387, 393, 396
Lubitz, R. 288
Lundberg, Erik 386
Luxemburg, Rosa 385

MacKinnon, James G. 246
Maróen, Atle 395
Marris, Stephen 492
Marstrand, E. 538
Marx, Karl 26
Mathiesen, Haagen 79
Mathiesen, H.C. 104
Mazier, J. 462, 467, 483
McKeown, Thomas 602, 606
Meltzer, Allan H. 238
Mikesell, Raymond F. 496
Milward 220–21, 232
Minde, K.B. 490
Mintz, I. 119
Mistral, J. 462
Moe, Thorvald 494, 499, 510, 512–16, 519, 525, 534–5
Moene, Karl O. 392
Möller, Peter 108
Moore, W.J. 539
Mueller, Dennis 597
Musgrave, Richard A. 597
Myrdal, Gunnar 324, 388, 621

Nguyen, Duk-Tho 399
Nickell, Stephen 387
Nielsen, Axel 308
Nissen, Gunhild 165
Nordby, Trond 388
Nordvik, H.W. 490
North, Douglas C. 408–10
Nurkse, Ragnar 597

Ohlsson, Ingvar 187
Ølgaard, Anders 155, 159
Olsen, Kristian A. 93
Olsen, P.B. 275
Olsson, S.-E. 646
Onsum, Oluf 93

Pearce, D.K. 539
Pedersen, H. Winding 328
Pedersen, Jørgen 33, 177, 325–6, 328
Pedersen, P.J. 539–40
Pencavel, J.H. 537, 539–40, 543
Pesaran, M.H. 246
Peston, Maurice 597
Pharo II 76
Phelps Brown, E. 523
Philip, Kjeld 327
Pollak, Robert A. 174
Pontusson, Jonas 400
Posner, M.V. 288
Prescott, Edward C. 242
Przeworski, Adam 385, 387, 389, 392, 398, 400

Quandt, R.E. 136–7
Quigley, John 510, 512–15, 534

Ramsóy, Rogoff 484
Ramstad, J. 472, 490
Ranis, Gustav 46
Ranki, Gyórgy 76, 88
Ravenstein, Edward 510, 530
Reagan 388
Risting, Sigurd 433
Rødseth, A. 388, 392–3
Ropeid, Andreas 99
Rosenberg, Margit 606
Rosenberg, Nathan R. 409–10, 420
Rostow, W.W. 6, 597
Rygg, N. 113, 124, 127

Saint-Simon, C.H. 89
Sargent, Thomas 253
Saul 220–21, 232
Scharling, William 13, 23, 143
Schmookler, J. 441
Schou, Halvor 91–3
Schumpeter, Joseph 106, 108, 111, 121, 143, 409–10
Schwartz, Anna 253
Schweigaard, Anton M. 52, 87
Seip, Jens A. 97
Sejersted, F. 113
Semmingsen, Ingrid 492, 506, 513
Sen, A.K. 636
Senghaas, Dieter 77, 80, 87, 92, 167, 169
Skancka, Gisle 494
Skånland, Hermod 495
Skedinger, Per 393
Skrubbeltrang, Fridlev 159, 175
Smith, Adam 87, 597–8

Smith, V.E. 206
Smout, T.C. 168–9
Söderlund, Ernst 101
Solhaug, T. 113
Solstad, Dag 93
Sørensen, R.S. 267
Sprague, John 400
Spree, R. 120
Stabell, Adolf B. 84, 88
Ståhlberg, A.-C. 644
Stang, Frederik 87
Stauffer, Robert F. 260
Steenstrup, P.S. 92–3
Steigum, E. 548
Steincke 271
Steinmo, Sven 400
Stølen, Nils M. 387, 395
Stoltz, G. 491
Stone, Richard 245
Stonehill, Arthur 497
Strang Petersen, O. 33
Strøm, Steinar 387, 395
Stuart, G.E. 641
Summers, Robert 388
Sundt, Eilert 85–6, 88

Taylor, D. 161
Teigen, Ronald L. 257
Theil, H. 144
Therborn, G. 633
Thilesen, G. 103
Thirlwall, A.P. 286
Thomsen, Nüchel 156, 159
Thue, Lars 106
Thurow, L. 634
Tietgen, C.F. 11, 306–7
Tinbergen, J. 206
Tinter, G. 205–6
Tobin, James 240
Tønnessen, J.A. 440, 448
Topp, Niels-Henrik 324, 329
Torp, Hege 387, 395
Torstendahl, R. 88
Tvethe, Braun 52

van Duijn, J. 288
Vernon, R. 288
Viby Mogensen, G. 264
Vinje, Aasmund O. 99

Wade, William W. 172
Wallerstein, Michael 392
Wallöe, Lars 606
Warming, Jens 24, 324–6, 538, 541
Warriner, Doreen 167
Wettergren, K. 112
Wilkinson, Maurice 510, 512–14, 534
Willerslev, Richard 9–10, 18, 27, 35, 37, 132
Williamson, Oliver E. 173
Witte, Jørgen 165–6
Wulff, Julius 324
Wunder, Sven 153

Zanden, J.L. van 157–61
Zeuthen, F. 324, 621
Zinser, James E. 496